D1317798

Planning and Administering
Early Childhood Programs
Second Edition

Celia Anita Decker
Northwestern State University

John R. Decker
Northwestern State University

Charles E. Merrill Publishing Co.
A Bell & Howell Co.
Columbus   Toronto   London   Sydney

To Kelcey and Keith, our twin sons, and Kristiana,
our daughter, who have brought delight to our
home as only very young children can.

Published by Charles E. Merrill Publishing Co.
A Bell & Howell Co.
Columbus, Ohio 43216

This book was set in Melior
Cover Design Coordination: Will Chenoweth
Production Coordination: Sandy Rawson Smith

Library of Congress Catalog Card Number: 80–80815
International Standard Book Number: 0–675–08160–2
Printed in the United States of America

1 2 3 4 5 6 7 8 9 10—85 84 83 82 81 80

Preface

This volume is a revision and extension of the first edition of *Planning and Administering Early Childhood Programs*. Much of the original writing remains timely. This book is built upon the conviction that thoughtful planning and administration are essential to the success of early childhood programs. Our main priority is to present the rationale for that thoughtful planning and administration. One of our goals is to provide a balance between current practices in early childhood education and conceptual approaches through which education and care of young children may be shaped in the future.

Another of our goals is to emphasize the leadership role in administration. We have raised issues and proposed changes to stimulate the early childhood leader to take another look at philosophy, policy, and practice, and to reexamine his own beliefs. Thus, we present examples of many options to help the leader choose alternatives or adapt suggestions to best fit the needs of the local program. Cookbook formulas are omitted, because single solutions will obviously not fit the needs of all programs. The necessity of making administrative decisions in keeping with the local program's chosen philosophy is the motif of the book.

A third goal is to provide information needed by all early childhood programs—for large and small centers and for private, public school, and federally funded centers. We have attempted to provide a balance between research and supported statements, applied ideas for implementation, and resources for further thought and consideration.

This revised and expanded edition differs from the original in several ways. Since the first edition was published, more early childhood professionals are (1) actively supporting programs for a broader age range, encompassing infants and toddlers through primary-grade children; (2) showing greater interest in day care; (3) planning for maximum development of all children, including the handicapped; (4) developing programs for a multicultural society; (5) encouraging parent participation and education as an integral part of early childhood programs; and (6) becoming involved in public policy, research, and professional ethics. The search continues for appropriate philosophies; the "best" comprehensive programming; effective methods of selecting, supervising, and evaluating staff and organizing the program; actions to fulfill regulations; functional and economical housing and equipment; and sources of funds and better fiscal planning. New chapters and expanded discussions in previous chapters have been given to these topics.

We continue to feel that a book on planning and administering early childhood programs should contain comprehensive resource information. We have expanded and updated information on equipment and materials used in early childhood programs; suppliers of early childhood equipment, books and materials; resources for program planning; overviews in chart form of many standardized tests and packaged curricular materials; synopses of professional organizations concerned with young children and additional organizations and publications of concern to early childhood educators; examples of records and reporting forms; ideas for working with parents and a sample parent's handbook; and extensive lists of additional readings for each topic.

We hope this edition will serve even better than the first as a guide for initial planning of early childhood programs and as a source of helpful information after programs are under way. The purpose of the book will be fulfilled when the reader makes wiser judgments about planning and administering early childhood programs.

Celia A. Decker
John R. Decker

Contents

1 Overview of Early Childhood Programs   1

Nature and Extent of Programs, 1
Nature of Planning and Administering Early Childhood
  Programs, 12

2 Determining Philosophy and Establishing Policies   16

Selection of a Systematic Philosophy, 16
Nature and Scope of Policies, 22

3 Planning the Program   26

Psychological Theories, 27
Programmatic Research, 28
The Child, 38
Planning and Implementing the Program, 38

4 Understanding Administrative Organization   47

Administrative Functions, 47
Administrative Organizational Patterns, 48

5 Considering Regulations   53

Regulations Governing Private Early Childhood Programs, 54
Proprietorship, Partnership, and Corporation Regulations, 64
Regulations Governing Public Early Childhood Programs, 67
Regulations Governing All Early Childhood Programs, 74
Accreditation, 82

6 Staffing   85

Trends in Staffing, 85
Roles and Qualifications of Personnel, 87
Personnel Communication, 93
Selecting Personnel, 95
Improving Personnel Qualifications, 97
Personnel Services and Records, 103

7 Supervising   111

Historical Synopsis of Supervision, 111
Functions of Supervision, 112
Qualifications of Supervisors, 118

8 Housing   122

Entry-Exit Area, 124
Outdoor Space, 140
Insurance, 146

9 Equipping   151

Purchasing Equipment and Materials, 151
Arranging Equipment and Materials, 155
Caring for Equipment and Materials, 156
Specific Equipment and Materials, 157
Community Resources, 179
Professional Library, 180

10 Planning and Scheduling Children's Activities   183

Grouping, 184
Daily Plans, 187
Special Plans, 195

11 Nutrition and Health Services   202

Nutrition, 202
Health and Safety Services, 211

12   Working with Parents   **217**

Values and Problems in Working with Parents, 217
Legal Rights of Parents, 221
Parent Involvement, 222
Parent Education, 242

13   Assessing, Recording, and Reporting Children's Progress   **256**

Assessing, 256
Recording, 268
Reporting, 276

14   Financing and Budgeting   **287**

Costs of Early Childhood Programs, 288
Financing Early Childhood Programs, 290
Budgeting, 305

15   Contributing to the Profession   **310**

Influencing Public Policy, 310
Becoming Involved in Research, 312
Developing a Code of Ethics, 313
Helping Others Find a Place in the Profession, 314

Appendix 1   State Licensing and Certification Agencies   **317**

Appendix 2   Resources for Program Planning   **320**

**Appendix 3   Professional Organizations Concerned with Young
Children**   **330**

**Appendix 4   Additional Organizations and Publications of Concern
to Early Childhood Educators**   **345**

**Appendix 5   Suppliers of Early Childhood Equipment, Books, and
Materials**   **351**

Appendix 6   Instructional Kits and Sets   **357**

Appendix 7   Parent's Handbook   **376**

Appendix 8   Tests   **389**

Index   **463**

1

Overview of Early Childhood Programs

Among the extensive and varied programs concerned with the total development of human potential, early childhood programs are in the forefront. Although these programs have had continuous appraisal based on hard data and subjective opinion, those involved with early primary programs differ sharply —and have engaged in divisive debates—concerning the ideal program for young children. The plenitude of "answers" appears today in the many forms of these programs now in the conception, planning, or operation stages.

We do know, however, that no matter which type of program is best for young children, it has a better chance of success if it is properly planned and administered. The necessity for adequate planning and administration seems self-evident; yet, judging by the frequent lack of a rational, conceptual, and systematic approach, planning and administration are often considered irrevlevant to program quality. Careful attention to the planning and administrative aspects of programs for young children can prevent costly, frivolous, and counterproductive mistakes.

Nature and Extent of Programs

Effective planning and administering begin with some perspective of the nature and extent of early childhood programs. An overview of the influential factors and the status and types of programs for young children will provide a setting from which to view the nature of their planning and administration.

FACTORS INFLUENCING EARLY CHILDHOOD PROGRAMS

Early childhood programs are the products of their exciting heritage and an expression of our society's determination to provide its young with the best.

1

Several factors appear to influence the nature and extent of today's programs. First, recent literature—stimulated by the theoretical writings of Bruner[1], Hunt[2], Bloom[3], and Piaget[4] and supported by data derived from over 200 research-based projects—reveals the growing conviction that a child's early years are crucial to the remainder of development. Because of evidence that early life experiences, including those of the newborn, influence later development, the quality of early childhood experiences is felt to determine, to a large extent, how effective later development can be. Consequently, programs designed to meet the needs of young children are receiving high priority.

Further, more and more children need care in productive group environments. Today, more than one million children come to school each year so educationally handicapped that failure is a natural consequence; there are more than one million handicapped children below the age of six, and state and federal laws now make schools responsible for these children; an increasing number of women with preprimary children are entering the work force; many unwed mothers are keeping their children and going to work or school; and there is recognition of the incapability of many parents to provide a stimulating home environment for their children. Simultaneously, on the social and research fronts, early childhood programs are no longer seen as depriving mothers of their nurturing functions, usurping the rights of the family, and producing the developmentally deprived "institutionalized" child. These programs now offer the dual possibility of providing an essential service to families and an enriched, productive environment for young children.

Finally, early childhood programs have been influenced by today's social problems. In some ways, these programs have come full circle. They are seen today, as they were under the leadership of Jean Oberlin, Friedrich Froebel, Elizabeth Peabody, Susan E. Blow, Kate Wiggin, Patty S. Hill, Maria Montessori, and Rachel and Margaret McMillan, as the best hope for reducing a significant social problem—poverty of mind and body. Until recently, except for periods of crises—wars and the depression of the thirties—most programs in the United States were private operations enrolling children from middle- and upper-class families. Of course, there were kindergartens in some of the more affluent public school systems and a few day care programs offered by philanthropic organizations in the inner cities, but it was not until the 1960s, when poverty of certain dispossessed groups of individuals was viewed as a nationwide crisis, that universally available early childhood programs were considered relevent to our economic and social needs.

There is some concern, however, over expecting our early childhood programs singlehandedly to provide panaceas or quick answers to our problems. Biber states:

> Everyone cares about education, at last—parents, businessmen, Congress, even psychologists; but who does not worry, as we scan each new legislative act, about the overloading on the school's magic, the shortsighted expectation that the school, almost alone, can erase the damages of poverty, racism, and dehumanization.[5]

Kamii also states that "it is absurd to think that we can institute 500–750 hours of preschool education without changing the 10,000 hours of compulsory education that follow preschool and kindergarten."[6] Nevertheless, the order is still large—the best preparation possible for all young children for the realities and demands of our time.

Most parents, even the advantaged—economically, educationally, and physically and emotionally healthy—often feel inadequate in trying to meet the demands of our rapidly changing society. Early childhood programs need to offer support to these parents as they help their children develop during the early years. Support for these "healthy" families may be given in the form of encouragement and guidance.

STATUS OF EARLY CHILDHOOD PROGRAMS

Early childhood programs, it would seem, come in all sizes, shapes, and philosophies, and, like most things, with all degrees of excellence. Young children and early childhood programs are big business from almost every standpoint. In fact, the 1960s and 1970s may well be recorded as the decades when early childhood programs came into their own. No longer are early childhood programs the additional service of a more affluent public school system, the special project of a philanthropic organization, an undertaking of a state welfare agency, or of a federal program. Currently, more states are providing monies for universal public school kindergartens; the federal government is funding many projects such as Head Start, the Parent-Child Center Program, and the Education Professions Development Act, as well as providing grants for research projects; businesses are operating early childhood programs; parent cooperatives are growing in numbers; universities are bombarding the scholarly market with research about young children and their programs and are producing professionals and paraprofessionals for child service programs; and the burgeoning commercial market, with its educational toys, equipment, and books, is benefiting from the present early childhood scene.

Although we know early childhood programs have greatly expanded since the 1960s, Goodlad and others find a "paucity of data regarding the whole field of preschool activity."[7] The following statistics, however, indicate increasing activity in programs for young children. For the 1976 school year, 49.2 percent of three-, four-, and five-year-olds, 31.3 percent of three- and four-year-olds, and 81.4 percent of five-year-olds were enrolled in nursery school and kindergarten. Because of a decrease in the number of births, the number of three- through five-year-olds has declined from 12.2 million in 1967 to 9.7 million in 1976. Enrollments in nursery schools and kindergartens increased from approximately 3.9 million in 1967 to 4.8 million in 1976. Nursery school enrollment doubled during this period, while increases in kindergarten enrollment was not significant. The proportion of children ages three through five years enrolled in nursery schools and kindergartens increased from approximately 32 percent in 1967 to 49 percent in 1976. For three- and four-year-olds, the increase was from

14 percent to 31 percent, and for five-year-old children, from 65 percent to 81 percent for the same time span. Black three- and four-year-old children were more apt to be enrolled than white children of the same ages, but the reverse was true for five-year-old children. There are two reasons for the growth in nursery school enrollments. First, twice as many three-year-olds were attending nursery schools. Second, the proportion of the enrolled four-year-olds in kindergarten, which was rather evenly split between nursery schools and kindergartens in 1967, shifted downward from 52 percent to approximately 36 percent enrolled in kindergarten.[8] Elementary school enrollment has been declining since the mid 1960s.[9] Statistics indicate that the proportion of mothers of three- to five-year-old children in the labor force increased from 32 to 42 percent.[10] Of Caucasian children of full-time employed mothers, approximately 54.1 percent are cared for in their own homes, 36.8 percent are cared for in other's homes, 6.6 percent in day-care centers, and the remaining have other arrangements or are not reported. Of black children of full-time employed mothers, approximately 57.7 percent are cared for in their own homes, 35.5 percent are cared for in others' homes, 2.8 percent in day-care centers, and the remaining have other arrangements or are not reported.[11] These statistics tend to indicate that more young children will be involved in early childhood programs, unless there is a decline in birthrates and/or a possible reduction in federal or state funding. Although these statistics do not tell the whole story, they are a partial indication of the present status of programs for young children.

TYPES OF EARLY CHILDHOOD PROGRAMS

One of the first problems encountered in trying to differentiate among the various types of early childhood programs is that the term *early childhood* has not been precisely defined. Educators usually define the term with equally vague synonyms, such as *young children, preschool, preprimary,* and *early primary.* Child psychologists usually define early childhood in terms of chronological age or developmental milestones, but here the agreement ends. For example, some psychologists include the chronological ages of 3.0 through 8.0 years,[12] 1.0 through 6.0 years,[13] or 2.0 through 5.0 years.[14] Others define early childhood according to the child's acquisition of the rudiments of language[15], or mastery of certain tasks in the affective[16] or cognitive domains.[17]

One simple classification of early childhood programs is by their source of funding. Generally, early childhood programs are under the jurisdiction of one of the following: (1) public schools (e.g., kindergartens); (2) private control (e.g., nurseries, kindergarten, parent cooperatives, business-operated day-care programs, and programs for young children sponsored by churches, service organizations, and charities); (3) federal programs (e.g., Head Start and Parent-Child Center Program); (4) national private agency programs (e.g., American Montessori schools); and (5) university laboratory programs (e.g., nursery, kindergarten, and primary-level schools). Closely paralleling the sources of funding are the legal forms of organization: proprietorships, partnerships, corporations, and public agencies. (For details on these legal forms of organizations, see chapters 3 and 4.)

Early childhood programs may also be described according to their origin. The following types can be historically traced: day care, Head Start and Follow Through, kindergartens, Montessori schools, nursery schools, and primary schools.

Day Care.   The term *day care* generally refers to programs that operate for extended hours (often twelve hours), and that offer services for children from 3.0 years or younger through school age. Most programs for young children are of the day-care type because they involve the care and education of children who are separated from their parents for all or part of the day. The exception to this is the night-care program.

The forerunners of day-care centers in the United States were the Infant Schools of Europe. Although these schools were conducted by social reformers in an attempt to help the poor, educators in the United States saw them as important for all young children. These Infant Schools, based on the writing of Comenius, Rousseau, and Pestalozzi, hoped to take advantage of the fact that young children learn rapidly and retain easily, to develop character, and to lay the foundation for good mental health.[18]

Medical discoveries of the mid-1800s brought greater concern with children's sanitation and health. In 1854, a Nursery School for Children of Poor Women was established in cooperation with the Child's Hospital of New York City. It was patterned after the 1844 French crèche, which was designed as day care for working French women and as a method of reducing infant mortality rates. Concern for physical well-being soon included concern for habits, manners, and vocational skills.[19]

As immigrants settled in urban areas, settlement-house day nurseries opened (e.g., Hull House nursery in 1898). These day nurseries were considered necessary to counter many social evils (such as the exploitation of women and children in the labor force) and to help alleviate immigrants' cultural assimilation problems. Education was deemed essential for true social reform. Thus, some day nurseries added kindergartens, and some were sponsored by boards of education and opened in public schools (e.g., Los Angeles, California). Parent education became a component of the day nursery's educational program. Parents were taught various household skills and management, and the care of children.[20]

Some social reformers began to feel the day nurseries might supplant the role of the family in child rearing. Consequently, emphasis was placed on the importance of mothering (i.e., nurturing), and mothers were encouraged to remain in the home. In order to help mothers "afford" to stay in the home, the Mother's Pension Act was enacted in 1911. Enthusiasm for day nurseries further declined when the National Federation of Day Nurseries drew attention to the poor quality of some programs. Concern over the appropriateness of day nurseries stimulated the development of nursery schools in the 1920s.[21] (The history of nursery schools is discussed later in this chapter.)

Day nurseries regained their status during the Depression, when the government provided its first direct subsidy through the appropriation of monies for all day programs to combat the problems imposed by the Depression on children and on unemployed school teachers. Although they were called Works Progress Administration (WPA) nursery schools, we include them here because of their all-day schedule. Early childhood nursery school educators associated with the National Association of Nursery Education, the Association of Childhood Education, and the National Council on Parent Aid became active in supervising and training teachers for WPA nursery schools by forming an advisory committee to assist the Washington Office in field services and in developing guides and records.[22]

Federal funds for all-day child care were again provided by P.L. 137 (the Lanham, or Community Facilities, Act) of 1942. The purpose of the funds was to provide for the child's physical needs, and nursery school educators again assisted. Outstanding examples of such centers were the two Child Service Centers established by Kaiser Shipyards in Portland, Oregon, and directed by Lois Meek Stolz and James L. Hymes, Jr.[23] Support ended with termination of the Act in 1946. During the Korean War, appropriation of funds under the Defense Housing and Community Facilities and Services Act (1951) was negligible.[24]

The Economic Opportunity Act (1964) funded Head Start, day-care services for migrant workers, and day care for children whose parents were involved in the various manpower projects. The Housing and Urban Development Act, Title VII (1965), The Model Cities Act (1966), and the Parent and Child Centers (funded with Head Start monies) also assisted the day-care efforts.

There is not total agreement as to the differences in day nurseries and nursery schools. Some writers indicate that in the 1930s, day care was an essential part of child welfare programs. Efforts were made to differentiate between day care as a philanthropic activity and nursery school as an educational activity, as noted in the following statement: "this purpose (care and protection), the reasons for which a family and child may need it, and the responsibilities shared with parents distinguish a day-care service from educational programs."[25] Others believe that nursery school thinking was assimilated by workers prior to World War II, in that day-care programs, in keeping with nursery school philosophy, see the teacher as assisting the child in each developmental stage, use play as the core of their curriculum, and seem to place language and intellectual development slightly behind children's physical and affective well-being.[26] There are perhaps more theoretical similarities than differences, and some advocate that there should be none.[27]

With the exception of the federally-funded Head Start program (which may not be classified as day care by some professionals, although it falls under a broad definition of day care), most day-care centers are profit-making, privately-operated efforts. The remaining day-care programs are sponsored by various organizations such as state and local governments, industries, labor unions, women's organizations, parent cooperatives, churches, university campus organizations, hospitals, and small businesses, such as those found in shopping centers. These day-care centers are operated on a for-profit or not-for-profit basis. Some variations in day-care programs are:

1. *After-school programs.* These programs are for older children from ages 6.0 to 12.0 years who need care after school hours.[28]

2. *Drop-in centers.* Drop-in centers provide occasional, part-time care for preschoolers. For example, they may be located in shopping areas for the temporary convenience of customers.[29]
3. *Family day-care homes.* Family day care usually refers to care given in a child's own home or in someone else's home. The care giver may be a relative or nonrelative. The Westinghouse/Westat attitudinal and satisfaction surveys of day-care users indicate the importance of family day-care homes. According to the study, parents use these criteria, in descending order of preference, in choosing among local options: closeness to home, cost, convenience of hours, sick child care, and program (i.e., education).[30] Legally, the family day-care program is under the supervision of the state social service agency,[31] but as noted in chapter 4, many family day-care homes are not in compliance with this regulation.
4. *Infant group-care programs.* These are day-care programs for babies and toddlers under 2.0 years. Good programs in infant group care provide for at least two qualified people for each group of four to six infants.[32]
5. *Play schools.* Play schools, usually administered by a city's recreation department, offer supervised play experiences for preprimary children.[33]
6. *Parent cooperatives.* Parent cooperatives have these unique features: (a) they are not-for-profit programs; (b) cooperative nurseries are operated and administered by parents; (c) on a rotating basis, mothers assist a qualified teacher in the program; (d) there is often an adult education program; and, (e) they are financed through fees, tuition, and fund-raising projects.[34]
7. *Public school centers.* These centers may serve children of teachers, of migrant workers, mothers on welfare who are seeking employment or training for jobs, or parents who work nights and need daytime rest.[35]

Head Start and Follow Through Programs.   In 1964, the federal government asked a panel of child development experts to develop program guidelines to help communities overcome the handicaps of disadvantaged preschool children. The report became the blueprint for Project Head Start, launched as an eight-week summer program by the Office of Economic Opportunity in 1965. Today, Head Start serves children from age three to school entry in a full-year program. In 1969, Head Start was delegated from the Office of Economic Opportunity to the Office of Child Development (HEW), and now has become a program within the Office of Human Development (HEW). The program is now authorized by the Head Start Economic Opportunity and Community Partnership Act of 1974 (P.L. 93-644). Head Start is locally administered by grantees within community-based organizations such as Community Action Agencies and public school systems.

The four major components of Head Start are education, health, parent involvement, and social services. Head Start programs provide these additional services:

1. Head Start has carried out a 1972 Congressional mandate requiring that at least 10 percent of its national enrollment consist of handicapped children, and is now applying that mandate on a state-by-state basis.
2. Head Start also provides career development and training. Local Head Start programs inform the HEW Regional Office of Child Development or the

Head Start Indian and Migrant Programs Division of their training needs. Also, the Head Start Supplementary Training Program gives professional and nonprofessional employees the opportunity to study at colleges and universities in courses that lead to degrees in early childhood education or to Child Development Associate credentials.

3. Head Start launched a series of experimental demonstration programs. Many of these programs are still in existence, although some were completed as "demonstration" projects:

    a. Home Start—a three-year demonstration project, completed in 1975, provided services to children and parents in their homes.

    b. The Child and Family Resource program—makes family-type services available for children from birth to age eight. Selected Head Start programs are used to develop community-wide systems linking services to children and families.

    c. The Developmental Continuity Project—pilot programs involve Head Start staff meetings with school administrators, teachers, and parents to plan programs to insure Head Start children continuity in curriculum, parent involvement, and social services through the third grade.

    d. Child Development Associate training in pilot programs is funded by the Office of Child Development and in Head Start Supplementary Training programs.

    e. Parent and Child Centers in 33 communities provide comprehensive services to low-income families with children to age three.

    f. Head Start has worked with the Social and Rehabilitation Service of the HEW to help make early and periodic screening available to Medicaid-eligible Head Start children.

Research indicated that the initial eight-week summer program of Head Start did not have enough impact on the enrollees' developmental lag. One of the problems was that kindergartens and primary grades were not prepared to build on the educational benefits of the Head Start experience. Thus, President Johnson requested Congress to "preserve the hope and opportunity of Head Start with a 'follow through' program in the early primary grades."[36] Follow Through was legislated in conjunction with Head Start in the 1967 amendment to the 1964 Economic Opportunity Act. This has now been superseded by the Community Services Act of 1974, P.L. 93-664—Title V, entitled, "The Head Start-Follow Through Act." Because Follow Through was directed toward children already enrolled in school, the U.S. Office of Education administers the program.

Appropriations for Follow Through were much smaller than had been anticipated. Consequently, Follow Through was originally research- and demonstration-oriented. Follow Through is now emerging as both a research-oriented and social action program because local school districts are absorbing more and more of the program's costs.

Kindergartens.   Kindergartens are publicly or privately operated programs for four- and five-year-old children. More specifically, the term *kindergarten* is used to define the unit of school which enrolls five-year-olds prior to entrance into the first grade.

Historically, the kindergarten (children's garden) was an 1837 German institution which enrolled children 3.0 through 7.0 years and provided teaching suggestions to mothers of infants. As the founder of the kindergarten, Friedrich Froebel's farsighted contributions included: (1) freedom of movement for the child; (2) a planned sequence of activities centered on the "gifts" (i.e., small blocks for building, developing mathematical concepts, and making designs), reinforced by the "occupations" (i.e., craft work) as well as other activities, and surrounded by a verbal envelope (i.e., poems, songs, storytelling, and discussions); (3) the emphasis on the relationship and orderliness among ideas; (4) the education of mothers, nurses (babysitters), and prospective kindergarten teachers; and (5) the desire that the kindergarten become a state-supported institution.

Kindergartens came to the United States in 1855 via a German immigrant, Margarethe Meyer (Mrs. Carl) Schurz. Although many kindergartens became English-speaking institutions, following the endeavors of Elizabeth Peabody, the kindergartens were philosophically a Froebelian transplant. When the progressive child study movement began in the early 1900s under the direction of G. Stanley Hall, a divisive debate ensued between the conservative, Froebelian kindergarten leaders (under the direction of Susan E. Blow) and the progressive kindergarten leaders (headed by Patty S. Hill). The progressives gained control of the kindergarten leadership and replaced the Froebelian curriculum with a more nonstructured curriculum, which lasted virtually unchanged until the 1960s' emphasis on more academic-type programs for young children.

Kindergartens have increasingly become an integral part of public school education. In the decade between 1870 and 1880, there were only two public school kindergartens, in St. Louis, Missouri, and Forrestville, Illinois. However, the number of public school kindergartens grew at a more rapid rate between 1890 and 1900.[37] By 1925, 40 states had enacted laws for the establishment of kindergartens.[38] Along with increased legislation favorable to the kindergartens, there was a numerical expansion of the kindergarten. Because of the expansion from 1900 to 1930, many efforts were made to determine the role of kindergarten in primary education.[39]

During the Depression, kindergartens were dropped out of school systems in a wholesale fashion, or were maintained under over-crowded, understaffed, and inadequately equipped conditions. Carr[40] discusses the reasons school boards gave for eliminating or maintaining kindergarten services. Many organizations, such as the Association of Childhood Education, tried to prevent the loss of public school kindergartens;[41] however, the Depression was devastating to the growth of the public school kindergarten.

Since the 1940s, there has been steady and vigorous growth in enrollment in public school kindergartens.[42, 43] Because theory and research published in the sixties have indicated the importance of early education for all children, there has been increased state and local financial support for public school kindergartens in the last two decades. Although 81 percent of five-year-olds are enrolled in group settings, kindergarten enrollment has slowed somewhat during the last decade, because four-year-olds previously enrolled in kindergartens are now enrolled in nursery schools.[44] As kindergartens become a more integral part of primary education, the "best" programs for five-year-olds must be sought. Headly has stated that the use of the "K" has made the kindergarten appear to be an "integral part of the education program" and yet "somewhat different than grade-school education,"[45] when the span of education is referred to as K–3, K–6, et cetera.

Montessori Schools.   Maria Montessori, an Italian medical doctor who had become interested in mentally handicapped children, founded the *Casa dei Bambini* (Children's House) in Rome in 1907. Slum children, between the ages of 2.6 and 7.0 years, attended the all-day program. Some of Montessori's contributions included the ideas that: (1) parents should be given training in child development and regulations for extending the principles taught to their children; (2) parents collectively owned the "Children's House"; (3) children taught themselves through self-correcting materials with minimal guidance from adults; (4) children worked with Montessori-designed didactic materials (i.e., materials of various graded stimuli, such as weighted wooden tablets), engaged in realty-oriented practical-life exercises (i.e., care of the environment and of self), and were instructed in the skill areas of language, reading, writing, and mathematics; and (5) children could grasp academic-type learning. Although Montessori's ideas met with sudden death in the United States in the 1920s, an Americanized version was introduced with the opening of the Montessori School in Greenwich, Connecticut (1958) and with Rambusch's publication, *Learning How to Learn: An American Approach to Montessori* (1962).[46]

Nursery Schools.   *Nursery school* is the term applied to facilities planned for three- and four-year-old children, although some nursery schools serve two-year-olds and others provide services for five-year-olds, where kindergartens are not available. However, the term *nursery school* is difficult to define. Goodlad, Klein, and Novotney state:

> This country's nursery schools appear to constitute a loose array of individual institutions about which relatively little is known, over which no governmental body exercises clear-cut authority, among which communication is minimal, and within which there are few signs of an intellectual expertise of self-study and improvement.[47]

Nursery schools developed in the twentieth century. Rachel and Margaret McMillan worked in the slums of London several years prior to the passage of the Education Act of 1918 to provide tax money for services to children aged two to five years. These nursery schools, as they were named by the McMillan sisters, attempted to meet the basic needs of young children which could not be provided by families living in the slums, and to educate each child.[48] The English nursery schools emphasized the necessity of working with mothers; cooperation between home and school was needed "to provide a suitable environment for the child's growing mind."[49]

With the advent of nursery schools came the decline of day nurseries and the beginning of scientific child study. Day nurseries declined when mothers were encouraged to keep their children home. However, those involved in scientific child study felt that parents at all socioeconomic levels failed to provide the "best" for their children. In contrast to day nurseries and even to the English nursery schools, nursery schools in the United States were a middle- and upper-class institution. Common philosophies of these nursery schools were that: (1) young children have a developmental need for group association with peers; (2) play is beneficial for investigation of environment and for alleviating emotional stress; (3) children should begin the process of social weaning, that is, becoming detached from parents; (4) routine bodily functions of sleeping, eating, and eliminating should be managed; and (5) teachers should provide guidance and guard against emotional stress.[50] Parent education and participation, often an admission requirement, emphasized child development and observation in home and school.[51]

Because the scientific child study movement attracted people from many disciplines, nursery schools had somewhat different objectives. In 1915, in New York City, Eva McLin opened the Child Education Foundation, which was operated according to Montessori theory and method. Also opened in 1915 was the Parent Cooperative Nursery School, operated by faculty wives at the University of Chicago.[52] In 1919, Harriet Johnson, a nurse, established a nursery school in the City and County Schools in New York City, sponsored by the Bureau of Educational Experiments (later called Bank Street), and structured its program according to facts of growth and development.[53] Patty S. Hill, leader of the reform kindergarten movement, helped initiate a laboratory nursery school at Columbia Teachers College in 1921, for the purpose of curricular research.[54] Abigail Eliot, a social worker, began Ruggles Street Nursery School in Boston in 1921 for physical, educational, and guidance purposes. Many children who were under the care of Dr. Douglas Thom, a child psychiatrist, attended the Ruggles Street Nursery School. The nursery school operated according to his direction, and helped mothers follow the psychiatric advice.[55] Research in child development was the major objective of the University of Iowa's Child Welfare Research Station, opened in 1921.[56] The Merrill-Palmer Institute was begun in 1922 by a home economist, Edna Noble White, who used the nursery school as a laboratory for training in child care.[57] The Yale Guidance Nursery, founded in 1926 by Gesell, was for purposes of helping children with emotional problems. The nursery school operated in conjunction with the Yale Psycho-Clinic.[58]

As mentioned before, nursery school educators provided leadership for the Works Progress Administration nursery schools and for those established under the Lanham Act during World War II. Thus, nursery schools have assisted all classes of children, have been funded privately and through federal, state, and local legislation, and have operated in research centers, universities and colleges, public schools, and privately owned centers.

Primary Schools.   The original purpose of primary schools in America was to instruct children in the 3 R's, especially in reading. This purpose was expounded in the Preamble to the Puritan School Law of 1647 (commonly referred to as the "Old Deluder Satan Law"). The methodology was rote memorization and recitation. During the eighteenth century, the schools were seen as a unifying force for the emerging America. State support of education and the concept of free, universal education were born during this century. Curriculum and methodology changed in the primary schools of the nineteenth century. The schools began to add aesthetic education, nature study, geography, and physical education to the 3 R's curriculum. The Pestallozzian system of an activity-oriented methodology was accepted and the still frequently-used unit-system of teaching evolved from the nineteenth century Herbartian method. "Normal schools" began teacher-training programs as the need for trained teachers emerged. Although primary schools have continued to change with the demands of the time, many people still consider them the level at which skill subjects of reading, writing, and arithmetic must be mastered and content subjects (e.g., science and social studies) introduced in a more structured atmosphere than is found in most preprimary programs.

Summary.   Regardless of whether an early childhood program is classified according to its source of funding or its legal form of organization, or whether it is historically traced, most programs tend to fit into one of these three categories:

Custodial—a program concerned with the child's physical well-being and safety, without any direct attempt to educate or to provide for psychomotor, cognitive, and affective developmental needs.

Developmental care—a program interested in the child's developmental needs, such as psychomotor development, cognitive development, language, self-concept, and social relationships.

Comprehensive child care—a program which provides developmental care and also includes a full range of support services, such as health care, parent training, family social services, and special teacher training.

Nature of Planning and Administering Early Childhood Programs

Variety among the early childhood programs is commonplace, although there is general consensus regarding the importance of the child's early years and the need for early childhood programs. Many unresolved issues have arisen from this kaleidoscope of programs for young children, such as choice of goals, policies, content of the curricula, methodology, types of equipment, housing specifications, personnel matters, and evaluation, recording, and reporting practices. Research may eventually resolve many of these issues with a one-answer solution or, more likely, indicate the necessity for alternative patterns to meet the needs of our diversified population. We are thus left with many decisions; it becomes the responsibility of those organizing early childhood programs to plan and organize their programs in ways consistent with their chosen philosophical stances.

Adequate planning and administration will mean that the environment provided and the services rendered are efficiently managed in ways that are in keeping with the program's goals and the legal and/or funding agency's regulations, and which are stimulating and supporting to those involved. Planning and administering local early childhood programs must be commensurate with contemporary needs and available resources. Planning entails the following five-step process: (1) identifying legitimate goals for the local early childhood program; (2) communicating these goals to those who will help in planning and administering the program; (3) determining the process by which these goals will be met; (4) operationalizing the means for their achievement; and (5) providing for feedback and evaluation.

The first step in planning an early childhood program is to develop a philosophical foundation and incorporate its goals into the curriculum. From this point, there is no linear progression in planning an early childhood program. In fact, all other aspects of planning should be considered simultaneously, because all facets influence and operate on each other.

Although the remaining chapters of this book offer no cookbook formulas, we feel that ingredients must match the label. In short, there should be a sense of congruity between the philosophy and each of the other aspects of the local program.

NOTES

1. Jerome S. Bruner, *The Process of Education* (Cambridge, Mass.: Harvard University Press, 1960).
2. J. McV. Hunt, *Intelligence and Experience* (New York: Ronald Press, 1961).
3. Benjamin S. Bloom, *Stability and Change in Human Characteristics* (New York: John Wiley & Sons, 1964).
4. Jean Piaget, *The Psychology of Intelligence* (Patterson, N.J.: Littlefield, Adams and Co., 1963).
5. Barbara Biber, *Challenges Ahead for Early Childhood Education* (Washington, D.C.: National Assn. for the Education of Young Children, 1969). p. 1.
6. Constance Kamii, "An Application of Piaget's Theory to the Conceptualization of Preschool Curriculum," *The Preschool in Action*, ed. Ronald K. Parker (Boston: Allyn and Bacon, 1972), p. 127.
7. John I. Goodlad, M. Frances Klein, and Jerrold M. Novotney, *Early Schooling in the United States* (New York: McGraw-Hill Book Co., 1973), p. 145.
8. Marquis Academic Media, *Standard Education Almanac*, 11th ed. (Chicago, Ill.: Marquis Who's Who, Inc., 1978–79), pp. 155–63.
9. Ibid., pp. 164–65.
10. Ibid., pp. 155–63.
11. U.S. Bureau of the Census, *Statistical Abstract of the United States: 1978*, 99th ed. (Washington, D.C.: U.S. Government Printing Office, 1978), p. 364.
12. Elizabeth M. Fuller, "Early Childhood Education," *Encyclopedia of Educational Research*, 3rd ed., ed. Chester W. Harris (New York: Macmillan Co., 1960).
13. Willard C. Olson, *Child Development* (Lexington, Mass.: D.C. Heath and Co., 1959).
14. R. I. Watson, *Psychology of the Child* (Somerset, N.J.: John Wiley & Sons, 1960).
15. Boyd R. McCandless, *Children and Adolescents* (New York: Holt, Rinehart and Winston, 1961).
16. Erik H. Erikson, *Childhood and Society*, 2d ed. (New York: W. W. Norton and Co., 1963).
17. Piaget, *Psychology of Intelligence*, 1963.
18. A. L. Kuhn, *The Mother's Role in Childhood Education: New England Concepts 1830–1860* (New Haven, Conn.: Yale University Press, 1947), p. 27.

14   Overview of Early Childhood Programs

19. I. Forest, *Preschool Education: A Historical and Critical Study* (New York: The Macmillan Co., 1927).
20. G. M. Whipple, ed., "Preschool and Parental Education," *The Twenty-Eighth Yearbook of the National Society for the Study of Education* (Bloomington, Ill.: Public School Publishing Company, 1929).
21. Forest, *Preschool Education: A Historical and Critical Study.*
22. M. D. Davis, "How NANE Began," *Young Children* 20 (1964): 106–9.
23. J. L. Hymes, Jr., "The Kaiser Answer: Child Service Centers," *Progressive Education* 21 (1944): 222–23, 245–46.
24. V. Kerr, "One Step Forward, Two Steps Backward," *Child Care Who Cares?* ed. P. Roby (New York: Basic Books, Inc., 1973), p. 166.
25. Child Welfare League of America, *Standards for Day Care Service* (New York: The League, 1960), p. 2.
26. K. H. Read, *The Nursery School: Human Relationships and Learning*, 6th ed. (Philadelphia: W. B. Saunders Company, 1976), p. 32.
27. L. B. Murphy, "The Consultant in a Day-Care Center for Deprived Children," *Children* 15 (1968): 97–102.
28. *Day Care—What and Why* (New York: Metropolitan Life Insurance Company, 1972), p. 7.
29. Ibid.
30. Westinghouse Learning Corporation and Westat Research Inc., *Day Care Survey—1970* (Washington, D.C.: Government Printing Office, 1971), Introduction.
31. *Day Care—What and Why*, p. 6.
32. Ibid., p. 7.
33. Ibid.
34. *Is This for My Child?* (Quebec: Parent Cooperative Preschools International, 1969).
35. *Day Care—What and Why*, p. 7.
36. U.S. 90th Congress, 1st Session, February, 1967. *Congressional Record*, Vol. 113, pt. 2, p. 2882.
37. N. C. Vandewalker, *The Kindergarten in American Education* (New York: The Macmillan Company, 1908), pp. 194–99.
38. N. C. Vandewalder, "Facts of Interest About Kindergarten Laws," *Childhood Education* 1 (1925): 323–25.
39. A. Temple, "The Kindergarten in America: Modern Period," *Childhood Education* 13 (1937): 358–63.
40. W. G. Carr, "The Status of the Kindergarten," *Childhood Education* 10 (1934): 425–28.
41. Association for Childhood Education, *Suggested Procedure When Elimination of Kindergartens Is Proposed* (Washington, D.C.: The Association, 1934).
42. U.S. Department of Health, Education, and Welfare, *Biennial Survey of Education in the United States* (Washington, D.C.: U.S. Government Printing Office, 1954).
43. K. A. Simon and W. V. Grant, *Digest of Educational Statistics*, 1969 ed. (Washington, D.C.: Government Printing Office, 1969).
44. Marquis Academic Media, *Standard Education Almanac*, 11th ed., pp. 155–63.
45. N. E. Headley, *Education in the Kindergarten* (New York: American Book Co., 1966), p. 42.
46. Nancy McCormick Rambusch, *Learning How to Learn: An American Approach to Montessori* (Baltimore: Helicon Press, 1962).
47. Goodlad, Klein, and Novotney, *Early Schooling*, pp. 127–28.
48. H. M. Christianson et al. *The Nursery School: Adventure in Living and Learning* (Boston: Houghton Mifflin Co., 1961).
49. Forest, *Preschool Education: A Historical and Critical Study*, p. 269.
50. Ibid., pp. 301–2.
51. M. D. Davis, *Nursery Schools: Their Development and Current Practices in the United States* (Washington, D.C.: United States Department of the Interior, Office of Education, Bulletin, No. 9, 1932).
52. Whipple, "Preschool and Parental Education."
53. H. Johnson, *Children in Nursery School* (New York: John Day Co., 1928).

54. Whipple, "Preschool and Parental Education."
55. Ibid.
56. Ibid.
57. Ibid.
58. Ibid.

For Further Reading

Almy, M. *The Early Childhood Educator at Work.* New York: McGraw-Hill Book Co., 1975.

Braun, Samuel J., and Edwards, Esther P. *History and Theory of Early Childhood Education.* Worthington, Ohio: Charles A. Jones. Publishing Co., 1972.

Evans, Ellis D. *Contemporary Influences in Early Childhood Education.* New York: Holt, Rinehart and Winston, 1971.

Fallon, Berlie J., ed. *40 Innovative Programs in Early Childhood Education.* Belmont, Calif.: Fearon Publishers, 1973.

Fein, G. G., and Clarke-Steward, A. *Day Care in Context.* New York: John Wiley & Sons, 1973.

Frost, Joe L., ed. *Revisiting Early Childhood Education—Readings.* (New York: Holt, Rinehart, & Winston, 1973.

Goodlad, J.; Klein, M.; Novotney, J. M. et al. *Early Schooling in the United States.* New York: McGraw-Hill, 1973.

Hunt, J. McV. "Revisiting Montessori." In *Early Childhood Education Rediscovered—Readings,* edited by Joe L. Frost, pp. 102–22. New York: Holt, Rinehart & Winston, 1968.

Katz, L. G., ed. *Current Topics in Early Childhood Education,* Vol. I. Norwood, N.J.: Ablex Publishing Company, 1977.

———. *Current Topics in Early Childhood Education,* Vol. II. Norwood, N.J.: Ablex Publishing, 1979.

King, Edith W. *Educating Young Children—Sociological Interpretations.* Dubuque, Iowa: William C. Brown Co., 1973.

Montessori, Maria. *The Montessori Method.* Cambridge, Mass.: Robert Bentley, 1966.

Parker, Ronald K. *The Preschool in Action.* Boston: Allyn and Bacon, 1977.

Publications Committee of the National Association for the Education of Young Children, eds. *Montessori in Perspective.* Washington, D.C.: National Assn. for the Education of Young Children, 1966.

Read, Katherine H. *The Nursery School—A Human Relationships Laboratory.* 6th ed. Philadelphia: W. B. Saunders, 1976.

Snyder, Anges. *Dauntless Women in Childhood Education—1856–1931.* Washington, D.C.: Assn. for Childhood Education International, 1972.

Weber, Evelyn *The Kindergarten: Its Encounter with Educational Thought in America.* New York: Teachers College Press, Bureau of Publications, Columbia University, 1969.

2

Determining Philosophy and Establishing Policies

Few of us have a systematic philosophy about the education of young children or early childhood programs. Some broad philosophical differences in these programs were identified in chapter 1. Because research is incomplete, we do not know which is the best program. The eclecticism in philosophy prevents tidy classifications of programs. Variation in programs is also a function of the staff member's own philosophy and competence, with a good deal of tradition and habit involved.

An identifiable philosophy is the key to any successful early childhood program. The purpose of discussing the prominent characteristics of various programs is to enable those involved in program development to assess potential relevance to local needs. Once a philosophy has been developed or selected, specific program goals and objectives must be written in keeping with that philosophy.

After the philosophy and goals are determined, policies must be established. "Policies are statements of preferred means for achieving goals."[1] Thus, policies facilitate goal implementation.

Selection of a Systematic Philosophy

A philosophy is what we believe about the experiences of teaching and learning and the choices we make in controlling those experiences. Educational philosophy includes what we believe about children's growth and development and how to guide them; the broad goals of what children should learn, that is, curriculum; the methods by which they should be taught; and how we should plan and administer the program, including staffing; housing and equipping; scheduling; providing nutrition and health services; working with parents;

assessing, recording, and reporting children's progress; and financing and budgeting. In most cases, the individuals involved in early primary programs are free to choose their own philosophy; however, in some cases, federal or state guidelines may determine all or part of the program's philosophy. Regardless of the philosophy's origin, all decisions about an early childhood program should be based on that philosophy. For example, to avoid inconsistencies, the philosophy of an early childhood program is relevant in making these (as well as other) decisions:

1. What are the goals and objectives of your early childhood program—to provide an environment conducive to the development of the whole child? to teach young children academic skills? to provide intensive instruction in areas of academic deficits and thinking skills? to develop creativity? to build a healthy self-concept? to spur self-direction in learning?

2. What provisions for children's individual differences are consistent with your program's philosophy—as children develop at their own rates, should you expect the same or varying levels of achievement? are individual differences accepted in some or in all academic areas? in some or all developmental areas (psychomotor, affective, cognitive)? are activities child-chosen and appropriate to his own interest and developmental level or staff-tailored to meet individual differences? activities presented for one or several learning styles?

3. What grouping strategy is in accord with your program's rationale—homogeneous (chronological age, mental age, achievement, and/or interest) or heterogeneous groups? fixed or flexible? staff-determined or child-interest? large or small?

4. What staff roles are necessary to implement the learning environment as set forth in the philosophy of your program—persons who dispense knowledge, resource persons, or persons who prepare the environment? persons who use positive or negative reinforcement? group leaders or individual counselors? academic content specialists or social engineers? persons who work almost exclusively with young children or who provide parent education?

5. What staff positions (director, care-givers, teachers, aides, and/or volunteers) are needed to execute your program? what academic or experiential qualifications are required or desired? what type of orientation or in-service training is needed? what child-staff ratio is required?

6. What equipment and materials are required—items and materials that are self-correcting or that encourage creativeness? equipment and materials designed to stress one concept (color paddles) or many concepts (blocks)? which require substantial or minimal adult guidance? are designed for group or individual use? provide for concrete experiences or abstract thinking?

7. What physical arrangement is compatible with the educational philosophy and goals of your program—differentiated or nondifferentiated areas of specific activities? fixed or flexible areas? outside area used primarily for

learning or for recess? equipment and materials arranged for self-service by the child or for teacher distribution?

8. What schedule format is needed to facilitate your program's philosophy and objectives—a full- or a half-day schedule? same session length for all children or length of session tailored to each child's and/or parent's needs? a predetermined or flexible daily schedule based on children's interests?

9. What evaluation procedures and instruments are consistent with your program's philosophy—evaluation of staff planning, care-giving or teaching performance? of physical arrangement, utilization of space, equipment and materials? continuous or specified times for evaluation? locally developed or standardized evaluation instruments?

Many of these choices are not either/or decisions, but involve alternative choices or combinations consistent with the chosen philosophy.

DEVELOPMENTAL THEORIES INFLUENCING PHILOSOPHIES

Our decisions as to program goals, methods for coping with individual differences in children, ways to group children, nature of the staff roles, staff selection and training, type of equipment and materials, housing arrangements, scheduling format, and evaluation, are influenced by our beliefs about what is best for children. Our beliefs about children's psychomotor, cognitive, and affective development are the root of our day-to-day actions.

The staff and consultants of Educational Products Information Exchange Institute's Western Project Office identified and described three main schools of thought regarding psychological development. The first school is the *behavioral-environmental* view, in which development is seen as an accumulation of learnings. The elicited, and reinforced, responses and patterns of responses are verbal, perceptual, and motoric rather than mental behaviors. The theory receives its name, behavioral-environmental, because the environment has the dominant role in development. Two teaching approaches are based on this view. First, wait for desired behaviors to occur and reinforce them with praise or object-type rewards. Second, communicate the desired behavior verbally, or physically model the behavior, and reinforce the child for making the appropriate response following the cue. It should be noted, however, that the behavioral-environmental view places at least these two limitations on teaching: (1) what is reinforcing to one individual may not be so to another person, and, consequently, adults may be rewarding (or punishing) behavior without being aware of it; and (2) because there is a variety of reinforcement sources, there may be stronger reinforcement for certain responses outside of the room.[2]

In the *maturational-nativist* view, development is seen as the result of the maturation of structures within the individual. The dominant aspect of development is genetic make-up. Although the genes guide the process of maturation, teaching or nurturing determines the specific content of what an individual learns (e.g., naming of colors, riding a bicycle, or using proper table manners) and influences the rate and/or extent of learning. The maturational-nativist view holds that teaching is to provide educative experiences when the child shows interest, or by using direct instruction when the child is ready.[3]

In the third school of psychological theory, the *comprehensive-interactional* view, theorists see genes and environment as more or less equal in shaping development. The child develops as a result of continual coping transactions with his environment. The five main influences shaping an individual's transactions throughout his development are (1) maturation, or mainly genetic factors; (2) experience, or environmental input; (3) developmental tasks with which an individual carries on transactions with his environment; (4) consultations with other people; and (5) interaction of all the foregoing influences. There are two subdivisions of the comprehensive-interactional view:

1. The *psychosexual-personality* view emphasizes affective and personality development. The individual develops via developmental drives which he must learn to handle in socially approved ways.
2. The *cognitive-transactional* view emphasizes cognitive or intellectual aspects. The individual develops via physical and mental interactions with objects in his environment and via consultations with people. The individual's transactions with his total environment can be stored in memory, retrieved, clarified, extended, and shared with others.[4]

SCHEMATA FOR GROUPING EARLY CHILDHOOD PROGRAMS

Each type of program is based on a specific theory of psychological development. There are several schemata for grouping early childhood programs, one of which is to consider the various programs on a continuum for psycho-social to behavioral views of development. Psycho-social programs have a minimum of formal structure, and children are encouraged to select many of their own activities. Conversely, behavioral programs tend to be structured and teacher-directed.[5]

The Office of Child Development assigns early childhood programs to one of three categories, based on the degree of teacher-child interaction. These categories are (1) preacademic models, which advocate high teacher direction; (2) discovery models, which require the teacher to provide a stimulating classroom environment; and (3) cognitive discovery models which require a broad curriculum framework but no set daily structure.[6]

Bissell[7] identifies four different program types, based on the objectives of the program, the teacher-directed or child-determined strategy, and the structure or the degree of external organization:

1. The *permissive-enrichment* program has multi-faceted objectives directed toward development of the whole child. The children's needs determine the types of informal experiences provided. These programs are "essentially adaptations of adjustment-centered preschools designed for middle class children."[8]

2. The *structured-cognitive* program has objectives "oriented towards the development of aptitudes and attitudes related to learning processes and with heavy emphasis on language growth."[9] The learning activities are prescribed by the teacher and, in many of these programs, concepts taught during structured periods are reinforced and expanded during directed play periods.

3. The *structured-informational* program aims at teaching information, especially language patterns. Similar to the structured-cognitive program, the learning activities are teacher-prescribed. However, because the major objective of the structured-informational program is to convey specific information, it is more structured than the structured-cognitive program.

4. The *structured-environment* program, or *prepared-environment* approach, has as its objective the development of learning processes. Structure results from the children's use of self-instructing or self-correcting classroom materials, and flexibility comes from the children's freedom to choose among the materials.

Another way of grouping curriculum models was developed around the initiating and responding roles of both teacher and child. The four groupings are (1) the *child-centered* curriculum, in which the teacher is the guide and resource person and the child the initiator of activities; (2) the *programmed* approach, in which the teacher initiates and implements the program and the child responds to teacher and materials; (3) the *open-framework* curriculum, in which the teacher both initiates ideas and responds to the child's activities; and (4) the *custodial* program, centered around protection rather than education of the child.[10]

Mayer[11] made a comparative analysis of preschool curriculum models which led to these four groupings:

1. The *child-development* model, which has been the pattern for most preschools serving middle-class populations, is based on the psychological belief that affective development fosters cognitive development. The curriculum consists of activities in interest centers and field trips in the community. Teachers do not prescribe the activities, and children are free to choose and change activities according to their own desires. In the child-development model, teacher-child interaction is low, child-material interaction is high, and child-child interaction is moderate.

2. The *sensory-cognitive* model, generally a Montessori-type program, is based on the psychological assertion that cognitive development influences affective development. The classroom is one of quiet activity, where children may choose any of the materials for perceptual and conceptual development and work at their own pace. Because most of the materials are self-instructing, the teacher only occasionally demonstrates the use of a particular item. Teacher-child interaction is low, child-material interaction is high, and child-child interaction is moderate.

3. The *verbal-cognitive* model has taken the stance that there is a mutual relationship between cognitive and affective development. The interest

centers of the verbal-cognitive model are essentially like those of the child-development model. In the verbal-cognitive model, however, learnings and the sequence of learnings are somewhat prescribed by the teacher, because the teacher plans the activities to be presented in the interest centers and develops activities for small-group and whole-class presentation. Teacher-child, child-material and child-child interactions are all high in the verbal-cognitive model.

4. The *verbal-didactic* model, a teacher-prescribed curriculum, is based on the position that cognitive development fosters affective development. Children, who are ability-grouped, receive direct instruction in language, reading, and arithmetic, and have shorter blocks of time for music and semistructured play. Teacher-child interaction is high, child-material and child-child interactions are low.

Ellis[12] notes four basic philosophies stemming from developmental theories:

1. The *cognitive-interactionist* model focuses on the theory of Jean Piaget. In the Piagetian model, the child is an active learner who adapts to his environment. Some of the programs associated with this model include the Montessori, the Weikart Cognitively Oriented Curriculum, the Nimnicht Response Model, and the British Primary Open School Models.

2. The *affective-interactionist* theoretical framework is based on Erikson's theory of psychosocial development that encompasses the learning of basic attitudes and ways of interacting with others. The model advocates the child's matching a skill to a learning task. Curriculum models that reflect Erikson's theory are the Bank Street program and the Educational Development Center.

3. The *behavioristic-theoretical* framework's most notable proponents include Skinner, Bereiter, and Englemann. They view the nature of the learning process as observable, measurable change in behavior directly transmitted through teaching. The child operates on his environment in response to cues and discriminative stimuli. The role of the teacher is to prescribe objectives and tasks, use direct teaching, and selectively reinforce specific behavior. The Demonstration and Research Center in Early Education and the Academically Oriented Preschool are examples of this model in action.

4. The *development-maturationist* model was developed by such theorists and researchers as Gesell, Ilg, and Ames. These researchers feel the learning process is best aided by a rich, nonoppressive environment supportive of natural development. Discovery, traditional, and play schools best exemplify this model.

As you have undoubtedly noticed, the foregoing classifcations indicate considerable differences in the amount of formal structure found in early childhood programs. Such an indication of real differences in programs lends credence to the necessity for considering various philosophies as a first step in planning an early childhood program. For more information on the specifics of the various early childhood models, the following may be consulted:

Chow, S. H. L., and Elmore, P. *Early Childhood Information Unit*. New York: Education Exchange (EPIE) Institute, 1973.

Evans, Ellis. *Contemporary Influences in Early Childhood Education*, 2nd ed, New York: Holt, Rinehart & Winston, 1975.

Fallon, Berlie J., ed. *40 Innovative Programs in Early Childhood Education*. Belmont, Calif.: Fearon Publishers, 1973.

Hechinger, Fred M., ed. *Pre-School Education Today*. Garden City, N.Y.: Doubleday and Co., 1966.

Hess, Robert D., and Bear, Roberta Meyer. eds. *Early Education*. Chicago: Aldine Publishing Co., 1968.

Maccoby, Eleanor E., and Zellner, Miriam. *Experiments in Primary Education*. New York: Harcourt Brace Jovanovich, 1970.

Parker, Ronald K. *The Preschool in Action*. Boston: Allyn and Bacon, 1977.

Weber, Evelyn. *Early Childhood Education: Perspectives on Change*. Worthington, Ohio: Charles A. Jones Publishing Co., 1970.

Nature and Scope of Policies

Policies are judgments which express a program's intentions for achieving certain purposes (e.g., in-service education of staff, budgetary priorities, and program evaluation). Although practices exist in any early childhood program regardless of whether or not written policies exist, policies establish the bases for authoritative action. Specific courses of action based on policies are referred to as regulations, procedures, and practices.

Formulation of policy is the responsibility of the board of directors or the board of education, and execution of policy in the responsibility of the program's director. There is a great deal of interchange between the board and the director. For example, the director should inform the board of needs for additional policies or changes in existing policies, of inconsistencies in policies, and of the community's attitudes and values; the board should provide adequate written and verbal reasons for and explanations of policies to facilitate execution, and should suggest methods of executing policy.

REASONS FOR POLICY ESTABLISHMENT

1. In many states, the state licensing agency and the state board of education require that programs under their respective jurisdictions have written policies covering certain aspects of the local program, and these policies must be in keeping with the restrictions and authorizations of state law.
2. Policies provide guidelines for achieving the program's goals. Inadequate policies or their absence result in: (a) hesitancy on the part of the director, because he never knows whether his decisions will result in endorsement or admonishment; (b) running from emergency to emergency; and (c) inconsistency in making decisions.
3. If policies are constant and apply equally to all, they assure fair treatment. Policies thus protect the program, staff, children, and parents.
4. Policies provide a basis for evaluating exisitng plans and for determining the merit of proposed plans, and are thus usually required by various funding agencies.
5. Policies may be requested by auditors.

CHARACTERISTICS OF VIABLE POLICIES

Developing viable policies requires that boards examine their potential reliability in facilitating achievement of the program's goals, overcome the frequently prevailing tradition of operating a program by expediency, understand the technique of policy making, and devote the time required for planning and evaluating policy. Some of the characteristics of viable policies are as follows:

1. Local program policies must conform to state law, to the policies of the funding agency, and/or the policies of any other regulatory agency. The autonomy of local programs in providing care for and education of young children (i.e., developing local policy) has given way, in varying degrees, to policy and regulations of federal and state agencies (e.g., Federal Interagency Day Care Regulations). Some of these regulations may provide a needed protective role, but they also place serious constraints on the local program, for example, by assessing children's progress by a specified assessment device, which in turn shapes the program accordingly, or by limiting funds for staff and equipment, which makes it impossible to operate "the best" program. (Additional discussion of how programs are affected by the policies of funding agencies are included in chapter 3; some of the ways in which early childhood leaders can affect public policy are discussed in chapter 15.)

2. Policies should cover all aspects of the local program, or at minimum, should cover those situations which occur frequently.

3. Internally consistent (noncontradictory) policies should be developed for the various aspects of the program. There is greater likelihood of consistency among policies if the philosophy and goals have been previously determined.

4. Generally speaking, policies should be followed consistently. When exceptions are necessary, they should be stated or allowed for in the policy. Many requests for exceptions often indicate a need for policy changes.

5. Policies should not be highly specific, as they are guidelines for establishing administrative consideration and action. The administrator should be allowed discretion in solving the day-to-day problems. Furthermore, if policies are specific, they must be changed frequently. The "specifics" should be stated in the rules, regulations, and procedures developed from the policies. For example, the fee policy should indicate criteria for assessing fees, and the fee regulation should state the specific amount charged.

6. Policies should be written and made readily available, so they can be interpreted with greater consistency by those concerned. A written policy minimizes the probability of sudden changes. Because the board formulates policy, the board can make changes at its discretion; however, the board feels the necessity for explanations more frequently when policies are written than when they are not.

7. Policies should be relatively constant. Policy should not change with changes in the membership of the board. As has been noted, the "specifics" (rules, regulations, and procedures) can change without resulting in a change of policy.

8. Local program policies should be subject to review and change, as their validity rests on current state laws and regulations of other agencies. Because of the necessity of having adequate and current policies, a procedure requiring periodic review of all policies may be written, or certain policies may be written containing a stipulation that they be reviewed by the board a year from the date they go into effect.

POLICY CATEGORIES

As mentioned, policies should cover all aspects of the local early childhood program. Because of variations in programs, the categories of policies, and especially the specific areas included in each category, differ from program to program. Most early childhood programs use the following five categories:

1. *Administrative policy.* Some specific areas included are the make-up of the board and procedures for selecting or electing board members; the appointment and functions of the director and supervisory personnel; and the administrative operations, such as the "chain of command" and membership and functions of various administrative councils and committees.
2. *Staff-personnel policy.* Areas covered often involve: recruitment, selection, and appointment; qualifications; job assignment; evaluation; tenure; separation; salary schedules and fringe benefits; absences and leaves; personal and professional activities; and who on the program staff has access to which kinds of records.
3. *Child-personnel policy.* This category may comprise: admission; attendance; program services; termination of program services; assessing and reporting children's progress; provisions for child welfare (e.g., accidents and insurance); and special activities (e.g., field trips and class celebrations).
4. *Business policy.* Some areas included are sources of funding; nature of the budget (e.g., preparation, adoption, and publication); categories of expenditures; guidelines and procedures for purchasing goods and services; and system of accounts and auditing procedures.
5. *Records policy.* Some areas included are the types of records to be kept; designation of "official" records versus "staff-members" notes; place where records are kept; which official will be responsible for records; and basic procedures for handling provisions of P.L. 93–380, "Family Educational Rights and Privacy Act of 1974."
6. *Parents' policy.* This category may comprise: ways of meeting parents' needs for participation and education; staff involvement with parents; and basic procedures for parents to follow in making contact with the director or staff for various purposes (e.g., children's admission or withdrawal, obtaining progress reports, participation in the program, parent education, and suggestions or complaints).
7. *Public relations policy.* This category relates to: participation by the public (e.g., citizens' advisory committees and volunteers); use of program facilities; relations with various agencies and associations; and communication with the public.

NOTES

1. Van Miller, George R. Madeen, and James B. Kincheloe, *The Public Administration of Public School Systems*, 2d ed. (New York: Macmillan Co., 1972).
2. *Early Childhood Education: How to Select and Evaluate Materials* (New York: Educational Products Information Exchange Institute, 1972), pp. 11–12.
3. Ibid., pp. 12–13.
4. Ibid., pp. 13–14.
5. J. W. Klein, "Making or Breaking It: The Teacher's Role in Model (Curriculum) Implementation," *Young Children* 28 (1973): 359–66.
6. Joan S. Bissell, *Implementation of Planned Variation in Head Start. Review and Summary of the Stanford Research Institute Report: First Year of Evaluation* (Washington, D.C.: Office of Child Development, 1971).
7. Joan S. Bissell, "The Cognitive Effects of Preschool Programs for Disadvantaged Children," *Revisiting Early Childhood Education*, ed. Joe L. Frost (New York: Holt, Rinehart & Winston, 1973), pp. 223–41.
8. Ibid., p. 225.
9. Ibid.
10. David P. Weikart, "Relationship of Curriculum Teaching and Learning in Preschool Education," *Preschool Programs for the Disadvantaged: Five Experimental Approaches to Early Childhood Education*, ed. J. C. Stanley (Baltimore: John Hopkins Press, 1972).
11. Rochell Selbert Mayer, "A Comparative Analysis of Preschool Curriculum Models," *As the Twig Is Bent*, ed. Robert H. Anderson and Harold G. Shane (New York: Houghton Mifflin Co., 1971), pp. 286–314.
12. D. Ellis, "Focus on Philosophies for Educating Young Children," paper presented at the Annual Convention of the International Reading Association, May 2–6 1977. (ERIC ED 142 283)

For Further Reading

Biber, Barbara. "A Learning-Teaching Paradigm Integrating Intellectual and Affective Processes." In *Behavioral Science Frontiers in Education*, edited by Eli M. Bower and William C. Hollister. New York: John Wiley & Sons, 1967.

Butler, A. L. *Current Research in Early Childhood Education: A Compilation and Analysis for Program Planners*. Washington, D.C.: American Assn. of Elementary-Kindergarten-Nursery Educators, 1970.

———. "Early Childhood Education: A Perspective on Basics." *Childhood Education* 50 (1973): 21–25.

Cunningham, Luvern L. "The Process of Educational Policy Development." *Administrator's Notebook* 7 (1973).

Weber, Evelyn. "The Function of Early Childhood Education." *Young Children* 28 (1973): 265–74.

3

Planning the Program

Providing leadership in program planning, implementation, and evaluation is undoubtedly the major task of the early childhood administrator. Staff, housing, equipment, assessment practices, parent education programs, and everything else involved in operating a program can be justified only in terms of their contributions to the child's development. And, although program planning is the pivot for all other administrative functions, perhaps no other aspect of early childhood planning is beset with so many problems and confusions.

Problems and confusion arise from these and other factors:

1. The broadened scope of program planning is a problem to most administrators. Several years ago, programs were conceived as planned classroom experiences; the term *curriculum* was used to refer to these experiences. Today, programs still include classroom experiences, but have been extended to include planned home and community experiences; thus, the term *program* is used more frequently than *curriculum* to refer to this more comprehensive approach. Regardless of the term used, the expanded scope of the program makes planning more difficult.

2. As we will see in the next section, numerous factors determine the program. There are often conflicts among these factors, such as the discrepancies that sometimes occur between expressed parental values, especially as expressed by parents who serve on advisory boards, and professional "expertise" on what is best for children. There are also conflicts within a factor, such as the basic schisms in psychopedagogical thought concerning young children's educational needs.

3. Theories are often psychological, that is, concerned with the investigation of human behavior and development, rather than pedagogical, concerned with content and methodology of the teaching/learning process. Adapting theoretical conceptions to program goals, objectives, and activities is a major problem.

4. There are difficulties involved in comparing program results, such as research methodological problems and the discrepancy that may occur between publicized objectives and actual practice.
5. Some educators believe that curriculum content or other program aspects are secondary to factors such as staff enthusiasm and commitment.
6. Program planning and assessment have not reached maturity. In 1969, Hunt[1] stated that an early childhood program which permits the child to develop his full potential has yet to be conceived, and that it will be two decades before assessment instruments are capable of measuring true gains in I.Q.

Factors Determining the Program

The great amount of activity in program planning, implementation, and evaluation during the last two decades results, at least in part, from the fact that more people are concerned about the care and education of young children. And, although concerned adults want "the best" for the child, there is no consensus as to what is "best" (i.e., what type of intellect, skills, knowledge, and values should be fostered in the child), how we should achieve it (i.e., the type of pedagogical methodology to be used), the setting of the delivery system (e.g., the home or center), the timing of the experiences (i.e., age at which children will be involved), or how to evaluate the program. Because these problems are so complex, simple solutions are not forthcoming; however, early childhood administrators must provide leadership in deciding among the alternatives.

Many factors influence these decisions, including psychological theories, programmatic research, teachers, parental values, the profession, continuity between present and later programs, assessment, policies of funding agencies, and the child.

PSYCHOLOGICAL THEORIES

The sixties saw a great number of programs planned and implemented. Programs burgeoned for two reasons:

1. Psychological research resulted in new concepts about: the modifiability of human intelligence;[2] the significance of the early years;[3] and the variables that affect cognitive development.[4] On the other hand, more recent research [5,6,7,8] indicates that early experience is important only as a link in the developmental chain of a life span. Thus, even "the best" early experience is not sufficient for maximum development unless there is both continuity in the early experiences and a potent environment. For a discussion of the "strong early experience position" versus the "strong life span position," see:

   Goldhaber, D. "Does the Changing View of Early Experience Imply a Changing View of Early Development?" In Current Topics in Early Childhood Education, Vol. II, edited by L. Katz. Norwood, N.J.: Ablex Publishing Corp., 1979.

2. National urgency for social reform to ameliorate the problems of poverty and for academic reform for purposes of excelling in the international scientific community resulted in intervention or compensatory programs.

Thus, there was interest in cognition and learning, and curriculum reform involved greater emphasis on mathematics, science, and reading.

Early childhood educators looked to psychological theories for guidance in program planning. The theories most often used were Piaget's cognitive-developmental theory and Skinner's behavioral-reinforcement theory. In the cognitive-developmental theory, cognitive and developmental stages provided information about what to expect of children in each stage of development, furnished insight for teacher's observation of children's development, and assisted the program planner in "matching" activities to the child's developmental level. Learning theories, especially the behavior-reinforcement theory, provided insight into procedures for breaking down complex learnings into simple, sequenced steps, frequently stated as behavioral objectives, used drill and other direct teaching techniques, gave tangible rewards for reinforcement, and thus demonstrated methodology for achieving short-term objectives quickly.

In the seventies, psychologists were still interested in cognitive processes, but gave more attention to motivation and affect. Piaget,[9] Harvey,[10] and Loevinger and Wessler[11] proposed theories in which affective development can be viewed in the context of cognitive development. Limited empirical evidence[12, 13] seems to support these theories.

There are problems in adapting theories for program use, because theories are psychological rather than pedagogical in nature. In extreme efforts to "match" theory to classroom activities, children are taught tasks designed by the theorist for research purposes. Furthermore, no single theory can cover all education problems. Baldwin states:

> ... At certain points the theories deal with the same subject matter in different terminologies, but these points of contact are less common than the place where they are non-overlapping.[14]

Thus, the program planner may need to consider which theories apply to which situations. However, in adopting an eclectic theory, the greatest problem is in achieving consistency.

PROGRAMMATIC RESEARCH

Some of the early childhood programs of the sixties were thought to develop the whole child, but most were designed to correct perceived language, perceptual, and conceptual deficits of poverty children. Proponents of academically-oriented programs argued that their programs were most important in enhancing intellectual and school achievement. Discovery, or informal method, advocates see social skills and autonomy as areas of major importance to the young child. Taking a midpoint view were those who looked to Piagetian theory as a basis of curriculum design. These programs tried to influence the child's thinking and processing skills. Programs were also extended upward (e.g., Follow Though) and downward (e.g., infant and toddler programs). Interest in the effectiveness of the many programs has led to research attempting to evaluate them.

Most of the programmatic research in early childhood education dates from the mid-1960s. Because of the impetus of Head Start and other intervention programs, research was and is limited primarily to the economically disadvantaged served in these programs. Furthermore, because of the interest in cognitive development, and because the most reliable assessment devices measure cognitive functioning, program evaluations were based primarily on cognitive variables.

Major Research Studies.   Program evaluation has resulted in a wealth of information about specific programs, some generalizations, and insight into methodological problems involved in programmatic research. There are countless studies; only a few are discussed here.

1. *The Westinghouse Study—Head Start* (1968–69).[15] The Westinghouse Learning Corporation and Ohio University study revealed that Head Start programs did not appear to affect cognitive and affective development if the child attended only during the summer session; changed cognitive development but not affective development if the child attended the full-year program; did not succeed to the point that Head Start children were at or above norms on standardized tests; and were generally successful in getting parent approval of and participation in the program.

2. *Planned Variations in Head Start* (1969–70; 1970–71; and, 1971–72). Ten programs were compared in the Planned Variations:
   a. Academically-Oriented Programs:
      Englemann-Becker Distar Program
      Bushell Applied Behavior Analysis (ABA)
      University of Pittsburg Individually Prescribed Instruction (IPI)
   b. Cognitive-Discovery Programs:
      Weikart's High Scope Model
      Tucson Early Education Model (TEEM)
      Nimnicht Responsive Model
      Gordon Parent Education Model
      Responsive Environment Corp (REC)
   c. Discovery Programs:
      Bank Street
      Education Development Center (EDC) Model

Results were discussed in three annual reports corresponding to the three waves of children. Bissel's[16] first-year report showed no significant differences among the programs. Smith[17] reported these results for the second year: (a) "academically-oriented" programs significantly enhanced children's recognition of shapes, numerals, and letters; (b) children in Weikart's High Scope Model scored higher on the Stanford-Binet; and

(c) there were no significant differences between programs on pre-science or pre-math concepts or on comprehensive measures of achievement. For the third year, Weisenberg[18] found that: (a) Weikart's High Scope Model no longer appeared superior; (b) children in "academically-oriented" programs performed better than children in the other programs on certain subtests (e.g., matching and recognizing letters, reading numerals, and counting); and (c) there were no differences in results on comprehensive preschool achievement tests.

3. *Ypsilanti Curriculum Comparison Project* (1965).[19] Weikart compared a teacher-directed, language-based curriculum (Bereiter-Englemann), a cognitive-discovery curriculum (The Piagetian-Based Cognitively-Oriented curriculum); and a unit-based curriculum (traditional program). Children were randomly assigned to each of three groups, and the experiment was replicated in the following two years. The groups were compared on language and intellectual development. Weikart found that: (a) although there were no significant differences among groups, all made statistically significant increases on the Stanford-Binet; (b) differences between groups posttest scores on the Leiter International Performance Scale and the Peabody Picture Vocabulary Test were nonsignificant; and (c) children in the Bereiter-Englemann program did markedly worse than children from the other two programs on the California Achievement Test. Weikart concluded that different curricular approaches, if there is high-quality implementation, will have essentially the same impact.

4. *Karnes' Curriculum Comparison Study* (1965).[20] Karnes hypothesized that the effects of preschool education on language functioning would increase with increased structure (i.e., the degree of specificity and intensity of the teacher-child interaction). Five programs were selected for comparison. Two programs, Traditional and Community-Integrated, were less-structured; a Montessori program was moderately structured; and the Ameliorative and Bereiter-Englemann programs were highly structured. The effects of these programs on global intellectual development, language growth, academic readiness skills, and perceptual-motor development were assessed.

Results at the end of the preschool were:

a. Children in the Ameliorative and the Bereiter-Englemann performed significantly better on the Stanford-Binet than did children in the Community-Integrated or Montessori groups, but the mean score of the Bereiter-Englemann and Ameliorative groups was not significantly higher than the mean of the Traditional group.

b. In perceptual-motor development, children in the Ameliorative group had significantly better scores on the Frostig Test of Visual Perception than did the children in the other programs.

c. The Ameliorative and Bereiter-Englemann groups were superior to all other groups on the number readiness subtests of the Metropolitan Readiness Tests.

d. Children in the Ameliorative program performed significantly better

than the Community-Integrated and the Montessori groups, but not
differently from the Bereiter-Englemann and Traditional programs on
the "verbal encoding," "auditory-vocal automatic," and "auditory-
vocal-association" of the Illinois Test of Psycholinguistic Abilities. No
significant differences were found between the Bereiter-Englemann and
Traditional programs, but Montessori children had significantly poorer
scores in language than did any of the other groups.

e. No significant differences were found on the Peabody Picture Vocabulary Test.

In the second year, all children, with the exception of the Bereiter-
Englemann group, entered regular kindergarten. Results indicated that:

a. Bereiter-Englemann group was superior to other groups on the Stanford-Binet and Illinois Test of Psycholinguistic Abilities.

b. Bereiter-Englemann and Ameliorative children were superior to other
   groups on the number readiness section of the Metropolitan Readiness
   Tests.

c. The Ameliorative group was superior on the reading readiness section
   of the Metropolitan Readiness Tests.

At the end of the first grade, results of tests for the Bereiter-Englemann,
the Ameliorative, and Traditional programs were studied. Findings were:

a. No significant differences among the programs were found on the Stanford-Binet, Illinois Test of Psycholinguistic Abilities, or Frostig Test of
   Visual Perception.

b. The Bereiter-Englemann and Ameliorative groups were ahead of the
   Traditional program in the reading readiness and arithmetic sections of
   the California Achievement Tests and the Metropolitan Readiness
   Tests.

5. *Miller and Dyer's Planned Variations Study* (1968).[21] Miller and Dyer used
   four types of Head Start programs to assess effects of the program on
   cognitive, motivational, and social development. The Head Start Programs
   used were the Bereiter-Englemann program, emphasizing linguistic and
   numerical skills; the Demonstration and Research Center in Early Education program, which emphasized verbal and conceptual abilities, motives,
   and attitudes; the Montessori program, which worked with independence
   and conceputal skills via sensory stimulation; and traditional Head Start,
   which emphasized socioemotional functioning and language. Findings
   were:

   a. On the Stanford-Binet and the Preschool Inventory, there were only
      small significant differences among groups.

   b. Children in the Demonstration and Research Center in Early Education
      showed greater gains in achievement motivation, independence, and
      inventiveness than did children in other groups.

   c. Higher (but not significantly different) scores were obtained on the
      Arithmetic Test, the Basic Concept Inventory, and the Parallel Sen-
      tence Production Test by children in programs oriented toward specific
      skills; group means for each test were ordered from highest to lowest as

follows: Bereiter-Englemann and Demonstration and Research Center for Early Education, Montessori, and Traditional.

   d. Children in the Demonstration and Research Center for Early Education and Montessori programs, both of which have low amounts of corrective feedback, were superior in inventiveness as compared with children in the other programs.

Following the pre-kindergarten year, the children entered a regular kindergarten or a Follow Through kindergarten in which the Bushell Applied Behavior Analysis model was used. The findings were:

   a. Children benefited more from the Follow Through kindergarten than from regular kindergarten.

   b. Traditional Head Start experience resulted in the best long-term effects as measured by the Metropolitan Readiness Tests when the traditional program was followed by intensive-achievement oriented Follow Through.

   c. For males entering kindergarten, any type of Head Start was better than none at all.

6. *A Comprehensive Assessment of the Impact of Schooling* (1969).[22] The effects of two different types of classroom experiences on advantaged fourth-grade students were compared by Minuchin, Biber, Shapiro, and Zimiles. Children in "discovery" classes were compared with children in "academically-oriented" classes on I.Q., achievement, problem solving, moral development, imaginative thinking, and self-concept. These results emerged:

   a. Children in the "academically-oriented" groups scored significantly better than those in "discovery" groups on achievement tests and group (but not individual) intelligence tests.

   b. No differences were found between the two types of classrooms on measures of self-concept and individual problem solving.

   c. Children in "discovery" classes did better on group problem solving tasks than did children in the "academically-oriented" classrooms.

   d. No differences were found in the amounts of imaginative thinking, but responses appeared to be more "child-oriented" in "discovery" programs and more "adult-oriented" in "academically-oriented" programs.

7. *The Soar and Soar Study of Follow Through* (1972).[23] Soar and Soar chose seven types of kindergarten and first-grade Follow Through programs representing the varied philosophical types of programs from the "academically-oriented" (Bereiter-Englemann) to "discovery" (Education Development Center) for their research. They found that:

   a. Highly-focused learning resulted in pupil growth in concrete concepts.

   b. Abstract-complex development seemed to be related to optimal levels of "pupil-selected" versus "teacher-directed" activity and of "pupil initiation" versus "drill."

   c. Abstract-complex growth was related to high levels of teacher talk.

8. *Planned Variations in Follow Through* (1975).[24] Stallings examined seven variations for differences in organization of equipment, instructional set-

tings, and teacher and child behaviors at the first and third grades and related these variables to child outcomes: the academically-oriented programs were the Englemann-Becker Distar Program and the Bushell Applied Behavior Analysis (ABA); the cognitive-discovery programs were the Nimnicht Responsive Model, the Tucson Early Education Model (TEEM), and Weikart's High Scope Model; and the discovery programs were the Education Development Center (EDC) and Bank Street. Stallings found that:

a. At both first- and third-grade levels, the degree of structure (i.e., models in which children worked rather independently and individually with adults versus models in which adults worked with children in large and small groups) differentiated the classrooms.

b. Programs which permitted children to select their own groups and activities and in which adults provided individual attention (i.e., Education Development Center and Nimnicht's Responsive Model) had children who were more independent than children in other programs.

c. Children were more persistent in classrooms where printed materials were used and in which adults interacted on an individual basis (i.e., Tuscon Early Education Model and Bushell Applied Behavior Analysis) than children in classrooms in which adults interacted on a group basis.

d. Classrooms with activities and manipulatives and with adults who worked with small groups (i.e., Bank Street, Weikart's High Scope Model, and Education Development Center) had children who were more cooperative than children in other groups.

e. Where teachers responded to children's questions (i.e., Nimnicht's Responsive Model, Bushell Applied Behavior Analysis, Weikart's High Scope Model, and Education Development Center), children questioned more than children in other programs.

f. Programs which allotted more time to reading and math instruction (i.e., "academically-oriented" programs) had children who performed better on achievement tests in these areas as compared with children in other programs.

g. Higher reading scores were found in classrooms where teachers provided information, questioned and used corrective feedback techniques where workbooks and programmed texts were used.

h. High computation scores (but not problem-solving scores) were found in structured models and negatively correlated with flexible, or "open" models.

i. Children in informal classrooms had better perceptual problem-solving ability as measured on the Raven Colored Progressive Matrices than those in other programs.

j. There were no significant differences in the self-concepts of children in the various programs, as measured by the Coopersmith.

k. Children in informal classrooms were more likely to accept responsibility for their success and less likely to accept responsibility for their failure than children in teacher-directed groups. The reverse was true for the teacher-directed groups.

1. Children in "cognitive-discovery" and "discovery" programs were absent from school less often, and were thus more likely to have learned from the activities presented in their classrooms than children in other groups, who were absent more frequently.

Other Research Studies.   There have been countless other studies concerning evaluation of programs. One group of researchers directing smaller projects has organized the "Developmental Continuity Consortium," funded by the Office of Child Development through the Education Commission of the States.[25, 26] The Consortium has reported these findings:

1. Children enrolled in Head Start programs scored higher on I.Q. tests than did control children, and maintained this advantage for as long as three years after the programs.
2. Fewer children in Head Start programs were placed in special education programs or were retained in a grade after leaving the program than were the control children.[27]

Other interesting research from varied sources indicates that:

1. Children enrolled in Parent-Child Centers seem to improve in their school readiness.[28]
2. Home Start appears effective in helping children gain in I.Q.[29] and in various cognitive areas, as measured by school readiness tests.[30]
3. Exceptional children appear to be better in academic areas in structured preschool programs as opposed to the traditional *laissez-faire* situation.[31] However, it should be noted that flexibility in goals, curriculum, methodology, and scheduling within the structured framework seem essential for success.[32]
4. Developmental Day-Care Centers have produced no gains, only modest gains, for middle-class infants.[33] With the possible exception of the intensive-intervention centers for infants,[34] group day care for disadvantaged infants does not seem successful. White states:

   Although there has been a general belief that the success of preschool projects would be increased if the age of intervention were lowered, there is little concrete support for this belief.[35]

   Some believe that the appropriateness of early intervention is questionable. Social class differences in children's intellectual functioning have not been noted prior to 18 months.[36]
5. Studies have been conducted of the televised "Sesame Street" and "The Electric Company." Ball and Bogatz[37] studied "Sesame Street" for two years. They found that:

... children learn more the more they watch—this holds true across age, sex, geographic location, socioeconomic status (SES), mental age (intelligence) and whether children watched at home or at school. In all eight goal areas in which children were tested, gains in learning increased steadily with amount of viewing.[38]

Gains during the first year were found mainly in letters, numbers, and classification skills. In the second year of "Sesame Street," Ball and Bogatz[39] found mixed results for the various goal areas. However, "Sesame Street" viewers gained more than nonviewers on the Peabody Picture Vocabulary Test. The Educational Testing Service evaluation of "The Electric Company,"[40] designed to help disadvantaged children in grades one through four with reading, found positive effects for second graders in several curriculum areas and on a standardized reading test.

Problems in Programmatic Research.   Research problems are a major reason for the lack of definitve answers as to the effects of different programs in early childhood education. According to Ball and Bogatz[41] and Cooley[42] some of research's major shortcomings include: assessing program implementation, inadequate measuring instruments, establishing comparable experimental and control groups, and limitations in interpretation of data. Attrition rates have minimized the effectiveness of many longitudinal studies. Seitz *et al.*, have argued that most of these studies "have had such serious methodological shortcomings that they have been virtually uninterpretable in regard to evaluating either the short-term or long-term effectiveness of intervention."[43] Aside from methodological problems, perhaps even the idea of comparing early childhood models has its limitations. Hanson[44] argues that we should not be testing models by comparing them. She believes we should test each model by manipulation of various parameters within the model (e.g., small group versus large group).
   More research is needed to study the relationship between process variables (e.g., teacher behavior, child behavior, and classroom environment) and child outcomes; to assess curriculum areas other than reading and math; to measure specific rather than global achievement; and to develop more assessment devices for the affective domain. As we reflect on completed research and plan future research, we must also remember that statistically significant differences cannot necessarily be equated with educational or social significance.

TEACHERS

In some cases, teacher participate in selecting a program—its philosophy, goals, and objectives; in other cases, the program is determined prior to staff selection. Regardless of the teacher's role in determining the program, the teacher is the key person in implementing it. The various programs perceive a teacher's role differently: as dispenser of knowledge, preparer of environment, presenter of problems and challenges, language and attitudes model, or group leader. The instructional aspects of the teacher's role seem to have become more important in recent years. For example, programs based on behavioral theory do a great deal of direct instruction. Also, programs centered around the child's interactions with other children and with the materials rather than with teachers use teacher questioning as a means of stimulating thinking. (British Infant Schools operate this way.) Even many infant programs involve infants in interaction with adults.

There is a need for more research on the relationship of teacher effectiveness and program success. Weikart[45] believes that teacher variables may be more important in determining the success of a program than are the program's philosophy and goals. Bennett's [46] research on the relationship of teaching style and children's progress tends to support the thesis that the teacher's role is a most important variable in program effectiveness. Bennett found that there was a defined continuum of teaching styles, rather than a polarity between "formal" and "informal" classrooms. The structure of the teaching style had these effects:

1. Disadvantaged children taught in programs with teacher-prescribed objectives and direct teaching show greater achievement than children taught by an informal teaching style.
2. Anxious and insecure children do better in the structured environment.
3. In general, the least effective programs were those at extreme ends of the continuum—the very structured and the very informal.

PARENTAL VALUES

By considering parental values in the process of determining the program, greater continuity between the early childhood program and the child's home life can be achieved. Keyserling[47] found that proprietary centers were more responsive to parents' values, probably because their funds are mainly tuition fees, than were not-for-profit early childhood programs. Many see active parent involvement as a basic component of any successful early childhood program.[48] (See chapter 12.)

THE PROFESSION

Early childhood education is an interdisciplinary field; its core derives from education and child development. However, many other professions contribute to the field, such as the health and social work professions. Because the early childhood "profession" is highly involved in research, child advocacy (discussed in chapter 15), and day-to-day direction of programs, the profession becomes a major factor in determing the curriculum. (It should be noted that the field of early childhood education does not meet all the criteria of a profession.)

CONTINUITY BETWEEN
PRESENT AND LATER PROGRAMS

Generally speaking, objectives of the present program should be consistent with programs that children will be involved in later. For example, the Follow

Through program was initiated to "continue" the work of Head Start, because children who went into a traditional program from the Head Start program soon lost the advantages they had gained. Also, Miller and Dyer found that participation in one type of preschool program may interfere with learning in a later program if the programs are greatly discrepant in approach.[49]

On the other hand, the goals of any program should center on the child's present benefit, and not merely on preparation for the future. For many years, the term *readiness* had been applied to many activities of the early childhood program (e.g., reading readiness and math readiness) and even to the names of some of the assessment devices used with young children (e.g., American School Reading Readiness Test and the Metropolitan Readiness Tests). These readiness skills were considered necessary to prepare children for later schooling. For example, some intervention programs, such as the Bereiter-Englemann, were based on a philosophy of overcoming specific "readiness" deficits. Although some "readiness skills" may be appropriate learnings, and continuity between present and future programs is achieved, planning a program solely on the basis of future content is questionable for several reasons. "Readiness skills" are not goals in themselves, but means to goals; the "advantage gained" in "crash" preparation may be lost; and formal readiness training may be detrimental in itself.[50]

ASSESSMENT

Assessment of children's progress in a program is essential. If the content of the assessment instruments and the techniques used in the assessment process relate closely to the program's objectives, assessment results may be used to add to or revise content or methodology to help meet stated objectives. One must avoid the pitfall of using assessment instruments that do not match the program's goals and of letting those instruments determine content or methodology. (See chapter 13.)

POLICIES OF FUNDING AGENCIES

Funding agencies have a great deal of control over the program:

1. Legislative control over curricular content of public school programs exists via legislation of what may or may not be taught and regulations regarding textbook adoptions.
2. The local school board or the board of directors/advisors can control program content and methodology by determining what may or may not be taught, what equipment will be used in the program, what curricular assistance will be given to teachers, and how the program will be staffed, as long as they stay within the restrictions and authorizations of federal, state, and local laws, directives, and guidelines.
3. Some federal programs have established goals for their programs, such as the "Performance Objectives" of the Head Start program.
4. Program content may also be determined by a State Task Force. Usually the state board of education and/or the superintendent of education, with

approval of the state legislature, asks a committee of early childhood professionals to write a master plan for statewide early childhood education. The recommendations and implementation guidelines are then presented to the state legislature for approval.

5. Printed information, such as a curriculum guide, from the state education agency or the department that licenses child care facilities often affects program content.
6. A program seeking funding must follow the agency's guidelines, including program guidelines, in order to be funded.

The Child

Program content has always been based on the needs of the child, or at least on what adults considered those needs to be. In the past, program content was determined almost exclusively on the basis of children's normative abilities. When programs are not adapted to individual needs, we end up teaching the "hypothetical child." Each child responds to a program in terms of his personal experiences. Almy[51] uses the analogy of "filters"—she describes the child's individuality in terms of individual and developmental "filters" through which that child responds to a particular program.

Because programs must coexist with children's experiences in their homes and communities, it is imperative that administrators assess program values for particular populations. Three popluations will be used as examples:

1. As a result of legislation (P.L. 94–142), early childhood program must meet the needs of the exceptional child. Handicapped children will require individual attention in the area of their handicaps and integration into other areas of the program.
2. In order to respond to individual needs in a multicultural society, program content must be sensitive to cultural values. This sensitivity is exemplified in pluralistic education, which is based on the belief that a school's expectations should reflect the values of minority cultures as well as those of the majority. Pluralistic education goes beyond merely accepting or coping with other cultures; it involves learning how to profit from cultural diversity.
3. Program content must also meet the needs of children of both sexes from various socioeconomic groups. Herzog, Newcomb, and Cisin[52] have demonstrated that a preschool program can affect boys differently than girls and can affect children from various socioeconomic groups differentially.

In short, effective program content must match the child's developmental and individual needs, in order that he may use his repertoire of behaviors in learning—"teaching must start where the learner is."[53]

Planning and Implementing the Program

In reviewing the factors that determine the program—psychological theories, programmatic research, teachers, parental values, the profession, continuity between present and later programs, assessment, policies of funding agencies, and the child—it becomes evident that no one approach is best for all children at all times. The various program models have different educational goals. Therefore, administrators and their staffs must learn how to assess program value for particular populations of children.

DECIDING AMONG ALTERNATIVES

After carefully considering all the factors that determine the program, the administrator and staff usually develop a preference for a particular "theoretical" stance. The "ideal" program they choose is one they feel is suited to their particular children and that they can implement.

Considering Alternatives.   The first step in determining any program is to consider the alternatives. Programs tend to fall along a continuum from informal to very structured. Child development programs tend to be more informal; the case for structured preschool programs is generally made in relation to the "disadvantaged child" as a way to counteract his supposedly disorganized environment. There is no consensus regarding the optimal amount of "structure." In fact the term *structure* takes on various meanings in various programs and may refer, among other things, to teacher-child interaction, time, content, or child-material interaction.

1. *Discovery Programs.* Most researchers consider early childhood education beneficial; however, others feel that formal, structured education may not only be ineffective in terms of long-range results, but may even be detrimental to development.[54] Rohwer reports Elkind's hypothesis that "the longer we delay formal instruction, up to certain limits, the greater the period of plasticity and the higher the ultimate level of achievement."[55] Rohwer finds as much evidence to support this hypothesis as to support early schooling.[56] Advocates of the self-discovery (or child-directed learning) approach include:

   Elkind, D. "Child Development in Educational Settings." *Educational Psychologists* 12 (1976): 49–58.

   Furth, H.G. *Piaget and Knowledge.* Englewood Cliffs, N.J.: Prentice-Hall, 1969.

   Kamii, C., and DeVries, R. "Piaget for Early Education," *The Preschool in Action*, 2d ed. Edited by M.C. Day and R.K. Parker. Boston: Allyn and Bacon, 1977. Pp. 365–420.

   Lavetelli, C. *Piaget's Theory Applied to an Early Childhood Curriculum.* Boston: American Science and Engineering, 1970.

   Sigel, I. "Developmental Theory: Its Place and Relevance in Early Intervention Programs." *Young Children* 27 (1972): 364–72.

Generally, those who advocate a more informal program believe in the benefits of play beyond its obvious importance to physical well-being. According to Piaget, play is prerequisite to all intellectual processes; play develops intellect. As play changes from exploratory encounters with people and objects, to physical play, and to logical and cooperative play in organized group games, a parallel development of thought occurs. Thinking and playing are interacting forces. Furthermore, play develops the social and intellectual skills of collaboration with one's peers.[57]

Children involved in the discovery programs tend to do as well as their peers in structured programs on intelligence tests and overall achievement; however, these children tend not to do as well as their counterparts in structured programs in specific areas of achievement. Research on children involved in discovery-based programs indicated that these children do better than those in structured programs on group problem-solving tasks, prefer child-oriented activities, have a higher level of moral development, and a better self-concept,[58] and that they may be more creative than those in structured programs.[59]

2. *Structured Programs.* Structured programs tend to be intervention programs for the "disadvantaged" child. Proponents of the more formally structured programs include:

Berlyne, D.E. "Curiosity and Education," *Learning and the Educational Process*, ed. J.D. Krumkoltz. Chicago: Rand McNally, 1965, pp. 67–89.

Blank, M. *Teaching Learning in the Preschool: A Dialogue Approach.* Columbus, Ohio: Charles E. Merrill Publishing Co., 1973.

Fowler, W. "Cognitive Learning in Infancy and Early Childhood." *Psychological Bulletin* 59 (1962): 116–52.

Hunt, J. McV. *Intelligence and Experience.* New York: The Ronald Press, 1961.

There has been a great deal of programmatic research on these compensatory programs. Bissell[60] has generalized from the research that:

1. Programs with goals for fostering cognitive growth, with specific emphasis on enhancing language abilities, and with teacher-prescribed activities, are more effective in producing measurable cognitive gains than programs that do not have these characteristics;
2. Programs with a high degree of quality control, such as a well-trained staff, a low child-staff ratio, and effective supervision, are the most effective programs in producing cognitive gains; and
3. Highly structured programs tend to be more effective with disadvantaged children and equally effective with all lower-class children. Less structured programs tend to be more effective with the less disadvantaged children.

Bronfenbrenner comes to the same conclusion:

With respect to the differential impact of various curricula there can be little doubt that the more structured programs are more effective for disadvantaged children at the preschool and primary level.[61]

Programs designed to produce gains in specific areas, such as math and reading, show greater gains in those areas than do discovery programs. Evidence that children learn specific skills through direct training was observed fifty years ago, in the Iowa Child Welfare Research Station.[62] Apparently, structure is effective in developing certain skills because: (a) activities are planned around and focus on the desired outcome; (b) test items and curricular content are similar; (c) the testing process is more similar to the structured program than to the "discovery" approach, which aids children in responding to the test items; (d) structured programs offer more opportunities for taking tests than do informal programs; and (e) children know what is important to learn because of the extent of direct teaching performed in the structured approaches as compared with that of the "discovery" approaches.

DEVELOPING THE PROGRAM

When the administrator and staff have decided whether to plan a program based on the discovery approach or on the formal, structured approach, and have considered other goals, such as the need for pluralistic education and the needs of handicapped children, they will want to analyze several program models compatible with their philosophical alternatives. Several formats are used to make specific analyses of program models, including:

Almy, M. *The Early Childhood Educator at Work.* New York: McGraw-Hill Book Co., 1974, pp. 55–77.

Lay, M., and Dopyera, J. *Analysis of Early Childhood Programs.* Urbana, Ill.: Educational Resources Information Center on Early Childhood Education, May 1971.

Mayer, R.S. "A Comparative Analysis of Preschool Curriculum Models." *As the Twig Is Bent,* eds. R.H. Anderson and H.G. Shane. Boston: Houghton Mifflin, 1971, pp. 286–314.

Smith, M., and Giesy, R. "A Guide for Collecting and Organizing Information on Early Childhood Programs." *Young Children* 27 (1972): 264–71.

Whether a discovery or a structured program has been chosen, the staff should develop some objectives. Objectives are essential because they serve as the rationale for the program and allow generation and sequencing of learning activities, serve as guides for selecting equipment and materials, suggest ideas for and arrangement of the prepared environment, and/or determine the form and content of assessment. However, the specificity of the objectives often varies with the amount of program structure; in some highly structured programs, all objectives are teacher-prescribed, and in some informal programs, children are involved in planning objectives. These books explain methods of writing objectives:

Butler, A.L.; Gotts, E.E.; and Quisenberry, N.L. *Early Childhood Programs: Developmental Objectives and Their Use.* Columbus, Ohio: Charles E. Merrill Publishing, Co., 1975.

Gronlund, N.E. *Stating Behavioral Objectives for Classroom Instruction.* New York: The Macmillan Company, 1970.

Mager, R.F. *Preparing Instructional Objectives.* Belmont, Calif.: Fearon, 1962.

(For a list of available resources on program descriptions and available curriculum materials, see Appendix 2.)

EVALUATING THE PROGRAM

Administrators are held accountable for the programs under their leadership and direction. In this day of rapid change in child care and education and of demand for excellence, evaluation has become one of the administrator's most significant responsibilities. Funding and legal sources require evaluation reports; accreditation is self-evaluation based on standards set by the accrediting agency, such as a professional group; the staff objectively and subjectively judges the program; many parents are questioning program quality; and there is heightened public interest, especially on the part of taxpayers, in program value. Administrators must answer to each of these groups.

Evaluation is made difficult because administrators must determine the appropriate type of evaluation to use. Most typical is *summative* evaluation, which determines the effectiveness of a program. Standardized tests are generally used to assess children's progress in certain model programs. Chapter 13 of this book and other sources[63,64] describe some of the problems in using standardized tests for summative evaluation. Furthermore, summative evaluation is used for federal and state programs to determine the worth of the "total" program, such as Head Start on a national basis, but not the effectiveness of a specific local program, such as Head Start in a particular city. Consequently, only the effectiveness of the national or state program, as measured by a specified instrument, has legislative and policy implications. A second type of evaluation is *formative* evaluation, which determines whether a specific program is meeting its own goals. If evaluation indicates weaknesses in the program, then means of attaining the goals are implemented, or the goals are changed. Formative evaluation is becoming more popular because it is concerned with a program's stated objectives.[65,66,67]

Furthermore, evaluation is difficult because of the many components, such as facilities, curriculum and staff, which constitute a program, and the fact that evaluation is often conducted on each separate component at different times by different people. When evaluation is conducted this way, it is difficult to view program effectiveness as a whole. Also, we have few valid and reliable evaluative instruments for measuring a program's many components, with the possible exception of some of those used for measuring children's development. (For discussions on evaluation of teachers, equipment, and children, see chapters 7, 9, and 13, respectively.) Consequently, we are only on the threshold of adequate program evaluation. A promising instrument has been developed by the Georgia Assessment and Improvement Program in Early Childhood Education (GAIP).[68] The GAIP, over a three-year period (1974 to 1977), developed and validated the Criterion-Referenced Early Childhood Education Program Assessment Instrument (CRI). The 32 criteria are standards by which the quality of a program is assessed and are grouped into five components:

1. The Learning Environment, or physical facilities
2. The Program, or scope and sequence of content, utilization of materials, and degree to which reality matches program intent
3. The Teacher (Personal), or health, personality, and character of teachers
4. The Teacher (Professional), or teaching and evaluating techniques employed
5. The Management System, or support given by nonprogram personnel to program development and implementation

Indicators, or signs that the criterion is being applied, are available for each criterion. Observers use these indicators to make summary judgments concerning each critierion.

Other sources of information on instruments used for assessing the total program include:

Day Care Checklist: Home Care, Family Day Care Homes, Day Care Centers. Washington, D.C.: Day Care and Child Development Council of America, 1972.

Spodek, B. *Teaching in the Early Years,* 2d ed. Englewood Cliffs, N.J.: Prentice-Hall, 1978, pp. 314–17.

Takanishi, R. "Evaluation of Early Childhood Programs: Toward a Developmental Perspective." In *Current Topics in Early Childhood Education*, edited by L.G. Katz, pp. 141–68 Norwood, N.J.: Ablex Publishing Corporation, 1979.

————. *Evaluation for Program Development: A Primer for Staff and Parents in Child Development Programs*. Paper presented at the California Association for the Education of Young Children Conference, Sacramento, Calif., 1976. ERIC ED 128 096

Pressures for answers from within and without the program will not seem so unbearable, or the difficulties involved in overcoming content and methodological problems so insurmountable, if one keeps in mind the major purpose of program evaluation. If evaluation is seen as a means for program improvement, it becomes a continuous process, and its results become starting points for future planning.

Notes

1. J. McV. Hunt, "Has Compensatory Education Failed? Has It Been Attempted?" *Harvard Educational Review* 39 (1969): 297.
2. ————. *Intelligence and Experience* (New York: The Ronald Press, 1961).
3. B.S. Bloom, *Stability and Change in Human Characteristics* (New York: John Wiley & Sons, 1964).
4. J. Piaget, *The Origins of Intelligence in Children* (New York: International Universities Press, 1952).
5. A.D.B. Clarke, "Learning and Human Development," *British Journal of Psychiatry* 114 (1968): 1061–77.
6. A.M. Clarke and A.D.B. Clarke, *Early Experience: Myth and Evidence* (New York: Free Press, 1976).
7. J. Kagan and R.E. Klein, "Cross-Cultural Perspectives on Early Development," *American Psychologist* 28 (1973): 947–62.
8. E. Zigler, *The Effectiveness of Head Start: Another Look* (Paper presented at the annual meeting of the American Psychological Association, San Francisco, Calif., 1977).
9. J. Piaget and B. Inhelder, *The Psychology of the Child* (New York: Basic Books, 1969).
10. O.J. Harvey et al., *Conceptual Systems and Personality Organization* (New York: John Wiley & Sons, 1961).
11. J. Loevinger and R. Wessler, *Measuring Ego Development* (San Francisco, Jossey-Bass, 1970).
12. T.G. DeCarie, *Intelligence and Affectivity in Early Childhood* (New York: International Universities Press, 1965).
13. L. Murphy, *The Widening World of Childhood* (New York: Basic Books, 1962).
14. A.L. Baldwin, *Theories of Child Development* (New York: John Wiley & Sons, 1967), p. 583.
15. Westinghouse and Ohio University, "The Impact of Head Start: An Evaluation of the Effects of Head Start on Children's Cognitive and Affective Development," *Revisiting Early Childhood Education*, ed. Joe L. Frost (New York: Holt, Rinehart, & Winston, 1973), pp. 400–4.
16. J.S. Bissel, "Planned Variation in Head Start and Follow Through," *Compensatory Education for Children, Ages 2 to 8*, ed. J.C. Stanley (Baltimore: John Hopkins University Press, 1973).
17. M.S. Smith, *Some Short-Term Effects of Project Head Start: A Preliminary Report on the Second Year of Planned Variation, 1970–71* (Cambridge, Mass.: Huron Institute, 1973).
18. H.I. Weisburg, *Short-Term Cognitive Effects of Head Start Programs: A Report on the Third Year of Planned Variation, 1971–72* (Cambridge, Mass.: Huron Institute, 1974).
19. D.P. Weikart, *Comparative Study of Three Preschool Curricula* (Paper presented at the biennial meeting of the Society for Research in Child Development, Santa Monica, Calif., March 1969).
20. M.B. Karnes, "Evaluation and Implications of Research with Young Handicapped and Low-

Income Children," *Compensatory Education for Children, Ages 2 to 8*, ed. J.C. Stanley (Baltimore: John Hopkins University Press, 1973).

21. L.B. Miller and J.L. Dyer, "Four Preschool Programs: Their Dimensions and Effects," *Monographs of the Society for Research in Child Development* 40 (1975): 5–6, Serial No. 162.

22. P. Minuchin, B. Biber, E. Shapiro, and H. Zimiles, *The Psychological Impact of School Experience* (New York: Basic Books, 1969).

23. R.S. Soar and R.M. Soar, "An Emperical Analysis of Selected Follow Through Programs: An Example of a Process Approach to Evaluation," *Early Childhood Education*, ed. I.J. Gordon. Chicago: University of Chicago Press, 1972.

24. J. Stallings, "Implementation and Child Effects of Teaching Practices in Follow Through Classrooms," *Monographs of the Society for Research in Child Development* 40 (1975): 7–8, Serial No. 163.

25. V.R. Hubbell, *The Developmental Continuity Consortium Study—Secondary Analysis of Early Intervention Research*. (Paper presented at the meeting of the American Association for the Advancement of Science, Denver, Colo., Feb. 1977).

26. H.W. Murray, *Early Intervention in the Context of Family Characteristics* (Paper presented at the meeting of the American Orthopsychiatric Association, New York City, April 1977).

27. I. Lazar et al. *Preliminary Findings of the Developmental Continuity Longitudinal Study* (Paper presented at the Office of Child Development "Parents, Children, and Continuity" Conference, El Paso, Tex., May 1977).

28. M. Holmes, D. Holmes, D. Greenspan, and D. Tapper, *The Impact of the Head-Start Parent-Child Centers on Children. Final Report* (New York: Center for Community Research, December 1973), DHEW/OCD Contract No. 2997A/H/O, pp. 11–17.

29. R.D. Hess, *Effectiveness of Home-Based Early Education Programs* (Paper presented at American Psychological Association, Washington, D.C., 1976).

30. J.M. Love, M.J. Nauta, C.G. Coelen, K. Hewett, and R. Ruopp, *National Home Start Evaluation, Final Report* (Cambridge, Mass.: Abt Associates, 1976).

31. Suzan Wynne et al., *Mainstreaming and Early Childhood Education: A Guide for Teachers and Parents. Final Report* (Washington, D.C.: Wynne Associates, 1975).

32. K.E. Berry, *Models for Mainstreaming* (San Raphael, Calif.: Dimensions Publishing Co., 1972).

33. H.N. Ricciuti, *Effects of Infant Day Care Experience on Behavior and Development: Research and Implications for Social Policy* (Paper presented for the Office of the Assistant Secretary for Planning and Evaluation, DHEW, 1976).

34. S.H. White et al., "Review of Evaluation Data for Federally Sponsored Projects for Children," Vol. 2, *Federal Programs for Young Children: Review and Recommendations* (Cambridge, Mass.: The Huron Institute, 1972), p. 109.

35. Ibid.

36. B. Birns and M. Golden, "The Implications of Piaget's Theories for Contemporary Infancy Research and Education," *Piaget in the Classroom*, ed. M. Schwebel and J. Raph (New York: Basic Books, 1973), pp. 114–31.

37. S. Ball and G.A. Bogatz, *A Summary of the Major Findings in "The First Year of Sesame Street": An Evaluation* (Princeton, N.J.: Educational Testing Service, 1970).

38. Ibid., p. 4.

39. ———. *The Second Year of Sesame Street: A Continuing Evaluation* (Princeton, N.J.: Educational Testing Service, 1971).

40. ———. *A Summary of the Major Findings from "Reading with Television: An Evaluation of the Electric Company"* (Princeton, N.J.: Educational Testing Service, 1973).

41. Ibid.

42. W.W. Cooley, "Evaluations of Evaluation Programs," *Evaluation of Educational Programs for Young Children: The Minnesota Round Table on Early Childhood Education II* (Washington, D.C.: CDA Consortium, 1975).

43. V. Seitz, N.H. Apfel, and C. Efron, *Long Term Effects of Intervention: A Longitudinal Investigation* (Paper presented at the Meeting of the American Psychological Association, Washington, D.C., 1976).

44. B. Hanson, *Trends and Problems in Comparison Studies of Early Childhood Education Models* (Washington, D.C.: National Institute of Education, Department of Health, Education, and Welfare, November, 1973).

45. Weikart, op. cit.
46. N. Bennett, *Teaching Styles and Pupil Progress* (Cambridge, Mass.: Harvard University Press, 1977).
47. M.D. Keyserling, *Windows on Day Care* (New York: National Council of Jewish Women, 1972).
48. G. Nimnicht, J. Johnson, Jr., and P. Johnson, "A More Productive Approach to Education than 'Compensatory Education' and Intervention Strategies," *Beyond Compensatory Education*, ed. G. Nimincht and J. Johnson, Jr. (Washington, D.C.: U.S. Government Printing Office, 1973), pp. 27–49.
49. L.B. Miller and J.L. Dyer, op. cit.
50. M. Stephen, *Policy Issues in Early Childhood Education* (Menlo Park, Calif.: Stanford Research Institute, 1973), p. 336.
51. M. Almy, *The Early Childhood Educator at Work* (New York: McGraw-Hill, 1975), pp. 119–24.
52. E. Hezog, C. Newcomb, and I. W. Cisin, "But Some Are More Poor than Others: SES Differences in a Preschool Program," *American Journal of Orthopsychiatry* 42 (1972): 4–22.
53. Hunt, *Intelligence and Experience*, p. 268.
54. R.S. Moore, R.D. Moon, and D.R. Moore, "The California Report: Early Childhood Schooling for All?" *Phi Delta Kappan* 53 (1972): 615–21, 677.
55. M. Stephen, *Policy Issues in Early Childhood Education* (Menlo Park, Calif.: Stanford Research Institute, 1973), p. 336. ERIC ED 088 595.
56. Ibid.
57. R.E. Herren and B. Sutton-Smith, eds., *Child's Play* (New York: John Wiley & Sons, 1971).
58. P. Minuchin, B. Biber, E. Shapiro, and H. Zimiles, op. cit.
59. E.P. Torrance et al., *The Creative-Aesthetic Approach to School Readiness and Measured Creative Growth* (Athens, Ga.: University of Georgia, Research and Development Center in Educational Stimulation, 1967). ERIC ED 017 344.
60. J. Bissell, "The Cognitive Effects of Preschool Programs for Disadvantaged Children," *Revisiting Early Childhood Education*, ed. J. Frost (New York: Holt, Rinehart & Winston, 1973), p. 238.
61. U. Bronfenbrenner, *A Report of Longitudinal Evaluation of Pre-School Programs* (Washington, D.C.: U.S. Government Printing Office, 1974), p. 19.
62. P.S. Sears and E.M. Dowley, "Research on Teaching in the Nursery School," *Handbook of Research on Teaching*, ed. N.L. Gage (Chicago: Rand McNally, 1963), p. 841.
63. R.H. Bradley and B.M. Caldwell, *Issues and Procedures in Testing Young Children* (Princeton, N.J.: ERIC Clearinghouse on Tests, Measurement and Evaluation, 1974.)
64. C. Kamii and D.L. Elliott, "Evaluation of Evaluations," *Educational Leadership* 28 (1971): 827–31.
65. L.A. McFadden, *Formative Evaluation: Parents and Staff Working Together to Build a Responsive Environment* (Washington, D.C.: Day Care and Child Development Council of America, undated).
66. M. Scriven, "The Methodology of Evaluation," *Perspectives of Curriculum Evaluation*, ed. R. Tyler, R. Gagne, and M. Scriven (Chicago, Ill.: Rand McNally, 1967), pp. 39–93.
67. R.B. Zamoff, *Guide to Assessment of Day Care Services and Needs at the Community Level* (Washington, D.C.: Urban Institute, 1971).
68. J.R. Cryan, C. Ellett, A.W. McConnell, and M. Atyeo, "The Development of Criterion Referenced Early Childhood Education Program Assessment Instrument," *Childhood Education* 55 (1978): 122–25.

For Further Reading

Anderson, R.H., and Shane, H.G., eds. *As the Twig Is Bent*. Boston: Houghton Mifflin, 1971.

Auleta, M.S., ed. *Foundations of Early Childhood Education: Readings*. New York: Random House, 1969.

Barber, T.X. "Pitfalls in Research: Nine Investigator and Experimenter Effects." In *Second Handbook of Research on Teaching*, edited by R.M.W. Travers. New York: Rand McNally, 1973, pp. 382–404.

Blackie, J. *Inside the Primary School*. London: Her Majesty's Stationery Office, 1967.

Day, M.C., and Parker, R.K., eds. *The Preschool in Action*, second edition. Boston: Allyn and Bacon, 1972.

Evans, E.D. *Contemporary Influences in Early Childhood Education*, second edition. New York: Holt, Rinehart, & Winston, 1975.

Frost, J.L., ed. *Revisiting Early Childhood Education: Readings*. New York: Holt, Rinehart & Winston, 1973.

Margolin, E. *Sociocultural Elements in Early Childhood Education*. New York: The Macmillan Company, 1974.

Mills, B.C., and Mills, R.A. *Designing Instructional Strategies for Young Children*. Dubuque, Iowa: William C. Brown Company Publishers, 1972.

Roland, B. *Open Education and the American School*. New York: Agathon Press, 1972.

Silberman, C.E., ed. *The Open Classroom Reader*. New York: Vintage Books, 1973.

Spodek, B. *Early Childhood Education*. Englewood Cliffs, N.J.: Prentice-Hall, 1973.

4

Understanding Administrative Organization

Programs for young children are both public and private, and are known by such titles as nursery schools, kindergartens, day care centers. Montessori schools, Head Start programs, and primary schools. Program titles mirror differences in the children served, the philosophy and goals of the program, and the sources of funding. Although there are certain common administrative functions, the several forms of administrative organization reflect the kaleidoscopic variation in early childhood programs.

Administrative Functions

Certain functions common to administration are separated for purposes of our discussion; however, each administrative function is affected by each of the other functions.

1. *Planning and evaluating services.* An administrator should plan services in consideration of the philosophy and policies of the program; delineate, clarify, and coordinate the responsibilities of the staff members in providing the services; and establish a procedure for evaluating each service.
2. *Conducting business affairs.* Business affairs may include obtaining financial backing or assistance, distributing funds, and accounting for income and outgo, as well as planning and budgeting for the building, equipment, and personnel.
3. *Initiating and maintaining personnel services.* This involves determining needed staff positions; recruiting, promoting, and compensating staff; providing in-service training and assistance, supervision, and staff evaluation; and keeping personnel records.
4. *Supervising, coordinating, and incorporating auxiliary services.* These

47

services vary from program to program, but tend to be important aspects of all early childhood programs. Usual auxiliary services include plant maintenance, food service, and transportation for children.

5. *Providing channels for communication and exchange of information.* Administrators advise the board of directors; relate and interpret the decisions of the board to staff, parents, children, and the public; assist staff and consultants with program planning, implementation, and evaluation; confer with parents; communicate with agencies involved in the program; and meet the news media.

Achieving these functions requires an organization staffed with competent administrators. An administrative organization with clearly defined functions increases the staff's effectiveness and efficiency and frees it from much time spent on "emergencies," from mechanical problems that result in delays in program implementation, from complaints that "no one informed me," and from uncoordinated efforts in providing services. The success or failure of an early childhood program depends on the administration's ability to fulfill its functions.

Administrative Organizational Patterns

Although there are many similarities from one to another, uniformity of the administrative organizational pattern is not an outstanding characteristic of early childhood programs. The administrative structure, the roles of each position, and the titles given to administrators and their staffs vary from program to program. Reasons for variation in the organizational patterns include the following:

1. The age group served may vary. Programs may be designed for infants, toddlers, young children, or a combination of any of these age groups.
2. The sources of authority and/or funds may be diversified. Programs may be private, public school, state, or federal.
3. The purposes and objectives of the program may vary. Program objectives may be only care-giving, or care-giving and educational in nature.
4. The classification of children served may differ. Programs may be open to virtually all children, or may serve special-interest groups, such as the economically disadvantaged or physically handicapped.
5. The traditional patterns of public school programs may vary. Public school programs differ because each state has developed its own pattern of organization, and each community or county school system guards the "home rule" principle of government. (Home rule refers here to the efforts of the community or system to retain as much power and control as possible.)

There are basically five administrative organizational patterns governing early childhood programs: public school, private school, federal and state, national private agency, and university laboratory programs.

PUBLIC SCHOOL EARLY CHILDHOOD PROGRAMS

Legally, public schools are public agencies. A public agency is an organization which is part of either the federal, state, or local government. The organizational structure of public education is similar in each of the states.

In most states, the chief state school officer is the superintendent of public instruction or the commissioner of education, who is either elected or appointed. Early childhood education programs in the public schools fall under his jurisdiction. The chief state school officer and the state board of education, composed of elected or appointed board members, are the policy-making group for public education in the state. With the state board's approval, the chief state school officer selects the personnel and operates the department of public instruction or state education agency. Within the department of public instruction is a bureau concerned with early childhood education programs. Duties of the bureau may include approving requests for state aid, evaluating teacher certification applications, responding to requests for information or assistance, supervising programs in the local school districts, appraising legislative proposals that affect early childhood programs, and publishing information on regulations or trends in early childhood education.

The local school district may be, according to each state's law, a large urban district, a small community district, a cooperative arrangement among several communities, or a county district. The board of education or trustees, an elected group which represents the district's interests, is the policy-making group. As authorized by state laws, the board approves all school expenditures, plans for building projects, makes personnel appointments, and determines the services offered to students and parents. The superintendent, appointed by the school board, is the administrative officer for the school district. His function is to execute, within limits of state law, the board's actions.

Directly over the early childhood education teacher is the building principal, who is the instructional leader and administrator of the school physic l plant, records, and personnel. Supervisors or supervisor-adminstrators may be assigned by the superintendent's office to supervise and assist early childhood education teachers. The early childhood education teacher is responsible for care-giving and instruction of the children assigned to her, for the management of the classroom, and for any assistant teachers or aides placed under her direction.

PRIVATE EARLY CHILDHOOD PROGRAMS

There are many types of private programs for young children. A private early childhood program may be a single class conducted by an individual or a multi-class school staffed by a large faculty. The private program may be not-for-profit or for-profit, with all varieties or combinations of financial support possible. A private program may be either care-giving or care-giving and educational in nature.

We described in chapter 1 the typologies of early childhood programs. Regardless of the type of program, however, state statutes require that legal responsibility be clearly defined. The three legal forms of private organizations, proprietorship, partnership, and corporation, are defined by state statutes as follows:

1. Under a *proprietorship,* a program is owned by one person. This individual has no partners and is not incorporated. Sole proprietorships may have a one-person owner and operator, or a large staff with one person as owner. In a proprietorship one individual is fully responsible and liable for all actions.
2. In a *partnership,* two or more persons join together for the purpose of operating a program. A partnership may involve minor children, a sole proprietorship, or even a corporation as partner. There are both general and limited partnerships.
   a. A *general partnership* is one in which each partner shares equal legal responsibility. Each partner has the right to make equal, but not necessarily the same kind of, contributions to the program. Since contribution is a right and not an obligation, it may be worked out in reality on an equal or unequal basis. A general partnership can be risky, because it makes the partners individually and collectively responsible for any decision made by any partner with or without the knowledge of the other.
   b. A *limited partnership* is one in which there is one or more general partners and one or more limited partners. There is no limit to a general partner's legal responsibility; however, a limited partner is legally responsible only to the extent of his original monetary or nonfinancial contribution, such as service rendered calculated on a monetary basis. Because of his limited liability, a limited partner participates only in decisions involving finances.
3. A *corporation* is a legal entity established on a for-profit or not-for-profit basis. The corporation protects its members from certain liability by creating a decision-making and accountable Board of Directors when the program is incorporated with the state. The members of the board of directors or governing board may be drawn from a single family, religion, profession, or the group of parents served by the program (as in parent cooperatives), or members may be chosen in ways similar to boards of large business corporations.

In most states, not-for-profit programs must have a board of directors or a governing board composed of the people the program serves. The board of directors is a corporate policy-making body whose responsibilities include establishing the corporate and legal existence of the agency; appointing the executive director and approving other personnel appointments; providing for adequate funding, staffing, and facilities; governing the agency by policies; representing their agency in the community; and conducting evaluations of the program. For a full discussion of the functions and organization of the board, you should consult the Child Welfare League of America's publication, *Guide for Board Organization and Administrative Structure.*

The functions of the director are to furnish necessary information to the board, to relate and interpret information and policies back to the staff, and to serve as the administrator of the staff. If the facility serves a large group of children, some staff members may be appointed as program leaders and administrators of the school physical plant, records, or personnel.

Franchises or chains fall under any of the three legal forms of private organizations, and are differentiated as follows:

1. A *franchise* is an organization that allows an individual or an entity to use its name, follow its standardized program and administrative procedures, and receive assistance (for example, in selecting a site, building and equipping a facility, and training staff), for an agreed upon sum of money and/or royalty.
2. A *chain* is ownership of several facilities by the same proprietorship, partnership, or corporation. These facilities are adminstered by a central organization.

OTHER EARLY CHILDHOOD PROGRAMS

Publicly funded programs are organized and administered according to the federal or state grant that establishes the program. Most federal programs for young children are funded by a grant to a local volunteer agency, which selects a board of directors, who, in turn, hire a director. The organizational pattern is stipulated in the proposal the agency made to secure the grant.

National private agency programs, such as the American Montessori Society, Inc., are governed by the national board and must meet its, as well as state, requirements. Although these local programs are organized similarly to other private programs, each local program must follow the guidelines established by the National board; for example, in the American Montessori Society, Inc., the prospective director of a local program is trained, supervised, and eventually receives the society's credential.

The administrative and organizational patterns of laboratory schools vary from state to state and program to program. They may be operated by private or state institutions of higher learning, typically under the home economics or child development department. Those with kindergartens and primary grades are usually under a director and operated by the college of education. If school-age children are taught, the laboratory programs, whether operated by public or private institutions, are under the jurisdiction of the state department of education.

For Further Reading

Anderson, Robert H. "Schools for Young Children: Organizational and Administrative Considerations." *Phi Delta Kappan* 50 (1969): 381–85.

Bartley, John A. *Administration as Educational Leadership.* Stanford, Calif.: Stanford University Press, 1956.

Campbell, Roald; Corbally, John E., Jr.; and Ramseyer, John A. *Introduction to Educational Administration.* 3rd ed. Boston: Allyn and Bacon, 1966.

Castetter, William B. *Administering the School Personnel Program.* New York: Macmillan Co., 1968.

Cherry, Clare. *Nursery School Management Guide.* Belmont, Calif.: Fearon Publishers, 1974.

Ellsbree, Willard; McNally, Harold; and Wynn, Richard. *Elementary School Administration and Supervision.* New York: Van Nostrand Reinhold Co., 1967.

5

Considering Regulations

.

The continuing growth of facilities and schools for young children has required greater emphasis on regulations for insuring that not only minimum standards are met, but that existing standards for quality care and instruction are raised. Regulations are the rules, directives, statutes, and standards that prescribe, direct, limit, and govern early childhood programs. These characteristics are generally representative:

1. Regulations cover all aspects of a program—administrative organization, facilities, personnel, funding, and services.
2. Various regulations apply to different types of early childhood programs. Some regulations govern private programs, for example, licensing and incorporation; others may affect federal and state programs, for example, direct administration and Interagency Day Care requirements; and some regulations must be met by virtually all programs—fire safety and sanitation requirements, zoning, transportation, the Civil Rights Act, local board regulations, and regulations concerning staff qualifications.
3. Regulations vary in comprehensiveness; for example, licensing regulations cover the total program, but certification requirements affect only the educational preparation of the staff.
4. Most regulations are mandatory; an exception is accreditation, which is self-regulation.
5. Regulations come from various sources. Federal agencies regulate some early childhood programs because they provide funds through various grants and titles.

In the 1960s, federal programs often dealt directly with community agencies; today, most federal programs do not by-pass state administration. There is thus more control at the state level. State agencies regulate some early childhood programs because they provide funds. State laws regulate public programs because public education is a state responsibility. Local governments regulate some programs through community ordinances and health and safety codes. The judiciary system regulates some early childhood programs through its decisions affecting civil rights and the responsibilities of agencies and schools. It is not always easy to determine which of several agencies has jurisdiction over some programs.

The various regulatory agencies assume protective roles by assuring parents that the early childhood program meets at least minimum standards. Although this protective role is necessary, there are at least four problems with regulations:

1. Regulations can keep early childhood programs at minimum levels and deter innovation. Regulations are often too concerned with uniformity.
2. In some states, there are gaps in regulation. Establishing state offices of child development may help remedy this situation.
3. Some regulations are simply "on record," with little or no enforcement, such as licensing of family day care homes.
4. Continuous consultation is often omitted. Continuous inservice training opportunities are necessary for providing and maintaining quality programs.

In the remainder of the chapter, we will discuss regulations governing private, public, all programs (i.e., private and public), and accreditation. In some cases, these regulations do not fit perfectly the category in which they were placed; for example, P.L. 94–142 is financed with public monies, but the law affects handicapped children in private as well as public schools.

Regulations Governing Private Early Childhood Programs

Licensing, registering, and incorporating are some of the regulatory procedures unique to private programs. They are means for insuring that minimum standards are met by those proposing to establish child care and/or instructional programs not funded, and hence not regulated, by federal or state agencies and through public school systems. Each state develops its own licensing, registration, and incorporation procedures, and defines what is meant by a private child care facility. This term usually refers to everything from a facility that accommodates a few children in the owner's home to one that may have several hundred children. Licensing, registration, and incorporation regulations tend to be comprehensive; that is, they usually include all aspects of planning and administering privately operated early childhood facilities.

LICENSING REQUIREMENTS

Licensing is the procedure by which an individual, association, or corporation obtains from its state child care licensing agency a license to operate or continue operating a child care facility. A licensed facility is recognized by the state agency as having met minimum standards for child care.

Protection of children is the basis for licensing. Private child care agencies are classified as either "voluntary or philanthropic" or "proprietary or commercial."[1] Licensing is not concerned with child care facilities under public auspices. Public agencies are expected to implement their own standards and exercise supervision of their own facilities. An outline for licensing private child care service would include "people, operations, structure, and materials—the accountable administering agency, the place in which the service takes place, and the program which is conducted there."[2]

Historical Note. Licensing originated in New England, when a board of charities was created in 1863 to inspect and report on various child care facilities. In 1873, the National Conference of Charities and Correction was created. The Conference urged state regulation of private agencies, including those concerned with child care.[3] The first licensing law was passed in Pennsylvania in 1885; however, general interest in licensing did not begin until the early 1900s, when public scandals arose over the abuse of children in some child care facilities. This concern led to regulations for minimum standard of care and supervision of the publicly subsidized agencies. The first White House Conference on the care of dependent children (1909) recommended that each state regularly inspect all agencies dealing with minor children and regulate the incorporation of new agencies.[4] Three years later, the U.S. Children's Bureau was created. The Bureau urged the establishment of standards for child care agencies. The Child Welfare League of America, established in 1920, developed such a set of standards.[5] By 1920, most states had some regulation of child care. As a result of the federal grant-in-aid funds of 1935, state child welfare departments were able to procure better-qualified personnel; day-care facilities were brought under child-care licensing statutes; social workers took an active interest in protective services; and licensing was identified as a state child welfare function.[6,7]

The bulletin *A Survey of State Day Care Licensing Requirements* reported:

1. There are three major categories of day-care facilities licensed in the United States: *family day-care homes,* a category in forty-eight state regulations; *group day-care homes,* a category in nine state regulations; and *day-care centers,* a category in fifty state regulations. The categories are not similarly defined in the various states, however.
2. State licensing of family day-care homes is not mandatory in eleven states. Licensing of day-care centers is voluntary in one state and the licensing regulation has been overturned in another state.
3. In some states, licensing requirements are not imposed for all cities and counties.[8]

The Licensing Agency. According to Class,[9] the licensing agency is a regulatory agency with both quasi-legislative and quasi-judicial authority. The quasi-legislative powers include responsibility for establishing standards, and the quasi-judicial powers include responsibility for making decisions to issue or deny a license application and for conducting hearings in grievance cases. The major tasks of the licensing agency are

(a) interpreting the fact that child care is an activity affecting public interests and is therefore recognized by the State as an area of regulation; (b) formulating and reformulating licensing standards which will reduce the risk of improper care; (c) evaluating each applicant's situation to decide whether or not to issue the license; and (d) supervisory activity to maintain conformity to standards and, usually, consultation to upgrade care.[10]

Licensing of child care facilities is the responsibility of a particular state department, such as the Department of Public Welfare, of Social Services, of Health, of Social Services and Health, and of Health and Welfare. Other departments, however, may be responsible for licensing; for example, each of these departments issue licenses in at least one state: Board of Pensions, Environmental and Community Services, Departments of Children and Family Services, of Employment and Social Services, of Institutions and Agencies, of Institutions, and of Human Resources. (See Appendix 1.)

Child-Care Service License.   The different types of child-care facilities may be covered by a general or differential licensing law. Differential licensing laws have varying standards for these types of programs: day care (family day-care homes, group day-care homes, and day-care centers); educational facilities (private kindergartens and programs that carry the term *school* in their title); foster care (foster homes and group foster homes); child placing institutions; residential facilities; children's camps; and handicapped children's centers.

In most states, the term *day-care center* includes an early childhood program with these characteristics:

1. Operated as either not-for-profit or for-profit by any person(s), association, corporation, institution, or agency.
2. Opened for all or any part of the daylight hours, but less than twenty-four hours.
3. Enrolling a specified minimum number of children not related to the operator and/or conducted away from the children's homes. (The minimum number of children and place of operation is used to make a distinction between day-care services and baby-sitting services.)

The term *day-care center,* in most states, does not include the following:

1. Kindergartens and/or nursery schools operated under public school auspices.
2. Kindergartens and/or nursery schools registered with the state department of public instruction. (These are usually operated in conjunction with private and/or parochial elementary schools.)
3. Nurseries or other programs in places of worship during religious services.
4. Day camps as defined by the various state codes.

Thus, in most states, privately operated nursery schools and kindergartens that are individually owned and/or church-supported programs are considered day-care centers and are under the licensing regulations of their state. If the state code includes the local nonpublic school nursery and/or kindergarten as an educational institution, and provides for registration of the program with the state department of public instruction, then the privately owned nursery school and/or kindergarten is exempt from licensing regulations as a day-care center.

Features of Day-Care Center Licensing Laws.   For this discussion of licensing laws, we will focus on regulations for day-care centers. The features of these regulations are similar to those of family and group day-care homes, differing only in regard to the number of children regularly enrolled. Regulatory laws governing day-care centers differ widely from state to state; to learn the specific regulations of a state, you should contract the state's licensing agency and request a copy of the regulations. Although state regulations vary, there are two common features. First, licensing regulations in most states are specific in areas pertaining to physical health and safety, and are more lax in the area of program content. For example, health and safety regulations may state the required room temperature or specific items to be included in the first aid kit, while a program regulation may be that the program content "contribute to total development." Second, licensing regulations in most states cover the following areas: licensing law and procedure, organization and administration, staffing, plant and equipment, health and safety, and program.

Licensing Laws and Procedures. Each state manual contains information concerning the law which gives the licensing agency its quasi-legislative and quasi-judicial authority. A section of the manual on procedure contains all or some of the following items:

1. Terms such as *day-care center* and *care-giver* are defined.
2. Institutions which must be licensed and those which are exempted are delineated; the penalty, usually a misdemeanor, for operating without a license is also stated.
3. Procedures are described for obtaining and submitting an application for a license.
4. Statements of fees, if any, charged for license application are given. Renewal fees are charged in some states.
5. Bases for application approval are explained. In most states, the applicant must show need for the program; demonstrate that minimum standards for child care or instruction have been met; give evidence of adequate financial stability; and indicate the probability of permanence in the proposed organization. In some states, a center that does not meet all requirements but is actively engaged in meeting them may obtain a provisional license.
6. The duration of a license and explanation of the procedure required for renewal are explained. In most states, a license must be renewed each year; a few states require renewal every two years. In some states, a provisional license must be renewed every three or six months; in other states, it cannot be renewed.
7. Bases for revoking a license are explained, and statements concerning grievance policies or appeals are given. There is a penalty for operating after a license has been revoked.
8. A statement is made that a license must be posted in the center.

9. Conditions that require notification of the licensing agency are outlined, such as changes in location of the facility, in administrators, in services offered, or in enrollment after the license is granted; serious accident; fire; civil action taken against an institution or an employee; and closing of the center.

Organization and Administration. State licensing laws require an applicant to indicate the purposes and sponsorship of the organization and whether the program is for-profit or not-for-profit.

All state licensing laws require that administrative authority be clearly placed. In for-profit organizations, the requirement may be that the authority reside in one person, or that an advisory board be formed, comprised of individuals who can be of professional assistance. Usually, not-for-profit organizations must operate under a governing board composed, at least in part, of the people it serves.

Policies concerning children must be included in a description of the center's organization. Although these policies vary from state to state, they usually embody these details:

1. The center's admission and termination of service policies must be stated and conform with state regulations. Once an admission policy is adopted by the center and approved by the licensing agency, a change in this policy by the center requires application for another license. In some states, day-care centers cannot serve children under a minimum age, which ranges from four weeks to three years, and over a maximum age, which ranges from school age to sixteen years. Not all regulations use age as a criterion for receiving services of a center, but may use phrases such as "ready for group activity," "children who are likely to benefit from the services available," or "consideration must be given to children who need care."
2. Procedures for admission must be written; for example, some states require an interview with a parent before admission.
3. In most states, a nondiscrimination provision with respect to race, sex, creed, color, or religion must be adopted before a license can be issued.
4. A fee policy must be written and made available to parents. Fees charged depend on services offered, and on whether the organization has been established for-profit or not-for-profit purposes. Often in not-for-profit organizations, fees are charged in keeping with a parent's ability to pay and in keeping with the actual cost of operation.
5. A center must state its child-staff ratio and the maximum number of children to be cared for or instructed in one group. Those numbers must conform to state licensing regulation.
6. Finally, state licensing laws require a center to show financial solvency for immediate and continuous operation. Continuous operation is often defined as three months.

Staffing. Regulations concerning staffing usually include categories of personnel; child-staff ratio; age, educational, health, character, and temperament requirements; and personnel records which must be kept. Current trends in staffing requirements are as follows:

1. Personnel needed include a director, who must be in charge and who must assume total responsibility for the center. One state requires that centers with forty or more children hire a nonteaching director. Most states stipulate that two or more care-givers or instructors be on duty at all operating times. In all states, auxiliary staff must be hired when their services are required (e.g., for meals) or offered (e.g., for transportation). Some states mandate and others suggest the use of parent volunteers.

2. The child-staff ratio is based on care-giving or instructional staff only. The ratio is always smaller when services are offered for younger or handicapped children than for older or nonhandicapped children. The maximum size of the group is often specified. Usually when a combination of ages is provided with services under one care-giver or instructor, the ratio is calculated on the basis of the youngest child in the group. Here are two representative examples of child-staff ratios and maximum group sizes:

Age of Children	Child-Staff Ratio	Maximum Group Size
Birth – 18 months	3:1	6
19 – 35 months	4:1	8
36 – 53 months	7:1	14
54 – 71 months	10:1	20
2½ – 4 years	10:1	10
4 – 5 years	20:1	20
5 – 6 years	20:1	20
School-age children	25:1	25

3. Each member of the staff must meet certain personal qualifications:
   a. *Age.* In most states, the minimum age required for directors and main care-givers or instructors is eighteen or twenty-one years, and the maximum age permitted is sixty-five or seventy years. Assistant care-givers or instructors, who are never alone with children, must be a minimum of sixteen or eighteen years of age.
   b. *Education and experience.* Minimum educational and experience requirements are given in most state licensing manuals. In most states, directors and main care-givers or instructors must have a high school certificate; a few states require two years beyond high school, with courses in child development and nutrition; one state requires a bachelor's degree and two years teaching experience; another state requires that centers called schools have at least one teacher with a high school certificate and college hours in child psychology, family relations, nursery school curriculum and procedures, and student teaching. In many states, assistant care-givers or instructors must be able to read and write. In all states, auxiliary professional staff must have the educational competencies required in their fields. For example, many states

certifying school nurses require some experience and/or training in public health services. Licensing requirements for personnel working in social and psychological services may be obtained from the following sources:

Houghton, A.W. *Certification Requirements for School Pupil Personnel Workers.* Washington, D.C.: U.S. Government Printing Office, 1967.

Stinnet, T.M. *A Manual on Standards Affecting School Personnel in the United States.* Washington, D.C.: National Education Association, 1974.

Finally, most states require that a plan for staff training and development be submitted to the licensing agency.

c. *Health.* All states require a physical examination, including evidence that a staff member is free of tuberculosis. Results of the examination must be signed by a physician and placed on file in the center.

d. *Character and temperament.* Some of the terms used to describe the character and temperament of employees are "mature," "warm," "friendly," and "have a liking for children." Most states do not permit hiring of a staff member who has a record of criminal conviction.

4. Personnel record keeping is a requirement in all states. Personnel records, containing information on each regulation concerning the staff, are kept in the day-care center and must be made available to the licensing agency upon request.

Plant and Equipment. Many licensing regulations concerning the physical plant begin with descriptive statements, such as that the plant should be "safe, sanitary, and comfortable," "roomy, conducive to the development of children," or "not where any condition exists which would be injurious to the moral or physical welfare of a child or children."

Before applying for a license, a potential applicant must meet local zoning, health, fire department, and state health department requirements. Although the licensing agency has no authority over these local and state requirements, it can make further location requirements. Some statements found in various licensing laws include: "front must be twenty feet or more wide with a door," "not located with aged, infirmed, or incapacitated," and "programs for children under two and one-half years must be on the ground floor."

A majority of the states have regulations concerning both size and number of rooms needed for care-giving or instruction, and other rooms needed in the center. States vary on the amount of indoor space required; generally, a minimum of twenty-five to thirty-five square feet per child is stated. A separate care-giving or instructional room is required for each maximum number of children who can be under one care-giver or instructor. In cases where law mandates that children of certain ages be separated, a room must be provided for each age group. Most states prescribe separate bathrooms for children and staff, isolation quarters for an ill or disturbed child, a kitchen, and office space.

Environmental control is included in licensing, with heating and cooling regulations, such as "central heating and air conditioning" and "no fireplaces," amount of window space, room temperature requirements, and light intensity.

Regulations for drinking water and sanitary facilities are included in all licensing laws. Drinking fountains or separate or disposable glasses are required in all states. In most states, minimum regulations for bathroom facilities vary between ten to fourteen children per toilet and basin. Facilities for bathing children are suggested in the licensing standards of some states.

Outdoor-space regulations often stipulate the amount of space required. Most states prescribe a minimum of forty to one hundred square feet per child. Other regulations (or recommendations, in some states) for outdoor space include that the grounds be adjacent to the indoor area, be clean, drained, and fenced in, have various types of surfacing, for example, both sand and grass; and have open and shaded areas.

Other physical plant regulations that most, if not all, licensing manuals incorporate are that kitchen facilities conform to health and sanitation requirements, telephones be installed, and medicines and/or cleaning equipment be stored where children cannot reach them.

Equipment regulations, on the whole, are not as specific as physical plant requirements. Many states require one chair per child and prescribe one cot (or sometimes a mat) per child who remains in the center during a resting time. Other equipment regulations are that the center be "equipped adequately" or "suitable for the age range," have "suitable furniture and arrangement," have "low shelves," and use "easily cleaned equipment." Some licensing manuals provide a list of suggested equipment for use with children of certain ages or developmental stages.

Health and Safety. All early childhood programs, both public and private, are charged with the protection of children under their care. Licensing agencies are concerned with this protection mandate and have required many health and safety standards be met before they license a private institution. Trends in health and safety requirements are as follows:

1. All states have regulations concerning the health of staff and enrolled children, and required that appropriate written records covering these regulations be on file. In most states, employees are required to have a general physical examination before being hired, and an annual tuberculosis examination thereafter. Some states require certain immunizations for the staff, and all states require food handlers to obtain a permit. In short, all staff members must obtain a physician's statement that they are in good physical and mental health. In all states, a child must have had a general physical examination, specified immunizations, and a tuberculosis examination before admission to a center. A daily check of each child is required, for a center cannot care for a child with an acute illness or communicable disease. When a child becomes ill at the center, he must be isolated from other children until the parents can remove him. All states have strict requirements concerning staff members' administering medicine to a child. Accurate and current medical records must be kept on file in all states. When handicapped children are admitted to a center, adequate staff must be provided to care for their specific needs.

2. Local and state health and sanitation requirements must be met before application can be made for a license. (Other sanitary regulations were discussed under "plant and equipment.")

3. Transportation regulations must be followed. All states require that each driver and vehicle be properly licensed. Other transportation regulations are not uniform from state to state. Most states require off-street loading and unloading; set a maximum number of children who can be transported in various types of vehicles; set a minimum number of supervisors who must ride in the transporting vehicle; state that a child cannot be left unattended in a vehicle; and require the center to have proper insurance coverage. Some states specify the maximum amount of time, ranging from thirty minutes to one hour, that a child can ride to and from the center. Many other safety precautions are found in the licensing manuals, such as safety locks on vehicle doors and seat belts for each occupant.

4. Emergency medical care must be planned. Although regulations vary, most states require that emergency-assistance phone numbers be posted by the telephone. Some states require that centers not employing full-time medical staff have at least one staff member who has a current American Red Cross Standard First Aid Certificate or its equivalent; and some states specify supplies to be included in a first aid kit. One state requires that a center have no more nonambulatory children or infants than can be carried by adults.

5. Nutritional requirements must be met. All states prescribe a fraction or percent, usually one-third to one-half, of daily food needs a child must receive at the center; types of food which must be served; length of time between meals and snacks, which is usually one main meal every four or five hours and a snack two to two and one-half hours after a meal; and that menus be posted and kept on file. States permitting enrollment of infants in centers specify the time periods for feeding infants and require that infants be held while taking a bottle. Finally, all state health and sanitation requirements must be met in preparing and serving food.

Program. As previously mentioned, program regulations tend to be more lax than other areas of licensing regulations. General areas of program regulations include content, scheduling and planning, and guidance of children.

Infants are to receive verbal stimulation, cuddling, encouragement, and play. Program content for young children is described in most licensing manuals in terms of suggested activity areas, such as art, language development, music, block building, dramatic play, science, and manipulative play. Some states specify "no formal learning experiences" and no television viewing.

Common planning and scheduling regulations include adequate play periods, outdoor playtimes, free-choice and teacher-determined activities, and rest periods. Posting of the schedule and regularity of program is required in several states.

Many states stipulate "no harsh discipline" and give suggestions for guidance of children. Examples of these suggestions are: discipline cannot be associated with food, rest, or toileting; children should be given choices; staff members should use positive remarks; and corporal punishment should not be used.

Improving Licensing Laws. There are some problems associated with licensing laws: First, licensing laws represent the combination of state commitments to more than 60 federal programs, each with its own goals and philosophy, concerned with day care. Second, states requirements vary greatly. Only recently has there been much concern over national day-care regulatory policy, which has resulted in, among others, these five national studies:

1. *A Survey of State Day Care Licensing Requirements* (Day Care and Child Development Council of America, Inc., 1971.) This survey defined day care and surveyed teacher education and child/staff ratio in all the states and Washington, D.C.
2. *Abstracts of State Day Care Licensing Requirements*, Part 2: Day Care Centers. (Office of Child Development (DHEW), 1971.) Abstracts all requirements from every state and Washington, D.C.
3. *A Comparison of Provisions in State and Federal Standards for Institutional Day Care* (Central Midwestern Regional Lab, 1972.) This survey included pre-employment physical, minimum age required, minimum education, specified responsibilities, annual physical, and child/staff ratio.
4. *Day Care Licensing Policies and Practices: A State Survey*, July, 1975 (Education Commission of the States, Early Childhood Report No. 13, 1975.) In a telephone survey conducted during July, 1975, of licensing directors of the 50 states, New York City, and the District of Columbia, information on the status of state day care licensing statutes and regulations, classification of facilities and licenses, organization of day care licensing, licensing unit duties and staff, and various licensing data was obtained.
5. *A Comparative Evaluation of State Day Care Personnel Requirements.* (Francis Michael McCormick, Master's Thesis, University of Wisconsin at Madison, 1977.) This survey found that standards for personnel requirements were highly variable across states. Generally, health requirements were most important and personality traits were least important.

Third, until recently, many state laws were 15 to 30 years old. As of 1975, approximately 13 states have licensing regulations dated prior to 1971.[11] And fourth, many states do not have the licensing personnel and/or funds necessary to provide technical assistance for upgrading early childhood programs under their jurisdiction.* In the 1975 survey,[12] program staff training and licensing staff training were listed as top priority for improving state day care licensing statutes, regulations, and practices.

---

*For a discussion of educational background and experience, specific training, and caseloads of Illinois licensing staff, which may be somewhat typical of staff situations in other states, see: *Day Care Licensing and Regulation: A Program Evaluation.* Springfield, Ill.: Illinois Economic and Fiscal Commission, 1974. ERIC ED 110 178

These recommendations would increase licensing effectiveness:

1. There should be greater coordination among the various state agencies involved in licensing early childhood programs.[13]
2. Regulations must be brought up to date.
3. Regulations must be clearly stated.
4. There must be a sufficient number of trained persons to carry out the licensing function, and licensing representatives must interpret standards uniformly. Without uniformity, some children may not be protected, and questions as to legal "equal protection" may arise when some operators are treated more severely than others.
5. Licensing processes must proceed rapidly and efficiently.
6. Enforcement procedures must be consistent.

REGISTRATION REQUIREMENTS

There has been a move toward registration rather than licensing of family day-care homes. Eighty-five to ninety percent of family day-care homes have remained unlicensed because: (1) Most day-care regulating efforts are in terms of center care; (2) Licensing seems to have little to do with the quality of care families look for in choosing among alternative facilities; (3) More legal problems are encountered in licensing homes than centers (state laws, for example, cover privacy of the home); and (4) Licensing is difficult to manage because of the great numbers of day-care homes.

Registration is the process by which a state's licensing agency maintains records of all family day-care homes, publishes regulations, and requires the operator to certify that he or she has complied with the regulations. In short, the operator of a family day-care home self-certifies substantial compliance at the time of registration. The Michigan "Registration Project,"[14] a study of registration rather than licensing as possibly a more effective, efficient, and economic regulatory method, found that: (1) The registration process resulted in a greater number of regulated homes than did licensing; (2) Registration incurs less cost than licensing; and (3) When compared to licensing, the percentage of registered homes in violation of one or more rules is greater than the percentage of licensed homes in violation.

For registration to work, the community must be informed of the need for registration, the agency's location, and the method of reporting concerns. Parents of "day-care children" should be given a copy of the rules and the method of reporting complaints of substandard care. Registration should also be combined with offers of technical assistance by the licensing bureau.

PROPRIETORSHIP, PARTNERSHIP, AND CORPORATION REGULATIONS

Proprietorship, partnership, and corporation are legal categories for three types of private ownership. Legal requirements for operating an early childhood program under one of these categories vary from state to state; we will focus on common features of the laws. Legal assistance should be sought before establishing a private early childhood program.

Proprietorship.   As explained in chapter 4, a sole proprietorship is ownership by one individual or family, without partners and without incorporation. The legal requirements are simple: to create a proprietorship, the owner must file with the city clerk a "True Name Certificate," or what may be called by other names, such as "Fictitious Name Registration," if the center is to be called by any name other than the person's own name, such as "Jack and Jill Center." The "Assumed Name Law" informs clients and creditors of true ownership of the business.

Partnership.   In a partnership, usually two or more individuals join together for purposes of ownership. However, a partnership may involve minor children, a sole proprietorship, or a corporation as partner. (The sole proprietor and the corporation would be involved in their own business, as well as in the business owned by the partnership.) The law recognizes two types of partnerships:

1. In a *general partnership,* the law makes the partners individually and collectively responsible for the actions of any one partner. As with a proprietorship, the partners must file a "True Name Certificate." The partnership operates without any other legal documents.
2. In a *limited partnership,* one or more partners has limited responsibility and financial liability. A "Limited Partnership Certificate" spells out the limitations of responsibility and liability. The document is written and filed with the Secretary of State or publicized according to the state's laws. Each partner faces risks identical to those of a general partnership. Parners must also file a "True Name Certificate." Many partnerships find it desirable, though not mandatory, to prepare a "Partnership Agreement," a document containing facts about how a program is to be operated and terminated.

Corporation.   A corporation is a legal entity, it has a legal existence separate from the people involved in the corporation. The corporation protects individuals from certain liability by creating a decision-making and accountable Board of Directors. Although the Board may delegate decision-making power to a director, it is still responsible. Individual board members can be held personally liable only in certain areas, such as failure of the corporation to pay withholding taxes on employees' salaries and fraud. In short, personal financial liability is greatly diminished in a corporation as compared to the proprietorship or partnership.

In addition to diminished personal financial liability, regulations governing taxation may provide incentive to operate a program as a corporation. There is often a monetary advantage in paying corporate taxes rather than paying all the taxes on the program's profits as personal income. Furthermore, not-for-profit centers must be incorporated to be eligible for tax-exempt status; proprietorships and partnerships are not eligible for a tax-exempt status. Some states require day-care centers to be incorporated before they can receive federal monies, such as Title XX funds.

Because the corporation is a legal entity, several documents are required. The forms are usually somewhat different for "for-profit" and "not-for-profit" corporations. Three documents required in the process of incorporating are:

1. "Articles of Incorporation" or "Certificate of Incorporation." The organization's legal creators, or incorporators, give information about the corporation, such as the name and address of the agency; its purposes, and whether it is a "for-profit" or "not-for-profit" corporation; its powers, for example, to purchase property and make loans; membership, if the state requires members; names and addresses of the initial Board of Directors; initial officers; and the date of the annual meeting.
2. "Bylaws." The Internal Revenue Service requires "bylaws" if the corporation is seeking tax-exempt status. "Bylaws" simply explain how the corporation will conduct its business, its power structure, and how the power may be transferred.
3. "Minutes of the Incorporator's Meeting." After the incorporators prepare the aforementioned documents, an "Incorporator's Meeting" is held. The name of the corporation is approved, and the "Articles of Incorporation" and "Bylaws" are signed. The incorporators elect officers and the Board of Directors, who will serve until the first meeting of the members. In profit-making corporations, they vote to authorize the issuance of stock. Formal minutes of the "Incorporator's Meeting," including votes taken, are written and signed by each incorporator.

These documents, along with payment of a fee, are filed with the Secretary of State or publicized according to state laws. Once the state approves the proposed corporation, a corporate charter is issued. The incorporators no longer have power. Board members carry out the purposes of the organization, and the members own the organization. When corporations dissolve, they must follow state laws, if they are "for-profit" corporations, or federal regulations, if they are "not-for-profit" corporations.

Early childhood programs may operate either as "for-profit" or "not-for-profit" corporations. Although the titles are somewhat descriptive, they are often misleading, particularly when incorrectly called "profit-making" and "nonprofit" corporations, respectively.

"For-profit" corporations are organized for purposes of making a profit. Early childhood programs in this category, as well as proprietorships and partnerships, are businesses. A "for-profit" corporation may be a "closed corporation," in which members of a family or perhaps a few friends own stock, or an "open corporation," in which stock is traded on stock exchanges. If the corporation makes a profit, it pays taxes on the profits; individual stockholders file personal income tax forms listing items such as salaries and dividends received from the corporation. In a closed corporation with a sub-chapter "S" status, granted by the Internal Revenue Service, the corporation may distribute its profits or losses in accordance with the proportion of stock held by each individual, who in turn pays taxes or files a depreciation schedule.

"Not-for-profit" corporations are not organized for purposes of making a profit, but are permitted to make a profit. However, any surplus, or "profit," must be used to promote the purposes of the organization as set forth in the "Articles of Incorporation." In other words, the "profit" may be used for housing, equipping, or merit raises in the present or future. Proprietary operators have also organized "not-for-profit" corporations, which gives them certain advantages such as "rent" money for the facility, a salary for directing the program, and free surplus food for children in the program.

Under child care, there are two types of "not-for-profit" corporations: those organized for "charitable, educational, literary, religious, or scientific" purposes under section 501 (c) (3) of the Internal Revenue Code; and those organized for social welfare purposes under section 501 (c) (4) of the Internal Revenue Code. Tax-exempt status is not automatic. The "not-for-profit" corporation must file for and be granted tax-exempt status at both federal and state levels.

Besides incorporation regulations, several additional regulations should be noted. Separate bank accounts should be obtained for any early childhood program. Corporations are required to have separate accounts, and some government agencies will not send funds to a program that does not have a separate account. Also, a "banking resolution," which states the name of the individual authorized to withdraw funds, is required of corporations (and in some states of partnerships). Not-for-profit corporations with a certain income level, and other programs receiving monies from certain funding sources, are required to have an audit. In most states, not-for-profit corporations are required to file an annual "Financial Report" following the audit.

Regulations Governing Public Early Childhood Programs

Publicly-funded early childhood programs are not subject to licensure. Instead, all publicly-funded programs, such as public school and federally supported early childhood programs, receive regulations from a state or federal agency, respectively. A specified state or federal agency is required by law to prepare regulations. Because publicly-funded programs are self-monitoring, or answerable only to elected officials, program quality depends upon citizen involvement.

PUBLIC SCHOOL REGULATIONS

Public school education in the United States is a state function. State control is exercised through legislation and through guidelines or directives from the state department of education. As discussed in chapter 4, the states delegate portions of the school's operation to local school districts. State control appears in the following areas:

1. The state creates local school districts and grants them specific legislative powers.
2. The legislature controls curricular content by deciding what may or may not be taught, approving course offerings, and regulating textbook adoption.
3. Certification of administrators and teachers is delegated to the state education agency by legislative authority.
4. Except in Mississippi and South Carolina, state legislatures have established compulsory attendance laws.
5. State aid comes to local schools with regulations regarding expenditures; local noncompliance can mean the withholding of state aid.
6. Building construction programs are regulated by various state agencies.
7. There are state regulations concerning transportation of children.
8. The state legislature delegates authority to the state board of education, the chief state school officer, and/or to the state department of education to approve or accredit local school systems. Local school systems are accredited on the basis of meeting state standards, although some state education agencies may work with regional accrediting agencies.

FEDERAL INTERAGENCY DAY-CARE REQUIREMENTS

The federal government became involved in early childhood programs in 1933, under the Federal Emergency Relief Administration. Today, an increasing number of early childhood programs receive federal support and are thus subject to federal regulations. Because government involvement is of a funding nature, one type of government regulation is funding standards. These standards, which are levels of quality for which the government is willing to pay, are ultimately a form of direct regulation.

The Federal Interagency Day-Care Requirements (FIDCR) contain requirements to be met as conditions of federal financing of day-care services under certain programs. Currently, the FIDCR apply to the following programs that provide day care: (1) Department of Health, Education, and Welfare: Social Services, Child Welfare Services, Work Incentive (WIN), and Vocational Education programs; and (2) Department of Agriculture: Childcare Food program in situations where there are no State standards. The FIDCR do not currently apply to federally financed day-care services provided by these programs: Head Start and Aid to Families with Dependent Children, under the Department of Health, Education, and Welfare; all programs under the Department of Defense; Comprehensive Employment and Training Act (CETA) program, under the Department of Labor; or to programs under the Department of Housing and Urban Development.

The Interagency Day Care Requirements are mandatory; that is, they have the force of law. There are also "Interagency Recommendations" an optional policy based on what is known or generally held valid for care and education of children. These "Recommendations" are seen as a goal for administering agencies. The "Requirements" and the "Recommendations" constitute the "Federal Interagency Day Care Standards."

Historical Note.[15]   The FIDCR were originally required by the provisions of the Economic Opportunity Amendments of 1967 (P.L. 90–222), which directed the Secretary of HEW and the Director of the Office of Economic Opportunity to "coordinate programs under their jurisdictions which provide day care, with a view to establishing, insofar as possible, a common set of program standards and regulations, and mechanisms for coordination at the state and local levels."

The Secretary first published the FIDCR on September 23, 1968, jointly with the office of Economic Opportunity and the Department of Labor. The FIDCR were reaffirmed by the Economic Opportunity Amendments of 1972 (P.L. 94–424, sec. 19). The Secretary was made solely responsible for carrying out the directives to coordinate and regulate day-care programs by the provisions of the Community Services Act of 1974 [P.L. 93–644, V, sec. 8(b)].

In 1975, Public Law 93–647, which enacted Title XX, incorporated the FIDCR as the minimum standards to be met whenever Federal funds are received by Title XX day-care providers. Title XX modified certain of the 1968 provisions. It permitted the federal government to recommend but no longer require educational services, revised child-staff ratios for school-age children, and, for the first time, authorized the Secretary to establish staffing ratios for children under 3 years of age. Congress also placed requirements on care provided in the child's own home and purchased by Title XX funds. Finally, the Law called for reports of appropriateness of the requirements. Later amendments imposed a moratorium on child-staff ratio requirements for care of children 6 weeks to 6 years of age in day-care centers, group homes, and family day-care homes.

Content of the FIDCR.[16]   The FIDCR are organized according to nine categories of day-care services:

1. Day-Care Facilities—types of facilities; grouping of children and child-staff ratios; and licensing or approval of facilities.
2. Environmental Standards—location of day-care facilities; safety and sanitation; and suitability of facilities.
3. Educational Services—educational opportunities, activities, and materials, supervision by trained or experienced staff member.
4. Social Services—coordinated provision of social services, counseling and guidance to parents, assessment of child's adjustment in day-care program.
5. Health and Nutrition Services.
6. Training of Staff.
7. Parent Involvement.
8. Administration and Coordination.
9. Evaluation.

The Appropriateness Study.   The FIDCR have been in force for over a decade. The Department of Health, Education, and Welfare, as well as many agencies, organizations, and individuals, have recognized the need to revise the FIDCR. Revised FIDCR were prepared by HEW in 1972, in connection with proposed welfare reform, but the legislation was defeated in Congress.

In 1974, Congress amended the FIDCR for incorporation into Title XX and called for a study of the appropriateness of FIDCR. The Report was submitted to Congress in May, 1978. The present schedule for developing new standards calls for public meetings on regulations options papers in every state for public input on regulations and consultation with appropriate federal agencies. In the winter of 1978–79, the Notice of Proposed Rulemaking (NPRM) in the Federal Register was published and disseminated. Regional and national hearings on the NPRM and publication of final regulations in the Federal Register were accomplished in the spring, 1979.

HEAD START PERFORMANCE OBJECTIVES

As a result of a three-year study begun in 1973, new performance standards, in the areas of education, health, nutrition, social services, and parent involvement, were tested and made mandatory for all Head Start programs. Self-assessment tools were prepared to help programs assess their ability to meet these standards. Local grantees were encouraged to adopt variations to the standard classroom-based Head Start Model. The Head Start Performance Standards, available from the Office of Child Development, now constitute official policy, which local Head Start programs must meet to receive future funding.

EDUCATION FOR ALL HANDICAPPED CHILDREN ACT

The Education for All Handicapped Children Act, Public Law 94–142, was signed on November, 1975. The formula for financial assistance to state educational agencies and school districts was implemented in the 1978 fiscal year. The scope and comprehensiveness of this act make it the most significant piece of legislation enacted to meet the needs of handicapped children.

Historical Note.   The first school for the mentally retarded was established in 1848. Samuel Howe, director of the Perkins Institution for the Blind, opened an experimental school for "idiot children" in the Perkins Institution. Other residential schools for handicapped children followed. The federal government became involved in special education in 1864, with the establishment of Gallaudet College for the Deaf in Washington, D.C.

In 1896, the first special education class for mentally handicapped was opened in the public schools of Providence, Rhode Island. The federal government established a Section on Exceptional Children and Youth in the Office of Education in 1930. Because parents saw the need to educate their handicapped children, and because the federal government has provided matching funds to state and local agencies and has supported special education with monies for research, dissemination of information, and consultative services, there has been a rapid increase in the number of special education classes in public schools since World War II.

Special education began to receive extensive federal support in 1965 with passage of Public Law 89–10, the Elementary and Secondary Education Act (ESEA), a bill for the "educationally disadvantaged." Three amendments to ESEA, Public Law 89–313 (1965), Public Law 89–750 (1966), and Public Law 90–247 (1967), provided more aid to exceptional children in state-operated and state-supported institutions. Public Law 90–538, Handicapped Children's Early Education Assistance Act of 1968, authorized experimental preschool programs for handicapped children to demonstrate that handicapping conditions might be eliminated or alleviated in over half of the cases by early and comprehensive help.

Litigation has also been an important part of the history of publicly-supported education for handicapped children. The constitutional right of extending equal educational opportunities to all children, including the handicapped, was settled by the United States Supreme Court in the case of *Brown* v. *Board of Education* (1954). More recent litigation has been concerned with methods of extending "equal educational opportunity." In *Madera* v. *Board of Education, City of New York* (1967), *Arreola* v. *Board of Education* (1967), and *Covarrubias* v. *San Diego Unified School District* (1970), parents were to participate (with legal counsel, in the *Madera* case) in and be informed of placement decisions. As a result of *Diana* v. *California State Board of Education* (1970), children must be tested in their primary language and in English, reevaluated within a specified length of time, and additional services must be provided those students who return to the regular class following special class placement. Two precedent-setting cases were decided in the early 1970s. In a federal district court action, *Pennsylvania Association for Retarded Children (PARC)* v. *Commonwealth of Pennsylvania*,[17] parents invoked the equal protection clause of the Fourteenth Amendment. The clause requires that, if the state provides a publicly-supported program of education, it must be made available on an equal basis. PARC showed that inappropriate assessment instruments and labels had led to incorrect placement or exclusion of children from school, and that it was more economical to educate retarded children in the public schools than to provide special institutions or welfare assistance. As a result of this case, the Pennsylvania State Board of Education agreed to provide handicapped students with equal educational opportunity and to implement due process hearings concerning a child's placement. The outcome of the second especially significant judicial decision, *Mills* v. *Board of Education*,[18] was similar to that of the Pennsylvania case. In this case, however, the plaintiffs included not only mentally handicapped, but all children with special needs.

Provisions of P.L. 94–142. The specific provisions of P.L. 94–142 are the culmination of a long history of legislation and litigation, but the provisions are so comprehensive and significant that they go beyond their history. P.L. 94–142 is a revision of Part B of the Education of the Handicapped Act. The law is administered through the Bureau of Education for the Handicapped (USOE-HEW). If certain stipulations are met, children in private as well as public schools may receive assistance under this Act. These are some of the major details and stipulations of the Act:

1. Handicapped children are defined as:

   mentally retarded, hard of hearing, deaf, speech impaired, visually handi-capped, seriously emotionally disturbed, orthopedically impaired, or other health impaired, or children with specific learning disabilities, who by reason thereof require special education and related services. (Section 602)

2. All children aged 3 to 21 years are included under this act. There is also provision for federal monies for early identification and screening. Free public education was to be made available to handicapped children aged 3 to 18 by the beginning of the school year in 1978, and must be made available to all handicapped childred aged 3 to 21 by September 1, 1980. For children in the 3-to-5 and 18-to-21 age ranges, such mandate does not apply if such a requirement is inconsistent with state law or practice or any court decree. Some state laws mandate special education services from birth.

3. Priorities will go to children who are not receiving an education and those with the most severe handicaps who are inadequately served. These priorities must be adhered to by both state and local education agencies.

4. To prevent "over-counting" of children for entitlement purposes, the law requires that the total number of children should not be greater than 12 percent of the total school-age population between the ages of 5 and 17 inclusively. No more than one-sixth of those deemed handicapped (or 2 percent of the total school population) may be children with specific learning disabilities (SLD).

5. Extensive child identification procedures are required.

6. Evaluation must not be culturally or racially discriminatory. More spe-cifically, tests must be conducted in the child's primary language, admin-istered by a qualified individual, validated for the specific purposes for which it was intended, and given in conjunction with other assessment devices.

7. Parents must be informed and give their permission for evaluation of their child. The state education agency must guarantee maintenance of due process procedures for all handicapped children and their parents or guardians with respect to all matters of identification, evaluation, and educational placement, whether for initiation or change of such place-ment, or for refusal to initiate or change.

8. An individualized program for each child must be developed. The law specifies that the program be based on:

   ... (A) a statement of the present levels of educational performance of such child; (B) a statement of annual goals, including short-term instructional objectives; (C) a statement of the specific educational services to be provided to such child, and the extent to which such child will be able to participate in regular educational programs; (D) the projected date for initiation and anticipated duration of such services; and (E) appropriate objective criteria and evaluation procedures and schedules for determining, on at least an annual basis, whether instructional objectives are being achieved. [Section 4(a) (19)]

9. Special education must be provided in the "least restrictive environment." This simply means that handicapped children must be integrated into regular classes—the "mainstream" of education. Mainstreaming is thus the organizational answer to the mandate. Special classes and schools may be used for educating handicapped when integration is not best for the child.

10. Related services must be provided for the handicapped child. These are comprehensive, and include:

transportation, and such developmental, and other supportive services (including speech pathology and audiology, psychological services, physical and occupational therapy, recreation, medical, and counseling services, except such medical services shall be for diagnostic purposes only) as may be required to assist a handicapped child to benefit from special education, and includes the early identification and assessment of handicapping conditions in children. [Section 4(a) (17)]

11. A document must be developed at the state level in the form of an annual state plan to meet the specific mandates of P.L. 94–142, and submitted to the U.S. Commissioner of Education. The state education agency monitors compliance by its local school districts with respect to the stipulations, and the U.S. Commissioner monitors the degree of compliance by the state education agency. The Commissioner may cut off funds to a state education agency if that agency is in substantial noncompliance with any of the major stipulations. Noncompliance may result in termination of funds for special programs for handicapped children.

12. The U.S. Commissioner of Education will evaluate the impact of the Act on an annual basis and provide a complete report to Congress on the effectiveness of individualized instruction, educating handicapped children in the least restrictive environment, and procedures to prevent erroneous classification of children.

P.L. 94–142 established a payment formula based upon a gradually escalating percentage (5%, FY 1978 to a permanent 40% FY 1982) of the national average expenditure per public school child times the number of handicapped children served in the school districts of each state. Of course, actual appropriations are determined by Congress.

A multimedia package published by the Council for Exceptional Children explains P.L. 94–142 in depth. In addition to using this multimedia package or any other general source of information, one should become familiar with the laws of one's particular state.

Regulations Governing All Early Childhood Programs

Although private and public early childhood programs each have their unique regulations, various types of minimum regulations are common to all programs. These regulations concern physical safety, prevention of discrimination, the Internal Revenue Service, program standards, and staff qualifications. [Mandatory state unemployment insurance and the Federal Insurance Contributions Act (Social Security) are discussed in chapter 6.]

There is some overlap in the regulations imposed by the various agencies of the federal, state, and local governments. When there are regulations of a similar nature under more than one jurisdiction, an early childhood program must be in compliance with each regulation. For example, a private early childhood program is subject to the fire safety standards of the local city code and the state licensing law. Furthermore, to help insure that both standards are met, most state licensing agencies require that an application for licensure of an early childhood program include proof of compliance with all applicable city ordinances.

FIRE SAFETY AND SANITATION REQUIREMENTS

The statutory base for fire safety and sanitation requirements rests in public safety and public health laws, which may be municipal ordinances or state regulations with local enforcement. All public and private early childhood facilities must meet fire safety and sanitation requirements. Certificates of public safety and public health inspections are usually required by licensing authorities as preconditions for the license.

ZONING REGULATIONS

Zoning, a local regulation, regulates the location of an early childhood facility. Early childhood programs are often zoned out of residential neighborhoods because of noise, and out of commercial areas because they are not considered good places for children. Generally, zoning regulations become more stringent as population density increases.

TRANSPORTATION

In each state, whichever agency regulates matters pertaining to motor vehicles has the legal mandate to protect those who are transported in buses and private vehicles. Some states have devised special regulations for day-care transportation. These regulations are in addition to those required for licensure.

THE CIVIL RIGHTS ACT OF 1964, TITLE VI

Any program which uses federal funds must sign an "Assurance of Compliance to the Civil Rights Act," promising that there will be no discrimination on the basis of color, race, national origin, or sex in employment of staff or admission of children. Since much of state licensing is indirectly paid for with federal funds, if the Civil Rights Office finds that any child is excluded from a licensed facility on the basis of discrimination, the exclusion is a denial of his rights, for he has not benefited from federal funds used to license the facility. If an early childhood program refuses to comply with this act, it could lose its federal funds.

TITLE VII OF THE CIVIL RIGHTS ACT OF 1964 AND AS AMENDED BY THE EQUAL OPPORTUNITY ACT OF 1972

Fair Employment practices are mandatory for organizations, companies, and individuals having a contract with the federal government. The practices are also mandatory for any entity that employs or is composed of 15 or more individuals. Employers subject to this act and its amendment must not discriminate against an individual on any factor over which he does not have control, such as race, creed, color, sex, national origin, or age. Employment practices involved in this regulation include, but are not limited to, recruiting, transfer, promotion, training, compensation, benefits, layoffs, and termination of employment. Employment practices must be based on merit and competence and the relevant measures of these. The employer must also develop job qualifications upon bona fide occupational qualifications (BFOQ); thus, job descriptions must clearly specify the tasks to be performed.

FAIR LABOR STANDARDS ACT

The *Fair Labor Standards Act* of 1938, as amended, applies equally to men and women. Employees subject to this Act and its amendments must pay, as a minimum, the current minimum wage; pay overtime at the rate of one-and-a-half times the employee's regular rate of pay for all hours worked over the forty-hour work week; pay regular wages and overtime pay for attendance at required training sessions, whether the sessions are conducted at the place of work or at another site; and must pay equal wages for equal work.

INTERNAL REVENUE SERVICE REGULATIONS

All early childhood programs must comply with Internal Revenue Service Regulations. Fraud and/or failure to comply results in serious consequences. Some IRS regulations specific to certain legal program categories have been mentioned; the following regulations apply to most, if not all, early childhood programs.

Employer Identification Number.   All programs are required to obtain a federal *Employer Identification Number.* One cannot file for a tax-exempt status without first having obtained this number (IRS Form SS-4).

Withholding Exemption Certificates.   These certificates, IRS Form W-4, are required for each employee. The certificates are used for determining the amount to withhold for federal, state, and city income taxes. Employees must sign new forms if more of their wages are to be withheld. Annual statements of taxes withheld from employee's earnings (W-2 forms) are sent to him no later than January 31 of the year following the year in which the employee was paid.

Form 1099.   Occasionally, early childhood programs hire someone to do a temporary specific job, such as plumbing or electrical work. Because withholding taxes would not have been deducted from their wages, all centers which pay $600 or more to any individual who is not an employee must file Form 1099.

Tax Returns.   Employers file quarterly tax returns, IRS Form 941. This form is filed with the Regional Federal IRS Service Center. There is a penalty for late filing.

All centers must file annual tax returns. Sole proprietors and partnerships with other incomes file the appropriate schedule of Form 1040; partnerships without other incomes file Form 1065; for-profit corporations file Form 1120; and not-for-profit corporations file Form 990.

LOCAL BOARD REGULATIONS

Each faculty and staff member employed by an early childhood program is governed by the regulations of its governing board, which must be in keeping with the restrictions and authorizations of federal, state, and local laws, directives, and guidelines. The governing board's regulations may include such things as: (1) educational requirements in addition to state certification requirements; (2) salary and related benefits; (3) absences and leaves granted; (4) promotions; (5) evaluations of staff; (6) grievance policies; (7) housing of programs; (8) equipment used in program; (9) curricular assistance given to teachers, in the way of detailed course outline, in-service training, resource personnel, or no curricular assistance; (10) plan of staffing for instruction whether self-contained classroom, team teaching, or departmentalized staffing; (11) teaching and nonteaching duties; (12) nature of communication with the public, through publicity, citizens' visits or participation in schools; (13) administrative, instructional, and discipline requirements to be employed in working with children, such as attendance regulations, methods of determining and reporting children's progress, and discipline, including punishment guidelines; and (14) each administrative and supervisory employee's responsibility in giving direction to faculty and staff.

REGULATIONS CONCERNING ADMINISTRATOR
QUALIFICATIONS

Administrators of public school early childhood programs must hold a state administrator's certificate, which grants legitimate authorization to administer a school program. Administrators of private early childhood programs need not hold an administrator's certificate unless the program is educational in nature. The state education agency issues various types of administrator certificates, such as an elementary principal's certificate, secondary principal's certificate, general principal's certificate, and superintendent's certificate. Several states are working toward certification requirements for an early childhood education administrator's certificate. Generally, administrators must have for certification:

1. Teaching experience (usually three years);
2. From fifteen semester hours of graduate work to a master's degree in school administration, with courses in curriculum, supervision, general adminis-tration, and specialized fields of administration such as school law and school finance; and
3. Two or three years of school administrative experience (for a superinten-dent's position only).

Administrators must meet any other qualifications established by the local board or accrediting agency to which the program belongs.

Directors of private early childhood programs must meet the educational and experience requirements of their state's licensing law. In some states, the mini-mum educational requirement for a director is a high school diploma, but other states require two or more years of college work. Minimum experience require-ments range from no experience to two years of successful experience in an early childhood program. Voluntary certification by child care administrators was implemented in 1978. The Alliance of Child Development Associations, through the National Association of Child Care Administrators (NACCA) and the relevant state provider associations, will issue the credential. Major require-ments are that: (1) administrators have three years of supervisory or administra-tive experience, plus 50 units or hours of training for initial certification, or ten additional units of training for each year of experience less than three years; (2) administrators complete 30 hours or 30 units each year after initial certification; and (3) at least 10 hours each for the initial and renewal requirement be earned by workshops conducted by a state provider association and approved by the NACCA. Other units may be obtained by participation in board meetings where training is part of the meeting, accredited as a Child Development Associate, and passing a test on state licensing standards.[19]

REGULATIONS CONCERNING TEACHER AND PARAPROFESSIONAL QUALIFICATIONS

A teacher of young children performs many roles every day, including those of language model, arouser of artistic sensitivity and creativity, relater of knowl-edge, questioner, stimulator of curiosity, learning diagnostician, guidance coun-selor and mediator of conflicts, diplomat with parents, classroom administrator, and more. Because the teacher also has total responsibility for all that happens to children in the school setting and for the quality of education, regulations help to insure that qualified teachers and paraprofessionals are placed with young children.

Certification of Teachers in Public School Early Childhood Education Pro-grams.   Certification is the function of granting authorization to teach. Certifi-cates may be standard or provisional, and are limited to special fields and/or

levels of instruction. In most states, the legislature delegates certification responsibilities to the state department of education (see Appendix 1). These responsibilities usually include the power to issue, renew, or revoke a certificate, and the
task of writing minimum requirements for each type of certificate or of developing guidelines for colleges and universities to follow in planning a program for
prospective teachers. Although the bases for certification are left to each state,
most certification standards specify United States citizenship, age and health
requirements, earned college degree with special course requirements, and
possibly a recommendation from the college or university.

Historical Note. When American kindergartens were first established, prospective kindergarten teachers received their training in Germany and other
European countries. The growing kindergarten movement, however, necessi-
tated establishing kindergarten training schools in the United States. The first
training institution was founded in Boston in 1868. These schools offered
instruction in Froebelian theory and methods and on-the-job training in kindergarten classrooms. "The training given emphasized the kindergarten as a unique
form of education apart from and having nothing in common with the school."[20]
In the decade from 1890 to 1900, many public schools adopted kindergartens.
The kindergarten training schools were continued as private, self-supporting
institutions, because the normal schools were not able to supply the increasing
demand for trained teachers.

Many educators realized the desirability of employing state certified kindergarten teachers rather than having the kindergarten work "carried on by people
who play a piano and love dear little children."[21] Consequently, many colleges
and universities reorganized to meet the needs of students preparing to teach
kindergartens. By 1925, in the forty states which had kindergarten legislation, all
states had teacher certification laws for kindergarten except Alabama, Kentucky,
Louisiana, Oklahoma, and Tennessee. Most of the certificates were based upon a
high school diploma and a two-year professional program, and were special
subject certificates valid only for teaching in the kindergarten. In California,
Illinois, Michigan, Ohio, and Wisconsin, however, kindergarten-primary certificate, based on a two-year professional program, was issued.[22] Recently, the
following profile was developed concerning certification for early childhood
personnel:

- 20 states have certification requirements for prekindergarten teachers
- 2 states have certification for prekindergarten paraprofessionals
- 47 states have certification for kindergarten teachers
- 6 states have certification for kindergarten paraprofessionals
- 11 states require state certification for day-care personnel
- 31 states accept elementary certification for kindergarten and/or prekindergarten,
  usually with an additional endorsement.[23]

Certification of preschool handicapped children is offered in 12 states and
additional states are working on certification guidelines.[24]

Special Features of Certification Requirements. There are several types of early childhood education teaching certificates. A few states offer a nursery or nursery-kindergarten certificate; others offer a kindergarten or kindergarten-primary (K-2 or K-3) certificate. Thirty-one states accept an elementary (K-6, K-8, or K-9) certificate or an elementary certificate with an additional endorsement. Requirements for an endorsed elementary certificate usually include two or more early childhood education courses and student teaching in an early child-hood program in addition to the requirements for an elementary certificate. This type of certificate is becoming more popular as educators begin to realize that early childhood education personnel need specialized training within the elementary education framework. Most states offer only one type (elementary or endorsed elementary) of early childhood education certificate; however, in some states more than one type (K-6, N-2, or K-3) of certificate is granted.

Generally, early childhood education certification requirements are as follows:

1. Approximately sixty semester hours in the areas of physical and biological sciences, language and literature, mathematics, the social and/or behavioral sciences, and humanities.
2. Between twenty-four and thirty semester hours of professional education courses, including: (a) introduction to education and/or early childhood education, including history and philosophy; (b) human growth and development including guidance; and (c) curriculum content, methods of teaching, and materials and equipment used in teaching.
3. At least three (or five to eight in some states) semester hours of student teaching in an early childhood education program and additional student teaching in a primary or intermediate level or grade.
4. Course electives in the areas of psychology of the exceptional child, abnormal psychology, psychology of learning, mental hygiene, parent/community relationships, linguistics, nutrition, speech correction, and school administration and/or supervision.

Prospects for Upgrading Requirements. Professional preparation for an elementary certificate is considered by the Task Force on Early Childhood Education of the Education Commission of the States as the best preparation for working with young children. In the 1971 report, *Early Childhood Development: Alternatives for Program Implementation in the States,* they urged all states to establish credentials within the preparation of an elementary education certificate.[25]

An *ad hoc* committee on the preparation of nursery school and kindergarten teachers, composed of the National Education Association's Department of Elementary-Kindergarten-Nursery Education, the NEA's National Commission on Teacher Education and Professional Standards, the American Association of Colleges for Teacher Education, the American Home Economics Association, the Association for the Education of Young Children, the National Association of State Directors of Teacher Education and Certification, the National Kindergarten Association, and Project Head Start, was convened to explore problems of providing competent personnel for nursery schools and kindergartens. The committee recommended the following ideas for further study:

1. Certification dependent upon demonstrated competence.
2. Recognition of differentiated staff roles (e.g., teacher aide).
3. Elimination of permanent certificates.
4. Greater opportunities for in-service education for all personnel.
5. Emergency-type certificates should be granted to permit able people to pursue the requirements while working within the profession.[26]

Hansen's analysis of forty-four kindergarten teacher-training institutions indicated that these institutions planned changes toward more appropriate student-teaching programs, additional early childhood courses, better screening of candidates, increased observation and participation in kindergarten programs, efforts to strengthen related subject-matter courses, and provisions for more materials for teaching methods courses.[27]

Because today's teacher must be prepared to teach children en masse—the advantaged and disadvantaged, the handicapped and nonhandicapped, the majority culture and minority culture—teachers must have special training. Most programs were not designed to prepare teachers for meeting the needs of these diverse groups.[28] Today, many institutions are attempting to train teachers to meet the needs of specific populations.[29]

Staff Qualification Required by Licensing Regulations.   The educational qualifications of personnel employed in child care facilities under private control are determined by each state's licensing regulations. In most states, directors and care-givers or instructors must have a high school certificate; a few states require a college education, usually two years, with course work in child development, curriculum, organization and administration, and methods and materials used with young children.

Licensing regulations often require that assistant care-givers or instructors be able to read and write or have a high school diploma. Professional personnel on the auxiliary staff, such as the nurse or psychologist, must meet the requirements of their respective specializations.

American Montessori School Certificate.   Because the American Montessori Society, Inc. is a national private agency, the instructional staff of a Montessori school would have to meet the licensing code requirements of the state or, in some states, the requirements of the state board of education. In addition to the state's regulations, the American Montessori Society has its own certification requirements:

1. A degree from an accredited four-year college or equivalent foreign credential is required, but no specific field of study is stipulated.
2. About 300 clock hours of academic work, including workshops or seminars in the historical and philosophical foundations of American education and the relationship of Montessori education to current knowledge

of child development; knowledge of Montessori theory, philosophy, and materials for instruction as presented in seminars and as seen in observation of laboratory classes; and training in language arts, mathematics, science, art, music, social studies, and motor perception.

3. An internship of nine months in a site approved by the "course director" under the approved "American Montessori Society supervisor" during which the intern is observed by a "training program representative."[30]

Child Development Associate.   In an effort to maximize the competence of persons working with young children in Head Start, Follow Through, and day-care centers, but who lack formal education in child development and early childhood education, the *Child Development Associate Consortium* was founded in 1972 (see Appendix 3). The Consortium's goals were to establish competencies needed for working in early childhood education, to develop methodologies for assessing such competencies, and to issue appropriate credentials. On March 27, 1975, the Board of Directors formally adopted the Credential Award System and authorized the awarding of the Child Development Associate (CDA) credential to anyone who could demonstrate competence by completing the requirements of the Consortium. The Consortium has now expanded the CDA credential to include a bilingual/bicultural component to accommodate paraprofessionals needing those competencies.

The prospective CDA may receive training through college-planned programs, field work-study, supervised field-work programs, and independent study; however, regardless of the training received, he will have to demonstrate competence in terms of performance with young children. The CDA is a person able to meet needs of a group of children aged three to five in a child development setting. The CDA must be able to nurture the child's total development, establish and maintain a proper child care environment, and promote good relations between parents and the program.

Six general categories of competencies were developed, on the assumption that these broad competencies would not violate divergent educational views or cultural backgrounds of various child care programs:

1. Setting up and maintaining a safe and healthy learning environment
2. Advancing physical and intellectual competence
3. Building positive self-concept and individual strength
4. Organizing and sustaining the positive functioning of children and adults, in a group, in a learning environment
5. Bringing about optimal coordination of home and center child-rearing practices and expectations
6. Carrying out supplementary responsibilities related to children's programs[31]

To earn a CDA credential, a person must enroll in the Consortium's Credential Award System, complete each phase of the process, and be recognized as competent by the assessment team.

Accreditation

Accreditation is a voluntary process of self-regulation. It means that the educational or child care facility has met minimum standards set by the accrediting agency. There are no legal penalties for inability to meet accreditation standards; rather, it means failure to gain professional status. Early childhood programs which are accredited by a particular association or agency are not necessarily superior to other programs, although they may be because accredited programs have voluntarily pursued a degree of excellence.

In order to receive accreditation, the personnel of an early childhood program must: (1) apply to the accrediting association; (2) evaluate its facility, staff, and program to be sure it meets or exceeds the association's standards; (3) request a visit and be reviewed by a committee selected by the accrediting association; and (4) accept accreditation when approved by the accrediting association. Accreditation is a continuous process, because programs are accredited only for a short period of time. Before the expiration date, a program that desires to remain accredited must repeat the process.

Public schools are necessarily accredited by the state education agency. Because early childhood programs in public schools are considered part of the elementary school, these programs are accredited with the elementary schools in a local school district. In addition to the various state education agencies, early childhood programs that are part of elementary schools may be accredited by the Southern Association of Colleges and Schools. (Among the six regional accrediting associations, only the Southern Association of Colleges and Schools has an arrangement for accrediting elementary schools.)

The Child Welfare League of America, Inc., has an accreditation program. League accredited membership is open to public and private child welfare agencies. Local private early childhood programs licensed by these accredited agencies warrant public confidence in their administration and professional competence.

NOTES

1. Norris E. Class, *Licensing of Child Care Facilities by State Welfare Departments* (Washington, D.C.: U.S. Department of Health, Education, and Welfare, Office of Child Development, Children's Bureau, 1968), p.7.
2. *Survey of State Day Care Licensing Requirements* (Washington, D.C.: The Day Care and Child Development Council of America, 1971), p. 6.
3. Norris E. Class, *Basic Issues in Day Care Licensing* (Washington, D.C.: U.S. Department of Health, Education, and Welfare, Office of Education, 1972), p. 58.
4. Children's Bureau, U.S. Department of Health, Education, and Welfare, *Spotlight on Day Care* (Washington, D.C.: U.S. Government Printing Office, 1966), pp. 4–5.
5. Class, *Basic Issues in Day Care Licensing*, pp. 58–59.
6. Class, *Licensing of Child Care Facilities*, pp. 56–60.
7. *A Survey of State Day Care Licensing Requirements*, pp. 5–6.
8. Ibid., pp. 11–13.

9. Class, *Licensing of Child Care Facilities,* p. 6.

10. Ibid., p. 9.

11. Education Commission of the States, *Day Care Policies and Practices: A State Survey, July, 1975* (Denver, Colo.: The Commission, August, 1975), p. 4.

12. Ibid., p. 5.

13. Social and Administrative Services and Systems Associations/Consulting Services Corporation, *A Survey of State Day Care Licensing Requirements* (Washington, D.C.: Day Care and Child Development Council of America, 1971).

14. J.D. Harrold, "Day Care Licensing Improvement Project, Final Report" (Lansing, Michigan: Michigan State Department of Social Services, 1976) ERIC ED 129 038.

15. For the legislative history of FIDCR and Title XX Day Care Requirements, see:
P.L. 90–222, sec. 107(a) Dec. 23, 1967
P.L. 92–424, sec. 19 Sept. 19, 1972
P.L. 93–644, sec. 8(b) Jan. 4, 1975
P.L. 93–647, sec. 2 Jan. 4, 1975
P.L. 94–120, sec. 3 Oct. 21, 1975
P.L. 94–401, sec. 2 Sept. 7, 1976
P.L. 95–171 Nov. 12, 1977

16. For the complete text of the FIDCR, see HEW Publication No. (OHDS) 78–31081.

17. *Pennsylvania Association for Retarded Children v. Commonwealth of Pennsylvania,* 344. F. Supp., 1275 (E.D. Pa. 1971)

18. *Mills v. Board of Education of the District of Columbia,* 348. F. Supp., 866 (D.D.C. 1972)

19. The Alliance of Child Development Associations, "Certification of Child Care Administrators," *Child Care Newsletter* (1978): 1–3.

20. Margaret Cook Holmes, "The Kindergarten in America: Pioneer Period," *Childhood Education* 13 (1937): 270.

21. "Marked Kindergarten Progress in the Northwest," *Childhood Education* 1 (1925): 303.

22. Nina C. Vandewalker, "Facts of Interest About Kindergarten Laws," *Childhood Education* 1 (1925): 325.

23. "Where Are We Now?," *Young Children* 28 (1973): 288–M.

24. A. Hirshoren and W. Umansky, "Certification for Teachers of Preschool Handicapped Children," *Exceptional Children* 44 (1971): 191.

25. Education Commission of the States, Task Force of Early Childhood Education, *Early Childhood Development: Alternatives for Program Implementation in the States* (Denver: The Commission, 1971)

26. Helen H. Hartle, "Early Childhood Programs in the States," *Compact* 3 (1969): 19.

27. Harlan S. Hansen, "Analysis of Forty-Four Kindergarten Teacher-Training Programs in Five Upper-Midwest States—Iowa, Minnesota, North Dakota, South Dakota, Wisconsin," *Childhood Education* 47 (1971): 281–82, 284, 286.

28. J.C. Stone, *Breakthrough in Teacher Education* (San Francisco: Jossey-Bass, 1968).

29. R.F. Peck and J.A. Tucker, "Research on Teacher Education," *Second Handbook of Research on Teaching,* ed. R.M.W. Travers (Chicago: Rand McNally, 1973), pp. 940–78.

30. *Approved Teacher Training Programs* (New York: American Montessori Society, 1973).

31. "The Development of the Child Development Associate (CDA) Program," *Young Children* 28 (1973): 140

For Further Reading

Aikman, W.F. *Day Care Legal Handbook: Legal Aspects of Organizing and Operating Day Care Programs.* Washington, DC: Day Care and Child Development Council of America, 1977. ERIC Ed 145 925.

Boguslawski, D. B. *Guide for Establishing and Operating Centers for Young Children.* New York: Child Welfare League of America, 1975.

Class, Norris E. *Licensing of Child Care Facilities by State Welfare Departments.* Washington, D.C.: U.S. Department of Health, Education, and Welfare, Office of Child Development, Children's Bureau, 1968.

Committee on Infant and Preschool Child of the American Academy of Pediatrics. *Standards for Day Care Centers for Infants and Children Under 3 years of Age.* Evanston, Ill.: The American Academy of Pediatrics, 1971.

Costin, L.B. "New Directions in Licensing of Child Care Facilities." *Child Welfare* 49 (1970): 64–71.

Morgan, Gwen G. *Regulation of Early Childhood Programs.* Washington, D.C.: The Day Care and Child Development Council of America, 1973.

National Association for the Education of Young Children, "Preparation Standards for Teachers in Early Childhood Education." *Young Children* 23 (1967): 79–80.

A Survey of State Day Care Licensing Requirements. Washington, D.C.: The Day Care and Child Development Council of America, 1971.

6

Staffing

The quality of the staff determines, to a high degree, the excellence of an early childhood program. To most people, a job is more than a means of earning money; it is a work situation in which an individual feels secure and accomplished in utilizing his skills. To obtain program quality and job satisfaction, three criteria must be met in staffing any program: (1) the personnel must meet at least minimal qualifications for their specific duties, although an employer hopes to select employees who seem to have the most potential; (2) those selected must be willing to work within the philosophical framework of the program; and (3) personnel must believe in the program's philosophy and goals in order to work together effectively and harmoniously.

Trends in Staffing

Sociocultural factors and psychological and educational research and their concomitant programmatic effects have resulted in new staffing patterns. There has been an increase in the number of staff needed, for several reasons. First, more early childhood programs are becoming comprehensive in nature, which necessitates additional staff to provide educational, nutritional, health, and social services to children and their families, and to assess programmatic results. Second, housing arrangements often necessitate additional staff. For example, more staff are needed to supervise facilities with multiple rooms or spatially separated outdoor areas and indoor activity rooms. Third, although Federal Interagency Day Care Requirements have not been set for center care of children under three years, programs that offer center care for infants and toddlers must meet state licensing regulations and requirements. *The Appropriateness of the Federal Interagency Day Care Requirements: Report of Findings and Recommendations*[1] finds a consensus that child-staff ratio for children under three years of age should not exceed a maximum of 5:1, and many individuals affiliated with day care recommend more age breaks, such as birth to 12 weeks, 13 weeks to 1 year or walking, 1 to 2 years, and 2 to 3 years, in determining the ratio for infants and toddlers. Typically, one ratio is used for children up to 6 weeks of age, then another is applied for children 6 weeks to 3 years of age. The recommended child-staff ratio for programs that include handicapped children ranges from 5:1 to 8:1.[2] (Some child-staff ratios may change in the near future as a result of the National Day Care Study.)

With increases in staff, more supportive services have been included. With the trend toward mainstreaming, supportive services will be needed for identifying and screening handicapped children and helping to integrate them into the regular classroom. Teachers have not only indicated their need for these services,[3,4,5] but seem willing to take the exceptional child if supportive services are available.[6,7,8] Several models have been proposed to show how supportive specialists should serve in early childhood programs. Four of these models are described in these sources:

Bailey, D.B., Klein, T.L., and Sanford, A.R. *A Model for Resource Services to the Young Handicapped Child in a Public School Setting.* Chapel Hill, N.C.: Chapel Hill Training-Outreach Project, 1974.

Buktenica, N.A. "A Multidisciplinary Training Team in the Public Schools." *Journal of School Psychology* 8 (1970): 220–25.

Ferguson, D.H. et al. "Models for Pupil Services in Elementary Schools." College Park, MD: Interprofessional Research Commission on Pupil Personnel Services, University of Maryland, 1969. ERIC ED 040 504.

Malcolm, D.D. "The Center/Satellite Model: Grand Strategy for Change." *The Personnel and Guidance Journal* 52 (1974): 303–8.

More men are being recruited for early childhood staff positions, although the ratio of men to women is far from balanced. The NEA Research Division Estimates that fewer than two percent of teachers at third grade and below are men.[9] There are several reasons for the trend in recruiting male personnel. Many young children are being raised in one-parent, female-dominated homes, and father absence seems to be most disruptive to boys under five years of age.[10] Perhaps father substitutes, such as the male teacher, can ameliorate some of the consequences of father absence.[11] For example, Mischel[12] predicted that male teachers should facilitate the imitation of masculine behaviors by boys. Also, Lynn[13] noted that the presence of male nursery-school teachers facilitates masculine sex identification of nursery-aged boys.

Boys do not see school as congruent with their sex role. Children are more inclined to imitate behaviors of same-sex models[14] and tend to sex-type school related objects.[15] Boys also have more problems in achievement.[16,17,18] For example, mathematical ability in boys has been associated with their fathers and male teachers.[19,20,21] Smith[22] believes that male teachers would enable boys to develop their academic achievement more fully. Kohlberg[23] predicted that boys will value and model their male teachers' values and academic behavior.

Another advantage to the presence of male teachers is that boys seem to be "disapproved of" by their female teachers.[24] Sexton's[25] study found that female teachers showed biases against their male students more frequently than they did against female students. Female teachers have expectations of children's behavior that are more in harmony with female behavior. These biases are thought to cause boys to rebel against the school system and, consequently, become underachievers. Girls from father-absent homes may also need male teachers to facilitate their development. Father-absent girls are more anxious than father-present girls and have more problems relating to males in early and middle adolescence.[26] Lack of male models also affects their intellectual abilities.[27]

Volunteer services are more frequently used in early childhood programs, and volunteers are no longer confined to peripheral tasks such as office help or drivers for field trips, but are involved in every aspect of the program.[28] About one-fourth of the nation's volunteers serve as tutors.[29] Stimuli for volunteering is coming from several directions. For example, the "Administration on Aging" (HEW) proposed a program to employ the aging poor as social aides in wards, cottages, and kitchens of children's institutions. The results are shown in the Foster Grandparent Program, which began in 1965. These "grandparents" serve in correctional institutions, mental health clinics, Head Start, day-care programs, and homes for handicapped children. In addition, some corporations grant employees time off for volunteer work. This concept was put into action in 1966 when the Philadelphia Board of Education requested the business community's participation in a tutorial program, and the Philadelphia Gas Workers immediately responded. Other "release time" programs have involved Michigan Bell Telephone and the Chrysler Corporation. Corporate executives have also helped school administrators with management problems. Finally, students as young as nine years through college-age are participating in volunteer programs. Some student volunteers are underachievers, who are helping others while increasing their own skills as well. To most, volunteering is personally satisfying because they are helping others, are gaining better understanding of various problems, and are putting their dormant talents to work.

Roles and Qualifications of Personnel

An individual's qualifications for participation in an early childhood program depend upon his specific role. All personnel, employees and volunteers, must be free from any psychological or physical illness which might adversely affect the children or other adults, and must have the personal qualities necessary to work with young children.

Personnel may be classified as either program or nonprogram personnel. Program personnel such as directors and teachers provide services in the realm of care-giving or instruction, and nonprogram personnel such as dietitians and office workers furnish services that support or facilitate the care-giving or instructional program. Although a staff member is classified by his major role, he may occasionally function in another capacity. For example, a teacher may occasionally clean the room or serve food, or a dietitian might discuss with children good eating habits or console a child who drops a food tray.

PROGRAM PERSONNEL

The major role of program personnel is to provide care-giving or instructional services to children. This personnel category includes the director, child care staff, teachers and assistants, and volunteers.

Director.   The title of director is a general term given to a person who may or may not be in charge of the total program. Directors of early childhood education programs in public schools are often supervisors and/or helping or resource personnel. In Montessori programs, teachers were traditionally given the title of director or directress. The title of director is frequently given to the person legally responsible for the operation of a public or private day-care center, a private nursery school or kindergarten, a university or college laboratory nursery school or kindergarten, or a Head Start program.

For our purposes, director refers to the person or persons legally responsible for the total program and services. More specifically, the director's responsibilities may include providing professional assistance to the board of directors or advisory board by supplying needed information, recommending changes in policy, and assisting in program evaluation; developing program philosophy and goals and providing leadership for program planning; planning school policies concerning children and parents; demonstrating awareness of current laws and regulations affecting children, families, and education, and insuring that regulatory standards are maintained; recruiting, employing, supervising, and training staff, delegating responsibility to and terminating employment of staff members; supervising building maintenance and managing the program and auxiliary services; representing the institution in the community; establishing and maintaining school records; and preparing an annual budget for the board's consideration, keeping the board informed of financial needs, and operating within the budget.

The ability to communicate effectively with the board, staff, parents, and community seems to be the major personal qualification of successful directors. The professional qualifications of directors vary depending on the program's organizational pattern.

Directors of private early childhood programs must meet their state's licensing requirements concerning age and educational qualifications. Licensing standards, however, are minimum requirements. A professional group, the Committee on Infant and Preschool Child of the American Academy of Pediatrics, has recommended that:

1. A director of a day-care center for more than eight children should have completed twenty-four semester hours in child development and early childhood education courses or have equivalent experience acceptable by the state's licensing agency; and
2. A director of a day-care center for eight or fewer children shall have a high school diploma, one course in child development, and two years of experience in direct child care in a day-care center and shall have regular, scheduled consultation from a supervising agency approved by the licensing board.[30]

As discussed in chapter 5, *The Alliance of Child Development Associations,* through the *National Association of Child Care Administrators* and the relevant state provider associations will certify child care administrators who meet their requirements.

In public school early childhood programs, those responsible for the children and the program include the superintendent of schools, the assistant superintendents, and the building principal. Although these individuals are not usually called directors, they are in reality directors who have been delegated their responsibility by the local school board. The public school directors must hold the administrator's certificate of their state and meet any other qualifications as established by the state department of education, the local school board, and/or the accrediting agency to which the school belongs. Several states have considered developing certification requirements for an administrator of early childhood education.

Child Care/Instructional Personnel. Child care/instructional personnel include child care personnel, teachers and assistant teachers, resource teachers, and volunteers. Personal qualifications of these staff members should include the ability to work with adults, such as other program personnel, nonprogram or support personnel, and parents; an enjoyment and appreciation of children; warm and nurturant personalities; a great deal of patience; exuberance; the ability and willingness to set and maintain reasonable limits; "available, well-directed energy;"[31] the ability to "flow" from the mentally concrete to the abstract;[32] and good health and stamina.

Child Care Personnel. Child care personnel are noninstructional (that is, not responsible for formal learning activities) care givers usually employed in family day-care homes and day-care centers. Their primary role is to perform the everyday tasks that would ordinarily be parents' responsibilities, including caring for children's physical needs; helping them grow emotionally and socially; and stimulating intellectual development, by answering questions, talking with them, and reading stories to them. Other responsibilities may include conferring with other staff members and representing the institution at meetings such as parents' groups.

Child care personnel in private early childhood programs must meet their state's licensing requirements. The Committee on Infant and Preschool Child of the American Academy of Pediatrics recommends that child care personnel should have completed high school and one course in early childhood education; or be at least eighteen years of age, enrolled in high school, and have taken one course in early childhood education or child development; or be at least eighteen years of age, have completed a child care program, and be enrolled in training courses.[33] Finally, as described in Chapter 5, the Child Development Associate Consortium authorizes the Child Development Associate (CDA) credential to anyone who demonstrates competence by completing the Consortium's requirements.

Teachers and Assistant Teachers. Teachers and assistant teachers are usually considered instructional personnel; however, under the law, supervision, or protection from physical harm, is the main responsibility of all those who work with young children. Teachers and assistant teachers are responsible for child care and academic instruction, while child care personnel informally enhance children's learning experiences as well as provide care-giving services, so the distinction between these two groups of personnel is somewhat blurred. The major distinction is that teachers and assistant teachers provide academic instruction in addition to carrying out the role of child care personnel. It would thus seem reasonable that teachers be well-informed in interdisciplinary areas such as psychology, child development, prediatrics, nutrition, sociology, and anthropology, as well as in the broad field of education.

Teachers in public school early childhood education programs must hold teaching certificates appropriate for this level of instruction and must meet all other qualifications established by their local school boards. Some state licensing standards require personnel holding the title of teacher or working with school-age children in a day-care center to meet the state's teacher certification requirements.

The Teacher Education Committee of the Association for Childhood Education International recommends the following standards of academic preparation for teachers of children three through eight years of age:

1. The teacher should have studied in the areas of physical and biological sciences, mathematics and philosophy, language and literature, social and behavioral sciences, and fine arts.
2. The teacher should have a minimum of twenty-four semester hours of professional preparation in the field of early childhood education, including courses in human growth and development; school, parent, home, and community relationships; history and philosophy of education; and school administration.
3. The teacher should have supervised experiences with young children for approximately 360 clock hours.
4. For professional advancement, teachers should be required to take refresher courses and to keep active affiliation with professional organizations.[34]

Some Head Start Teachers have a four-year college degree with a major in nursery, kindergarten, or early childhood education. Degrees in other areas concerning children, such as child development, child psychology, child welfare, or medicine, may provide the necessary academic preparation for Head Start positions. Head Start teachers who do not have a four-year college degree are encouraged to obtain the Child Development Associate credential.

The assistant teacher's role includes carrying out, under supervision, some of the teacher's responsibilities. Assistant teachers are helpful in several ways: they may know the community better than the teacher; they may have special talents to share; and they serve as an additional adult needed for supervision and instruction of children. Assistant teachers in private early childhood programs must meet the licensing standards in their respective states. The Child Development Associate credential is appropriate for many assistant teachers.

Resource Teachers. Resource teachers are often used in programs that integrate handicapped and nonhandicapped children. The resource teacher, who possesses state special education certification and meets all other qualifications established by the local school board, delivers special education services to children in the district.

Volunteers. Supervised volunteers may work directly with children. Parent volunteers can help the teacher meet the needs of individual children, plan greater variety of learning activities, interpret neighborhood culture to the teacher, and provide additional personalities and resource people in the classroom. "Drafting the help of parents is the only solution that will overnight let the boys and girls in school today have the teacher-pupil ratio that decent education demands."[35]

Licensing standards of most states require that volunteers be a minimum of sixteen or eighteen years of age and able to read and write. All volunteers should have adequate orientation to the program and be willing to participate in in-service education.

NONPROGRAM PERSONNEL

The major role of nonprogram personnel is to furnish services that support or facilitate the care-giving or instructional program. This group includes dietitians and food-service personnel, medical staff, psychologists, caseworkers, maintenance staff, general office staff, transportation staff, and volunteers. Personal qualifications include the ability to work with other adults, such as program personnel, other nonprogram or support personnel, and parents, as well as the ability to communicate with and be knowledgeable about age-level expectations of young children.

All must meet licensing standards in their states; in addition, professional nonprogram personnel must have the qualifications of their respective professions.

Dietitians and Food-Service Personnel.   The dietitian is responsible for all food service, including recommending the quantity, quality, and variety of food to be purchased; directing work assignments and schedules of all dietary personnel; and providing in-service training to employees responsible for preparing and serving the food and for cleaning the food area. Other food service personnel carry out, under supervision, some of the dietitian's responsibilities. If a registered dietitian is not employed on a full-time basis, the program should seek such services on a consultant basis.

A registered dietitian must have undergraduate education in dietetics and clinical experience in the form of a dietetic internship.* Other food service personnel should have some training and experience in dietetics.

Medical Staff.   Most medical services are supplied on an "as needed" basis or through contractual arrangements. Preferably, physicians would be pediatri-

---

*More information can be obtained from The American Dietetic Association, 620 North Michigan Avenue, Chicago, Illinois 60611.

cians, and would have backgrounds in public health. The physician's duties may include acting as a consultant to the institution in formulating and carrying out its policies for health care and planning, and supervising the medical staff's services.

Depending on the number of children in a program, a nurse may be employed as a full- or part-time staff member. Duties of the nurse may include inspecting the children as they enter the program each day, referring children who need special medical attention, conferring with other staff members and parents about the children's health, administering medical care during the day, and keeping health records.

In addition to a physician and nurse, a dentist should be retained. Dental services may include a dental inspection of children and conferences with other staff members and parents about the children's dental needs.

Psychologist.   The services of a qualified child psychologist should be available. Most early childhood programs would employ a psychologist who has specialized in school, educational, or clinical psychology. A person with a doctoral degree in psychology is eligible for license after examination by the Board of Examiners of the State Psychological Association, and a person who has a master's degree in educational or school psychology may be certified by the State Board of Education in some states. Duties of the psychologist may include psychological evaluation of children and the promotion of guidance techniques. Recent studies have been conducted concerning the specific training needed by the school psychologist[36] and evaluation of his performance.[37]

Caseworkers.   Some institutions hire persons trained in social work or use caseworkers from a local government agency. Their services include explaining to parents the problems children may face upon entering day-care programs; helping a mother with her problems in finding a job or assuming her role as a full- or part-time mother; explaining to the parents the agency's requirements for admitting a child to a program and the opportunities offered; introducing the mother to the day-care staff; and helping the family understand their child.[38]

Maintenance Staff.   Staff must be employed for housekeeping and for maintaining the building and grounds. At least one staff member should be on duty throughout the day for any work that must be done immediately. Major cleaning and maintenance must be performed when the children are not present.

General Office Staff.   They perform secretarial and clerical duties, including maintenance of records, correspondence, and bookkeeping. The size of the staff and the specific skills needed will vary according to the size of the program.

Transportation Staff.   Programs offering transportation services must employ staff in this area. Transportation staff may include drivers and mechanics.

Volunteers.   Besides serving as program personnel, volunteers provide nonprogram services such as securing equipment, interpreting the program to the community, working with the office staff, and providing transportation services. Nonprogram volunteers may be needed on either a regular or an irregular basis.

Personnel Communication

What are the qualities that make a good administrator? Although there are personality tests, matrices for analysis, and models for explaining the factors necessary to effective administration, success rests on a foundation of good communication. Communication is an elusive concept, involving a circular process of presenting one's ideas and feelings to another person and interpreting the feedback. The term *communication* is derived from the Latin *communis*, meaning to share or make common. The theory behind communication is that through the exchange of information and feelings, people can develop common understandings. Communication is also intricately bound up with personality. Consequently, communication is difficult at best, because people react to the same situation in different ways. Nonetheless, the lack of clear communication undermines the effectiveness of any administrator.

PROCESS OF COMMUNICATION

In a team approach, no one should act unilaterally; however, the administrator must define the primary task and see that it is carried out. Because leaders make decisions, they take risks and live with the consequences. Morale is usually low when administrators are indecisive. Thus, administrators should not hesitate to take a stand,[39] yet must avoid assuming a lordly manner.

Staff participation in decision making is highly important.[40] Staff members feel more secure and are more apt to follow through, when decision making is decentralized. The administrator cannot successfully share his thoughts with others unless he is willing that staff members share theirs with him. Administrators must also recognize that the purpose of leadership is to help staff members maximize their personal potential. Information sharing is vital. The administrator is a generalist, who must recognize that some of his staff have more information on a particular subject than he does. He must not mistakenly believe that some people are less able than they really are. (This is most apt to happen when an administrator works with inexperienced professionals and paraprofessionals, such as assistant teachers and volunteers.) In short, an effective administrator considers and appraises all germane information from all concerned. He listens not only to words, but to emotional undertones as well.

An effective administrator respects his staff's worth[41] and is willing to publicly acknowledge their accomplishments.[42,43] Failure to appreciate is an age-old problem,[44] not simply a product of our hurried society. One must also remember that praise is not just the absence of criticism, and for praise to be effective, a spirit of appreciation must be present—not just the form.

Effective administrators also exhibit these qualities in their communication:

1. They have a high degree of empathy—they put themselves in their staff members' shoes.
2. Their communication is optimistic, and optimism unleashes staff energy.

3. They are consistent in words and actions, and know the importance of integrity.
4. They accept some conflict. Issues are put on the table, and each staff member has a chance to influence a decision.
5. Staff humiliation—in the form of condescension, criticism in front of others, gossiping, or belittling—are not part of their communication repertoire.
6. They are committed to the welfare of children; thus, communication never ceases, for final goals are never reached.
7. The administrator never loses his personal identity in the communication process, and his unique communication style contributes to his effectiveness.

FLOW OF COMMUNICATION

Most communication is conducted informally, as need arises. This flow of communication is essential to any organization, including an early childhood program, but there may be gaps in the flow of communication in all but the smallest programs unless a more formal method of communication is established.

Exclusive use of communiqués from administrator to staff violates the principle of team decision making. Staff meetings are thus essential. For staff meetings to be effective, they must be carefully planned and executed, so the following tips should be kept in mind:

1. Have a purpose for calling a staff meeting. Don't call meetings unless there is a need for discussion. Routine announcements may be made in other ways.
2. If decisions to be made pertain only to a few staff members, do not call a general staff meeting.
3. Schedule meetings at times suitable to the staff. Generally, a regular time should be set aside during work hours.
4. Prepare and distribute an agenda a few days before the scheduled meeting. If certain materials are to be discussed, they should be available prior to the meeting. The agenda should indicate the name of the person presenting an item and the amount of time allocated for the presentation. Additional time for discussion and voting should be included.
5. Stay within time limits. (Agenda items may be omitted or added and time allocations changed with group consensus.)
6. Listen to each staff member's ideas during a discussion.
7. Start and stop the meeting on time.
8. Distribute minutes of the meeting to staff members. Minutes should be read and approved before sending them to the Board of Directors and/or filing them.

LINES OF COMMUNICATION

The lines of responsibility and communication should be clear. Confusion arises and staff morale drops when the communication structure is not clear. Although each job description should indicate placement in the "chain of command," an organizational chart indicates the interrelationships of the various positions, both program and nonprogram (see the chart below for an example).

ORGANIZATIONAL CHART

Board of Directors
or
Board of Advisors

Director

Program Personnel	Nonprogram Personnel
Teachers (including Resource Teachers) and/or Child Care Personnel	Dietitians and Food-Service Personnel
	Psychologists
Assistant Teachers and/or Assistant Care-givers	Medical Staff
	Caseworkers and Home Visitors
Teacher Aides or Child Care Helpers	Office Staff
	Maintenance Staff
Volunteers (where applicable)	Transportation Staff
	Volunteers (where applicable)

Although responsibility lines should be delineated, there should be a plan for shifting responsibility when a staff member is unavailable.

Occasionally, large early childhood programs have a special communication structure for handling employees' questions and complaints, usually referred to as "grievance procedures" and incorporated into the personnel policies. Grievance procedures should allow for documentation and corroboration by others to determine whether fair and equitable solution of grievances has been achieved. To leave grievances unresolved results in low efficiency and moral on the part of the staff.[45, 46]

Selecting Personnel

After developing a philosophy and program on paper, the administrator is faced with the tasks of determining the staff needed and of matching job requirements with staff. This task is a continual one; staffing patterns change as a program expands or changes and as vacancies occur.

ASSESSMENT OF NEEDS AND OTHER CONSIDERATIONS

The administrator must first assess the staff needs and desires for particular services. Since the budget is usually limited, the administrator must also determine priorities among needs. Other considerations may include the potential staff available, the amount of space needed for staff offices and other facilities, and the amount of training and/or supervision that will have to be conducted. The necessary positions must then be translated into job descriptions (to be discussed later).

PROCEDURE FOR RECRUITING STAFF

The director or personnel administrator is responsible for advertising the positions. Many programs must follow affirmative action guidelines[47] in recruiting and hiring. The director should first notify those already involved in the program of the opening, then make the advertisement public. The advertisement should be in keeping with the job description. State all nonnegotiable items, such as education and experience, so that unqualified candidates can be quickly eliminated. The advertisement should state the method of applying and the deadline for application. The method of applying and accepting applications will depend on the abilities and experiences of the likely candidates and the administrator's time. Thus, the method of application may vary from a telephone call or completion of a simple form to a lengthly application form, a vitae, and a letter requesting transcripts and credentials.

After the deadline for applicaion, the director or other staff member in charge of hiring will screen applications to eliminate the unqualified. The administrator is required by affirmative action guidelines to list reasons for rejection and to notify these individuals.

The remaining candidates should be interviewed. The administrator must determine, or follow established board policies concerning, who will conduct the interview, the nature of the interview, the setting of the interview, and who will make the final decision regarding selection of the candidate. Those conducting the interview and the candidates should be prepared. The nature and setting of the interview depends greatly on the position to be filled and the information available in the application form. In the case of highly trained, experienced personnel, the interview may center more on their philosophies concerning programs for children and whether their experiences and abilities match the present program. On the other hand, methods of selecting paraprofessionals for training are usually based on the idea of finding those individuals who appear to have the greatest potential to learn after being employed. Thus, interaction with children, reaction to videotapes of classroom situations, or verbally-described situations are often part of the interview for a paraprofessional position. The interviewer should also discuss and answer such questions about the program as its philosophy, the ages of enrolled children, how children are evaluated, the guidance and discipline practices, the degree of parent involvement, salary, length of day and school year, complete description of the job, opportunities for promotion, fringe benefits, sick leave and retirement plans, consulting and supervisory services, and the nature of the evaluation procedures that will be used to determine the level of job performance and how those results will be used. (For future reference, a staff handbook containing such information should be made available to those employed.) A word of caution—the interviewer must not make any inquiries of the candidate on any matter, such as sex or marital status, not directly related to the job description. For the current status of laws and litigation, contact the Equal Opportunities Commission.[48]

At a given date and in a specified manner, the candidates are informed about the selection. The candidate who is hired must usually sign a contract and other required personnel papers. If no candidate is selected, the recruitment process is repeated.

Improving Personnel Qualifications

Analyses of a program's strengths and weaknesses provide a basis for improving personnel qualifications. All personnel need to refresh their present skills and learn new skills. Because early childhood programs and their personnel differ in many ways, methods of improving qualifications differ from program to program. Four methods for improving personnel qualifications are formal education, orientation and in-service education, membership in professional organizations, and performance evaluation for improvement.

FORMAL EDUCATION

Since institutions of higher education first began offering early childhood education courses in the early 1900s, there has been a tremendous growth in the number of colleges and universities that offer these courses. Many institutions offer both undergraduate and graduate degree programs in early childhood education, and with the growth of day-care centers that often employ the paraprofessional, some institutions are offering associate degree programs in child development and/or early childhood education. From the number of individuals enrolled in these programs throughout the nation, formal education is undoubtedly one of the major methods for improving personnel qualifications.

Care-givers who have not met minimum licensing requirements and teachers who hold provisional certificates must enroll in courses to overcome their educational deficiences. Boards of education may also require their teachers to obtain additional college hours periodically or to work toward more advanced degrees; many teachers enroll in college courses because they feel the need to refresh their skills and/or because professional advancement leads to subsequent salary increases. As has been noted, the Association for Childhood Education International recommends that teachers be required to take refresher courses for professional advancement.[49] Katz[50] indicates that teachers in the stages of renewal and maturity (after three to five years of experience) are in need of college work.

ORIENTATION AND IN-SERVICE EDUCATION

Other methods for improving personnel qualifications are orientation and in-service education. An adequate orientation program is essential for all personnel. Formal orientation procedures vary from program to program. In some programs, the orientation is a short conference with the director and a tour of the facility; in other programs, the orientation procedures, consisting of individual conferences, group meetings, and written materials, continue for a year or longer.

Although orientation procedures should fit the needs of the personnel, there are several desirable features of all general orientation programs.

1. Beginning the orientation procedure with a social event, in which staff members are introduced to other personnel and perhaps to parents, sets the mood for cordial relationships.

2. Explanations should be given to all personnel concerning the program's philosophy and goals, the general organizational structure, and the clientele served.

3. Written information should include the employee's job description, the organizational structure with names of personnel, information on any procedure the employee might need in the near future, such as accident or fire procedures, and securing office supplies or audiovisual equipment, and information on the day-to-day operation of the program, such as work hours and special duties. Conversely, employees should not be burdened with information they will need in the more distant future, such as instructions for end-of-school reports.

4. Demonstration teaching, observation of other teachers, and workshops or seminars on particular methods or materials are helpful even to veteran teachers.

5. Orientation procedures should permit employees to ask questions as well as to receive information.

In addition to that given to all personnel, orientation may be needed for special reasons. For example, the new teacher needs a specific type of orientation. Katz[51] states that the teacher in stage 1, "Survival" (beginning through the first several months to one year), needs on-site support in the overall teaching task—instruction in specific skills and guidance in understanding child behavior. Orientation which includes exchange of ideas with teachers at the same stage is beneficial at stage 2, "Consolidation" (first year through three to five years).

Teachers involved in mainstreaming will need assistance in understanding the needs of and how to work with handicapped children integrated into the regular classroom. The following materials are useful in preparing for in-service training:

Latane, J. et al. *Progress Report of Training Inservices to Handicapped Head Start Children in Region IV*. Washington, D.C.: U.S. Office of Child Development, Bureau of Education for the Handicapped, Chapel Hill Training Outreach Project, 1974.

Lawrence, L. *Films Relevant to Child Development, Early Childhood Education, and Preschool Education of Handicapped Children: An Annotated Listing*, Vol. 111, No. 1, the Staff Training Resource Series. Austin, Texas: University of Texas, Department of Special Education, 1973). ERIC ED 133 934

Sanford, A. R. et al. *The Chapel Hill Model for Training Head Start Personnel in Mainstreaming Handicapped Children*. Washington, D.C.: U.S. Office of Education, Bureau of Education for the Handicapped, Chapel Hill Training-Outreach Project, 1974.

Paraprofessional personnel will also need orientation. For example, they will need information on the motoric, sensory, perceptual, cognitive, language, and affective development of the young child; on how classroom space and grounds, materials and equipment, learning and assessment activities, adult-child interaction techniques, and auxiliary services are used to meet developmental needs in the specific program; and on nutrition, health, and safety. This information must be presented over an extended period of time and in a variety of ways, through discussion, demonstration, and films.

A bulletin from the Office of Economic Opportunity states that regardless of the type of service provided, the following items should be included in volunteers' orientation: information about the program; an opportunity to absorb the general staff approach to children; descriptions of their duities and the line of authority; and assistance in recognizing differences between various socioeconomic groups, between majority and minority groups, and between the various minority groups. Inexperienced volunteers will have to have their duties explained carefully, and will need information concerning schedules, policies, procedures, and so forth.[52] In many cases, it is as necessary to orient teachers to the use and supervision of volunteers as it is to orient volunteers to program philosophy and operation. Historically, education has been a closed-door business; consequently, many teachers are unaccustomed to having somone in the room. Some of them express concern about the reliability of volunteers. Thus, orientation will be beneficial to the teacher as well as to the volunteer.

In-service education is actually a follow-up to a good orientation program and should be offered to all personnel to help them understand the program and auxiliary services and to improve their skills. Observing other staff members in action or demonstration teaching, viewing films and videotapes, using consultants, and participating in case conferences on particular children are a few of the many methods used in in-service education. In developing an in-service education program, these criteria should be considered: (1) in-service education should meet the specific needs of personnel in the program; (2) it should be conducted when teachers are not too tired to be receptive; (3) the method of presentation should be varied to fit the interest and level of understanding of the personnel; and (4) it should be ongoing.

MEMBERSHIP IN PROFESSIONAL ORGANIZATIONS

Membership in professional organizations offers various opportunities for personnel to improve their qualifications. All international and national organizations publish literature which contains pertinent information; most have regional, state, or local branches and workshops; some offer research assistance and provide resource materials to members; and a few have consultation programs available to members.

Appendix 3 presents alphabetically-arranged synopses of many of the international and national organizations concerned with the development of young children. Each synopsis consists of a brief history, its purposes, the journal name and special publications, and membership requirements and/or types of membership available. (Since publication of the first edition of this book, two of the oldest professional organizations, the American Association of Elementary-Kindergarten-Nursery Educators and the National Kindergarten Association, have discontinued their activities.)

In addition to the organizations listed in Appendix 3, there are other professional organizations that serve children, including the handicapped, and many newsletters and journals containing articles about the education of young children. These additional organizations and other helpful publications are listed in Appendix 4.

PERFORMANCE EVALUATION FOR IMPROVEMENT

Performance evaluation for improvement, the method by which a person's performance is evaluated, is another way to improve personnel qualifications. In the area of evaluation, there seem to be only two points of consensus: (1) the practice of evaluation of personnel is more prevalent today than a decade ago; and (2) evaluation of personnel effectiveness is recognized as a complex task.

A 1963 survey by the National Education Association[53] found that one-half of all school systems followed formal evaluation procedures; written ratings or evaluations were required in three-fourths of the schools for probationary teachers and in two-thirds of the schools for teachers after their probationary term; the principal was responsible for evaluation in most of the schools; and three-fourths of the adminstrators had confidence in their school's program of evaluation, but a majority of teachers did not share this confidence. With regard to purposes of evaluation, Stemnock[54] found that 93 percent of the teachers favored evaluation for assisting teacher-performance; 54 percent favored it for retaining and firing; and 17 percent favored it for merit-pay purposes.

Purpose of Evaluation.   The first question in considering a personnel evaluation program is: What is the ultimate purpose of evaluating personnel? Evaluation may be used for such decisions as continuance of employment, offering tenure, advancing merit pay, and/or personnel improvement. For our purposes, we will consider only performance evaluation for improvement, because all other purposes of evaluation, such as tenure and merit pay, should be based on performance.

Selection of Evaluation Criteria.   The next question which arises is: What are the steps to follow in initiating a program of evaluation? The first step is to determine whether all personnel should be evaluated by the same criteria and what criteria should be used. Generally, personnel who provide similar services should be evaluated according to the same criteria, but personnel serving in dissimilar roles should be evaluated according to different criteria, although some evaluation items might be the same.

Each early childhood program should develop its own criteria for evaluating personnel performance, rather than secure criteria developed for another program. In developing criteria, the policy-making body should keep in mind the philosophy and policies of the program, the roles of the personnel, and the personnel characteristics that constitute successful performance. Characteristics frequently evaluated are (1) physical characteristics, or the physical health and vitality conducive to effective performance which the position demands; (2) mental ability, or the ability to conceptualize the philosophy of the program, the needs of the children and adults involved in the program, and the employee's role and the roles of others as they relate to his position; (3) professional qualifications, or knowledge of methods and materials used in performing one's role; and (4) personal attributes, such as enthusiasm, poise, ability to adjust to frustrations, ability to cooperate with colleagues, and ability to accept constructive criticism.

Selection of an Evaluator.   The second step is to decide who should evaluate. In most early childhood programs, the director, supervisor, or building principal evaluates all personnel, although in some large programs, a personnel director is charged with the responsibility of evaluation. There is a growing trend toward self-evaluation. If individuals were able to evaluate themselves objectively and decide on target areas for improvement, self-evaluation might be the most effective means of improving performance. However, as we will see in the next section, self-evaluation has not been successful.

Selection of an Evaluation Instrument.   Another step in performance evaluation is to ascertain the type of instrument to be used. When criteria for evaluating personnel performance have been determined, they must be incorporated into an appraisal instrument. Locally-devised evaluation procedures may include observations, interviews, questionnaires, or check sheets and rating scales.

During observation, the evaluator observes the staff member performing his role and notes specific strengths and weaknesses of the performance based on the criteria selected for that particular job category. The staff member may also be asked to make a self-evaluation based on his own memory or by viewing a videotape of the performance. After appraisal, target areas for improvement should be chosen and a timetable for improvement considered.

Self-ratings have not been too successful. Research indicates that teachers may not perform better even when they view themselves privately on videotapes and have their lessons accompanied by guide sheets for self-appraisal.[55,56]

Interview procedures or questionnaires may be developed as evaluation instruments. Interviews may take the form of an open-ended discussion concerning strengths, performance areas needing improvement, and discussions on how to make improvements. On the other hand, interview forms and question forms may be, in actuality, verbal rating scales.

Check sheets and rating scales usually list evaluation criteria in categories of characteristics, such as physical characteristics and professional qualifications. Many check lists and rating scales also include an overall evaluation for each category of characteristics and/or for total performance evaluation. Although check sheets and rating scales are written evaluation instruments, each instrument has a distinctive style, as shown in the following examples:

1. The check sheet is used to indicate those behaviors satisfactorily completed by a staff member. The evaluator may check "yes," "no," or "not applicable."

	Yes	No	Not Applicable
Was prepared for lesson	____	____	____
Used a variety of teaching materials	____	____	____

2. A rating scale, a qualitative evaluation of performance, represents successive levels of quality along an inferior-superior continuum.
   a. Levels of quality may be described in words.

Use of step-by-step presentation			
Excellent	Good	Fair	Poor

   a Excellent
   b Above average
   c Average
   d Below average
   Creative in teaching   a b c d

   b. Levels of quality may be indicated with numerals. Directions given on the rating scale must indicate whether numeral "1" is the most inferior or the most superior evaluation.

Kept the children's attention				
1	2	3	4	5

   c. Levels of quality may be described in words and numerals.

Lesson was organized		
1	2	3
Usually		Never

```
Overall evaluation

  Superior      Excellent       Good        Average        Fair
  10      9      8      7      6      5      4      3      2      1
```

Cohen and Brawer[57] discuss problems in using rating scales for measuring staff performance.

An early childhood program may secure a standarized evaluation instrument to use as part of or as the total evaluation program. An example of a standardized evaluation instrument for evaluating teacher performance is the *Social-Emotional Climate Index,* which categorizes teacher verbalizations into types, such as commendatory, problem-structuring, and reproving.[58] A more recent observation instrument is the *Teacher Practices Observation Record.*[59] Many recent techniques for evaluation are based on "interaction analysis," the impetus for such developed by Flanders.[60] Other popular evaluation methods are called "contract plans," based on student gains,[61,62] but there are many problems involved in teacher accountability.[63]

Other excellent readings on the problems and development of teacher-evaluation instruments include:

Biddle, B.J., and Ellena, W.S., eds. *Contemporary Research on Teacher Effectiveness.* New York: Holt, Rinehart and Winston, 1964.

Brown, B.B., "Bringing Philosophy Into the Study of Teacher Effectiveness." *The Journal of Teacher Education,* 17 (1966):35–40.

Flanders, N.A., and Simon, A., "Teacher Effectiveness." In *Encyclopedia of Educational Research,* edited by R.L. Ebel, pp. 1423–37. New York: The Macmillan Company, 1969.

Rosenshire, B., and Furst, N., "Research on Teacher Performance Criteria." In *Research in Teacher Education: A Symposium,* edited by B.O. Smith, pp. 37–72. Englewood Cliffs, N.J.: Prentice-Hall, 1977.

Simon, A., and Boyer, E.G., eds. *Mirrors for Behavior II: An Anthology of Observation Instruments,* Vol. A. Philadelphia: Research for Better Schools, Inc., 1970.

Frequency of Evaluation.   Informal evaluation, especially self-evaluation, should be conducted continuously; however, the policy-making body should plan, determine the frequency of, and schedule formal evaluation. Frequency of evaluation must be planned before the instrument is written or selected, because this affects wording of evaluation criteria. For example, "uses chalkboard effectively" might be an appropriate evaluation criterion for a single lesson, but "uses a variety of audiovisual equipment effectively" would be suitable as an evaluation criterion for several informal or formal observations.

Personnel Services and Records

The state board of education and state licensing agency require that certain personnel services be provided and records kept by early childhood programs under their respective jurisdictions. In addition to those mandated personnel services and records, the local board of education or the board of directors may provide additional services and require other records permitted by state law.

CONTRACT AND TERMS OF EMPLOYMENT

A contract is an agreement detween two or more parties. In early childhood programs, a contract is an agreement between each staff member and the board of education or board of directors specifying the services a staff member must provide and the specific sum of money to be paid for services rendered. All contracts should conform to the following guidelines:

A written agreement as opposed to an oral one
Specific designation of the parties to the contract
Statement of the legal capacity of the parties represented
Provision for signatures by the authorized agents of the board of education or board of directors, and by the teacher or child care worker
Clear stipulation of salary to be paid
Designation of date of contract, duration, and the date when service is to begin
Definition of assignment[64]

In signing a contract, an employee indirectly consents to obey all rules and regulations in force at the time of employment or adopted during the period of employment. Policies which most directly affect employees may include hours per day and days per week; vacation; specific requirements, such as a uniform or driver's license; sick, emergency, and maternity leaves; substitutes; insurance; salary increases and fringe benefits; and retirement plan. Potential and present employees should have a written copy of all current policies.

The employee may receive a contract for some specified period of time, perhaps an annual contract or a continuing contract. Contracts for a specified period of time must be renewed at the end of such time period. The two types of continuing contracts are notification and tenure. An individual having a notification continuing contract must be notified on or before a given date if the contract is not to be renewed. A tenure contract guarantees that an employee cannot be dismissed except for certain specific conditions, such as lack of funds to pay salaries, neglect of duty, incompetency, failure to observe regulations of the board, and immorality; furthermore, a dismissed, tenured employee has the right to a hearing in which the board must prove "just cause" for the dismissal. Boards which offer tenure require that an employee serve a probationary period of a given number of years (usually three or five) before receiving a tenure contract.

JOB DESCRIPTION

A job description for each personnel category should be written, kept current, and include the following: (1) job title; (2) duties and responsibilities; (3) semi-regular additional duties; and (4) placement in the "chain of command." Job descriptions should be specific to the particular center and/or position, rather than adopted from another program. A potential employee should be permitted to review a job description before signing a contract, and all employees should keep their job descriptions in their files.

INSURANCE AND RETIREMENT PLANS

There are various kinds of insurance and retirement plans to protect employees and organizations. Adequate coverage is expensive but essential. Some types of insurance and retirement plans may be mandated by state or federal laws, whereas other types may be voluntary.

Federal Insurance Contributions Act (FICA).   Most centers are required to pay the FICA, or Social Security, tax. The FICA tax is generally used for retirement purposes. Tax rates are set at a percentage of the employee's salary. The employer desposits quarterly the amount of the employee's contributions collected as payroll deductions, plus an equal amount from the employer. (This money is deposited in a separate account, because comingling of federal funds is prohibited by law.) A quarterly report on FICA taxes is also required.

Until recently, tax-exempt organizations did not pay FICA tax, but changes were made in this law in October, 1976, so tax-exempt corporations should keep in contact with the District Office of the Internal Revenue Service.

Workman's Compensation Insurance.   Workman's compensation insurance is a liability insurance required by law in many states. State laws determine the kind of benefits and amounts. This insurance covers medical and hospital expenses (and may pay for time off work) to compensate employees for an initial injury or for aggravation of a preexisting condition sustained from accidents arising out of, or in the course of, their employment.

State Unemployment Insurance.   State unemployment insurance is required in most states and varies considerably from state to state. A questionnaire must be completed about the employees' activities and the tax-status of the early childhood program. The insurance rates are figured as a percentage of total wages and will be different for for-profit and not-for-profit corporations.

Liability Insurance.   Liability insurance protects the organization or employee from loss when persons have been injured or property damaged as a result of negligence (rather than accident) on the part of the institution or its employees; however, almost any "accident" that occurs is usually considered the result of negligence. The extent to which an institution or its employees can be held liable varies from state to state, and a liability policy should cover everything for which an institution is liable.

In most states, programs providing transporation services are required to have vehicle insurance. One type is liability insurance, which is coverage of liability for injury to persons or damage to property. Minimal auto liability insurance should be from $50,000 to $100,000.

Health Insurance and Hospital-Medical Insurance. Health insurance, whether fully or partially paid for by the employer or taken on a voluntary basis and paid for by the employee, may assume any of three forms: (1) medical-reimbursement insurance; (2) medical service or prepaid medical care; and (3) disability income benefits. Hospital-medical plans fall into three groups: (1) basic hospitalization and medical coverage; (2) major medical insurance; and (3) closed-panel operation, that is, service available from a limited number of physicians, clinics, or hospitals.

Crime Coverages. Protection against loss resulting from dishonesty of employees or others is available under four forms of coverage: (1) fidelity bonds; (2) board-form money and securities policy; (3) "3-D policy" (dishonesty, disappearance, and destruction); and (4) all-risk insurance.

Retirement Programs. Federal social security coverage, FICA tax, is usually mandatory. Generally, the tax is used as a federal "retirement program." Most public school program personnel are also under state retirement programs, paid on a matching-fund basis by employer and employee. Private institutions may have retirement programs in addition to federal social security coverage.

PERSONNEL RECORDS

Personnel administration involves keeping records and making reports in accordance with state laws, program governing-body requirements, and federal legislation concerning privacy of personal information. Public and private schools must keep personnel records on each regulation pertaining to employees—both program and nonprogram personnel. In most cases, personnel records are kept by the local programs and reports are submitted to their respective state governing boards (licensing agency or state board of education); however, the governing board may inspect locally-kept records.

Personnel records is a collective term for all records containing information about employees. Although these records vary from program to program, they usually embody these details:

1. Personnel information records are kept by all early childhood programs. Most of the personal information is given by a potential employee on the application form, and the information is kept current. Personal information includes name, age, sex, address and telephone number, marital status, social security number, and names and addresses of those who will give references.
2. Personal health records signed by an appropriate medical professional are required by all early childhood programs. These records may be detailed, requiring specific medical results of a physical examination, or may be a general statement that the employee is free from any mental or physical illness which might adversely affect the health of children or other adults.

In addition to records on general health, an annual tuberculosis test is required by most programs.

3. Emergency information is required by many programs. This information includes names, addresses, and telephone numbers of one or more persons to be contacted in a emergency; name of physician and hospital; and any medical information deemed necessary in an emergency situation, such as allergies to drugs or other conditions.

4. Records of education and other qualifications are required by all programs. They must include the names of schools attended; diplomas or degrees obtained; transcripts of academic work; and the registration number and type of teacher's or administrator's certificate or any other credential needed by an employee (such as a chauffeur's license).

5. Professional or occupational information records are kept by all programs, which include the places and dates of employment, names of employers, and job description.

6. Professional or occupational skill references and character references are included in the personnel records. In most cases, these references are for the confidential use of the employer.

7. Service records are kept by some programs. These records contain information concerning date of present employment; level or age of children cared for or taught, or program directed; absences incurred or leaves taken; in-service education received and conferences attended; committees served on; salary received; and date and reason for termination of service.

8. Insurance records are kept by all programs involved in any group insurance.

9. Evaluation records are placed on file in many programs. Evaluation records should not be kept after they have fulfilled the purposes for which they were intended.

10. Because an individual's legal right to privacy must be guarded, administrators must keep abreast of the laws pertaining to record keeping and record security. For example, the Privacy Act of 1974 (P.L. 93–579) requires federal agencies to take certain steps to safeguard the accuracy, currentness, and security of records concerning individuals and limit record keeping to necessary and lawful purposes. Individuals also have a lawfully enforceable right to examine federal records containing such information and to challenge the accuracy of data with which they disagree.[65] In accordance with the Privacy Act, the Office of the Federal Register has published a digest of the names of various record systems maintained by the federal government; categories of individuals about whom individual record systems are maintained; and procedures whereby an individual can obtain further information on any record system covered by the Privacy Act.[66] Personnel of many early childhood programs, such as Head Start and others receiving federal funding, are covered under the Privacy Act of 1974.

NOTES

1. U.S. Department of Health, Education, and Welfare, *The Appropriateness of the Federal Interagency Day Care Requirements: Report of Findings and Recommendations* (Washington, D.C.: U.S. Government Printing Office, 1978), p. 28.

2. S. Wynne et al., *Mainstreaming and Early Childhood Education for Handicapped Children: A Guide for Teachers and Parents. Final Report* (Washington, D.C.: Wynne Associates, 1975), p. 23. ERIC ED 119 445

3. E. Barngrover, "A Study of Educator's Preference in Special Education Programs," *Exceptional Children* 37 (1971): 754–55.

4. A. Beeler, "Integrating Exceptional Children in Preschool Classrooms," *BAEYC Reports* 15 (1973): 33–41.

5. J.R. Shortel, R.P. Iano, and J.F. McGettigan, "Teacher Attitudes Associated with the Integration of Handicapped Children," *Exceptional Children* 38 (1972): 677–83.

6. A.M. Edelman, *A Pilot Study in Exploring the Use of Mental Health Consultants to Teachers of Socially and Emotionally Maladjusted Pupils in Regular Classes* (Philadelphia: Mental Health Association of Southeast Pennsylvania, 1966). ERIC ED 026 292

7. W.A. Johnston, *A Study to Determine Teacher Attitude Toward Teaching Special Children with Regular Children* (DeKalb, Ill.: Northern Illinois University, 1972). ERIC ED 065 950

8. S. Yule, "Kindergarten Children with Handicaps," *Australian Preschool Quarterly* 4 (1963): 4–7.

9. NEA Research Division, "New Profile on the American Public School Teacher," *Today's Education* 61 (1972): 14–17.

10. E.M. Hetherington and J.L. Deur, "The Effects of Father Absence on Child Development," *Young Children* 26 (1971): 233–48.

11. P. Wohlford, J.W. Santrock, S.E. Berger, and D. Liberman, "Older Brothers Influence on Sex-Typed, Aggressive, and Dependent Behavior in Father-Absent Children," *Developmental Psychology* 4 (1971): 124–34.

12. W. Mischel, "Sex Typing and Socialization," *Carmichael's Manual of Child Pyschology*, ed. P.H. Mussen (New York: John Wiley & Sons, 1970), pp. 3–72.

13. D.B. Lynn, *Parental and Sex-Role Identification, a Theoretical Formulation* (Berkeley, Calif.: McCutchan Publishing Corp., 1969).

14. C. Madsen, "Nuturance and Modeling in Preschoolers," *Child Development* 39 (1968): 221–36.

15. R.L. Kellogg, "A Direct Approach to Sex Role Indentification of School-Related Objects," *Psychological Report* 24 (1969): 839–41.

16. American Association of School Administrators and Research Division of NEA, "Pupil Promotion Policies and Rate of Promotion," *Educational Research Service Circular*, No. 5., 1958.

17. F. Bentzen, "Sex Ratios in Learning and Behavior Disorders," *National Elementary Principle* 46 (1966): 13–17.

18. B.R. McCandless, A. Roberts, and T. Starnes, "Teachers' Marks, Achievement Test Scores, and Aptitude Relations with Respect to Social Class, Race, and Sex," *Journal of Educational Psychology* 63 (1972): 153–59.

19. K.G. Kuckenberg, *Effect of Early Father Absence on Scholastic Attitude* (Cambridge, Mass.: Ph.D. diss., Harvard University, 1963).

20. M.M. Shinedling, and D.M. Pederson, "Effects of Sex of Teacher and Student on Children's Gain in Quantitative and Verbal Performance," *Journal of Psychology* 76 (1970): 79–84.

21. D.F. Smith, *A Study of the Relationship of Teacher Sex to Fifth Grade Boys' Sex Role Preference, General Self Concept and Scholastic Achievement in Science and Mathematics* (Miami, Fla.: Ph.D. diss., University of Miami, 1970).

22. Ibid.

23. L. Kohlberg, "A Cognitive-Developmental Analysis of Children's Sex-Role Concepts and Attitudes," *The Development of Sex Differences*, ed. E. Maccoby (Stanford, Calif.: Stanford University Press, 1966), pp. 82–173.

24. H.H. Davidson and G. Lang, "Children's Perceptions of Their Teachers' Feelings Toward Them Related to Self-Perception, School Achievement, and Behavior," *Journal of Experimental Education* 29 (1960): 107–18.

25. P. Sexton, *The Feminized Male* (New York: Random House, 1969).

26. E.M. Hetherington, "Effects of Father Absence on Personality Development in Adolescent Daughters," *Developmental Psychology* 7 (1972): 313–26.

27. F. Landry, B.G. Rosenberg, and B. Sutton-Smith, "The Effect of Limited Father Absence on Cognitive Development," *Child Development* 40 (1969): 941–44.

28. B. Carter and G. Dapper, *School Volunteers: What They Do and How They Do It* (New York: Citation Press, 1972).

29. ———. *Organizing School Volunteer Programs* (New York: Citation Press, 1974), p. 8.

30. Committee on Infant and Preschool Child, *Standards for Day Care Centers for Infants and Children Under 3 Years of Age* (Evanston, Ill.: American Academy of Pediatrics, 1971), p. 7.

31. S. Farnham-Diggory, *Cognitive Processes in Education* (New York: Harper & Row, 1972), p. 590.

32. O.J. Harvey et al., "Teacher Belief Systems and Preschool Atmospheres," *Journal of Educational Psychology* 57 (1966): 373–81.

33. *Standards for Day Care Centers for Infants and Children Under 3 Years of Age*, p. 7.

34. Association for Childhood Education International, Teacher Education Committee, *Standards for Teachers in Early Childhood Education* (Washington, D.C.: The Association, 1958), pp. 65–66.

35. James L. Hymes, Jr., *A Child Development Point of View* (Englewood Cliffs, N.J.: Prentice-Hall, 1961), p. 96.

36. N. Fairchild, "An Analysis of the Services Performed by School Psychologist in an Urban Area: Implications for Training Programs," *Psychology in the Schools* 11 (1974): 275–81.

37. A. Conti and J.I. Bardon, "A Proposal for Evaluating the Effectiveness of Psychologists in the Schools," *Psychology in the Schools* 11 (1974): 32–9.

38. Children's Bureau Publication, *Day Care Services* (Washington D.C.: U.S. Department of Health, Education, and Welfare, 1970).

39. M. Silverman, "Principals—What Are you Doing to Teacher Morale?" *Educational Adminstration and Supervision* 43 (1957): 205.

40. T.H. Briggs, "Morale," *The Educational Forum* 22 (1958): 148.

41. M.V. Campbell, *Self-Role Conflict Among Teachers and Its Relationship to Satisfaction, Effectiveness, and Confidence in Leadership* (Chicago, Ill.: Ph.D. diss., University of Chicago, 1958).

42. F.W. Bewley, *The Characteristics of Successful School Superintendents* (Los Angeles, Calif.: Ph.D. diss., University of Southern California, 1960).

43. Silverman, "Principals—What Are You Doing to Teacher Morale?"

44. *The Bible*, St. Luke 17: 11–17.

45. R.E. Sibson, "Handling Grievances Where There Is No Union," *Personnel Journal* 35 (1956): 56.

46. W. Gellhorn, *Ombudsmen and Others: Citizens Protectors in Nine Countries* (Cambridge, Mass.: Harvard University Press, 1966).

47. Affirmative action is a program under which early childhood programs which receive public monies must eliminate any discriminatory practices. For more information consult the following source: Equal Opportunity Commission, "Affirmative Action Guidelines," *Federal Register* 44 (14), January 19, 1979.

48. Director, Office of Public Affairs, Equal Employment Opportunity Commission, 2401 E. Street NW, Washington, D.C. 20506 (Tel: 202-634-6930)

49. Association for Childhood Education International, *Standards for Teachers*, pp. 65–66.

50. L. Katz, "Developmental Stages of Pre-School Teachers," *Elementary School Journal* 73 (1972): 50–54.

51. Ibid.

52. Office of Economic Opportunity, *Project Head Start—Volunteers* (Washington, D.C.: Government Printing Office, 1967).

53. National Education Association, Research Division, *Evaluation of Classroom Teachers Research Report, 1963—R14* (Washington, D.C.: NEA, 1964).

54. S.K. Stemnock, *Evaluating Teaching Performance*, Educational Research Service Circular, No. 3 (Washington, D.C.: NEA, 1969).

55. B. Weiner and A. Kukla, "An Attributional Analysis of Achievement Motivation," *Journal of Personality and Social Psychology* 15 (1970): 1–20.

56. G. Solomon and F.J. McDonald, "Pretest and Posttest Reactions to Self-Viewing One's Teaching

Performance on Video Tape," *Journal of Educational Psychology* 61 (1970): 280–6.

57. A.M. Cohen and F.B. Brawer, *Measuring Faculty Performance* (Washington, D.C.: American Association of Junior Colleges, 1969).

58. John Withall, "The Development of a Technique for the Measurement of Social-Emotional Climate of Classrooms," *Journal of Experimental Education* 18 (1949).

59. B.B. Brown, *Systematic Observation: Relating Theory and Practice in the Classroom* (Gainesville, Fla.: Florida University, Institute for Development of Human Resources, 1969). ERIC Ed 031 444

60. N.A. Flanders, *Interaction Analysis in the Classroom* (revised edition) (Ann Arbor, Mich.: School of Education, University of Michigan, 1966).

61. R. Goldhammer, *Clinical Supervision* (New York: Holt, Rinehart & Winston, 1969).

62. J.D. McNeil, *Toward Accountable Teachers: Their Appraisal and Improvement* (New York: Holt, Rinehart & Winston, 1971).

63. M. Lieberman, ed., "8 Articles on Accountability," *Phi Delta Kappan* 52 (1970): 194–239.

64. Willard S. Elsbree and E. Edmund Reutter, Jr., *Staff Personnel in the Public Schools* (Englewood Cliffs, N.J.: Prentice-Hall, 1954), pp. 421–22.

65. Title v, Section 552a, *U.S. Code 1976 Edition: Containing the General and Permanent Laws of the U.S., In Force on January 3, 1977*, Vol. 1. (Washington, D.C.: U.S. Government Printing Office, 1977).

66. Office of the Federal Register, *Protecting Your Right to Privacy—Digest of Systems of Records, Agency Rules, and Research Aids* (Washington, D.C.: U.S. Government Printing Office, 1977).

For Further Reading

Association for Childhood Education International, Teacher Education Committee. "Preparation Standards for Teachers in Early Childhood Education—Nursery, Kindergarten, Primary." *Young Children* 23 (1967): 79–80.

Bacmeister, Rhoda W. *Teachers for Young Children—The Person and the Skills.* New York: Early Childhood Council of New York, 1968.

Early Childhood Education: How to Organize Volunteers; How and Where to Find Volunteers. Los Angeles: Los Angeles City Schools, Office of Volunteer and Tutorial Programs, 1973. ERIC ED 104 560

Fletcher, Margaret I. *The Adult and the Nursery School Child.* Toronto, Canada: University of Toronto Press, 1958.

Gross, Dorothy. "Teachers of Young Children Need Basic Inner Qualities." *Young Children* 23 (1967): 107–10.

Milgram, J.I. "Sources of Manpower for the Preschool Classroom." *Childhood Education* 49 (1972): 187–89.

Schmitthauser, C.M. "Professionalization of Teaching in Early Childhood Education.' *Journal of Teacher Education* 30 (1969): 188–90.

Spodek, Bernard. "Constructing a Model for a Teacher Education Program in Early Childhood Education." *Contemporary Education* 40 (1969): 145–49.

Stinnett, T.M. *A Manual on Standards Affecting School Personnel in the United States.* Washington, D.C.: National Education Association, 1974.

7

Supervising

Supervision is generally viewed as a component of administration and, thus, is executed by administrators. Because supervisors have been called upon to do many jobs, such as to provide leadership in program planning and implementation, to work with teachers, including beginning and student teachers, and to evaluate teachers, supervision has been defined in various ways, such as program leadership and personnel development. Just as supervisors' job descriptions vary from program to program, titles also vary. The supervisor may be called a director, principal, program or curriculum consultant, or helping teacher.

Supervision is in an embryonic stage of development; it has only recently become a discipline in its own right. There is, consequently, little research on the functions and problems of supervision, or on the methods and qualities of supervisors. Most information about supervision and supervisors is based on extrapolation of the experiences of people who write in this field. Because of the recency of supervision as a distinct field, there are few professionals at state or local supervisory levels—especially in early childhood education.

Historical Synopsis of Supervision

Supervision was traditionally seen as an adjunct of administration. Until 1920, the primary purpose of supervision was inspection of the schools.[1] Improvement of instruction was recognized as an additional objective of supervision in the 1920s.[2]

One theory of supervision saw supervisors and teachers as having separate and distinct jobs. Their respective functions on the school staff were described in this way:

It was the supervisory staff which was to have the largest share in the work of determining proper methods. The burden of finding the best methods was too great and too complex to be laid on the shoulders of teachers. The teacher was expected to be the specialist in the practice that would produce the "product"; the supervisor was to specialize in the science relating to the process. Supervisors were to: (1) discover best procedures in the performance of particular tasks and (2) give these best methods to teachers for their guidance.[3]

A second and differing theory had its roots in the Progressive Movement. Democratic supervision, as it was called, held that a teacher's ability must be endorsed by avoiding the threat of supervision as "inspection," or evaluation. In short, under the "democratic supervision" theory, supervisors and teachers were viewed as equal partners in policy formulation.[4]

Functions of Supervision

In just over half a century, supervision of education has progressed from an inspection role to a highly sophisticated leadership role. The analysis of supervisory functions which follows is somewhat lacking in precision, attributable in part to the fact that the study of supervisory functions is relatively new. There are ambiguities and voids in our knowledge of supervisory functions, and supervisory functions are not restrictive in nature. Because supervisors are educational leaders, their leadership role may be exercised in many ways and with many people, in addition to the classroom teacher, such as officials of state and federal regulatory and/or funding agencies, board members of the local program, the director, specialists involved in the program, nonprogram personnel, and other supervisors. Keeping in mind the dynamic role of supervision, present literature suggests that supervision is composed of three functions: (1) improving the quality of instruction; (2) mutual growth of supervisor and teacher; and (3) evaluation.

IMPROVING THE QUALITY OF INSTRUCTION

Improving the quality of instruction is the most important function of supervision, because the only purpose of any program is to help the children and their parents. The quality of any program is determined by content and staff. Supervision should become the pivotal activity around which to manage program and staff development. Program development requires specific training or retraining of staff, because new knowledge, methodological techniques, and even attitudes are required for implementation and maintenance of program changes. Staff development itself can cause changes in the program, too. Thus, supervisors must be involved in program and staff development in order to change the quality of instruction for the better.

Program Development.   The close relationship between supervision and program development is implied in the title of one of the major professional organizations for supervisors, the Association for Supervision and Curriculum

Development. Supervisors are needed to help establish the direction of an early childhood program. The last two decades have seen a proliferation of new curricular ideas and model programs. Supervisors may keep abreast of new ideas, try some of these ideas as pilot projects with a few teachers or in demonstration centers, and serve on committees that choose from among alternatives that seem best for the local program. After program decisions are made, supervisors must provide professional assistance while the staff develops knowledge and skills for implementing the new program; and, more importantly, supervisors must help the staff develop a commitment to a particular action. (An example of the assistance needed in mainstreaming was given in the preceding chapter.)[5,6,7,8]

Staff Development.   Programs are not "teacher proof." When new programs are developed, all staff members must have assistance and support in the implementation process if the programs are to be successful. Continuous supervisory assistance is needed even when new program development is not being undertaken. Katz[9] describes the need for supervisory help in each of four stages of teacher development. Besides promoting staff development for all teachers, supervisors must attempt to salvage inadequate and failing teachers. Wiles[10] identifies the "lazy," "colorless," "older," "inadequate," "disagreeing," and "failing" teacher and discusses supervisory approaches that may help these teachers. In short, staff development improves the quality of instruction.

MUTUAL GROWTH OF SUPERVISOR AND TEACHER

Developing programs and working out implementation problems should be an experimental process for both supervisor and teacher. This process will result not only in improving the quality of instruction, but also in the supervisor's and teacher's mutual growth. Supervisors are not all-knowing authorities, nor are teachers "blank slates" to be written upon. Both must be committed to a relationship that fosters growth, learning, and exchange of ideas. Without this commitment on the part of even the most potentially talented supervisors and teachers, supervision will become a game played by the supervisor for putting in a day's work, and by the teacher for getting a degree, tenured status, or a raise.

EVALUATION

There is some disagreement as to whether supervision and evaluation can be successfully accomplished by the same person. Some feel that one cannot be both a helping hand and a judgmental figure. Many teachers call this "snoopervision," and many supervisors feel the evaluation function breaks the lines of communication between supervisor and teacher. Evaluation can also create fear and produce teacher conformity, and may be seen as an invasion of academic freedom. Finally, protective tenure laws can reduce evaluation to nothing more than paper-and-pencil exercises for tenured staff. On the other hand, others argue that if the supervisor evaluates, the teacher will most likely perform to his maximum ability.

Regardless of the pros and cons of the supervisor's evaluation function, supervisors are usually called upon to evaluate because protection of the client (in this case, the child and his parents) justifies evaluation. In the past, teachers were often felt to have high success-potential if they were neat, displayed good conduct, and were friendly and cheerful.[11] More objective approaches are used today.[12] As noted in the preceding chapter, there are problems in evaluation as a result of the lack of definitive research on teaching effectiveness and objective methods of teacher assessment.[13, 14] Flanders[15] and others[16, 17] have developed methods for analyzing teaching which may relate significantly to student learning. Some of the best research on supervision is recent and includes use of audio- and videotapes for feedback purposes[18] and development of instruments for analyzing the supervisory conference.[19, 20] However, until there are more advancements in the fields of teacher effectiveness and evaluation, and until these methods become more widespread, the situation will continue to give rise to statements of professional equalitarianism and to resistance to evaluation.

Finally, one hopes the process engaged in during supervision will be continued by the teacher beyond the period of formal supervision. An effective teacher must continue to evaluate his own teaching processes. Both creativeness and self-reliance are facilitated when self-evaluation is primary and evaluation by others secondary.[21] Thus, supervisors should help the teacher become self-supervising by serving as a role model for the evaluation process.

PROBLEMS IN THE SUPERVISOR-TEACHER RELATIONSHIP

Both supervisor and teacher bring their respective knowledge and assumptions, skills, and attitudes to their relationship. Although the relationship is complex, communication between supervisor and teacher is essential to effective supervision. Sharing knowledge and attitudes to arrive at common understandings is a two-way process. The essence of supervision is communication, yet the literature is replete with hints at and discussions on the barriers and problems in the supervisor-teacher relationship, as seen in the following readings:

Blumberg, A. *Supervisor and Teacher: A Private Cold War.* Berkeley, Calif.: McCutchan Publishing Company, 1973.

Blumberg, A., and Amidon, E. "Supervisory Behavior and Interpersonal Relations." *Educational Administrational Quarterly* 4 (1968): 34–45.

Wiles, K. *Supervision for Better Schools,* 3d ed. Englewood Cliffs, N.J.: Prentice-Hall, 1967, pp. 51–90.

The supervisor-teacher relationship can be more effective when both parties recognize some of these barriers and problems.

PRESCRIPTIVE SUPERVISION

Traditionally, supervision of teachers has been an authority-subordination relationship. The idea behind this relationship was that through innate qualities and experience (but rarely special training), the supervisor knew best, and all the teacher need do was follow directions. Prescriptive supervision, which often involves on-the-spot judgments, is usually of negative value. The objective was apparently to oversee the teacher and use competition with other teachers as a stimulus.

The attitude toward supervision now is that it is collaboration in a problem-solving effort. In order to have collaboration, the supervisor-teacher relationship must be collegial rather than hierarchial. In this partnership, alternatives are sought by each professional and both assume responsibility for decisions. Thus, in a nonprescriptive relationship, there is heavy emphasis on the teacher's responsibility for analysis of and solutions to the instructional process. Teachers feel freer to discuss their problems with supervisors in a colleague relationship. Once the teacher sees the supervisor as a source of help, he will be more willing to understand and accept the analysis of his teaching, which, in turn, should result in more effective teaching.

TIME SPENT IN "TELLING"

Closely related to prescriptive supervising is the amount of time supervisors spend in "telling." Blumberg and Cusick[22] analyzed fifty separate supervisor-teacher tape-recorded conferences involving total conference time of over eleven hours. Analyses of the tapes indicated that supervisors spent only .04 percent of their talking time (1.2 minutes out of five hours) questioning teachers as to how they would go about solving their instructional problems, and that teachers spent only .06 percent of their talking time (2.2 minutes out of every six hours) asking the supervisor any kind of question. These analyses show that the bulk of the supervisor's behavior was "telling" in nature. Supervisors seldom ask teachers for ideas about how to solve problems, and teachers rarely ask supervisors questions. Teachers sometimes see supervisors' questions as attempts to "box them in" rather than to help them. Negative behavior on the part of the teacher was met in kind 13 percent of the time.[23] Supervisors should listen a lot, for when teachers have been heard, they are better able to hear.

OTHER PROBLEMS

There are many other problems with the supervisor-teacher relationship. Consider the following situations:

Supervisor "Takes Over" Class.   The supervisor should not take over the teacher's class to show how he would do it himself. This procedure may help the class, but will not help the teacher. The teacher will feel resentful or inadequate and may feel he must teach the same way the supervisor does. If the supervisor does not take over the classroom, the teacher can either follow or ignore the supervisor's suggestions. How can teachers be told when, what, and how to teach, then be told to feel free to use their own imaginations?

Supervision Concerned with Trivia.   A supervisor may concern himself only with trivia—whether or not chalkboards are clean, desks straight, shades evenly drawn, students' chairs, desks, or tables straight, whether paper is off the floor, and whether or not children walk in "straight" lines. Is not teacher-learning a more complicated process?

Supervisor Does Not Develop a Cognitive "Match."   Much has been written about the importance of teachers' "matching" the functioning levels of the children with whom they work. Yet, many supervisors work as though the teacher knows nothing; the idea that teachers are "blank slates" is the basic assumption of prescriptive supervision. Should not the supervisor develop a cognitive match with the teacher's level of functioning?

Supervisors Often Serve Two Masters.   As previously mentioned, there are problems for the supervisor in being both a helping hand and a judgmental figure. In fact, administration may sensitize the supervisor to the "problem" or "deviant" teacher. When pressed for time, the supervisor may depend on the administration, such as the principal, for a teacher's evaluation. Supervisors often fulfill the function of legitimatizing certain administrative procedures and at the same time serving as spokesman for the teachers. (A parallel situation is found between the superintendent or director of a school system or program and their boards and staffs.) Can a person serve two masters?

Too Little Time.   "Too little time" seems to be everyone's problem today. This problem is readily apparent in the infrequent, unscheduled, and short time of some supervisory visits and the haste of supervisory conferences. The medical profession uses the case conference as a means of professional development, and time is allotted for this process. Should not our cases have this same benefit of time for thoughtful consideration?

Excluding the Teacher as a Person.   Because so much of supervision tends to be aimed at the curricular and methodological aspects of teaching, there is a tendency to forget the human being behind the process. Do we not need more emphasis on personal and career goals?

The Personality Clash.   Ideally, supervisors are expected to work with any teacher. Occasionally, however, the relationship between supervisor and teacher is one of stress and negative behavior. If the relationship continues, one or another of these things happens: the supervisor quits supervising—physically or psychologically; the supervisor and teacher go through the motions but ignore each others' ideas; the supervisor avoids confrontations to keep the relationship trouble free, at least on the surface; or the supervisor rationalizes to cover his inadequacies. Are there not some cases in which the supervisor-teacher relationship is worthless? Can any supervisor be expected to help every teacher anymore than any teacher can help every child?

Methods of Supervision

Supervisors may work with teachers individually or in groups. The individual conference is the most common method of supervision. There are no hard and fast rules for conducting such a conference. Certainly, how the conference is conducted depends on the teaching situation and the level of functioning for both supervisor and teacher. Nonetheless, certain pointers can make a supervisory conference worthwhile:

1. Supervisor and teacher should plan together prior to the teaching. Planning should include:
   a. Rethinking lesson objectives, content, and methodology. (It is assumed that the teacher has preplanned.)
   b. Proposing other strategies (by both supervisor and teacher) and predicting how children will respond.
   c. Choosing a final teaching strategy.
2. The supervisor should observe the teacher and record in detail both the presentation and the children's response.
3. The children's response should be studied by both supervisor and teacher prior to the conference.[24] Questions may include:
   a. How did the children respond to the lesson objectives?
   b. Was classroom management smooth or disorganized?
   c. What was the affective relationship between teacher and children?
4. The conference should not be held immediately after observation; the teacher's feelings may be too sensitive, and both parties need time to think about what went on in the classroom.
5. The conference should focus on patterns that tend to recur during the teaching period. Two prerequisites are essential:
   a. The supervisor should have extensive evidence to document a problem; and
   b. He should be able to summarize the problem in language devoid of vague educational jargon.
6. Most of the conference time should be spent with supervisor and teacher presenting alternate ideas for solving each problem, keeping in mind that:
   a. The supervisor should elicit and accept the teacher's ideas and feelings and positively reinforce the teacher;[25] and
   b. The teacher should be allowed to make the final decision among the alternatives discussed.
7. Plan the next lesson on the basis of the conference.
8. Observe the following practices:
   a. Discuss only four or five topics in a conference, of which the first and last should be the teacher's strong points;[26]
   b. Do not refer to a teaching technique as "bad" or "good," but rather as "appropriate" or "inappropriate" for the objectives and/or children.

c. Reinforce successful teaching techniques with praise, which will not only make the teacher feel more adequate, but will cause him to repeat the successful techniques. (The absence of criticism is not praise!)

If the early childhood program is a less structured one in which children interact with the teacher on an individual basis or in small groups, supervision may follow this format:

1. Supervisor and teacher should discuss, demonstrate, and/or practice how to reinforce and extend the children's learning experiences in a training session.
2. The supervisor should observe the teacher's performance to compare with that practiced in the training session.
3. In the supervisory conference, teacher and supervisor should discuss the teacher's perceptions of his interactions with the children. If the interactions were successful, the teacher should be praised; if not, a plan of action should be developed.

Supervisors also work with teachers in groups. Orientation and in-service are examples of group supervision. There are also group supervisory conferences, identical to the individual supervisory conferences, except that the teacher usually discusses his own teaching first, followed by analyses from other teachers and the supervisor, all of whom have observed the teaching. Group supervision permits multiple perspectives to be introduced and is especially effective when nonprogram professionals, such as physicians or psychologists, are included.

A quasi-supervisory idea has taken form in the "Teachers' Centers."[27] Teachers' centers are physical facilities and self-improvement programs organized and operated by teachers themselves. These Centers break with tradition because, in the past, initiative for change has always come from the outside, from such sources as political officials, boards, administrative officers, supervisors, textbook publishers, and professors. The Teachers' Centers promise change from within. Teachers have always learned from other teachers and through their own experiences, and a cooperative effort is likely to be a successful alternative among supervisory methods.

Regardless of the structure of the classroom or the method of supervision, supervisors need to help teachers reach two broad goals:

1. Are teachers learning to consider the relationship between their actions and children's learning? Is the teacher developing a style that is both effective with children and appropriate to his personality?
2. Are teachers becoming more self-reliant? Do they draw on their own resources, or do they merely see the supervisor as a "bearer of gifts" in the form of materials or an assistant teacher?

Qualifications of Supervisors

There are many personal styles found among supervisors. Perhaps less is known about supervisor effectiveness than about teacher effectiveness, but successful supervisors appear to have some common characteristics:

1. They have been excellent teachers, with the personal and professional qualities of a good teacher.
2. They are sensitive to problems often not obvious to others. These problems may be in the areas of program objectives, methodology, or teacher-child interrelationships.
3. They are accepting individuals who can empathize with the difficulties of a new teacher, the challenges of mature teachers, and the problems of "failing" teachers.
4. They have excellent communication skills and have learned the arts of timing and feedback.
5. Knowing the importance of self-evaluation, they help the teacher become his own critic.
6. They are willing to take the responsibility of protecting a child, even if it means terminating a teacher's position.

The professional qualifications of supervisors depend on whether the supervisor is serving a program regulated by the state education agency or by the state licensing agency. In general, supervisors in public schools hold state certificates. There is great variation in supervisory certificates.[28] Supervisors of day-care centers and other early childhood programs that are not part of public schools have to meet the standards of their regulatory agency. (The director is usually the supervisor of these programs.)

Two additional references may be of help to those interested in supervisory competencies and their assessment:

Harris, B.M., and King, J.D. *Professional Supervisory Competencies.* Austin, Texas: Report of Special Education Training Project, University of Texas, 1974.

McIntyre, K.E., and Bessent, E.W. *New Form Knowledge Assessment Test (KAT-NF), revised: A New Test for Assessment of Professional Supervisory Competencies.* Austin, Texas: Department of Educational Administration, University of Texas, 1976.

NOTES.

1. W.H. Lucio and J.D. McNeil, *Supervision: A Synthesis of Thought and Action* (New York: McGraw-Hill Book Co., 1962), pp. 3–21.
2. J.B. Gwynn, *Theory and Practice of Supervision* (New York: Dodd, Mead and Co., 1961), p. 9.
3. Lucio and McNeil, *Supervision: A Systhesis of Thought and Action,* p. 8.
4. Ibid., p. 11.
5. C.T. Jacobs, *Comparison of Teacher Attitudes and Certain Other Variables in Three School Settings for the Educable Mentally Handicapped* (Kalamazoo, Mich.: Ph.D. diss., Western Michigan University, 1974).
6. J.E. Jordan and D.I. Proctor, "Relationship Between Knowledge of Exceptional Children, Kind and Amount of Experience with Them, and Teacher Attitudes Toward Their Classroom Integration," *The Journal of Special Education* 3 (1969): 433–41.
7. J.R. Yates, "Model for Preparing Regular Classroom Teachers for 'Mainstreaming,'" *Exceptional Children* 39 (1973): 471–72.
8. A.M. Edelman, *A Pilot Study in Exploring the Use of Mental Health Consultants to Teachers of Socially and Emotionally Maladjusted Pupils in Regular Classes* (Philadelphia: Mental Health Association of Southeast Pennsylvania, 1966). ERIC ED 026 292

9. L. Katz, "Developmental Stages of Pre-School Teachers," *Elementary School Journal* 73 (1972): 50–54.

10. K. Wiles, *Supervision for Better Schools*, third edition (Englewood Cliffs, N.J.: Prentice-Hall, 1967), pp. 124–33.

11. J.D. McNeil and W.J. Popham, "The Assessment of Teacher Competence," *Second Handbook of Research on Teaching*, ed. R.M.W. Travers (Chicago: Rand McNally and Co., 1973), pp. 218–44.

12. R.F. Peck and J.A. Tucker, "Research on Teacher Education," *Second Handbook of Research on Teaching*, ed. R.M.W. Travers (Chicago: Rand McNally and Co., 1973), pp. 940–78.

13. S.J. Domas and D.V. Tideman, "Teacher Competence: An Annotated Bibliography," *Journal of Experimental Education* 19 (1950): 99–218.

14. J.W. Getzels and P.W. Jackson, "The Teacher's Personality and Characteristics," *Handbook of Research on Teaching*, ed. N.L. Gage (Chicago: Rand McNally and Co., 1964), pp. 506–82.

15. N.A. Flanders, "Some Relationships Among Teacher Influence, Pupil Attitudes, and Achievement," *Contemporary Research on Teacher Effectiveness*, ed. B.J. Biddle and W.P. Ellena (New York: Holt, Rinehart & Winston, 1964), pp. 196–231.

16. A.A. Bellack et al., *The Language of the Classroom* (New York: Teachers College Press, 1966).

17. J.B. Hough, "An Observational System for the Analysis of Classroom Instruction," mimeographed paper (Columbus, Ohio: Ohio State University, College of Education, 1965).

18. H. Schueler and M. Gold, "Video Recordings of Student Teachers: A Report of the Hunter College Research Project," *Journal of Teacher Education* 15 (1964): 358–64.

19. R.H. Weller, *An Observation System for Analyzing Clinical Supervision of Teachers* (Cambridge, Mass.: Ph.D. diss., Harvard University, 1969).

20. J.W. Seaver and L.S. Orlando, *An Observation Protocol for Early Childhood Settings* (University Park, Pa.: The Pennsylvania State University, 1977).

21. C. Rogers, *Freedom to Learn* (Columbus, Ohio: Charles E. Merrill Publishing Co., 1969).

22. A. Blumberg and P. Cusick, "Supervisor-Teacher Interaction: An Analysis of Verbal Behavior," *Education* 91 (1970): 126–34.

23. Ibid.

24. M.V.S. Yonemura, "Supervision in Early Childhood Education," *Young Children* 24 (1968): 104–9.

25. A. Blumberg and E. Amidon, "Teacher Perceptions of Supervisor-Teacher Interaction," *Administrator's Notebook* 14 (1965): 1–8.

26. G.C. Kyte, "The Effective Supervisory Conference," *California Journal of Educational Research* 13 (1962): 160–68.

27. S.K. Bailey, "Teachers' Centers: A British First," *Phi Delta Kappan* 53 (1971): 146–49.

28. H.R. Hallberg, "Certification Requirements for General Supervisors and/or Curriculum Workers Today-Tomorrow," *Educational Leadership* 23 (1966): 623–25.

For Further Reading

Amidon, E.J. et al. "Group Supervision." *National Elementary Principal* 45 (1966): 54–8.

Blocker, C.E., and Richardson, R.C. "Twenty-five Years of Morale Research: A Critical Review." *Journal of Educational Sociology* 36 (1963): 200–10.

Blumberg, A. "A System for Analyzing Supervisor-Teacher Interaction." In *Mirrors for Behavior, VIII*, edited by A. Simon and G. Bower. Philadelphia: Research for Better Schools, 1970.

Blumberg, A., and Amidon, E. "Teacher Perception of Supervisor-Teacher Interaction." *Administrator's Notebook*, 14 (1965).

Cox, J.V. "Selection and Recruitment of Supervisors." *Educational Leadership* 24 (1966): 47–51.

Downing, G. "A Supervision Experiment with the Disadvantaged." *Educational Leadership* 21 (1964): 433–35.

Lucio, W.H., ed. *Supervision: Perspectives and Propositions.* Washington, D.C.: Association for Supervision and Curriculum Development, 1967.

MacDonald, J.B. "Knowledge About Supervision: Rationalization or Rationale?" *Educational Leadership* 61 (1965): 161–63.

Mosher, R.L., and Purpel, D.E. *Supervision: The Reluctant Profession.* Boston: Houghton Mifflin Co., 1972.

Ogletree, J.R. et al. "Preparing Educational Supervisors." *Educational Leadership* 20 (1962): 163–66.

Wiles, K. *Supervision for Better Schools,* 3d ed. Englewood Cliffs, N.J.: Prentice-Hall, 1967.

Willover, D.; Cistone, P.; and Packard, J. "Some Functions of the Supervisory Role in Educational Organizations." *Education* 92 (1972): 66–68.

8

Housing

There is, in many adult minds, a fixed image of a school building—a grey, gritty asphalt playground surrounded by high walls or iron railings; blocks of lavatories and cloakrooms; long corridors with unfriendly doors; rows of classrooms with high windows and with lines of desks facing the teacher's platform and the blackboard; partitions fretted with small panes of glass; heating pipes, radiators and tall cupboards; green and brown paint and glazed tiles.[1]

In most facilities for today's young children, such a gloomy atmosphere no longer exists. Environments have changed as a result of alterations in philosophy—more profound understanding of how children develop and more accurate interpretations of adult-child and child-adult relationships. Despite major differences in philosophies of early childhood programs, most facilities are physically and psychologically comfortable. The homelike atmosphere of today's facilities comes about because staff members move among the children, rather than stand or sit behind a permanent station in front of the room; children move around, rather than sit in a year-long work place; furnishings and equipment are like the rugs, couches, and tools of home; and there is more floor and ground space because of curricular expansion and greater variety of opportunities for learning.

Before contemplating the specifics of housing, one must remember that:

1. Regardless of the type of program, most of the occupants will be young children, so the facility should be child-oriented.
2. Safety of the children and staff members is of maximum importance. Protection can be insured by using fire-resistant materials, allowing for several fire exits, mounting fire extinguishers on the walls, equipping the building with fire alarm systems, and by making sure that exit doors have emergency hardware and swing outward.

3. Determining the right type of housing begins with an understanding of the children's developmental needs. Objectives must be defined in terms of environmental features which make the program possible. Design should be aesthetically pleasing and in keeping with the program's philosophy.

   Sensitive architects can impart to working space a character which promotes a particular attitude to a job done in it; privacy for quiet study; intimacy for quiet group-listening; workmanlike and messy spaces; clinical spaces to cope with noise. The colour, texture and finishing of the walls; the cold, warmth or hardness of floors; carpets, rugs, and cushions; tables to read and write at, and working surfaces for many kinds of jobs; chairs, stools and bench seating, hard and upholstered, for adults as well as for children; all these contribute to the quality and character of the environment. Light from windows, casting oblique shadows and giving shape and texture to the many interesting objects and materials within the building; delightful prospects of clouds, trees, and building shapes seen from inside; all these contribute to the learning environment which we call school.[2]

   Not every early childhood program will be so fortunate as to have a new building. Many will necessarily be housed in an old structure, or in a new addition to an older building. Renovated buildings are fine, if they are renovated. to meet the needs of the program and are not just hand-me-downs or cast-offs which do not fit. A problem of sharing the children's activity room or building with other groups, such as a church or civic group, is that of clearing the room or building, storing equipment, and setting up again.

4. Housing is an important consideration in planning for the handicapped. Special architectural plans and room arrangements are needed for the physically handicapped and visually impaired.[3,4] Also, noise and activity levels must be more controlled when learning disabled and hyperactive children are integrated into the regular classroom.[5] P.L. 94-142 authorizes Congress to appropriate monies for awarding grants to pay all or part of the costs of remodeling existing buildings to eliminate architectural barriers for handicapped children.

5. Variations in arrangement of space and materials contribute to the effectiveness of housing. There should be differences in the placement of objects in space, such as high, eye-level, and low places; size of areas, such as large areas for running and small areas for squeezing through; sound levels, such as noisy places and quiet areas; and light and color, such as cheerful, busy color schemes and quiet, relaxing hues.

6. Flexibility is essential. Housing should be planned to accommodate both individual and group pursuits. "The early childhood program requires that the site and the space, as well as the furniture and equipment, be so adaptable as to permit activities to expand, shrink, disappear completely or even move outdoors."[6]

7. Cost must be considered. The building or physical facilities require a large initial investment; however, when good facilities are amortized over forty years, the investment represents only eight or twelve cents of the total dollar spent on the program.[7]

8. Location of the facility is an important aspect of planning, since local zoning laws may include restrictions. Much thought should be given to potential sites.

> The first criterion for the location of a facility should not be administrative convenience or saving plumbing costs. Physical facilities to house a well-defined, well-executed program for children will not be limited to formalized school settings, but will be found in individualized thoughtfully developed setting appropriate for achieving the child development ends you seek.[8]

To summarize, the philosophy and objectives of your local program should determine the housing facilities. For example, the housing facilities probably would be somewhat different for "academically-oriented" and "discovery" programs. Once housing facilities are constructed or selected, they may determine staff members' abilities to supervise children, the types and convenience of activities, the accessibility of equipment and materials and of places to work and play, the ease of seeing and hearing, and the safety of children. One should never have to adapt the program to the building; rather, the building should always serve the purposes of the program. Of course, in reality, some facilities must "wait" for renovation; in the meantime, programs often make extremely successful adaptations.

There are several logical steps in planning a facility for an early childhood program, once it is determined that a building is needed; (1) a committee, or several committees, must be appointed to investigate special needs and consider preliminary plans; (2) specific needs of the program must be outlined, including maximum enrollment, ages of children, special needs of children, and program objectives; (3) trips should be planned to buildings housing similar programs; and (4) preliminary plans should then be submitted to the board of directors (or local school board) for action. (Many of these steps for planning a new building are equally appropriate when planning an addition to an existing building.)

Entry-Exit Area

Because the entry-exit area serves as the first and last picture of the facility that children and parents see every day, the area may be a major factor in communicating the attitude, "It's nice here!" or "This is a good place for my child!" The entry-exit area is also the view most often seen by the public, and its opinion of a program may be based on what it sees—even from street distance.

An entry-exit area should be a bright, welcoming area, because blind corners and dimly-lit places are frightening to the young child. The entry-exit area could be a mall, with views of indoor and outdoor activity areas, a porch, a courtyard, or a gaily-decorated interior room. Because the acclimatized child will want to enter on his own, the entry door should operate easily. There should be a parking lot near the entry-exit area for parents who drive and a shelter for walking parents to watch until their children enter the building or outdoor activity area.

Indoor Space

The amount and types of indoor space vary from program to program. Most public school kindergartens are housed in a single activity room with an emergency-use restroom. The kindergarten shares the cafeteria, main restrooms, isolation area, and other facilities with elementary-age children also housed in the building. A day-care center is usually housed in a separate building, so some of the following suggestions are not equally applicable to all early childhood programs.

ACTIVITY ROOM

Space affects the quality of living and learning within a center:

> the higher the quality of space in a center, the more likely were teachers to be sensitive and friendly in their manner toward children, to encourage children in their self-chosen activities, and to teach consideration for the rights and feelings of self and others. Where spatial quality was low, children were less likely to be involved and interested, and teachers more likely to be neutral and insensitive in their manner, to use large amounts of guidance and restriction, and to teach arbitrary rules of social living.[9]

The children's activity room is perhaps the single most important area of the building, because it is in this room that children work and play for most of their day.

Room-Directional Orientation.   Generally, a southern or eastern exposure is better than a western exposure. A northern exposure is not recommended by most building planners,[10] although a northern exposure may be preferable in hot climates where there is no air conditioning.[11] Of course, programs housed in renovated buildings will not have a choice as to directional orientation; however, if the orientation is incorrect, the resulting light-reflection problems can be partially overcome by use of certain color schemes.

Room Size.   Forty to 60 square feet per child is recommended for the children's activity room,[12] although many states use 35 square feet per child as the minimum square footage in licensing regulations. Thirty-five square feet can be very workable if additional indoor space is available for active play. If the group of children is small, the space per child should be increased.[13] If a nap period is planned for an all-day program, as much as 30 square feet per child may be needed in addition to the suggested 40 to 60 square feet. Regardless of the number of children or length of the session, the children's activity room should be a minimum of 900 square feet of clear floor space, exclusive of restrooms, dining area, and separate napping area.[14]

There is a marked increase of negative and idle behavior under high density and low resources, or equipment. On the other hand, positive and constructive behavior was prevalent in day-care centers with low density (of at least 48 square feet per child) and high resources. The quality and quantity of resources should be increased if high density is unavoidable.[15] Arrangement becomes very important in low density situations. Shapiro[16] found that some lower density centers (over 50 square feet per child) had poor arrangement.

When floor space is small and ceilings are high, space can be stretched vertically. Balconies with railings or cargo net can be built over cot storage or other storage; they can be the second floors of two-story houses; or housekeeping centers can be arranged on balconies with block centers below. A balcony built against a wall, particularly corner walls, is most stable and economical. On the other hand, free-standing platforms give more freedom of placement. Various apparatus, such as stairs, ladders, and ramps, can be installed for ascending and descending. For safety purposes, a railing must be provided for stairs greater than three steps, stationary ladders are safer than rope ladders, ladder rungs should extend above a platform for easy mounting and dismounting, and ramps covered with friction material and railings are safer than stairs or ladders, but can be used only with platforms less than four feet high.

Room Arrangement.   An activity room that is slightly longer than it is wide is less formal looking and easier to arrange.[17] The room arrangement should be such that there are no hidden areas, for these cannot be supervised. Children have privacy and staff members can supervise as long as dividers and storage cabinets are not over four feet high. When two rooms are joined by a mall, or when a small room opens off the main room, glass panels or openings in the wall at adult height facilitate supervision.

A well-organized activity room cuts down on time loss by children and staff and reduces confusion and discipline problems. Room organization also helps communicate the general atmosphere of the program to the child; for example, in early childhood programs where staff members are engaged in direct instruction of children, small spaces defined by walls should be utilized. Conversely, for child-initiated activity programs, there should be a maximum amount of open space.

Many building planners recommend covering the floor space with furniture and equipment; for example, Kritchevsky and Prescott[18] state that good space organization is found where the surface is between one-half and two-thirds covered. However, children may not prefer the covered floor surface. In one study of room arrangement, nursery school children were permitted to arrange their activity room as they pleased and were permitted to leave the equipment in the main classroom or in the adjoining room or hall. In this way, children could structure their own environment rather than adjust their activities to the prearranged environment. Instead of choosing a covered-floor arrangement, the children returned equipment and materials to the adjoining room and hall after each activity. They seemed to enjoy roominess and openness in their environment.[19]

INTEREST CENTERS

Certainly, the program philosophy determines whether interest centers will become the basis for room arrangements. If interest centers are to be used, the types and arrangement of the centers should be in keeping with the program's objectives. We will discuss interest centers because they are used in most early childhood programs. Such centers are a series of working areas that have a degree of privacy but are related to the whole activty room. The distinctiveness and integrity of each interest center can be maintained by defining space, allowing sufficient space, and providing acoustical seclusion. There are specific ways to achieve distinctiveness and integrity in each center. An interest center should be a defined space. Shapiro[20] notes the importance of organizing space and clear boundaries between activity areas. The space should remain flexible, but there should be enough space definition to provide a feeling of place. This definition of space may be accomplished by placing dividers or storage units in L, U, or other configurations, or by using dividers or storage units in conjunction with corners and walls to create two or more areas (Such configurations permit traffic flow but also provide containment.):

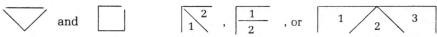

Space can also be defined by differences in colors or shades of wall paint or carpet in adjoining centers, by differences in light intensity in adjacent centers, and by manipulation of the floor plane, with wells, pits, or platforms. Adjoining centers can also be visually separated with dividers. (A four-foot high divider will provide enclosure to a standing or sitting child, and a two-foot high divider will provide enclosure to a sitting child.)

Before deciding how to define space for an interest center, one must decide whether or not the space is to be permanent. Differences in colors or shades of wall paint, carpet colors, and manipulation of floor plane are more or less permanent, while placement of movable dividers or storage units and light intensity are less so. There are advantages in being able to change interest centers; for example, an interest center may be infrequently used, and must be eliminated or made more attractive to the children. The teacher may wish to create an interest center to fit a new curriculum topic, or a popular interest center may need to be enlarged, or another similar interest center must be created to accommodate additional children. There may also be problems with traffic flow or storage, or the activity room may be too small to house all activities at one time, and need to be rearranged during the day.

There should be sufficient space for the type of activity the interest center is intended to accommodate. More space is required in interest centers that have group play, that have large items of equipment and/or materials to spread out, or that have materials or equipment tending to cause aggressive acts among children.

Noise levels from one center should not interfere with activities in another interest center. Seclusion may be achieved by using adequate acoustical materials on the floors, walls, or ceilings, by providing headsets, by locating interest centers with similar noise levels, such as library and concept centers adjacent to each other, and by placing extremely noisy centers, like the workshop, outside. Most of the literature suggests that noisy and quiet areas be separated. However, Nilsen[21] recommends mixing noisy and quiet areas to resemble more accurately a real-life situation and to help prevent areas of the activity room from appearing to be more "for boys" or "for girls."

In addition to the objectives of the program, other factors enter into the arrangement of interest centers in the room and arrangement of equipment and materials within each interest center, such as type of floor covering required, size and quantity of equipment and materials, special requirements, such as a water source, electrical outlet, a specific intensity of light, or a certain type of storage, the level of noise, and the maximum number of children working in each center at one time. To prevent problems of overcrowding, popular interest centers may be widely separated to distribute children throughout the room.

The following comments are not intended as specific solutions on the arrangement of interest centers (or even a comprehensive list of all interest centers); rather, the statements are a mixture of pertinent factors to consider in arranging interest centers.

Block Center. In block play, there is a tendency toward expansive aggression and solitary retreat; therefore, the block center should accommodate a child who wants to work alone, with another child, or with a group of four or five children. The working areas in the block center should be fluid enough to encourage a regrouping of children as they desire. There are several ways of accommodating various group sizes: block centers may be housed both inside and outside, on a terrace or other firm, flat surface; or block centers can be divided into large or small areas. A center should be twenty-five square feet to accommodate one or two children; for three to five children, seventy-five square feet are necessary. These block center sizes can be created by subdividing a large block center with dividers or shelves, placing block centers throughout the room, perhaps a small center near the entrance for a timid child and a larger center adjacent to the dramatic play center, and using a raised platform or pit for small centers and open floor space for large centers.

Since block constructions are easily knocked over by fast-moving traffic, block centers should be placed in areas where traffic moves at a slower pace, or should have protection via storage units or dividers almost enclosing the centers in configurations such as ⌐‾‾‾⌐ or ⌐‾‾‾⌐ . Finally, the block center requires acoustical materials to lessen the noise of falling or banging blocks. A dense, low-pile carpet should cover the floor, and block shelves could be carpeted to reduce noise.

Dramatic Play Center. The most common type of dramatic play center is the housekeeping corner. Because of the size of the furniture (stoves, doll beds, chairs, and tables), the housekeeping corner requires approximately 75 to 100 square feet of floor space. If a dress-up area is included, additional space is required. Carpeting is not needed for acoustical control in this area and should not be used if children use water in their miniature kitchen. Although the housekeeping corner needs to be enclosed to give a homelike atmosphere, the openings should be wide enough to accommodate doll buggies. Alcoves often serve for housekeeping centers.

Some early childhood programs attempt to expand dramatic play beyond prestructured areas such as housekeeping. Staff members provide basic materials, such as boxes, bottles, cans, pillows, ropes, wheels, and hardware gadgets, and encourage children to dramatize any experience they wish. Unless prestructured areas are desired, there are two solutions for housing the dramatic play center: do not provide a specific center, but,instead, permit children to play in other centers or in multipurpose area; or provide a specific space and equip it with materials conducive to many types of dramatic play.

Art Center. The art center should have places for individual and group work. Work surfaces include the wall (chalkboards and murals), tilted (easels), and flat surfaces (tables). Movable stand-up tables should be approximately twenty inches high and sit-down/stand-up tables about eighteen inches high. Built-in work surfaces should be twenty inches high and between two and three feet deep.

A sink in the art center or one in an adjacent restroom with plenty of counter space on both sides is essential for mixing paints and for clean-up. The sink should have a faucet twenty-three inches above the floor[22] and should be equipped with a disposal drain for catching clay and paste.[23] The sink counter and the wall behind the sink should be covered with an easily cleaned surface.

Surfaces in the art area should be impervious to water, paint, paste, and clay, and should be easy to clean. Floors should not be slippery when wet, and all surfaces should dry quickly. Linoleum, Formica, or a vinyl cloth should cover the tables; ceramic tile, vinyl-coated wallpaper, or waterproof paint should cover the walls; and the floor should have a vinyl covering.

The art center needs many storage shelves for art supplies. To protect poster and construction paper from light and dust, these storage shelves should have doors, although other storage shelves may be open. Drying art products will require lines and racks for paintings and mobiles, and shelves for three-dimensional products.

Music Center. Children can listen to music in any of the quiet areas with the use of listening stations and headsets; however, the area for dancing and singing should be physically separate or acoustically treated to focus sound within. Carpeting the rhythm/dance area does not permit as much freedom of movement as vinyl flooring does, but minimizes dangers from falls. The piano should not be placed near windows or doors or heating or cooling units.

Sand Play Center. A stand-up sand table should be twenty-two inches high and a sit-down sand table should be sixteen inches high. Because there may be many conflicts at the sand table, provide a flat working surface, such as an eight-inch wide board down the center of the table, from end to end, and station the children about two feet apart. Sand tables may be permanently installed or movable; the advantage of having a movable unit is that it can be pushed out of the way when not in use or taken outdoors. Because sand tracks and is slippery underfoot, the sand play center should be carpeted (and sand removed by a heavy-duty vacuum), or a metal grate with a collecting pan should be installed flush with the floor.

Water Play Center. The indoor water play center should be close to a water source and drain, out of the main flow of traffic, and somewhat enclosed. Water table height should be between twenty and twenty-four inches. Children should be stationed about two feet apart and, if both sides of the table are to be occupied, the table should be three feet wide. For toys, shelving should be made of material unaffected by water and adjacent to the water play area. The water play center should have a slip-proof surface—a grate with a pan for collecting water or a rubber mat.

Concept and Manipulative Centers. The concept and manipulative centers are characterized by quietness and by children working alone or in groups with staff members' assistance. For individual or small-group work, quietness can be created by using a corner with tables, using built-in alcoves, or creating alcove-like spaces. The teacher can arrange shelves or screens to give a sense of enclosure, use study carrels modified to accept audiovisual machines, or have special lighting, acoustical, or other design treatments. If a separate room is used for group sessions, the room should be no larger that 100 square feet and unaffected by outside sounds.

Places for Animals and Plants. Many programs for young children include the keeping of animals and plants. A major problem in having animals and plants is that young children disturb living things. Places for living things should be carefully planned to provide for their safety and for children's learning. Such planning requires housing each animal and plant on an appropriate table; placing animal homes out of the flow of traffic; providing a sturdy table (preferably child-sitting height, with a surface larger than the base of the container and covered with Formica); and providing chairs or stools around the table. Plants need varying amounts of light and humidity, which must be considered in placing them in the room.

Other Areas. In addition to interest centers, a children's room should have places to watch from and special interest areas. Places to watch from (small block centers, a rocking horse, a windowseat, playhouse, a ride-on toy) should be close to ongoing activities, while providing the child with a sense of enclosure. Children enjoy special interest areas, such as an aquarium or terrarium, rock, mineral or shell collections, a garden seen from the window, a hanging basket, an arboretum, egg incubators, books, and displays connected with specific curriculum themes.

Figure 1, a floor plan of a children's activity room, illustrates some of the principles we have discussed. Because floor arrangements must fit the needs of the local program, the floor plan is intended for illustration only, not as an ideal arrangement of a children's activity room.

Floors, Ceilings, and Walls. These components must be both functional and durable, and the materials used on their surfaces must be coordinated so that they are aesthetically pleasing and comfortable.

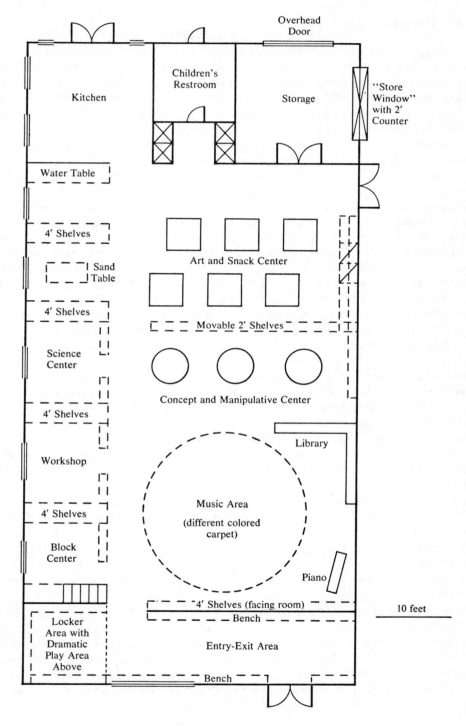

FIGURE 1
Children's Activity Room

Young children are accident-prone; they get floors wet from play activities, spilling, and bathroom accidents. When choosing floor covering, one must keep in mind that floors must be kept dry, sanitary, and warm for children's play. Flooring materials should be easy to clean, suited to hard wear, and sound deadening. Because children enjoy working on the floor, good floor covering can reduce the number of tables and chairs needed.

Resilient flooring and carpet are the most prevalent materials used. Resilient flooring includes various types of vinyl floors and linoleum. Carpeting is superior to resilient flooring in softness, in noise absorption, and in minimizing injuries and breakage; however, carpeting presents problems in cleaning-up spills, germ and static-electricity retention, moving cabinets or bins equipped with casters, using toys with wheels, and allergies to carpet fiber. Of the soft floor coverings, wall-to-wall carpeting is probably the most desirable, but large carpets, area rugs, throw rugs, carpet remnants joined together with tape, artificial grass, or astroturf may be suitable. To temporarily cover wall-to-wall carpeting, lay down plastic sheeting, then inexpensive boards, such as 1 × 12's or 4' × 8' plywood sheets. Make sure boards are free of splinters. Most early childhood programs use resilient flooring for areas that will have rugged use or get wet, and carpet for areas that will have passive or noisy, but nonwet activities.

Many programs have begun using platforms or wells to facilitate floor use as a place to work and play. Children enjoy exploring the spaces created by raised and sunken areas, but such areas are less flexible in use. Platforms or wells can be built into the activity room during its construction, or less permanent structures can be built with wooden boxes attached to a plywood base and carpeted, or a platform on rollers. If platforms or wells are used, one should consider that raised or lowered areas should be out of the main flow of traffic; changes in floor levels should not exceed two or three feet and the steps should not be steep—five or six steps for a well two feet deep; in some cases, a railing may be needed to partially surround the well, if the well is used in programs for the very young child or if wells are located near areas of fast-moving traffic; and electrical outlets should be provided near the wells or platforms if electric teaching equipment will be used.

A final problem is keeping floors warm and free from drafts. Radiantly heated floors have been used, but this kind of heat does not solve draft problems. A perimeter wall system as a supplementary heating source provides floor warmth and freedom from drafts.

Ceilings should be of differing heights, to accommodate equipment of various heights. Variation in ceiling height helps with noise control and is aesthetically pleasing. Seven-foot ceilings are too low, unless the space is for children only. Low ceilings make staff members appear excessively large because of the nearness of the adult to the ceiling. Such an illusion makes children feel dominated by the adult, and the continued presence of a reassuring adult may cause more aggression on the part of the children. Millar states:

> in the relatively strange laboratory setting at least, normal nursery-school children play less aggressively where there is no supporting adult present. Where there is a consistently friendly, encouraging and reassuring adult, the overall score of aggressive acts increases from session to session and play becomes less stereotyped.[24]

The recommended ceiling height would be ten to eleven feet. In order that the adult provide supervision yet further minimize his presence during free play times, there should be some play areas with low-ceilinged spaces, approximately four feet, which exclude the adult. Low-ceilinged areas may be created by building a two-story playhouse, or by using a balcony along an entire wall with interest centers on and under the balcony.

Although permanent walls provide acoustical privacy, fewer interior walls give greater flexibility in room arrangement. Supervision becomes less of a problem when dividers and storage units delineate space rather than floor-to-ceiling walls. Just as low ceilings make an adult appear excessively large, so do nearby walls. If program planners desire to minimize the adult's presence, they should include fewer walls.

Soft greens or other pastels are the best wall colors for a southern or western exposure. Rooms with a northern exposure will probably need a shade of yellow, a strong light-reflecting color.[25] Equipment, art work, and the children themselves add to the room's brightness. In painting any surface that children can reach, use only those paints marked: "Conforms to American Standard Z66.1-9: For use on surfaces that might be chewed by children."

Walls may be covered with various types of materials rather than painted. Wall finishes of soft porous materials or soft pine will deaden sound.[26] Tackboard walls permit the use of any area for display purposes.

Storage and Display Facilities.   In an early childhood program facility, there must be storage:

> to keep the indoor and outdoor materials in daily use—blocks, cars, trucks, housekeeping materials, crayons, paints, paper
>
> to keep the things that may or may not be used on a daily basis, but which need to be readily available—musical instruments, additional books, picture file, math and science materials
>
> to store equipment and materials for seasonal use—sled, snow shovels, water spray, wading pool
>
> to keep consumable supplies safe, fresh, and inviting—assortments of papers, collage materials, chalks and crayons, collections of waste materials
>
> to keep auxiliary equipment easily accessible—corn popper, portable oven, cooking equipment, egg incubator, fish tanks, animal cages
>
> to keep audiovisual equipment and materials—cameras, film, projectors, film strips, records, tapes.[27]

There should be many storage cabinets, low enough for children to secure their own materials. Shelves without doors or with removable doors are excellent, but bins are not as suitable for young children. In addition to obvious storage, such as cabinets and shelves, design storage in less evident places, such as underneath raised platforms. Shelf height should be approximately three feet. When you want to store materials out of reach of children, place unlocked cabinets or shelves at a minimum of four and one-half feet, lock cabinets, or use high doorknobs on closets and storage rooms.

Shelves or racks should be placed near the area in which they will be used. If children have to walk across the room to get supplies or equipment, there will be many temptations along the way. Unnecessary additional steps are not easy on teachers, either. The design of storage units and materials used in their construction should be compatible with their use, such as steeply-slanted shelves for books, resting-cot cupboards with louvered doors to allow air circulation, and shelf materials resistant to water damage in water-play centers. Different storage designs (slanted vertically and horizontally partitioned cabinets, drawers and shelves of varying depths) help in arranging, finding, and protecting materials and equipment, and are also aesthetically pleasing. Equipment and materials should be displayed like wares in a market so that children can window shop or buy. How materials are arranged and their accessibility to children are almost as important as the materials themselves. Door and window arrangement should permit many large spaces for bulletin boards. "An abundance of 'pinning space' at the eye level of the child is desirable."[28] Backs of storage units may be covered with corkboard or pegboard for displaying children's work. Chalkboards should be on a level children can reach. Portable chalkboards are more functional than permanent ones.[29]

ADDITIONAL AREAS FOR CHILDREN

Learning is going on all the time in an early childhood program: in the shared activity area, the restrooms, the dining area, the napping area, and the isolation area as well as the children's activity room. The children use many of the additional areas to take care of their physical needs, and staff members emphasize the necessity for children's becoming self-reliant in taking care of these needs. Thus, designing additional areas must be done with as much care as planning the children's activity room.

Shared Activity Areas. In some early childhood programs, several children's activity rooms open into a shared activity area, usually a large room, an exceptionally long and wide hallway, or a covered patio. Shared activity areas are often used for physical education, music, rhythmic activities, and drama.

Resource Room. Early childhood programs involved in mainstreaming of handicapped children may have a resource room. This room is equipped with special education materials needed by the enrolled handicapped children. Usually, the special education teacher uses the resource room in working with the special child for part of his day.

Children's Lockers or Cubbies. It is important for children to have their own individual cubbie for storing personal belongings, because their use emphasizes personal possessions, helps the children learn proper habits for caring for their belongings, and reduces the danger of spreading contagious disease. The locker or cubbie area should not be part of the entry-exit area, but should be close to this area and to the outdoor space. The children's locker area should be large enough to facilitate easy circulation of staff members when they help children with wraps. The floor covering in the locker area should be easily cleaned, since it will get quite dirty during inclement weather.

Various combinations of storage are possible for children's possessions. Outdoor garments, extra clothing and aprons, blankets or rest mats, and personal possessions, such as crayons, show-and-tell treasures, and art work to take home, may be stored together or separately. Lockers usually provide places to hang garments, and overshoes are placed on the floor of the locker. Such a locker may be modified by adding one or two top shelves to accommodate a shoe box or a tote tray (usually 7″ × 8″ × 15″) for personal possessions, and a blanket or rest mat. Another shelf about ten inches from the bottom of the locker provides a place for the child to sit while putting on overshoes or changing clothes. Garment hooks are attached to the bottom of the lower top shelf or to the sides or back of the locker. The overall dimensions of this locker would be approximately fifty-six to sixty inches high, by twelve inches wide, by fifteen inches deep. Lockers seldom include doors, as these catch little fingers, are always in the way, and are never closed.

Jefferson[30] suggests that inexpensive lockers can be created by installing two parallel horizontal shelves about twelve inches apart, with upright partitions dividing the shelves into ten-inch compartments. A hook is placed under each compartment for wraps. If there is no sitting place in the locker itself, stools or benches permit off-the-floor sitting.

Three other considerations need attention in planning children's lockers or cubbies:

1. If the lockers or cubbies are not designed with partitions between the wraps, hooks should be spaced so that one child's wraps are not against those of another;
2. Hangers on clothes rods are difficult for children, as wraps have a tendency to fall off, and a child may, intentionally or unintentionally, use a hanger as a weapon; and
3. Name tags or symbols on cubbies or tote trays further emphasize personal possessions and help staff members locate a child's cubbie when the child is sick, a parent comes to pick up a child's possessions, or when, during after hours straightening of the room, the staff members finds a child's misplaced possession.

Children's Restrooms.   Children's restrooms should have two doors, one off the activity room and one into the outdoor area. Each restroom should be approximately five square feet per child when in maximum use.[31] When a large building houses more than thirty-five children, there should be restrooms in different areas. Early childhood programs for children under school age do not generally provide separate restrooms for boys and girls. Because some children like privacy, unlocked, low partitions between and in front of toilets provide this feature and permit easy supervision. The restroom should be cheerful, with windows for sunlight and ventilation, bright wall colors, and potted plants.

Different ratios are suggested for the number of toilets to the number of children, such as 1:10,[32] 1:8,[33] and 1:5.[34] Toilet seats should be between ten and thirteen inches from the floor. These toilet-seat heights may be too high for the toddler or very young child; thus, the restroom may need portable "potties," a step installed to the child-sized toilets, or toilets set into the floor. Urinals, especially trough rather than floor-mounted types, keep the toilet seats and floors clean.

Lavatory bowls should be adjacent to, but outside of, toilet areas, and placed near the door. The ratio of the number of bowls to the number of children should be 1:10[35] or 1:8.[36] Bowl heights should vary between one and one-half to two feet. The water heater should be set to provide lukewarm water, thus preventing scalded hands. (Because the thermostatic control must be set higher for the diswasher, another water heater must be installed for kitchen water.) Bowls must be equipped with disposal drains to catch clay, sand, and so forth;[37] mirrors, preferably of safety glass or metal, should be placed at child's height over them. If cloth towels are used, the hooks should be far enough apart so that hanging towels do not touch each other;[38] however, paper towels are more sanitary. If the budget permits, a bathtub is helpful, especially in an all-day program or one serving younger children.

Drinking fountains should be located near the restrooms and out of the path of fast-moving traffic. They should be made of vitreous china or stainless steel,[39] be between twenty and twenty-three inches high.[40,41] Water-bubbling level should be controlled. It takes time for young children to learn to get enough water from a fountain to quench their thirst; thus, paper cups should be available for children while they are learning to drink from a fountain.

Details frequently overlooked in designing restrooms for children are:

The need for a cleanout to allow retrieval of flushed toys that have blocked the drain;
Sound isolation of flushing—especially if the group play environment is used for napping;
Placement of toilet paper, hand towels, mirrors at child height; and
The need for a seamless floor in the toilet area to minimize retention of water and germs, i.e., liquid plastic, ceramic tile, or sheet vinyl. . . . Raw concrete is not a good material since the urine will find its way into the "hairline" cracks and produce odors.[42]

Dining Area.   Kitchen facilities need not be extensive for programs that serve mid-morning or mid-afternoon snacks. A kitchenette needs one or two heating elements, a refrigerator with a small freezer compartment, a sink with hot and cold water, a diswasher (unless disposable utensils are used), work-counter space, and storage units for food and eating utensils. For programs that serve main meals, selection of food service equipment should follow the pattern, or a similar pattern, found in the publication, *Equipment Guide for Preschool and School Age Child Service Institutions.*[43] For a child to be able to serve himself snacks or a main meal, the serving counter should be two feet or less in height and as close as possible to dining tables.

The dining area should be bright, cheerful, and airy, with screens on the windows. All surfaces should be made of materials that are soap-and-water scrubbable and resistant to water damage. In planning the dining area, allow plenty of space per child for manipulating trays, sliding chairs back, and so forth.

Napping Area.   A separate napping area should be considered for all-day programs. Sleeping areas should be isolated from noise in adjacent areas, and lighting should be controlled. If a separate napping room is used, efficient use of space can be achieved by placing cots end-to-end in rows, with an aisle approximately four feet wide between the rows. Small screens may be used to separate cots.

Programs that do not have separate napping areas must provide for resting in the children's activity room. The disadvantages of locating cots throughout the activity room are that more space is required, in comparison to placing cots head-to-toe; supervision is difficult; and cots must be moved at the beginning and end of each session. Cots must be stored in a well-ventilated storage unit, because stacked cots in the corner of the room make an attractive but dangerous climbing apparatus.

Isolation Area.   An isolation area is necessary for caring for ill or hurt children until parents arrive. It should contain a bed or cot and have a small play space, since a cheerfully decorated room with a few toys reduces the hospital-like atmosphere. A small bathroom adjacent to the isolation area is helpful.

ADULT AREAS

Although the early childhood facility is planned primarily for the needs of young children, housing must also meet the requirements of staff members and parents. The two major criteria to meet in planning adult areas is that they be scaled to adult size, and that the type and specific design of each area fit the needs of the program.

Parent Reception Area.   A parent reception area should make parents feel welcome, and encourage exchange of information between parents and staff members. A separate area adjacent to the children's activity room has these advantages: (1) a parent has a place to sit and wait until the child completes his activity or puts on his coat; (2) a parent does not have the feeling of being stranded in the middle of the children's room while he is waiting; (3) interruptions of children's activities are minimized; and (4) a parent can speak confidentially to a staff member. The parent reception area should be well-defined, comfortable, and invite the parent to view the materials arranged on the bulletin board, to browse through the materials placed on various tables, or to visit.

If an observation room is provided for parents, it should be adjacent to or part of the parent-receiving area. When the observation room is part of the parent reception area, one-way glass rather than screen should be used for the observation window, because talking can be heard through a screen. If the observation room has a curtain drawn across the one-way glass, it can serve as a room for showing films. Observation rooms may also be balconies, which have the advantage of not taking up valuable floor space.

Staff/Parent Lounge. A staff/parent lounge should be provided for resting and visiting. Comfortable chairs and a place for preparing and eating a snack should be considered in designing a staff/parent lounge. For greater privacy, adult restrooms should not be part of the lounge, but should be located nearby. The staff lounge may be combined with the parents' lounge; however, in all-day programs where the staff may need a period of relaxation, separate lounges should be considered.

Office and Workroom. When early childhood programs are housed with other programs under the same administrative control, office and workroom areas are usually shared. Conversely, early childhood programs that are housed in separate buildings or in buildings with other programs not under the same administrative control usually have office and workroom areas designed especially for their program.

The design of the office and workroom area should fit the needs of the local program. For most early childhood programs, space will be needed for desks or tables and chairs, cabinets for filing professional materials and records, office machines, large work tables, high stools, and a sink, and storage units for office supplies and other work materials. Additional offices are needed if the program employs special-service personnel.

ENVIRONMENTAL CONTROL

An important consideration in constructing any early childhood facility is environmental control, including lighting, heating, cooling, ventilating, and acoustics. Lack of adequate environmental control results in a number of problems, such as eye strain from glare, or discomfort from heat or cold. It can also contribute to poor behavioral patterns not only in children, but adults as well. Adequate environmental control can also save money. Become familiar with good energy-saving practices by reading some of the many pamphlets on this topic; one such example is the Edison Electric Institute's *104 Ways to Save on Your Electric Bill* (1140 Conneticut Ave., Washington, D.C. 20036).

Lighting. Illumination is highly important because of the amount of time spent on visual tasks. Also, approximately one-fifth of the enrolled children will have below-normal vision. Not only does lighting affect our physical well-being, but it also has a psychological and aesthetic impact.

Defused light, such as fluorescent bulbs above plastic defusing panels, should be considered for use with young children, because it provides nonglare lighting with very little heat. Fluorescent lighting is less expensive to operate, although more expensive to install, than incandescent light. However, the "cool" shades of fluorescent lighting should not be used; the best shades are the warm ones—

"delux warm white," similar to light emitted by incandescent, or "vita lite," similar to light emitted by the sun. Because incandescent is a concentrated source of light, it is useful for spotlighting interest areas. Regulatory agencies frequently specify the minimum amount of light intensity for various parts of the facility. Usually 50 to 60 foot-candles of glare-free illumination is recommended.[44] After 50 foot-candles, the amount of light must be doubled or redoubled to increase visual efficiency; thus, task lighting is more efficient than general illumination when more than 50 foot-candles of illumination is needed. For additional recommendations concerning brightness, see:

Gwynne, S.K., ed. *Guide for Planning Educational Facilities.* Columbus, Ohio: Council of Educational Facility Planners, International, 1976, pp. 1–4.

Because lighting should be tailored to the needs of children working in each interest center, variable light controls should be provided in each area. For example:

the art area could have sun-free directional light from skylights or windows, the reading area could have soft incandescent light and a view of the window, and the plant area could be a small greenhouse.[45]

Local lighting in an interest center should not be so bright as to make other interest centers appear dim and hence unattractive.

Window areas should be approximately one-fifth of the floor area.[46] Approximately 50 percent of the required window area should be openable, and those that open should be screened. A windowsill twenty-four inches high permits children to see out. Windows, when properly placed, are important for these reasons:

Light from a window, even a small one, falls horizontally across the room making a useful contribution to modeling and softening the shadows cast by overhead lighting. A view through a window provides a distant visual release and avoids an oppressive sense of enclosure.
The sun and sky, clouds and winds, and the play of light and shade outside are never static, and a window is a link with the interest in the constantly changing world out of doors.[47]

Reflective surfaces in the room will determine the efficiency of illumination. Light-color shades on walls and ceilings are important reflecting factors. Walls should be light enough to reflect 50 percent of the light, and ceilings light enough to reflect 70 percent of the light.[48] There should be as little contrast as possible between ceiling and light source. Tables and counter tops should reflect 35 to 50 percent of the light.[49] Even light-colored floors increase the efficiency of illumination. Louvers, blinds, and overhangs control excessive light from windows and help prevent glare. Glare is also reduced by covering work surfaces with a matte finish. Peripheral lighting helps keep the level of illumination uniform and thus helps prevent glare.[50]

Heating, Cooling, and Ventilating.   The temperature of the room should be between 68° and 72° Fahrenheit (20° to 22° Celsius) within two feet of the floor.[51] Thermostats should be at the eye level of seated children. Many early childhood facilities are finding it necessary to have central air conditioning. Because it costs nore to cool than to heat air, "there is a tendency to close in the space, make it more compact, increase the insulation, reduced the perimeter, and reduce the amount of window area."[52] There should be a circulation of ten through thirty cubic feet of air per child per minute.[53] For comfort, the humidity should be from 50 through 65 percent.[54] If a humidifying system is not installed, an open aquarium or water left in the pans at the water table will add humidity to the room.

Acoustics.   There is better acoustical control in a nearly square room than in a long narrow room.[55] Acoustical absorption underfoot is more effective, and thus more economical, than acoustical absorption overhead.[56] Interest centers that generate the greatest amount of noise should be designed and decorated for maximum acoustical absorption. Sand and grit on the floor increase noise as well as destroy the floor covering. Leeper et al.[57] suggest reducing noise by using tablecloths on luncheon tables, area rugs, padding on furniture legs, removable pads on tabletops used for hammering, and doors to keep out kitchen noises.

Outdoor Space

Outdoor space is too often wasted. Because of inadequate planning outdoor space has been referred to as the "sea of asphalt" or the "sterile square." Regardless of the type of program, outdoor space should meet these criteria:

1. The design should be based on the needs of the children. Ellis[58] notes that children play for stimulation, need increasingly complex activities, and learn in social groups. Dattner[59] states that children need graduated challenge, choice in activities, exercise in fantasy, and separation from adults. Sutton-Smith[60] believes that play serves three functions: exploration, testing, ane creative needs. Playgrounds must also meet the needs of the handicapped child.[61]
2. Outdoor space should provide opportunities for activities similar to those conducted in the indoor space. There should be places that challenge the children to mental activity, social interaction, and physical activity. Almost every activity that can be carried on indoors is equally appropriate outdoors; thus, the outdoor space is more than a place to run or stand about. In short, the indoors must be extended outside.
3. Merely establishing a playground does not ensure that children will use it. A playground must compete with other attractions. Outdoor space should be aesthetically pleasing.

    A playground should be a sensuous textile woven of touch, smell, sight, hearing and (be that it could!) taste. Areas of differing color, varying textures and resonance should be built into the armature of topography. There is a conscious approach to tactile variation in the use of different materials. Wood and stone provide contrast to the sense of touch; there is cold, hard concrete and sun-warmed sand. In the frame bordering this setting there could be planted flowers to smell! There might be walls for banners to be hung and murals to be painted. For something to listen to, a series of oil drums of different heights, each producing a different sound, can be jumped or banged upon.[62]

4. The outdoor space must be safe. Enclosure of the space, proper arrangement of equipment, appropriate surfacing, and adequate supervision are basics that help mitigate danger; however, over-concern for safety can eliminate challenge.

A playground should be safe but not at the expense of experience, for play is a part of the preparation for the reality of mature life with its built-in dangers. As a child grows, he must sometime learn to cross a street, climb a stair, fly a plane. But all of these activities are done within rational limitations.[63]

5. Initial cost and maintenance expenses should be considered. There are some possibilities of working out arrangements between the early childhood program and the local department of parks and recreation.

SPECIFICATIONS FOR OUTDOOR SPACE

Specifications for the outdoor space should be sufficiently flexible to meet local needs and requirements, and should include considerations such as location, size, enclosing, surfacing, and sheltering.

Location. Outdoor activity areas should not surround the building, because supervision becomes almost impossible. The area is best located on the south side of the building where there will be sun and light throughout the day.[64] The outdoor space should be easily accessible from the inside area. To minimize the chance of accidents as children go from inside to outside, or vice versa, a facility should have: (1) a door threshold flush with the indoor/outside surfaces, or a ramp, if there is an abrupt change in surface levels; (2) adjoining surfaces covered with material that provides maximum traction; (3) a sliding door or a door prop; and (4) a small glass panel in the door to prevent collisions.

Indoor restrooms and lockers should be adjacent to the outdoor area. If this is impossible, there should be one restroom opening off the playground. "Cold weather and winter clothing, hard to manage quickly, make speedy access to a toilet important."[65] A drinking fountain should be easily accessible to children during outdoor play.

Size. There is not total agreement as to the ideal size of the outdoor activity area. Most licensing regulations require a minimum of 75 square feet per child. One authority says there should be 75 to 200 square feet per child[66]; another authority suggests a minimum of 200 square feet per child, but says 250 square feet per child is better.[67] A minimum of 15 square feet per child should be added for a sheltered area or terrace. Approximately one-third the square footage of the outdoor area should be used for passive outdoor play, as in a sand pit or outdoor art center, and the remainder for active outdoor play such as climbing and running. "Adventure" or junk playgrounds may be one-half to two and one-half acres in size.[68]

Enclosing. Enclosure of the outdoor area relieves the staff member of a heavy burden of responsibility, gives the child a sense of freedom without worry,[69] and prevents stray animals from wandering in. A nonclimbable barrier approximately four feet high is adequate as boundaries that adjoin dangerous areas (parking lots, streets, or ponds), but minimum barriers such as large stones or shrubbery are adequate in areas where the outside has no potential dangers.

In addition to the entry from the building, the outdoor area should have a gate opening wide enough to permit trucks to deliver sand or large items of play equipment. If children are allowed to use the outdoor area for after-program hours, a small gate should be installed and benches placed on the periphery to give adults a place to relax while watching and supervising.

Terrain. Flat terrain, especially one with hard surfacing, provides no curb to the children's random movement, and random movement is dangerous. A rolling terrain has several advantages. Mounds are an ideal place for active games of leaping and running and are a natural shelter for passive games such as sand or water play. Mounds can be used in conjunction with equipment; for example, slides without ladders can be mounted to a slope so the children can climb the mound and slide down the slide. Ladders and boards can connect the mounds. Tricycle paths can wind on a rolling terrain.

Surfacing. The outdoor area should have a variety of surfaces and be well-drained, with the fastest-drying areas nearest the building. It is desirable to have one-half to two-thirds of the total square footage covered with grass, and about 1,000 square feet covered in concrete or asphalt.[70] The open areas can be grassy, with sand or dirt around each piece of equipment; paths can be asphalt or wood, as grass will not grow with a concentration of traffic. Changes in types of surfacing should be level to prevent tripping. Some areas should be left as dirt for gardening and for realizing "a satisfaction common to every child—digging a big hole!"[71]

Sheltering. The building, trees and shrubs, or a rolling terrain should protect children from excessive sun and wind. Knowledge of snow patterns and prevailing winds may lead to use of snow fences or other structures to provide snowy hills and valleys.[72] A covered play area should be planned as an extension of the indoor area. The shelter's purpose is for passive play during good weather and for all play during inclement weather. It should be designed to permit a maximum amount of air and sunshine.

OUTDOOR SPACE ARRANGEMENT

As we have noted, the outdoor space should not be barren but should be aesthetically pleasing, safe, and designed to further the purposes of the early childhood program. Because the outdoor space is an extension of the indoor area, there must be areas for active and passive play. There is no clear-cut distinction between the two types of play. Large-muscle play is usually active, but walking on a balance beam may be passive; water play is usually passive, but running from a squirting hose is active.

In passive play, children need protection from excessive wind or heat and from other fast-moving children. Passive play areas should be enclosed and protected from more active play areas. Enclosure may be accomplished with shrubbery or large stones, with small openings between these areas, by changing the terrain, or by providing a sheltered area. Additional protection may be obtained by building a slightly winding path or by separating the two types of play areas.

Play areas must be separated for safety reasons. Space around each piece of equipment must be equal to the child's potential action outward, or the maximum distance children can jump, slide, or swing forward from any position on the equipment. Children also need space to bypass a piece of equipment. Paths should be three to five feet wide, adjoin safety areas, and be slightly curving. Very curvy paths cause children to cut through one play area to reach another, and necessitate quick movement by the supervising staff.

Similar pieces of play equipment, such as climbing apparatus, should be scattered throughout the area rather than placed side-by-side or clustered. This arrangement has several advantages: (1) a child may be able to select a piece of equipment that is not in the hot sun; (2) it is aesthetically more pleasing; (3) children will have more contrasting types of muscle activity during one play session, because they tend to move from one play area to an adjacent one; and (4) dare-devil competition may be lessened or eliminated.

Often in outdoor areas, there is a great deal of physical inactivity; thus, in outdoor areas, children need places to cluster and sit. Boulders or logs are perhaps more enjoyable for young children than park or picnic benches.

The types of activities conducted in the outdoor area are perhaps more extensive than those conducted in the indoor space. Because many of the interest centers are identical, factors to be considered in their outdoor arrangement would be similar to those suggested for the indoor design. The following suggestions should be considered in planning interest centers unique to the outdoor area.

1. *Road for vehicles.* A hard-surfaced area can form a tricycle, wagon, or doll buggy road extending through the outdoor space and returning to its starting point. The road should be wide enough to permit passing. A curvy road is more interesting, but there should be no right-angle turns, as these cause accidents.[73]

2. *Sand pit.* Because the outdoor sand pit involves the child's whole body, a sand pit for twenty children must be approximately 250 square feet. To prevent overlap of the sand area (and hence child aggression), the sand pit should be narrow. A winding river of sand is more aesthetically pleasing than an oblong-shaped box. Children should have flat working surfaces, such as wooden boards or flat boulders, beside or in the sand.

   An outdoor sand pit should have a boundary element which "should provide a 'sense' of enclosure for the playing children, keep out unwanted traffic, protect the area against water draining from adjacent areas, and help keep the sand within the sand play areas."[74] Boundaries can be built or created by a rolling terrain.

The sand pit should be partially shaded, but with exposure to the purifying and drying rays of the sun. Water should be available so the sand is not bone dry, and the water source should be at the periphery of the sand pit with the runoff flowing away from the sand.

3. *Wading pool and water spray area.* Outdoor water play activities should allow for more energetic play than indoor water activities. Concrete wading pools must have slip-proof walking surfaces and a water depth of one-half foot. Water temperature should be between 60° and 80° Fahrenheit (16° and 27° Celsius). In colder weather, a drained wading pool makes an excellent flat, hard surface for passive play. For programs on a meager budget, an inflatable pool can be used instead of a permanent one and a garden hose with a spray nozzle or water sprinkler attached can serve as a water spray.

4. *Garden.* An outdoor garden should be fenced to protect it from animals or from being accidentally trampled. The garden should be narrow, perhaps two feet wide, to minimize the need for the child gardener to step into the garden (especially important when the plot is muddy). A narrow garden can take on an aesthetically pleasing shape as it parallels straight fences or encircles large trees.

5. *Outdoor animal cages.* Outdoor animal cages should be built to meet the specific needs of each animal; located in a well-drained area sheltered from excessive heat and wind; and near a water source and the delivery gate. Because of vandalism, programs should take animals on a one-day basis only.

Figure 2, a plan of an outdoor activity area, illustrates some of the principles we have discussed. Because the plans for an outdoor activity area must fit the needs of the local early childhood program, the plan is only illustrative and is not necessarily an ideal arrangement.

OUTDOOR STORAGE

Outdoor storage can be attached to the main building, perhaps next to a terrace where the storage can provide shelter. If detached from the building, outdoor storage should be of a design and material to fit with the main building and not detract from it. Also, if a separate building is used, it should serve as a windbreak to the outdoor activity area.[75]

Outdoor storage twelve feet long, ten feet wide, and seven to eight feet high will be sufficient for most early childhood programs. The doorway should be six feet wide and should be a tilt- or roll-a-door garage-type. Hooks or pegs for hanging can be installed four and one-half feet above the floor along one side of the storage shed, and shelves for storing equipment in daily use can be built two or three feet above the floor along the back of the shed. A high shelf can be used for storing seasonal items or items for staff use.[76] Outdoor storage areas should have slightly raised flooring to prevent flooding after a substantial rain-

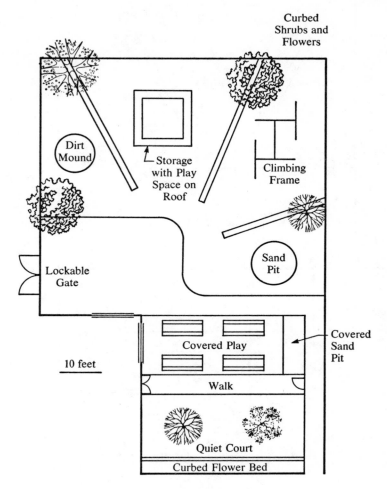

FIGURE 2
Outdoor Activity Area

fall. A ramp would facilitate moving equipment in and out of the storage shed and minimize tripping over different levels.

A storage shed can also serve as a prop for dramatic play. The roof of a storage shed might be fenced to serve as an additional play area, and the inside could serve as a place to play during inclement weather and for some daily play activities, like block building, that require a firm surface.

Figure 3 illustrates the arrangement of the children's activity room, the outdoor activity area, and the other children's and adults' areas of an early childhood facility. The illustration of the physical plant layout shows only one possible arrangement of the various areas. Figure 3 is not intended as a model layout but is presented to graphically depict some of the ideas discussed in the chapter.

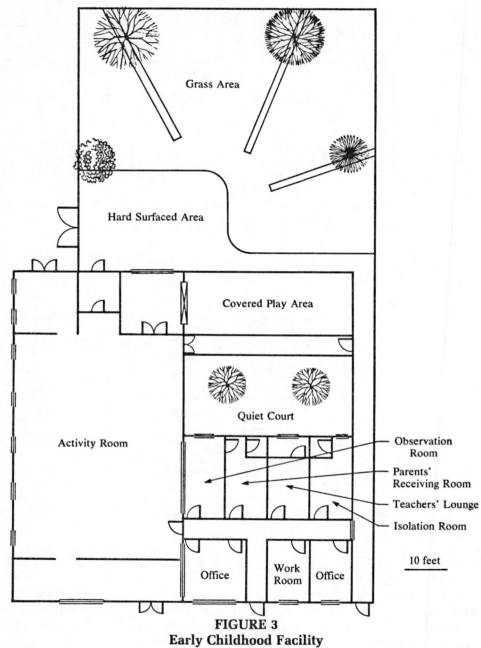

FIGURE 3
Early Childhood Facility

Insurance

Adequate insurance for a facility and its equipment and materials is of utmost importance, is required for mortgaged buildings, and is recommended for all owned buildings and for the contents of rented buildings. Basically, fire insurance covers the perils of fire and lightning. Most policies can have an extended-coverage endorsement attached that covers such things as losses from wind, hail, explosion (except from steam boilers), civil commotion, aircraft, vehicles, smoke, vandalism, and malicious mischief. If the program moves equipment and materials to various buildings, the insurance should include a floater policy to protect against loss rsulting from such transportation. In order to have adequate fire insurance (basic or extended coverage endorsement), the administrator must maintain up-to-date property records that reflect current values.

Two other types of insurance may be necessary. Boiler and machinery insurance is designed to protect against losses resulting from the explosion of pressure-type vessels or partial or complete breakdown of certain types of machinery. If the program owns vehicles, insurance should be secured to protect against losses from material damage or the destruction of the vehicle and its material contents.

NOTES

1. Eric Pearson, *Trends in School Design* (New York: Citation Press, 1972), p. 29.
2. Ibid., pp. 20–21.
3. A. Beeler, "Integrating Exceptional Children in Preschool Classrooms," *BAEYC Reports* 15 (1973): 33–41.
4. J. S. Evans, "Classroom Planning for Young Special Children," *Teaching Exceptional Children* 4 (1972): 56–62.
5. A. Beeler, "Integrating Exceptional Children in Preschool Classrooms."
6. Dwayne E. Gardner, "An Ideal Environment for Learning," *Housing for Early Childhood Education*, eds. Sylvia Sunderland and Nan Gray (Washington, D.C.: Assn. for Childhood Education International, 1968), p. 5.
7. Charles D. Gibson, "Preschool Educational Housing," *Housing for Early Childhood Education*, eds. Sylvia Sunderland and Nan Gray (Washington, D.C.: Assn. for Childhood Education International, 1968), p. 20.
8. Gibson, "Preschool Housing," p. 21.
9. Sybil Kritchevsky and Elizabeth Prescott, *Planning Environments for Young Children-Physical Space* (Washington, D.C.: National Assn. for the Education of Young Children, 1969), p. 5.
10. James R. Foster and Lorene R. Rogers, *Housing Early Childhood Education in Texas* (College Station, Tex.: Innovative Resources, 1970), p. 5.
11. Clarice Wills and Lucile Lindberg, *Kindergarten for Today's Children* (Chicago: Follett Educational Corp., 1967), p. 111.
12. Sarah H. Leeper et al., *Good Schools for Young Children* (New York: The Macmillan Co., 1968), p. 407.
13. Ruth E. Jefferson, "Indoor Facilities," *Housing for Early Childhood Education*, eds. Sylvia Sunderland and Nan Gray (Washington, D.C.: Assn. for Childhood Education International, 1968), p. 41.
14. Foster and Rogers, *Housing Early Childhood Education*, p. 4.
15. E. Prescott and T. G. David, "Effects of Physical Environments in Child Care Systems" (New York: Paper presented at the Annual Meeting of the American Education Research Association, April, 1977). ERIC ED 142 284
16. S. Shapiro, "Preschool Ecology: A Study of Three Environmental Variables," *Reading Improvement* 12 (1975): 236–41.
17. Neith E. Neadley, *Education in the Kindergarten*, 4th ed. (New York: American Book Co., 1966), p. 79.
18. Kritchevsky and Prescott, *Planning Environments*, p. 21.

19. L. W. Pluger and Jessie M. Zola, "A Room Planned by Young Children," *Young Children* 24 (1969): 337–41.
20. Shapiro, "Preschool Ecology: A Study of Three Environmental Variables."
21. A. P. Nilsen, "Alternatives to Sexist Practices in the Classroom," *Young Children* 32 (1977): 53–58.
22. Foster and Rogers, *Housing Early Childhood Education*, p. 9.
23. Leeper et al., *Good Schools*, p. 410.
24. Susanna Millar, *The Psychology of Play* (Baltimore, Md.: Penguin Books, 1968), p. 150.
25. Headley, *Education in Kindergarten*, pp. 80–81.
26. Leeper et all., *Good Schools*, p. 408.
27. Sophie Rosner, "A Place in Space," *Housing for Early Childhood Education*, eds. Sylvia Sunderlin and Nan Gray (Washington, D.C.: Assn. for Childhood Education International, 1968), p. 68.
28. Foster and Rogers, *Housing Early Childhood Education*, p. 7.
29. Leeper et al., *Good Schools*, p. 408.
30. Jefferson, "Indoor Facilities," p. 50.
31. Wills and Lindberg, *Kindergarten for Today's Children*, p. 119.
32. Foster and Rogers, *Housing Early Childhood Education*, p. 8.
33. Jefferson, "Indoor Facilities," p. 43.
34. Leeper et al., *Good Schools*, p. 410.
35. Foster and Rogers, *Housing Early Childhood Education*, p. 8.
36. Jefferson, "Indoor Facilities," p. 43.
37. Leeper et al., *Good Schools*, p. 410.
38. Jefferson, "Indoor Facilities," p. 43.
39. Wills and Lindberg, *Kindergarten for Today's Children*, p. 113.
40. Ibid.
41. Foster and Rogers, *Housing Early Childhood Education*, p. 9.
42. Fred Osmon, *Patterns for Designing Children's Centers* (New York: Educational Facilities Laboratories, 1971), p. 57.
43. U. S. Department of Agriculture, Food and Nutrition Service, Child Nutrition Division, *Equipment Guide for Preschool and School Age Child Service Institutions* (Washington, D.C.: U.S. Government Printing Office, 1972).
44. C. Stein, "School Lighting Re-evaluated," *American School and University* 48 (1975): 70–78.
45. Osmon, *Patterns*, p. 97.
46. Headley, *Education in Kindergarten*, p. 80.
47. Osmon, *Patterns*, p. 98.
48. Wills and Lindberg, *Kindergarten for Today's Children*, p. 112.
49. Educational Facilities Laboratory, *SER 2 Environmental Evaluations* (Ann Arbor, Mich.: University of Michigan, Architectural Research Laboratory, Department of Architecture, 1965), p. 120.
50. F. K. Sampson, *Contrast Rendition in School Lighting* (New York: Educational Facilities Laboratory, 1970).
51. Wills and Lindberg, *Kindergarten for Today's Children*, p. 112.
52. Gardner, "An Ideal Environment," p. 6.
53. Wills and Lindberg, *Kindergarten for Today's Children*, p. 112.
54. Ibid.
55. Jefferson, "Indoor Facilities," p. 44.
56. Leeper et al., *Good Schools*, p. 407.
57. Ibid.
58. M. J. Ellis, "The Rational Design of Playgrounds," *Education Product Report* 3 (1970): 3–6.
59. R. Dattner, "Playgrounds Aren't for Playing: Playgrounds Are for Growing and Learning," *American School Board Journal* 160 (1973): 30–31.
60. B. Sutton-Smith, "A Psychologist Looks at Playgrounds," *Educational Product Report* 3 (1970): 22–27.

61. Orange County Board of Public Instruction. *An Adaptive Playground for Physically Disabled Children with Perceptual Deficits: The Magruder Environmental Therapy Complex* (Orlando, Fla.: The Board, 1969). ERIC ED 036 941

62. M. Paul Friedberg, *Playground for City Children* (Washington, D.C.: Assn. for Childhood Education International, 1969), p. 9.

63. Ibid.

64. Katherine Read Baker, "Extending the Indoors Outside," *Housing for Early Childhood Education*, eds. Sylvia Sunderlin and Nan Gray (Washington, D.C.: Assn. for Childhood Education International, 1968), p. 60.

65. Baker, "Extending the Indoors," p. 62.

66. Leeper et al., *Good Schools*, p. 411.

67. "Planning the Playground," *Housing for Early Childhood Education*, eds. Sylvia Sunderland and Nan Gray (Washington, D.C.: Assn. for Childhood Education International, 1968), p. 72.

68. F.C. Thompson and A.M. Rittenhouse, "Measuring the Impact," *Parks and Recreation* 9 (1974): 24–26, 62–63.

69. Baker, "Extending the Indoors," p. 60.

70. Foster and Rogers, *Housing Early Childhood Education*, p. 14.

71. Baker, "Extending the Indoors," p. 61.

72. The University of the State of New York, *Design for the 70's: Planning Educational Facilities in the Elementary School for Very Young Children* (Albany, N.Y.: The State Education Department, Bureau of Child Development and Parent Education, 1973). ERIC ED 086 375

73. Baker, "Extending the Indoors," p. 61.

74. Osmon, *Patterns*, p. 77.

75. Foster and Rogers, *Housing Early Childhood Education*, p. 15.

76. "Planning the Playground," p. 75.

For Further Reading

Aaron, D., and Winawer, B.P. *Child's Play: A Creative Approach to Playspace for Today's Children.* New York: Harper & Row, Publishers, 1965.

Abramson, Paul. *Schools for Early Childhood.* New York: Educational Facilities Laboratories, 1971.

American Association of School Administrators. *Open Space Schools.* Washington, D.C.: The Association, 1971.

Bartholomew, R. et al. *Child Care Facilities Planning.* Ithaca, N.Y.: Cornell University, College of Human Ecology, 1973.

Bengtsson, A., ed. *Adventure Playgrounds.* New York: Praeger Publishers, 1972.

————. *Environmental Planning for Children's Play.* New York: Praeger Publishers, 1970.

Berson, M.P., and Chase, W.W. "Planning Preschool Facilities." *Early Childhood Education Rediscovered: Reading.* Edited by Joe L. Frost. New York: Holt, Rinehart & Winston, 1968, pp. 547–51.

Boles, Harold W. *Step by Step to Better School Facilities.* New York: Holt, Rinehart & Winston, 1965.

Campbell, W.J., ed. *Scholars in Context: The Effects of Environments on Learning.* New York: John Wiley & Sons, 1971.

Crowley, M.B. "Education Architecture." *Encyclopedia Britannica* 7 (1970): 1020–21.

Dattner, R. *Design for Play.* Cambridge, Mass.: The MIT Press, 1974.

Friedberg, M. Paul. *Playgrounds for City Children.* Washington, D.C.: Assn. for Childhood Education International, 1969.

————, with E.P. Berkeley. *Play and Interplay*. New York: The Macmillan Publishing Co., 1970.

Hanson, R.F. "Playgrounds Designed for Adventure." *Journal of Health, Physical Education, and Recreation* 40 (1960): 34–36.

Hewes, J.J. *Build Your Own Playground! A Sourcebook of Play Sculptures*. Boston, Mass.: Houghton Mifflin Co., 1974.

Kritchevsky, Sybil, and Prescott, Elizabeth. *Planning Environments for Young Children —Physical Space*. Washington, D.C.: National Assn. for the Education of Young Children, 1969.

Mittelstaedt, A.H., Jr. "Planning School Grounds." *Journal of Health, Physical Education, and Recreation* 40 (1969): 37–40.

Orange County Board of Public Instruction. *An Adaptive Playground for Physically Disabled Children with Perceptual Deficits: The Magruder Environmental Therapy Complex*. Orlando, Fla.: The Board, 1969. ERIC ED 036 941

Osmon, Fred. *Patterns for Designing Children's Centers*. New York: Educational Facilities Laboratories, 1971.

Passantino, E.D. "Adventure Playgrounds for Learning and Socialization." *Phi Delta Kappan* 56 (1975): 329–33.

Pearson, Eric. *Trends in School Design*. New York: Citation Press, 1972.

Roeper, A. *Planning Tomorrow's Nursery School Structures*. Bloomfield Hills, Mich.: Roeper City and Country School, 1965.

Sunderlin, Sylvia, and Gray, Nan, eds. *Housing for Early Childhood Education*. Washington, D.C.: Assn. for Childhood Education International, 1968.

"Taking Play Seriously: The Experimental Playground." *American School and University* 48 (1976): 22–27.

"Today's Playground: Designed for Chimp or Child? Q. and A. with M.J. Ellis." *American School and University* 43 (1971): 21–23.

Tonigan, R. et al. *Housing for Early Childhood Education*. Washington, D.C.: Association for Childhood Education International, 1965.

9

Equipping

Equipment and materials have a major influence on both staff and children; consequently, the task of deciding on specific equipment and materials should be determined by the educational objectives of the local early childhood program. They should be planned and budgeted for at the conception of the early childhood program for two reasons. First, if budgeting for equipment and materials is an afterthought, these items may be purchased with what remains after other expenditures are determined. Although the budget distribution in industries and schools should not necessarily be analogous, there is an interesting inverse relationship in their capital outlay budgets—industries use 10 percent of their capital outlay for structures and 90 percent for equipment, while schools spend 90 percent of their capital outlay for buildings and 10 percent for equipment.[1] A second reason for planning equipment and materials at the outset of a program proposal is that furnishing an architect with information about the types and quantities of equipment and materials that will be purchased can help him plan an adequate design.

Purchasing Equipment and Materials

The purchasing of equipment and materials is of immeasurable significance, for items that do not meet the needs of the program or that are insufficient in quantity for the activities planned hamper, rather than facilitate, the early childhood program. Moreover, careful purchasing of equipment and materials helps insure quality, and thus lengthens the time for replacement. Finally, in today's inflationary world, careful planning is essential if the items are to be secured within budgetary limitations.

PURCHASING GUIDELINES

Many considerations must be given to purchasing equipment and materials for an early childhood program. The following suggestions are only minimal guidelines.

1. Purchase equipment and materials that will facilitate meeting local program objectives. Sequenced materials are needed for programmed instruction; self-correcting materials are used in Montessori programs; materials for learning about the physical and social environment are used in child development programs; and some programs use materials that encourage creativity. There are materials available to meet the needs of handicapped children. There are also materials to teach multicultural, nonsexist concepts, such as dolls and hand puppets with a range of skin tones or characteristic features, and books, puzzles, and picutres depicting various ethnic and racial groups and nontraditional sex-role behavior. If program objectives are written in keeping with the ages and needs of the children, to be served, with the care-giving or teaching-learning methods to be employed, and with the number and qualifications of the staff to be hired, the equipment and materials secured to meet the program objectives should be appropriate. Item usefulness is of prime importance.

2. Check on the amount of money available and the procedures for purchasing. The building administrator has the budget and knows the procedures regarding the use of monies.

3. Maintain a perpetual inventory and a list of items needed. The inventory and list help to insure that the most essential pieces of equipment and materials have priority and that unwanted duplications will be avoided.

4. Consider your building space for using and storing equipment, and any additional building specifications for use of the item (e.g., electrical outlet or water source). Because equipment and materials require space for use and storage, the facility should be designed after the major pieces of equipment and materials are selected.

5. Be economical: Price an item in several distributors' catalogs, negotiate prices with distributors, and put purchases of substantial amounts up for bids; Always ask the question, "Can I make the item or adapt a previously purchased item?" The cost of making an item should be carefully calculated to include both raw materials and staff labor; and Work out plans for sharing equipment and materials in programs that have several groups of children under the care of various staff members.

6. Do not overbuy consumable items (food, paste, paint, paper, and clay). As a general rule, consumables are more susceptible to deterioration than are permanent pieces of equipment and materials.

7. Use equipment and materials on trial plans, offered by many reputable companies.

8. Check the "consumer's guide" for purchasing suggestions. The consumer's guide for early childhood programs consists of the opinions of personnel employed by the state education or welfare agency and local

universities, reports on research projects using the items, observations of displays at conventions, and discussions with other staff members.

9. Purchase safe equipment and materials. Standards for safety of equipment and materials are partially regulated by the Child Protection and Toy Safety Act (1969), the Child Safety Committee of the National Safety Council, and the Toy Manufacturers of America. In judging equipment and material safety: Avoid equipment and materials that have sharp edges and protrusions, brittle plastic parts, and parts easily pulled off, such as trimmings on doll clothes, squeakers that fall out of plastic toys, and so forth; Look for electrical equipment and materials that have the Underwriters' Laboratories (UL) seal, fabric products labeled nonflammable, flame-retardant, or flame resistant, stuffed toys filled with hygienic, washable and nonflammable materials, and items that use nontoxic paints; All playground equipment should be the right size for the children, standing playground equipment should be firmly anchored in concrete, with anchoring devices placed below ground level (up to 18 inches in depth is required by some licensing laws) to prevent equipment from falling or children from tripping; equipment should be installed over soft materials; bolt-ends on equipment should have protective end caps; swing sets should be installed a minimum of six feet away from fences, other structures, walkways, and other play areas; moving parts of swing sets should have wide spaces to avoid pinching fingers or toys; swing chains should not have open-ended S hooks; swinging rings should have a diameter smaller than five inches or larger than ten inches to avoid entrapping a child's head; climbing bars should not turn; attachments at the fulcrum of the seesaw should be enclosed to protect hands and a block should be placed under each end of the board to protect feet; climbing nets should be in good repair; and adventure or junk playground equipment should be free from splinters and projecting nails. Although the following source does not provide information for public playground equipment, the information is certainly helpful:

   Safety Requirements for Home Playground Equipment, American National Standard Z 304.1–1975. Washington, D.C.: U. S. Department of Commerce, National Bureau of Standards, 1976. ERIC ED 145 964

10. Select durable and relatively maintenance-free equipment and materials. Factors that contribute to durability are the types and quality of raw materials, the care given to fabricating the equipment and materials, and the reliability of working parts.

11. As much as possible, choose materials that are comprehensive in nature. Because both budget and space are usually limited, staff members should consider equipment and materials that can be used in a variety of situations, that are suitable for individual differences, and that will need to be stored infrequently. Pragnell states: "Flexibility can be gained when each object has not only its obvious function but also a certain ambiguity, so that, in different circumstances it can be used in a variety of different ways."[2] Materials that can be used in many ways also stimulate creativity.

Of course, many pieces of equipment and types of materials are designed for specific purposes, and staff members must not overlook these items in making decisions.

12. Select equipment and materials that are aesthetically pleasing. Young children are keenly aware of color, texture, size, form, brightness, sound, odor, and temperature; thus, equipment and materials should be appealing to the senses.

13. Choose equipment and materials that actively involve the child. Equipment and materials should not make the child a spectator, nor should all items call for the same repetitive activity.

14. The "acid test," of course, is whether the children like it over a period of time.

PURCHASING PROCEDURES

Most early childhood programs, whether federal, public school, or private, have similar procedures for purchasing, with the possible exceptions that publicly-funded programs are subject to more restrictions than are privately owned programs, and that early childhood programs with large enrollments follow a more formal procedure for purchasing than do programs with small enrollments. Because of the similarity in purchasing procedures, the following description of the basic purchasing procedure followed by public schools should apply, more or less, to other early childhood programs.

The needs of each division within a school system, including food service, transportation, instructional, and personnel, are made known to the division administrators, who submit their budgetary needs to the superintendent. Working with this information (and perhaps with the demands of pressure groups), the superintendent develops a budget and offers it to the board of education. If the budget is approved by the board of education, the board authorizes the obligating of the school district funds for the purchase of equipment and materials, as well as for services and other goods. Adoption of the operating budget—which must be done within legal procedures, tax limitations, and the approved outline of the program—authorizes the superintendent to spend the funds allocated for the fiscal year. Various restrictions may be placed on the general authorization, such as that the superintendent cannot trasfer funds allotted for purchases within one category to another category without authorization.

Specifications are prepared to determine whether bids on quotations should be secured or whether the item should be purchased by brand name. (Specifications can be helpful whether or not bidding will be the result.) Questions to answer include: Is the cost sufficiently high to justify bidding? Does the quantity of the single purchase or the possibility of repetitive purchases justify bidding? Is the item available from multiple sources? When purchases involve substantial amounts and are available from several manufactures, companies are asked to submit bids. Requests for bids are announced publicly, extended to all companies that might have the specified items, and contain the rules that regulate receiving and approving such bids. On a specified date, the sealed bids are opened during the meeting of the local board. Bids are announced, and the contract awarded to the lowest bidder able to provide the items as specified. In cases where purchases do not involve substantial amounts or where there is no prospect of competition in the bidding, purchases are negotiated. If small centers in close geographic proximity would purchase as a group, they could probably obtain better prices and reduced shipping costs, and would have more clout in dealing with companies that sell inferior equipment.

In large school systems, purchased equipment and materials are stored in warehouses that must be free from moisture, insects, vermin, or extremes in temperature. Allocation of equipment and materials to each building is initiated by a requisition from an authorized staff member. When the items are delivered, a copy of the signed requisition form is placed on file and serves as a receipt.

The inventory record is an essential aspect of the purchasing procedure. This record should list and identify all equipment and materials that have been purchased and delivered. The inventory record should indicate date of acquisition, current cost of replacement (often more than the initial cost), and what maintenance was provided. The inventory serves as a record of the quantity of materials purchased and of the location of items, and becomes the basis for preventing duplication, for determining what equipment and materials need to be replaced, for deciding insurance needs, for calculating loss or theft of items, and for assisting in budget planning with yearly readjustments.

Arranging Equipment and Materials

If interest centers are used, equipment and materials for daily use should be arranged in them. Portable objects should be placed on low shelves or in cabinets, so children can get them out and put them back. Open shelves encourage children to return their items. Heavy or nonportable objects should be placed on tables or shelves where they can be used without moving them, since children who attempt to move heavy or nonportable equipment and materials can hurt themselves or damage the items.

Many early childhood facilities lack enough shelf space. According to Osmon,[3] economy of shelf use can be achieved by creating distinctiveness in the items placed on the shelves. Distinctiveness is increased by using various types of shelving (inclined, slotted, stepped, and drawers) in one storage unit and by placing items with contrasting properties (color, size, shape, and texture) next to each other.

Equipment and materials for regular but not daily use should be readily available and stored to prevent deterioration and damage. If space permits, equipment and materials should be stored in or near the interest center where they will be used. Labeling also helps staff members locate equipment and materials quickly. Special care must be exercised in storing consumable items, such as food, paper, paste, and paints, audiovisual equipment, science materials, musical instruments, recordings, and any breakable objects.

Caring for Equipment and Materials

Caring for equipment and materials teaches children good habits and helps prevent expensive repairs and replacements. Keep the following suggestions in mind:

1. Arrange room and shelves to minimize the chance of accidents and to maximize housekeeping efficiency. Equipment and materials should be shelved close to the working space; objects susceptible to damage should be used in areas out of the main flow of traffic; breakable items or those likely to spill should be placed on shelves within easy reach (if there are frequent accidents involving the same item, try setting it in a different place); and there should be enough open space to prevent accidents.
2. Teach children how to care for equipment and materials. Staff members should establish a routine for obtaining and returning equipment and materials and for using facilities. To establish a routine, every item must have a place, and time must be allowed for returning all items to their places.
3. Clean up spilled materials. In some cases, you can create a science lesson on "how to clean it up."
4. Set a good example in caring for equipment and materials.
5. Be where the action is. Staff members should station themselves properly for adequate supervision.
6. Remove children from an area when they deliberately destroy or damage equipment or materials.
7. Repair equipment and materials as soon as possible and do not use items until they are repaired.
8. Clean equipment regularly. Toys for infants and toddlers should be cleaned with a disinfectant daily, and equipment for preschoolers should be cleaned weekly.
9. Periodically check equipment and materials. Tighten loose nuts, bolts, clamps, and other hardwear; replace rusted parts or sand and repaint rusted tubing; oil metal parts; sand wooden equipment where splinters are found; paint or use clear protective coatings on wooden equipment and remove loose paint; repair torn fabric and secure fasteners on doll or dress-up clothes; and replace broken-off or sharp plastic equipment. To report a product you believe to be unsafe, write to:

Standards Development Service Section
National Bureau of Standards
Washington, D.C. 20234
or
U.S. Consumer Product Safety Commission
Washington, D.C. 20207
(Toll Free, 800-638-2666, or Maryland residents only, call 800-492-2937)

10. Consider what heat, light, moisture, and storage method may do to your equipment and materials.

11. Have plenty of equipment and materials, so that each child has something to do and does not have to wait his turn too long. Tempers flare and damage occurs when children are not constructively involved.

12. Store these chemicals where children cannot get to them: ammonia, antifreeze, aspirin, bleach, camphor, cement and glue, detergent, drain cleaner, dry cleaning fluid, fabric softener, floor wax, furniture polish, gasoline, ink, insecticide, kerosene, kindling or prepackaged illuminating preparations, laundry bluing, leather polish and dye, lighter fluid, lye, metal polish, methanol, moth repellent, oil of wintergreen, oral prescription drugs, paint and thinner, putty and rust removers, rat poison, room deodorizer, rug cleaner, shoe cleaner, shoe polish, sulfuric acid, turpentine, typewriter cleaner, varnish, and washing soda. To request information about a product, call: Consumer Product Safety Hot Line 800-638-2666 (Maryland residents only, call 800-492-2937). Post the telephone number of the local poison control center.

Specific Equipment and Materials

Most of the specific equipment and materials used in an early childhood program are instructional. Instructional materials are representations of everyday life "which have been produced or selected for their educational relevance and arranged so that they are accessible for use."[4] One classification of instructional materials is as follows: (1) simple objects; (2) models, facsimiles, dolls, and mock-ups; (3) pictures, diagrams, photographs, filmstrips, maps, and globes; (4) language samples, oral and print, such as recordings and books; (5) motion pictures, video broadcasts, and tapes; and (6) combinations of the foregoing.[5] In fact, almost anything can be an instructional material.

One source claims there is a wider variety of instructional materials in use in early childhood programs that at any other level of education.[6]

> Some of the claims made for sets and for individual items could give the proverbial "Man from Mars" the impression that the curriculum of schools for young children in this country is entirely contained in such materials. Many items are offered for sale to parents as well as teachers, and many are described as self-instructing, or as containing instructions for use that are so complete that even relatively untrained laymen could use them successfully to achieve the described objectives with children.[7]

Appendix 5 contains a list of names and addresses of many suppliers of early childhood equipment and materials.

FURNITURE

Furniture for young children should be of the proper height and proportions, durable and lightweight, and have rounded corners. If space is at a premium, furniture, especially children's chairs, should be stackable. Tables accommodating from four to six children are advisable for kindergartens and nursery schools. For groups of one- and two-year-old children, it is advisable also to have some tables for two children. Although tables are designed in many geometrical shapes, rectangular tables accommodate large pieces of paper for art and craft work, and round tables are attractive in the library center.[8] Trapezoidal tables are quite versatile, because they can be arranged in many configurations. All table surfaces should be scrubbable. Portable drawing and writing surfaces, such as clipboards and cut-outs from formica countertops, are also being used. Cut-outs from formica countertops can be used for finger painting, play dough, and cooking experiences.

Children's chairs should have a broad base to prevent tipping and a full saddle seat with a back support approximately eight inches above the seat. So that chairs can be carried safely by children, chair weight should not exceed eight to ten pounds. The distance between the seat height of the chairs and the table surface should be approximately seven and one-half inches.[9] Chairs used at tables should not have arms. In addition to regular school chairs, rocking chairs, easy chairs, stools, or benches may be used. There is a movement today toward the use of pillows, hassocks, beanbag chairs, inflatable cushions, and inner tubes instead of traditional chairs. These nonrigid chairs add to the softness of the room and are important to the children's sensual-tactile development.

In addition to children's tables and chairs, the activity room must be equipped with storage units and dividers. Staff members should have comfortable furniture, work surfaces for making instructional aids, and places for filing and storing records and other materials.

In summary, furniture should be suited to the children's physical development and to the objectives of the program. Some of the necessary furniture might be:

adult chairs
adult rocking chair
children's chairs (8"–12" seat height)
children's rocking chairs, easy chairs, stools, or benches
children's tables (15½"–19½" high)
filing cabinets
flag
pencil sharpener
portable or built-in children's cubbies
portable and/or built-in storage units (or bins) for instructional materials
portable dividers (bulletin boards, chalkboards, flannel boards, or screens)
sofas, easy chairs, and occasional tables in adult areas
staff member's desk or table
staff member's locker or cupboard
staff members' cubbies for mail
stapler
wastebasket

AUDIOVISUAL EQUIPMENT

Though early childhood programs have used audiovisual equipment for years, recent growth in both quantity and quality of material has broadened its use. Of course, "more" use is not necessarily better, if vicarious experiences via audiovisual equipment are substituted for available real experiences. Audiovisual equipment that might be needed includes:

    camera (35mm and/or Polaroid)
    filmstrip projector and filmstrips
    headsets or earphones and listening stations
    "Language Master"
    loop (8mm)
    movie projector (16mm) and film
    overhead projector and transparencies
    projection table
    record player and records
    screen (36" × 48")
    slide projector and slides
    stereoscope and stereoscope reels (Viewmaster)
    still pictures and graphic representations
    storage cabinets for tapes, slides, etc.
    tape recorder(s) (cassette and/or reel-to-reel) and blank tapes
    television
    three-dimensional models
    videotape equipment

In addition to the foregoing equipment, a manual for operating and adjusting audiovisual equipment might be helpful, such as *Audiovisual Equipment: Self-Instruction Manual.*[10]

INTEREST CENTERS

Because of the wide variety of equipment and materials, it would be impossible to list all the items available for interest center. The following lists name some of the basic equipment and materials exclusive of textbooks, workbooks, and instructional kits and sets.

Language Arts.   The equipment and materials needed for language arts frequently envelop the specific curricular areas of listening, speaking, preparation for reading and writing, and literature. Although some early childhood programs have a language arts center, many programs place their language arts materials in several interest centers, such as the library, manipulative center, and concept development center. Regardless of the arrangement of equipment and materials, items needed for language arts instruction include:

    alphabet letters (alphabet insets, kinesthetic letters, letters to step on, etc.)
    books and recordings of stories
    filmstrips and/or slides of children's stories
    flannel board
    lotto (covering many subjects)
    objects and pictures depicting rhyming words and/or initial sounds
    perceptual and conceptual development games (absurdities, missing parts, sequenc-
        ing, go-togethers, opposites, and classification)
    picture dominoes

pictures and graphic representations of finger plays, poems, and stories
puppets and a puppet theater
puzzles (jigsaw, sequencing, etc.) and puzzle rack
recordings of sounds, such as animal, city, and home sounds
signs and labels
typewriter

Mathematics.   Concepts frequently taught in mathematics include: numbers, number combinations, and numerals; geometric concepts; size; position (i.e., ordinals); and patterns. Some early childhood programs have a mathematics center; others include mathematical equipment and materials in several interest centers, such as the concept-development center and the block center. Articles that help in children's mathematical development include:

abacus (or counting frame)
balance scales for developing an understanding of simple number operations
beads for pattern work and for developing an understanding of geometric concepts
"Broad Stair" for developing size concepts (Montessori)
calendars, thermometers, clocks, scales, etc. which have numerals
counting discs
"Cuisenaire" materials for developing number and geometric concepts
cylinders which are graduated in diameter and/or height (Montessori)
design cubes
dowel rods in graduated lengths, for developing serial concepts
fabric, wallpaper, and cabinet- and floor-covering samples for pattern work
flannel board objects, numerals, and illustrations of finger plays and stories with
    mathematical concepts
fraction plates or cards
geometric shape insets and solids
"Golden Beads" for developing place value concepts (Montessori)
lotto (number and geometric shapes)
measuring cups and spoons for developing size concepts
number cards, dominoes, puzzles, and sorter
numerals (cards, insets, kinesthetic, puzzles, numerals to step on, etc.)
objects to count
pegboards and pegs for developing number and geometric concepts
picture books, poems, and finger plays which have mathematical concepts
pictures of objects for grouping into sets and of geometric shapes
"Pink Tower" for developing size concepts (Montessori)
sorting box for geometric shapes
stacking and nesting blocks for developing size concepts
unit blocks and/or parquetry blocks for developing geometric and size concepts

Social Studies.   Areas frequently covered in social studies include home and family; community workers; concepts from geography, sociology, and economics; and holidays. Though the block and housekeeping centers can be considered social studies centers, they are usually arranged separately and their equipment and materials will not be listed here. Equipment and materials needed for social studies include:

books, poems, and finger plays with the following themes: (1) home and family; (2) community workers; (3) self-awareness (needs of security, self-confidence, achievement, belonging to groups, etc.); (4) holidays; and (5) family living in other parts of the world

doll house, dolls, and miniature furniture

globe and maps (primary globe and a simple map of the area)

holiday decorations (although most decorations are child-made)

pictures, posters, and flannel boards with the following themes: home and family; community workers; people in other parts of the country and in other parts of the world; various geographical land and water areas; and holidays

    (some multicultural and nonsexist pictures and posters include

    "Home and Family" (pictures), by The Instructo Corporation;

    "Mothers Do Many Kinds of Work" (posters), by Scott, Foresman and Company;

    "People at Work" (photos), by Women's Action Alliance, Inc., a Nonsexist Child Development Project;

    "People at Work Photo Packet" (photos), by Change for Children;

    "Resource Photos of Men in Nuturing Role" (photos), by Women's Action Alliance, Inc., a Nonsexist Child Development Project;

    "Resource Photos of Women in Community Jobs" (photos), by Feminist Resources for Equal Education;

    "Resource Photos of Women in Professional Jobs" (photos), by Feminist Resources for Equal Education;

    "We Are a Family," an Exploring Childhood Program by Educational Development Center; and

    "Women at Work" (photos), by Change for Children.)

puppets (family, community workers, and holiday characters such as Santa Claus)

    puzzles and lotto: family, community workers, and holidays

    (some multicultural and nonsexist puzzles and lotto include:

    "The City," "The Park," "Safety," and "The Doctor" (floor puzzles), by Judy Publishing Company;

    "Play Scenes Lotto" by the Milton Bradley Company; and

    "Occupational Series" (puzzles), by Judy Publishing Company.)

    village (miniature)

Blocks and Building Structures.   Blocks and building structures may be set up in one center; however, smaller building materials, such as Tinker Toys and Lego blocks are often used in the manipulative center, and larger building materials, such as hollow blocks, are placed in an outdoor activity center. Unit blocks, so named because each block is the size of the unit or a multiple or fraction of that unit, and larger floor blocks are most commonly placed in block and building centers. Other materials to include in block and building centers are:

accessories for bloc building, such as animals and peovle (wood, rubber, or plastic), wheel toys for pushing on floor, steering wheel, and block attachments (Two examples of multicultural and nonsexist block accessories are "My Family Play People" and "Our Community Helpers" by the Milton Bradley Company.)

block bin or cart (unless shelves are used)

giant blocks (made of polyethylene and corrugated cardboard)

indoor blocks[11]

100 units	1⅜″ × 2¾″ × 5½″
180 double units	1⅜″ × 2¾″ × 11″
200 quadruple units	1⅜″ × 2¾″ × 22″
36 ramps	1⅜″ × 2¾″ × 5½″
25 roof boards	⅜″ × 2¾″ × 11″
10 curves (eliptical)	1⅜″ × 2¾″ × 13¾″
10 curves (circular)	1⅜″ × 2¾″ × 7¾″
10 Y-Switches	1⅜″ × 8¼″ × 11″
20 cylinders	2¾″ diam. × 5½″
20 pillars	1⅜″ × 1⅜″ × 5½″
25 half-units	1⅜″ × 2¾″ × 2¾″
20 pairs triangles	1⅜″ × 2¾″ × 2¾″

interlocking planks
"Lego" blocks and other miniature interlockers (a wide assortment is available in wood and plastic)
out-of-door hollow blocks[12]

36 units	12″ × 12″ × 6″
36 double units	12″ × 24″ × 6″

planks, boxes, wooden sawhorses, barrels, etc.
Tinker Toys (miniature and giant)
traffic sign set

Housekeeping and Dramatic Play.　In dramatic play, children act out the roles of family members and community workers, reenact school activities and story plots, and learn social amenities such as table manners and telephone courtesy. Dramatic play may occur in almost any interest center; however, one or more centers are usually arranged specifically for dramatic play. Necessary equipment and materials are:

costumes, especially hats and tools of the trade (e.g., doctor's bag and stethoscope) of community workers and costumes for reenacting stories

doll items (table and two to four chairs; doll furniture—high chair, bed or cradle, carriage, chest of drawers, refrigerator, stove, sink, cabinet for dishes, and washer-dryer; doll wardrobes and linens; pots, pans, dishes, flatware [all items should be unbreakable]; ironing board and iron; housekeeping articles—broom, dust mop, dustpan, and dust rag; artificial food; clothesline and clothespins; and dishpan).

dolls (baby and teenage dolls representing both sexes and various ethnic groups, such as the dolls manufactured by Childcraft Education Corporation and Mattel, Inc.)

dress-up clothes for men and women (long skirts; blouses; dresses; shirts; shoes; caps; hats; boots; small suitcase; scarves and ribbons; flowers; jewelry; purses; neckties; and pieces of material)

fabric (several strips two or three yards in length, which can be used imaginatively)

gadgets, such as rubber hose, steering wheels, pipe, old faucets, door locks, springs, keys, pulleys, bells, scales, alarm clock, cash register and play money, cartons and cans, paint brushes, paper bags, light switch, and paper punch (for tickets)

For specific prop equipment, see:

Bender, J. "Have You Ever Thought of a Prop Box?" *Young Children* 26 (1971): 164–69.

In addition to the occupation props described by Bender, develop prop equipment for parent occupations.

miniature doll house, community, farm, service station, etc.

mirrors (full-length and hand-held)

playscreens, cardboard houses, etc.

puppets and stages

rocking chair

stuffed animals

telephone

Science. Both biological and physical science concepts are presented to young children. Because of the diversity of science equipment and materials, they are rarely all housed in a single interest center. Some of the equipment and materials include:

animal and insect cages (container for small insects, cocoon holder, cage with treadmill, rabbit hutch, container for praying mantis, large walk-in cages, etc.)

animals, insects, and fish

aquarium (equipped with air pump and hose, filter, gravel, fish net, light, thermometer, medicine and remedies, and aquarium guide)

balloons

bird and suet feeders, and bird house

books and pictures with the following themes: animals, plants, natural phenomena, and machinery

bubble pipes and soap

butterflly net

chick incubator

collections (rocks, bird nests, insects, sea shells, etc.)

color wheel, color paddles (i.e., glass or plastic paddles in the primary colors), and prisms

compass

dry cell batteries, flashlight bulbs, bells, light receptacle, and electrical wire

gardening tools (child-sized)

kaleidoscope

magnets (bar, horseshoe, and bridge)

magnifying glasses (hand-held and tripod)

measuring equipment (measuring cups and spoons; scales—balance, bathroom, postal; time instruments—sun dial, egg timer, clocks; thermometers (real indoor/outdoor and play); and lineal measuring instruments (English and metric)

miscellaneous materials (string, tape, hot plate, bottles of assorted sizes, pans, buckets, sponges, and hardware gadgets)

models (animals, space equipment, machine, solar system, etc.)

pin wheels

plants, seeds, and bulbs (with planting pots, soil, fertilizer, and watering cans)

pulleys and gears

puzzles or science themes, such as "Bodies," by Childcraft Education Corporation)

seed box

wheelbarrows (child-sized)

sound-producing objects

terrariums (woodland and desert)

vases and "frogs" for vases
weather vane

Water, Sand, and Mud.   Water, sand, and mud interest centers are found both in the indoor and outdoor areas. Some items are:

mops and sponges for clean-up
sand (white and brown)
sand and mud toys (trucks, jeeps, trains, bulldozers, tractors, cartons, cans, gelatin or
   sand molds, cookie cutters, spoons, pans, cups, dishes, strainers, watering cans,
   shovels, blocks, sand dolls, sieves, pitchers, sand pails, ladles, sifters, screens, sand
   combs, planks, and rocks)
sand table
siphon tubes
soap (floating) and soapflakes
straws
water play table
water plays toys (small pitchers, watering cans, measuring cups, bowls of various sizes,
   plastic bottles, detergent squeeze bottles, medicine droppers, funnels, strainers,
   hose, corks, squeeze bottles, sponges, washable dolls, wire whisks, butter churns,
   and shaving brushes)
water pump for indoor water table

Cooking.   Few programs have a permanent cooking interest center; however, most programs do provide children with occasional cooking experiences. If the facility has a kitchen or kitchenette, separate cooking equipment is not essential. Items that may be needed for cooking experiences include:

baking pans (cookie sheets, muffin tins, cake pans, and pie pans)
dishcloth and dish towels
dishes and flatware
electric, counter-top oven/broiler
hot plate
kitchen utensils (stirring spoons, spatula, tongs, and paring knife)
measuring spoons and cups
mixing bowls
napkins
pitcher, serving dishes and baskets, and trays
place mats
popcorn popper
pot holders
recipes written for young children
sauce pans
serving cart equipped with wheels
skillet
tea kettle

Woodworking or Carpentry.   The woodworking or carpentry interest center may be set up in either the indoor or outdoor area. This is a popular center for young children. Equipment and materials needed for woodworking or carpentry are:

C clamps (variety of)
cloth, leather, styrofoam, cardboard, cork, bottle caps, and other scraps to nail on wood
drill (hand)
glue
hammers (claw) of differing weights and sizes
magnet (tied to a string for picking up dropped nails)
nails (thin nails with good-sized heads, because thick nails tend to split wood)
paints (water-base)
pencils (heavy, soft-leaded)
pliers
ruler and yardstick used as a straight edge more than for measuring
sandpaper of various grades (wrapped around and tacked to blocks)
sawhorses
saws (crosscut and coping)
scraps of wood (soft wood such as white pine, poplar, fir, and basswood with no knots), doweling, wood slats, and wooden spools
soap (rubbed across the sides of a saw to make it slide easier)
tacks
tri-square
vises (attached to workbench)
wire (hand-pliable)
worktable or workbench (drawers for sandpaper and nails are desirable)
Note: Young children cannot handle and/or do not need a rasp, screwdriver and screws, a plane, a brace and bits, a file, an ax or hatchet, metal sheets, tin snips, or power tools.

Music.   Young children respond to music by listening, singing, playing rhythm instruments, and dancing. Equipment and materials for music may include:

autoharp
capes and full skirts for dancing
chromatic bells
chromatic pitch pipe
headsets and listening stations
music books for singing, rhythms, and appreciation
music cart
piano and piano bench
pictures of musicians, musical instruments, and dancers
record player
record rack or cabinet and/or cassette rack
records and cassettes
rhythm instruments (drums, claves, triangles, tambourines, cymbals, tom-toms, handle bells, jingle sticks, wrist bells, ankle bells, shakers, maracas, rhythm sticks, tone blocks, castanets, sand blocks, sounder, finger cymbals, and gong bell)
scarves (5′ × 3′)
stories (e.g., picture books) about music and sound
xylophone

Art.   Using various art media, children create graphic and three-dimensional works and learn concepts of color, form, texture, and size. Art equipment and materials include:

apron or smock (snaps preferred, because ties can knot)
chalk (various colors, ⅝" to 1" diameter)
clay (powdered and/or "Play Doh" or "Plasticine")
clay boards
color paddles (three paddles—red, yellow, and blue)
crayons (red, yellow, blue, orange, green, purple, black, and brown)
design block sets
display boards and tables
drying rack
easels (two working sides with a tray for holding paint containers on each side)
erasers (art gum and felt for chalkboard)
geometric shapes (insets, etc.)
gummed paper in assorted shapes for making designs and pictures
junk materials for collage work (beads, buttons, cellophane, cloth, flat corks, wallpaper
    scraps, wrapping paper scraps, and yarn)
magazines for collage
markers (felt-tip, various colors)
mosaics
mounting board (22" × 28")
pails (plastic with covers for storing clay)
paint (powdered or premixed tempera paint in various colors and finger paint)
paint jars (some are now made which do not spill)
paint and varnish brushes (camel hair or bristle, ½" and 1" thick with long handles)
paper (corrugated paper; newsprint, 24" × 36"; finger paint paper or glazed shelf paper;
    construction, tissue, and poster papers of various colors; manila paper, 18" × 24";
    metallic paper, 10" × 13"; wrapping paper; and tag board, 24" × 36")
paper bags
paper cutter
parquetry
paste brushes and sticks
paste and glue
pictures of children engaging in art activities and of famous artists
printing blocks or stamps
recipes for finger paints, modeling materials, etc.
reproductions of famous paintings and pictures of sculpture and architecture
ruler
scissors (adult shears and right- and left-handed scissors for children)
scissors rack
sorting boxes for sorting colors and shapes
staff members' supplies (art gum erasers; masking, cellophane, and mystic tapes;
    shellac or a fixative; liquid starch; dishwashing detergent; straight pins; shears;
    stapler; paper punch; and cutter)
stories and poems with themes of color, shape, size, beauty of nature, etc.
tape (masking, mending, and transparent)
textured materials
yarn (various colors)
yarn needles

Manipulative Activities.   Manipulative activities help young children develop
eye-hand coordination. Equipment and materials for manipulative activities
include:

art materials
beads for stringing
blocks (small, interlocking)
dressing doll, dressing frames, and/or dressing vests (equipped with buttons, raincoat
    snaps, zippers, bows, snaps, and buckles)
insets (geometric shapes, numerals, and letters)
lacing boards (or cards)
latch frames
pegs and pegboards
pounding boards
puzzles
sewing cards

Large-Muscle Play.   Because professionals concerned with young children are realizing the multifaceted benefits of large-muscle play, the equipment and materials designed for vigorous activity have undergone several major changes. One change is the emphasis on developing an outdoor area that takes advantage of and enhances the beauty of the natural landscape. The Kansas State Child Development Laboratory has developed creative outdoor equipment that fits not only the objectives of their program but accentuates the beauty of the rolling terrain.[13]

A second change is the prevalent use of adventure, or creative or junk playgrounds. The idea of an adventure playground was first conceived by C.T. Sorensen, a landscape architect in Copenhagen. Sorensen noticed that children did not play on the playgrounds he designed; instead, they played with discarded building materials. Disadvantages of traditional equipment are that it does not stimulate the imagination; chileren may use it in ways other than those intended, so that it becomes dangerous; children have to wait turns; metal equipment is affected by weather, and it is expensive—from less than a hundred to several thousand dollars per item. Although adventure playgrounds are not without their problems (drainage, lack of enclosure, and unsightliness), many writers feel these playgrounds will be prevalent in the future. A study by Reid[14] found that in comparing the enthusiasm of children, parents, school personnel, and people of the community for adventure playgrounds, children are most enthusiastic and school personnel least enthusiastic. Parents like the idea of these playgrounds, but are concerned about their children's clothing. Thompson and Rittenhouse[15] show that social skills increase as children participate in adventure playgrounds. All types of materials seem to have an irresistible fascination for children; thus, adventure playgrounds can include items to climb, such as ropes, rope nets, and walls; to crawl through, such as foxholes or culverts, with some opening straight up in an escape manhole; to balance on, such as balance logs or roll barrels; to walk or run on, such as stepping stones or tire walks; for stair-stepping or island hopping, such as stepping stones or log pieces; to swing on, such as tire swings and ropes; to slide on, such as boards or aluminum roofing; to stack, balance, and build, such as pieces of scrap lumber or plastic pipe; to bounce on, such as car springs with platform or a used innerspring mattress; for water, dirt, and mud play; and for make-believe play, such as tree houses or forts, old cars, boats, or airplanes, and lookout towers or foxholes.

It is interesting to note that manufacturers of play equipment are deigning free-form climbing units and other structures somewhat like those of the adventure playgrounds.

A third change is the increase in equipment and materials available for large-muscle activity. Some items are:

balls (inflatable; 14″, 8½″, and 5″ diameters)
bean bags
blocks (hollow and/or large floor blocks)
bridges (platform)
doll carriages
gardening tools
horizontal ladder
horse (broomstick variety)
inner tubes (rubber)
jumping boards
jungle gym (approximately 5′ high)
kegs (wooden)
ladder box
ladders (cleats or hooks on each end; 3′, 4′, and 5′ lengths and 14″ wide)
mattresses for jumping (innerspring)
packing cases (wooden, 42′ × 30″ × 30″)
pedal toys (e.g., tricycles)
pictures of children playing and people engaging in physical activities and sports
planks (cleats at ends to hold place on climbing structure, 6′ × 10″)
platform and steps (each step, 6″ × 18″ × 6″ high; landing 12″ × 18″)
ringtoss game and rings
rocking boats
rope ladder
ropes (jumping, 10′ long)
sand pit
sand play toys
sawhorses (24″ long, 12″ to 24″ high, and 24″ wide at the base to prevent tipping)
seesaw
singing game recordings
slide
stories with physical activity themes
swings with canvas seats or tire swings
wagons (and other pull/ride-in toys)
walking beam
walking boards
water play equipment

MATERIALS FOR INFANTS AND TODDLERS

The number of infant and toddler programs is increasing, both because more mothers of even the youngest children are employed, and because of the hope that infant and toddler programs will provide maximum developmental stimulation. Similarly to securing equipment and materials for any age group, criteria for selection should include program objectives, health and safety, staffing patterns, and budget limitations.

Basic Equipment.   Basic equipment includes items for the health, safety, and comfort of infants and toddlers, and for general visual and auditory stimulation (audiovisual equipment):

bibs, or polyback dental towels for disposable bibs

blankets (receiving and crib blankets)

bottles

bottle warmers

carriers (molded plastic)

car seats, infant and toddler (if transporting)

clocks, wall (preferably with nursery motif)

cloths, 45-inch square vinyl (to cover floor during meals or snacks or during art activities)

clothes hamper

crib bumper pads

crib mattresses

crib pads (water resistant)

cribs, portable (cribs should fit through doorways, and those which can be reassembled into play pens are good)

crib sheets, fitted

cups, plastic (for drinking)

decorations, wall and freestanding

diaper-changing equipment (bath-table replacement tops that are foam-cushioned and plastic-covered, diaper pails with deodorant cakes, and paper towel dispenser)

diaper changing supplies (diapers, disposable diaper bags or plastic trash bags, washcloths—preferably disposable towelettes, oils/lotions/powders, extra transparent tape for disposable diapers or pins for cloth diapers, liquid germicidal soap, and paper towels)

dividers or screens (for privacy at naptime)

dustcovers for cribs (muslin fabric)

feeding dishes (electric or hot water), cups, and spoons (and forks, if appropriate for age . group)

gates, safety

housecleaning equipment and supplies (vacuum, floor cleaners, mops, sponges, and disinfectants)

labels, iron-on (name tapes for linens)

lap pads (water resistant)

mirrors (preferably unbreakable)

mobiles

pads, 26″ × 54″ × 2″ foam (for cushions under indoor climbing apparatus)

"Play n' Feed Table" (a Sears item, although similar items found under other brand names are just as appropriate) or high chairs (molded plastic—for easy cleaning)

range and oven for cooking or heating meals and snacks

record player

records (suitable for infants and toddlers)

refrigerator (counter-size is sufficient for small group)

rocking chair (adult-sized)

safety harnesses (especially in high chair)

safety equipment for room (safety latches for cabinets, safety door knobs, and electrical outlet covers)

smocks (worn by care-givers)

sponge, for changing diapers or clothing or for bathing
sterilizer with bottle brushes, etc.
storage units
strollers
towel clips, chrome (used by dentists; holds disposable bib)
towel racks, hooks, or pegboards
towels and washcloths
training chairs
tub, baby
walker

Play Equipment and Toys.   In addition to safety considerations, equipment and toys should fit the program objectives and the children's ages. The following lists are divided for approximate stage-appropriateness.

1. Crib equipment and toys:
    animals and dolls, stuffed and washable
    ball (or another object with chime)
    balls (easy to clutch)
    beads, large plastic
    blocks, foam with pictures and blocks that rattle, make sounds when squeezed, etc.
    books (often cloth, wooden, vinyl, or plastic-coated; some are the "turn-the-page-type" and others are accordian-folded)
    "Busy Box" (a Sears item, but similar items are found under other brand names and are equally appropriate)
    cradle gym (most are a single unit, but some are modular, such as Childcraft's "Modular Crib Rod")
    cylinder roller, inflated vinyl (such as the "Peek-In Roller" by Walt Disney Productions)
    mirror, unbreakable
    mittens (to help infants discover their hands)
    mobiles (some revolve and some have music boxes)
    music-box toys (plastic and stuffed animal variety available; often attached to cribs, play yards, etc.)
    rattles (hand-held, and attached to sides of crib, play yard, or walls)
    stacking rings
    squeeze toys
    swings (with canvas seats)
    teething rings
2. Older infant and toddler equipment and toys:
    animals, farm and zoo
    balls, soft rubber, sponge, cloth (approximately 5 inches in diameter)
    bathtub, infant, or dishpans for water play
    beads, stringing
    blocks (cloth, vinyl, or small wooden)
    books (often cloth, wooden, vinyl, or plastic-coated)
    bottles or jugs, plastic
    bowls, plastic
    boxes and other containers (baby cereal and oatmeal and plastic ice cream containers; medium and large cardboard boxes)
    building equipment (such as "Bristle Blocks" or "Jumbo Lego")

cans, coffee and juice
cookie cutters, plastic
cups, measuring (plastic or metal)
dishpans, plastic
doll bed
doll bedding
doll carriage
dolls (cloth or vinyl)
dolls (for learning to dress)
drum
fabric pieces (clothing and upholstery fabrics)
fill and dump toys (such as a dump truck)
fingerpaints and pudding for fingerpainting
floating objects
gym, indoor and outdoor
hats (men's and women's)
kiddie cars (double-wheel)
lacing shoe
lock boxes
lotto (simple farm, zoo, and object)
nesting and stacking toys
objects of various shapes and textures and feely boxes
painting easel
pegs and pegboard
people, family and community
play dough
pounding bench
pull toys
purses, ladies'
puzzles, wooden jigsaw and "see into"
rocking chairs (child-sized)
rocking boat
rocking horse
sandbox
sandbox toys (plastic)
scoops, plastic (sugar or coffee)
slides and cubes
sorting boxes or balls (for sorting shapes)
spice shakers, plastic
spools, for stringing
spoons, plastic and measuring
swings
telephone, play
top, spinning
tricycles
trucks, small
wagons, including walker wagon
xylophone

(Although these toys are listed for infants and toddlers, many are appropriately used across a wide span of ages. It is our feeling that too many teachers put away toys after toddlerhood and bring out textbooks, workbooks, and audiovisual hardware.)

EQUIPMENT AND MATERIALS
FOR HANDICAPPED CHILDREN

A growing number of materials is advertised as being designed for children with a variety of disabilities; however, there is little research about their value. Before reading the list of equipment and materials, please note that:

1. Many types of handicaps require therapy with equipment and materials that can only be handled by a trained professional. The items listed below are examples of equipment and materials for the less severely handicapped, those most apt to be "mainstreamed."
2. Most regular early childhood equipment is suitable for the less severely handicapped. In fact, early childhood and "special education" equipment and materials are often listed in the same section of suppliers' catalogs. However, "special" children do need additional and sometimes different equipment and materials for their comfort and safety, and for therapy.
3. Kits for young handicapped children are listed with the other kits in Appendix 6.

The following legend indicates suppliers of the listed equipment and materials:

CP—Community Playthings
DLM—Developmental Learning Materials
I—Ideal
M—Markham
P—Preston
TR—Teaching Resources

Basic Equipment. Basic equipment and materials include furniture and other helps for the handicapped child:

carrel, "Portable Study Carrel" (I)
chairs
  "All-Adjustable Child's Commode Chair" (P)
  "Floor Sitter" (M)
  "Halpern Wheeler" (M)
  "Rifton Adjustable Chair" (CP)
  "Rifton Straight Chair" (CP)
  "Rifton Transport Chair" (CP)
matting, "No-Slip Matting" (P)
tables
  "Curved Martian Canal" (M)
  "Cut Out Tables" (P)
  "Picnic/Work Table" (M)
  "Rifton Adjustable Table" (CP)
  "Rifton Body Support Table" (CP)

"Stand-in-tables" (P)
trays
   "Art Tray" (M)
   "Mess N' Play Tray" (M)
walker, "Rifton Adjustable Walker" (CP)

Perceptual-Motor Equipment and Materials.   Perceptual-motor equipment and materials are basic needs of most handicapped children. Skills are usually subdivided into gross and fine perceptual-motor tasks:

Materials/Equipment for Gross Perceptual-Motor Skills:
   ball
      "Cage Ball" (P)
      "Delux Safety Play Batting Set" (P)
      "Developmental Exercise (Vestibular) Ball Program" (P)
      "Neuro-Developmental Training Ball" (P)
      "Successball" and "Successball, Jr." (M)
   bean bags
      "Bean Bags" (DLM)
      "Shape Beanbags" (TR)
   body position materials
      "Body Position Cards" (TR)
      "Developlay Person" (M)
   climbing equipment
      "Net Climber" (M)
      "Stacking Climbers" (M)
      "Staircase" (P)
      "Tot Tent" (M)
   jumping equipment
      "Harmon Jump Board" (I)
      "Safety Bouncer" (M)
   punching bag
      "Early Years Puncher" (M)
   "rocking" equipment
      "Balance Disk" (I)
      "Dyna-Balance Rocking Platform" (DLM)
      "Rocker Balance" (P)
      "Vestibular Board" (P)
   shapes
      "Soft Spongy Shapes" (DLM)
      "Sponge Balls" (DLM)
   slide
      "Safety Slide" (M)
   swing
      "Tireswing" (M)
   vehicular equipment
      "Chain Drive Tricycle" (P)
   crawlers (P)
      "Irish Mail" (P)
   "Padded Scooter" (M)

"Rifton Combination Prone and Scooter Board" (CP)
"Roll-a-Mat" (M)
"Round Scooter Board" (P)
"Super Irish Mail" (M)
"Super Saf-T-Trike" (M)
tumbling equipment
cylinders, wedges, and crash pads (M, P)
walking equipment
"Directional Mat" (TR)
"Dyna-balance Walking Board" (DLM)
"Great Shapes" (TR)
"Harmon Walking Rail" (I)
"PerceptoMats" (TR)
"Swingbeam" (M)
"Tac Tracks" (DLM)
"Walkalong" (M)
"Wheelthru Arcade"—"gym" for children in wheelchair (M)

Materials and Equipment for Fine Perceptual-Motor Skills:
blocks
"Builder Blocks" (M)
crayons
"Chubbi Stumps" (TR, DLM)
"Chublets" (DLM)
"Door and Latch Frame Set" (P)
drawing and writing equipment
"Happy Hoppy Chalkboards" (I)
"Tactile Drawing Board" (DLM)
dressing equipment
"Dressing Frame Set" (P)
"Lacing Cards" (CLM)
"Lacing Shoe" (L)
form boards
"Form Boards" (P)
"Form Frames" (I)
"Geometric Sponge Shapes" (P)
Montessori didactic (sensory) materials (P)
parquetry
"Jumbo Parquetry and Patterns" (I)
"Pathway School Program" (TR)
pegs and pegboards
"Easy-Grip Pegs" (I)
"Large Pegboard" (DLM)
"Jumbo Pegs for Stringing" (I)
"Jumbo Tactilmat Pegboards" (I)
pegboards, many types (P)
"Pencil Grips" (DLM, I)
puzzles
"Large Knobhead" (P)
scissors
"Double-Handed Scissors" (DLM)
"Easy Grip Scissors" (DLM, TR)
"Loop the Loop Scissors" (P)

"Tactile Surface Ball" (P)
"Threading Board" (DLM, TR)
tracing stencils and templates (DLM)
weights
    "Wrist and Ankle Weights" (DLM, P)

TEXTS AND WORKBOOKS

Because most prekindergarten children cannot read and because many professionals consider book-learning activities inappropriate prior to first grade,
textbooks are not frequently used at these levels; however, beginning at the
first-grade level, they become frequently-used instructional materials. With
the exception of reading textbook series, textbook series in the various curriculum areas, such as mathematics, social studies, science, spelling, English, and
health, include one textbook (and possibly some supplementay materials) per
grade or instructional level. Instructional materials for developing reading skills
are usually referred to as basal materials, which often include readers to be read
by the child (first, second and third preprimers, primer, first reader, first and
second parts of the second-grade reader, and one reader per year thereafter); a
teacher's guide; one workbook per reader; and supplementary materials such as
word cards, pocket charts, tests, big charts, and various audiovisual aids. Instructional manuals or teacher's guides usually accompany each textbook, and
may include: objectives of the materials; an itemized list of new vocabulary,
concepts, and/or skills to be introduced; assessment questions or activities; a
suggested sequence or time plan for presentation of materials; and supplementary enrichment activities. The manuals are printed in one of these forms:

1. The *teacher's annotated edition* (T.A.E.) is a two-part manual. One part is
   an annotated edition of the children's textbook that includes the children's
   text with added comments printed in red in the margins, vocabulary words
   circled, and so forth. In short, the authors have made notes on the teacher's
   copy of the children's text—hence the name, teacher's annotated edition.
   Before or after the annotated part, another section describes objectives of
   the materials, assessment tasks, and supplementary activities.
2. Some instructional manuals are not annotated, but contain two parts. One
   part is the children's textbook without annotations, and the other part
   contains information for the teacher.
3. Some textbook series publish an instructional manual with information for
   the teacher, but do not include the children's text. Because the size of the
   manual is reduced when the children's text is not included, the manual is
   often a paperback.

Workbooks and worksheets provide paper-and-pencil activities for children.
Although many professionals do not approve of these types of activities for
young children, workbooks and worksheets that may not require reading are
more often found in prekindergarten and kindergarten programs than are textbooks. Characteristics of workbooks and worksheet are as follows:

1. Workbooks are published in paperback. Individual pages are occasionally
   perforated so that children can handle them as worksheets rather than as

booklets. Worksheets are one page in length and are sold in class-size packages of twenty-five or thirty copies. Some published worksheets are available as ditto masters.

2. Many textbook series have an accompanying children's workbook. If a textbook-workbook combination is not available, the publisher may suggest a particular workbook as supplementary instructional material.
3. Many workbooks and worksheets are written without reference to a textbook.
4. A workbook or worksheet may contain paper-and-pencil tasks for a curricular area at one instructional level, such as kindergarten mathematics, or for subcurricular areas at one instructional level, such as four kindergarten mathematics workbooks with one for each subarea: number concepts, spatial relationships, geometric concepts, and patterns.

INSTRUCTIONAL KITS AND SETS

The available kits and sets of early learning materials cover a range of psycho-motor-, affective-, and cognitive-developmental tasks, and embody the contents of various curricular areas. Kits and sets differ from singly-packaged items in several ways: (1) the materials are collected and arranged so as to provide for a range of individual and/or group activities; (2) various learning methods are employed while working with materials (listening to records and stories, manipulating objects, viewing books, pictures, and filmstrips, and talking); (3) a manual or teacher's guide provides guidance in using the kit; (4) components of the kit or set are sold as a unit although components may be sold separately in kits that divide materials into distinct instructional units or that have consumable materials; (5) kits are rather expensive, with one survey reporting a price range of $3.00 to $500.00;[16] and (6) the materials are encased in a drawer-, cabinet-, or luggage-type storage container. Some kits or sets are published with staff training materials, supplementary materials for children's activities, and/or evaluation materials.

The specific kits and sets listed are not evaluated, because the value of a kit or set depends on the objectives of the local program, the children involved, and the use made of the kit. As is true of all instructional materials, however, kits or sets should be carefully evaluated by the user. Before purchasing a kit or set, ask:

1. How does the philosophy of the program match the rationale of the kit or set in both content and methodology?
2. Are the materials in the kit or set appropriate for the methods and rationale stated in the accompanying manual?
3. Why were the materials gathered into a kit or set? Are they gathered simply to save the teacher time? Are the various components used together in such a way that some materials present concepts and other materials reinforce and extend the concepts?
4. Is the teacher's manual adequate and easy to handle? Are directions clear and easy to find? Are there suggestions for enrichment activities and for evaluation and diagnosis? How much teacher planning is necessary? Is the manual a "cookbook," a suggestion book, or both?
5. Can the local staff use the kit or set with or without training?

6. How many kits or sets are required for the local program?
7. Are all the components sold only as a unit, or can you purchase replacement parts and consumable items?
8. Are other pieces of equipment necessary when using the kit or set? If so, are these additional items already owned by the local program or must they also be purchased?
9. Are special services, such as training of staff, evaluation, installation, and maintenance, provided with the kit or set?
10. Are the materials, including storage case and manual, durable? Are the components safe for young children and easily maintained? Are they large enough that they are not easily lost?
11. How much physical space is required to use the kit or set? Is it easily stored and is storage space available?
12. What is the total cost of purchase, including tax and shipping charges, of replacement and consumable parts, of other equipment necessary for using the kit or set, and of maintenance and staff training?
13. How does the kit or set fare in terms of research results or subjective opinion by those who have used it in a program similar to yours?
14. Are there other kits or sets on the market similar in rationale to this one? If so, how do they compare to this one on all of the above points?

Additional guidelines for analyzing kits or sets are found in the following sources:

Dick, W. "A Methodology for the Formative Evaluation of Instructional Materials." *Journal of Educational Measurement* 5 (1968): 99–102.

Eash, M.J. "Assessing Curriculum Materials: A Preliminary Instrument." *Educational Product Report* 2 (1969): 18–24.

Educational Products Information Exchange Institute. *How to Select and Evaluate Materials.* Educational Products Report No. 2. New York: EPIE Institute, 1972, pp. 71–78.

Appendix 6 describes some of the many kits and sets of published early learning materials. The variety of purposes given, of learning methods employed, and of types of materials packaged can be readily discerned. The kits and sets are grouped under the headings of learning skills and/or multi-curricular areas; language arts and reading; mathematics; social studies; science; art; and self-concept. It should be noted, however, that some of the kits and sets do not exclusively fit one heading

RAW OR PRIMITIVE MATERIALS

Raw or primitive materials are any materials that do not duplicate reality—a lump of clay, a scrap of cloth, a bead, and so forth. Many programs use, and many professionals see, this type of material as excellent for instruction, because children with various degrees of competence and differing interests can use the materials, and because raw materials permit children to use various symbols to stand for a real object.

STAFF-MADE AND COLLECTED MATERIALS

There is no consensus about whether one should purchase equipment or make it. Some have related good experiences with homemade equipment[17,18] while others are not so enthusiastic about a "do-it-yourself" job.[19] Certainly, professionally-customized play areas are incredibly expensive, as noted in the Friedberg report.[20] "Do-it-yourself" projects are certainly in vogue, as evident in the publication of these and other books:

Cherner, N. *How to Build Children's Toys and Furniture.* New York: McGraw-Hill Book Co., 1954.

Maginley, C.J. *Toys You Can Build.* New York: Hawthorne Books, 1973.

Nelson, L.W. *Instructional Aids: How to Make Them,* 2d ed. Dubuque, Iowa: William C. Brown and Co., 1970.

Sunset Books and Sunset Magazine. *Children's Rooms and Play Yards,* 2d ed. Menlo Park, Calif.: Lane Books, 1976.

Toys to Build, current catalog. Van Nuys, Calif.: U-Bild Enterprises.

Workshop for Learning Things, Inc., current catalog. Watertown, Mass.: Workshop for Learning Things, Inc. (Catalog for making things from cardboard.)

In some early childhood programs, staff membees make almost all of their equipment and materials; but generally, staff members make or collect the following materials:

1. Raw materials (egg cartons, cloth scraps, string, wire, clay, etc.);
2. Picture files. Each picture should fit the objectives of the program, be accurate in content, be large enough and of good quality, be mounted, and laminated, if possible, for protection, and be filed. The most frequent topics for picture collections are: animals (forest, zoo, farm, pets, birds, fish, insects, reptiles, and amphibians); plants; holidays; scenery (land and seascapes); toys; nursery rhymes and children's stories; transportation; foods; houses and buildings (inside and outside); household articles and tools; schools; occupations; and self-concept;
3. illustrations for songs, poems, finger plays, and stories. These illustrations may be pictures, puppets, and/or flannel board figures; and
4. Other small teaching aids, such as flash cards, charts, posters, bulletin boards, etc.

Four guides to securing free and inexpensive materials are: Monahan's *Free and Inexpensive Materials for Preschool and Early Childhood;*[21] Schain and Polner's *Where to Get and How to Use Free and Inexpensive Teaching Aids;*[22] Suttles's *Elementary Teacher's Guide to Free Curriculum Materials;*[23] and, also by Suttles, *Educators Guide to Free Teaching Aids.*[24]

OTHER EQUIPMENT AND MATERIALS

Other equipment and materials that do not seem to fit under the foregoing headings but which should not be forgotten in equipping an early childhood program are

bathroom supplies
clock (large, wall-mounted)
first aid cabinet with recommended supplies
flashlights
food service equipment (see: *Equipment Guide for Preschool and School Age Child Service Institutions*)[25]

housekeeping supplies
office machines and supplies
radio or TV (for latest weather information)

Community Resources

Since the early 1900s, early childhood programs have utilized community resources. Undoubtedly, with emphases on career education and use of parents as hired staff and volunteers, community resources will be even more widely utilized by taking children to the community through field or study trips, bringing the community to the children through resource people, and by getting families involved in community projects and services. Staff members should keep a perpetual inventory of local places to visit and of resource people suitable to their program's needs. In compiling such an inventory, one should list: name of place, telephone number, person at location in charge of hosting visitors, age limitations, time of day visitors are welcomed, number of children the place can accommodate, how long a tour takes, and additional comments as to preferable apparel, whether advance notice is required, what children can see or do and what the host provides for the children, and number of adults requested to accompany the group. The following list of places is provided only to start staff members thinking about local community resources:

airport
art and craft museums
bakery
bank
beauty shop
brick plant
buildings under construction
dairy
dentist's office
doctor's office
fast food chain
pizza shop
vocational high school (classes and equipment in cosmetology, mechanics, graphics, etc.)
dry cleaner
electric company
elementary school
farm (tree, animal, and crop)
feed store
fields
fire station
gas company
grocery store (corner market and supermarket)
hospital
ice cream plant
library
manufacturing companies

milk processing plant
neighborhood walk
newspaper office
parks (neighborhood, city, state, or national)
pet shop
photography studio
police station
post office
telephone company
television cable company
television studio
water plant
zoo

Professional Library

Every early childhood program should have a professional library to keep staff members informed and to help them in their planning. The library should contain:

1. Journals, newsletters, and special publications of professional organizations concerned with young children;
2. Instructional manuals in addition to those regularly used;
3. Curriculum guides printed by the state board of education, state department of public welfare, local school system, and/or other early childhood programs that have similar objectives;
4. Professional books and audiovisuals concerned with various aspects of early childhood—child development, curriculum, guidance, and administration;
5. Catalogs and brochures from distributors of equipment and materials;
6. Newsletters or information on current legislation pertaining to child care and education (obtained by being on your congressman or senator's mailing list);
7. Information from local community resources—health department, dental association, March of Dimes, Heart Fund, Sickle Cell Anemia, and SIDS groups; and
8. Bibliographies of pertinent topics in child development, care and education, and parenting skills.

NOTES

1. Harold Boles, *Step by Step to Better School Facilities* (New York: Holt, Rinehart, & Winston, 1965), p. 190.
2. P. Pragnell, "The Friendly Object," *Harvard Educational Review* 39 (1969): 39–40.
3. Fred Osmon, *Patterns for Designing Children's Centers* (New York: Educational Facilities Laboratories, 1971), p. 48.
4. *Early Childhood Education: How to Select and Evaluate Materials* (New York: Educational Products Information Exchange Institute, 1972), p. 43.

5. Ibid.

6. Ibid.

7. Ibid., pp. 42–43.

8. Ruth E. Jefferson, "Indoor Facilities," *Housing for Early Childhood Education*, eds. Sylvia Sunderland and Nan Gray (Washington, D.C.: Assn. for Childhood Education International, 1968), p. 47.

9. Neith E. Headley, *Education in the Kindergarten*, 4th ed. (New York: American Book Co., 1966), p. 96.

10. Stanton C. Oats, *Audiovisual Equipment: Self-Instruction Manual* (Dubuque, Iowa: William C. Brown and Co., 1972).

11. Esther B. Starks, *Blockbuilding* (Washington, D.C: Department of Kindergarten-Primary Education, N.E.A., 1960).

12. Ibid.

13. Ivalee H. McCord, "A Creative Playground," *Young Children* 26 (1971): 342–47.

14. M.J. Reid, *An Evaluation of Creative/Adventure Playgrounds and Their Use by Pupils of Elementary Schools* (British Columbia: Vancouver Board of School Trustees, 1971). ERIC ED 057 108

15. F.C. Thompson and A.M. Rittenhouse, "Measuring the Impact," *Parks and Recreation* 9 (1974): 24–26, 62–63.

16. *Early Childhood Education: How to Select and Evaluate Materials*, p. 42.

17. J. Seker, "Your School Can Have This Scavenger Playground," *Grade Teacher* 87 (1970): 62–64.

18. P.E. Lueck, "Planning an Outdoor Learning Environment," *Theory Into Practice* 12 (1973): 121–27.

19. A.B. Etkes, "The Case for Buying Your Playground," *Educational Product Report* 3 (1970): 3–6.

20. M.P. Friedberg, *Playgrounds for City Children*. (Washington, D.C.: Association for Childhood Education International, 1969).

21. Robert Monahan, *Free and Inexpensive Materials for Preschool and Early Childhood* (Belmont Calif.: Fearon Publishers, 1973).

22. Robert L. Schain and Murray Polner, *Where to Get and How to Use Free and Inexpensive Teaching Aids* (New York: Teachers Practical Press, 1966).

23. Patricia H. Suttles, ed., *Elementary Teachers Guide to Free Curriculum Materials*, 28th ed. (Randolph, Wis.: Educators Progress Service, 1971).

24. Patricia H. Suttles and Raymond H. Suttles, eds., *Educators Guide to Free Teaching Aids*, 19th ed. (Randolph, Wis.: Educators Progress Service, 1971).

25. *Equipment Guide for Preschool and School Age Child Service Institutions* (Washington, D.C.: U.S. Department of Agriculture, Food and Nutrition Service, Child Nutrition Division, 1972).

For Further Reading

Allen, William H. "Audio-Visual Materials." *Review of Educational Research* 26 (1956): 125–56.

Apter, Michael J., and Boorer, David. "Skinner, Piaget, and Froebel: A Study of Programmed Instruction with Young Children." *Programmed Learning* 6 (1969): 164–77.

Coursen, D. *Playground Facilities and Equipment*. ACSA School Management Digest, Series 1, No. 7 ERIC/CEM Research Analysis Series, No. 34 Eugene, OR: Eric Clearinghouse on Educational Management, U iversity of Oregon, 1977. ERIC ED 146 662.

Early Childhood Education: How to Select and Evaluate Materials. New York: Educational Products Information Exchange Institute, 1972.

Educational Development Center. "How to Equip a Classroom: the EDC Guidelines." In

The Open Classroom Reader, edited by C.E. Silberman. New York: Random House, 1973.

————. "How to Scrounge for Materials." In *The Open Classroom Reader*, edited by C.E. Silberman. New York: Random House, 1973.

Educational Products Information Exchange Institute. *How to Select and Evaluate Materials*, Educational Products Report No. 2. New York: EPIE Institute, 1972.

Erickson, Carlton W. *Fundamentals of Teaching with Audiovisual Technology*. New York: The Macmillan Co., 1965.

Nichols, M.S., and O'Neill, P. *Multi-Cultural Resources for Children: A Bibliography of Materials for Preschool through Elementary School in the Areas of Black, Spanish-Speaking, Asian American, Native American, and Pacific Island Cultures*. Stanford, Calif.: Multicultural Resources, 1977. ERIC ED 152 394.

Passantino, E.D. "Adventure Playgrounds for Learning and Socialization." *Phi Delta Kappan* 56 (1975): 329–33.

Tyler, L.L.; Klein, M.F.; and Associates. *Evaluating and Choosing Curriculum and Instructional Materials*. Los Angeles: Educational Resource Associates, 1976.

10

Planning and Scheduling Children's Activities

Careful planning and scheduling are essential to all early childhood programs. When programs take on a laissez-faire posture, chaos is inevitable. Planning and scheduling are not done in order that children will simply have fun or keep busy and out of mischief; their main purpose is to meet the objectives of the program. Planning and scheduling should facilitate the presentation to children of what they must learn in all developmental areas—psychomotor, cognitive, and affective—in such a way that they will be able to learn and will want to learn. More specifically, in order to meet program objectives, planning and scheduling are essential:

1. To provide continuity in learning. Learning experiences must be organized so that each experience contributes to total development.
2. To help children overcome learning deficits. Using evaluation data from informal observations and standardized tests, teachers need to plan and schedule special remedial activities.
3. To help meet children's special needs.
4. To balance the day between skill areas such as preparation for reading, writing, and mathematics and content areas such as social studies, science, music, and art, between times of strenuous activity and of relaxation, and between occasions for self-expression and for group conformity.
5. To improve coordination of staff tasks. The responsibilities of the staff members must be coordinated so that each staff member's work reinforces and extends the efforts of others.
6. To expedite the use of materials and equipment. Without proper planning, some quality materials may go virtually unused and other materials may be overused; too many types of equipment and materials may be out at one time, causing children to "window shop"; or too few types of equipment and materials may be out, causing children to fight over "the bargain table."

7. To prevent emergencies that arise because activities are either too easy or too difficult, or children are too tired or too excited, because of inadequate supervision, or because too many, too few, or the wrong materials and equipment have been made available.

Because each early childhood program has its unique philosophy, planning and scheduling will differ from program to program. Planning and scheduling must be based on answers to three philosophical questions:

1. What do you want children to learn, in scope and sequence, in each area of development?
2. How do you want children to learn skills, information, values, and attitudes—through drill or gamelike tasks, prescribed or free-choice activities, or through individual effort or group work?
3. How will you determine whether the child has learned the skill—that is, what will you use for assessment?

And, as part of planning and scheduling, decisions must be made as to grouping. Grouping arrangements help provide the best ways to meet the needs of individuals and of the group via scope and sequence of content, methodology, and assessment techniques.

Grouping

Our society recognizes the importance of the individual by encouraging and recognizing individual achievement and by granting and protecting the individual right to think, speak, and act in accordance with personal beliefs; yet, a chaos-free society must have some conformity—some group-mindedness. From birth until a child enters an early childhood program, his individuality is fostered, tempered only to some extent by the "group needs" of his family. In contrast, because of the numbers of children involved and the time limits imposed, the school is forced to consider group needs. In fact, we often say that a child enrolling in an early childhood program is entering a "group setting."

Grouping, or organizing children for learning, is an attempt to aid individual development in a group setting. Grouping has been devised to make caring for and teaching children more manageable and effective. There is no consensus as to the "best" grouping practice, but because instructional plans and scheduling are determined to a great extent by grouping procedures, the administrator must choose grouping practices that are in keeping with the program's philosophy.

VERTICAL GROUPING

Vertical grouping is concerned with how children move from year to year, in either a graded or nongraded approach.[1] The graded system was based on the concept that children of similar ages were most homogeneous in ability. Thus, a child entered the graded system at a specified age (usually 6.0 years for first grade) and, at the end of a year's instruction, was promoted to the next level. A variant of this practice was to "double promote" children who far exceeded age and grade expectations, and to retain children who failed to meet the expectations. Although this approach has been and is the most typical practice of elementary schools, nursery schools and other programs for the younger child have also admitted children on an age-basis and "promoted" some of them on the same basis, rather than according to developmental gains.

Because children of similar ages are not necessarily homogeneous in achievement, nongraded approaches have been used especially at the preprimary and primary levels. The "traditional" nursery schools of the 1950s, Montessori schools, and the British Infant Schools all use this grouping approach. Goodlad and Anderson[2] define the nongraded approach as a plan that enables children to advance in the sequenced curriculum at their own rate. The nongraded approach uses multiage, or "family" grouping. Such grouping forms a microsociety of many abilities and achievement levels. Ideally, in this approach, teachers plan instruction according to a child's ability rather than his age-grade level. Advanced children tutor the less advanced children. Flexible groups that are homogeneous in at least one subject area (often reading or math) are formed for small-group instruction. The concept behind the nongraded approach is that the "cognitive match" between instruction and ability will motivate children, reduce boredom and frustration problems, and permit students to master skills or content before moving on. Furthermore, advanced or older children gain confidence from helping less able or younger children, and advanced or older children serve as a model for others.

Two major problems seem to be that instruction may not be adapted to ability and that the flexible homogeneous ability groups become more or less permanent to the extent that ability in one subject area replaces age, as in the graded approach.

HORIZONTAL GROUPING

Horizontal grouping is concerned with how students are assigned to instructional groups, which may be self-contained, departmentalized, team taught, intraclass ability groupings or individualized.[3]

Self-contained Groups. The self-contained approach, in which a group of children is under the direction of one care-giver or teacher, is the most frequently used plan in public school early childhood programs and small private programs. In a self-contained room, the head care-giver or teacher is responsible for all program services, although he may assign certain tasks to assistant care-givers, teachers, or to volunteers, Snyder[4] believes this approach is best for children's affective needs and for correlation of curriculum areas. On the other hand, Stoddard[5] notes a major disadvantage to the approach is that one teacher cannot know all subject-matter areas.

Departmentalized Groups. Departmentalized instruction is not common in early childhood programs. The nearest approach to departmentalization at this level is a variation of the self-contained classroom. In this variation, the teacher of the self-contained classroom has assistants for special subjects such as physical education, speech, music, art, foreign language, remedial reading, and library. In some private early childhood programs, special-subject teachers give children religious training. Unlike the pure departmentalization approach, in early childhood programs the main care-giver or teacher is responsible for all program services except those offered by special-subject teachers.

Team Teaching or Care-giving.   A team teaching or care-giving plan places a group of children under the direction of two or more teachers or care-givers. The team plan is most frequently employed in large day-care centers, in college or university nursery schools or kindergartens, and in public schools with multiage groups of children. Assistant care-givers or teachers, volunteers, and/or special-subject teachers may be employed in the team plan, and are responsible for certain program services on a regular basis. For example, one teacher may teach in the academic areas of the curriculum and another may work with creative activities, or they may exchange duties periodically. Each person's specific responsibilities may be mutually agreed upon or delegated by a team leader. Advantages of this approach are that teachers can plan together, correlate teaching, and have flexibility in grouping and scheduling. There are, however, indications that teachers often do not really plan together. An excellent collection of articles on "Cooperative Teaching" appeared in a special issue of the *National Elementary Principal* (January, 1965).

Ability Grouping.   Ability grouping is really achievement-level grouping and is widely practiced in elementary schools in such areas as reading and math. Ability or achievement grouping is practiced when schools form transitional groups, such as a class of children whose chronological age is 6.0 years or older but who seem to lag in certain developmental areas essential for achievement on a first-grade level. Ability grouping is also common in the verbal didactic models in early childhood education, such as the Englemann approach. This approach is based on the assumption that both children and teachers profit from a homogeneous-achievement group. Several problems with ability grouping are that: (1) there is still a wide range of abilities;[6] (2) such grouping may be associated with lower achievement scores on the part of slower students;[7,8] (3) the quality of instruction may be inferior in lower groups;[9] (4) children are likely to remain in the same ability group to which they are originally assigned;[10] and (5) slow learners may feel the stigma associated with such placement.

Individualized Teaching.   Since the mid-sixties, individualized teaching has become the most discussed grouping approach. Technological advances such as computer-assisted and programmed instruction have made individualized approaches more feasible. Two well-known early childhood projects in which technology became a part of instructional methodology were Patrick Suppes's Computer-Assisted Instruction and Omar K. Moore's Autotelic Responsive Environment, better known as the "talking typewriter." The *Individually Prescribed Instruction System*[11] (IPI) also fits this approach.

Daily Plans

The long-range goals contained in a program's philosophy are explicitly defined in terms of objectives and reflected in daily plans. These plans become the teacher's tools in realizing these goals, and a periodic review of daily plans serves as a check on the variety of activities, teaching-learning approaches, and materials used in implementation.

BASIC CONSIDERATIONS

In developing daily plans, certain points need to be considered. For programs with developmental philosophies, one consideration is the developmental levels and needs of both individuals and groups of children. What are the children's ages? What understandings, skills, and attitudes do they have? How long are their attention spans and what are their degrees of perserverance? Are they having to cope with special problems or excitements?

Another consideration is the quality of the care-giving or teaching assistance. Does each staff member understand and accept the program's basic philosophy? Does each staff member recognize the rationale of each activity as a step in realizing long-range goals? Is the program adequately staffed in terms of the number and needs of the children, the physical layout of the building and grounds, and the nature of the activities?

A third consideration is the amount and arrangement of indoor and outdoor space. Is it adequate for the planned activities? Is supervision of children difficult because of the vastness of space or its arrangement? Is much time spent in moving equipment and materials between each activity? Do accidents occur frequently because of the amount or arrangement of space?

Availability of resources is a fourth consideration. Are appropriate equipment and m$terials available in sufficient quantity for the activities? Are community resources available?

The fifth consideration is time. Are too many or too few activities planned? How much time is involved in getting out and putting away, in going to the restroom or to lunch, and in conducting administrative duties such as attendance and lunch counts? Are the blocks of time suitable for the various types of activities?

PLANNING ACTIVITIES

Planning activities is essential regardless of the type of early childhood program. Formally structured programs, of course, are planned, but planning must also take place in informal, nonstructured programs if they are to be effective.

Planning daily activities begins with developing a philosophical foundation for the program. Once the basic philosophy is formulated by the board of directors, it becomes the staff's responsibility to formulate specific objectives in keeping with the philosophy. These objectives become the basis for prearranging activities in the interest centers, for designing learning episodes, and for using interest centers and learning episodes. Although the following discussion uses a single objective, naming shapes, in practice one would use several objectives and a variety of materials to meet multiple objectives.

Prearranging Activities for Interest Centers.   As noted in chapters 8 and 9, equipment and materials are usually arranged in interest centers such as dramatic play, library, science, art, and music. In a few early childhood programs, no activities are planned for the interest centers. Each child is permitted to use any materials and equipment not being used by other children. Because plans have not been made, children's needs are likely to go unmet.

Planning activities for the interest centers should begin with the specific objectives of the program. For example, one or more specific objectives are chosen for several days' work, the appropriate equipment and materials are selected and arranged in interest centers, and all unneeded supplies are stored until they are needed to accomplish other objectives. Consequently, regardless of which interest center a child chooses in spontaneous play, he will be working with equipment and materials that will help him achieve the objectives. For example, if a specific objective is for the children to be able to name a circle, rectangle, and triangle, the following materials could be prearranged in the interest centers:

1. In the art center, precut construction paper circles, rectangles, and triangles are provided. The child may make a collage with these geometric shapes.
2. In the manipulative center, sorting boxes for geometric shapes are placed on the table.
3. In the block center, blocks of various geometric shapes are available for building.
4. In the mathematics center, materials for fishing for shapes, lotto games using shapes, and a flannel board with felt shapes for making or extending patterns are arranged.
5. In the active or physical play center, bean bags of different geometric shapes are tossed at geometrically-shaped targets.

Designing a Learning Episode.   A learning episode is any form of direct teaching involving one child, a small group of children, or the whole class. In designing a learning episode around the foregoing objective, the teacher could read a children's book, perhaps *Shapes*, by M. Schlein, teach a game, and/or use a piece of equipment, developing a modified activity based on the Cuisenaire Company's geoboard, for example. Learning episodes can serve several purposes: (1) teachers do not have to wait to take advantage of children's spontaneous activities; (2) it is easier for inexperienced teachers to become familiar with a concept in a learning episode rather than in a spontaneous learning situation; (3) learning episodes can be used to introduce something new to the children and to evaluate their progress; and (4) they can be used to determine the appropriateness of equipment and materials.[12]

Using Interest Centers and Learning Episodes. Many early childhood programs use a combination of interest centers and learning episodes to help the child achieve each specific objective. However, the various programs do not give equal emphasis to spontaneous activities in interest centers and to learning episodes. Nonstructured programs and/or programs for younger children generally place more emphasis on free activity in interest centers than on learning episodes, while in the more formally structured programs and/or programs for older children, there is more direct teaching than child-initiated exploration in interest centers.

SCHEDULING

Although scheduling is only one aspect of planning, it is one of its more critical aspects, for decisions about scheduling greatly influence the children's feelings of security, the accomplishment of objectives, and the staff's effectiveness. Scheduling involves planning the length of the session and timing and arranging activities during the session.

Length of Session. Early childhood programs have traditionally been half-day sessions. Exceptions have been full-day sessions in day nurseries and day-care programs, which are becoming increasingly popular because more mothers have jobs outside the home and because of the awareness of the needs of disadvantaged children. Some day-care programs have incorporated kindergarten objectives and activities into their programs, because parents cannot leave work to transport their children to and from kindergartens that operate on half-day sessions.

There is a great deal of controversy concerning the length of the session. Advocates of half-day sessions cite these advantages: (1) children do not get as tired; (2) the staff member has more time for planning, evaluating, and working with parents (unless the teacher is employed for two half-day sessions) and helps prevent staff "burnout"; (3) no provisions have to be made for lunch or rest activities; and (4) young children have an opportunity to be with their parents for part of the day. Supporters of full-day sessions enumerate these advantages: (1) fewer transportation problems; (2) longer blocks of time for lengthy activities; (3) more staff influence, which is especially important for children without a rich home life; (4) the staff can get to know the children better; and (5) more time for academic experiences, or more time for emphasis on play (a point of disagreement among those advocating a full-day session). Other individuals, rather than advocating a half-day or a full-day session for all children, support an individualized schedule to meet the needs of each child. Berson states: "Kindergartens and their timetables are not sacred; children are."[13]

Timing and Arranging Activities. Regardless of whether the session is half-or full-day, good schedules for early childhood programs have certain characteristics:

1. A good session begins with a friendly, informal greeting of the children. Staff members should make an effort to speak to each child individually during the first few minutes of each session. A group activity such as a greeting song also helps children feel welcome.
2. Children's physical needs, such as toileting and eating, should be cared for at regular intervals in the schedule. Special times should be set aside for toileting early in the session, before and after each meal or snack, and before and after resting. Meals should be served every four or five hours, and snacks should be served midway between each mealtime; however, each child's individual needs must be considered.
3. The schedule must provide a balance between physical activity and rest. Young children are prone to become overtired without realizing their need for relaxation.
4. The schedule should fit the philosophy of the program and the needs of the children as individuals and as a group. There should be a balance between indoor and outdoor activities, group and individual times, and child-selected and staff-determined activities.
5. The schedule must be flexible under unexpected circumstances, such as inclement weather, children's interests not originally planned for, and emergencies.
6. A good schedule should be readily understandable to the children so they will have a feeling of security and will not waste time trying to figure out what to do next.
7. A good session ends with a general evaluation of activities, straightening of indoor and outdoor areas, a hint about the next session, and a farewell. Children need to end a session with the feeling they have achieved something and with a desire to return. These feelings are important to staff members, too!

Examples of Schedules.   Every program should devise its own schedule. Programs that serve children of different age groups, perhaps infants, toddlers, and young children, must prepare more than one schedule, so that each age group's needs will be met.

Some early childhood programs place more emphasis on the individual by having flexible schedules, and by requiring that children conform to the group for some routine procedures, such as the morning greeting, and for short periods of group "instruction," such as music and listening to stories. Other programs place more emphasis on group conformity by having fixed schedules, and by expecting children to work and play with others at specified times and to take care of even the most basic human differences, their appetites and bodily functions, at prescribed times except for "emergencies." Flexibility within specific blocks of time refers to periods during which children are relatively free to choose activities. Another way to achieve flexibility is to balance periods of activities like free play, dramatic play, or creative activities with periods of specific learning and instruction. The following schedule examples are only suggestions; they are not to be considered prescriptive.

Day-care centers have perhaps the most flexible schedules of all early child-hood programs, because of their longer hours of operation, the children's staggered arrivals and departures, and the varying ages of the children the center serves. One example of a day-care center schedule might be:

7:00–9:00 A.M.	Arrival, breakfast for children who have not eaten or who want additional food, sleep for children who want more rest, and child-initiated play (which should be relatively quiet) in the interest centers.
9:00–9:30 A.M.	Toieting and morning snack.
9:30–11:45 A.M.	Active work and play period, both indoor and outdoor. Field trips and class celebrations may be conducted in this time block.
11:45 A.M.–12:00 noon	Preparation for lunch, such as toileting, washing, and moving to dining area.
12:00 noon–1:00 P.M.	Lunch and quiet play activities.
1:00–3:00 P.M.	Story, rest, and quiet play activities or short excursions with assistants or volunteers as children awaken from naps.
3:00–3:30 P.M.	Toileting and afternoon snack.
3:30 P.M. until departure	Active work and play periods, both indoor and outdoor, and farewells as children depart with parents.
5:00 P.M.	Evening meal for those remaining in center, and quiet play activities until departure.

Nursery schools serve prekindergarten-age children (usually exclusive of infants) and are frequently operated for half-day sessions. Children arrive and depart at approximately the same times. Generally, nursery school schedules have short group times and longer blocks of time for active work and play periods. An outline of a nursery school schedule might be:

9:00–9:15 A.M.	Arrival, group time activities, such as attendance count, greeting song, and brief exchange of experiences.
9:15–10:15 A.M.	Active work and play period with child-selected activities in the interest centers.

10:15–10:30 A.M.	Toileting and snack.
10:30–10:45 A.M.	Group time for story, finger play, music, or rhythmic activities.
10:45–11:15 A.M.	Outdoor activities.
11:15–11:30 A.M.	Rest.
11:30–11:45 A.M.	Cleaning up and discussing the next session; "What we will do tomorrow . . ."
11:45 A.M.–12:00 noon	Quiet activities and farewells as children depart.

Kindergartens are usually half-day programs, with children arriving and departing at approximately the same times. Kindergartens usually schedule longer group times than nursery schools, because kindergartens have more structured activities. An example of a half-day kindergarten schedule is as follows:

8:15–8:30 A.M.	Arrival and greeting of individual children.
8:30–9:00 A.M.	Greeting of group, opening exercises, such as good morning song and flag salute, sharing of experiences, and planning for the day.
9:00–10:00 A.M.	Active work and play in interest centers (with small-group learning episodes in some kindergarten programs) and cleanup.
10:00–10:30 A.M.	Music and rhythmic activities.
10:30–10:45 A.M.	Toileting and snack.
10:45–11:15 A.M.	Group time for stories and other quiet activities (with full-class learning episodes in some kindergarten programs).
11:15–11:45 A.M.	Outdoor activities.
11:45 A.M.–12:00 noon	Evaluation of day, preparing for next session, straightening of room, and farewells.

Some kindergartens have full-day sessions. An example of a schedule for a full-day session is as follows:

8:15–8:30 A.M.	Arrival, greeting of individual children, and toileting.
8:30–8:45 A.M.	Greeting of group, opening exercises, sharing of experiences, and planning for the day.
8:45–9:45 A.M.	Active work and play in interest centers (with small-group learning episodes in some kindergarten programs) and cleanup. Field trips and class celebrations may be conducted during this time block.
9:45–10:15 A.M.	Outdoor activities.
10:15–10:45 A.M.	Music and rhythmic activities.
10:45–11:00 A.M.	Toileting and preparation for lunch.
11:00–11:45 A.M.	Lunch.
11:45 A.M.–12:15 P.M.	Rest and toileting.
12:15–12:45 P.M.	Outdoor or indoor activity.
12:45–1:30 P.M.	Active work and play in interest centers and cleanup.
1:30–1:45 P.M.	Toileting and snack.
1:45–2:00 P.M.	Evaluation of day, preparing for next session, cleanup of room, and farewells.

An infant and toddler schedule needs to be the most flexible and adaptable of all. The schedule revolves around the children's feeding and sleeping periods, but should include some manipulative toy activities, outside play, and singing and story time. An example of a schedule for a full-day session is as follows:

7:00–8:30 A.M.	Arrival, changing or toileting, and dressing babies who are awake, and individual activities.
8:30–9:00 A.M.	Breakfast snack, songs, stories, and fingerplays.
9:00–10:00 A.M.	Manipulative toy activities conducted by staff, and changing or toileting.

10:00–11:00 A.M.	Naps for those who take morning naps and outside play for others. (Children go outside as they awaken.)
11:00–11:45 A.M.	Lunch and changing or toileting.
11:45–1:00 P.M.	Naps.
1:00–2:00 P.M.	Changing or toileting as children awaken and manipulative toy activities.
2:00–2:30 P.M.	Snack, songs, stories, and fingerplays.
2:30 P.M. until departure	Individual activities.

Toileting was placed in the foregoing schedules; however, toileting should be conducted on an "as needed" basis, unless building plans do not permit, as when the toilet is "down the hall," or when toilets may not be available for a short period of time, as when the children are leaving to go home or on a field trip. Also, the feeding and resting schedule must be flexible enough to meet the needs of a hungry or sleepy child.

DETERMINING THE RESPONSIBILITIES OF PROGRAM PERSONNEL

In making daily plans, coordination of the responsibilities of program personnel is essential. Without careful planning, there will be duplication of tasks, omissions in services, and a general lack of staff efficiency. Criteria to consider in planning the responsibilities of the staff are (1) the philosophy of the program as it reflects the needs of the children; (2) specific organizational policies (i.e., the way children are grouped for care or instruction); (3) the number of program personnel involved and the qualifications and skills of each individual; (4) the layout of the building and grounds and the nature of equipment and materials; and (5) the specific plans for the day.

The responsibilities of program personnel must be in keeping with legal authorizations and with the policies of the board of education or board of directors. The director usually determines the responsibilities of program personnel; however, in some cases, head care-givers or teachers may assign duties to assistant care-givers or teachers and to volunteers. Specific responsibilities may be delegated by the director or "lead" teacher or care-giver, but mutually agreed-upon responsibilities in keeping with the basic job descriptions are usually more satisfactory. Both people will understand the plans for the day, and the day's program will thus function more coherently and smoothly; a periodic exchange of some duties lessens the likelihood of staff "burnout" and the frustration of always having less popular responsibilities, such as straightening the room; and staff morale will be higher when all personnel are involved in the program from planning to execution.

Special Plans

Special plans must be suitable to the children's needs, and must be as carefully developed as daily plans. Although daily plans should be changeable, special plans require even more flexibility. Certain routines—especially eating, toileting, and resting—should always be followed as closely as possible. Planning for first days, field trips, class celebrations, and substitute personnel are discussed in this chapter because of the almost universal need for making special plans for these situations.

FIRST DAYS

Whether the first days represent a child's first experience in an early childhood program or denote his entry into a different program, the child views the first days with a mixed feeling of anticipation and anxiety. The first days should be happy ones, for they may determine the child's feeling of security and his attitude toward the program.

Initiation of children into an early childhood program is often done gradually. Preliminary orientation of the children to the staff and routine may be handled in several ways:

1. If the group is small, all the children may attend for half the normal session.
2. If it is a large group, two plans could be used: the daily session could be divided into two sections, with half the children coming to each; or two evenly-divided groups could attend alternate-day sessions, full- or half-time.
3. A few children may come the first day for the full session or for half the session. Each day additional children are added. This plan works well with multiage groups. Children who know the routine assist the staff in helping new children make initial adjustments.
4. If all children enter on the same day, additional paraprofessional or volunteer assistance should be secured for the first days.

Generally speaking, planning for first days requires that more time and individual attention be given to greeting children and their parents, to establishing regular routines, and to familiarizing the children with care-givers or teachers and with the physical plant. These suggestions will facilitate children's orientation to an early childhood program:

1. Name tags help staff members become acquainted with the children.
2. For the first days, use equipment and materials and have activities that most children of that age are familiar with and enjoy, and that require minimum preparation and clean-up time.
3. Begin to make mental notes (if not written) on strong and weak points in your plans. Also, begin to note the children's strengths and problems, but be careful not to pass judgment too fast or compare a fall group to last year's spring group.
4. Plan what to do about children who will not leave their parents or who cry

after their parents leave. Salot and Leavitt say that forcing children who are upset to remain makes the child feel more frightened and insecure, and that crying is highly contagious. Consequently, a child who is reluctant to leave his mother or who cries after his mother leaves should return home for several days. When the other children are more oriented to the program, the care-giver or teacher can give more individual attention to the child or the mother can stay without causing other mothers to want to stay.[14] Not all who work with early childhood programs agree with Salot and Leavitt. Many believe parents should stay if the child is reluctant to leave the parent (or the parent the child) until the child is oriented to the program. Furthermore, parents may feel more welcomed if they are not "pushed away" on the first days. Regardless of the program's philosophy, parents should be informed of the policy so they will know what to expect, and can thus facilitate rather than hinder the child's orientation to the program.

FIELD TRIPS

A field trip is a planned journey to somewhere outside the school building or grounds, although teachers sometimes use the term field trip in reference to journeying on foot to a destination on the school property, such as the carpenter's room or the kitchen area of the cafeteria. Thoughtful planning of field trips is important because of their benefits to children's learning and because of the added dangers of taking children beyond the building and grounds.

Field trips require a great deal of planning and supervision. The teacher must:

1. Develop specific objectives that help children achieve the goals of the program.
2. Make arrangements with those in charge at the point of destination. Know the rules of the host: date and time preferred, size of group recommended, safety rules, and parking space. Furnish all needed information to the host, such as the purpose of the trip, age and number of children, date and time of proposed arrival, and time of proposed departure. Arrange for children to see and hear; if the host is to give explanations to the children, be sure he can communicate with them. Make arrangements for care of the physical needs of children, staff, and other adults assisting with the field trip, such as location of places to eat and restrooms. One staff member should visit the destination before making final plans.
3. Provide enough qualified supervisors. Good judgment and experience in working with young children are qualities to look for in supervisors. There should be one adult for every four or five children. Supervisors should have a list of the names of children under their care; when they do not know the children, name tags should be worn for easier identification.
4. Obtain written parental consent for each field trip and keep the signed statement on file. Note the example of a field trip form.

Dear Mom and Dad,

Our class will be making a field trip to the _____ bakery on May 13. A baker will take us on a tour of the bakery. We hope to learn how bread and rolls are made. We will be leaving school at 9:00 A.M. and will be returning in time for lunch. We will ride on a bus to the bakery and back to our school. We all think it will be fun to ride on the bus with our teacher, Mrs. Smith, and three mothers. Please sign the form below to give your permission for me to take the trip.

Jody

I, _____ , give my permission for

_____ to attend a field trip to

_____ .

My child has permission to travel _____ .
(in a parent's car, on a school bus)

I understand that all safety precautions will be observed.

Date _____ Signature _____

The signed form is essential, because the signature serves as evidence that the parent has considered the dangers of his child's participating in the field trip experience. There should be no statement on the form relieving the care-giver or teacher and director of any possible liability for accidents. Such a statement is worthless, because a parent cannot legally sign away the right to sue (in the child's name) for damages, nor can the staff escape the penalty for its own negligence.[15, 16]

5. Obtain permission for the children to participate in the field trip from the director or building principal. Policies of early childhood programs often require that care-givers or teachers complete forms giving the specifics of the field trip.

6. Become familiar with the procedures to follow in case of accident or illness. Take children's medical records and emergency information records along, in case an accident or illness requiring emergency treatment occurs during the field trip.

7. Make all necessary arrangements for transportation, and determine

whether all regulations concerning vehicles and operators are met.

8. Prepare the children by helping them understand the purposes of the field trip and the safety rules to be observed. In some cases, the host may send information or may come and talk to the children before they make the field trip. After the field trip, provide follow-up activities.
9. Evaluate all aspects of planning the field trip and the field trip itself.

CLASS CELEBRATIONS

Class celebrations of birthdays and holidays are traditional in early childhood programs and require special planning. Celebrations should relate the program's objectives, because "tacked on" celebrations may be counterproductive. A policy should be written to cover the following points:

1. The specific celebrations the children will observe should be determined. Which celebrations are most appropriate to the program's objectives and learning activities? Will children's birthdays be celebrated? Which holidays will be celebrated?
2. The amount of time during the session that can be used for the celebration should be regulated by policy.
3. The number of celebrations which can be observed during one session should be included in the policy. Can there be two or more birthday celebrations, or a birthday and a holiday celebration, during one session? If there are two or more celebrations during one session, are they to be conducted jointly, successively, or with a time interval? The foregoing decision may affect the amount of time allotted for each celebration.
4. If birthdays are observed, these decisions should be made: the nature of and responsibility for birthday celebrations; whether a parent is responsible or can help; the policy on treats, favors, decorations, and entertainment; type and quality (homemade or purchased) of food, advance notice needed by the staff; and use and clean-up of kitchen and dishes. If the staff has full or part responsibility, the foregoing decisions, plus the amount of money to be spent, also need to be noted.
5. If holidays are to be observed, all policy decisions mentioned for birthday celebrations need to be considered; in addition, a policy on card and/or gift exchanges among children and/or between staff and children needs to be stated. If allowed, a limit on the number of gifts and amount spent per gift should be specified. If your program has room mothers, decisions need to be made concerning their responsibilities.
6. The places in which celebrations can take place should be regulated. Are certain areas of the building more suitable for celebrations than others? Can the outdoor space be used, or can children be taken to places beyond the organization's property for celebrations?

SUBSTITUTE PERSONNEL

Plans for a substitute care-giver or teacher are most essential in a self-contained situation and in programs where special-subject teachers are hired. In programs that use a team teaching approach or have paraprofessional assistance, plans for substitute personnel are not as necessary.

Directors of early childhood programs must develop a list of potential substitute care-givers or teachers who meet the qualifications required by the state licensing agency or the state board of education, respectively. Each program must establish a procedure for obtaining substitute personnel; usually, the absent care-giver or teacher contacts the director who, in turn, secures the substitute.

The care-giver or teacher has an important responsibility in planning for substitute personnel. Because there are few advance warnings of impending illness or emergency plans must be made soon after the care-giver or teacher begins employment, and the plans must be kept current. Some suggestions for planning for substitute personnel are:

1. As soon as the children are secure in the early childhood program, prepare them for the possibility of a substitute. Young children are often frightened of a substitute care-giver or teacher unless they are prepared in advance. One way to prepare children for substitutes is to have prospective substitutes visit (or even employ them to work) before they are needed. The visitation can also serve as an orientation of the prospective substitute to the program, or as a check to determine whether this person seems to fit into the program.

2. In as much detail as possible, write information on the procedures for: greeting the children, such as where to meet them and the greeting ritual; meals, snacks, and toileting; types of activities planned in each major block of time on the schedule; moving the children from one activity to another within the room, such as a verbal, light-blinking, or musical signal; moving children outdoors and to other parts of the building; emergencies, such as evacuation of the building and illness of the child; conducting the administrative functions, such as attendance or meal counts or sending notes home to parents; and departure of the children, such as the method of getting home and the exit door.

3. Write care-giving or teaching plans for a minimum of two or three days. Plans should be ideas appropriate anytime of the year and should not burden substitute personnel by requiring extremely careful supervision or extensive preparation or clean-up time.

4. Provide a shelf or cabinet for the specific equipment and materials needed for the care-giving or teaching plans, such as a storybook and record for rhythmic activities. Large pieces of equipment like record players and playground balls may be left in their usual places. Because substitute personnel do not know the children's names, name tags should be placed with the equipment and materials.

5. Keep an up-to-date list of the children and note those with special problems, physical, intellectual, or emotional, and what you do to work with these problems.

6. Keep a note taped to your desk or in some other obvious place telling where to find the information and materials for substitute personnel.

7. Leave on the desk the schedule of semiregular activities such as library time, special duty, or times for special-subject teachers or other personnel to work with children.

8. If the substitute did a good job, it is especially nice to call and express your appreciation. The substitute should inform you of any special problems that occurred. Inform the director or building principal of the quality of the substitute's work so a decision can be made about rehiring the substitute at a future date.

NOTES

1. J.I. Goodlad, *Planning and Organizing for Teaching* (Washington, D.C.: National Education Association, 1963).

2. J. Goodlad and R.H. Anderson, *The Nongraded Elementary School*, re. ed. (New York: Harcourt Brace Jovanovich, 1963).

3. Goodlad, *Planning and Organizing for Teaching*.

4. E.R. Snyder, ed., *The Self-Contained Classroom* (Washington, D.C.: Association for Supervision and Curriculum Development, 1960).

5. G.D. Stoddard, *The Dual Progress Plan* (Scranton, Pa.: Harper & Row Publishers, 1961).

6. J.I. Goodlad, "Classroom Organization," *Encyclopedia of Educational Research*, ed. C.W. Harris (New York: The Macmillian Co., 1960), pp. 221–26.

7. W.R. Borg, *Ability Grouping in the Public Schools*, second edition (Madison, Wisc.: Dembar Educational Research Services, 1966).

8. G. Heathers, *Organizing Schools Through the Dual Progress Plan* (Danville, Ill.: Interstate, 1966).

9. Ibid.

10. J.C. Daniels, "Effects of Streaming in the Primary School II: A Comparison of Streamed and Unstreamed Schools," *British Journal of Educational Psychology* 31 (1961): 119–27.

11. "The Individually Prescribed Instructional Systems," Pace Learning Systems, P.O. Box AG, University, Ala. 35486.

12. Glen Nimnicht, "Planning in a Head Start or Kindergarten Classroom," *Curriculum Is What Happens*, ed. Laura D. Dittmann (Washington, D.C.: National Assn. for the Education of Young Children, 1970), pp. 10–11.

13. Minnie Perrin Berson, "The All-Day Kindergarten," *Today's Education* 57 (1968):29.

14. Lorraine Salot and Jerome E. Leavitt, *The Beginning Kindergarten Teacher* (Minneapolis, Minn.: Burgess Publishing Co., 1965).

15. *School District No. 23 v. McCoy*, 30 Kan. 268, 1 Pac. 97, 46 Am St. Rep. 757.

16. *Miller v. Jones*, 224 NC 783, 32 SE (2nd) 594.

For Further Reading

Borg, W. *Ability Grouping in the Public Schools*. Madison, Wis.: Dembar Educational Research Services, 1966.

Carbone, R.F. "A Comparison of Graded and Non-Graded Elementary Schools." *Elementary School Journal* 62 (1961): 82–88.

Douglas, J.W.B. *The Home and the School: The Study of Ability and Attainment in the Primary School*. London: MacGibbon and Kee, 1964.

Drews, E.M. *Student Abilities, Grouping Patterns, and Classroom Interactions*. East Lansing, Mich. Michigan State University Press, 1963.

Eash, M.J. "Grouping: What Have We Learned?" *Educational Leadership* 18 (1961): 429–34.

Ferguson, Eva D. "An Evaluation of Two Types of Kindergarten Attendance Programs." *Journal of Educational Psychology* 48 (1957): 287–301.

Franseth, J., and Koury, R. *Grouping Children in the Elementary School: Research and Implications.* Washington. D.C.: U.S. Office of Education, 1963.

————. *A Guide to Research and Informal Judgment in Grouping Children.* Washington, D.C.: U.S. Office of Education, 1964.

Goldberg, M. et al. *The Effects of Ability jgrouping.* New York: Teachers College, Columbia University, 1966.

Goodlad, J.I., and Anderson, R.H. *The Nongraded Elementary School,* rev. ed. New York: Harcourt Brace Jovanovich, 1963.

Halliwell, J.W. "A Comparison of Pupil Achievement in Graded and Nongraded Primary Classrooms." *Journal of Experimental Education* 32 (1963): 59–64.

Hillson, M., ed. *Change and Innovation in Elementary School Organization.* New York: Holt, Rinehart & Winston, 1965.

————. "A Controlled Experiment Evaluating the Effects of a Nongraded Organization on Pupil Achievement." *Journal of Educational Research* 57 (1964): 548–50.

Hopkins, K.D. et al. "An Experimental Comparison of Pupil Achievement and Other Variables in Graded and Nongraded Classes." *American Educational Research Journal* 2 (1967): 207–15.

Hosley, Eleanor M. "The Long Day." *Young Children* 20 (1965): 135–39.

Liston, C.W. "Managing the Daily Schedule." In *Perspectives on Infant Care,* edited by R. Elrado and B. Pagon. Orangeburg, S.C.: Southern Association for Children Under Six, 1972, pp. 51–57.

Mills, Belen C., and Mills, Ralph A. *Designing Instructional Strategies for Young Children.* Dubuque, Iowa: William C. Brown and Co., 1972.

Morganstern, A., ed. *Grouping in the Elementary School.* Belmont, Calif.: Fearon-Pitman Publishers, 1966.

Nimnicht, Glen; McAfee, Oralie; and Meier, John. *The New Nursery School.* New York: The General Learning Press, 1969.

Office of Economic Opportunity. *Project Head Start-Daily Program 1.* Washington, D.C.: U.S. Government Printing Office, 1967.

Passow, H.A. "The Maze of Research on Ability Grouping." *Educational Forum* 26 (1962): 281–88.

Shane, H.G. "Grouping in the Elementary School." *Phi Delta Kappan* 41 (1960): 313–19.

Shaplin, J.T., and Olds, H.F. Jr., eds. *Team Teaching.* Scranton, Ill.: Harper & Row, Publishers, 1964.

Snyder, E.R., ed. *The Self-Contained Classroom.* Washington, D.C.: Association for Supervision and Curriculum Development, 1960.

Thelen, H.A. *Classroom Grouping for Teachability.* New York: John Wiley & Sons, 1967.

Tronick, E., and Greenfield, P.M. *Infant Curriculum: The Bromley-Health Guide to the Care of Infants in Groups.* New York: Media Projects, 1973.

Weisdorf, Pearl S. "A Comparison of Two, Three, and Five Days of Nursery School." *Young Children* 21 (1965): 24–29.

Yates, A., ed. *Grouping in Education.* New York: John Wiley & Sons, 1966.

11

Nutrition and Health Services

Increasing emphasis on health in our society has resulted in an expanded health program for young children. Today's emphasis is on total health rather than the control of contagion only. One aspect of the expanded health program is that of developing concepts and attitudes toward good health. Curriculum books are replete with understandings young children should acquire in the areas of nutrition, personal hygiene, clothing, exercise, relaxation, and safety. Another aspect of today's health program is the provision for a healthful school environment, as discussed in chapter 8.

A health program for young children also involves a comprehensive nutritional program and additional health services. Nutrition programs include more than food preparation, serving, and clean-up activities, and the health service program of today involves more than meeting various health regulations.

Nutrition

Early childhood programs are becoming more concerned about nutrition. Adequate nutrition is essential for maintenance of biological integrity. During periods of rapid growth, the child is especially unprotected against malnutrition. Thus, permanent effects from malnutrition on brain size and composition would be most likely before 4.6 years of age and especially before 1.0 year of age.[1] The effects of malnutrition depend not only on the point at which deprivation occurs, but also on the severity of deprivation and the nutrients involved in the deprivation. Because malnutrition interferes with development of the central nervous system, it also affects mental functioning; it can impair learning during critical periods and can change motivation and other aspects of behavior. A few of the many studies indicate these problems from malnutrition:

1. Poor sensory integration was found in children suffering from protein deficiency. Protein affects the organs of perception and thus visual-auditory-kinesthetic abilities, with definite implications for reading and writing.[2] The National Nutrition Survey found that protein-calorie malnutrition is a prevalent form of malnutrition in the United States.[3]
2. Pyridoxine (vitamin B_6) deficiency causes severe irritability and uncontrolled convulsive seizures.[4]
3. Although definitive research is still not available, Minimal Brain Dysfunction (MBD) and the associated hyperkinetic syndrome may be due to nutritional imbalances and metabolic dsyfunction. Prescriptions of mega-vitamins,[5] elimination of foods containing artificial colors and flavors,[6] and inclusion of foods rich in compounds containing salicylates[7] have all been tried with some success.
4. Apathy and accompanying irritability are a syndrome of nutritional stress.[8]
5. Nutrition is important in determining resistance to disease.[9]

Nutritional habits, like many others, are formed during the early years of life. Because young children living in poverty are subject to nutritional risks, the Planning Committee for Project Head Start emphasized that it is essential that Head Start programs "establish sound nutritional practices by providing food to program participants as well as educating families in the selection and preparation of food in the home."[10] Besides impoverished children, many from nonpoor families are also nutritionally handicapped.

DEVELOPING OBJECTIVES FOR A NUTRITION PROGRAM

The nutrition program does not consist only of food preparation, serving, and cleanup. The program must provide for a nutritionally adequate diet, offering one-half to two-thirds of the recommended daily allowances during the six- to eight-hour period the child spends in the program. Although licensing regulations contain minimum nutritional requirements, a 1969 White House Conference on Food, Nutrition, and Health recommended that day-care centers provide 80 percent of the child's total nutritional requirements. A study conducted by the Tulane University Early Childhood Research Center found that after six months, children who ate both breakfast and lunch had major nutritional improvement as compared with little improvement among those who had only lunch, lending support to the White House Conference recommendation.[11] Furthermore, the nutritional program should expose the child to a wide variety of foods, so he will develop a taste for many foods; provide for direct dietary consultation to meet special needs of some of the children; and provide menus to parents to aid them in food selection for the remaining part of the child's diet.

The staff should identify children's nutritional problems such as overweight, underweight, iron deficiency anemia, food allergies, and faulty food habits. Referral for medical and dental examinations and laboratory tests will reveal nutritional conditions that need remediation. If treatment is necessary, the staff should follow the recommendations while the child is in the center; if necessary, assist the family in carrying out the care plan; and ascertain whether the child has received follow-up assessment. The staff should be provided with in-service training to make them more aware of the specific nutritional problems.

The program should include nutrition education for the children. Children should talk about foods and good diets; learn about food origins, storage, and preparation; have cooking experiences, to help them learn to measure, follow directions, cooperate with others, coordinate eye-hand movements, use language as a means of expression, recognize differences in food preferences of the various ethnic groups, and eat foods prepared in different ways; and develop socially acceptable eating behavior and adaptability to various meal situations—family-style meals, snacks, restaurants, and picnics. There are many curricular resources available, such as:

Association for Childhood Education International. *Cooking and Eating with Children—A Way to Learn.* Washington, D.C.: The Association, 1974.

Good Times with Good Foods: Classroom Activities for Young Children—Idea Exchange, Vol. 6, No. 3. Greensboro, N.C.: A LINC Publication, 1976.

How Children Learn About Food. Ithaca, N.Y.: Visual Communications Office, Cornell University. (Slides or flashcards)

Project Head Start, Rainbow Series 3F. *Nutrition Education for Young Children.* Washington D.C.: U.S. Department of Health, Education, and Welfare, Office of Child Development, 1976.

Schlick, M. *Good Food for Life.* Seattle, Wash.: Washington STATO, University of Washington, 1973.

Yakima Home Economics Association. *Kim Likes to Eat* (Food Is Good, Book 1); *Food Helps Kim Grow* (Food Is Good, Book 2), *Kim Remembers to Wash* (Food Is Good, Book 3); and, *Kim Helps Care for Food* (Food Is Good, Book 4). Yakima, Wash.: The Association, 1973–1975.

Of the many cookbooks available for children, some contain recipes children like, and others are designed to teach them how to cook:

Bruno, J., and Dakan, P. *Cooking in the Classroom.* Belmont, Calif.: Lear Siegler/Fearon Publishers, 1974.

Cannamore, S. et al. *Snacks for Young Children,* Vol. II, No. 4, The Staff Training Monograph Series. Washington, D.C.: U.S. Department of Health, Education, and Welfare, Office of Education, Bureau of Education for the Handicapped, 1973. ERIC ED 133 935.

Children Can Cook. New York: Bank Street Films. (Filmstrip and record)

Ferreira, N.J. *The Mother-Child Cook Book,* Menlo Park, Calif.: Pacific Coast Publishers, 1969.

Foster, F.P. *Adventures in Cooking: A Collection of Recipes for Use in Nursery Schools, Day Care Centers, Head Start Programs, Kindergartens, and Primary Classrooms.* Westfield, N.J.: The Author, 1971. ERIC ED 069 360.

Little Miss Cookbook. San Francisco, Calif.: Del Monte Corp., 1971.

The nutrition program should also meet the special needs of a child with a handicapping condition. Children with delayed feeding skills may need special help; children with metabolic problems, such as phenylketonuria, will need a carefully planned diet; and approaches used in nutrition education may have to be modified for the deaf and blind. Several available resources are:

Feeding the Child with a Handicap (Publication N. HSM 735609). Rockville, Md.: U.S. Department of Health, Education, and Welfare, Health Services Administration, Maternal and Child Health Services, Bureau of Community Health Services, 1967.

Garton, N.B., and Bass, M.A. "Food Preferences and Nutrition Knowledge of Deaf Children." *Journal of Nutrition Education* 6 (1974): 60.

McWilliams, M. *Nutrition for the Growing Years,* 2d ed. New York: John Wiley & Sons, 1975, pp. 347–50.

Smith, M.A., ed. *Feeding the Handicapped Child*. Memphis, Tenn.: *University of Tennessee Child Development Center, Department of Nutrition, 1971.*

Sofka, D. *Nutrition and Feeding Techniques for Handicapped Children Series*. Sacramento, Calif.: Developmental Disabilities Program, Room 892, California State Department of Health, n.d.

Thompson, R.J., and Palmer, S. "Treatment of Feeding Problems—A Behavioral Approach." *Journal of Nutrition Education* 6 (1974): 63.

U.S. Department of Health, Education, and Welfare. *Nutrition Training Guide for Classroom Personnel in Head Start Programs*. Washington, D.C.: The Department, Office of Human Development, Office of Child Development, 1976, pp. 52–53.

Parents need to be informed on various topics concerning nutrition for their children, including:

What kinds of foods are needed for a healthy child?; how to plan meals and buy foods economically; how to prepare varieties of food; how to serve and store food; how to establish food cooperatives; new foods; eating problems of children; food allergies; the purchase and preparation of surplus foods; what are food plans?; can a freezer save me money?; and others.[12]

The staff needs to know the social realities of the families with whom they work, or they may make nutritional demands that families cannot meet.[13,14] Parents can be reached in parent's meetings, demonstration classes, home visits, and through newsletters. Some specific suggestions:

1. Aid parents in planning nutritious meals using the basic four food groups. A list of foods in each of the four groups may help parents plan adequate meals or may help those who are already planning adequate meals see how they can vary their food choices;
2. Newsletters can contain information about food planning and preparation and recipes as a way of developing the young child's interest in foods and snacks;
3. Menus should be posted for parents;
4. Other information on nutrition should be made available, such as the nutrient content of foods in relation to cost, the nutrient content of food after storage and preparation, and the relationship between nutrition and health of infants and young children; and
5. Volunteer work in the food area may be helpful in informing parents.

The staff will need to develop basic competencies to meet the foregoing objectives; one helpful resource is:

U.S. Department of Health, Education, and Welfare. *Nutrition Training Guide for Classroom Personnel in Head Start Programs*. Washington, D.C.: The Department, Office of Human Development, Office of Child Development, 1976.

REGULATIONS REGARDING NUTRITION PROGRAMS

All early childhood programs must meet state and local health and sanitation requirements. Specific nutrition program requirements depend upon the type of the early childhood program, that is, the source of its funds. Nutrition programs for both preschool and school-age children in public and nonprofit private institutions, except in-residence service institutions, must meet the requirements of the Special Food Service Program for Children authorized in 1968 by Public Law 90–302. Child care programs may be eligible for reimbursement from the U.S. Department of Agriculture (USDA), Special Food Service Program (SFSP). The SFSP is administered directly by the USDA Regional Office in some states, and in other states, by the State School Lunch Program.[15]

All private early childhood programs, including those nonprofit private programs which meet the requirements of the Special Food Service Program for Children, must meet the minimum standards of the state licensing law. As we have already discussed, licensing requirements prescribe: (1) the fraction of the recommended daily food allowances a child must receive at the center; (2) the length of time between meals and snacks; (3) the posting and filing of menus; and (4) the qualifications of individuals who prepare and serve food. Several licensing manuals suggest types of foods and menus.

PROVIDING AND SERVING NUTRITIOUS MEALS AND SNACKS

Providing and serving nutritious meals and snacks is important for two reasons: to feed the child's body and mind; and to provide an opportunity for the child to learn about new foods, ways foods can be served, and social amenities. Before personnel plan meals and snacks, every child should have a nutritional assessment. (Nutritional assessment is now part of the final regulations of the Department of Health, Education, and Welfare's Early and Periodic Screening, Diagnosis and Treatment program for children under 21.0 years.)[16]

Infants.   Medical advice should be followed in providing foods for infants in child care centers. Formula or fluid whole milk is the central food in an infant's diet. In addition to milk, infants receive cereals (especially prepared for infants) and strained fruits, vegetables, and meats. Infants six months to a year old eat a variety of strained foods and dried bread or toast. When the infant has enough teeth, he can chew mashed vegetables and fruits. For additional suggestions for infant meals and snacks, see:

Maternal and Child Health Service. *Nutrition and Feeding of Infants and Children Under Three in Group Day Care.* Washington, D.C.: Day Care and Child Development Council of America, 1971.

Young Children.   One habit young children must learn is to eat a variety of nutritious foods. Meal and snack patterns are often based on the four basic food groups: (1) meat (two or more servings); (2) vegetables and fruits (four or more servings); (3) milk and milk products; and (4) bread and cereal (four or more servings). Two examples of meal and snack patterns are found in tables 1 and 2. For additional suggestions, see:

Hillie, H.M. *Food for Groups of Young Children Cared for During the Day.* Washington, DC: Children's Bureau Publication No. 386, U.S. Department of Health, Education, and Welfare, 1960.

Project Head Start, Rainbow Series 3. *Nutrition, Better Eating for Head Start.* Washington, DC: U.S. Department of Health, Education, and Welfare, Office of Human Development, Office of Child Development, 1965.

TABLE 1
Regulations of the Special Food Service Program for Children

	CHILDREN	
PATTERN	1 up to 3 years	3 up to 6 years
Breakfast		
Milk, fluid[1]	½ c	¾ c
Juice or fruit	¼ c	½ c
Cereal and bread,[2]		
enriched or whole grain		
Cereal	¼ c	⅓ c
Bread	½ sl	½ sl
Mid-morning or Mid-afternoon Supplement		
Milk, fluid[1]; or juice; or fruit; or vegetable	½ c	½ c
Bread or cereal,[2]		
enriched or whole grain		
Bread	½sl	½ sl
Cereal	¼ c	⅓ c
Lunch or Supper		
Milk, fluid[1]	½ c	¾ c
Meat and/or alternate[3]		
Meat, poultry, or fish, cooked[4]	1 oz	1½ oz
Cheese	1 oz	1½ oz
Egg	1	1
Cooked dry beans and peas	⅛ c	¼ c
Peanut butter	1 T	2 T
Vegetables and fruits[5]	¼ c	½ c
Bread,[2] enriched or whole grain	½ sl	½ sl

Source: *A Supplement to A Guide for Planning Food Service in Child Care Centers*. Washington, D.C.: U.S. Department of Agriculture, Food and Nutrition Service, 1974.
[1]Includes whole milk, lowfat milk, skim milk, cultured buttermilk, or flavored milk made from these types of fluid milk which meet state and local standards.
[2]Or an equivalent serving of an acceptable bread product made of enriched or whole grain meal or flour.
[3]Or an equivalent quantity of any combination of the above listed foods.
[4]Cooked lean meat without bone.
[5]Must include at least two kinds.

There are some other practices to follow in planning enjoyable meals and snacks for young children:

1. Large portions of food are overwhelming to children; serve food in small portions and permit second helpings.
2. When serving an unpopular food, serve a tiny portion with a more generous portion of the popular one.
3. Plan special menus for holidays and birthdays.
4. Do not serve the same food, or virtually the same food, such as meatballs and hamburgers, on consecutive days.

TABLE 2

Meal and Snack Plan Published by the Office of Economic Opportunity

Breakfast
Juice or fruit
Cereal   OR
Milk (part used for cereal)
Butter or margarine, as needed.

Snack—one or more of the following:
Milk or fruit, vegetable or juice, or protein-rich food

Lunch or Supper
Protein-rich food (main dish)
Vegetable and/or fruit (at least 2 kinds)
Bread, enriched or whole grain
Butter or fortified margarine as needed
Milk

	Juice or fruit			
	Protein-rich food			
	Bread, enriched or whole grain			
	Milk			

		AGES		
		1	2–3	4–6
Milk		½–1 c	½–1 c	¾–1 c
Bread		½ sl	½–1 sl	1–1½ sl
Cereal		¼ c	⅓ c	½ c
Vegetable	Vitamin A source	2 T	3 T	4 T
	Other	2 T	3 T	4 T
Fruit	C source	¼ c	⅓–½ c	½ c
	Other	2 T	3 T	4 T
Meat, lean cooked without bone		½ oz	1–1½ oz	1½–2 oz
Egg		1	1	1
Dried peas or beans, cooked		1 T	2–3 T	3–4 T
Peanut butter		1 T	2–3 T	3–4 T
Cheese, cheddar		½ oz	1–1½ oz	1½–2 oz
Cottage cheese		1 T	2–3 T	3–4 T
Butter or margarine		½ t	1 t	1 t

SOURCE: Office of Economic Opportunity. Handbook for Local Head Start Nutrition Specialists. Washington, D.C.: U.S. Department of Health Education, and Welfare. Office of Human Development, Office of Child Development, 1975, pp. 12, 14.

5. Consider children's ethnic backgrounds, and plan menus to include familiar foods.

6. Take advantage of children's likes and dislikes as to how foods are prepared and served. Young children generally like a variety of foods (foods of different sizes, shapes, colors, textures, and temperatures); foods prepared in different ways; foods served in bite-sized pieces or as finger foods; vegetables with mild flavors; strong-flavored vegetables served only occasionally and in small portions; fruit (but not vegetable) combinations; good texture (fluffy, not gooey, mashed potatoes); and foods that are not too hot or cold.

7. Provide a good physical and emotional climate by having adults set a good example of eating; having an attractive room setting with furniture, dishes, silverware, and serving utensils suited to young children; avoiding serving delays or using activities such as singing and fingerplay while waiting; providing a quiet time before meals; making meal time pleasant; permitting the child to have choices and recognizing that young children occasionally go on food sprees (wanting the same food every day or even several times a day); and understanding that young children do not have an adult's sense of time and are not prone to hurry to finish.

PLANNING OTHER ASPECTS OF FOOD SERVICE

Besides providing and serving nutritious meals and snacks, at least four other aspects of food service must be planned: staffing, equipping, purchasing food, and meeting sanitation requirements. Careful consideration of all of these aspects will upgrade meal and snack quality.

Staffing. Programs with a large enrollment and/or programs that serve a main meal should have a staff dietitian who is registered with the American Dietetic Association. If it is not possible to hire a full-time dietitian, one should be hired as a consultant. Enough personnel should be employed so that meals and snacks can be prepared in the time allowed. Each state's licensing standards or other state and federal regulations indicate the qualifications necessary for a private or public program's food service personnel, respectively.

Equipping. Meals and snacks must be prepared and served with the facilities and equipment available. A registered dietitian can help plan the equipment and kitchen layout. An excellent publication concerning food service equipment is the booklet, *Equipment Guide for Preschool and School Age Child Service Institutions,* published by the U.S. Department of Agriculture. Some equipment, such as the automatic dishwasher, must meet local and state health agency regulations.

Purchasing Food. Planning food purchases helps control costs and reduces waste. The following suggestions should be considered when purchasing food:

1. Check several food companies or stores in the area for quality food at

reasonable prices and for services such as credit or delivery.

2. Know food products. Purchase U.S. Government inspected meats, fish, and poultry; pasteurized, Grade A milk and milk products; breads and pastries that are properly sealed; and frozen foods that are kept hard-frozen and perishable foods that are kept under refrigeration. Notice which brand names prove most satisfactory.

3. Carefully calculate quantities of food needed. Use standardized recipes that always yield a given amount. One source of this kind of recipe is the U.S. Department of Agriculture's publication, *Quantity Recipes for Type A School Lunches.* A standardized recipe can be adjusted to provide the number of servings needed for a meal or snack.

4. The types of food (perishable or nonperishable) and the amount of storage space must be carefully considered in determining when to purchase.

5. Keep accurate records of food purchased, quality of food purchased, when and how food was used in the program, the cost, and any other notes that will be useful for other food purchases.

For additional suggestions, see:

Sadow, S. *Food Buying Guide and Recipes for Project Head Start Centers.* Washington, D.C.: U.S. Department of Health, Education, and Welfare, Office of Human Development, Office of Child Development, 1965.

Meeting Sanitation Requirements.   All sanitation requirements must be rigidly enforced to avert disease. Sanitation must be considered in all aspects of food service:

1. All food service employees must meet state and local health requirements, must be free of infections on the skin and from contagious diseases, and must be clean.

2. Preparation and serving utensils and dishes must be thoroughly washed, sterilized, and properly handled. A dishwasher should be set for a water temperature of 160° to 165°F, and use 0.25 percent detergent concentration, or one ounce of detergent per three gallons of water. Follow these four steps if washing by hand:

    Wash with soap or detergent in hot water (110°–120°F);

    Rinse in warm water;

    Sanitize by immersing for at least one minute in clean hot water (at least 170°F) or by immersing for at least three minutes in a sanitizing solution of one tablespoon household bleach per two gallons of water; and

    air dry—do not wipe dry.

3. Foods should be checked upon delivery, protected in storage, used within the specified time, and kept at appropriate serving temperatures: hot foods at 140° Fahrenheit (60° Celsius) or above and cold foods at 40° Fahrenheit (4° Celsius) or below.

4. Wash raw foods carefully and cook other foods properly.

5. Dispose of all foods served and not eaten.

6. Help children develop habits of cleanliness.

For additional suggestions, see:

Handbook for Food Preparation. Washington, D.C.: American Home Economics Association,

U.S. Department of Agriculture. *Storing Perishable Foods in the Home.* Home and Garden Bulletin, No. 78.

U.S. Department of Agriculture, Extension Service. *It's Good Food—Keep it Safe; The Invaders— Keep it Clean;* and, *Watch the Temperatures/Every Minute Counts.* Wheaton, Ill.: Double Sixteen Company. (Slides)

Health and Safety Services

There are several reasons for providing comprehensive health and safety services so vital to every early childhood program:

1. Several studies indicate that the longer children attend school, the more physical defects they manifest. It is not known to what extent the school environment contributes to development of these defects; however, health services can help eliminate conditions that may be conducive to the development of physical defects and ailments.
2. Many children enter school with physical defects that interfere with their progress. Screening children for possible physical defects is an important health service.
3. Public health nursing in the schools began as the result of concern with controlling contagion. Prevention of communicable diseases is another aspect of today's comprehensive health services.
4. Procedures must be developed to take care of emergencies such as accidents, sudden illnesses, and disasters.
5. A health and safety education program should be included for the benefit of the staff and for the guidance of parents.

Health and safety services should be provided through the cooperative efforts of the program staff, parents, local health department personnel, and medical professionals in the community. A health consultant should evaluate the physical facility. The American Academy of Pediatrics suggests that the health profession provide consultation on program policies, implementation, and training of staff.[17]

Most centers only offer minimal health and social services. Suggestions are being made to offer comprehensive preventive and curative health care and social services. Peters believes all programs should screen and identify handicaps and problems and provide follow-up services. She describes two models for providing these services: in the first model,[18] a part-time pediatrician and a pediatric nurse practitioner would serve several centers and a licensed practical nurse would be housed in each center; the second model[19] consists of a physician, a public health nurse, and a social worker, who would provide regular consultation services to several programs.

DEVELOPING HEALTH AND SAFETY POLICIES

Policies should cover all health services of an early childhood program. Each state has various health regulations that public and private programs must meet.

In addition to state regulations, the governing board of an early childhood program may write other health policies.

Health Admission Policies.   These policies stipulate what information the parent must provide before a child is admitted to the program. The following items are included:

1. A statement concerning the maximum time lapse between the required medical examininations and date of admission. Such a statement insures that the health information on the admission forms is based on recent evaluation. Generally, medical examinations completed between one month prior to school entry to two weeks after entry provides maximum protection for all children.
2. A statement concerning the child's ability to participate in the program's activities and any special health needs, such as food allergies or restrictions of physical activities signed by the child's physician.
3. Requirements concerning immunizations and a test for tuberculosis at the appropriate age. The American Academy of Pediatrics guide, *Report of the Committee on Infectious Diseases,* may be used to verify adequate immunizations. Another helpful guide is *Parents' Guide to Childhood Immunization* (Washington, D.C.: U.S. Department of Health, Education, and Welfare, Public Health Service, 1977).
4. A health history form regarding diseases the child has had, dates of immunizations, and health habits, such as brushes teeth, eats a variety of foods, and so forth (see Appendix 7).
5. An emergency information form to be completed and signed by parents. This form usually includes names, addresses, and phone numbers of parents and other persons who can accept responsibility for the child when parents cannot be contacted; name and phone number of the physician to be contacted; and name and address of the hospital to which the child may be taken (see Appendix 7).
6. Description of pupil accident insurance coverage. This insurance provides protection against financial losses resulting from accidents that happen to students while engaged in school activities or in going to and from school. There is no consideration of fault and no concern as to who is liable. Some private and public institutions purchase pupil accident insurance. When institutions do not or cannot legally purchase the pupil accident insurance, such coverage may be mandatory or optional on the part of parents.

Other Policies.   Health policies should include procedures to be followed in case of accident or sudden illness. Medical consultation should be sought in developing health policies concerning:

1. *Routine procedures for minor illnesses and accidents.* Most licensing standards and policies of other types of programs exclude sick children. The American Academy of Pediatrics recommends the following change in policy, if the early childhood program has adequate personnel:

Children who are tired, ill, or upset should be given a chance to rest in a quiet area under frequent observation. Ill children should be given a health appraisal by the regular staff in attendance. These children need not be discharged home as a routine policy; they may be cared for during minor illness at the discretion of the parent.[20]

As indicated in the chapter on regulations, some state's licensing laws require that at least one staff member have a current American Red Cross Standard First Aid Certificate or its equivalent. Regardless of the regulations, such knowledge is important. One excellent source is M.I. Green's *Sigh of Relief: The First Aid Handbook for Childhood Emergencies* (New York: Bantam Books, 1977).

2. *Procedures for disasters.* Some licensing regulations require disaster plans, while others do not. Certainly, plans for evacuating children in the event of fire or explosion or measures to take during tornadoes, flash floods, smog alerts, or civil defense emergencies are important.

3. *Procedures for serious accidents and illnesses.* Plans should be made for prompt care of any serious accident or illness. Quick access to the telephone numbers on the emergency information form is essential.

Health policies should also include procedures for conducting daily observations for symptoms of communicable diseases, and for notifying parents when communicable diseases have occurred among children in the program. Safety policies must include daily inspection of the indoor and outdoor areas and equipment. Be constantly alert for dangerous substances, and check equipment, especially playground equipment, which was responsible for 118,000 injuries in 1974.[21] The staff should be well-educated in strategies to prevent accidents. Not only is the well-being of the child involved, but the courts have also ruled that there is no contributory negligence on the part of a young child.[22]

DESIGNING A HEALTH EDUCATION PROGRAM FOR ADULTS

Medical consultation should be secured for in-service first aid education of staff; at least one or more staff members should be so trained. Furthermore, the staff needs guidance in discovering children's health needs and problems, in following and evaluating the school's health policies, and in helping parents meet their children's health needs.

The staff of an early childhood program must work with parents to promote the child's health. A meeting with the parents before the child is enrolled will familiarize them with the health admission, sick-child, and other policies of the program. Throughout the school term, some of the parents' meetings can focus on such topics as health problems of young children, health and safety practices, and health services. The staff could distribute free and inexpensive health or safety materials to parents. Some sources for these materials include:

American Academy of Pediatrics
1801 Hinman Avenue
Evanston, IL 60204

American Medical Association
533 North Dearborn Street
Chicago, IL 60610

American National Standards Institute
1430 Broadway
New York, NY 10018

American Red Cross
17th and D Streets, NW
Washington, DC 20006

Child Study Associates of America, Wel/Met
835 Broadway
New York, NY 10003

Food and Nutrition Information and
Educational Materials Center
Nutritional Agricultural Library
Room 304
Beltsville, MD 20705

Metropolitan Life Insurance Company
Health and Welfare Division
One Madison Avenue
New York, NY 10010

National Dairy Council
6300 North River Road
Rosemont, IL 60018

National Safety Council
444 North Michigan Avenue
Chicago, IL 60611

Society for Nutrition Education
2140 Shattuck Avenue
Suite 1110
Berkeley, CA 94704

The U.S. Consumer Product Safety
Commission
Washington, DC 20207
(Telephone: 800-638-2666; Maryland
residents, 800-492-2937)

State and local health depts.
State agriculture extension agencies

NOTES

1. H.G. Birch and J.D. Gussow, *Disadvantaged Children: Health, Nutrition, and School Failure* (New York: Harcourt Brace Jovanovich, 1970).

2. J. Cravioto, E.R. Ciardi, and H.G. Birch, "Nutrition, Growth and Neurointegrative Development: An Experimental and Ecological Study," *Pediatrics* (Supplement) 38 (1966): 319–72.

3. U.S. Department of Health, Education, and Welfare, Maternal and Child Health Service, *Maternal and Child Health Information* (Washington, D.C.: The Department, 1970).

4. D.B. Coursin, "Relationship of Nutrition to Central Nervous System Development and Function," *Federation Proceedings* 26 (1966): 134–38.

5. A. Cott, "Megavitamins: The Orthomolecular Approach to Behavior Disorders and Learning Disabilities," *Academic Therapy* 7 (1972): 245–58.

6. B.F. Feingold, *Why Your Child Is Hyperactive* (New York: Random House, 1974).

7. H.W.S. Powers, Jr. "Dietary Measures to Improve Behavior and Achievement," *Academic Therapy* 9 (1973–74): 203–14.

8. Birch and Gussow, *Disadvantaged Children*.

9. Ibid.

10. Office of Economic Opportunity, *Project Head Start-Nutrition* (Washington D.C.: U.S. Government Printing Office, 1967), p. 2.

11. Office of Economic Opportunity, "Hungry Children Lag in Learning," *Opportunity* 1 (1971): 10–13.

12. R.E. Rockwell and J. Endres, "Nutrition in Day Care Centers," *Young Children* 25 (1969): 22.

13. R. Hamlin, R. Mukerji, and M. Yonimura, *Schools for Young Disadvantaged Children* (New York: Teachers College Press, Columbia University, 1967).

14. R.R. Zimmerman and N. Munro, "Changing Head Start Mothers' Food Attitudes and Practices," *Journal of Nutrition Education* 4 (1972): 66.

15. U.S. Department of Agriculture Food and Nutrition Service Regional Offices are: Northeast: 729 Alexander Road, Princeton, N.J. 08540; Southeast: 1100 Spring Street, N.W., Atlanta, Ga. 30309; Midwest: 536 S. Clark Street, Chicago, Ill. 60605; West–Central: 1100 Commerce Street, Room 5-D-22, Dallas, Texas 75202; West: Appraiser's Building, Room 734, 630 Sansome Street, San Francisco, Calif. 94111.

16. *Federal Register* 44 (May 18, 1979), 29,424–26.

17. American Academy of Pediatrics, *Standards for Day Care Centers for Infants and Children Under Three Years of Age* (Evanston, Ill.: The Academy, Committee on Infant and Preschool Child, 1971).

18. A.D. Peters, "Health Support in Day Care," *Day Care Resources for Decisions*, ed. E.H. Grotberg (Washington, D.C.: Office of Economic Opportunity, 1971), pp. 328–30.
19. A.D. Peters, "The Delivery of Health and Social Service to Child and Family in a Daytime Program," *Early Childhood Development Programs and Services: Planning for Actions*, ed. Dennis W. McFadden (Washington, D.C.: National Association for the Education of Young Children, 1972), pp. 72–3.
20. American Academy of Pediatrics, *Recommendations for Day Care Centers for Infants and Children* (Evanston, Ill.: The Academy Committee on Infant and Preschool Child, 1973), p. 28.
21. Consumer Product Safety Commission, *Hazard Analysis of Injuries Relating to Playground Equipment* (Washington, D.C.: The Commission, 1975). ERIC ED 120 102.
22. *Fowler v. Seaton* (61 C 2d 681; 39 Cal. Rpts. 881, 394 p. 2d 697).

For Further Reading

Bettelheim, B. *Food to Nurture the Mind*. Washington, D.C.: Children's Foundation, 1970.

Birch, Herbert G., and Gussow, Joan D. *Disadvantaged Children: Health, Nutrition, and School Failure*. New York: Harcourt Brace Jovanovich, 1971.

Breckenridge, M.E., and Murphy, M.N. *Growth and Development of the Young Child*, 8th ed. Philadelphia, Pa: W.B. Saunders, Co., 1969. Pp. 178–202; 203–16.

Deutsch, R.M. *The Family Guide to Better Eating and Better Health*. Des Moines, Iowa: Meredith Corp., 1971.

Equipment Guide for Preschool and School Age Child Service Institutions. Washington, D.C.: U.S. Department of Agriculture, 1972.

Fomon, S.J. *Infant Nutrition*, 2d ed. Philadelphia, Pa.: W.B. Saunders, Co., 1974.

Fontana, V. *Parent's Guide to Child Safety*. New York: Thomas Y. Crowell Co., 1973.

A *Guide for Planning Food Service in Child Care Centers*. Washington, D.C.: U.S. Department of Agriculture, 1971.

Infant Care. Washington, D.C.: Office of Child Development, 1973.

Martin, E.A. *Nutrition in Action*, 3d ed. New York: Holt, Rinehart & Winston, 1971.

———. *Robert's Nutrition Work with Children*. Chicago: University of Chicago Press, 1954. (Midway Print, 1974).

A Menu Planning Guide for Breakfast at School (FNS-7). Washington, D.C.: U.S. Department of Agriculture, 1970.

A Menu Planning Guide for Type A School Lunches (PA-719). Washington, D.C.: U.S. Department of Agriculture, 1970.

Meyer, H.F. *Infant Foods and Feeding Practice*. Springfield, Ill.: Charles C. Thomas, 1960.

Nutrition Foundation, Inc. *Food a Key to Better Health*. New York: The Foundation, 1970.

Project Head Start. *Nutrition*. Washington, D.C.: U.S. Department of Health, Education, and Welfare, Office of Human Development, Office of Child Development.

Reinsch, E.H., and Minear, R.E. *Health of the Preschool Child*. New York: John Wiley & Sons, 1978.

Sunderlin, S., ed. *Nutrition and Intellectual Growth in Children*. Washington, D.C.: Association for Childhood Education International, 1969.

U.S. Department of Agriculture, U.S. Department of Health, Education, and Welfare, and Grocery Manufacturers of America and Advertising Council. *Food Is More Than Just Something to Eat*. Pueblo, Colo. Consumer Information, Department 45, 1976.

The Yakima Home Economics Association. *Road to Good Health*, 3d ed. Yakima, Wash. The Association, 1974.

Your Child From 1 to 6. Washington, D.C.: Office of Child Development, 1972.

Resource Materials Available:

Food and Nutrition Information and Educational Materials Center
National Agricultural Library
Room 304
Beltsville, Md. 20705
(Tel: 301-344-3719)

Society for Nutrition Education
2140 Shattuck Avenue
Suite 1110
Berkeley, Calif. 94704

The U.S. Consumer Product Safety Commission
Washington, D.C. 20207
(Tel: 800-638-2666; Maryland residents 800-492-2937)

12

Working with Parents

In the past, instructions to parents have frequently been: get your child to school regularly, on time, clean, fed, and ready to learn; make your child do his homework; come to PTA and Open House; and come and discuss problems. In short, parents were asked to support school policies and remediate their child's learning or social problems. Even the foregoing instructions have been given hesitantly, because many staff members respond with alarm to parental involvement. These staff members see home teaching of academics as confusing to the child, visits to the facility disruptive, and critiques of the program's curriculum and methodology as unqualified judgments of professionals by nonprofessionals. Nevertheless, with research showing the significance of the family in a child's total development, enlightened people are increasing pressure for parent involvement in children's programs. Parent groups and other taxpayers are concerned with the rising costs of education. Parents and business people are concerned with the seeming dichotomy between the real world and school life. Some federal programs require parent participation as a prerequisite for funding.

Values and Problems in Working with Parents

People do not usually commit themselves strongly to any program in which they are not involved. Historically, many early childhood programs had parental involvement. Friedrich Froebel, founder of the kindergarten, developed activities and materials for mothers to use with their infants. From the late 1800s through the early 1900s, kindergarten teachers in the United States taught children in the mornings and spent the afternoons visiting mothers in their homes. Since that time, those concerned with programs for young children have continued to insist on the importance of parental involvement and services to parents.

Many benefits stem from parental involvement in early childhood programs. These benefits may be described for the school, the child, and the parent.

School:
1. Parent involvement frequently enables the school to comply with federal and/or state guidelines.
2. Through parent involvement, schools achieve a better adult-child ratio.
3. Using parents is more economical than hiring additional professional help.
4. The care-giver or teacher benefits from direct assistance by parents. In some early childhood programs, parents assist in the classroom and help gather or make instructional or play materials. The Ameliorative Preschool Program, Champaign, Ill., and the Ferguson/Florissant Home/School Program for Four-Year-Olds, St. Louis County, Mo., have parents teaching in the classrooms.
5. Parents can serve as resource people. Their special talents and interests can be useful to the program.
6. Parents can explain to other parents the program's services and problems in ways that no other form of communication can. For example, the Parent Education Program of the Institute for Development of Human Resources, University of Florida, uses parent educators (i.e., parents from a background similar to those parents being trained) to work with parents of children from three months through eight years of age. These educators are trained to demonstrate toy making and specific activities for parents to do with their children, to model language patterns to be used with the activities, to explain the rationale for the activities, materials, and language patterns, and to stress the importance of parents in their children's development.
7. In addition to sharing teaching responsibilities with professionals in the classroom and in the home, parents are serving in decision-making capacities. Many early childhood programs have a parent advisory council. In some cases, parents are asked to make decisions regarding the objectives of the program; for example, in the Far West Laboratory for Educational Research and Development, Berkeley, Calif., Nimnicht feels that parents should make decisions concerning the amount of culturally relevant material to be included in the child's curricula and the teaching method to be employed in language development.
8. When parents are available to "explain" the culture to the teacher, the teacher may become more empathetic.
9. Parents have a chance to see other children of the same age and gain a more realistic picture of their child's strengths and weaknesses.

Child:
1. More adult attention increases the chance for greater achievement on the part of the child.

2. The child has the opportunity of developing a greater understanding of various cultures because of his social interaction with more adults from diverse backgrounds.
3. The child may develop a more positive self-concept from the increased frequency of individual attention in group settings that have a more adequate adult-child ratio.
4. Children see their parents in new roles and can see that parents and staff members are working together for them. This relationship stimulates in the child wholesome attitudes toward the staff and the program.

Parent:
1. Parents learn their importance in their child's education and how to help the schools maximize educational benefits.
2. Parents can profit from the educational expertise the early childhood program offers in child guidance and carry these skills into the home. Most early childhood research projects have programs designed to help parents understand the effects of the home environment on the child's development and to assist parents in helping their children at home. For example, staff members of the Bank Street Early Childhood Center, New York, hold classes for parents in child care; Miller and Camp, directors of the Demonstration and Research Center for Early Education, Nashville, Tenn., have developed curricula for other members of the child's family; Nimnicht, director of the Far West Laboratory for Educational Research and Development, Berkeley, Calif., lends games and toys from the "Parent/Child Toy Library" and offers a ten-week course of instruction in the use of these materials; and Schaeffer and Aaronson stress the need for family-centered programs, as a result of the analyses of data gathered in their Infant Education Research Project, Washington, D.C.

> I assume that no influence upon the child's early years is as powerful as that of the home. With such an assumption, it is obvious that the school has a responsibility for doing whatever it can to help the home help the child learn effectively in school.[1]

3. Parental involvement often results in a change in parental attitudes toward the schools. Research indicates that parental attitudes changed as a result of involvement in Head Start and Follow Through. The impact has been in terms of parent satisfaction with their child's educational achievements, of parents' own progress in understanding development, and of parents' general self-confidence.[2,3]
4. Parents learn to work in schools in a responsible, professional way.
5. Employment of parents will increase their incomes, provide them with training, and may lead them to seek further training.

Conversely, there are some inhibiting factors in parent-staff communications. Some parents, particularly those from lower socioeconomic classes, feel inhibited or even inferior around staff personnel because of their limited and unsuccessful school experiences, and the great socioeconomic distance between staff and parent. They may have a negative attitude toward school because they recall their own unhappy experiences, and some may fear that the staff blames them for their children's shortcomings; the staff cannot handle the child; the program does not devote enough time to certain areas of development; taxpayer money (for public schools and government-subsidized programs) is wasted on educational frills; or the staff is not disciplining children properly.

Parents may also feel helpless about their ability to contribute in a meaningful way to the program; some programs, in reality, fail to promote the idea that parents must become an integral part of the program.

Indeed, a major obstacle the school must seek to overcome through honest and direct communication is the pervasive sentiment that there is little parents can do to effect change in the quality of the classromm experience. It is precisely this feeling of impotency and alienation from the classroom lives of their children that has precipitated for some the moderate to angry cries for community control of the schools. Partisan sympathies aside, surely involvement and commitment are better than the passive withdrawal of many parents.[4]

The parent may be afraid the staff will see something that indicates parental failure. This may be especially true when parents are faced with special problems, such as those of the single parent, of the handicapped child, of child-abusing parents, or highly mobile parents. Communication with the staff can be difficult or embarassing for parents who cannot read or write, who do not have paper or pencil, who work during school hours, who cannot get to school because of transportation or babysitting problems, or who feel intimidated by the school.

The staff, on the other hand, may feel that parents are not qualified to make judgments of them as professionals, while some feel their jobs become vulnerable when parents assume an instructional role in the classroom. The staff may not want to surrender its policy-making power by having parents serve on curriculum planning committees or advisory boards.

Staff members may also blame parents for a child's failures, and may feel the parents do not do what they are taught to do by the professional in parent-education or parent-staff conferences, yet the staff member may feel insecure with the highly-educated parent. And, the staff may feel it is in competition with the parents for the "good" of the child. Staff members may not realize the parent role is different from the teacher role, and that schools and other institutions cannot make up for all functions of parenting. M. Gerzon's book, *A Childhood for Every Child*,[5] discusses the dangers of an institution overstepping its role.

Legal Rights of Parents

The legislative and judicial branches of our government have recognized the need for parent involvement. Consequently, legislation and litigation have been a part of the history of parent involvement in schools for young children. Because of the extent of this history, only a few key examples of parents' legal rights will be discussed,

Public schools are funded and advised by the local school district. The concept of local control is fundamental to public school organization, and parents, as citizens and taxpayers, have a right to be involved in the decision-making process.

In the statutes of most states, the teacher stands in loco parentis to the child. This legal terminology is replaced in some state statutes by another phrase meaning the same thing, such as teachers "stand in the relation of parents and guardians to pupils."[6] In states without such a provision, the court affirms the in loco parentis position of the teacher. In order to more appropriately assume this role, teachers should know what parents want for their children.

To some extent, the teacher stands in loco parentis with respect to punishment of children. Until recently, there was no clear distinction between legal and illegal punishment, particularly in regard to the rights of schools to administer corporal punishment,[7] but decisions of the U.S. Supreme Court have clarified the rights of the public schools. On October 20, 1975, the U.S. Supreme Court upheld a lower court decision handed down in Greensboro, North Carolina, that the schools had a right to use corporal punishment without parental consent. The Court insisted that corporal punishment not be used as a first line penalty, not be used without prior warning, and be conducted in the presence of another teacher.[8] The second decision, in Ingram v. Wright, was rendered on April 20, 1977. The majority opinion was that the "cruel and unusual punishment" clause of the Eighth Amendment is not applicable outside the criminal process (and thus does not extend to public school disciplinary practices), and that the procedural safeguards imposed by the "due process" clause of the Fourteenth Amendment could not be employed because due process would jeopardize the schools' ability to handle discipline problems and only "marginally" reduce the infliction of unjustified corporal punishment.[9] These decisions have polarized the educational community. Supporters of corporal punishment see it as a necessary means of keeping order in the classroom, although they do admit that corporal punishment may be occasionally misused. On the other hand, nonsupporters see it as a continuation of the puritanical, authoritarian tradition, as legalized child abuse, and as a potential for increasing rather than decreasing dicipline problems. (Excellent discussions of the pros and cons of corporal punishment, and more specifically of these cases, are found in ERIC ED 145 535 and ERIC ED 151 664.)

All educational agencies that receive funds under any federal program administered by the U.S. Office of Education must allow parents access to their child's official records. Due process is also granted if parents wish to challenge the records on the grounds that they are inaccurate, misleading, or inappropriate. Parents must give written permission for the release of their child's records to a third party. Under this law, commonly referred to as the "Buckley Amendment," parents must be informed of their rights to access, to use the due process provision, and to determine whether a record may be released.[10]

Finally, as discussed in chapter 5, parents have specific rights under P.L 94-142, including a role in yearly diagnosis, in placement decisions, and in development of the individual educational plan (IEP). A due process provision is also a part of P.L. 94-142.

Parent Involvement

The movement toward greater parent involvement in programs for young children has come about for several reasons. In a democracy, we believe all citizens have the right to be involved in the operation of their social institutions, including the schools. Throughout the history of public education in the United States, we have professed and defended the benefits of community control over educational policy and decision making.

Second, the importance of the role of the family in a child's overall development is more fully understood. The school working in isolation is likely to be impotent. Cooperation between parent and school gives the child a sense of security, knowing that both institutions are working together for his welfare. It also helps both parties recognize each other's competencies and weaknesses and thus be able to help each other meet the common goal of a successfully functioning child.

Early childhood educators promote early involvement of parents in their children's programs because, for maximum impact, cooperation must start early. Also, when parents are involved from the beginning, there is a chance for lasting concern and identification with a program. In fact, it might be said that perhaps all organizations concerned with young children have recognized the importance of and encouraged parent involvement. Some organizations, such as the Parent Cooperative Preschools International (P.C.P.I.) and the Parent-Teachers Association (P.T.A.), have directly promoted cooperation between parents and the schools. Other organizations, such as The National Committee for Citizens in Education (N.C.C.E.),[11] have as their major purpose parent participation in educational programs. Parents of handicapped children may receive help through the National Association of Retarded Citizens (N.A.R.C.),[12] which works in an advocacy capacity on the national and state levels and provides direct services on the local level. Besides these nationally established organizations, many local parent groups, not affiliated with a national organization, work for parent involvement in the schools.

Not all parents will want to be involved in the early childhood program in the same way or to the same degree. Gordon[13] found five levels of parental involvement in compensatory programs: (1) minimal parental involvement (parents simply received information about the program); (2) parent was used as a teacher in the home setting; (3) parent worked in the program in an untrained capacity;

(4) parent served as a trained worker in the program; and (5) parent participated in a policy-making process. There is little data specifying which type of parent involvement is most beneficial, so programs should appreciate all roles parents are willing to take.

Involvement with parents includes parent-staff communication and parent participation. Maximum returns in the area of parent-staff communication require various channels through which information may be exchanged, (such as conferences, home visits, and written communication; various ways of promoting dialogue, such as individual and small-group conferences, demonstrations, and formal programs; and plans for acting upon the information received, that is, methods of adjusting the services of the program to fit the needs of the child and a referral system.

Parent participation includes parents serving in various planning and advisory capacities and parents working as volunteers, either program or nonprogram, and as resource people.

PARENT-STAFF COMMUNICATION

"The happiest and most successful teacher is the one who regards parents as partners and friends in the program of educating the child."[14] In approaching parents, staff members should interpret the philosophy of the program; for example, the beliefs of a particular program might be stated as follows: (1) the staff is concerned about the child's overall welfare; (2) the program is designed to fit each child's special needs; and (3) parents are wanted and needed to fulfill the goals of the program. The following discussion will give you some ideas to use in communicating with parents.

Parent Reception Area. This area helps parents feel welcome and encourages an exchange of information between parents and staff members. Such an area should be well-defined and inviting, with adequate lighting, ventilation, comfortable chairs, a place to write, and materials with information about child development and about the early childhood program. Suggested materials are:

1. Periodicals published by organizations concerned with young children;
2. Guidelines for helping parents choose appropriate literature, toys, and other materials for young children;
3. Suggestions for good movies, television shows, local events, and any community happenings designed for children and/or parents;
4. Information about the program's services, basic schedule, names of staff members, special events, and vacation periods;
5. Directions for making things, such as finger paint, flannel boards, and bulletin boards;
6. Materials that serve as preparation for or follow-up to parents' meetings— for example, if you are introducing a new mathematics approach in your program, put some books and materials about this new approach on display; and
7. Information of concern to all parents on childhood diseases, safety in home

and other play areas, warnings on products used by children, and discipline and guidance. Free or inexpensive booklets can be secured from the American Red Cross, local pediatricians, and insurance companies.

The parent reception area should invite relaxed communication among parents and between parents and staff members, in addition to providing information. Some other suggestions for a parent reception area are as follows:

1. If there is an observation room for parents, it should be adjacent to or part of the parent reception area.
2. Photographs of the children engaged in the program's activities and samples of the children's art and other work can be displayed in this area.
3. Items for viewing, such as the photographs and samples of children's work, and informational materials should be changed frequently. Each child's work should be displayed from time to time, rather than only "the best" work.
4. Refreshments may be placed in the parent reception area on special occasions, (at holiday seasons and at the beginning and end of the term).

Spring or Autumn Orientation.   Many early childhood programs have an orientation meeting for parents who will be enrolling children. This is an excellent means of establishing a cooperative relationship between parents and staff. Although the orientation meeting is usually held in late spring, it can be held in early autumn. The purposes of the meeting are to orient parents to the services and requirements for admission to the program, and to the techniques they can use in preparing their children for entrance.

Parents should be greeted as they arrive. An orientation meeting that begins with an informal presentation of activities, such as songs, finger plays, rhythmic activities, or other typical activities, by the children presently enrolled, gives insight into some of the program's activities. If enrolled children are not available for a presentation, a slide-tape presentation is mose effective. If children are invited to come with their parents, presentation of a few activities by young children is not only entertaining, but also gives the new children something to look forward to next fall or next week. Following the presentation, the new children should be asked to join the enrolled children and several staff members or volunteers in activities to be conducted in another room or in the outdoor area. Reluctant children can remain with their parents.

The director and other program and nonprogram personnel should explain the program's services in an interesting way. Written, take-home materials are usually appreciated by the parents, who should be given an opportunity to ask questions about the program's services.

Requirements for admission to the program should be carefully described and included in a parent's handbook; if the handbook is not distributed at the orientation, the requirements should be in written form for parents to take home. Requirements for admission usually include: (1) age requirememts and verification of age through presentation of a birth certificate or an acceptable alternative; (2) residence in a certain attendance area (often required by public school early childhood programs); (3) fees; (4) proof of adequate immunizations and tuberculosis test; (5) medical statement concerning the child's ability to participate in the program; (6) emergency information form completed and signed by each child's parents; and (7) parental needs for and ability to pay for the child's enrollment (sometimes required by government-subsidized programs). In addition to admission requirements, parents should be informed about what kind of clothing the child should wear and whether he is to bring a change of clothing, along with suggestions about what kinds of clothing children can most easily manage. Finally, if the parent is to purchase any supplies, a list of these supplies should be included. The supplies can be displayed so parents can see exactly what to purchase. A note on the supply list can remind the parent to put his child's name on each article, thus reducing loss of property. Some programs provide a list with children's and parents' names, addresses, and telephone numbers, so parents can get acquainted and arrange car pools, if they wish.

Parents often want to know how to prepare their child for an early childhood program. They should be discouraged from engaging in a "crash course" of academic preparation, because young children are unlikely to gain long-lasting learnings and likely to develop an unfavororable attitude toward learning. The staff member, to allay parents' fears of no longer being needed in helping their children's development, should have a list of suggestions for helping their children to be better prepared for the program, such as places to visit, home experiences that would be beneficial, techniques and activities for developing listening skills and oral expression, and ways to encourage independence in young children. The staff can also indicate some of the materials that will be used in the early weeks of the session, so the parent can familiarize the child with them. An excellent article to help the staff prepare for the orientation is:

Anderson, L.S. "When a Child Begins School." *Children Today* 5 (1976): 16–19.

The informal meeting should last no longer than an hour. A social time following the meeting gives parents a chance to visit with each other and with the staff. A tour of the facility is appropriate during this time.

Parent's First Individual Visit.   The first individual visit to an early childhood program is often to register the child. The initial, individual contact between parent and staff member must go beyond the mechanics of registration, however. The parent's first visit to the program's facility is a time of direct learning and impressions for both parent and staff members.

The parent should bring the child. The conference room should contain a child-sized table and chair, books, crayons and drawing paper, and/or manipulative toys. In order that the parent may observe his child and the child may watch his parent, the child's table should be close to the table provided for parent and staff member. Also, the close proximity of the child makes it possible for the staff member to observe the child informally.

From the parent, a staff member should obtain: (1) an impression of the relationship between parent and child; (2) an impression of how the child reacts to the new situation and how the parent feels about putting his child in the program; (3) a personal and social history of the child; (4) all necessary admission forms; and (5) tuition and/or fees. The parent should obtain from the staff member: (1) an impression of the staff member; (2) an overview of the philosophy of the program and of the facility and equipment; (3) a handbook or mimeographed information sheet; (4) a list of items (clothing and/or supplies) needed before the child begins attending; and (5) receipts for tuition and/or fees paid.

Handbook for Parents.   The major purposes of the handbook are to help the parent become oriented to the program and to serve as a reference during the child's first year of enrollment. In planning a handbook, there are several points to consider:

1. Information in the parent's handbook should be consistent with the program's philosophy and policies. If the program is based on a specific model, this should be stated. Because philosophy and policies differ from program to program, the staff of each program must develop its own handbook.
2. At a minimum, the handbook should contain: an introduction to the philosophy and the services of the program; information about the program's policies that directly concern parents, such as hours of operation, fees, and children's celebrations; and information on requirements that must be met before admission to the program, such as proof of age, record of immunizations, completion of the emergency information, the personal information, and the health history forms. Other information the handbook might contain includes: developmental characteristics of young children; ways parents can help their child's development; health and safety of young children; how the staff members will report the child's progress; list of supplies parents need to purchase; ways parent can be involved in the center; and dates of scheduled meetings, such as Board and parent meetings.
3. Before writing the handbook, the frequency of revision should be determined. If annual revisions are not planned, include only a minimum of variable information, such as names of staff members, fees, and hours of operation. Because much of the variable information is essential, blank spaces can be left in the handbook and completed in handwriting each year; for example:

Lunch Period

A hot lunch will be served in the cafeteria every day. It costs _____¢ a day, or you may pay $___ . ___ a week. (Checks may be made payable to _____.) If your child wishes to bring his lunch, milk will cost _____¢ a day. Those who wish to know whether their children qualify for free or reduced-cost lunches may secure forms in the central office.

For partial revision, a plastic spiral bidding or a stapled handbook can be easily dismantled.

4. Information in the handbook should be arranged logically. A table of contents, each section printed on paper of a different color, and/or pages of each successive section cut longer or wider than the preceding section for a tab effect are three devices to facilitate locating specific information.
5. Information in the handbook should be concise. The handbook is a reference—not a novel!
6. The parents' levels of understanding should be considered in wording the handbook. Wording should not sound condescending, nor should it be educational jargon. Bilingual handbooks should be available if the program serves children in a mixed culture area.
7. The handbook should be attractive and the writing style interesting. Various colors of paper, readable printing, and/or photographs, cartoons, or children's drawings help make the handbook attractive. The writing might be in various styles or voices; for example, a staff member may "talk" to the parents:

Dear Parents:

We wish to extend a warm welcome to you and your child. We want to make this kindergarten year a pleasant one for parents as well as for children. You, as parents, will influence, to a large degree, your child's success in this venture.

Your help and cooperation will assist us in helping your child. Please feel free to talk with us anytime you feel it is necessary. You are welcome to visit and to get to know us and the program better.

Sincerely,

_____
(Staff member's signature)

The child may "talk" to his parents:

I am ready, if . . .

I know my name and address.
I know the safest way to school.
I know how to put on and take off my clothes.

The parent may "talk" to the child:

I will keep you home, when you have . . .

    Temperature over 99.6° Fahrenheit (37.6° Celsius)
    Sore throat
    Pain
    Chills
    Diarrhea
    Rash
    Earache
    Vomiting

A previously enrolled child may "talk" to a new child:

In kindergarten, you'll draw and paint. The teacher told my mom that drawing and painting help children symbolize their everyday world, express their feelings, develop creativity, and coordinate eyes and hands. It sounds serious, but drawing and painting are fun.

Or, the wording may be impersonal:

A child is eligible to enroll in the kindergarten of the Hubbard Suburb's Public School if he is five years old on or before September 1 of the year he enters.

Although different styles of wording are usually not combined, some combinations add to he cleverness of the writing; for example:

I can enter, if . . .

    I have my birth certificate.
    I have all my immunizations.

P.S. To parents:

*If you do not have a birth certificate, write to:

> Bureau of Vital Statstics
> State Capitol Building

| _____ | _____ | _____ |
| (Capital city) | (State) | (Zip code) |

*All immunizations are available through your doctor or the Public Health Center, _____ .
                                                    (Address)

To request information or an appointment call _____ .

---

8. In designing a handbook, costs must be considered. Since the handbook can become an expensive project, be sure to explore various typesetting and printing techniques, including typewritten camera-ready copy, and get several estimates. Ditto or mimeograph may be least expensive, and more than adequate for the program's needs.

The staff of each early childhood program should develop a handbook to fit its unique philosophy and policies. Appendix 7 presents an example of a kindergarten handbook.

Large-Group Conferences.   Although individual conferences are most common, large-group conferences may be conducted. A popular type is the "get acquainted" and "preview of what's to come" conference. Unlike the spring or autumn orientation, the get acquainted conference is held a few weeks after the beginning of the term. It is especially important when staff members do not conduct an orientation meeting. For a "get acquainted" conference, you should:

1. Send invitations to parents. If you include an RSVP, you can follow up on parents who do not respond, perhaps by telephone for a personal touch. A night meeting is preferable to an afternoon one, because it permits working parents to attend. Tuesdays, Wednesdays, and Thursdays are usually the best days for meetings, but check the community calendar before setting a date. Plan the conference to last a maximum of one hour, followed by a social period.
2. Set the conference date after you know the children, so you can associate parents with children.
3. Plan simple refreshments and ask volunteer parents to serve.
4. Arrange the room to show your program to best advantage; for example, put

the program's schedule on the chalkboard, arrange materials and equipment around the room, and display some of the children's work.
5. Make a specific outline of your presentation; for example,
   a. When most of the guests have arrived, greet them as a group.
   b. Introduce other staff members.
   c. Briefly describe your background and express confidence in the year ahead.
   d. Outline the purpose of the conference. Explain that there will be individual conferences scheduled and that parents can call anytime about their own child.
   e. Explain the purposes of the program, using specific examples. An excellent way to communicate objectives and activities is to take parents through a "typical day."
   f. Review the policies of the program. Parents may be asked to bring their "Parent's Handbook" for reference.
   g. Suggest ways parents can help their children.
   h. Have a short question and answer period, but remind parents that a child's particular problems are discussed in individual conferences.
   i. Circulate paper or ask for parents who will serve as resource people, etc.
   j. Invite parents to have refreshments, visit with each other, and look around the room. Thank them for coming.[15]

In addition to the get acquainted conference, a large-group conference is an appropriate setting for explaining new policies and changes in previous policies, for introducing new program services, and for outlining and explaining new methods or curricular content. The large-group conference is also an excellent medium for sampling parents' opinions about and attitudes toward the program.

Small-Group Conferences.   Three or four parents can be invited to a small-group conference, for which a topic may or may not be predetermined. In small-group conferences without predetermined topics, each parent might describe a situation that bothers him in relation to his own child. The staff members and other parents can discuss the situation and make suggestions. The director might invite an authority to lead the discussion on a topic selected by interested parents or by the program director. Observation of the program before the conference is another stimulus to discussion. Small-group conferences help parents who feel uneasy in an individual or large-group conference and reassure them that others have similar problems.

Scheduled Individual Conferences.   Based on the point of view that parental rights and responsibilities must not be usurped or violated by the early childhood program, individual parent-staff conferences help the parent know what is going on in the program and how his child is developing. Although the conference setting may be informal, parents can expect staff members to discuss in depth the program's objectives and methodology and the child's life in the program. If the question or problem is not under the staff member's jurisdiction, she should direct the parent to appropriate channels, so the question or problem can be properly handled. Suggestions for preparing and conducting individual conferences are to:

1. Send out a brief newsletter explaining what individual conferences are, what parents can contribute, and what staff members hope to accomplish as a result of the conferences. The point of the conference is to share with parents the ways the staff is helping the child meet program objectives and to elicit parental concerns for the child. If certain topics are to be covered, inform the parents.[16] It is necessary to send a newsletter if information about scheduled individual conferences is included in the handbook.
2. Specify appointment times and invite parents to make an appointment; for example:

Dear _____ ,

   Let's get together and talk. I would like to discuss with you:

   1. Bedtime _____   5. Sharing toys _____

   2. Breakfast _____   6. General

   3. Bathroom habits _____   adjustment _____

   4. Crying _____   7. _____

   Please list below some of the things you would like to talk to me about.

   _____

   _____

   _____

   A babysitter will be available for your enrolled child and younger children. Please indicate the day(s) and time(s) you could come for a twenty minute conference by circling one or more of the following time periods:

Oct. 7 Mon.	Oct. 8 Tues.	Oct. 9 Wed.	Oct. 10 Thurs.	Oct. 11 Fri.
3:00–3:20	3:00–3:20	3:00–3:20	3:00–3:20	3:00–3:20
3:30–3:50	3:30–3:50	3:30–3:50	3:30–3:50	3:30–3:50
4:00–4:20	4:30–4:20	4:00–4:20	4:00–4:20	4:00–4:20
4:30–4:50	4:30–4:50	4:30–4:50	4:30–4:50	4:30–4:50
5:00–5:20	5:00–5:20	5:00–5:20	5:00–5:20	5:00–5:20
5:30–5:50	5:30–5:50	5:30–5:50	5:30–5:50	5:30–5:50

I will confirm a time for your appointment.

Sincerely,

_____

(Staff member's signature)

3. Construct a schedule of appointments, allowing a few minutes break between each conference to jot down notes and prepare for the next conference.[17] Although the example schedule is designed for 20-minute conferences, many find 30 minutes minimal to cover the purposes of the conference and to avoid an assembly-line appearance.
4. Confirm the conference time with each responding parent.
5. In your letter requesting parents to make appointments, explain whether they are to bring their enrolled child and other young children. If an aide or volunteer can baby-sit, more parents may be able to participate in an individual conference.
6. Provide an attractive, private place for the conference. The staff member should not sit behind a desk. It might be advantageous to hold the conference in some parent's home rather than in the school. (Individual conferences with all parents in one home is not to be confused with the home visit.)
7. Provide early-arriving parents with a place to wait and have an aide or parent volunteer chat with them until time for the conference. If no one can wait with them, provide professional or popular reading material.[18]
8. Have a clear picture of the child in terms of the objectives of your program. Also, list information to collect from parents; for example, you may want to obtain a developmental history of the child. Plan to elicit parental concerns for the child early in the conference. Stein[19] found these types of questions helpful in working with parents: What were your worries and fears as a child? The discussion of childhood memories may lead to a discussion of their children's feelings and the expression of these feelings.

When did the child's trouble start? Most parents find that trouble starts when the child starts walking and yelling "No!" It is helpful for parents to learn to laugh at their child's behavior and to know that all children behave in similar ways. How did your infant show you that he was a healthy, happy child? When parents respond by saying that the infant smiled, cooed, and so forth, they can be led to see that the child's "No!" is a step toward independence. What type of guidance do you think your child will respond to favorably? Usually, the parents' answers can be translated into these principles of child rearing: Children need and want limits; therefore, parents have to set up certain rules and regulations which they can stick to. Children also need some freedom and a chance to make occasional choices. If we give them these, it is easier for them to obey the necessary rules. Children will obey better when they know the reasons for the rules set by their parents. Children need praise, and they will do better if we praise them for the things they do well. It is easier for children to obey when rules are geared to developmental stages.[20]

9. Greet parents cordially. Explain what you are doing with and for the child. In talking about the child, use your file of anecdotal and achievement records and samples of the child's work. Point out strengths or positive areas first, then weaknesses.

10. Never put the parent on the defensive. Negative expressions will often do so; for example, instead of calling a child a "troublemaker," say he "disturbs others by . . . ." A staff member needs to recognize the attitudes a parent may take when his child is having problems, so the staff member does not respond argumentatively. The most frequent defensive attitudes a parent has are projection and denial. In projection, the parent insists the problem must be that the staff member doesn't know how to handle the child. In denial, the parent considers the problem small or feels the child is just active or going through a state. With either defensive attitude, the parent is protecting himself from the possibility that he has failed in some way, or that he doesn't know what to do.[21]

11. Be careful about talking down to parents, using educational jargon, or giving long-winded, complicated explanations. Conduct conferences in the parent's native tongue, using a translator, if necessary.

12. Do not expect to have an answer to every problem and do not expect parents to solve all problems. Decisions should be reached during the discussion by: listening to parents' suggestions for solving the problem; offering suggestions; suggesting referral to special services, if necessary; and making arrangements to follow through. Follow-up is most important. If the parent knows he has your help he will not feel helpless.

13. Practice professional ethics. Respect parents' confidences and do not belittle the director of the program, other staff members, other families, or other children.

14. Do not make the parent feel rushed; however, in fairness to waiting parents, conferences must end on schedule. If necessary, the parent can make another appointment to continue the discussion.

15. Make notes on the conference and file them in the child's folder.

Nonscheduled Individual Conferences.   Unlike large-group, small-group, and scheduled individual conferences, which are usually staff-initiated and noted on the program calendar, nonscheduled conferences may be initiated by parent or staff member and held when the need arises. These conferences should be encouraged for any number of reasons: learning more about the program, questioning the meaning of activities observed, or dicsussing a present or foreseeable problem.

If the staff member initiates the conference to discuss a child's problems (and certainly many conferences have been initiated for that reason only!), he should have suggestions to give parents for solving a problem. It is most important that the staff member begin and end the conference on a positive note. In discussing a problem, the staff member should show evidence to support his statements and use tact. Finally, the staff member and parent should concentrate on one or two suggestions, not a long list.[22]

Home Visits.   Home visits demonstrate acknowledgement of the home as a source of change in children's lives. Jones[23] identifies four roles or combinations of roles a staff member can use in making home visits: (1) the *teacher-expert*, who enlists parental help by teaching the parent how to teach the child; (2) the *teacher-learner*, who seeks information from the parent about the child, such as the child's abilities and interests; (3) the *student-researcher*, who questions parents about their beliefs about child rearing; and (4) the *bringer of gifts*, who, like the *teacher-expert*, enlists parental help in the educative process but who brings, in addition to instructional procedures, materials such as games, books, and toys. There are several advantages to home visits: (1) the staff member is seen as a person who cares enough about a child to visit his family. (2) the staff member may obtain valuable information about the child that will help in meeting program objectives for that child; (3) children are proud because their teacher came to see them; (4) the staff member sees the child in his home environment; (5) at home, the parent is more likely to do the talking; conversely, at the program's facility the staff member is likely to do more talking; (6) the staff member can note alternative courses of child rearing open to the parents rather than just criticizing; (7) if a home visit is made prior to enrollment, there may be fewer tears shed on the first day; and (8) the staff member is seen as "just an individual" when he makes home visits. (Home visitation for the purpose of parent education will be discussed later in the chapter.)

Parent Visitation.   Parent visitation helps make parent-staff conferences more meaningful. The parent has the opportunity to observe the program and to see his child functioning in the program with peers and adults. The staff member has the opportunity to observe parent-child interaction in the program setting and the parent's expressed attitudes toward the program. When a parent visits the room, the staff member or a volunteer and the visitor's child should greet the parent. The parent can watch various groups of children engaging in activities, or may even initiate an activity, such as reading a story. If a parent wants to see his child in action without the child's knowledge, invite the parent to use the observation room or gallery.

Parents should be encouraged to visit the program; however, many parents do not visit unless their children have special problems. Sending a special invitation often results in more visitations and may even initiate greater involvement in the program; for example:

Dear Parents,

The PTA will meet on Tuesday, October 8, at 3:00 P.M. Won't you try to attend? The program will be on "Children's Phobias." Before the PTA meeting, our kindergarten class would like you to visit us at 2:00 P.M. Won't you please visit our class, and then we can attend PTA as a group? A babysitter will be available for your enrolled child and younger children.

Sincerely,

_____

(Teacher's signature)

"Open House" is a parent visitation in which parents and other family members view samples of the children's work, (e.g., art work, stories children have "written," and block structures they have built), examine equipment and materials, and visit with staff members and other guests. It is held at a time when the program is not in session. Here is an example of an invitation to an open house:

Dear Parents,

We are having Open House, Thursday, October 24, at 7:30 P.M. Examples of your child's work will be on display. We hope you will come and see some of the things your child has done in school.

We will be looking forward to visiting with you. Refreshments will be served in the auditorium.

Sincerely,

_____

(Staff member's signature)

Telephone Conversations. These may be initiated by either parent or staff member. A parent may use telephone conversations to help staff members better understand his child during the day. Perhaps the child was sick during the night, is worried, or is excited. Some parents may be more at ease talking over the telephone than in a face-to-face encounter.

Staff members can use telephone conversations as a means of making a positive contact, which can serve as a pleasant event for the child, too. These are examples of positive telephone contacts:

1. The staff member explains to the parent something interesting or successful the child did; parents are then able to reinforce the child immediately.
2. The staff member can call to inquire about the health of family members.[24]

Other Methods. There are several other methods of aiding parent-staff cooperation. A short note praising a child's effort can be sent to the parent. Newman[25] gives this example:

_____ is a good helper. She helped her friend put the blocks away.

When staff members have casual contacts with parents outside of school, the contacts should be friendly, and never used for serious conferences. A shopping center or a community affair is not the place for a conference. If a parent wants to talk about his child, the staff member should suggest an appointment time.

A newsletter can be sent home on a regular or irregular basis. It can be duplicated and sent to each parent via the child. A newsletter helps the parent communicate with his child and develops a liaison between staff members and parents.[26] Information that might be included in newsletters are announcements about the program or about daily or special activities in the program; suggestions for home-learning activities and methods that may be conducive to learning; information on new books, play materials, and television shows for children; articles to help parents; announcements about community events; and ideas for summer fun. The following is an example of a newsletter to parents about television:

Dear Parents,

Television plays a big part in your child's life. He enjoys watching television in his spare time. Of course, it is important that he does not stay "glued" to the TV. Playing outside in the fresh air, visiting with his friends, looking at books, and getting to bed early are important.

> Because there are many TV shows which are educational and enjoyable, television can be a wise use of some leisure time. Each week I will send home a schedule of some shows from which your child might profit. Your child might tune in these shows if they are convenient for your family.
>
> Sincerely,
>
> _____
>
> (Staff member's signature)

An excellent example of a newsletter format is found in:

Harms, T.O., and Cryer, D. "Parent Newsletter: A New Format." *Young Children* 33 (1978): 28–32.

Some schools have tried materials workshops for parents and staff members. In a materials workshop, parents and staff members analyze instructional materials for concepts and develop original equipment and material for presenting these instructional concepts.[27] Workshops may also be held in the evening for doing repair jobs on the building and grounds or on equipment and materials.

Program objectives were communicated to parents in the New Rochelle prekindergarten program when parents were present for their children's pretesting; thus, parents saw the objectives the teacher would pursue during the program.[28] Social meetings, such as picnics for the whole family, a coffee for parents, or a mother's or father's recognition night stimulate good relationships between parents and staff members. Sending cards or notes when a child has a birthday or is ill or when a parent is ill show that staff members care. Parents can be given feedback on the child's progress when they drop off or pick up their children; this is also a good time for staff and parents to get to know one another as people.

Parent Participation

Involvement with parents includes parental participation in the program. The early childhood program must initiate and maintain programs that enlist the worthwhile services and resources of the community. Parents and other community citizens must feel the program is their own, and not off limits. Early childhood programs must revise the old conception of the parent's role as exclusively a guest at a holiday presentation, homeroom mother, or field trip supervisor.

Parents as Members of Planning and Advisory Groups.   Many include parents as well as other community citizens as members of planning and advisory groups. Including parents in planning and advisory groups is in accordance with democratic principles of citizen's rights and responsibilities in formulating public policy, works as a two-way public relations committee, and constitutes a partnership between professional and nonprofessional.

Parent involvement is a major component of the Head Start program. Parents are considered major contributors to the program and to their communities. Parents are specifically involved in making decisions concerning program planning and operations, and serve as members of Head Start policy groups such as Head Start Center Committee, Head Start Policy Committee, and Head Start Policy Council.[29]

Most state licensing laws require that a nonprofit, private early childhood organization operate under a governing board composed, at least in part, of the people it serves, and public school early childhood programs are under the jurisdiction of the local board of education or trustees, an elected, policy-making group representing the community's interests.

For parents to be effective members of planning and advisory groups, these committees and councils must have the following characteristics:

1. The committee or council must be an educational group, not a pressure group. Although politically-minded individuals may serve on the committee or advisory council, their input should not necessarily be considered the thinking of the majority.

2. The director must show members of the committee or council how a decision will affect the program, and make sure parents have appropriate information on which to base their decisions. Parents must then have input into the decision-making process, because one cannot convince parents to become involved if the most important decisions have already been made—for example, decisions regarding goals of the program, the program's delivery system, staffing policies, fiscal matters, and program evaluation.

3. The parents and all other board members must be trained. Programs have failed because of problems at the committee or council level. Training must be given in identifying problems, investigating possible solutions, understanding regulations, learning decision-making processes, and communicating recommendations to the power structure.

4. The committee or council must be small enough to be manageable (twelve or fewer members), and membership should be rotational.

Several programs with effective parent participation in policy making are:

Freedom School for Young Black Children
Dr. Martin Luther King Family Center
Institute for Juvenile Research
124 North Hoyne Avenue, Apt. 113
Chicago, Ill.

National Capital Child Daycare Association
1020 3rd Street, N.W. and 14th and Independence Avenue, S.W.
Washington, D.C. 20001

New Rochelle Prekindergarten Program
60 Union Avenue
New Rochelle, N.Y. 10801

Preschool Program, Oakland Unified School District
Children's Center Preschool Programs
831 East 14th St.
Oakland, Calif.

Parents as Volunteers. Parents can also participate as volunteers, on a regular, semiregular, or occasional basis. For a volunteer program to work, the administrator must support the program by providing general guidance in planning, although parents can organize and operate the program itself. In effective programs, all parents are given a change to participate, a choice of roles, and the freedom to determine the extent of their participation. Some parents will choose not to participate.

Programs that have used volunteers successfully include:

A Demonstration Project in Group Care of Infants and Toddlers
The Institute for Child and Family Development
The University of North Carolina at Greensboro
Greensboro, N.C. 27412

Omaha Parent-Child Center
1702 Grace Street
Omaha, Neb. 68110

Parent-Child Educational Centers[30]

Parent Cooperative Nursery School[31]

Thayer Lindsley Nursery
Robbins Speech and Hearing Clinic
Emerson College
168 Beacon Street
Boston, Mass. 02116

Program and Nonprogram Volunteers. Parents are valuable as program volunteers because they know and understand parents' working hours, transportation situations, and community mores; they can serve as cultural models for the children; help staff members understand the children's likes and dislikes, strengths and weaknesses, and home successes and failures; act as interpreters in bilingual programs; assist staff members in program activities such as storytelling, art, music, and gardening; assist in positive control of the children by understanding the values of positive guidance, by using consistent, positive reinforcement and kindness, and by solving minor concerns before they develop into major disciplinary problems; accompany staff members in home-visitation programs; and serve as ambassadors to the neighborhood. Specific expectations of volunteers should be determined by the program's needs and the volunteers' abilities. Some basic considerations are as follows:

1. Volunteers should have an orientation to the program's facility and staff, to professional ethics, and to state and local laws regarding personnel qualifications and activities. Orientation could include a broad overview of the program's philosophy and objectives, rules and regulations, specific tasks and limits of responsibility, classroom management (if involved with children), and a "hands on" experience with materials. Their response to the orientation will benefit future programs.
2. Staff members should be oriented toward using volunteers. After orientation, staff members should be given a choice of whether or not to use volunteers.
3. A handbook is helpful for staff and volunteers, reiterating much of the information given during the orientation program.

4. The staff member should plan specific activities for the volunteer. Teaching activities require most careful planning; the staff member should set up the activities for the volunteers so that only one child or a small group of children works with the parent volunteer at one time; and, before demonstrating teaching techniques, the staff member should briefly explain the rationale for and the plan of the activity, the material to be used, and the expected learnings.
5. The volunteer must be evaluated by the administration and staff, and should be encouraged to discuss his involvement.

Parents can serve as nonprogram volunteers as lunchroom workers, aides to program nurses, aides in the library-media center, assistants in distributing equipment and materials, workers in transportation services, office workers, and as resource people to locate or gather services or items.

Parents as Occasional Volunteers. Many parents cannot serve as volunteers on a regular or semiregular basis; however, they often can and are willing to help on several occasions during the year. They may be needed for transportation and/or supervisory services on field trips, and can be invited to volunteer by letter:

Dear Parents,

We are planning a trip by bus to the zoo on Thursday, April 4.

We need at least four parents to go with us as guides. Would you please help us? We will be leaving the building at 9:00 A.M. and will return at 1:30 P.M. If you can go with us, please let us know by April 2.

Yours truly,

_____

(Staff member's signature)

Parents often help with class celebrations, if invited:

Dear Parents,

Our kindergarten class is planning five parties this year. The parties will be for Halloween, Thanksgiving, Christmas, Valentine's Day, and Easter. I hope that you will be able to help with one of them. We will need refreshments consisting of cupcakes or cookies and something to drink. If you want to help with a party, please indicate which one.

Sincerely,

_____

(Staff member's signature)

They can also help with money-raising projects:

Dear Parents,

Our kindergarten will be having a bake sale on Friday, April 26, from 10:00 A.M. until noon. The sale will be at the end of the hall in our school. The money made from the sale will be used to buy materials for our room.

We need our parents to make cookies, fudge, cupcakes, brownies, popcorn balls, and just anything else that is good to eat. Your children will love to help you prepare the goodies. Everything must be cut in servings and wrapped individually. If you can help, will you please send a note to me stating "what type" and "how many" goodies you plan to make.

We also need several parents to help us sell our goodies. If you will be able to help, please send a note to me at school. You will need to be at the school around 9:15 A.M. to help prepare for the bake sale.

Thanks so much for helping in any way you can.

Sincerely,

_____

(Teacher's signature)

Parents can serve as resource persons, since they frequently enjoy sharing their talents with young children. Survey parents for their special talents and encourage them to participate in your program. Ask parents to serve as resource persons representing various occupations and hobby groups.

Parent Education

Parent education has had a long and exciting history.[32] Parent education and home visitations began early in the century as a way to help immigrants. The Children's Bureau was founded in 1913 to eradicate some child labor practices, but began to publish materials on child rearing, most of it middle-class oriented.

Parent education for the middle class thrived in the 1920s with the development of the Progressive Education Movement. Many parent and lay programs were developed during this period, such as the child study movement, the Parent-Teachers Association, mental health associations, and parent cooperative nursery schools. In the 1960s, the shift of emphasis was away from the middle class. Parent education became part of the intervention programs set up with federal monies, and today, a great deal of effort is expended on evaluating parent education programs.

PURPOSES OF PARENT EDUCATION

The basic assumption of parent education is that if the parent's role as teacher is enhanced, the parent will be able to help maximize the child's level of functioning. Reisman[33] listed certain family-related factors that contribute to inadequate school performance: (1) the absence of an "educational tradition" in the home; (2) lack of motivation to pursue the long-range educational program required for many careers; (3) poor self-concept; (4) displeasure with schools and educators; and (5) uncorrected health problems, malnutrition, and a noisy, disorganized home environment. Parents communicate their expectations and attitudes about education, which in turn shapes the child's expectations and attitudes. Garber and Ware[34] believe these expectations and attitudes may be the single most important influence on the intelligence quotient. Finally, extreme family inadequacy is present at all socioeconomic levels as indicated by the present incidence of child abuse.[35]

Specific purposes of parent education are to:

1. Learn more about child growth and development;
2. Develop general concepts of effective child rearing practices;
3. Acquire an understanding of the philosophy, objectives, and methodology of the early childhood program;
4. Become an important part of the educative process by expressing good attitudes about the program and staff and about education in general; reinforcing the child's achievement; providing continuity between activities at home and in the program; and extending the child's knowledge and skills; and
5. Increase education, formally and informally, and perhaps earning power, and develop self-confidence as a parent.

EFFECTS OF PARENT EDUCATION

Vast amounts of research have emphasized the importance of parent-child relationships in the early years of a child's life. Such research suggests that the influence of parental involvement at early ages significantly contributes to achievement motivation and other factors associated with educational success. The objectives of recent parent education programs are now being studied in terms of the impact on the growth and development of the child and the impact on parents, the type of delivery system used, and the temporal extensiveness of the program.

Impact on Child and Parent.   Some studies indicate a significant impact on the child's overall development.[36,37,38,39] Parent behavior influences early language and cognitive development, and perhaps later development.[40,41,42,43] Jencks[44] asserts that the home enviornment may be more important than the school on children's academic achievement. Although some believe we may be treating only symptoms, Goodson and Hess[45] found lasting effects of increased intellectual and academic functioning.

Delivery System.   Investigations assessing the effect of a parent education program found no discernible differences in children's intellectual functioning, but positive changes in the mother's attitudes.[46,47] One study did indicate that a parent education component is important if the child is to continue to benefit from the compensatory preschool program.[48] Another study found that parent education programs preceding a child's enrollment in a classroom-based program had the most potential for producing the greatest gains.[49]

There is literature concerning the effects of parent education programs that used home visits and others that used small-group work as the delivery systems; some findings are as follows:

1. Levenstein[50] found that her Toy Demonstration Project resulted in significant increases in the child's intellectual functioning.
2. Love et al.[51] found that children participating in Home Start performed better than nonparticipating children on tests of school readiness, language development, and task orientation. No significant differences were noted in dietary habits or immunizations.
3. The Demonstration and Research Center for Early Education (DARCEE) Home Visitor Program[52] was successful in raising children's motor and intellectual functioning. Because of "vertical diffusion," children other than the target-age child also benefited from the parent's training.
4. Karnes, Teska, Hodgins, and Badger[53] designed a weekly, two-hour, small-group program. At the end of the two-year program, the experimental-group children scored higher in intellectual functioning, but there was no intrafamily diffusion.
5. Badger, Elsass, and Sutherland[54] compared the effectiveness of an intensive group parent education model with a less intensive home visitor

model. The group model proved very effective with adolescent mothers, because of its structure, specific directions, and peer support. On the other hand, home visit models appeared an equally potent delivery system for older mothers.

Negative results have been found in several cases. For example, Chilman[55] and White et al.[56] have noted that traditional parent programs involving case-work and community organization strategies have not been very effective. Lambie et al.[57] argue that "canned" objectives and activities must not be used; rather, objectives must be based on the needs and knowledge of specific groups of parents. There should also be a "match" to the existing parent-child relation-ship; for example, fathers were included in some activities of the Houston Parent Child Development Center, because of the father's instrumental role in the Chicano family. Lambie et al. summarized their research by stating that negative results occurred in programs with minimal treatment, high turnover rate of visitors, little supervision, and no or inappropriate objectives.

Temporal Extensiveness of Programs.   We do not know how extensive parent education programs must be to yield maximal and lasting results. Long-term consultation (that is, a minimum of 18 to 24 months) seems to produce the most significant effects.[58,59] Gordon and Guinagh,[60] in the Florida Parent-Infant Edu-cation Project, found that a home visitation program of less than two years was ineffective. Two years of home visitation and one year of participation in the home learning center was most effective in changing maternal attitudes toward schooling.

TYPES OF PARENT EDUCATION PROGRAMS

There are many types of parent education programs. Their nature depends on program needs, parental needs and wishes, and on program philosophy. For example, programs that use many parent volunteers need more emphasis on parent education, Spanish-speaking parents may need bilingual education, and some early childhood programs may want to train parents to reinforce the program's concepts and language models. Techniques may vary as well. Ser-vices for parents may be either staff-directed or parent-initiated; they may have one focus or be multifaceted; and they may be direct, using organized class-rooms, or indirect, with parents observing teaching and guidance techniques during program visitations. Programs may be sponsored by school systems, uni-versities, various community agencies, or handled through a cooperative, inter-agency approach.

Orientation Programs.   Perhaps the most common service for parents of chil-dren enrolled in an early childhood program is orientation to the program. Parents receive their orientation through handbooks for parents, by attending meetings, and by becoming members of parent-teacher associations. Most orien-tation programs are designed by the staff members in local programs; however, some materials on orientation of parents are available, such as the National

Education Association Publication workshop materials published under the title, *Parents and Teachers Together (for the Benefit of Children).*[61]

The Parent-Child Center (PCC) Program.　The PCC was developed in response to research on the importance of prenatal and infancy periods on a child's later development. The program, financed by the Office of Economic Opportunity and administered by the Washington office of Project Head Start, was designed to provide services to low-income families with children under 3.0 years, and to expectant mothers. The PCC objectives were to overcome physical, cognitive, and affective deficits; to improve parent skills, motivations, and confidence; to strengthen family organization; to encourage a community spirit; to provide training and experience for professionals and nonprofessionals; and to conduct research and evaluation of progress toward the above-stated objectives. Four major program components were developed: (1) programs for children including a home-visiting program, a home-care program, and a center-based program; (2) programs for parents in areas such as home economics, child development, adult education, and job counseling; (3) health and nutrition services, including medical services for children and their parents, classes in child care, safety, and nutrition; and (4) social services, such as referral, recreational, and assistance in finding adequate housing and in providing food and clothing.[62]

Home Visiting Programs.　Home visiting programs were designed to help parents learn how to teach their young children, including how to prepare and collect educational materials. In home visiting programs, a paraprofessional, often a trained parent, or a professional models the teaching/reinforcing style to parents in the home. The parent may later plan to teach the activities, because many program planners feel that parents should learn to set their own goals for their children. In some home visiting programs, parents are taught in groups without children present. After the group consultation, parents return home and present activities to their children. The exact nature of home visiting programs depends on the number of families to be visited, the number and frequency of visits per family, and the program's financial resources. Consider these programs:

1. *The home* visits at the Demonstration and Research Center for Early Education (DARCEE) project[63] were used as a supplement to Head Start and/or the first grade curriculum, or as the only intervention technique. Mothers received help once weekly in physical training and cognitive tasks. Gray's[64] study contrasting a preschool program with one taught by mothers showed equal effectiveness, but the home program was lower in cost and resulted in vertical diffusion to younger children in the family and horizontal diffusion to the neighborhood.

2. Gordon[65] presented materials and exercises to mothers, and the mothers also learned to make simple toys. Issues of *Life* and *Ebony* were taken to the homes for family reading materials and for use in picture identification.

3. Karnes's[66] program consisted of a weekly, two-hour program with mothers

of disadvantaged infants between 1.0 and 2.0 years. The mothers learned teaching principles for various educational toys. A mother-centered activity, such as a discussion of discipline techniques, was also part of the session.

4. The Ypsilanti Home Teaching Project[67] explored the feasibility of sending home tutors for the preschool child and of providing assistance with teaching techniques, language development, and child management for the mothers without an accompanying classroom project. The project was effective.

5. "Sesame Street" and other television programming, such as the Appalachian Preschool Project, is a major method of reaching children in their homes, and is thus a quasi-home visiting project.

There are excellent resources available for parent education:

Appalachian Educational Laboratory. *Home-Oriented Preschool Education: Home Visitors' Handbook.* Charleston, W.V.: AEL, 1972. ERIC ED 082 846.

Bell, T.H. *Your Child's Intellect: A Guide to Home-Based Preschool Education.* Salt Lake City, Utah: Olympus Publishing Company, 1972.

Coleman, L.V.; Smith, B.C.; and Hodges, W.L. *BOPTA Home-Instruction Manual: The Child Learns At Home.* Atlanta, Ga.: Department of Early Childhood, Georgia State University, 1972.

Levenstein, P. *Toy Demonstrator's "Visit" Handbook.* Mineola, NY: Family Service Association of Nassau County, 1969. ERIC ED 059 788.

Levenstein, P.; Adelman, H.; and Kochman, A. *Verbal Interaction Project: Manual for the Replication of the Mother-Child Home Program.* Mineola, N.Y.: Family Service Association of Nassau County, 1971. ERIC ED 059 790.

Snider, M. *Home-Oriented Preschool Education: Curriculum Planning Guide.* Charleston, W.V.: Appalachian Educational Laboratory, 1972. ERIC ED 082 848

Other materials may be obtained from:

Parenting Materials Information Center
Southwest Educational Development Laboratory
211 East 7th Street
Austin, TX 78701

Parent Discussion Programs.   In a discussion program, parents identify an area of concern, and a resource person knowledgeable in the area of concern leads a discussion group. The resource person must be able to relate information from theory and research to practice. Guidelines for developing parent discussion groups are found in the following sources;

Auerback, A.B. *Parents Learn Through Discussion: Principles and Practices of Parent Group Discussion.* New York: John Wiley & Sons, 1968.

Pickart, E., and Fargo, J. *Parent Education: Toward Parental Competence.* New York: Appleton-Century-Crofts, 1971.

These are specific programs that have been used successfully.

1. The Bowdoin Method[68] is a ten-lesson course focusing on the parent as a partner in the teaching process. Course materials include filmstrips, cassette tapes, educational games, and a manual.

2. Education for Parenthood[69] was designed by the office of Child Development in cooperation with the Office of Education to improve the competence of the adolescent for prospective parenthood. The course develops skills in the areas of health, educational, and affective needs of children through the use of materials and through interaction with young children.
3. Parent Effectiveness Training, developed by Gordon, is based on the idea of "listening," the expression of feelings, and a dialog between parent and child.[70]
4. Systematic Training for Effective Parenting (STEP) was developed by Dinkmeyer and McKay,[71] to help parents use democratic rather than autocratic methods of child rearing. Materials in the program include cassette tapes, a parent's handbook, discussion guide cards, posters, charts, invitational brochures, and a manual. Topics for the nine sessions are: (1) "Understanding Children's Behavior and Misbehavior"; (2) "Understanding How Children Use Emotions to Involve Parents"; and "The 'Good' Parent"; (3) "Encouragement"; (4) "Communication: Listening"; (5) "Communication: Exploring Alternatives and Expressing Your Ideas and Feelings to Children"; (6) "Developing Responsibility"; (7) "Decision Making for Parents"; (8) "The Family Meeting"; and (9) "Developing Confidence."

Parent discussion programs can be particularly beneficial to parents of handicapped children. Peer support helps these parents adjust to their children's handicaps, and to the problems of facing a seemingly endless number of "experts"—psychologists, physicians, and counselors—involved in decision making. These parents often need information about diagnosis, prognosis, and treatment of the handicap and management of the child. Several helpful resources include:

Bennett, L.M., and Henson, F.O., II. *Keeping in Touch with Parents: The Teacher's Best Friends.* Austin, Texas Learning Concepts, 1977.

Dardig, J.C., and Howard, W.L. *Sign Here: A Contracting Book for Children and Their Parents.* Bellevue, Wash. Edmark Associates, 1976.

D'Audney, W., ed. *Giving a Head Start to Parents of Handicapped.* Omaha, Neb.: Meyer Children's Rehabilitation Institute, 1976.

Stewart, J.C. *Counseling Parents of Exceptional Children.* Columbus, Ohio: Charles E. Merrill Publishing Company, 1978.

Resource Centers.   A rather popular type of resource center for children are toy lending libraries. The purposes of toy lending libraries are to help parents provide intellectual stimulation for their children with toys and to offer guidelines in using these toys. Nimnicht[72] set up a toy lending library to develop concepts and verbal fluency in children ages 3.0 to 9.0 years. The toys were loaned to parents who enrolled in an eight-week course. Specifics on establishing and operating a toy lending library may be found in:

McNelis, J.R. *A Practical Guide for Planning and Operating a Toy Lending Library.* Washington, D.C.: American Institute for Research, 1974. ERIC ED 145 962.

Adult resource centers have also been used for parent education. For example, in Montgomery County, Maryland, the Adult Education Department has established a Parent Education Resource Center. The facility has four areas: (1) a children's discovery corner with books and toys; (2) an adult area with publications of interest to parents; (3) an area for using multimedia equipment; and (4) a record and toy lending library.[73] Materials will be needed in the resource center to explain concepts of child development and early childhood education. For example, parents need to understand something of what children are like physically, cognitively, and affectively; what tasks the child is trying to accomplish, what experiences retard and facilitate development, and what evidence is indicative of progress. Parents are also concerned about the normality of certain behaviors or stages and the length of time each should last.

Parents need to understand the interacting influences of various aspects of development. Certain behaviors are incompatible; for example, toilet training is most difficult when a toddler is at the peak of his run about stage and doesn't want to sit, which is a necessity for toilet training. Other behaviors are compatible; for example, when the young child begins to imitate sounds in his physical environment, like those of motors and animals, he enjoys hearing stories and poems that have onomatopoeic words like buzz and hiss.

Parents need knowledge about several approaches to guiding a child based on the child's developmental stage. If parental demands are not geared to development, disharmony between adult and child results. If parent expectations are too low, the child sometimes shows permanently dependent behavior; if too high, the child displays agonizing frustration. Parents also need to understand the child's interests, what types of experiences are meaningful, and which play equipment and materials help the child develop. As parents become more enlightened, they can reinforce the practices of the early childhood program and can become more discriminating consumers of equipment and materials, movies and television shows, and other things marketed for children. The parent also needs help with the specific skills children should develop, with teaching techniques, such as activities, language models, questioning techniques, and reinforcement methods, and with teaching equipment and materials.

The following list of current materials will be of interest to parents, and should thus be part of an adult resource center:

Armstein, H.S. *The Roots of Love; Helping Your Child to Learn to Love in the First Three Years of Life.* Indianapolis, Ind.: Bobbs-Merrill Co., 1975.

Bell, T.H. *Active Parent Concern: A New Home Guide to Help Your Child Do Better in School.* Englewood Cliffs, N.J.: Prentice-Hall, 1976.

Bert, D.K. *The Parent as Teacher.* New York: Parents Magazine Films, 1975.

Brazelton, T.B. *Infants and Mothers.* New York: Delacorte Press, 1969.

————. *Toddlers and Parents. A Declaration of Independence.* New York: Delacorte Press, 1975.

Caldwell, B.M. *Home Teaching Activities.* Little Rock, Ark.: Center for Early Development, University of Arkansas, 1971.

Cheavens, F. *Creative Parenthood.* Word Books, Publisher, 1971.

Church, J. *Understanding Your Child From Birth to Three: A Guide to Your Child's Psychological Development.* New York: Random House, 1973.

Cole, A. et al. *Recipes for Fun.* Winnetka, Ill.: Parents as Resources Project, 1970.

————. *Workshop Procedure. A Comparison Guide to Recipes for Fun.* Winnetka, Ill.: Parents as Resources Project, 1970.

Dodson, F. *Dare to Discipline.* Wheaton, Ill.: Tyndale House Publishers, 1970.

————. *How to Parent.* New York: Signet Books, 1970.

Dreikurs, R. *The Challenge of Child Training: A Parent's Guide.* New York: Hawthorn Books, 1972.

————. *Coping with Children's Misbehavior: A Parent's Guide.* New York: Hawthorn Books, 1972.

Dreikurs, R., and Grey, L. *A Parent's Guide to Child Discipline.* New York: Hawthorn Books, 1970.

Dreikurs, R., and Cassel, P. *Discipline Without Tears.* New York: Hawthorn Books, 1972.

Dreikurs, R.; with Soltz, V. *Children: The Challenge.* New York: Hawthorne Books, 1964.

Eimers, R., and Artchson, R. *Effective Parents, Responsible Children: A Guide to Confident Parenting.* New York: McGraw-Hill Book Co., 1977.

Fisher, S., and Fisher, R.L. *What We Really Know About Child Rearing.* New York: Basic Books, 1976.

Fraiberg, S.H. *The Magic Years.* New York: Charles Scribner's Sons, 1959.

Ginnot, H. G. *Between Parent and Child.* New York: The Macmillan Co., 1965.

————. *Teacher and Child.* New York: The Macmillan Co., 1972.

Gordon, I.J. *Baby Learning Through Baby Play: Parent's Guide for the First Two Years.* New York: St. Martin's Press, 1970.

————. *The Infant Experience.* Columbus, Ohio: Charles E. Merrill Publishing Co., 1975.

Gordon, I.J. et al. *Child Learning Through Child Play: Learning Activities for Two- and Three-Year Olds.* New York: St. Martin's Press, 1972.

Jones, S. *Good Things For Babies.* Boston: Houghton-Mifflin Co., 1976.

Lamb, M. *The Role of the Father in Child Development.* New York: John Wiley & Sons, 1976.

Lane, M.B. *Education for Parenting.* Washington, D.C.: National Association for the Education of Young Children, 1975.

Lathrop, J.C. *Infant Care.* Washington, D.C.: U.S. Government Printing Office, 1973.

LeShan, E.J. *Natural Parenthood.* New York: The New American Library, 1970.

Levine, J.A. *Who Will Raise the Children? New Options for Fathers (and Mothers).* New York: J.P. Lippincott Co., 1976.

Lillie, D.L., with Trohanis, P.L. eds. *Teaching Parents to Teach.* New York: Walker and Co., 1976.

Lynn, D.B. *The Father: His Role in Child Development.* Monterey, Calif.: Brooks/Cole Publishing Co., 1974.

Maddox, B. *The Half Parent.* New York: M. Evans and Co., 1975.

Rabinowitz, M. *In the Beginning: A Parent Guide of Activities and Experiences for Infants from Birth to Six Months,* Book 1. New Orleans, La.: Parent Child Development Center, 1975.

Retting, E.B. *ABCs for Parents.* Van Nuys, Calif.: Associates for Behavior Change, 1973.

Segal, M. *You Are Your Baby's First Teacher.* Fort Lauderdale, Fla.: Nova University, 1973.

Spock, B. *Baby and Child Care.* New York: Pocket Books, 1968.

Stott, D.H. *The Parent as Teacher: A Guide for Parents of Children with Learning Difficulties.* Belmont, Calif.: Lear Siegler, Fearon Publishers,

Other resource materials are listed in:

Parenting in 1977
SEDL-PMIC
211 East 7th Street
Austin, Texas 78702

Parent Self-Improvement Programs.   Finally, services can include instruction for parent self-improvement in the areas of basic adult education, English for speakers of other languages, consumer education, nutrition, clothing, health, community resources, home repairs, and family life. Such instruction may be in the form of formal courses for high school credit or informal workshops, and are usually offered by the public school system for the benefit of all adult residents of a community. Several programs that have effective parent self-improvement components are:

Central Harlem Association of Montessori Parents, Inc. (CHAMP)
220 West 143rd St.
New York, N.Y. 10030

Community Cooperative Nursery School
Laurell Street
Menlo Park, Calif. 94025

Demonstration and Research Center for Early Education
George Peabody College for Teachers
Nashville, Tenn. 37203

Pre-School and Primary Education Department
State Department of Public Instruction and Welfare
Harrisburg, Pa. 17126

NOTES

1. John H Niemeyer, "Home-School Interaction," *Profile of The School Dropout*, ed. Daniel Schrieber (New York: Vintage Books, 1968), p. 352.
2. A.J. Mann, A. Harrell, and M. Hunt, *A Review of Head Start Research Since 1969, and an Annotated Bibliography* (Washington, D.C.: Social Research Group, the George Washington University, 1977).
3. Milton Babitz, "Parents in Early Childhood Education," *California Education* 3 (1966): 5.
4. Jeanne W. Quill, "Working with Parents," *Parents-Children-Teachers Communication* (Washington, D.C.: Assn. for Childhood Education International, 1969), p. 46.
5. M. Gerzon, *A Childhood for Every Child* (New York: E.P. Dutton and Co., 1973).
6. *The School Code of Illinois*, 1967, sec. 23-24, p. 253.
7. N. Edwards, *The Courts and the Public Schools*, rev. ed. (Chicago: University of Chicago Press, 1955), pp. 610–15.
8. *Baker v. Owen*, 395 F. 294 (M.D.N.C. 1975) aff'd per curiam 423 U.S. 907, 96 S. Ct. 210 (1975).
9. *Ingraham v. Wright*, 97 S. Ct. 1401 (1977).
10. Title IV of P.L. 90–247 (General Education Provision Act) Sec. 438, added by Sec. 513 P.L. 93–380 (August 21, 1974) and amended by Senate Joint Resolution (Sen. J. Res. 40) (1974).
11. National Committee for Citizens in Education (N.C.C.E.) was founded in 1962, but was called the National Committee for Support of the Public Schools until 1970. The Committee disseminates information, gives legal advice, and conducts "Citizens Training Institutes." For more information, the address is Wilde Lake Village Green, Suite 410, Columbia, Maryland 21044 or call toll free, 800 NETWORK.
12. National Association for Retarded Citizens (N.A.R.C.) was founded in 1950, but was called the National Association of Parents and Friends of Mentally Retarded Children until 1952 and the National Association for Retarded Children until 1974. For more information, the address is 2709 Avenue E, East, Arlington, Texas 76011.
13. I.J. Gordon, *Parental Involvement in Compensatory Education* (Urbana, Ill.: Published for the ERIC Clearinghouse on Early Childhood Education by the University of Illinois Press, 1970).
14. Sarah H. Leeper et al. *Good Schools for Young Children* (New York: The Macmillan Co., 1970), p. 388.
15. *Conference Time for Teachers and Parents* (Washington, D.C.: National School Public Relations Assn., 1961), pp. 14–19.
16. Ibid, p. 21.
17. Ibid, p. 22.
18. Ibid.
19. Lisa S. Stein, "Techniques for Parent Discussions in Disadvantaged Areas," *Young Children* 22 (1967): 210–17.
20. Ibid., p. 215.
21. Eleanor C. Crocker, "Depth Consultation with Parents," *Young Children* 20 (1964): 91–99.

22. *Conference Time*, pp. 23–24.

23. Elizabeth Jones, "Involving Parents in Children's Learning," *Childhood Education* 47 (1970): 126–30.

24. Lassar G. Gotkin, "The Telephone Call: The Direct Line from Teacher to Family." *Young Children* 24 (1968): 70–74.

25. Sylvia Newman, *Guidelines to Parent-Teacher Cooperation in Early Childhood Education* (New York: Book-Lab, 1971), p. 83.

26. Ibid., pp. 78–79.

27. Quill, "Working with Parents," p. 46.

28. A.E. Boehm, "One Model for Developing a Prekindergarten Assessment Program," *Exceptional Children* 37 (1971): 523–27.

29. *Federal Register*, 40 (126) (June 30, 1975).

30. H.E. Moore and I.W. Stott, *A Plan of Action for Parent-Child Educational Centers* (Tempe, Ariz.: Arizona State University, 1968). ERIC ED 027 959.

31. The Juniper Gardens Children's Project (Kansas City, Mo.: The Project, 1968).

32. S.M. Gruenberg, "Parent Education in Six White House Conferences," *Child Study* 37 (1959–1960): 9–15.

33. F. Riessman, *The Culturally Deprived Child* (New York: Harper & Row, Publishers, 1962) p. 4.

34. M. Garber and W.B. Ware, "Relationship Between Measures of Home Environment and Intelligence Scores" (Miami Beach, Fla.: Proceedings of the 78th Annual Convention of the American Psychological Association, 1970), pp. 647–48.

35. Report of the Joint Commission on Mental Health of Children, *Crises in Child Mental Health: Challenge for the 1970s* (New York: Harper & Row, Publishers, 1969), pp. 344–45.

36. I.J. Gordon, *Parental Involvement in Compensatory Education*.

37. E.S. Schaefer, "Learning From Each Other," *Childhood Education* 48 (1971): 2–7.

38. J.H. Stephens, Jr., "Current Directions in the Study of Parental Facilitation of Children's Cognitive Development," *Educational Horizons* 50 (1971–72): 62–66.

39. A.P. Streissguth and H. Bee, "Mother-Child Interactions and Cognitive Development in Children," *The Young Child: Reviews of Research*, Vol, II, ed. W.W. Hartup (Washington, D.C.: National Association for the Education of Young Children, 1972), pp. 158–83.

40. J. Rubenstein, "Maternal Attentiveness and Subsequent Exploratory Behavior of the Infant," *Child Development* 38 (1967): 1089–1100.

41. T. Moore, "Language and Intelligence: A Longitudinal Study of the First Eight Years. Part II: Environmental Correlates of Mental Growth," *Human Development* 11 (1968): 1–24.

42. J.W. Douglas, *The Home and the School. A Study of Ability and Attainment in the Primary School* (London: MacGibbon and Kee, 1964).

43. W. Fowler, "Cognitive Learning in Infancy and Early Childhood," *Psychological Bulletin* 59 (1962): 116–52.

44. C. Jencks et al., *Inequality: A Re-Assessment of the Effect of Family and Schooling in America* (New York: Basic Books, 1972).

45. B. Goodson and R. Hess, *Parents as Teachers of Young Children: An Evaluative Review of Some Contemporary Concepts and Programs* (Stanford, Calif.: Stanford University Press, 1975).

46. C. Adkins, *Programs of Head Start Parent Involvement in Hawaii* (New York: Paper presented at the meeting of the American Education Research Association, 1971).

47. M.B. Karnes, *Final Report: Research and Development Program on Preschool Disadvantaged Children* (Urbana, Ill.: Institute for Research on Exceptional Children, 1969).

48. N. Radin, *Three Degrees of Parent Involvement in a Preschool Program: Impact on Mother and Children* (Ann Arbor, Mich.: School of Social Work, University of Michigan, 1971).

49. U. Bronfenbrenner, *A Report on Longitudinal Evaluations of Preschool Programs, Vol. 2: Is Early Intervention Effective?* (Washington, D.C.: Department of Health, Education, and Welfare Publication No. (OHD) 74–25, 1974).

50. P. Levenstein, *A Message From Home: A Home-Based Intervention Method for Low-Income Preschoolers* (Mineola, N.Y.: Family Services Association of Nassau County, 1974). ERIC ED 095 992.

51. J.M. Love, M.J. Nauta, C.G. Coelen, K. Hewett, and R.R. Roupp, *National Home Start Evaluation: Final Report. Findings and Implications.* (Ypsilanti, Mich.: High Scope Educational Research Foundation and Abt Associates, 1976).

52. B. Gilmer, J.O. Miller, and S.W. Gray, *Intervention with Mothers of Young Children: Study of Intra-Family Effects* (Nashville, Tenn.: Demonstration and Research Center for Early Education, George Peabody College, 1970).

53. M.B. Karnes, J.A. Teska, A.S. Hodgins, and E.D. Badger, "Educational Intervention at Home by Mothers of Disadvantaged Infants," *Child Development* 41 (1970): 925–35.

54. E. Badger, S. Elsass, and J.M. Sutherland, *Mother Training as a Means of Accelerating Childhood Development in a High Risk Population* (Washington, D.C.: Paper presented at the Meeting for Pediatric Research, 1974). ERIC ED 104 522.

55. C.S. Chilman, "Programs for Disadvantaged Parents," *Review of Child Development Research,* Vol. III, ed. B.M. Caldwell and H.N. Riccuiti (Chicago, Ill.: Univeristy of Chicago Press, 1973) pp. 403–65.

56. S.H. White, M.C. Day, P.K. Freeman, S.A. Hantman, and K.P. Messenger. *Federal Programs for Young Children: Review and Recommendations. Vol. II: Review of Evaluation Data for Federally Sponsored Projects for Children* (Cambridge, Mass.: Huron Institute, 1973).

57. D.Z. Lambie, J.T. Bond, and D.P. Weikart, *Home Teaching with Mothers and Infants* (Ypsilanti, Mich.: High Scope Educational Research Foundation, 1974).

58. I.J. Gordon and B.J. Guinagh, *A Home Learning Center Approach to Early Stimulation, Final Report* (Gainesville, Fla.: Institute for Development of Human Resources, Florida University, 1974). ERIC ED 115 388.

59. P. Levenstein, *A Message From Home: A Home-Based Intervention Method for Low Income Preschoolers.*

60. I.J. Gordon and B.J. Guinagh, *A Home Learning Center Approach to Early Stimulation, Final Report.*

61. *Parents and Teachers Together (for the Benefit of Children)* (Washington, D.C.: National Education Assn. Publication, 1973).

62. *Parent and Child Centers* (Washington, D.C.: Office of Economic Opportunity, OEO Phamplet 6108–11, 1969), Forward and Introduction.

63. S.W. Gray and R.A. Klaus, "The Early Training Project: A Seventh Year Report," *Child Development* 41 (1970): 909–24.

64. S.W. Gray, *Home Visiting Programs for Parents of Young Children* (Boston: Paper presented at the meeting of the National Association for the Education of Young Children, 1970).

65. I. Gordon, *Early Stimulation Through Parent Education: Final Report* (Gainesville, Fla.: University of Florida, 1969). ERIC ED 033 912.

66. M.B. Karnes et al., *An Approach for Working with Mothers of Disadvantaged Children: A Pilot Project* (Urbana, Ill.: University of Illinois, 1968). ERIC ED 017 335.

67. D. Weikart and D.Z. Lambie, "Preschool Intervention Through Home Teaching Program," *Disadvantaged Child,* Vol. II, ed. J. Hellmuth. (New York: Brunner/Maxel, 1968), pp. 435–500.

68. R. Bowdin, *The Bowdin Method* (Nashville, Tenn.: Webster's International Tutoring Systems, 1976).

69. *Education for Parenthood.* (Washington, D.C.: Office of Child Development, Department of Health, Education, and Welfare, 1972).

70. T. Gordon, *Parent Effectiveness Training* (New York: Peter H. Wyden, Publishers, 1970).

71. D. Dinkmeyer and G.D. McKay, "Systematic Training for Effective Parenting," *Leader's Manual* (Circle Pines, Minn.: American Guidance Service, 1976).

72. G.P. Nimnicht and E. Brown, "The Toy Library: Parents and Teachers Learning with Toys," *Young Children* 27 (1972): 110–17.

73. P. Edmiston, "Establishing a Parent Education Resource Center," *Young Children* 54 (1977): 62–66.

For Further Reading

American Association of Elementary-Kindergarten-Nursery Educators. *Parents: Active Partners in Education.* Washington, D.C.: National Education Association, 1971.

Applegate, Maureen. *Everybody's Business—Our Children.* Evanston, Ill.: Row, Peterson, and Co., 1952.

Auerback, A.B. *Parents Learn Through Discussion: Principles and Practices of Parent Group Education.* New York: John Wiley and Sons, 1968.

————. *Trends and Techniques in Parent Education.* New York: Child Study Press, 1960.

Bailey, Virginia, and Strang, Ruth. *Parent-Teacher Conferences.* New York: McGraw-Hill Book Co., 1964.

Batelle Memorial Institute. *Early Childhood Development Programs and Services: Planning for Action.* Washington, D.C.: National Association for the Education of Young Children, 1972.

Becker, W.C. *Parents are Teachers.* Bellevue, Wash.: Edmark Associates, 1971.

Brock, H.C., III. *Parent Volunteer Programs in Early Childhood Education.* Hamden, Conn.: Shoe String Press, 1976.

Butler, A.L. *Current Research in Early Childhood Education: A Compilation and Analysis for Program Planners.* Washington, D.C.: American Association of Elementary-Kindergarten-Nursery Educators, 1970.

Cansler, D.P., and Martin, G.H., eds. *Working With Families: A Manual for Developmental Centers.* Washington, D.C.: Office of Education, Bureau of Education for the Handicapped, Chapel Hill Training-Outreach Project, 1974.

Chilman, C.S. "Some Angles on Parent-Teacher Learning." *Childhood Education* 48 (1971): 119–25.

Conference Time for Teachers and Parents: A Parent's Guide to Successful Conference Reporting. Washington, D.C.: National Public Relations Assn., 1970.

Cooper, J.C. *Parenting: Strategies and Educational Methods.* Columbus, Ohio: Charles E. Merrill Publishing Company, 1978.

Early Childhood Programs in the States: Report on a December 1972 Conference. Denver, Colo.: Educational Commission of the States, 1973.

Fullmer, Daniel, and Bernard, Harold W. *Family Consultation.* Palo Alto, Calif.: Houghton Mifflin Co., 1968.

Gilkerson, Elizabeth. *Teacher-Child-Parent Relationships.* New York: Early Childhood Education Council of New York, 1969.

Gordon, I.J. "Developing Parent Power." In *Critical Issues in Research Related to Disadvantaged Children,* edited by E. Grothberg. New Jersey: Educational Testing Service, 1969.

————. *Parental Involvement in Compensatory Education.* Urbana, Ill.: Published for the ERIC Clearinghouse on ECE by the University of Illinois Press, 1970.

Hess, R.D; Block, M.; Costello, J.; Knowles, R.T.; and Largay, D. "Parent Involvement in Early Education." In *Day Care: Resources for Decisions,* edited by E. Grothberg. Washington, D.C.: Day Care and Child Development Council of America, 1971. Pp. 265–98.

Hess, R.D.; Beckman, L.; Knowles, R.T.; and Miller, R. "Parent Training Programs and Community Involvement in Day Care." In *Day Care: Resources for Decisions,* edited by E. Grothberg. Washington, D.C.: Day Care and Child Development of America, 1971. Pp. 299–312.

Hess, R.D., and Shipman, V.C. "Early Experience and the Socialization of the Cognitive Modes in Children." *Child Development* 36 (1965): 869–86.

Hoffman, D.R.; Jordan, J.S.; and McCounich, F. *Parent Participation in Preschool Daycare.* Washington, D.C.: National Center for Educational Research and Development,

Department of Health, Education, and Welfare, and Office of Education, 1971. ERIC ED 054 863.

Honig, A.S. *Parent Involvement in Early Childhood Education.* Washington, D.C.: National Association for the Education of Young Children, 1975.

Hymes, James L., Jr. *Effective Home-School Relations.* New York: Prentice-Hall, 1953.

Ilg, Frances L., and Ames, Louise B. *The Gesell Institute's Parents Ask.* New York: Dell Publishing Co., 1975.

Kremer, B. *Parent Education: Abstract Bibliography.* Urbana, Ill.: Educational Resources Information Center, Clearinghouse on Early Childhood Education, 1971.

Kroth, R.L. *Communicating with Parents of Exceptional Children.* Denver, Colo.: Love Publishing Company, 1975.

Langdon, Grace, and Stout, Irving W. *Teacher-Parent Interviews.* Englewood Cliffs, N.J.: Prentice-Hall, 1954.

Levenstein, P. "Learning Through (and From) Mothers." *Childhood Education* 48 (1971): 130–34.

Lillie, D.L. *Parent Programs in Child Development Centers.* Washington, D.C.: Day Care and Child Development Council, 1972.

Lillie, D.L., and Trohanis, P.L., eds. *Teaching Parents to Teach.* New York: Walker and Company for Technical Assistance Development System, the University of North Carolina at Chapel Hill, 1976.

McBride, A.B. *The Growth and Development of Mothers.* Scranton, Pa.: Harper and Row Publishers, 1973.

Mechan, W.M. *Introduction to Child Development and Parent Education.* New York: Vantage Press, 1969.

Miller, Gordon W. *Educational Opportunity and the Home.* London: Hazell Watson and Viney, 1971.

Mok, Paul P. *Pushbutton Parents and the Schools.* New York: Dell Publishing Co., 1964.

Morrison, G.S. *Parent Involvement in the Home, School, and Community.* Columbus, Ohio: Charles E. Merrill Publishing Co., 1978.

Newman, Sylvia. *Guidelines to Parent-Teacher Cooperation in Early Childhood Education.* New York: Book-Lab, 1971.

Parents-Children-Teachers: Communication. Washington, D.C.: Assn. for Childhood Education International, 1969.

Pickarts, E.M., and Fargo, G. *Parent Education: Toward Parental Competence.* New York: Appleton-Century-Crofts, 1971.

Public Relations Ideas for Classroom Teachers. Washington, D.C.: National School Public Relations Assn. in cooperation with the Assn. of Classroom Teachers, National Education Assn., 1964.

Radkin, N. *Three Degrees of Parent Involvement in a Preschool Program: Impact on Mothers and Children.* Washington, D.C.: Bureau of Elementary and Secondary Education, Department of Health, Education, and Welfare, Office of Education, 1971. ERIC ED 052 831.

Reeves, Charles W. *Parents and the School.* Washington, D.C.: Public Affairs Press, 1963.

Schaefer, E.S. "Learning from Each Other." *Childhood Education* 48 (1971): 2–7.

———. "Need for Early and Continuing Education." In *Education of the Infant and Young Child,* edited by V.M. Denenberg. New York: Academic Press, 1970.

Streissguth, A.P., and Bee, H. "Mother-Child Interactions and Cognitive Development in Children." In *The Young Child: Reviews of Research*, Vol. II, edited by W.W. Hartup. Washington, D.C.: National Association for the Education of Young Children, 1972. Pp. 158–83.

Wagonseller, B.R. et al. *The Art of Parenting*. Bellevue, Wash.: Edmark Associates, 1979.

Weikart, O.P. "Learning Through Parents: Lessons for Teachers." *Childhood Education* 48 (1971) 135–37.

Working with Parents-A Guide for Classroom Teachers and Other Educators. Washington, D.C.: National School Public Relations Assn. in cooperation with the Assn. of Classroom Teachers, National Education Assn., 1968.

13

Assessing, Recording, and Reporting Children's Progress

Assessing, recording, and reporting children's progress is one of the most controversial aspects of program development for young children. Among the various types of early childhood programs, there is perhaps greater diversity in the area of assessment than in almost any other aspect of the programs. The controversy revolves around (1) the purposes of evaluation and the methods used in assessment; (2) the staff time spent in recording children's progress, the possibility that records will negatively typecast children, and indiscriminate release and use of information about children and their families; and (3) the problem of what and how much to communicate to parents who are not professionally trained in interpreting assessment results and who are emotionally involved in their children's development. At the same time, assessing, recording, and reporting children's progress serve as a basis for many worthwhile functions, such as planning and implementing all program services, guiding each child's development, and communicating with parents, public, and regulatory agencies.

Assessing

Assessment involves three separate processes. First is the gathering of qualitative and quantitative evidence, by whatever method, such as writing an anecdotal record or administering a paper and pencil test. Second is processing the evidence so as to permit formation of value judgments, perhaps by using anecdotal records to write a case study or converting a raw score into a percentile. Third is making decisions based on these value judgments. Thus, assessment goes beyond measurement, grading, or classifying. Whether using informal methods such as observation, interviews, samples of children's work, and staff-contructed tests and/or standardized tests, the nature of the evidence gathered should be in keeping with the local program's objectives. In short assessment should ultimately improve the chances of obtaining the program's objectives.

Assessment of progress should be used to help boards of directors or education and staff members implementing their programs. Specifically, assessment should serve these functions:

1. Determine each child's present status in relation to program goals and the child's progress in attaining the goals.
2. Provide evidence of developmental progress, and thus serve as an effective tool in parent-staff communication.
3. Serve as a basis for guidance and placement.
4. Be useful in making administrative decisions such as planning additions to or revisions of services; determining changes in philosophy and activities; ascertaining staffing needs; and reporting progress and problems to the community and regulatory agencies.

Thus, the two basic functions of assessment are formative evaluation—assessment used to modify curriculum and/or methodology; and summative evaluation—assessment used to determine the effectiveness of curriculum and methodology.[1]

Although assessment of progress can serve many useful functions, it also has the potential to do harm. One of its greatest dangers is that assessment itself can determine the program, rather than the program determining the why and how of assessment. Assessment may "do more to influence student learning and teacher practices than the other educational procedures that we regard as the substance of education."[2] Negative aspects of assessment include the fact that parents and staff may tend to see the integrative nature of a child's behavior in a compartmentalized way, considering psychomotor, cognitive, and affective aspects of development as separate entities. Assessment can also result in premature labeling of a child. Evaluation devices usually assess only a restricted range of development, and test scores are subject to error from both human and environmental factors. They also tell use little about rate of learning, modalities used in learning (visual, aural, etc.), or about the reasoning process. One must also guard against using assessment as a beginning or end-of-year task, then failing to use the results to benefit the child's development, or giving greater weight to information from a single test than to patterns that emerge from accumulated evidence. Finally, adminstrative decisions based on assessment results will be less than valid when assessment does not consider all the program's objectives; when too much emphasis is placed on norms, especially when the norming population reported by the test publishers is dissimilar to that of the children enrolled in the local program; and when the importance of timing is overlooked. For example, young children enrolled in a program for only a short time may not show measurable progress, and time is required for staff members to become effective in presenting unfamiliar concepts or in using new methods.

PLANNING ASSESSMENT

Because assessment is not a supplementary activity but an integral aspect of a program, decisions concerning assessment of children's progress should be based on the program's long-range goals and philosophy. For one thing, assessment techniques must match the program. Kamii and Elliott[3] state that there must be a match between program objectives and instructional content, between instructional content and assessment instruments, and between program objectives and assessment instruments. Some instruments for measuring intelligence, vocabulary, visual perception, and psycholinguistic abilities were constructed for classifying children and diagnosing problems. Unless the content of the assessment instruments, that is, knowledge and skills assessed, and the assessment techniques, whether verbal, manipulative, paper-and-pencil, or feeding back facts vs. reasoning, relate closely to the program's objectives, you are not likely to obtain valid assessment of the children's status and progress in the program, as individuals or as a group. One cannot assess all objectives, so priorities must be determined. On the other hand, care must be taken to avoid having broad, vague goals and narrow, specific evaluation in one or two areas. Some of these problems result from the lack of assessment devices. (The lack of availability of valid and reliable assessment devices in the affective domain and in adult-child interaction is apparent.) Consequently, the first and most important task in planning assessment is to create a list of possible instruments and techniques to use in assessing growth toward each major program objective.

The staff must determine whether a norm-referenced or a criterion-referenced test is most appropriate for the local program. A *norm-referenced* measure is one in which an individual's behavior is interpreted against the behavior of others (hopefully but not always of similar background) on the same testing instrument. The norm-referenced measure is typically designed to spread people out along some dimension of behavior. The *criterion-referenced* measure is one in which an individual's behavior is interpreted by comparing it to a preselected or established standard or criterion of performance. Because minimal absolute standards of competence have been established, the performance of others is irrelevant. On criterion-referenced tests, such as Englemann's *The Basic Concept Inventory*,[4] scores are translated into statements of behavior typical of people with that score. The test should be relevant to children from different backgrounds and abilities represented in the local program. One must take special care in selecting instruments and techniques to assess the handicapped for screening, placement, and general progress, and in developing articulated guidelines. The following sources will help in developing such guidelines:

Bardwell, A.; Krieg, F.J. and Olion, L.D. *Knowing the Child with Special Needs: A Primer.* Chicago: Head Start, Office of Child Development, Region V, 1973.

Hobbs, N., ed. *The Futures of Children: Categories, Labels and Their Consequences.* San Francisco: Jossey-Bass, Publishers, 1975.

———. *Issues in the Classification of Children: A Sourcebook on Categories, Labels, and Their Consequences.* San Francisco: Jossey-Bass, Publishers, 1975.

Jordan, J.B., ed. *Not All Little Wagons are Red: the Exceptional Child's Early Years.* Reston, Va.: Council for Exceptional Children, 1975.

Randolf, L. "OCD's Policy Issuance to Local Head Start: Identify, Recruit, and Serve Handicapped Children." *Exceptional Children* 40 (1973): 46–47.

Responding to Individual Needs in Head Start: A Head Start Series on Needs Assessment. Part 1: Working with the Individual Child. Department of Health, Education, and Welfare Publication No. (OHD 75–1075). Washington, D.C.: Department of Health, Education, and Welfare, Office of Child Development, 1974.

The assessment technique should measure aspects of children's functioning that appear related to later school success, and children should have opportunities to develop a repertoire of test-taking skills. Testing itself is always a problem with young children. For example, the child may not be familiar with the setting; he could perhaps be tested in two or more settings, allowed to become familiar with the test setting prior to testing. Another problem is that the measurement tool may be obtrusive, that is, the assessment process intrudes into the child's usual environment, in which case unobtrusive measurement strategies should be considered.[5]

Any assessment device should provide information that enables teachers to meet specific needs. The staff must be able to recognize and break down the learning tasks. In short, the question is, "What test can be most effectively used in a certain way for a designated purpose in a specific school setting?"[6] Selection of an assessment instrument must be made on that basis. Additional considerations in planning an assessment program involve these questions:

1. How willing and knowledgeable are staff members to administer the assessment instruments and interpret the scores?
2. How much time and money are budgeted for assessment? What instrusions on staff, children, and parents can be accommodated for collecting, analyzing, recording, and preparing the data for use?
3. How much useful information will be derived from the process?
4. Who will coordinate the assessment program?
5. Will the services of resource persons such as psychologists and guidance workers be needed?
6. How will children's progress be interpreted to parents and to the community?
7. Will the assessment program be rigid, using specified instruments administered at scheduled times, or flexible, using selected instruments administered as staff members feel the need?
8. Are the assessment procedures in line with the "Ethical Standards for Research with Children"?[7]

INFORMAL METHODS

For purposes of this book, informal methods of assessing children's progress include all methods of assessment except standardized tests. Because the definition is broad, these informal methods may range from general observation of children while they engage in activities, to staff-constructed tests designed to measure specific knowledge and skills. In most early childhood programs, informal assessment is more common than the use of standardized tests.

Observations.   Undoubtedly, observation is the most frequently used informal method of assessing young children's progress. Recently, even greater emphasis has been placed on observation.[8] Among the many methods used in observation, these three are popular:

1. In a *specimen-description*, the observer records all events within a given situation. The observer uses an audio- or videotape to record the "stream of

behavior." At a later time, the observer codes the behavior, noting antecedents and consequences of target behavior.

2. *Time-sampling* involves coding the occurrence of previously defined, targeted behavior within discrete time units.

3. The recording of critical incidents that have been previously determined as targeted behaviors is referred to as *event sampling.*

Detailed descriptions of these and other observation techniques are found in the following sources:

Barker, R.G., ed. *The Stream of Behavior.* New York: Appleton-Century-Crofts, 1963.

Baumrind, D. *Naturalistic Observation in the Study of Parent-Child Interaction.* Berkeley, Calif.: California University, Department of Psychology, 1968. ERIC ED 027 073.

Boyer, E.G.; Simon, A.; and Karatin, G., eds. *An Anthology of Early Childhood Observation Instruments,* Vols. 1–111. Philadelphia: Research for Better Schools, 1973.

Carbonara, N.T. *Techniques of Observing Normal Child Behavior.* Pittsburg, Pa: University of Pittsburg Press, 1961.

Cohen, D.H., and Stern, V. *Observing and Recording.* New York: Teachers College Press, Columbia University, 1958.

Coller, A.R. *Systems for the Observation of Classroom Behavior in Early Childhood Education.* Urbana, Ill.: ERIC Clearinghouse/Early Childhood Education, 1972.

Gordon, I.J., and Jester, R.E. "Techniques of Observing Teaching in Early Childhood and Outcomes of Particular Procedures." In *Second Handbook of Research on Teaching,* edited by R.M.B. Travers. Chicago: Rand McNally, 1973. Pp. 184–217.

Wright, H.F. "Observational Child Study." In *Handbook of Research Methods in Child Study,* edited by P.H. Mussen. New York: John Wiley & Sons, 1960. Pp. 71–139.

The popularity of observation may be attributed to these factors: an individual can simultaneously work and observe children (unfortunately, many look and do not see!); observations may be conducted by skilled and unskilled observers; they may be conducted for long or short intervals of time; observations may be used in conjunction with any other assessment methods—both informal methods and standardized tests; and observation is suitable for use in any type of program, because one child or a group of children may be observed, and any aspect of development can be assessed. Disadvantages in using observations for assessment are that the validity of observation depends on the skill of the observer; the observer's biases are inherent in the observation; the soundness of the observation may depend upon the behavior observed, because some aspects of development, such as motor skills, are easier to observe than others, such as thinking processes; when an individual is simultaneously working with children and observing them, it can be difficult to "see the forest for the trees"; and one-way mirrors used in observation rooms, and hidden audio- or videotapes may not be ethical.

Interviews.   Because of the emphasis on their involvement, the interview with parents is now used with greater frequency in early childhood programs. The interview method permits a more comprehensive picture of the child's life at home and with peer groups. The interview method of assessment generally has these characteristics:

1. Questions used in the interview are usually developed by staff members, although interview questions are available in publications such as the

Preprimary Profile,[9] the *Early Detection Inventory,*[10] the *Preschool Attainment Record,*[11] and the *Vineland Social Maturity Scale.*[12]

2. Parents of the child are usually interviewed; however, others familiar with the child are occasionally interviewed.
3. Specific questions in the interview commonly include background information about the child: birth history; self-reliance; development, especially affective development and motor skills; previous experiences that aid concept development, such as places the child has visited in the community, trips he has taken, and previous group experiences; problems, such as handicaps and illnesses, fears, and accident proneness; and interests, such as televsion shows, books and toys, pets, and games. Occasionally, questions are asked about the family situation, family relationships, and parental attitudes, and may encompass family income, housing, occupations, educational level, aspirations for their children, and views of child rearing. Answers to the questions help in assessing needs and potential program services.[13]
4. Interviews may be structured, as in the psychometric method, or semistructured, as in the exploratory method. Kamii and Peper contrast the structured and semistructured methods:

> In the psychometric method, the examiner is required to follow a standard set of procedures specified in a manual, without any deviation. The wording of a question cannot be changed, and the number of times instructions can be repeated is specified. In the "exploratory method," on the other hand, the examiner has an outline and a hypothesis in mind at all times, and he tests these hypotheses by following the child's train of thought in a natural conversational way. The examiner uses his ingenuity to make himself understood by the child in any way possible.[14]

Advantages of the interview as an assessment technique are that valuable information—both verbal and emotional—may be gleaned; interviews can be used in conjunction with other informal assessment methods and with standardized tests; they are suitable for use in any type of early childhood program; and interviews can help clarify and extend information found on written forms. The interview method also has disadvantages: the information obtained may not be comprehensive or accurate because the questions were unclear or not comprehensive and/or because the interviewee was unable or unwilling to answer; the interviewee's and the interviewer's biases are entwined in the information given and in the interpretation of the information, respectively; and the interview method is very time consuming.

Samples of Children's Work.   Samples of children's work serve as an excellent informal method of assessment if they meet the following criteria:

1. Samples of various types of children's work should be collected: dictated or tape-recorded experiences told by children; drawings, paintings, and other two dimensional art projects; photographs of children's projects (for example, three-dimensional art projects, block constructions, or a

completed science experiment); tape recordings of singing or language activities; videotapes of any action activities; and/or writing or math worksheets, if this type of formal activity is conducted in the program.
2. Samples are collected on a systematic and periodic basis.
3. Samples are dated with notes on the children's comments and attitudes.

Among the advantages to using samples of children's work as an assessment technique are that the evidence is simply a collection of children's real, ongoing activities or products of activities, and not a contrived experience for purposes of assessment; collecting is not highly time-consuming; collecting samples works for all aspects of all programs; samples can be used as direct evidence of progress; if samples are dated and adequate notes taken about them, interpretations can be made later by various people; some samples can be analyzed for feelings as well as concepts; and samples can be used in conjunction with other informal methods of assessment and with standarized tests. Disadvantages are that samples may not be representative of the children's work; samples of ongoing activities are more difficult to obtain than two-dimensional art work; some children do not like to part with their work; storage can be a problem; photographs, magnetic tapes, and videotapes are expensive; and staff members often try to read too much into the samples.

Staff-Constructed Tests.   Many staff-constructed tests are administered to children in early childhood programs; however, most of these tests are not the conventional paper-and-pencil variety, administered to all children at the same time. Characteristics of staff-constructed tests are:

1. Most tests are administered to individual children, although a few tests are given to small groups or to the entire class at one time.
2. Administration of the tests is usually conducted by observing the skills and concepts exhibited as children engage in the program's activities, by asking questions, and by requesting demonstrations of skills and concepts. For example, a staff member might note which children can measure during a cooking experience; point to a red ball and ask, "What color is this ball?"; or request that a child skip, or count beads set out on a table.
3. In most staff-constructed tests, the content of each test covers one skill, or a group of related skills, and is administered for the purpose of assisting staff members in planning activities. Some staff-constructed tests are inventories of many skills and concepts, with the information used for referral, placement, or retention.
4. Scoring of staff-constructed tests usually consists of checking the skills and concepts each child has mastered, or by rating the level of mastery achieved.

The advantages of staff-constructed tests are that if the tests are carefully constructed, there will be a match between test items and program goals, and between test items and developmental levels; they are more adaptable to the program's time schedule than are standardized tests; they lend themselves to many types of responses, such as gross motor, manipulative, and verbal; they can be used in conjunction with other assessment methods and tests; and they are inexpensive, and do not require the services of a psychometrist for administering, scoring, and/or interpreting. Some disadvantages of staff-constructed tests are that the match between program goals and test items depends on the skill of the staff members; developing adequate test items is highly time-consuming; and, with the exception of a few locally-normed tests, no normative data are available.

STANDARDIZED TESTS

Standarized tests are formal methods of assessing children's progress, and have these characteristics:

1. Specific directions for administering the test are stated in detail, usually including even the exact words to be used by the examiner in giving instructions, and specifying exact time limits. By following the directions, teachers and counselors in many schools can administer the test in essentially the same way.
2. Specific directions are provided for scoring. Usually a scoring key is supplied that reduces scoring to merely comparing answers with the key; little or nothing is left to the judgment of the scorer. Sometimes carefully selected samples are provided with which a student's product is to be compared.
3. Norms are supplied to aid in interpreting scores.
4. Information needed for judging the value of the test is provided. Before the test becomes available for purchase, research is conducted to study its reliability and validity.
5. A manual is supplied that explains the purposes and uses of the test, describes briefly how it was constructed, provides specific directions for administering, scoring and interpreting results, contains tables of norms, and summarizes available research data on the test.[15]

There are some advantages in using standardized tests. The tests are developed by people familiar with test construction, and before marketing, research is conducted to study test reliability and validity; specific instructions are given for administering and scoring; the manuals contain quick methods for converting raw scores into normative data; the examiner can compare a child's most recent performance with an earlier one; one can compare the performance of children in the local program against that of other children of similar ages and backgrounds; scores provided by good standardized tests are usually reliable and stable, although the younger the child, the more unstable the score; some tests provide diagnostic information; test manuals usually summarize available research data on the test; and the tests may be used with any other form of assessment. Among the disadvantages of using standardized tests are that the score for a particular child may be invalid—the examiner may not have had the child's attention and interest; the child may not have understood what he was supposed to do; there may have been a general lack of rapport between examiner and child; or the child may have been penalized because of his cultural orientation. The content of the tests and the form of the responses (paper-and-pencil, verbal, or motor) may bear little resemblance to the program's curriculum, and some of the many tests available are of poor or inferior quality, especially in terms of validity (i.e., the test measures what it purports to measure) and reliability (i.e., it gives approximately the same numerical score for an individual each time). Most standardized tests now available do not encompass far-ranging behaviors in all areas of development, particularly affective development. There is also the danger that the curriculum of some early childhood programs may be determined by achievement test items. Often, a test's published norms are based on population samples dissimilar to the children in the local program, and normative data may be used to label a child. The test may not provide diagnostic information; the services of a psychometrist may be required for administering the test and interpreting results, particularly some of the individual aptitude and personal-social adjustment tests. Also, tests are an additional expense, and the negative attitudes of some staff members and parents toward the appropriateness of standardized tests may be difficult to overcome.

There has been a staggering proliferation of new assessment instruments, most of which are conventional. Several trends in standardized testing may be considered innovative:

1. Because of our emphasis on identifying handicaps at an early age, there are more screening procedures used at entry level (e.g., prekindergarten). Some screening devices are developed by the local school district while others are standardized procedures.[16]
2. With growth of infant programs, there has been a corresponding development of assessment instruments for measuring cognitive and sensory-motor development in infants.[17]
3. Because of increased emphasis on the desirability of culturally fair tests, more tests are available for measuring individual differences along cultural-linguistic dimensions.
4. More assessment instruments are available for evaluating children's language.
5. There has been an obvious gap in our assessment instruments for measuring the affective domain; however, more instruments are now available.

The specific standardized tests described in Appendix 8 are not evaluated, because the values of a test depend on the objectives of the local program, the children involved, and the use made of the test. However, those proposing to use a test should carefully evaluate its appropriateness for local use. Questions to consider before using a standardized test include:

1. For what purpose do we need to administer this test? Will it help us meet the objectives of our program? Is the test required by the funding agency? Is the test to be given for research purposes?
2. How will the test data be used?
3. Is the rationale of the test appropriate to the objectives of our program?
4. What is the degree to which this test measures our objectives accurately and reliably?

5. Is the response form required by the test (paper-and-pencil, verbal, manipulative, or gross motor performance) familiar to the children?
6. Is the printed matter in the test of good quality?
7. Is the norming population similar to the children in our program?
8. Will the children be penalized because of their cultural orientation?
9. Which children need the test?
10. Does the test have diagnostic cues, such as subscale scores or other pattern data?
11. Is the information as to mental age or grade equivalent yielded by the test appropriate for our purposes?
12. Is the test an individual or group test? Will additional staff be needed when the tests are administered?
13. Who can administer the test? Will an expert be needed to interpret the scores?
14. Are the directions clear and sufficient for administering and scoring the test?
15. What is the length of the test and is it appropriate for the children? What schedule will be followed on testing days?
16. What facilities are needed for administering the test? Using the present facilities, how will this be arranged?
17. Will there be any foreseeable negative attitudes on the part of the children, staff, or parents as a result of administering this test? If so, how will these be handled?
18. What is the cost of the test?
19. Are there other services, such as scoring or training, provided with the test?
20. Are there other tests on the market similar in rationale to this test? If so how do they compare to this one on all of the above points?

Because young children may find a standardized test situation strange, staff members may find testing somewhat difficult. Although specific directions for administering are given with each test, the following suggestions may help alleviate children's uneasiness: (1) make the testing area attractive and comfortable; (2) keep materials not in immediate use out of sight; (3) be completely familiar with the test; (4) develop a rapport with the child before testing; (5) encourage the child throughout the testing situation; and (6) make sure the child's responses reflect his full cooperation, because valid test results can only be obtained when the child actively engages in the tasks.

Scores on standardized tests and the normative data supplied to aid in interpreting the scores are given in technical terms used in educational and psychological measurement. The following terms are frequently used in reporting or interpreting scores on standarized tests for young children:

1. *Age equivalent.* The age equivalent score is expressed as a year and month of chronological age; for example, 5.11 is five years, eleven months. The age equivalent for a raw score represents the year and month of chronological age for which that raw score is the median for the norming group for

the same year and month. Some of the age equivalents reported on various tests are language, psycholinguistic, attainment, and social.

2. *Anticipated achievement.* Anticipated achievement is a predicted score on an achievement test. When the predicted score is compared with the child's actual score, children who are falling significantly below levels of achievement attained by students with similar sex, age, and grade characteristics can be identified.

3. *Diagnostic profile.* This is a graphic representation of the child's performance on test items or categories of test items. The profile permits easy identification of areas of strength and weakness.

4. *Class record sheet.* The class recored sheet provides an analysis of an individual's performance and a description of the group's performance.

5. *Grade equivalent.* The grade equivalent score is expressed as a year and month of school; for example, 2.3 is second grade, third month. The grade equivalent for a raw score represents the year and month of school for which that raw score is the median for the norming group for the same year and month. Because a grade equivalent is based solely on the number of items answered correctly, it does not mean the child has mastered all concepts taught in his school up to the year and month indicated by the grade equivalent. Language and reading tests are likely to have a wider range of scores than mathematics tests.

6. *Grade level indicator.* The grade level indicator is read or interpreted in much the same way as the grade equivalent. To determine grade equivalent, the publishers make interpolations (that is, set grade equivalents for the months that fall between the times the test was actually given) and extrapolations (that is, inferences of grade equivalents above and below the grades in which the test was given). The grade level indicator is based on more empirical evidence, as opposed to statistical charting, because students used in norming actually take the tests on a range of levels, and the tests are normed several times per year.

7. *Intelligence quotient.* The intelligence quotient, referred to as IQ, is a measure that takes into account the raw score on the intelligence test and the child's chronological age. Specifically:
   a. The *ratio intelligence quotient* is the ratio of an individual's mental age (MA) to his chronological age (CA), or the ratio of an individual's mental age to the mental age normal for chronological age. In both cases, the ratio is multiplied by 100 to eliminate the decimal.
   b. The *deviation intelligence quotient* is a measure of mental capacity based on the difference (i.e., deviation) between an individual's score and the score that is normal for that individual's chronological age.
   c. The *verbal, performance, or full-scale intelligence quotients* measure an individual's mental capacity on language, nonlanguage, or all test items, respectively.

8. *Intelligence quotient equivalent.* The intelligence quotient equivalent is an expression of a comparable score on other intelligence tests.

9. *Mental age.* Mental age (MA) is interpreted as the performance on an intelligence scale which is typical of a given chronological age group.

10. *Norms.* Norms are statistics that describe the average performance on a specified test for a particular age, socioeconomic level, geographic area, grade, and/or sex group.
11. *Percentile.* A percentile is a value on a scale of 100 that indicates the percent of a distribution that is equal to or below it. (A percentile score of 25 is a score equal to or better than 25 percent of the scores.)
12. *Percentile rank.* A percentile rank is the percentage of scores in a distribution equal to or lower than the score gained. Thus, a child's percentile rank may be explained as the percentage of children in the norm group who scored equal to or lower than he. A scale of percentile ranks is not a scale of equal measuring units; in terms of raw score units, a given percentile difference is greater near the extremes of the distribution than it is near the middle.
13. *Raw score.* A raw score is a quantitative but uninterpreted, unconverted result obtained in scoring a test. It usually represents the number of items on the test answered correctly.
14. *Standard score.* A standard score is usually used as a general term denoting several varieties of converted scroes. Examples of converted scores include percentile rank, age and grade equivalents, and so forth.
15. *Stanine.* A stanine is a standard score from a scale of nine units (STAndard score—NINE units; hence STANINE). The mean stanine of the norming population is 5.0 and the standard deviation is 2.0. The scale ranges from 1.0 through 9.0 with 1.0 as the lowest level and 9.0 as the highest level. The units are equal, with each representing approximately one-half a standard deviation.

The following deliminations should be noted in reading the descriptions of the standardized tests described in Appendix 8:

1. These tests represent only some of the many available standardized tests; consequently, staff members of an early childhood program will want to review the latest edition of the *Mental Measurements Yearbook*, edited by Oscar K. Buros, for a more comprehensive listing. However, examples of both typical and atypical types of items included in standardized tests for young children may be readily discerned by reading test descriptions in our listing.
2. No attempt is made to evaluate or compare the tests. It is suggested that the following sources, among others, be consulted for critical reviews of tests: (a) Buros' *Seventh Mental Measurements Yearbook;*[18] (b) CSE-ECRC *Preschool/Kindergarten Test Evaluations;*[19] (c) Stott and Ball's "Infant and Preschool Mental Tests: Review and Evaluation";[20] (d) Educational Testing Services' *An Annotated Bibliography of References to Tests and Assessment Devices;*[21] (e) CSE *Elementary-School Test Evaluations;*[22] Johnson and Bommarito's *Tests and Measurements in Child Development: A Handbook;*[23] and (f) *Measures of Maturation: An Anthology of Early Childhood Observation Instruments.*[24]
3. The tests described are classified on the basis of content. The test classifications are (a) aptitude, (b) achievement and diagnostic, and (c) personal-

social adjustment. It should be noted that there are other bases for classifying tests and that some of these tests do not exclusively fit into one of the three content classifications.

Aptitude Tests.   An individual's aptitudes (capacities for learning) are the result of innate abilities and environmental learning, both direct experience and social transmissions. Aptitude tests are designed to evaluate an individual's ability to progress in cognitive activities; they may measure an aggregation of abilities or one or more discrete abilities. Items on aptitude tests are "(1) *equally unfamiliar* to all examinees (that is, novel situations) or (2) *equally familiar* (in the sense that all students have had equal opportunity to learn, regardless of their pattern of specific courses)."[25] There are aptitude tests of (1) general mental ability, (2) special aptitudes (for example, motor performance or articulation), and (3) prognostic tests, (such as reading readiness). Appendix 8 describes some standardized tests for use with young children.

Achievement and Diagnostic Tests.   Achievement tests measure the extent to which an individual has mastered certain information or skills as a result of specific instruction or training. Diagnostic tests pinpoint specific weaknesses. Achievement and diagnostic tests are given most frequently in the areas of reading, language, and mathematics. Appendix 8 describes some standardized tests for assessing young children's achievements and specific weaknesses.

Personal-Social Adjustment Tests.   These tests are, in reality, tests of good mental health. Generally, an individual is considered to have good mental health if his behavior is typical of his own age and cultural group. Appendix 8 describes some standardized tests for assessing the personal-social adjustment of young children.

Recording

Record keeping, the developmental record of a child or a group of children, has always been an important aspect of a staff member's duties; today, record keeping is becoming even more important and prevalent. Most early childhood programs have a philosophy of providing for children's individual differences, and record keeping allows the program to assess and improve the services it provides. There is greater involvement with parents, and increasing mobility of both children and staff members. In addition, funding agencies, citizens' groups, boards of directors or school boards, and parents often require "proof" of the early childhood program's effectiveness in meeting its stated objective, which is often best demonstrated by its records.

Naturally, though, record keeping also presents problems:

1. A staff member can spend more time keeping records than in planning and working with children;
2. A staff member can make a prejudgment based on records, and become positively or negatively biased towards a child;

3. Records may cause staff members to mentally picture a particular chrono-logical age group homogeneously. For example, a staff member may notice that his records indicate that most five-year-olds can count by rote to ten, and thus assume that all her five-year-olds can do so;
4. Parents can challenge inaccurate, inappropriate, misleading, and irrele-vant information and unsubstantiated opinions (see section on P.L. 93–380, pp. 275–76); and
5. Record keeping may become a meaningless activity because the types of data required to be kept may not be congruent with the objectives of the local program or because records may be filed and forgotten or may not be used effectively.

USES OF RECORDS

There are many effective uses for records. They are especially valuable to staff members as guides for planning the types of experiences each child needs. By studying a child's records, a staff member can find evidence of strengths and weaknesses, and can better judge when to push, when to step aside, when to go back, or even when to look further. Developmental records of a child's progress are like medical records that contain information about what has been done in the way of examinations and treatment, and that form the basis for further diagnosis and prescription. Again, records should not used as instruments for typecasting children; rather, they should help staff members formulate a realis-tic but open-ended picture of a child. Good records also permit independent evaluation of a child by more than one individual.

The process of recording data causes staff members to think about each child more profoundly. Staff members are forced to consider each child, not just categories like "children with problems," "extra-bright children," or "creative children." Their records thus make the work of specialists (guidance counselors, physicians, or caseworkers) more efficient by helping them determine whether a problem is transient or continuous, in knowing when a problem began, in ascertaining how pervasive its effects are in the child's development, and in suggesting possible solutions to the problem.

Records can help staff members see each child's progress; because they work daily with a child, they may not be able to see progress except through a review of the records. The child can also see his progress in records—especially in col-lected samples of his work.

Records can also be used as a basis for discussion with parents, and can become a defense in dealing with a dissatisfied parent. In working with parents, it is the staff member's use of records that determines their value.

Records can be invaluable in home–school contacts if the school personnel know how to use its records wisely and constructively in dealing with parents. No school device is more effective when wisely used, but no material is more likely to antago-nize parents if wrongly used. On the whole, no school record should just be handed to parents for them to look over. Selected parts of records should be shown to parents by a member of the school staff who is competent to interpret this material construc-tively.[26]

Recent legislation, permitting parents to view the records of their children, should make staff members more aware of their responsibilities in determining the nature of records to be kept. (A more comprehensive discussion of P.L. 93–380 appears later in this chapter.)

Records are beneficial to children who change programs frequently. Records of a child who has recently transferred makes it easier for staff members to assist the child in the new situation. Recognition of the benefits of a record keeping and record transferring system for the transient child can be seen in the formation of the Migrant Student Record Transfer System which disseminates data from the Migrant Data Bank at Little Rock, Arkansas.[27] The local program's regulatory agency requires various records. These records of children's progress toward a program's stated goals may determine whether subsequent funding will be forthcoming. Other uses for records are referral conferences, to help teachers see results of new teaching techniques or services, and as data for research.

TYPES OF RECORDS

The information contained on records may be classified (1) on an objective-subjective information continuum; (2) on the basis of written information about children or samples of children's work; (3) according to the individual who provided the information (child, parent, staff member, physician, or psychometrist); (4) according to the contents of the record (whether social behavior, medical information, and/or cognitive achievement); or (5) in keeping with the purposes of the record, such as grouping, placement, referral, reporting to parents, and/or information for the regulatory agency. We will discuss background information, anecdotal, achievement, guidance and placement, referral, and cumulative records.

Background Information Records. Boards of directors or local school boards and staff members are realizing that home background, early experiences in the home and neighborhood, and language experiences all affect what a child can accomplish from experience in an early childhood program. Many programs now ask for considerable information from parents. Sometimes these records are supplemented by additional information obtained by a caseworker, or volunteered at a later date by the parents or the child.

Basic information about the child and his family is always part of background information records, including the child's legal name, home address, and telephone number; birth date, birthplace, and birth certificate number; number of siblings; marital status of parents, and whether both parents are living; and the father's and mother's or guardian's legal names, home address and telephone number, occupation, place of business, and business telephone number.

Medical information is also included in the background information records, and completion of medical information records is required before a child is admitted to a program. (See the section entitled "Forms" in the Parent's Handbook found in Appendix 7.) Usually, parents complete health history form, which asks for a general evaluation of the family's health, a history of the child's illnesses (especially communicable diseases); frequent illness or complaints, such as colds, headaches, or styes, and any physical or personal-social handicaps that might affect the child's participation in the program. Medical professionals must complete records of recent physical and dental examinations and immunization records. These records may call for comments on any significant medical findings concerning eyes, ears, nose, throat, glands, heart, circulation, lungs, bones, joints, reflexes, and so forth; a statement as to whether the child can participate in the regular program or needs an adjusted program; the condition of teeth and gums; and dates of immunizations.

Finally, records on the child's personal-social history are frequently included as part of the background information records. This information may be supplied by a parent or by another adult who knows the child. Parents may record the information on forms, or a staff member may record the information during an interview. The child's personal-social history is likely to include information about his self-reliance, development, previous experiences, problems, interests, and family situation, relationships, and attitudes toward child rearing. The records may also ask parents to report guidance methods they have found effective.

Anecdotal Records.   An anecdotal record is an observational record of a significant incident in the child's life. Anecdotes are usually made during the child's participation in program activities, but can also be made during home visits. Characteristics of a good anecdote are that:

1. It gives the date, the place, and the situation in which the action occurred. We call this the setting.
2. It describes the actions of the child, the reactions of other people involved, and the responses of the child to these reactions.
3. It quotes what is said to the child and by the child during the action.
4. It supplies "mood cues"—postures, gestures, voice qualities, and facial expressions that give cues to how the child felt. It does not provide interpretations of his feelings, but only the cues by which a reader may judge what they were.
5. The description is extensive enough to cover the episode. The action or conversation is not left incomplete and unfinished but is followed through to the point where a little vignette of a behavioral moment in the life of the child is supplied.[28]

Anecdotal records should contain information as to what staff members and/or parents are doing about a problem. Information about attempts to solve a problem and their degree of success would be of value to others using the information.

A single anecdote usually contains no conclusive information. Unless the observer time-samples the child's behavior, there may be a tendency to look only at problem behavior. Anecdotal records are influenced by the staff member's expertise in observation, assumptions, and expectations. Finally, to write and study anecdotes is time-consuming. Even with these limitations, the accumulation of anecdotes contributes to an understanding of a child's typical behavior, his adjustment problems and sensitivity, and the adjustment mechanisms he employs, his interests and goals, his relationships with adults and peers, and the staff members' reactions to the child and specific methods they use in working with him.

Achievement Records.   These are invaluable for planning activities to assist the child in his development. Achievement records include facts, general under-standings, and skills the child has developed, a prognosis of his readiness for the next stage of development, and an indication of how the child compares with others in various areas of development (a comparison of the child's score with available normative data). Achievement records can take several forms:

1. They may be written as anecdotes.

Sept. 27. Tim and two other boys (David and Tom) were in the sand box using dump trucks for hauling sand. David remarked that this lot needed more sand than the lot to which they had just delivered one dump-truck load. Tim looked and asked, "How much more sand?" "Twice as much," replied David. "Then I'll drive my truck up once and give them a load and come back for one more load of sand," Tim commented.

---

2. Achievement may be recorded on check sheets.

_____
            (Child's name)

Art Concepts

Can recognize   red   _____
these colors: yellow   _____
                           blue   _____
                           green   _____
                           orange   _____
                           purple   _____
                           black   _____
                           brown   _____

Can arrange four varying grades
of sandpaper from rough to smooth.   _____

Can name the colors and point
to rough and smooth fruit in a
reproduction of Cezanne's painting.
Apples and Oranges.   _____

---

3. Rating scales may be used.

(Child's name)

1. Can put on his outdoor
   clothes.

Not   Sometimes   Always
Yet

---

4. Collected samples of children's work may be used. These records are more valuable if they are dated and contain comments regarding the situations in which the samples were collected.
5. Achievement records may consist of the raw or converted scores on staff-constructed and/or standarized tests. The scores may be recorded in a class record or grade book, a cumulative record form, an individual profile sheet, or a diagnostic profile sheet.
6. Achievement records may be in the form of a list. For example, a staff member may list songs a child can sing or nursery rhymes he can recite.

Guidance and Placement Records.   Guidance and placement records per se have not generally been used in prekindergarten and kindergarten programs. These records are more frequently used in early childhood programs that enroll school-age children (sometimes including kindergarten-age children), or in programs with academic objectives. Early childhood programs serving children younger than school-age and programs that are primarily care-giving customarily group children by chronological age. (Licensing requirements frequently specify such grouping.) Placement records are used when handicapped children are mainstreamed.

Guidance and placement records are used for ability groupings for learning or instruction in a graded system, or for placement in an appropriate learning or instructional level in a continuous progress approach. More specifically, placement and guidance records are used for initial placement in a group, for moving a child from group to group, and for keeping track of a child's present level of work. Certain dated records should be kept for guidance and placement:

1. Scores on aptitude tests;
2. Present level of work in academic areas in which children are grouped (usually skill areas of reading, mathematics, and writing). The level of work may be indicated by specific skills that are mastered or by books completed in a series, such as reading readiness, preprimer, or primer, and by other materials completed, such as labs or workbooks;
3. Achievement test scores; and
4. Staff member's comments about developmental characteristics and problems.

Referral Records.   All early childhood programs that employ specialists for purposes of working with children who need unique assistance need referral records. Specialists hired as full-time staff members or as part-time consultants may include medical professionals, psychometrists, guidance counselors, speech pathologists, and remedial reading specialists. If the program does not employ specialists for support services, it will be necessary to develop a community resource directory. In some cases, a directory may be available through the local Chamber of Commerce, the United Fund, the Community Council, or the State Department of Social Services. Administrators who must compile their own file of community resources should include in each description the basic service, that is, whether it is health, mental health, or recreation, the name of the agency, its address and phone number, the days and hours of operation, a detailed explanation of the services it provides, the eligibility requirements, the name of the person to contact.

Local early childhood programs should develop a separate referral form for each type of referral, for example, a form for medical referral, a form for referral to a psychometrist, or to a speech pathologist. The items on each form would differ, but each type should include the signed permission for referral from parent or legal guardian; date and person or agency to which referral is being made; the name of the staff member who is referring the child; specific reasons for referral; either a digest of, or the complete reports from, other referrals; comments or attitudes of parents, peers, or the child himself if these are available; length of time the staff member has been aware of the problem; and what staff members or parents have tried and with what success. Many referral records allow space for the specialist's report after he evaluates or works with the child.

Cumulative Records.   Cumulative records are permanent records of the child's progress and adjustment in a program. The purposes of cumulative records can be summarized as follows:

> Cumulative records serve as a basic pupil guidance tool for teachers, counselors, specialist-consultants, and administrators; provide assistance in planning school policy and curriculum; furnish a basis for planning pupil progress; and serve as a means for identifying pupil differences and group tendencies.[29]

The contents of the records should fit the program's requirements. For example, if a birth certificate is required to verify each child's age, the cumulative record form should contain a space for recording the birth certificate number. The contents of the cumulative record form should also meet the program's objectives. Some categories frequently found in the cumulative record are background information, such as personal family data; attendance records; records of assessment (aptitude, achievement, and personal-social adjustment); reports of special interests and goals; a digest of, or reference to, other records of the child's progress and adjustment; and objective specific comments of staff members. The form should be reviewed and revised periodically, and require minimal clerical work.

PUBLIC LAW 93–380

Children's records are now protected under the Family Educational Rights and Privacy Act of 1974, P.L. 93–380. This law provides that:

1. Parents of children who attend a school receiving federal assistance may see information in the school's official files. This information includes test scores, grade averages, class rank, intelligence quotient, health records, psychological reports, notes on behavioral problems, family background items, attendance records, and all other records except personal notes made by a staff member solely for his own use.
2. Records must be made available for review within 45 days after the request.
3. Parents may challenge information irrelevant to education, such as religious preference, or unsubstantiated opinions.
4. Contents of records may be challenged in a hearing. If the school refuses to remove material challenged by parents as inaccurate, misleading, or inappropriate, the parent may insert a written rebuttal.
5. With some exceptions (e.g., other officials in the same school, officials in another school to which the student has applied for transfer, some accrediting associations, state educational officials, some financial aid organizations, and the courts), written consent of parents is required before school officials may release records. Schools must keep a written record as to who has seen, or requested to see, the child's records.
6. Parents have the right to know where records are kept and which school officials are responsible for them.
7. Unless a divorced parent is prohibited by law from having any contact with the child, divorced parents have equal access to official records.
8. Most of the foregoing rights pass from parent to child when the child is 18.0 years of age.
9. School districts must notify parents (and the 18.0-year-olds) of their rights.

For more information about P.L. 93–380, or for assistance with problems about its provisions, correspondence with these sources could prove helpful:

Mr. Thomas S. McFee
Deputy Assistant Secretary for Management FERPA
Room 514E
Department of Health, Education, and Welfare
200 Independence Avenue, S.W.
Washington, D.C. 20201
Tel. 202–245–7488

National Committee for Citizens in Education
Wilde Lake Village Green
Columbia, Md. 21044
Tel. 800–638–9675

There are also books available on this law:

Gluckman, I.B., and Ackerly, R.L. *The Reasonable Exercise of Authority*—11. Reston, Va.: National Association of Secondary School Principals, 1976.

Levine, A., and Cary, E. *The Rights of Students*, rev. ed. New York: American Civil Liberties Union, 1977.

Schimmel, D., and Fischer, L. *The Rights of Parents.* Columbia, Md.: The National Committee for Citizens in Education, 1977.

Reporting

Reporting is becoming a more important aspect of early childhood programs, as programs seek to involve parents in their children's development and as they become more accountable to parents, citizens' groups, and funding and regulatory agencies. Some trends and emphases in reporting practices may be summarized as follows:

> Parent-teacher conference is the goal universally accepted and is spreading widely in actual use.
> Emphasis is on assessing the stage of development rather than on formal grades or ratings; failing grades are practically eliminated.
> Checklists, narrative reports, letters to parents are three commonly used media.
> The child as a citizen and the child as a scholar are not clearly distinguished; grades for achievement and grades for citizenship are frequently blurred.
> Great diversity of forms and formats is found at this level.
> Scattered attempts are made to involve the child in self-evaluation, with the help of the teacher.[30]

Many of the foregoing trends apply more to children of public school age than to children under public school age, where grading has never been used extensively.

As is true of all other aspects of an early childhood program, reporting practices should be based on program objectives. The first step in developing a reporting practice is to determine the purposes of reporting. Once these have been determined, the second step is to clarify ambiguous objectives (that is, objectives that cannot be assessed and for which progress cannot be reported) and put program objectives into categories. The third step is to determine reporting methods, whether informal reports, individual conferences, report letters, check sheets, and/or report cards, that best convey information about children's progress, that are understood and accepted by those receiving the reports, and that suit staff abilities and time. The final step is to experiment with the reporting practices, and revise them if necessary.

PURPOSES OF REPORTING

For most early childhood programs, the major purpose of reporting is to provide information to parents about their children's progress. Parents and staff jointly discuss each child's strengths and needs and plan the next steps in the educative process. In addition to parent-staff communication, there are other purposes of reporting:

1. Evaluating the evidence of each child's progress helps staff members plan experiences the child should have, and sometimes shows gaps in their knowledge about a child's progress.

2. Reporting progress helps obtain support for the program from parents and citizens' groups; and
3. Reporting progress, especially by group, is often required by regulatory and funding agencies.

METHODS OF REPORTING

One trend in reporting children's progress is the great diversity of methods; five common methods are informal reports, individual conferences, report letters, check sheets, and report cards. Many programs use more than one method.

Informal Reports.   Informal reports are perhaps the most common way of reporting, in fact, they are so common, staff members may not even be aware that they are communicating information about children's progress. This kind of report may be a casual conversation with a parent in which the staff member mentions that "Lori excells in mathematical concepts" or "Mark can't tie his shoes"; it might be a paper carried home by the child with corrections marked on it, or a star or a smiling or sad face; it might be praise or corrections of a child while a parent visits the program; or it might be reports from the child himself, such as "I learned to skip today."

Individual Conferences.   Many programs schedule individual conferences with each child's parents, because it permits face-to-face communication between parent and staff member. The staff must plan intensively for successful conferences. First, they need to send out a newsletter explaining the purposes of the conference and inviting parents to make appointments during specified times, construct a schedule of appointments and confirm them, provide a place for the conference, secure a baby sitter for enrolled and younger children, and plan a waiting area for early-arriving parents. (See "Scheduled Individual Conferences" in chapter 12.)

The next task is to develop a guide sheet for reporting children's progress. This sheet outlines points the staff member plans to cover in the conference. Although the staff member should concentrate on those items he feels to be most significant, he will want to present a well-rounded picture of the child, not just problem areas. The staff person should consult all records on the child, and carefully transfer to the guide sheet any information to be shared with parents. A report card or check sheet given to parents at the conference can be used as the guide sheet, although some supplemental material may need to be gathered.

The third step in preparing for individual conferences is to gather samples of children's work. A collection of samples that represents all or most areas of development gives parents a more comprehensive picture of their children's progress. The final step is to duplicate reports to give to parents, and plan a method for documenting the conference.

Report Letters.   Programs using report letters usually provide forms on which staff members write a few brief comments about a child's progress under each of several headings, such as psychomotor development, personal-social adjustment, cognitive development, language growth, work habits, problem-solving growth, aesthetic growth, self-reliance, and general evaluation. An example of a report letter form is as follows:

YOUR CHILD'S PROGRESS

Name _____ Level _____

Psychomotor development (motor skills):

George can gallop, skin, run, and throw and catch a rubber ball. He enjoys all games that use movement and his skills indicate that his attainment is high in this area of development.

Personal-social adjustment:

George does not initiate many aggressive acts; however he still has trouble keeping his hands to himself. He responds to negative overtures from his classmates by hitting.

Language growth:

George appears to enjoy new words. He uses rhyming words and makes up words to fit the rhymes. He has not been able to express his negative feelings toward others with words, however.

General evaluation:

George is progressing nicely. More opportunities to talk to others would help him learn to express himself. He performs well in the room and on the playground as long as he is kept busy and as long as others leave him alone.

The advantages of report letters are that the staff member can concentrate on a child's specific strengths and needs without ranking by letter grade or satisfactory/unsatisfactory ratings or checking progress in highly specific areas, such as "knows his address" or "ties his shoes." The disadvantages are that they are highly time-consuming, and staff members may develop stereotypical comments, especially after writing the first few letters.

Check Sheets.   Check sheets contain lists of desired achievements. The staff member indicates that the child has developed a particular skill or shown understanding of a particular concept by a checkmark—hence the name. Some programs use check sheets as the only method of reporting, but check sheets are more frequently used in conjunction with other methods of reporting. These sheets may be given to a parent during an individual conference or enclosed in the report card. Check sheets generally differ from report cards in these ways:

1. They are usually printed on sheets of paper rather than on cards.
2. Categories of items on check sheets are similar to those on report cards, but the items on check sheets tend to be more specific. For example, an item on a report card might read:

	Always	Sometimes
Shows self-reliance by putting on his own outdoor clothing.		

The same category listed on a check sheet might look like this:

Can button clothes.. _____
Can put on overshoes .... _____
Can zip a coat .... _____
Can lace and tie shoes .... _____

3. Items on report cards may rate a child as to degree of accomplishment, for example, satisfactory, progressing, and needs improvement, while check sheets indicate whether or not child has accomplished a specific task.

Report Cards.   The report card is more frequently used in early childhood programs that enroll kindergarten or primary children (and/or in programs that have an educational focus) than in programs that enroll prekindergarten age children (and/or in programs with care-giving focus). Although there are rumors that the report card is dead, or at least dying, the report card in fact survives, and finds its way into homes at monthly to semiannual intervals. "Traditional report cards coexist with new and innovating reporting procedures—frequently in the same school system, in the same school."[31]

Report cards usually list items such as academic subjects or activities and areas of personal-social adjustment, and have a blank space opposite each item for recording a symbol denoting progress. A key on the report card interprets the symbols, whether they are the traditional A, B, C, D and F symbols (rarely used) or others. Other specifics frequently included are the child's attendance record, a space for comments by the staff member and/or parents, and a parent's signature line for each reporting period.

Because the items selected for inclusion on the report card should fit program objectives, the items vary. The following list, compiled from a nationwide sampling of kindergarten report cards, indicates the wide range of evaluated achievements:

1. general well-being (e.g., alertness and ability to rest)
2. identity (e.g., writes name, knows address, and ties shoes)
3. social maturity (e.g., friendly, shares, and controls temper)
4. eye-hand coordination (e.g., able to use art and hand-tools and able to trace shapes)
5. perception of direction (e.g., shows consistent handedness and knows right–left)
6. work habits (e.g., has adequate attention span and follows directions)
7. language development (e.g., speaks clearly, has adequate vocabulary, and makes up stories)
8. reading readiness (e.g., understands sequence, shows interest in stories, and recognizes likenesses and differences both visually and aurally)
9. mathematics (e.g., counts rationally and recognizes numerals)
10. science (e.g., shows curiosity and classifies)
11. music (e.g., enjoys listening and singing and participates in rhythmic activities)
12. art (e.g., enjoys arts and crafts, recognizes colors, and handles tools correctly)
13. health, safety, and physical education (e.g., practices good health habits, obeys safety rules, participates in physical activties and shows good sportsmanship).[32]

There are various styles for report cards; one style may require the staff member to check a child's achievements. An understanding or skill the child has not developed is left unchecked. This style closely resembles the check sheet.

A Message to Parents:

   In kindergarten your child lives, works, and plays with other children of his age. He has learning experiences that are a foundation for all that follows in later school years. This card is a description of your child's development at this time. Each quality checked is evident in your child. You, as a parent, will help and encourage him by your interest in his growth.

BEHAVIOR	participates with confidence	
IN LARGE	usually follows others	
GROUP	participates in activities	
SITUATIONS	gets along well with others	

RESPONSE	cooperates when encouraged	
TO	accepts group decisions	
RULES		
	follows rules of the school	

Another style may require staff member to mark both understandings and skills the child has achieed and those he has not achieved. The following report card style might be used for a program that serves children of bilingual families:

Name (Nombre) _____

S   Satisfactory growth at this time.
Desarrollo satisfactorio al presente.
N   Not yet.
Todavia no es satifactorio el desarrollo.

Can hop Puede saltar		Puts on wraps Se pone el abrigo
Knows age Sabe su edad		Knows address Sabe su domicilio

The following two styles require the staff member to denote each child's progress by marking one of three or one of four choices:

Progress Report

Name _____

A check shows the child's performance	1st Semester			2nd Semester		
	Most of the time	Part of the time	Not at this time	Most of the time	Part of the time	Not at this time
Work Habits						
Takes care of materials						
Has good attention span						
Is able to work independently						
Follows group instruction						

THIS PRESCHOOL PROGRAM is designed to help each child: build self-confidence, sharpen his senses. learn to work with others, and enlarge his span of experiences.	FIRST				SECOND			
	COMMENDABLE	SATISFACTORY	NEEDS TO MAKE GREATER EFFORT	NEEDS MORE TIME TO DEVELOP	COMMENDABLE	SATISFACTORY	NEEDS TO MAKE GREATER EFFORT	NEEDS MORE TIME TO DEVELOP
READING READINESS First reporting period								
Is interested in learning to read								
Sees and hears likenesses and differences in words								
Follows directions most of the time								
Is becoming acquainted with books								
READING READINESS Second reporting period								
Can distinguish right and left								
Hears rhyming sounds								
Hears beginning sounds								
Knows the letters of the alphabet								
Can write most letters clearly								

Another style calls for the staff member to evaluate both effort and progress on each item:

EDUCATIONAL GROWTH	EFFORT		PROGRESS	
	Adequate	Needs to Improve	Shows Development	Shows Strength
PERSONAL ATTITUDES AND SKILLS				
Interest and contributions				
Can put on outdoor clothing				
Can tie shoes				
Can wait his or her turn				
Keeps hands to himself or herself (doesn't bother others)				
STORY PERIOD				
Retells stories and rhymes				
Refrains from disturbing others				
Sits quietly				
Shows interest in story				
Listens while story is read				

Yet another style requires the staff member to evaluate progress on each item on an inferior-superior continuum; such a style is actually a rating scale.

YOUR CHILD'S PROGRESS

_____   _____
Name of child   Year and class

_____   _____
School   Teacher

	RARELY				CONSISTENTLY
GROWTH AND DEVELOPMENT					
A. Considers ideas and points of view of others	.	.	.	.	.
B. Associates with a variety of people	.	.	.	.	.
C. Respects the feelings of each human being	.	.	.	.	.
D. Practices conservation of living things	.	.	.	.	.
E. Practices safety habits	.	.	.	.	.
F. Demonstrates good health habits	.	.	.	.	.

Staff members must recognize that regardless of the method of reporting, the report is only as accurate and comprehensive as are the assessment devices and recording. When the assessment plan matches program objectives and recording is accurate and thorough, reporting becomes a valuable facet of the early childhood program.

NOTES

1. M. Scriven, "The Methodology of Evaluation," *Perspectives of Curriculum Evaluation*, ed. R. Tyler, R. Gagné, and M. Schriven (Chicago: Rand McNally, 1967), pp. 39–93.
2. Benjamin S. Bloom, J.T. Hastings, and G.F. Madaus, *Handbook on Formative and Summative Evaluation of Student Learning* (New York: McGraw-Hill Book Co., 1971).
3. C. Kamii and D.L. Elliott, "Evaluation of Evaluations," *Educational Leadership* 28 (1971): 827–31.
4. S. Englemann, *The Basic Concept Inventory* (Chicago: Follett Educational Corp., 1967).
5. E.J. Webb, D.T. Campbell, R.D. Swartz, and L. Sechrest, *Unobtrusive Measures: Nonreactive Research in the Social Sciences* (Chicago: Rand McNally, 1966).
6. Martin Katz, ed., *Selecting an Achievement Test: Principles and Procedures* (Princeton, N.J.: Educational Testing Service, 1961), p. 6.
7. The Society for Research in Child Development, "Ethical Standards for Research with Children," *Directory* (1974); 151–52.
8. P. McReynolds, "An Introduction to Psychological Assessment," *Advances in Psychological Assessment*, Vol. 1, ed. P. McReynolds (Palo Alto, Calif.: Science and Behavior Books, 1968), pp. 1–13.
9. H.J. Schiff and M.I. Friedman, *Preprimary Profile* (Chicago: Science Research Associates, 1966).
10. F.E. McGahan and Carolyn McGahan, *Early Detection Inventory* (Chicago: Follett Publishing Co., 1967).
11. Edgar A. Doll, *Preschool Attainment Record* (Circle Pines, Minn.: American Guidance Service, 1966).
12. Edgar A. Doll, *Vineland Social Maturity Scale* (Circle Pines, Minn.: American Guidance Service, 1965).
13. E.H. Brady and D.G. McClain, *Assessing Day Care Needs and Services: Interview Procedures* (San Francisco: The Rosenberg Foundation, 1972).
14. C. Kamii and R. Peper, *A Piagetian Method of Evaluating Preschool Children's Development in Classification* (Washington, D.C.: Bureau of Elementary and Secondary Education, Office of Education, 1969). ERIC ED 039 013.
15. Georgia S. Adams, *Measurement and Evaluation in Education, Psychology, and Guidance* (New York: Holt, Rinehart, & Winston, 1965), p. 150.
16. M.M. Rogolsky, "Screening Kindergarten Children: A Review and Recommendations," *Journal of School Psychology* 7 (1968–69): 18–27.
17. H. Thomas, "Psychological Assessment Instruments for Use with Human Infants," *Merrill-Palmer Quarterly* 16 (1970): 189–223.
18. Oscar K. Buros, ed., *The Seventh Mental Measurements Yearbook*, 2 vols. (Highland Park, N.J.: The Gryphon Press, 1972).
19. R. Hoepfner, C. Stern, and S.G. Nummedal, eds., *CSE-ECRC Preschool/Kindergarten Test Evaluations* (Los Angeles: University of California, Center for the Study of Evaluation, 1971).
20. L.H. Stott and R.S. Ball, "Infant and Preschool Mental Tests: Review and Evaluation," *Monograph of Social Research in Child Development* 30 (1965): Serial No. 101.
21. Educational Testing Service, *An Annotated Bibliography of References to Tests and Assessments Devices* (Princeton, N.J.: Test Collection, ETS, undated [mineographed]).
22. R. Hoepfner et al., *CSE Elementary-School Test Evaluations* (Los Angeles: University of California, Center for the Study of Evaluation, 1970).
23. O.G. Johnson and J.W. Bommarito, *Tests and Measurements in Child Development: A Handbook* (San Francisco: Jossey-Bass, 1971).
24. *Measures of Maturation: An Anthology of Early Childhood Observation Instruments* (Philadelphia: Research for Better Schools, 1973).
25. Adams, *Measurement and Evaluation*, p. 182.
26. Ethel Kawin, "Records and Reports: Observations, Tests, and Measurements," *Early Childhood*

Education 46th Yearbook, National Society for the Study of Education (Chicago: University of Chicago Press, 1947), p. 290.

27. David A. Lewis, *Computer Aids Educationally Deprived Migrant Students* (Washington, D.C.: Automated Systems Corp., div. of Averbach Associates, 1970).

28. Daniel A. Prescott, *The Child in the Educative Process* (New York: McGraw-Hill Book Co., 1957), pp. 153–54.

29. Emery Stoops and James R. Marks, *Elementary School Supervision* (Boston: Allyn and Bacon, 1965), p. 118.

30. Ben Brodinsky, ed., *Grading and Reporting* (Arlington, Va.: National School Public Relations Assn., 1972), p. 64.

31. Ibid., p. 64.

32. Ibid., pp. 32–33.

For Further Reading

Almy, Millie C. *Ways of Studying Children.* New York: Teachers College, Columbia University, 1959.

Bloom, B.S.; Hastings, J.T.; and Madaus, G.F. *Handbook of Formative and Summative Evaluation of Student Learning.* New York: McGraw-Hill Book Co., 1971.

Bronfenbrenner, Urie, and Ricciute, H.N. "The Appraisal of Personality Characteristics in Children." In *Handbook of Research Methods in Child Development*, edited by P.H. Mussen. New York: John Wiley & Sons, 1960.

Butler, Annie L. "How to Evaluate and Report Individual Progress." *Nursery School Portfolio.* Washington, D.C.: Assn. for Childhood Education International, 1969.

Carbonara, Nancy T. *Techniques for Observing Normal Child Behavior.* Pittsburgh, Pa.: University of Pittsburgh Press, 1961.

Cohen, Dorothy H. *Observing and Recording Behavior of Young Children.* New York: Teachers College, Columbia University, 1958.

Deal, T., and Wood, P. "Testing the Early Educational and Psychological Development of Children." *Review of Educational Research* 38 (1968): 12–18.

Divorky, D. "Cumulative Records: Assault on Privacy." *Learning* 2 (1973): 18–23.

Gordon, Ira J. *Studying the Child in the School.* New York: John Wiley & Sons, 1966.

Hoffman, B. *The Tyranny of Testing.* New York: Crowell Books, 1962.

Rubin, Albert I. *Projective Techniques with Children.* New York: Greene and Stratton, 1960.

Suchman, S. Richard. *Observation and Analysis in Child Development: A Laboratory Manual.* New York: Harcourt Brace Jovanovich, 1959.

Walker, Deborah K. *Socioemotional Measures for Preschool and Kindergarten Children.* San Francisco: Jossey-Bass Publishers, 1973.

Witherspoon, R.L. "Studying Young Children." *Nursery School Portfolio.* Washington, D.C.: Assn. for Childhood Educational International, 1961.

14

Financing and Budgeting

Early childhood programs are expensive. Both the scope and the quality of services are interrelated with the financial program. Prescott and Jones[1] found that programs with similar hourly costs ranged in quality from poor to excellent. One would expect positive correlation between expenditure level and quality of a program. Exceptions to this generalization come in programs that spend money wastefully, or in programs that carefully budget meager funds. Even with careful budgeting, however, good programs cannot operate effectively for long periods of time on "leftovers" without weakening the quality and quantity of their services and without damaging the morale of those involved in the program.

Few early childhood administrators receive adequate training in fiscal management. Such training is important, because parents, funding agencies, and taxpayers who feel their early childhood programs are properly managed are more likely to be receptive to needs that require additional funding. As is true of all other aspects of planning and administration, fiscal planning begins with the philosophy of the local program. Unless the proposed services and the requirements for meeting those services, in the way of staff, housing, and equipment, are taken into account, how can a budget be planned? And, although program philosophy should be considered first, probably no early childhood program is entirely free of financial limitations.

Fiscal planning affects all aspects of a program; consequently, it should involve input from all of those involved in the program—board of directors or advisory board, director, program and nonprogram personnel, and parents. By considering everyone's ideas, a more accurate conception of budgeting priorities, of expenditure level, and of revenue sources can be derived. Furthermore, planning and administering the fiscal aspects of an early childhood program should be a continuous process. Successful financing and budgeting will only come from evaluating current revenue sources and expenditures and from advance planning for existing and future priorities.

Fiscal affairs are probably the most surveyed aspect of an early childhood program. Not-for profit programs are responsible to their funding agencies and for-profit ones are accountable to their owners, stockholders, or the Internal Revenue Service. Even if the average citizen doesn't understand the problems of fund management, any hint of fund misuse will cause criticism. It becomes the responsibility of administrators to budget, to secure revenue, to manage, account for, and to substantiate expenditures in keeping with the philosophy and policies of the early childhood program, in a professional and businesslike manner.

Costs of Early Childhood Programs

Reported costs of early childhood programs show extensive variation.[2] Costs vary with the type of program (whether custodial, educational, or educational with supportive services), the level of training and quantity of staff, sponsorship (whether a federal program, public school, or parent cooperative), the delivery system, (that is, whether center-based, home visitor, or television), and with the child enrolled (age, and whether handicapped or nonhandicapped). Another factor that can contribute to variations in costs is whether the program is new or is offering new, additional services and thus has "start-up costs"—such as salaries of planning personnel and initial expenditures for housing, equipping, and advertising—or whether the program is already underway and has continuing costs. Geographic location, the amount of competition, and the general economy all contribute to the varying costs.

ESTIMATES OF PROGRAM COSTS

Among other studies, the Senate Committee on Finance has estimated costs for different programs:

1. Day-care center costs range from $1,500 to $2,800 per year;
2. Costs for family day-care home programs range from over $1,700 to $2,900; and
3. After-school care ranges from over $300 to $800 per year.[3]

Similar to the Finance Committee's study, Keyserling[4] estimates that "good" day care costs between $2,000 and $3,000 per child per year. Ruopp et al.[5] estimate that day care with an educational program and supportive services costs $2,200 per child per year in 1970 dollars. Start-up costs (for needs assessment, selection and training of staff, location of facility, initial equipment and materials purchases, insurance, and legal and licensing fees) range from $1,000 to $3,700 per child per year in 1970 dollars. Because day-care center costs are approximately $2,000 per year per child, this is what many government agencies will pay,[6] and thus, to some degree, circularity is involved. In other words, because agencies pay a certain number of dollars, program designers plan the program around the expected amount of money. If funded the first year, the planners write a similar program the next year in hopes of being refunded. Thus, the agency pays approximately the same amount again, and the cycle is continued. So, the program is designed around a specific dollar value, whether or not it makes for the "best" program.

Early childhood programs subsidized by a church or community agency may cost a little less because facilities and even some personnel services are charged to the organization that supports the program. Parent cooperatives are even less expensive, usually 50 to 70 percent of the payments for other centers, because of the contributions in terms of services. Church-sponsored cooperatives may be the least expensive, because of contributions of services by parents and contributions of housing and equipment by the church. With their educational component, Child Development Centers of the Office of Economic Opportunity cost $3,300 per child per year.[7] Lewis[8] reports that the average public school prekindergarten program, operating two to three hours per day for 40 weeks, costs between $700 and $1,100 per child per year.

Mainstreaming increases the costs of early childhood programs. Frohreich [9] found that certain expenditure categories contributed significantly to cost differences between exceptional-child programs and regular programs: (1) instruction was the largest single component of expenditure; (2) transportation, especially for crippled children, was very high; (3) instructional support expenditures, for counselors, psychologists, and medical personnel, were major factors when the program used support personnel; and (4) regular classrooms that were converted to rooms for handicapped and nonhandicapped students together, resulting in fewer students per class, produced square footage per pupil and thus increased the cost. Rossmiller et al.'s study,[10] conducted for the National Education Finance Project, analyzed a nationwide sample of 24 school districts that reportedly provided high quality and comprehensive education programs for handicapped children. To compute the cost indices in each category of exceptionality, a foundation cost index of 1.0 corresponded to the amount a district was spending per child in its general elementary and secondary education programs. Cost indices for exceptional children were as follows:

Intellectually gifted	1.14
Speech handicapped	1.18
Educable mentally retarded	1.87
Trainable mentally retarded	2.10
Special learning disorders	2.16
Multiple handicapped	2.73
Emotionally disturbed	2.83
Visually handicapped	2.97
Auditorily handicapped	2.99
Physically handicapped	3.64

A study[11] to evaluate the costs of serving handicapped children in Head Start indicated that costs for the average handicapped child in a Head Start program were approximately 1.69 times the cost of serving a typical child, which averages over $1,600 per year. Two points were made in discussing the findings:

1. Because costs are a function of the type and degree of the handicap

involved, average costs are almost meaningless; and

2. Head Start costs cannot be used in computing costs for public schools because Head Start budgets allocate a smaller proportion of monies to teachers' salaries and a larger proportion to support personnel salaries than do public schools; public schools would add more credentialled teachers (rather than paraprofessionals) when a more intense teacher-child ratio was desired, while the reverse was true for Head Start; and public schools, with their emphasis on academic learnings, would require more instructional materials when handicapped children are involved in their programs, but Head Start programs, with their emphasis on psychomotor and affective activities, would not require as many additional materials for use with the mainstreamed child.

COSTS TO FAMILIES

It is estimated that only one percent of families can afford quality day-care costs for one child, and even fewer can afford quality care for more than one child.[12] Costs to families may differ from absolute program costs because of "direct subsidies," "foregone income," and monies made available for support of local programs. There are several types of direct subsidies, such as Aid to Families with Dependent Children (AFDC) and Project Head Start for families who qualify. Direct subsidy is also provided through the federal income tax deduction allowed for day-care services (IRS Form 2441).

Costs to families will vary according to the amount of income foregone when a family member provides child-care services rather than obtaining outside employment. The income is considered foregone when a family member provides child-care services without payment, or on an intrafamilial income transfer. In either case, the amount of foregone income depends on the care-giver's employable skills and availability of employment, or their potential income. (Of course, one should consider costs of outside employment, such as transportation, clothing, organization or union dues, and higher taxes, in calculating foregone income.)

Financing Early Childhood Programs

Early childhood programs receive funds from local, state, and federal resources, as well as from foundations, fees and tuition, and miscellaneous sources. Various regulations govern: (1) a program's eligibility to receive revenue from a source such as the federal government: (2) procedures for obtaining revenue; (3) use made of the revenue: and (4) which personnel are accountable for the expenditure. Because of the many types of programs and the intricacies and variations involved in funding, we will give only a brief description of sources of financing.

PUBLIC SCHOOL FINANCING

Public school programs are supported by local, state, and federal monies. Taxation is the major source of monies available for funding; consequently, revenues for public school programs are closely tied to the general economy of the local area, state, and nation.

Local Support.   Tax funds are used to maintain and operate the schools, and the sale of bonds is used for capital improvements and new construction expenses. The local school board's authority to set tax rates and to issue bonds for school revenue purposes is granted by the state—that is, authority is *not* implied. When granted the power to tax, state laws concerning tax rates and procedural matters must be followed by the local school board in an exacting manner. In this way, the state protects the public from misuse and mismanagement of public monies.

In most states, local school districts tax real and personal property based on some fraction of its market value. Only state laws can change the maximum tax rate for local schools. If a local board desires a tax rate increase, not in excess of maximum rates, it must follow state statutory procedures in presenting the tax increase issue to the voter. (Increases are usually requested when the budget exceeds the amount of revenue that will be collected under present tax rates or, occasionally, for accumulation of excess operating funds, which is limited by statute.) If the board needs the revenue for the proposed budget and the tax referendum fails, the school board must trim its budget or borrow from future tax receipts.

The sale of bonds is the main source of revenue for major improvements of the school plant or for construction of new schools. Bonds are certificates documenting a debt by the school district. A special election is called for the purpose of approving the sale of bonds; if the referendum passes, the bonds are sold and the revenues used for the specified purposes.

State Support.   The amount of state support for public schools varies widely from state to state. Almost every state has some form of a foundation program that is designed to equalize the tax burden and the educational opportunity among various school districts in a state. Generally, the foundation program begins with a definition of minimum standards of educational service that must be offered throughout the state. The cost of maintaining the standards is calculated and the rate of taxation prescribed. The tax rate may be uniform, or based on an economic index ability—the ability of a local school district to pay. If local taxes do not cover the cost of maintaining minimum standards, the balance of the costs is provided via state monies.

These monies come from three sources: (1) earnings from permanent school funds or lands; (2) taxes and fees specified for educational purposes, including license fees, occupational, inheritance and gift, and specific activity taxes; and (3) appropriations from the state's general revenue fund, the major source of support, obtained from state income and retail sales taxes.

States vary considerably in the machinery they use for channeling state monies to local school districts, the most common plans being flat and equalization grants. States which have *flat grant* plans require that local school districts meet minimum standards for local taxation. The state sets the standards for determining a minimum (and maximum) tax rate, expressed in mills or cents, of assessed valuation of taxable property. Local school districts desiring flat grants from state revenues are then awarded on the basis of average daily attendance (or on the basis of "per certified employee") in the local district and paid periodically during the fiscal year. *Equalization grants* are given on the basis of local need, in order to achieve some degree of equality in local district school funds throughout the state. States which use equalization grants have formulas that consider average daily attendance, local tax rates, and assessed property valuation.

Federal Support.   Since the 1940s, the federal government has become the chief tax collector. There has also been a trend toward unprecedented expenditures for education through the Office of Education, the Office of Human Development Service, and the Community Services Administration, as well as other federal agencies. Consequently, public schools (as well as other institutions, agencies, and organizations) are relying more and more on federal assistance programs to undergird their local and state resources. Federal funding of public schools is used for two purposes: (1) to improve the quality of education (e.g., research, experimentation, training, housing, and equipping); and (2) to encourage greater effort by states and local districts to improve the quality of education by providing initial or matching funds for a program.

FEDERAL FINANCING

In addition to programs receiving some federal fiscal support, such as the public schools, some early childhood programs, such as Head Start, and research and demonstration projects were conceived as federally-supported programs. The extent of federal involvement in early childhood programs is not easily determined. The lists of federal early childhood programs may include direct subsidies, monies to support local projects, and other miscellaneous types of support, such as milk subsidies or credit from the Small Business Administration. The purpose of most federal assistance programs was to accomplish particular educational objectives, or to meet the needs of specific groups. Most federal assistance programs require state and/or local support in varying amounts.

Funding Sources.   Federal funding sources are in a state of constant change.*
The reader should refer to the latest edition or update of the *Catalog of Federal Domestic Assistance* (Washington, D.C.: U.S. Government Printing Office), which describes some of the federal agencies administering various assistance programs and some of the projects and services funded under these agencies.

Department of Health, Education, and Welfare. The Department of Health, Education, and Welfare (DHEW) supports programs that include the funding of direct services, the training of personnel to provide services, conducting research, and using demonstration or pilot projects to discover ways to achieve program objectives. In the Department of Health, Education, and Welfare, the Office of Human Development Services and the Office of Education administer the major federal programs in early childhood education; however, other

*The impending division of the Dept. of Health, Education, and Welfare into two departments is testimony to the existing state of flux.

agencies are involved, also. A few of the many assistance programs (arranged alphabetically by federal agency only) are briefly described as follows:

Federal Agency: Health Care Financing Administration.

Authorization: Title XIX, Social Security Act as amended.

Purpose of Funding: Formula grants are provided for Early and Periodic Screening, Diagnosis, and Treatment (EPSDT) service to "Medicaid" children under 21.0 years. (Formula grants are provided for payments of Medical Assistance.)

Applicant Eligibility: State and local welfare agencies who operate under an HEW approved (Medicaid) State plan.

Federal Agency: Health Services Administration, Public Health Service.

Authorization: Social Security Act, P.L. 74–271, Title V, Sec. 503.

Purpose of Funding: Financial assistance to states to extend and improve services for reducing the incidence of infant mortality and improving maternal and child health. (For formula grants under Fund A, there is a 50 percent matching requirement for states; project grants, under Fund B have no matching requirement.)

Applicant Eligibility: Formula grants are available to state health agencies. Limited project grants are available to state health agencies and to institutions of higher learning.

Federal Agency: Health Services Administration, Public Health Service

Authorization: Social Security Act, P.L. 74–271, Title V, Sec. 504.

Purpose of Funding: Financial assistance to states to extend and improve services to crippled children and children suffering from conditions leading to crippling. (For formula grants under Fund A, there is a 50 percent matching requirement for states; project grants under Fund B have no matching requirement.)

Applicant Eligibility: Formula grants are available to state crippled children's agencies. Limited project grants are available to state crippled children's agencies and to institutions of higher learning.

Federal Agency: Office of Human Development Services.

Authorization: P.L. 93–644, Title V, Part A (Head Start Act).

Purpose of Funding: Provides grants for comprehensive health, educational, nutritional, and social services to preschool economically disadvantaged children and their families and for involvement of parents in activities with their children. (Federal funds pay for 80 percent with a 20 percent non-federal share supplied in cash or in kind—space, equipment, volunteer servcies, etc.)

Applicant Eligibility: Any public or private not-for-profit agency which meets the requirements.

Federal Agency: Office of Human Development Services.

Authorization: Title IV, Part B, Sec. 426.

Purpose of Funding: Funds for research and demonstration projects in the area of child and family development and welfare. (Grants pay for 95 percent of costs with the grantees providing 5 percent of direct costs.)

Applicant Eligibility: Institutions of higher learning and not-for-profit organizations and agencies engaged in research or child welfare activities.

Federal Agency: Office of Education.

Authorization: P.L. 93–644, Title V, Part B (Follow Through Act).

Purpose of Funding: Funds to sustain and augument in the primary grades the gains that children from low-income families make from Head Start and other quality preschool programs. (Discretionary grants or contracts and formula grants or contracts are provided.)

Applicant Eligibility: Discretionary grants or contracts to approved local education agencies, public and private institutions of higher learning, and educational and research organizations or agencies. Formula grants for state educational practices.

Federal Agency: Office of Education.

Authorization: Bilingual Education Act; Title VII of the Elementary and Secondary Education Act.

Purpose of Funding: Funds to help meet the needs of preschool and older children who have limited English speaking ability and to demonstrate effective ways of providing such children instruction designed to enable them, while using their native language, to achieve competence in English. (Project and formula grants and research grants and research contracts are funded. State education agencies are allowed up to 5 percent of the amounts awarded to the local education agency under the basic program during the preceding fiscal year.)

Applicant Eligibility: All states, District of Columbia, Puerto Rico, Guam, American Samoa, the Virgin Islands, the Trust Territory of the Pacific Islands and the Department of the Interior. Grants made to state education agencies, local education agencies, and institutions of higher education. Research contracts are available to public and private organizations.

Federal Agency: Office of Education

Authorization: Education of the Handicapped Act, Title VI, Part B.

Purpose of Funding: Provide grants to states to assist them in providing free appropriate education to all handicapped children. (After the state's "Annual Program Plan" is submitted and approved under the requirements of P.L. 94–142, a grant award document representing the total grant amount for that fiscal year or portion thereof is forwarded to the state department of education.)

Applicant Eligibility: State education agencies in the 50 states, District of Columbia, Puerto Rico, American Samoa, Guam, Virgin Islands, and Trust Territory of the Pacific Islands, and the Department of the Interior, Bureau of Indian Affairs.

Federal Agency: Office of Education.

Authorization: Education of the Handicapped Act, P.L. 91–230, Title VI, Part C, 20 U.S.C. 1423, as amended by P.L. 95–49.

Purpose of Funding: Funds to support experimental, demonstration, outreach and state implementation of preschool and early childhood projects for handicapped children. (Federal funds pay 90 percent with a 10 percent nonfederal share supplied in cash or in kind.)

Applicant Eligibility: Public agencies and private not-for-profit organizations.

Federal Agency: Office of Education.

Authorization: Title I; Elementary and Secondary Education Act, Part A.

Purpose of Funding: Provide formula grants to expand and improve public and private elementary and secondary educational programs to meet the needs of educationally disadvantaged children. (Formula grants with no matching funds requirement.)

Applicant Eligibility: Departments of Education in states and outlying areas; Bureau of Indian Affairs.

Federal Agency: Office of Education.

Authorization: Elementary and Secondary Education Act, Title IV, Part C, as amended by P.L. 93–380.

Purpose of Funding: Monies to support supplementary education centers and services, fund innovative projects, improve health and nutrition projects in schools, and strengthen state and local educational agencies. (Formula grants with no matching funds requirements.)

Applicant Eligibility: Any state which establishes a State Title IV Advisory Council and submits a state program plan designating the State educational agency as the sole administrator of the plan. The "Annual State Program Plan" must meet certain requirements.

Federal Agency: Office of Education.

Authorization: Title IV, Sec. 404, P.L. 93–380.

Purpose of Funding: Monies to support state and local planning, development, operation, and improvement of programs designed to meet the special education needs of gifted and talented. (Project grants with no matching funds requirements.)

Applicant Eligibility: The Commissioner is authorized to contract with public or private agencies for the establishment and operation of model projects. Grants may be made to state educational agencies (or consortia thereof) and local educational agencies. Grants may be made to institutions of higher learning for personnel training programs.

Federal Agency: Social Security Administration.

Authorization: Title IV, Part B, Sec. 426.

Purpose of Funding: Grants are provided for innovative research and demonstrations that are in keeping with Social Security Administration priorities in child welfare. (Federal funds pay 90 percent of costs with grantees sharing in 10 percent of total project costs.)

Applicant Eligibility: All states, District of Columbia, and not-for-profit organizations.

Department of Agriculture. The Department of Agriculture has assistance programs concerned with nutrition for maternal and child health. We will briefly describe some of the specific assistance programs.

Federal Agency: Food and Nutrition Service.

Authorization: National School Lunch Act of 1946, as amended.

Purpose of Funding: Funds to assist state, through cash grants and food donations, in making school lunch program available to all school children, and thereby promoting their health and well-being. (Formula grants and sale, exchange, or donation of property and goods are provided with various matching requirements.)

Applicant Eligibility: States and U.S. Territory agencies, and private schools, residential child care centers, and settlement houses which are exempt from taxes under the I.R.S. code.

Federal Agency: Food and Nutrition Service.

Authorization: Sec. 4 of the Child Nutrition Act, as amended.

Purpose of Funding: Funds to assist states in providing nutritious breakfasts for school children, through cash grants and food donations. (Formula grants and sale, exchange, or donation of property and goods are provided with various matching requirements.)

Applicant Eligibility: States and U.S. Territory agencies and private schools which are exempt from taxes under the IRS code.

Federal Agency: Food and Nutrition Service.

Authorization: Child Nutrition Act of 1966, as amended.

Purpose of Funding: Funds to encourage consumption of fluid milk through reimbursement to eligible schools and institutions that inaugurate or expand milk distribution service. (Formula grants with no matching requirement, but the cost of milk in excess of Federal reimbursement must be borne by sources within the state.)

Applicant Eligibility: States or U.S. Territory agencies or not-for-profit private schools or child care institutions.

Federal Agency: Food and Nutrition Service.

Authorization: Child Nutrition Act of 1966, as amended.

Purpose of Funding: Funds to make supplemental foods available to pregnant or lactating women, infants, and children up to 5.0 years of age. (Project grants are allocated on the basis of a modified DHEW, MCH, Title V formula with no matching funds required, but states and local agencies are expected to bear the administrative costs in excess of 20 percent of the total grant.)

Applicant Eligibility: Only local agencies qualifying under state agency applications submitted to the Department may operate "Women, Infants, and Children Program" (WIC Program).

Department of Labor. Programs relevant to early childhood care and education under the Department of Labor are primarily concerned with training adults in occupations that will allow them to support their families. Day-care services are made available so that parents can participate in the training programs. The following is an example of a specific program:

Federal Agency: Employment and Training Administration, Department of Labor in cooperation with the Office of Human Development Services.

Authorization: Title IV-A of the Social Security Act.

Purpose of Funding: Funds to provide needed child care for those participating in employment or training under Work Incentive Employment (WIN). (Federal funds are authorized to pay 90 percent of state costs for child care, with a 10 percent state matching amount in cash only.)

Applicant Eligibility: All states, the District of Columbia, Puerto Rico, Virgin Islands, and Guam.

Community Services Administration. The Community Services Administration funds some programs authorized under the Economic Opportunity Act of 1964, as amended by the Community Services Act of 1974. Two of these programs are as follows:

Federal Agency: Community Services Administration.

Authorization: Economic Opporutnity Act of 1964, as amended by Community Services Act of 1974, Title II, P.L. 93–644.

Purpose of Funding: Funds are available for project grants to community organizations. Projects may include day care and school-age education for children from low income families. (Usually a 30 percent nonfederal contribution for a community action agency receiving annual financial assistance of $300,000 or less, and 40 percent for a community action agency receiving more than $300,000 annually.)

Applicant Eligibility: A community action agency must be designated by the state, a political subdivision of the state, or a combination of such political subdivisions or Indian tribal governments. These governments may also designate themselves or a separate public agency or not-for-profit organization as a community action agency.

Federal Agency: Community Services Administration.

Authorization: Economic Opportunity Act of 1964, as amended by the Community Services Act of 1964, Title II, Sec. 222 (a) (5).

Purpose of Funding: Funds may be used for planning and establishing community nutrition programs only if it is understood that "Community Food and Nutrition" funds are available as seed money or for start-up costs. (No local matching of funds is required; however, grantees must guarantee community mobilization to assist in counteracting conditions of starvation and malnutrition.)

Applicant Eligibility: Not-for-profit corporations, public and private agencies, Indian tribal councils, and migrant and seasonal farmworker organizations.

Appalachian Regional Commission. The Appalachian Regional Commission funds assistance programs authorized under the Appalachian Regional Development Act of 1965. One of these assistance programs directly involves young children, as follows:

Federal Agency: Appalachian Regional Commission.

Authorization: Appalachian Regional Development Act of 1965.

Purpose of Funding: Funds to create a state and substate capacity for planning child development programs and a program to provide child development services in under served areas throughout the region, and to test innovative projects and programs for replicability. (For operating grants, a gradual scale of nonfederal cash support is required, with a minimum cash requirement of 5 percent in the second year, and 15 percent in the third and subsequent years. For grants for planning, program development, and evaluation, the federal share shall not exceed 75 percent of total cost. Equipment and construction projects are limited to a maximum of 80 percent federal participation.)

Applicant Eligibility: State interagency committees are eligible for planning grants. Public and private not-for-profit organizations are eligible for project grants, if the projects are consistent with the state plan and priorities.

Department of the Interior. The Department of the Interior funds early childhood programs for reservation Indian children. The assistance programs are authorized under the Snyder Act of 1921 and the Johnson-O'Malley Act of 1934. Two assistance programs are as follows:

Federal Agency: Bureau of Indian Affairs.

Authorization: Snyder Act, Nov. 2, 1921.

Purpose of Funding: Payments for foster-home care and appropriate institutional care for dependent, neglected, and handicapped Indian children residing on or near reservations, including those children living in jurisdictions under the BIA in Alaska and Oklahoma, where these services are not available from state or local public agencies. (Direct payments with unrestricted use.)

Applicant Eligibility: Dependent, neglected, and handicapped Indian children whose families live on or near reservations, including those children living in jurisdictions under BIA in Alaska and Oklahoma.

Federal Agency: Bureau of Indian Affairs.

Authorization: Johnson-O'Malley Act of April 16, 1934.

Purpose of Funding: Funds are made available to assure adequate educational opportunities for Indian children attending public schools and tribally-operated, previously private schools. (Direct payments are based on formula specified in 25 Code of Federal Regulations 273 for supplementary programs.)

Applicant Eligibility: Public school districts and previously private schools that have eligible Indian children in attendance and whose educational services meet established state standards.

Miscellaneous Federal Assistance Programs. As we have mentioned, the Internal Revenue Code provides deductions for child-care expenses incurred by fully-employed individuals and married couples. The Housing and Community Development Act of 1974 authorizes funds for services, including child care in community development programs. Finally, through the Small Business Administration, loans may be obtained to establish child care centers as a profit-making venture, with the federal government providing funds for up to 90 percent of the loan.

Obtaining Federal Funds.   There are several problems associated with obtaining federal assistance. As you can see, there is a bewildering array of funding agencies and assistance programs. Along with the problems of dealing with the number of federal sources, there is a jumble of rulings from agencies. Finally, assistance programs are constantly being deleted and added, and appropriations may fall below congressional authorization.

Most federal funds are obtained by writing and submitting a grant proposal and having the proposal approved and funded. One person on the early childhood staff should oversee the entire writing of the proposal, although input should be obtained from all those involved in the program. In fact, early childhood programs that plan to seek regular federal assistance may find it advantageous to hire a staff member with expertise in the area of obtaining federal as well as other funds, such as foundation grants, that require proposal writing. Proposal writing can vary according to an assistance program's particular requirements, but most require a similar format.

Preproposal Planning. Preproposal planning is, in essence, research. And, as is true with any research, problem identification is the first step. What need exists? If the assistance program sends out a "Request for Proposal" (RFP), the need is already defined in broad or general terms.

The next step is gathering documented evidence that needs exist in the population or potential population served by the early childhood program. Also, assessment must be made as to how critical or extensive the need is. Most proposals require that needs, and the degree of these needs, be described in terms of demographic, geographic, socioeconomic distribution, and racial/ethnic makeup. Because proposals often have to be written quickly (perhaps two to four weeks), keep an up-to-date notebook with this data available. You may secure such data from these and other sources:

Community Action Associations (local)

Department of Public Welfare (local and state)
Federal publications (found in the *Monthly Catalog of U.S. Government Publications*)
U.S. Department of Commerce, Bureau of the Census
U.S. Department of Labor, Bureau of Labor Statistics
U.S. Department of Labor, Employment and Training Administration

The literature must be reviewed to see whether others have handled the problem, and with what results. Research and evaluation studies may be found in such sources as:

Educational Resources Information Center (ERIC)
ERIC Document Reproduction Service
P.O. Box 190
Arlington, Va. 22210

Human Resources Abstracts
Sage Publications, Inc.
275 South Beverly Drive
Beverly Hills, Calif. 90212

Monthly Catalog of U.S. Government Publications
U.S. Government Printing Office
Washington, D.C. 20402

In order to prevent duplication of services in a local area, one must also present evidence as to whether the same or similar needs are being met by other local programs. Check with local social service organizations, which can be identified through the telephone directory, the Department of Public Welfare, and agencies served by the United Fund or Community Chest.

Finally, write a two- or three-page preproposal prospectus. The prospectus should contain a statement of the proposed problem, what will be done about the problem, the target group to be served, and whether there is a need for the proposed early childhood program. The prospectus is helpful in clarifying one's thinking and in getting the opinion of others, including reviewers of funding agencies. (Some federal agencies require a prospectus before accepting a complete proposal.)

Funding sources must also be identified. Compilations of federal assistance may be found in the following sources:

Annual Register of Grant Support
Marquis Academic Media
Marquis Who's Who, Inc.
200 East Ohio Street
Chicago, Ill. 60611

Catalog of Federal Assistance
Executive Office of the President
Office of Management and Budget
Washington, D.C. 20503

Federal Funds for Day Care Projects
Women's Bureau Pamphlet 14, revised
U.S. Government Printing Office
Washington, D.C. 20402

User's Guide to Funding Resources
Human Resources Network
Chilton Book Company
Radnor, Pa. 19087

Writing the Proposal.   Federal agencies have their own guidelines for writing a proposal; they differ from agency to agency, but should be followed exactly. Most guidelines wish these points to be covered in the body of the proposal:

1. Statement of problem—general and specific objectives, documentation of needs and degree of needs, review of literature of programs that have tried to meet the specified needs, and description of any local programs currently involved in meeting specified needs;
2. Program goals and objectives—description of broad program goals and specific, measurable outcomes expected as a result of the program;
3. Population to be served—What qualifications will children and/or parents need for inclusion in the program? Will you accept all who qualify? If not, how will you choose from among those who qualify?;
4. Plan of procedure—Were there several alternative approaches to solving the problem? If so, why did you select a particular alternative? How will you accomplish each objective?;
5. Administration of project—What staffing requirements are being proposed? Indicate how the program will be managed by including an organizational chart and writing brief job descriptions. Include a short vita of the program director. What is your program's capability to conduct the proposed project? Do you have community support? Show a time schedule of activities that will occur from the day of funding until project termination;
6. Program evaluation—What assessment devices will be used? Who will conduct the assessment?;
7. Future funding—How will you continue to operate the program at the conclusion of federal assistance?;
8. Budget—personnel and nonpersonnel costs; and
9. Appendices—job descriptions, director's vita, organizational structure of the early childhood program.

There are several available sources for ideas on proposal writing:

Hall, M. *Deveolping Skills in Proposal Writing.* Corvallis, Ore.: Continuing Education Publications, n.d.

Kush, G. *An Introduction to Proposal Writing: A Self Instructional Program Text.* Tempe, Ariz.: Cook Christian Training School, 1974.

MacIntyre, M. *How to Write a Proposal.* Washington, D.C.: Educational, Training, and Research Corporation, n.d.

A Manual for Obtaining Government Grants. Boston: Robert J. Corcoran Co., 1972.

Meyer, J. *Writing Action Proposals.* Houston, Texas: Center for Human Resources, University of Houston, College of Business Administraion, 1976.

Proposal Review Checklist. Washington, D.C.: Day Care and Child Development Council of America, 1973.

Stalking the Large Green Grant. Washington, D.C.: National Youth Alternative Project, 1976.

White, V.P. *Grants, How to Find Out About Them and What to Do Next.* New York: Plenum Press, 1975.

Some agencies also require completion of an application form, which usually asks for information about the general subject, to whom you are submitting the proposal, legal authorization, the project title, the name of the person submitting the proposal and/or the program director's name, address, and telephone number, the probable budget, the amount of funds requested, and the date the application is transmitted. Some agencies have a form for a proposal abstract, and usually require that this summary be no longer than two hundred words. You may also need to fill out forms assuring protection of human subjects and nondiscrimination.

FOUNDATION SUPPORT

Foundations are one of several kinds of nongovernmental, not-for-profit organizations that promote public welfare, including that of young children, through the use of private wealth.[13,14] Other similar organizations are trusts and endowments. Foundation aid is typically given to support research. Because of increased federal support of education, foundation grants to education have decreased in the past few years. Nevertheless, administrators of early childhood programs need to investigate foundations as a potential source of funds.

Several foundations support research projects concerned with young children and child advocacy programs, among them:

Carnegie Corporation of New York
437 Madison Avenue
New York, N.Y. 10022
   Awards grants primarily to academic institutions and national and regional organizations to improve education at all levels. Grants are not awarded to individuals, for building or endowment funds, or for operating budgets.

The Clark Foundation
250 Park Avenue, Room 900
New York, N.Y. 10017
   Grants are given to projects seeking to improve the chances of a permanent and stable family life for dependent and neglected children in institutional and foster care. There are no grants or loans to individuals for scholarships or fellowships. Endowments, capital expenditures for construction or equipment, or ongoing expenses are not funded.

The Commonwealth Fund
One East 75th Street
New York, N.Y. 10021
   Grants are given to medical schools and grants and fellowships are awarded to medical and biomedical students.

The Ford Foundation
320 E. 43rd Street
New York, N.Y. 10017
   Grants are awarded in many areas which advance public welfare. Early childhood programs conducting research on learning, or seeking ways to improve educational quality, may be eligible. Restrictions were not given in The Foundation Directory.

Foundation for Child Development
345 East 46th Street, Room 700
New York, N.Y. 10017

Grants are awarded for research, policy development, and selected service experiments designed to improve social institutions affecting the lives of children and their families. No grants are given to individuals, for endowments, or for operating budgets.

Gould Foundation for Children
126 East 31st Street
New York, N.Y. 10016

Grants are awarded for child welfare projects, with priority given to agencies affiliated with the Foundation. Grants are not given to individuals, for endowments, for building funds, or for operating budgets.

Ittleson Foundation, Inc. (formerly Ittleson Family Foundation)
660 Madison Avenue
New York, N.Y. 10021

Grants are awarded for projects in health, welfare, and education, with emphasis on mental health and psychiatric research. No grants are awarded for projects in the humanities, in general education, to social agencies offering direct service to people outside New York City, to individuals, for endowments, or for building.

Johnson Foundation
P.O. Box 2316
Princeton, N.J. 08540

Grants are awarded in the field of personal health care. Grants are not available to individuals, to finance biomedical research, to finance international activities, for endowments, or for construction or equipment costs.

The New World Foundation
100 East 85th Street
New York, N.Y. 10028

Grants are awarded for projects seeking improvements in the education of children. No grants are awarded for endowments, building-fund campaigns, capital investments, general operating budgets, or to individuals or institutions which discriminate.

Similar to the process of obtaining federal funds, foundation funds are also obtained through submission and approval of a proposal. The foundation's board of directors determines the guidelines for submitting proposals, sets a deadline for application, reviews proposals, and selects recipients. Several helpful sources for learning to secure foundation funds are:

Dermer, J. *How to Raise Funds from Foundations*. New York: Public Service Materials Center, 1977.
———. *How to Write Successful Foundation Presentations*. New York: Public Service Materials Center, 1977.
Foundation Center Information Quarterly. New York: The Foundation Center, n.d.
The Foundation Directory. New York: The Foundation Center, 1977.
Margolin, J.B. *About Foundations, How to Find the Facts You Need to Get a Grant*. New York: The Foundation Center, 1977.

FEES, TUITION, AND MISCELLANEOUS
SOURCES OF FUNDS

For-profit private programs usually operate almost exclusively on tuition and fees, and are usually the most expensive. In a few cases, they may sponsor fund-raising drives, such as carnivals and bake sales, receive donations, or they may be eligible for grants from foundations or the federal government. Although some parents pay up to 25 percent of their income for full-day care for one or more children, 10 percent of their combined gross incomes is a more reasonable and manageable figure. There are two ways to determine fees and tuition for early childhood programs. One can draw up a budget, and subtract monies received from other funding sources. The remaining costs (and profit, if this is a profit-making program) are then distributed among the children. The second method is to determine the amount of money on a fixed fee, a sliding scale, or two fixed fees for different income bracket bases and balance the budget with funds from other sources. One problem with this method is that information must be available as to family income. Your community's income distribution is available from the Bureau of Labor Statistics, and parents may be willing to supply this information. A second problem is that fixed fees may exclude lower-class families. On the other hand, a sliding scale requires enough higher-income families to balance the lower-income families. Higher-income families would have to be willing to contribute more money. Another problem is that the administrator needs an extremely accurate estimate of monies to be secured from other funding sources.

Rowe and Husby[15] explain that computing cost per child on the basis of enrollment underestimates the cost by 15 percent, because most children are not in attendance every hour the early childhood program is open and some children are enrolled part-time. To remedy this underestimation, Ruoff et al.[16] found that the baseline for determining cost should be cost per child hour.

In addition to carefully calculating fees and tuition, an early childhood program must have definite policies on fee payment. Loss of income may occur as a result of absenteeism or child turnover. These suggestions might be considered in establishing a fee policy:

1. Set a deposit fee at time of enrollment, to be returned at time of withdrawal if all monetary policies have been met (two- or three-weeks' tuition or fees is reasonable.
2. Several weeks' notice should be given to withdraw a child. (The fee deposit covers this if notice is not given in advance.)
3. Children on the waiting list must be enrolled within a stated period of time after notification, or their place on the waiting list will be forfeited.
4. Payments may be no more in arrears than the amount of the initial deposit.
5. Payments must be made when a child misses a few days, or a withdrawal notice should be given for an extended absence.

There are several miscellaneous sources of funds for early childhood programs.

1. Public support via a community campaign can help balance the difference between the program's anticipated income and its expenses. For example, some programs qualify for United Ways funds (which may be called by some other name). There are specific eligibility requirements for qualifying for such local funds.
2. In-kind contributions (that is, noncash contributions) are often available through some community resource, such as a charitable organization. In-kind contributions include program and nonprogram volunteer services, free rent, and payment of utility bills.
3. Endowments may be given in someone's memory or scholarships may be awarded.
4. The early childhood program may engage in fundraising projects to supplement income from other sources.

Budgeting

A budget is a list of all goods and services for which payment may be made. Budgets are important because no matter how good a program is, it cannot continue to operate if it is not on a sound fiscal foundation. Limited funds require making decisions about priorities, and funding and regulatory agencies require information about monetary functions. We will not attempt to project the expenditure level of a particular program, because costs vary with types and quality of services, with the extent of a program, and with the geographical area, but we can describe features of budgeting that apply to most programs.

REGULATIONS GOVERNING BUDGET MAKING AND ADOPTION

Public school programs are subject to many budget regulations. In setting up a budget, a local school district is subject to constitutional or statutory limitations. The superintendent of schools (or other administrative personnel under his direction) determines the budget, estimates the assessed valuation of taxable property (minus an estimated amount for delinquent taxes), computes the tax rate and other sources of revenue needed to meet the proposed budget, and presents it to the school board. In most states, after the school board has tentatively approved a budget, a revised budget that includes the board's changes is made available to the public and hearings are held. (The budget is invalidated if state procedure is not followed exactly.) After the hearings, the board can adopt additional changes, if it desires. (States rarely give the public the right to mandate changes.) Unless the state requires fiscal control by other government agencies, such as the city government, the budget adoption process ends with the printing of the final draft. Fiscally dependent school districts (those that rely heavily on federal and/or state funds) must have their budgets reviewed by the designated government agencies before the adoption process ends.

Budgets of private and federally-funded early childhood programs are developed by local program directors. Efforts are usually made to include the opinions of various personnel in the first draft of the proposed budget. The budgets are presented to their respective boards of directors or advisors for approval. In addition to the board's approval, regulations may require that the budget be presented to licensing and/or funding agency personnel before approval.

DEVELOPING A BUDGET

Budgets usually have three components: (1) a synopsis of the program; (2) specifically itemized expenditures for operating the program including direct costs (items that can be attributed to a particular aspect of the program, such as personnel salaries and indirect costs, or overhead items that cannot be attributed to a particular aspect of the program, such as interest on bank loans, utility costs, and advertising) and (3) anticipated revenues and their sources, including in-kind contributions. Before writing the budget, the administrators should list the program's objectives and needs. The program and the fiscal plan should be carefully related and in writing. Although there are many ways of presenting data, an effective way is to present it under the same headings as the proposed expenditures.

The proposed expenditures are careful estimates of the money required to operate the local program and should be organized under headings that fit the local program. These headings are referred to as the budget format, two types of which are:

1. The functional classification format, which assembles data in terms of categories for which money will be used, such as administration, child instruction, parent education, food and health services, and transportation. The advantage of the functional classification format is that one can readily link expenditure categories to program purposes. Disadvantages to this approach are that functional categories tend to be somewhat broad, raising questions as to expenditures within a classification, and there is not always a distinct classification for a particular item; for example, health services may be provided for within several other classifications.

2. The line-item classification format lists the sums allocated to specifics of the program (salaries of designated personnel, gas, electricity, water, telephone, postage, etc.). The major advantage of this approach is that it shows specific accountability of expenditures. On the other hand, if the categories are very fine, the director has little power to exercise changes in expenditures.

Regardless of the format used, an allowance for emergencies is reasonable. Some items which must be included are:

Personnel salaries and fringe benefits
> regular staff (program and nonprogram)
> consultant staff (health personnel, social workers, psychologists, educators, and business personnel hired on a semiregular basis as opposed to a consultant hired for in-service education)

Fees (licensing, incorporation)
Housing (mortgage or rent payments on buildings, insurance, money for repairs, utilities)
Furniture, equipment, materials, and supplies for:
    children
    office and workroom
    food service
    teacher/parent lounge
    housekeeping and maintenance
    repairs
Food and health services for children
Laundry
Vehicles:
    maintenance
    fuel
    insurance
In-service education:
    consultant fees
    travel costs
    supplies/equipment
    professional library
    professional conferences or workshops
Parent education:
    consultant fees
    supplies/equipment
Postage and telephone
Publicity costs
Bank and auditor fees
Emergency allowance (small amounts of petty cash for items not planned for)

After the expenditure section the administrators should furnish actual figures for the current fiscal year. Any significant difference between current services and expenditures and those proposed should be explained. In planning the expenditure section, administrators should keep in mind that:

1. Wages or salaries must be paid on time:
2. A desirable inventory level is one that will carry a program through two months of operation;[17]
3. A program may have cash flow problems. Federal funds do not pay ahead of time for expenses; receipts and proof of money spent are required for reimbursement, and even reimbursement checks may come irregularly.

To prevent cash flow problems:

1. Do not overestimate initial enrollment.
2. Do not purchase all equipment at the beginning. Also calculate equipment estimates on cost per use rather than on the purchase price. For example, it is more expensive to spend $100 on equipment and then not use it than to spend $500 on equipment that will be in constant use.
3. The number of staff hired should correspond to initial enrollment.

4. Expect enrollment variations, for example, a summer lull.
5 Check with the government agency for its reimbursement schedule, which may be six months or longer. Determine whether the local bank will give credit or a short-term loan to state or federally funded centers that receive government reimbursements.

The third part of the budget is an estimate of income or receipts. This section should clearly indicate monies earmarked for a specified purpose, such as staff training. Two excellent sources of useful budgeting information are:

Beyers, B.B. *A Planning and Budget Management System for Day Care.* Washington, D.C.: Educational Projects, 1974. ERIC ED 095 622

DeBies, R.C. *Budget, School Business Management Handbook No. 3 Revised.* Albany, N.Y.: New York State Education Department, 1968. ERIC ED 065 922.

An example of an actual budget for study purposes is found in:

Revels, V. *A Plan for Establishing a Child Care Center on the Campus of Bladen Technical Institute,* 1976. ERIC ED 125 708.

Examples of other actual budgets may be found in ERIC under descriptions of "budgets" and "early childhood education," or can be obtained by writing for the budgets of some model programs listed in Appendix 2.

NOTES

1. E. Prescott and E. Jones, *The "Politics" of Day Care* (Washington, D.C.: National Association for the Education of Young Children, 1972), p. 78.
2. T. Hu and K. Wise, *A Cost Analysis of Day Care Centers in Pennsylvania,* CHSD Report No. 21 (University Park, Pa.: Pennsylvania State University, 1973).
3. M. Stephen, *Policy Issues in Early Childhood Education* (Menlo Park, Calif.: Stanford Research Institute, 1973). ERIC ED 088 595.
4. M.D. Keyserling, "Day Care: Crises and Challenge," *Childhood Education* 48 (1971): 62.
5. R. Ruopp, B. O'Farrell, D. Warner, M. Rowe, and R. Freedman, *A Day Care Guide for Administrators, Teachers, and Parents* (Cambridge, Mass.: M.I.T. Press, 1973).
6. M.P. Rowe, "Economics of Child Care," Hearings on S. 2003 before Committee on Finance, United States Senate, 92nd Congress, 1st Session, 22–24 September 1971, p. 280.
7. "Federal Interagency Day Care Requirements," Code of *Federal Regulations,* Title 45, Subtitle A.
8. V. Lewis, "Day Care: Needs, Costs, Benefits, Alternatives," *Studies in Public Welfare* Paper No. 7, prepared for the Subcommittee on Fiscal Policy of the Joint Committee, Congress of the United States (Washington, D.C.: U.S. Government Printing Office, 1973), p. 124.
9. L. Frohreich, "Costing Programs for Exceptional Children: Dimensions and Indices," *Exceptional Children* 39 (1973): 517–18.
10. R. Rossmiller, J. Hale, and L. Frohreich, *Educational Programs for Exceptional Children: Resource Configurations and Costs* (Madison, Wisc.: Department of Educational Administration, University of Wisconsin, 1970).
11. Division of Special Education and Rehabilitation, *Costs in Serving Handicapped Children in Head Start: An Analysis of Methods and Cost Estimates, Final Report* (Syracuse, N.Y.: Division of Special Education and Rehabilitation, Syracuse University, 1974). ERIC ED 108 443.
12. M. Stephen, *Policy Issues in Early Childhood Education,* p. 30.
13. F.E. Andrews, *Legal Instruments of Foundations* (Scranton, Pa.: Russell Sage Foundation, 1958).
14. M.R. Fremont-Smith, *Foundations and Government* (Scranton, Pa.: Russell Sage Foundation, 1965).
15. M.P. Rowe and R.D. Husby, "Economics of Child Care: Costs, Needs, and Issues," *Child Care: Who Cares?* ed. P. Roby (New York: Basic Books, 1973), pp. 98–122.

16. R. Ruoff, B. O'Farrell, D. Warner, M. Rowe, and R. Freedman, *A Day Care Guide for Administrators, Teachers, and Parents.*

17. M.S. Host and P.B. Heller, *Day Care Administration* No. 7, Child Development Series (Washington, D.C.: Office of Child Development, 1971), p. 156.

For Further Reading

Abt Associates, Inc. *Cost and Quality Issues for Operators.* Washington, D.C.: Day Care and Child Development Council of America, 1972.

Alford, Albert L. *Nonproperty Taxation for Schools: Possibilities for Local Application.* Washington, D.C.: U.S. Office of Education, 1963.

Atkinson, Jonathan. *Day Care Costs: Day Care Accounting.* Washington, D.C.: 4-C Committee of the Housing and Urban Development 4-C Model Cities Project, 1973.

Auerbach, S. "Federally Sponsored Child Care." In *Child Care: Who Cares?* edited by P. Roby. New York: Basic Books, 1973. Pp. 172–90.

Benson, Charles S. *The Economics of Public Education.* 2d ed. Boston: Houghton Mifflin Co., 1968.

Boguslawski, Dorothy B. *Guide for Establishing and Operating Day Care Centers for Young Children.* New York: Child Welfare League of America, 1968.

Burkhead, Jesse. *Public School Finance.* Syracuse: Syracuse University Press, 1964.

Galambos, E.C. *A Cost Analysis System for Day Care Programs.* Atlanta, Ga.: Southeastern Day Care Project, Southern Regional Education Board, 1971.

Gauerke, Warren E., and Childress, Jack R. eds. *The Theory and Practice of School Finance.* Chicago: Rand-McNally., 1967.

Host, Malcolm S., and Heller, Pearl B. *Day Care Administration.* Child Development Series, no. 7. Washington, D.C.: Office of Child Development, 1971.

Johns, Roe L., and Morphet, Edgar L. *Financing the Public Schools.* Englewood Cliffs, N.J.: Prentice-Hall, 1960.

Jones, Howard R. *Financing Public Elementary and Secondary Education.* New York: Center for Applied Research in Education, 1966.

Mort, Paul R.; Reusser, Walter C.; and Polley, John W. *Public School Finance: Its Background, Structure, and Operation*, 3d. ed. New York: McGraw-Hill Book Co., 1960.

Mushkin, Selma J. "Cost of a Total Preschool Program in 1975." *Compact 3* (1960): 47.

Mushkin, Selma, and McLoone, Eugene P. *Local School Expenditures: 1970 Projections.* Chicago: Council of State Governments, 1965.

National Council of State Consultants in Elementary Education. *Education for Children Under Six.* Cheyenne, Wyo.: National Council of State Consultants in Elementary Education, 1968.

Peterson, LeRoy J. *Financing the Public Schools 1960–1970.* Washington, D.C.: National Education Assn., 1962.

Rowe, R., and Rowe, M. *The Costs of Child Care; Money and Other Resources.* Washington, D.C.: The Day Care and Child Development Council of America, 1972.

Ruoff, R. et al. *A Day Care Guide for Administrators, Teachers, and Parents.* Cambridge, Mass.: M.I.T. Press, 1973.

Tiedt, Sidney W. *The Role of the Federal Government in Education.* New York: Oxford University Press, 1966.

15

Contributing to the Profession

The role of the early childhood administrator, regardless of his official title, is one of leadership. As a leader, the administrator must be concerned with the quality of early childhood care and education. The concern for quality must go beyond the local program to an interest in the overall excellence of early childhood programs. Consequently, administrators as leaders can contribute to their profession by attempting to influence public policy, becoming involved in research, participating in the development of a code of ethics, and helping others find a place in the profession.

Influencing Public Policy

Historically, early childhood educators have not been involved in policy development; instead, they have entered the scene after programs were authorized. Noninvolvement can be drastic, as was evident when no group of early childhood specialists was ready to work with Project Head Start at its inception. Instead of taking a back seat, administrators must influence public policy on behalf of young children and their families.

Advocacy is one way to influence public policy. No special group is responsible for child/parent advocacy; to be effective, advocacy must be conducted by all early childhood professionals, including administrators, who practice in the field of early childhood education. The federal government recognized the importance of child advocacy when the Office of Child Development established a Center for Child Advocacy in 1971.

There are two types of advocacy—case and class advocacy. Case advocacy refers to a situation in which a particular child or family is not receiving services or benefits for which they are eligible. The advocate takes the necessary steps to right the situation. Class advocacy involves more than an isolated incident;

rather, it is advocacy on behalf of a group—migrants, handicapped, or minority groups—who need help in working with the agencies that were established for them.

ROLES IN INFLUENCING PUBLIC POLICY

Takanishi[1] indicates three roles in public policy formulation:

1. An *expert* assesses the research literature pertinent to some issue and evaluates the likely efficacy of a proposed procedure for achieving a goal. The expert makes judgments based on consideration of alternatives, costs and benefits of alternatives, and an analysis of the techniques necessary to bring about and maintain policy change.
2. The *advocate* pursues or defends a program believed to be in the best interest of the child or his family. The advocate stays close to the data base of the expert, but his main role is one of action. In a sense, professional practice itself is advocacy.
3. *Community members* must also be involved in policy making, in order to prevent encroachment on local autonomy. Services should respond to the needs expressed by people of the local community. Community involvement also increases accountability; thus, administrators must devise a process for community participation.

BECOMING AN EFFECTIVE ADVOCATE

There are several steps to becoming an effective advocate:

1. Know about the problems and the number of people in your area affected by a problem.
2. Determine the agency responsibile for correcting the problem, and the authority each level of government has. Those responsible may deny responsibility.
3. Be familiar with the institutions for policy making and how they operate.
4. Note legislative issues. Examine the Association for the Advancement of Psychology's *APA Monitor*. Know your congressional representatives and how lobbies are formed. Information on forming state lobbies is found in:

Hass, E. "Getting Support for Children's Programs: Organizing Child Advocacy." In *Rationale for Child Care Services: Programs vs. Politics*, Vol. 1. edited by S. Auerback. New York: Human Sciences Press, 1975. Pp. 125–35.

5. Translate your ideas into concrete terms. According to Fink and Sponseller, [2] child advocacy can be learned through simulation. Simulation can help in testing various alternatives and in clarifying thinking.
6. Do not duplicate the work of other child advocacy groups. A study of the role of child care information and referral throughout the U. S. will be conducted by the American Institute for Research in Cambridge, Massachusetts, sponsored by the Department of Health, Education, and Welfare, Office of Human Development Services, and the Ford Foundation.

The idea is to eliminate one-shot needs assessments conducted in local communitites, and instead locate a chain of child care information and referral programs across the U.S. These programs would not only serve local needs of parents and child care and education providers, but also serve as a public voice. Such a referral system could deter crisis-oriented legislation and assist in long-range planning and follow-up.

Another example of cooperation for effective advocacy is "Children's Cause," a strategy of the National Association for the Education of Young Children, which encourages active lobbying and coalitions with other organizations for the purpose of child advocacy.

7. Practice patience, but take the offensive. Advocacy is more than defensive in nature.

8. Follow through on plans for correcting a situation. Many plans have been delayed for further study or for lack of budget at the expense of child and family.

9. Enlist more child advocates by informing others. See:

Dittmann, L.L. "Affecting Social Policy in Community and Nation." *Childhood Education* 55 (1979): 194–204.

Duff, R.E., and Stroman, S.H. "Mobilizing Community Agencies in Coalitions for Child Advocacy." *Childhood Education* 55 (1979):210–12.

Organizing Your Community for Child Advocacy: The 4C Approach. Lansing, Mich.: Michigan Community Coordinated Child Care (4-C) Council, 1976. ERIC ED 131 944.

White, J.A., and Vernon, L. "Parents, Teachers and the Legislative Process—Texas Style!" *Childhood Education* 55 (1979) 207–10.

Wingfield, L.G.A. "How to Get Involved." *Childhood Education* 55 (1979) 205–7.

10. Join groups which are assuming an advocacy role, such as "Common Cause," and professional organizations listed in Appendix 3. For a list of many advocacy programs, see:

Child Advocacy Programs: 1975 (Report No. DHEW-OHO-76-30082). Washington, D.C.: National Center for Child Advocacy, 1975. ERIC ED 130 212.

Becoming Involved in Research

Contributing to the research and making sense of data and their interpretation for the benefit of children is part of the business of the administrator. Research has come to occupy a position of major importance in society. Tremendous advances have been made in business, industry, and medicine. Some businesses and industries allocate more than 50 percent of their budgets for research. Although educational advancement lags behind that of other areas and educational research has been conducted on a shoestring budget, research is now recognized as a major way to effect educational improvements. More groups are interested in and are financially supporting research, especially the federal government.

Early childhood education is involved in both psychological and pedagogical research. Educators must implement programs based on research, not on intuition, and must systematically evaluate program effectiveness. From the mid-sixties through the early seventies, research centered on cognitive and linguistic "deprivation" and effects of "compensatory action." Several of the new trends in early childhood education research include:

1. Focus on the child's early life and resultant developmental effects;
2. Effects of infant and toddler programs;
3. A holistic perspective, reflecting the desire for a comprehensive theory of child development;
4. Efforts to discover a program's enduring and indirect effects; and
5. Historical public policy research, exploring the impact of early education on the lives of American children, public attitudes toward education, the philosophical orientation of various professional organizations, and the development of private institutions for early education.[3]

More specific information on research trends and needs is found in the following sources:

Butler, A.L. "Areas of Recent Research in Early Childhood Education." *Childhood Education* 48 (1971): 143–47.

————.ed. *Current Research in Early Childhood Education: A Compilation and Analysis for Program Planners.* Washington, D.C.: American Association for Elementary-Kindergarten-Nursery Educators, 1970.

Chapman, J.E. *Early Childhood Research and Development Needs, Gaps, and Imbalances: Overview.* Washington, D.C.: George Washington University, 1972. ERIC ED 086 358.

Lazar, J.B. *The Present Status and Future Needs in Longitudinal Studies in Early Childhood Research and Development. A Preliminary Report.* Washington, D.C.: Office of Child Development, 1972. ERIC ED 093 457.

All early childhood educators should become involved in research efforts. You might begin by volunteering or cooperating with those conducting research, perhaps compiling observational records or completing questionnaires when requested. You can invite researchers into your program, and you can make your interest known at colleges and universities.

Developing a Code of Ethics

A code of ethics is one sign of a mature profession. Moore calls a code of ethics a "private system of law which is characteristic of all formally constituted organizations."[4] Practitioners of a profession share a code of ethics that highlights proper relations and responsibilities to each other and to clients or others outside the profession. A code of ethics is a statement of professional conduct. Katz[5] gives four reasons the early childhood profession is in special need of a code of ethics:

1. We, as practitioners, have almost unlimited power over children whose self-protective repertoire is limited. How shall they be protected?
2. The professional staff serves a multiplicity of clients—children, parents, regulatory/funding agencies, and the community. Who makes the final decisions?
3. Because of the unavailability and unreliability of empirical findings, there

are gaps in our knowledge of what is best. How can we avoid our seemingly "functional" orthodoxies or ideologies and remain open-minded?

4. We are responsible for the "whole" child, yet there are limits to our expertise and limits to our power. Parents, for example, are gaining more power in the decision-making process. What are the limits of our expertise and power?

For the foregoing reasons, and for the fact that an unwritten, or even an undeclared, code of ethics may not be known to practitioners except cases where a member of the profession has been charged with a violation,[6] the code should be written. One commendable attempt at writing a code of ethics is that of the Minnesota Association for the Education of Young Children.[7] Writing is, of course, only a formal step. Living the code is what counts. Friedson says the code of ethics "has no necessary relationship to the actual behavior of members of the occupation."[8] Perhaps when we, as professional practitioners, devote ourselves to the service of young children and encourage positive behavior in our fellow professionals and in all others involved with young children, we will make our finest leadership contribution to early childhood education.

Helping Others Find a Place in the Profession

Helping others find a place in the profession of early childhood education is a major leadership responsibility. This is certainly a form of advocacy, as others are encouraged to contribute to early childhood education. We can:

1. Provide places for student teachers, interns and others in our programs;
2. Write and verbally consult with others on careers in early childhood education, beginning by including childhood education as a career along with the other careers introduced to young children in your program;
3. Share skills and knowledge with others who work with young children; and
4. Encourage others to continue their education through independent study, conferences, short courses, formal degrees, and participation in professional organizations, and set an example by continuing your own education.

NOTES

1. R. Takanishi, *Public Policy for Children and Families: Who Shall Decide?* Report No. 3, (Rockville, Md.: National Institute for Mental Health, Department of Health, Education, and Welfare, 1977). ERIC ED 148 494.
2. J. Fink and D. Sponseller, "Practicing for Child Advocacy," *Young Children* 32 (1977): 49–54.
3. R. Takanishi-Knowles, *Federal Involvement in Early Childhood Education (1933–1973): The Need for Historical Perspectives* (Los Angeles: University of California, Department of Education, 1974). ERIC ED 097 969.
4. W.E. Moore, *The Professions: Roles and Roles* (New York: Russell Sage Foundation, 1970), p. 116.
5. L.G. Katz, *Ethical Issues in Working with Young Children* (Washington, D.C.: National Institute of Education, Department of Health, Education, and Welfare, 1977). ERIC ED 144 681.

6. R. Fox, *Experiment Perilous* (Glencoe, Ill.: The Free Press, 1959).

7. Minnesota Association for the Education of Young Children, *Code of Ethical Conduct Responsibilities* (St. Paul, Minn.: The Association, 1976).

8. E. Friedson, *The Profession of Medicine* (New York: Dodd Mead and Co., 1970).

For Further Reading

Becker, J. "On Defining the Child Care Profession." *Child Care Quarterly* 5 (1976): 165–66.

Bersoff, D.N. "Professional Ethics and Legal Responsibilities: On the Horns of a Dilemma." *Journal of School Psychology* 13 (1975): 359–76.

Berson, M.P. "Early Childhood Education." *American Education* 4 (1968): 7–13.

Bowers, G.A. "Emergent Ideological Characteristics of Educational Policy." *Teachers College Record* 79 (1977): 33–54.

Butler, A.L. "The Challenge of Young Children." *Theory Into Practice* 8 (1969): 158–63.

Eisenberg, L. "The Ethics of Intervention: Acting Amidst Ambiguity." *Journal of Child Psychiatry* 16 (1975): 93–104.

Feshback, N. et al. *APA Task Force on the Rights of Children and Youth*. Washington, D.C.: American Psychological Association, 1977.

Heath, D. "The Education of Young Children: At the Crossroads?" *Young Children* 25 (1969): 73–84.

Henry, N.B., ed. *Education for the Profession*, the 61st Yearbook of the National Society for the Study of Education. Chicago: University of Chicago Press, 1962.

Katz, L.G. "Early Childhood Education and Ideological Disputes." *Educational Forum* 3 (1975): 267–71.

Lane, M.B. "The Young Child: Priorities and Potentials." *Young Children* 22 (1967): 219–27.

Margolin, E. "Crucial Issues in Early Childhood Education." *Childhood Education* 45 (1969): 500–4.

Murphy, L.B. "Child Development: Then and Now." *Childhood Education* 44 (1968): 302–6.

Needle, P. *State of the Art Review in Early Childhood Education Research and Development*. Washington, D.C.: Office of Child Development (DHEW), 1970–71.

Prescott, E. *Politics of Day Care*. Washington, D.C.: National Association for the Education of Young Children, 1972.

Ratliff, P. *Organizing to Coordinate Child Care Services*. Washington, D.C.: The Day Care and Child Development Council of America, 1973.

Rosenberg, H., and Ehrgott, R.H. "Games Teachers Play." *School Review* 85 (1977): 433–37.

Schorr, A. "Family Values and Public Policy: A Venture in Prediction and Prescription." *Journal of Social Policy* 1 (1972): 33–44.

Senn, M.J.E. "Early Childhood Education: For What Goals?" *Children* 16 (1969): 8–13.

———. *Speaking Out for America's Children*. New Haven, Conn.: Yale University Press, 1977.

Siegel, A.E. *Current Issures in Research on Early Development*. Stanford, Calif.: A paper presented at the Raymond G. Kuhlen Memorial Symposium: Elements of Life Span Psychology, 1968. ERIC ED 028 813.

Sparling, J., and Gallagher, J., synthesizers. *Research Directions for the 70's in Child Development*. Chapel Hill, N.C.: Frank Graham Child Development Center, University of North Carolina, 1971.

Spodek, B. "From the President." *Young Children* 32 (1977): 2–3.

Steiner, G.A. *The Children's Cause*. Washington, D.C.: The Brookings Institution, 1976.

Toward a National Policy for Children and Families. Washington, D.C.: National Academy of Sciences, 1976.

Ward, E.H. "A Code of Ethics: The Hallmark of a Profession." In *Teaching Practices: Reexamining Assumptions*, edited by B. Spodek. Washington, D.C.: National Association for the Education of Young Children, 1977.

Young, D., and Nelson R. *Public Policy for Day Care of Young Children*. Lexington, Mass.: Lexington Books, 1973.

Appendix 1

State Licensing and Certification Agencies

STATE	STATE DEPT. RESPONSIBLE FOR LICENSING	STATE DEPT. RESPONSIBLE FOR CERTIFICATION
Alabama	Pensions and Security	Dept. of Education for nursery school through grade three in public schools; Dept. of Pensions and Security determines qualifications for personnel in other programs
Alaska	Health and Social Services	Day-care pesonnel—Health and Social Services; kindergarten teachers and administrators and prekindergarten teachers and administrators—Dept. of Education
Arizona	Health	Dept. of Education
Arkansas	Social and Rehabilitative Services	Dept. of Education
California	Public Health	Commission for Teacher Preparation and Licensing
Colorado	Social Services	Dept. of Education certifies kindergarten teachers; Dept. of Social Services determines day-care personnel qualifications for licensing purposes
Connecticut	Health	Dept. of Education
Delaware	Health and Social Services	Dept. of Public Instruction
District of Columbia	Human Resources	
Florida (Dade, Duval, Orange Counties only)	Health and Rehabilitative Services	Dept. of Education
Georgia	Human Resources	Dept. of Education, Div. of Teacher Certification

STATE	STATE DEPT. RESPONSIBLE FOR LICENSING	STATE DEPT. RESPONSIBLE FOR CERTIFICATION
Hawaii	Social Sevices and Housing	Dept. of Education; certification not required for non-DOE administered programs, but minimum qualifications are required for program to receive DSSH license to operate
Idaho	Environmental and Community Services	Board of Education
Illinois	Children and Family Services	Office of Supt. of Public Instruction
Indiana	Public Welfare	Dept. of Public Instruction, Div. of Teacher Education and Certification
Iowa	Social Services	Dept. of Public Instruction
Kansas	Health	Day-care and prekindergarten personnel—Dept. of Health; kindergarten personnel,—Dept. of Education
Kentucky	Human Resources	Dept. of Education, Div. of Teacher Education and Certification
Louisiana	Health and Social Rehabilitation Services	Dept. of Education
Maine	Health and Welfare	Dept. of Education
Maryland	Health and Mental Hygiene	Dept. of Education
Massachusetts	Office for Children	Dept. of Education
Michigan	Social Services	Dept. of Education
Minnesota	Public Welfare	Dept. of Education
Mississippi	Health	Dept. of Education
Missouri	Public Health and Welfare	Dept. of Elementary and Secondary Education and state-supported teacher training institutions certify kindergarten personnel; Dept. of Elementary and Secondary Education certifies early childhood special education teachers; Div. of Welfare licenses day care programs
Montana	Social and Rehabilitation Services	Supt. of Public Instruction
Nebraska	Public Welfare	Dept. of Education; certification not required for teachers in privately-owned prekindergarten programs
Nevada	Human Resources	Dept. of Education

STATE	STATE DEPT. RESPONSIBLE FOR LICENSING	STATE DEPT. RESPONSIBLE FOR CERTIFICATION
New Hampshire	Health and Welfare	Dept. of Education
New Jersey	Institutions and Agencies	Dept. of Education
New Mexico	Health and Social Services	Dept. of Education
New York	Social Services	Education Dept., and cities of Buffalo and New York
North Carolina	Office of Child Day Care Licensing	Dept. of Public Instruction
North Dakota	Social Services	Kindergarten—Dept. of Public Instruction; day care—Welfare Board
Ohio	Public Welfare	Kindergarten teachers, administrators, and paraprofessionals—Dept. of Education
Oklahoma	Institutions, Social and Rehabilitative Services	Dept. of Education, Teacher Education and Certification Section
Oregon	Human Resources	
Pennsylvania	Public Welfare	Dept. of Education
Puerto Rico		Dept. of Education
Rhode Island	Social and Rehabilitative Services	Dept. of Education
South Carolina	Social Services	Dept. of Education
South Dakota	Public Welfare	Div. of Elementary and Secondary Education
Tennessee	Public Welfare	Dept. of Education
Texas	Public Welfare	Education Agency
Utah	Social Services	Board of Education
Vermont	Human Services	Dept. of Education
Virginia	Welfare and Institutions	Dept. of Education
Washington	Social and Health Services	Dept. of Education certifies public school kindergarten teachers
West Virginia	Welfare	Dept. of Education
Wisconsin	Health and Social Services	Dept. of Public Instruction
Wyoming	Health and Social Services	Dept. of Education, Certification and Placement Div.

Appendix 2

Resources for Program Planning

INFANTS AND TODDLERS

Model Programs (that may disseminate information)

The Center for Child Development and
Education (the Kramer Project)
College of Education
University of Arkansas at Little Rock and
Little Rock School District
Little Rock, Ark. 72204

Early Intervention for High Risk Infants
and Young Children: Program for
Down's Syndrome Children at the
University of Washington
University of Washington
Seattle, Wash. 98195

Educational Intervention at Home
Institute for Child Behavior and
Development and Department of
Special Education
University of Illinois, Champaign-Urbana
Urbana, Ill. 61801

Florida Parent Education Infant and
Toddler Program
Institute for Development of Human
Resources
University of Florida
Gainesville, Fla. 32601

Hawkeye Model Day Care Center
University of Iowa
Iowa City, Iowa 52240

The Houston Parent Child Development
Center: A Parent Education Program
for Mexican American Families

Parent Child Center
University of Houston
Houston, Texas 77004

The Infant, Toddler, and Preschool
Research and Intervention Project
George Peabody College
Nashville, Tenn. 37203

Mothers' Training Program: Educational
Intervention by the Mothers of
Disadvantaged Infants
Institute of Research for Exceptional
Children
University of Illinois
Urbana, Ill. 61801

Oakland University Infant Parent
Program
Oakland University
Rochester, Mich. 48063

Syracuse University Children's Center
100 Walnut Street
Syracuse, N.Y. 13210

Verbal Interaction Project
Family Service Association
State University of New York at Stony
Brook
Stony Brook, N.Y. 11790

Ypsilanti-Carnegie Infant Education
Project
Eastern Michigan University
Ypsilanti, Mich. 48197

Books and other media

Anselmo, S., and J.D. Peterson. *A Manual for Caregivers of Infants and Toddlers.* Iowa
City, Iowa: University of Iowa, Early Childhood Education Center, 1976.

Arnote, T. *Learning and Teaching in a Center for the Care of Infants and Toddlers.* Greensboro, N.C.: University of North Carolina, 1969.

Badger, E. *Infant and Toddler Learning Programs.* Paoli, Pa.: Instructo/McGraw-Hill, 1971.

Chandler, C.A., R.S. Lourie, and A.D. Peters. *Early Childhood Care—The New Perspective.* New York, N.Y.: Atherton Press, 1968.

Deneberg, V. *Education of the Infant and Young Child.* New York, N.Y.: Academic Press, 1970.

Dittmann, L.L., ed. *The Infants We Care For.* Washington, D.C.: National Association for the Education of Young Children, 1973.

———. *What We Can Learn from Infants.* Washington, D.C.: National Association for the Education of Young Children, 1970.

Elrado, R., and B. Pagan. *Pespectives on Infant Day Care.* Orangeburg, S.C.: Southern Association for Children Under Six, 1972.

Evans, E.B., and G.E. Saia. *Day Care for Infants.* Boston, Mass.: Beacon Press, 1972.

Evans, E.B., G.E. Saia, and E.A. Evans. Designing a Day Care Center. Boston, Mass.: Beacon Press, 1974.

Frost, J. *Developing Programs for Infants and Toddlers.* Washington, D.C.: Association for Childhood Education International, 1977.

Frost, J., and M.D. Cohen, eds. *Understanding and Nurturing Infant Development.* Washington, D.C.: Association for Childhood Education International, 1976.

Furfey, P.H., ed. *Education of* Children Age One to Three: A Curriculum Manual. Washington, D.C.: The Catholic University of America, 1972.

Gordon, I.J. *Baby Learning Through Baby Play.* New York: St. Martins Press, 1970.

———. *The Infant Experience.* Columbus, Oh.: Charles E. Merrill Publishing Company, 1970.

Greenfield, P.M., and E. Tronick. *Infant Curriculum.* Santa Monica, Calif.: Goodyear Publishing Company, 1979.

Haith, M.M. *Day Care and Intervention Programs for Infants.* Atlanta, Ga.: Avator Press, 1972.

Hirshen, S., and J. Ouye. *The Infant Day Center.* Washington, D.C.: Day Care and Child Development Council of America, 1973.

Honig, A., and R. Lally. *Infant Caregiving.* New York: Media Projects, Inc., 1972.

———. *Infant Education and Stimulation. (Birth to 3 years): A Bibliography.* Urbana, Ill.: University of Illinois, College of Education, Curriculum Laboratory, 1973.

———. *Preparing the Child for Learning.* New York: Parents Magazine Films, 1973.

Howard, M., M. Hickman, and M. Hones. *Group Infant Care Programs.* Washington, D.C.: Sharing Project Cyesis Program Consortium, 1971.

Huntington, D., and S. Provence, eds. *Serving Infants.* Washington, D.C.: United States Government Printing Office, 1971.

Keister, M.E. *Beginning with Infants.* Greensboro, N.C.: The University of North Carolina Institute for Child and Family Development, 1972.

———. *The Good Life for Infants and Toddlers.* Washington, D.C.: National Association for the Education of Young Children, 1970.

Koontz, C. *Koontz Child Development Program Training Activities for the First 48 Months.* Los Angeles, Calif.: Western Psychological Services, 1974.

Kramer, R. *The First 18 Months from Infant to Toddler.* New York, N.Y.: Parents Magazine Films, 1975.

Kunkle, E., and G. Engstrom. *The Infant.* Milwaukee, Wisc.: The University of Wisconsin, 1970.

Lehane, S. *Help Your Baby Learn: 100 Piaget-Based Activities for the First Two Years of Life.* Englewood Cliffs, N.J.: Spectrum Books (Prentice-Hall), 1976.

Levenstein, P. *Toy Demonstrator's Visit Handbook.* Freeport, N.Y.: Family Service Association of Nassau County, 1969.

————. *Verbal Interaction Project: Mother-Child Home Program Manual for Replication of the Mother-Child Home Program.* Freeport, N.Y.: Family Service Association of Nassau County, 1969.

Levy, J. *The Baby Exercise Book.* New York, N.Y.: Pantheon Books, 1973.

Painter, G. *Teach Your Baby.* New York, N.Y.: Simon and Schuster, 1971.

Pizzo, P., and J. Manning. *How Babies Learn to Talk.* Washington, D.C.: Day Care and Child Development Council of America, 1973.

Pudden, S., and J. Sussman. *Creative Fitness for Baby and Child.* New York: William Morrow, 1972.

Ribble, M., M.D. *The Rights of Infants.* New York: Columbia University Press, 1967.

Saunders, M. *ABCs of Learning in Infancy.* Greensboro, N.C.: The University of North Carolina, Institute for Child and Family Development, 1971.

Saunders, M., and M.E. Keister. *Curriculum for the Infant and Toddler.* Greensboro, N.C.: The University of North Carolina, Institute for Child and Family Development, 1971.

Segner, L., and C. Patterson. *Ways to Help Babies Grow and Learn: Activities for Infant Education.* Denver, Colo.: University of Colorado Medical Center, John F. Kennedy Child Development Center, 1970.

Shearer, D. et al. *The Portage Guide to Early Education.* Portage, Wisc.: Portage, Wisconsin Cooperative Educational Service, 1974.

Smart, M.S., and R.C. Smart. *Infants.* New York: The Macmillan Company, 1973.

Sparling, J. et al. *Carolina Infant Curriculum.* Chapel Hill, N.C.: Frank Porter Graham Child Development Center, 1974.

Taylor, A., and M. Ryan. *Daily Programming for Infants in Day Care.* Cambridge, Mass.: Educational Day Care Service Association, 1973.

Tronick, E., and P.M. Greenfield. *Infant Curriculum: The Bromley-Heath Guide to the Care of Infants in Groups.* New York: Media Projects, 1973.

Wagoner, B. *Planning for Infants in Day Care: Developmental Activities for Infants.* Lubbock, Texas: Texas Tech University, Child and Parent Services, 1976.

White, B.L. *The First Three Years of Life.* Englewood Cliffs, N.J.: Prentice-Hall, 1975.

Willis, A., and H. Ricciuti. *A Good Beginning for Babies.* Washington, D.C.: National Association for the Education of Young Children, 1975.

YOUNG CHILDREN

Model Programs (that may disseminate information)

Bank Street Program
610 W. 112th Street
New York, N.Y. 10025

Behavioral Education Approach
University of Oregon
Eugene, Ore. 97403

Behavioral Analysis Approach
Department of Human Development
University of Kansas
Lawrence, Kansas 66044

Behavior-Oriented Prescriptive Teaching
  Approach
State College of Arkansas
Conway, Ark. 72032

California Process Model
California State Department of Education
State Education Building
721 Capitol Hall
Sacramento, Calif. 95814

Cultural Linguistic Approach
Northeastern Illinois State College
Chicago, Il. 60625

Demonstration and Research Center for
  Early Education
George Peabody College for Teachers
Nashville, Tenn. 37203

Early Childhood Project
Institute for Developmental Studies
School of Education
New York University
New York, N.Y. 10003

Education Development Center
  Approach
Education Development Center
Newton, Mass. 02160

Hampton Institute Nongraded Model
Hampton Institute
Hampton, Va. 23368

Home-School Partnership: A
  Motivational Approach
Southern University and A nd M College
Baton Rouge, La. 70813

Institute for Research on Exceptional
  Children
University of Illinois
Urbana, Ill. 61801

Interdependent Learner Model
New York University
Washington Square
New York, N.Y. 10003

Language Development—Bilingual
  Education Approach
Southwest Educational Development

Laboratory
Austin, Texas 78701

Learning to Learn School, Inc.
1936 San Marco Boulevard
Jacksonville, Fla. 32207

Mathemagenic Activities Program
University of Georgia
Athens, Ga. 30601

New School Approach
University of North Dakota
Grand Forks, N.D. 58201

Parent Educator Program
Institute for the Development of Human
  Resources
College of Education
University of Florida
Gainesville, Fla. 32601

Parent Implementation Approach
Alafram Associates, Inc.
103 E. 125th Street
New York, N.Y. 10035

Perry Preschool Project
Ypsilanti Public Schools
Ypsilanti, Mich. 48197

Piaget-Derived Preschool Curriculum
Ypsilanti Early Education Program
Ypsilanti, Mich. 48197

Precision Teaching
Behavior Research Corporation
Box 3351
Kansas City, Kansas 66102

Responsive Environment Approach
Far West Laboratory for Educational
  Research and Development
Berkeley, Calif. 94705

Responsive Environment Corporation
  Model
Responsive Environment Corporation
1025 Conneticut Avenue, N.W.
Washington, D.C. 20036

Systematic Use of Behavioral Principles
  Program
University of Oregon
Eugene, Ore. 97403

Tucson Early Education Model
University of Arizona
Tucson, Ariz. 85721

For information on other model programs, see:

"Early Childhood Information Unit"
(reports and filmstrips on 15 early
childhood programs)
Products Services
Far West Laboratory for Educational
Research
1 Garden Circle
Hotel Claremont
Berkeley, Calif. 94705

Books

Broman, B.L. *The Early Years in
Childhood Education.* Chicago: Rand
McNally Publishing Company, 1978.

Brophy, J.E., T.L. Good, and S.E. Nedler.
Teaching in the Preschool. New York:
Harper and Row, Publishers, Inc.,
1975.

Croft, D.J., and R.D. Hess. *An Activities
Handbook for Teachers of Young
Children,* second edition. Boston,
Mass.: Houghton Mifflin Company,
1975.

Lagenbach, M., and T.W. Neskora. *Day
Care: Curriculum Considerations.*
Columbus, Ohio: Charles E. Merrill
Publishing Company, 1977.

Leeper, S.H. et al. *Good Schools for
Young Children,* fourth edition. New
York: The Macmillan Publishing Co.,
Inc., 1979.

Mills, B.C. *Understanding the Young
Child and His Curriculum: Selected
Readings.* New York: The Macmillan
Company, 1972.

Nixon, R.H., and C.L. Nixon.
*Introduction to Early Childhood
Education.* New York: Random House,
1971.

Pitcher, E.G. et al. *Helping Young
Children Learn,* second edition.
Columbus, Ohio: Charles E. Merrill
Publishing Company, 1974.

Seefeldt, C. *A Curriculum Guide for
Child Care Centers.* Columbus, Ohio:
Charles E. Merrill Publishing
Company, 1973.

Spodek, B. *Teaching in the Early Years,*
second edition. Englewood Cliffs, N.J.:
Prentice Hall, Inc., 1972.

Robinson, H.F. *Exploring Teaching in
Early Childhood Education.* Boston:
Allyn and Bacon, Inc., 1977.

Wills, C.D., and L. Lindberg.
Kindergarten for Today's Children.
Chicago: Follett Educational
Corporation, 1967.

Todd, V.E., and H. Heffernan. *The Years
Before School: Guiding Preschool
Children,* third edition. New York: The
Macmillan Company, 1977.

For other curricular materials, see:

kindergarten curriculum guides
(available from State Department of
Education or similar department in
most states)
curriculum manuals and materials
available from the various publishers
kits (listed in Appendix 6)

HANDICAPPED CHILDREN: INTEGRATION OF HANDICAPPED AND NONHANDICAPPED YOUNG CHILDREN

Model Programs (that may disseminate information)

Accountable Re-entry Model (ARM)
Behavioral Sciences Institute
Carmel, Calif.

Center for Children
Univesity of Nebraska at Omaha and
Eastern Nebraska Community
Office of Retardation
Universiy of Nebraska
Omaha, Neb. 68132

Demonstration and Diagnostic
Intervention Model for Early
Childhood
Houston, Texas

Diagnostic Resource Unit
Martin Luther King, Jr. Child
Development Center
Atlanta, Ga.

Eliot-Pearson Children's School
Department of Child Study
Tufts University
Medford, Mass. 02155

Exceptional Child Research Program
Teaching Research Division
Oregon State System of Higher Education
Monmouth, Ore. 97361

Experimental Education Unit
University of Washington
Seattle, Wash. 98195

GOOD START
Washington, D.C. Public School System
Washington, D.C.

Handicapped Early Childhood
   Assistance Program
Child Care and Development Services of
   Los Angeles, California
Los Angeles, Calif.

High/Scope Educational Research
   Foundation
Ypsilanti, Mich. 48197

Human Services Associates
Sonoma County Office of Education,
   Santa Rosa Junior College, and
   California State College, Sonoma
Rohnert Park, Calif. 94928

National Children's Center
Washington, D.C.

The Nisonger Center
The Ohio State University
Columbus, Ohio 43210

Project Maine Stream
Cumberland Center, Maine

Project PAR
Saginaw Public Schools
Saginaw, Mich.

Project PEECH (Precise Early Education
   of Children with Handicaps)
University of Illinois
Urbana, Ill. 61801

Project RAAYHT (Retrieval and
   Acceleration of Young Handicapped
   and Talented)
University of Illinois
Urbana, Ill. 61801

Teaching Research Infant and Child Care
   Center
Monmouth, Ore. 97361

UNISTAPS Projects
Minneapolis Public Schools, University
   of Minnesota, and State Department of
   Education
Minneapolis, Minn. 55455

For information on other model programs, see:

Clark, V.L., and S.P. Johnston, compositors. *Description of Projects: Developing Strate-gies for Integrating and Delivery Services to Handicapped Children in Head Start Programs.* Chapel Hill, N.C.: University of North Carolina, Technical Assistance Development System, 1974. ERIC ED 136 505

Council fò. Exceptional Children. *Mainstreaming: Program Descriptions in Areas of Exceptionality. A Selective Bibliography.* Exceptional Child Bibliography Series No. 623. Reston, Va.: The Council, 1976. ERIC ED 129 004

Books

Bennett, L.M., and F.O. Henson, II. *Keeping in Touch with Parents: The Teacher's Best Friends.* Austin, Texas: Learning Concepts, 1977.

Birch, J.W. *Mainstreaming: E.M.R. Children in Regular Classes.* Reston, Va.: Council for Exceptional Children, 1974.

Braun, S.J., and Lasher, M.G. *Are You Ready to Mainstream? Preparing to Help Preschool-ers with Behavior and Learning Problems.* Columbus, Ohio: Charles E. Merrill Publishing Company, 1978.

Cohen, S.B. *Resource Teaching: A Mainstream Simulation.* Columbus, Ohio: Charles E. Merrill Publishing Company, 1978.

Dardig, J.C., and W.L. Howard. *Sign Here: A Contracting Book for Children and Their Parents.* Bellevue, Wash.: Edmark Associates, 1976.

Fairchild, T.N. *Counseling Exceptional Children: The Teacher's Role.* Austin, Texas: Learning Concepts, Inc., 1977,

————. *Managing the Hyperactive Child in the Classroom.* Austin, Texas: Learning Concepts, Inc., 1978.

Fairchild, T.N., and A.L. Parks. *Mainstreaming the Mentally Retarded Child.* Austin, Texas: Learning Concepts, Inc., 1976.

Fairchild, T.N., and O.H. Ferris, II. *Mainstreaming Exceptional Children.* Austin, Texas: Learning Concepts, Inc., 1976.

Fallen, N., ed., with J.E. McGovern. *Young Children with Special Needs.* Columbus, Ohio: Charles E. Merrill Publishing Company, 1978.

Gentry, D., and A.L. Parks. *Education of the Severely/Profoundly Handicapped: What Is the Least Restrictive Alternative?* Austin, Texas: Learning Concepts, Inc., 1977.

Guralnick, M.J., ed. *Early Intervention and the Integration of Handicapped and Nonhandicapped Children.* Baltimore, Md.: University Park Press, 1978.

Hanna, R.L., and D.L. Graf. *The Physically Handicapped Child: Facilitating Regular Classroom Adjustment.* Austin, Texas: Learning Concepts, Inc., 1977.

Hawisher, M.F., and M.L. Calhoun. *The Resource Room. An Educational Asset.* Columbus, Ohio: Charles E. Merrill Publishing Company, 1978.

Hayden, A.H., and B.K. Smith. *Mainstreaming Preschoolers: Children with Learning Disabilities.* Washington, D.C.: U.S. Government Printing Office, 1978.

Healey, A., and P. McAreavey. *Mainstreaming Preschoolers: Children with Health Impairments.* Washington, D.C.: U.S. Government Printing Office, 1978.

Heinich, R., ed. *Educating All Handicapped Children.* Englewood Cliffs, N.J.: Educational Technology Publications, 1979.

Henson, F.O., II. *Mainstreaming the Gifted.* Austin, Texas. Learning Concepts, Inc., 1976.

Henson, F.D., and T.N. Fairchild. *Mainstreaming Children with Learning Disabilities.* Austin, Texas: Learning Concepts, Inc., 1978.

Jordan, J., ed. *Not All Little Wagons Are Red: The Exceptional Child's Early Years.* Reston, Va.: CEC Information Center, Special Education, IMC/RMS Network, 1973.

Jordan, J., A.H. Hayden, M.B. Karnes, and M. Wood, eds. *Early Childhood Education for Exceptional Children: A Handbook of Ideas and Exemplary Practices.* Reston, Va.: CEC Information Center, Special Education, IMC/RMS Network, 1977.

Kieran, S.S., and F.P. Connor. *Mainstreaming Preschoolers: Children with Orthopedic Handicaps.* Washington, D.C.: U.S. Government Printing Office, 1978.

Klein, J. *Teaching the Special Child in Regular Classrooms.* Washington, D.C.: U.S. Department of Health, Education, and Welfare, Office of Child Development, 1977. ERIC ED 136 902

LaPorta, R.A., D.V. McGee, A. Simmons-Martin, and E. Vorce. *Mainstreaming Preschoolers: Children with Hearing Impairment.* Washington, D.C.: U.S. Government Printing Office, 1978.

Lasher, M.G., I. Mattick, and F.J. Perkins. *Mainstreaming Preschoolers: Children with Emotional Disturbance.* Washington, D.C.: U.S. Government Printing Office, 1978.

Liebergott, J., and A. Favors, Jr. *Mainstreaming Preschoolers: Children with Speech and Language Impairment.* Washington, D.C.: U.S. Government Printing Office, 1978.

Lowenbraun, S., and J.O. Affleck. *Education of the Mildly Handicapped Child in the Regular Classroom—A Handbook for Teachers.* Columbus, Ohio: Charles E. Merrill Publishing Company, 1976.

McCartan, K.W. *The Communicatively Disordered Child: Management Procedures for the Classroom.* Austin, Texas: Learning Concepts, Inc., 1977.

Orlansky, M.D. *Mainstreaming the Visually Impaired Child: Blind and Partially Sighted Students in the Regular Classroom.* Austin, Texas: Learning Concepts, Inc., 1977.

Orlansky, J.A. *Mainstreaming the Hearing Impaired Child: An Educational Alternative.* Austin, Texas: Learning Concepts, Inc., 1977.

Parks, A.L. *Behavior Disorders: Helping Children with Behavioral Problems.* Austin, Texas: Learning Concepts, Inc., 1976.

Parks, A.L., and M.K. Rousseau. *The Public Law Supporting Mainstreaming: A Guide for Teachers and Parents.* Austin, Texas: Learning Concepts, Inc., 1977.

Pasanella, A.L., and C.B. Volkmor. *Coming Back . . . or Never Leaving—Instructional Programming for Handicapped Students in the Mainstream.* Columbus, Ohio: Charles E. Merrill Publishing Company, 1977.

Schrag, J.A. *Individualized Educational Programming (IEP): A Child Study Team Process.* Austin, Texas: Learning Concepts, Inc., 1977.

Selected Readings in Early Education of Handicapped Children. Reston, Va.: CEC Information Center, Special Education IMC/RMS Network, n.d.

Stephens, T.M., A.C. Hartman, and V.H. Lucas. *Teaching Children Basic Skills: A Curriculum Handbook.* Columbus, Ohio: Charles E. Merrill Publishing Co., 1978.

Turnbull, A.P., B.B. Strickland, and J.C. Brantley. *Developing and Implementing Individualized Education Programs.* Columbus, Ohio: Charles E. Merrill Publishing Company, 1978.

Virginia Association for Retarded Citizens. *Young Children with Special Needs: A Television Series for Parents and Professionals.* Columbus, Ohio: Charles E. Merrill Publishing Company, 1978. (videotape or video cassettes)

Wynne, S., L.S. Ulfelder, and G. Dakof. *Mainsteaming and Early Education for Handicapped Children: Review and Implications for Research.* Washington, D.C.: Bureau of Education for the Handicapped, 1975.

NONSEXIST AND MULTICULTURAL

Resource Centers

Change for Children
532 Valencia Street
San Francisco, Calif. 94110

Far West Laboratories for Educational Research and Development
1855 Folsom Street
San Francisco, Calif. 94103

Non-Sexist Child Development Project
370 Lexington Ave.
New York, N.Y. 10017

Racism and Sexism Resource Center for Educators
1841 Broadway
New York, N.Y. 10023

Resource Center on Sex Roles in Education
National Foundation for the Improvement of Education
1201 16th Steet, N.W.—Room 701
Washington, D.C. 20036

Women's Action Alliance, Inc.
Non-Sexist Child Development Project
370 Lexington Avenue
New York, N.Y. 10017

Books

Banks, J. *Teaching Strategies for Ethnic Studies.* Boston: Allyn and Bacon, Inc., 1975.

A Bibliography of Multi-Cultural and Sex Fair Resource Materials. Springfield, Mass.: Massachusetts Department of Education, n.d.

Cohen, M., editor. *Growing Free: Ways to Help Children Overcome Sex-Role Stereotypes.* Washington, D.C.: Association of Childhood Education International, 1976.

Frazier, N., and M. Sadker. *Sexism in School and Society.* New York: Harper and Row, Publishers, Inc., 1973.

Greenleaf, P.T. *Liberating Young Children from Sex Roles: Experiences in Day Care Centers, Play Groups, and Free Schools.* Somerville, Mass.: New England Free Press, 1972.

Guttentag, M., and H. Bray. *Undoing Sex Stereotypes: Research and Resources for Educators.* New York: McGraw-Hill Book Co., 1976.

Harrison, B., *Unlearning the Lie: Sexism in Schools.* New York: Liveright Publishing Corp., 1973.

Help Wanted: Sexism in Career Education Materials. Princeton, N.J.: Women on Words and Images, 1975.

Johnson, L.O., ed. *Nonsexist Curricular Materials for Elementary Schools.* New York: Feminist Press, n.d.

National Education Association. *Combating Discrimination in Schools: Legal Remedies and Guidelines.* Washington, D.C.: The Association, 1973.

Racism and Sexism Resource Center for Educators. *Sexism and Racism in Popular Basal Readers 1964–1976.* New York: The Center, 1976.

Social Studies Staff of Educational Research Council of America. *Prejudice and Discrimination.* Boston: Allyn and Bacon, Inc., 1973.

Sprung, B., ed. *Guide to Non-Sexist Early Childhood Education.* New York: Women's Action Alliance, 1974.

———. *Non-Sexist Education for Young Children: A Practical Guide.* New York: Citation Press, 1975.

Stacey, J. et al. *And Jill Came Tumbling After: Sexism in American Education.* New York: Dell Publishing Company, Inc., 1974.

To Live in Freedom: Human Relations Today and Tomorrow. Norman, Okla. University of Oklahoma Press, 1972.

Films, Filmstrips, and Slides

Breitbarb, V., E. Breitbarb, and A. Jacobs. *At Your Fingertips: Sugar and Spice.* New York: Odeon Films.

Dick and Jane as Victims: Sex Role Stereotyping in Children's Readers. Princeton, N.J.: Women on Words and Images.

Free to Be—You and Me. Highstown, N.J.: McGraw-Hill Film Rental, Princeton Laboratory.

Golden, G., and L. Hunter. *Sex Role Stereotyping in Schools Film Series.* Berkeley, Calif.: Far West Laboratory, Media Extension Center, University of California.

National Education Association. *Sex Role Sereotyping EduPak.* Washington, D.C., The Association.

A Non-Sexist Curriculum for Early Childhood. New York: Educational Alliance Day Care Center (197 East Broadway).

Sex Role Development. Highstown, N.J.: Contemporary/McGraw-Hill Film Preview Library.

The Sooner the Better: Non-Sexist Education for Young Children. Non-Sexist Child Development Project. Cambridge, Mass.: Third Eye Films.

The Time Has Come: An Approach to Non-Sexist Parenting. New York: Odeon Films, Inc.

Guidelines for Evaluating Instructional Materials

Fairness in Educational Materials: Exploring the Issues. Chicago: Science Research Associates.

Guidelines for Creating Positive Sexual and Racial Images in Educational Materials. Riverside, N.J.: Macmillan Publishing Company, Inc.

Guidelines or Eliminating Stereotypes from Instructional Materials. Scranton, Pa.: Harper and Row Publishers, Inc.

Guidelines for Equal Treatment of the Sexes in McGraw-Hill Book Company Publications. New York: McGraw-Hill Book Company.

Guidelines for Evaluation of Instructional Materials for Compliance with Content Requirement for the Educational Code. Sacramento, Calif.: California State Board of Education.

Guidelines for Improving the Images of Women in Textbooks. Glenview, Ill.: Scott, Foresman and Co.

Guidelines for the Development of Elementary and Secondary Instructional Materials: The Treatment of Sex Roles. New York: Holt, Rinehart and Winston, Inc.

Images of Males and Females in Elementary School Textbooks. Washington, D.C.: Resource Center on Sex Role in Education.

Review Curriculum for Sexism. Albany, N.Y.: The State Education Department.

Appendix 3

Professional Organizations Concerned with Young Children

HISTORY	PURPOSES	PUBLICATIONS	MEMBERSHIP REQUIREMENTS
Alliance of Child Development Associations 303 Quill Drive E. San Antonio, Texas 78228			
The Alliance was founded in 1973.	1. To further knowledge, training, and skills of members in child development. 2. To educate the public in the value of and to promote licensed child care. 3. To conduct research and evaluation in any areas of possible benefit to children. 4. To foster optimum child growth and development. 5. To correlate the efforts of the members and associations within the Alliance for the benefit of children. 6. To conduct and sponsor workshops in child development for parents, teachers, directors, administrators and operators.	1. The *Child Care Newsletter*, published quarterly. 2. Other special publications.	Any individual interested in the objectives or purposes of the Alliance.

7. To publish and communicate results of research, evaluations, proposals, regulations, and events for possible benefit of children.

American Montessori Society (A.M.S.)
150 Fifth Ave.
New York, N.Y. 10011

The American Montessori Society was founded in 1960. Although Montessori's ideas held great interest for the American public between 1912 and 1918, there was no central organization to support them, and her psychological principles were dissonant with the times and frowned on by leaders of the educational community. It was not until 1958, when Nancy McCormick Rambusch opened a Montessori program at the Whitby School, and the first American Montessori teachers training course was offered in 1960, that the Montessori movement experienced an American revival.

331

The basic purposes of the Society are to promote better education for all children through teaching strategies consistent with the Montessori system and to incorporate the Montessori approach into the framework of American education. The purposes are implemented by:

  1. serving as a clearinghouse for information about Montessori methods, materials, teachers, and schools;

  2. accrediting programs for the training of Montessori teachers in pre-primary and primary levels, and issuing credentials to persons successfully completing accredited course

1. *AMS Bulletin* includes papers on innovative early childhood and alternative education and related subjects.
2. *AMS News* includes items and articles on Montessori education, schools, teachers, book reviews, etc.
3. *The Constructive Triangle* is a professional journal for teachers and schools.
4. *Board Briefs* is a digest of AMS board actions.
5. *Annual Report.*
6. *Teaching Opportunities* is a list of staff openings in AMS affiliates. The list is reserved for teacher members.

The Society is comprised of and supported by public, private, and parochial schools, Montessori teachers, and concerned individuals. Membership classes are:
1. Organizational Affiliates
  a) schools: furnish documentation of Montessori training of teachers, details of their organization, and evidence of compliance with state and local requirements. School affiliates are required to have a consultation the first or second year of affiliation and every four years thereafter.
  b) subscribers: an interim membership for ongoing programs, to assist and encourage them in converting

HISTORY	PURPOSES	PUBLICATIONS	MEMBERSHIP REQUIREMENTS
	requirements; 3. maintaining a consultation/resource service to assist member schools; 4. conducting an annual seminar/conference and regional workshops; 5. assisting research projects; 6. providing assistance to those interested in starting Montessori schools; and 7. maintaining a materials/publications center, with a full selection of Montessori and Montessori-oriented teaching aids and literature.		to full Montessori programs. c) associates: any group, or individual interested in starting a Montessori School. 2. *Individuals* a) Teachers' Section: open to teachers furnishing copies of a recognized Montessori credential and details of their academic background. b) General: no restrictions.

Association for Childhood Education International (A.C.E.I.). 3615 Wisconsin Ave., NW Washington, D.C. 20016

HISTORY	PURPOSES	PUBLICATIONS	MEMBERSHIP REQUIREMENTS
During the 1892 meeting of the National Education Association, the International Kindergarten Union (I.K.U.) was founded. In 1915, thirty representative educators in	1. To promote desirable living conditions, programs, and practices for children from infancy through early adolescence. 2. To support the raising of	1. *Childhood Education* (journal, published five times a year). 2. Other special publications.	Membership is open to all concerned with the well-being and education of children. Four types of membership: (1) individual; (2) local branches; (3) associate; and (4) student.

the kindergarten and primary fields met in Cincinnati, Ohio, and formed another association, the National Council of Primary Education. The I.K.U.'s official journal, *Childhood Education*, was launched in 1924. In 1930, the International Kindergarten Union and the National Council of Primary Education united under the title the Association for Childhood Education. The word "International" was added to the name in 1946. Today, the Association is a nonprofit, professional organization which is supported by dues and income from sale of publications. The national headquarters of the Association are in Washington, D.C.

standards of professional preparation.
3. To bring into active cooperation all organizations concerned with children in the home, the school, and the community.
4. To inform the public of the needs of children and how the educational program must be organized and operated to meet those needs.

Association Montessori Internationale (A.M.I.)
161, Koninginneweg, Amsterdam-Zuid
The Netherlands

In 1929, a Montessori congress was held in Helsingor, Denmark. At the Congress, the idea of the Association Montessori

1. To safeguard the integrity of the Montessori philosophy of child development and the methods of instruction.
2. To propagate, maintain, and

1. *Communications* (journal, published quarterly).

Membership is open to those interested in Montessori education. Two types of membership: ordinary and collective.

HISTORY	PURPOSES	PUBLICATIONS	MEMBERSHIP REQUIREMENTS
Internationale was born. From its beginning, the organization has had its headquarters in Amsterdam, Holland.	further the rights of the child in society by: (a) demonstrating the importance of young people in the progress of civilization; (b) propagating the Montessori method and knowledge of child development; (c) creating an atmosphere and opportunity for adults to work together; and (d) cooperating with other organizations concerned with human rights. 3. To establish training centers where the Montessori method is taught and to offer A.M.I. diplomas. 4. To encourage the publication of Montessori's books in different languages. 5. To supervise and approve the making of Montessori materials.		

The Child Development Associate Consortium
7315 Wisconsin Ave., Suite 601E
Washington, D.C. 20014

The Consortium was	1. To establish the	1. *Dateline CDAC,* [newsletter,	Each of 39 organizations

organized in June, 1972, as a private, not-for-profit corporation composed of 39 national groups and two public members. The Consortium represents a membership of half a million persons who are directly concerned with the education and development of young children. The Consortium became an operational credentialling agency in 1975. The Consortium has received its funds from the office of Child Development, a division of the Office of Human Development of Health, Education, and Welfare. The Office of Child Development initiated the concept of CDA and continues to direct CDA training programs.

competencies required by persons engaged in early childhood education.
2. To establish assessment methodologies.
3. To issue credentials.
4. To develop and disseminate principles and advice on programs for training.
5. To promote an understanding and acceptance of the credential.

published bimonthly).
2. Other special publications.

elects or appoints one individual to represent it in the Consortium. The organizations are grouped into nine separate categories according to their particular interest. These representatives vote, by categories, to elect the individuals who serve on the Board of Directors.

Child Welfare League of America, Inc. (C.W.L.A.)
67 Irving Place
New York, N.Y. 10003

The League was founded in 1920 with its national headquarters in New York. It is a nonsectarian federation of affiliated agencies in the

1. To devote its efforts to improvement of child care and services for deprived children.
2. To develop standards for

1. Child Welfare (journal, published monthly except in August and September).
2. C.W.L.A. Newsletter (newsletter, issued quarterly).

Memberships and associate memberships are given respectively to agencies accredited by the League or working toward accreditation.

HISTORY	PURPOSES	PUBLICATIONS	MEMBERSHIP REQUIREMENTS
United States and Canada. The League is financed from: (1) dues paid by member agencies; (2) restricted grants; (3) foundations; (4) United States federal government project grants; (5) United Way allocations; and (6) bequests and contributions. The Hecht Institute For State Child Welfare Planning, a division of CWLA, was launched in 1975. (1346 Connecticut Ave., NW, Washington, D.C. 20036).	services. 3. To conduct research and to publish professional materials. 4. To provide consultation to agencies and communities and to maintain a literary information service. 5. To cooperate with other organizations in an effort to improve child care and services for deprived children.	3. Other special publications. The journal was published under the title, *Child Welfare League of America Bulletin*, from 1922 to October 1948. The C.W.L.A. Newsletter was published from 1954 to 1968 under the title, *The President's Letter*; and, between 1969 and September, 1971, no newsletter was published. Newsletters from Hecht are: 1. *Child Welfare Planning Notes*. 2. *Washington Report on Children's Services*.	

Day Care and Child Development Council of America, Inc. (D.C.C.D.C.A.)
805 15th Street, NW, Suite 520
Washington, D.C. 20005

HISTORY	PURPOSES	PUBLICATIONS	MEMBERSHIP REQUIREMENTS
The Council began when a small group of interested individuals organized in 1959 at the National Conference on Social Welfare. In 1960, this group incorporated as the	1. To promote development of a locally controlled, publicly supported, and universally available child care program. 2. To formulate public child care policies.	1. *Voice for Children* (published bimonthly). 2. *Resources for Day Care* (publication list). 3. *Bulletin* (published when need indicates).	Membership is open to those interested in all facets of child care—parents, staffs of child care centers, and professionals in the field of child development. Three levels of

"National Committee for the Day Care of Children." The Committee published a newsletter and held two national day care conferences (1960, 1965). In 1967, the Committee reorganized to become a broad-based citizen action agency to work on behalf of children. It thus became known as the Day Care and Child Development Council of America, Inc., with national headquarters in Washington, D.C. The Council is private, nonprofit, and membership-supported.

3. To render assistance to local communities establishing child care programs.

4. To improve the life of the child, family, and community through a child care system.

4. Other special publications. The Council published 4-C from March-April, 1970 through January-February, 1971 and published four or five issues of Action for Children which came to an end in July, 1971.

membership: (1) individual; (2) agency; and (3) library.

National Association for the Education of Young Children (N.A.E.Y.C.)
1834 Connecticut Ave., NW
Washington, D.C. 20009

The organization began in 1926 as the National Committee on Nursery Schools. In 1931 it was organized under the title of the National Association for Nursery Education (N.A.N.E.). The N.A.N.E. became the National Association for the Education of Young Children in October, 1966, with

The expressed purpose of NAEYC is to serve and act on behalf of the needs and rights of young children, with primary focus on the provision of educational services and resources to adults who work with and for children. This purpose is accomplished through a variety of

1. Young Children (journal, published bimonthly). The official journal changed its title from the Journal of Nursery Education (begun in 1945–46) to Young Children in 1964–65.

2. NAEYC books—The Association offers more than 50 titles reflecting a broad base of information in the

Membership is open to persons engaged in work with young children. Two categories of membership: (1) individual—membership through the national headquarters; and (2) affiliate—membership through one of the state or local affiliated groups.

HISTORY	PURPOSES	PUBLICATIONS	MEMBERSHIP REQUIREMENTS
national headquarters in Washington, D.C. The Association has focused on the development and advancement of programs for children under eight years of age.	services—publications and conferences designed to expand the understandings and skills of adults working with and for children; sponsorship of the Week of the Young Child and dissemination of public policy information to assist members in speaking on behalf of the developmental needs of young children; and Affiliate Group activities which provide advocacy and growth opportunities in communities and states.	field of early childhood education.	
National Association of Child Care Administrators 303 Quill Drive E. San Antonio, Texas 78228			
The Association was organized in 1975 under the auspices of the Alliance of Child Development Associations.	1. To serve as a professional association for child care administrators. 2. To further the knowledge, training and skills of members in child development. 3. To educate the public in the value of and to promote	Child Care Newsletter, published quarterly, in conjunction with the Alliance of Child Development Associations.	Membership is open to individual child care administrators, including child care directors, assistant directors, head teachers, trainers, supervisors, and social services personnel, as well as officials or officers of

child care organizations and associations, and agency personnel.

licensed child care.
4. To conduct research and evaluation in any areas of possible benefit to children.
5. To foster optimum child growth and development.
6. To correlate the efforts of the members for the benefit of children.
7. To conduct and sponsor workshops in child development for parents, teachers, directors, administrators, and operators.
8. To publish and communicate results of research, evaluations, and events for the benefit of children.
9. To credential child care administrators in conjunction with state provider associations.

1. *Froebel Journal* (published three times a year); originally called the *Bulletin*.
2. Other special publications.

Individual membership is open to anyone interested in the education of children.

National Froebel Foundation

The Foundation was formed in 1938 by the amalgamation of the National Froebel Union, the examining body for Froebel students, and the Froebel Society, which had more general functions, such

1. To promote the raising of standards of education for children from two to thirteen years of age.
2. To disseminate information on principles and methods of teaching children.

339

HISTORY	PURPOSES	PUBLICATIONS	MEMBERSHIP REQUIREMENTS
as organizing lectures and operating the library. The name Froebel has been retained because the original societies were founded by men and women who received their inspiration from Froebel, and because of the main principles that underlay his work and proved themselves of basic value to education. (Friedrich Froebel founded the kindergarten in 1837.) The Foundation has its headquarters in London, England.	3. To conduct courses, conferences and lectures.		
Parent Cooperative Preschools International (P.C.P.I.) 20051 Lakeshore Road Baie d' Urfé, Quebec, Canada			
The first known cooperative nursery school in the United States was founded in 1916 by a group of faculty wives at the University of Chicago. The Berkeley Community Nursery School, established in 1927 by Katherine Whiteside Taylor	1. To strengthen and extend the parent cooperative movement and community appreciation of parent education and preschool education. 2. To promote desirable standards for the program	1. *Parent Cooperative Preschools International Journal* (published three times a year since 1970) 2. *Directory* (annual listing of membrships in the various categories). 3. Other special publications:	Membership in P.C.P.I. is open to all who accept the purposes of the organization. Six types of memberships: (1) individual; (2) student; (3) group; (4) council; (5) library; and (6) life.

(remaining a model co-op to date), was the earliest influence in California for use of Public Education funds for setting up parent participation nurseries, and for training parents and supervising programs. Councils were formed in the United States and Canada from the 1940s on, so that schools could learn and help each other on city, state, and regional levels. Katherine W. Taylor published *Parent Cooperative Nursery Schools* (now entitled *Parents and Children Learn Together*, Teachers College Press, 1965) and launched a quarterly newsletter, "The Parent Cooperative" (1958).

In 1960, at the first annual conference for parent cooperative nurseries, P.C.P.I. was founded under the name "American Council for Parent Cooperatives." With the spread of interests in memberships co-op centers in other countries, the present name was assumed in 1966. In 1969, the "Whiteside

practices, and conditions in parent cooperative projects, and to encourage continuing education for parents, teachers, and directors.
3. To promote interchange of information and help among parent cooperative nursery schools and kindergartens and other parent-sponsored preschool groups.
4. To cooperate with family living, adult education, and early childhood educational organizations in the interest of more effective service relationships with parents of young children.
5. To study legislation designed to further the health and well-being of children and families.

P.C.P.I. Journal was preceded by th *Parent Cooperative Newsletter* 1953–1968, (substance preserved in booklet, *Learning Together*, now in reprint); also by *Off Spring* (1968–1969) continuing to date as journal of the Michigan Council of Cooperative Nurseries.
4. *Service Materials*, to assist in establishing and operating parent cooperative preschools, available from P.C.P.I. Office.

HISTORY	PURPOSES	PUBLICATIONS	MEMBERSHIP REQUIREMENTS
Taylor Center" was opened at 20551 Lakeshore Road, Baie d' Urfé, Quebec, Canada, to serve as a model parent cooperative nursery, teacher training center for such nurseries, and international headquarters for P.C.P.I.			
Society for Research in Child Development (S.R.C.D.) 508 Ellis Avenue Chicago, Ill. 60637			
In 1922, a subcommittee was appointed on child development under the Division of Anthropology and Psychology of the National Research Council. The subcommittee became the Committee on Child Development in 1925. In 1933, the Committee was dissolved and replaced by the Society for Research in Child Development. The headquarters of the Society are located in Chicago,	1. To advance research in child development. 2. To encourage interdisciplinary consideration of problems in the field of child development. 3. To encourage study of the implications of research findings. 4. To enable specialists to share research tools and techniques. 5. To sponsor national and regional conferences.	1. *Child Development* (journal, published quarterly). 2. *Child Development Abstracts and Bibliography* (journal, published triannually). 3. *Monographs of the Society for Research in Child Development* (journal, published 4–6 times annually). 4. Newsletter. 5. A triennial directory. 6. Other special publications.	Membership application may be made by an individual who is engaged in research in child development or a related field, who is engaged in teaching undergraduate and graduate courses in child development, and who has published in the field of child development, or by an individual who is actively engaged in promoting the purposes of the Society. All applications are considered by the governing board of the Society. Three

Illinois, at the University of Chicago Press.

types of memberships: (1) individual; (2) graduate student; and (3) emeritus.

Southern Association on Children Under Six
Box 5403 Brandy Station
Little Rock, Ark. 72205

SACUS began as the Nashville Council for the Education of Children Under Six in September, 1948. During the third meeting of the group, in Louisville, Kentucky, in March, 1952, the participants voted to become the Southern Regional Association on Children Under Six and adopted a constitution. At the 1954 Conference in Biloxi, Mississippi, the constitution was amended to delete "Regional," and the official organization became SACUS.

The basic purposes of SACUS are to work on behalf of young children and to provide opportunities for the cooperation of individuals and groups concerned with the well-being of young children. Particular concerns are:

1. to further the development of knowledge and understanding of young children and the dissemination of such information;

2. to contribute to the professional growth of persons working with and for young children;

3. to encourage the provision of educational and developmental resources and services for young children;

4. to work to improve the standards for group care and

1. *Dimensions*, the quarterly journal, began as a regular publication in 1973.
2. The *Proceedings* of the annual conference were published each year except 1966.
3. Other special publications.

Membership is open to all persons concerned with infants and young children. Two classes of membership: (1) Affiliate (a member of a state affiliate association); and (2) Individual (a person not a member of a state affiliate association).

343

HISTORY	PURPOSES	PUBLICATIONS	MEMBERSHIP REQUIREMENTS
	education of children and improve the quality of life for them; and 5. to provide support for state associations in their work for these objectives.		

Appendix 4

Additional Organizations and Publications of Concern to Early Childhood Educators

Organizations

Alexander Graham Bell Association
  for the Deaf
1537 35th Street, NW
Washington, D.C. 20007

American Academy for Cerebral Palsy
University Hospital School
Iowa City, Iowa 52240

American Academy of Pediatrics
1801 Hinman Avenue
Evanston, Ill. 60204

American Alliance for Health,
  Physical Education and
  Recreation
Programs for Handicapped
1201 16th Street, NW
Washington, D.C. 20036

American Assoriation on Mental
  Deficiency
5101 Wisconsin Ave., NW
Suite 405
Washington, D.C. 20016

American Foundation for the Blind, Inc.
15 West 16th Street
New York, N.Y. 10011

American Medical Association
535 North Dearborn Street
Chicago, Ill. 60610

American National Red Cross
17th and D Streets, NW
Washington, D.C. 20006

American Orthopsychiatric Association,
  Inc.
7790 Broadway
New York, N.Y. 10019

American Psychiatric Association
1700 18th Street, NW
Washington, D.C. 20009

American Psychological Association
1200 17th Street, NW
Washington, D.C. 20036

American Speech and Hearing
  Association
10801 Rockville Pike
Rockville, Md. 20852

Association for Mentally Ill Children
12 West 12th Street
New York, N.Y. 10003

Bureau of Education for the
  Handicapped (BEH)
U.S. Office of Education
400 Maryland Avenue, SW
Washington, D.C. 20202

Closer Look
National Information Center for
  the Handicapped
P.O. Box 1492
Washington, D.C. 20013

Council on Education of the Deaf
Clarke School for the Deaf
Northampton, Mass. 01060

Council for Exceptional Children
1920 Association Drive
Reston, Va. 22091

Developmental Disabilities
330 C Street South, Room 3070
U.S. Department of Health, Education,
  and Welfare
South Building
Washington, D.C. 20201

Epilepsy Foundation of America
1828 L Street, NW
Washington, D.C. 20036

Family Services Association of America
44 East 23rd Street
New York, N.Y. 10010

Muscular Dystrophy Association
810 7th Avenue
New York, N.Y. 10019

National Association for Children
with Learning Disabilities
4156 Library Road
Pittsburgh, Pa. 15234

National Association for Retarded
Citizens, Inc.
2709 Aveune E, East
P.O. Box 6109
Arlington, Texas 76011

National Committee for Multi-
Handicapped Children
239 14th Street
Niagara Falls, N.Y. 14303

National Easter Seal Society for
Crippled Children and Adults, Inc.
2023 West Ogden Avenue
Chicago, Ill. 60612

National Foundation March of Dimes
1275 Mamaroneck Avenue
White Plains, N.Y. 10605

National Institute of Child Health
and Human Development
Public Health Service
National Institute of Health
U.S. Department of Health,
Education, and Welfare
Washington, D.C. 20201

National Society for the Prevention of
Blindness, Inc.
70 Madison Avenue
New York, N.Y. 10016

Office of Child Development
U.S. Department of Health, Education
and Welfare
P.O. Box 1182
Washington, D.C. 20013

Parents of Down's Syndrome Children
3358 Annandale Road
Falls Church, Va. 22042

Planned Parenthood Federation of
America
810 7th Avenue
New York, N.Y. 10019

Spina Bifida Association of America
343 South Dearhorn
Chicago, Ill. 60604

Social Rehabilitation Services
Children's Bureau
Office of Child Development
U.S. Department of Health, Education
and Welfare
Washington, D.C. 20013

United Cerebral Palsy Association, Inc.
66 East 34th Street
New York, N.Y. 10016

U.S. Public Health Service
Health Services and Mental
Health Administration
National Institute of Mental Health
5454 Wisconsin Avenue
Chevy Chase, Md. 22015

USDA
Director of Child Nutrition
Food and Nutrition Service
Auditors Building, Room 3405
Washington, D.C. 20250

Newsletters

Action for Children's Television News
Action for Children's Television
46 Austin Street
Newton, Mass. 02160

Advisory and Learning Exchange
Association for Renewal in Education,
Inc.
1101–15th Street, NW, Suite 11–80
Washington, D.C. 20005

*Agency for Instructional Television
Newsletter*
AIT
Box A
Bloomington, Ind. 47401

The Alaflaga Word
  Alabama-Florida-Georgia Early
    Childhood Institute
    Newsletter
  201 West Park Avenue, Rm. 104
  Tallahassee, Fla. 32304

Apple Pie
  Center for the Study of Parent
    Involvement
  5240 Boyd
  Oakland, Calif. 94618

Behavior Today
  Behavior Today
  Box 2993
  Boulder, Colo. 80302

Building Blocks
  Child Care Task Force
  1400 East 53rd Street
  Chicago, Ill. 60615

*Bulletin of the Center for Children's
Books*
  The University of Chicago Press
  5801 Ellis Avenue
  Chicago, Ill. 60637

The Calendar
  Children's Book Council, Inc.
  67 Irving Place
  New York, N.Y. 10003

Caring
  National Committee for the
    Prevention of Child Abuse
  Suite 510
  111 East Wacker Drive
  Chicago, Ill. 60601

Cartel
  Dissemination and Assessment
    Center for Bilingual Education
  6504 Tracor Lane
  Austin, Texas 78721

CEMREL Newsletter
  CEMREL
  10646 St. Charles Rock Rd.
  St. Ann, Mo. 63074

Child Care Information Exchange
  Child Care Information Exchange

  70 Oakley Road
  Belmont, Mass. 02178

CTW Newsletter
  Public Affairs
  Children's Television Workshop
  1 Lincoln Plaza
  New York, N.Y. 10023

DARCEE Newsletter
  Demonstration and Research
    Center for Early Education
  Peabody College, Box 151
  Nashville, Tenn. 37203

*Day Care and Child Development
Reports*
  Plus Publications
  2626 Pennsylvania Avenue, NW
  Washington, D.C. 20037

Diversity
  Center for Cross Cultural Education
  811 Lincoln
  Suite 6
  Denver, Colo. 80203

ECE Options
  ECE Options
  Box 3007
  Stanford, Calif. 94305

ECS Early Childhood Project Newsletter
  Early Childhood Project
  Education Commission of the States
  300 Lincoln Tower
  1860 Lincoln Street
  Denver, Colo. 80003

EDC News
  Education Development Corporation
  Publications Office
  55 Chapel Street
  Newton, Mass. 02160

Education Daily
  Education News Service
  Capitol Publications, Inc.
  2430 Pennsylvania Avenue, NW
  Suite G–12
  Washington, D.C. 20037

Education Recaps
  Education Recaps

Educational Testing Service
Princeton, N.J. 08540

Educational Researcher
American Educational Research
  Association
1126 Sixteenth Street, NW
Washington, D.C. 20036

(Various Publications)
ERIC Clearinghouse on Elementary
  Childhood Education*
University of Illinois
805 W. Penn. Ave.
Urbana, Ill. 61801

(Various Publications)
ERIC Clearinghouse on Rural
  Education and Small Schools
New Mexico State University
Box 3 AP
Las Cruces, N.M. 88003

(Various Publications)
ERIC Clearinghouse on Handicapped
  and Gifted Children
Council for Exceptional Children
1920 Association Drive
Reston, Va. 22091

(Various Publications)
ERIC Clearinghouse on Urban
  Education**
Teachers College
Columbia University
Box 40
New York, N.Y. 10027

Evaluation Comment
Center for the Study of Evaluation
145 Moore Hall
University of California
Los Angeles, Calif. 90024

Feed Kids—It's the Law
The Children's Foundation
1028 Connecticut Avenue, NW, Suite
  1112
Washington, D.C. 20036

Focus on Children and Youth
National Council of Organizations for
  Children and Youth
1910 K Street, NW, Suite 800
Washington, D.C. 20006

Growing Child and Growing Parent
Growing Child and Growing Parent
22 North Second Street
Lafayette, Ind. 47902

Head Start Newsletter
Project Head Start
Office of Child Development
Department of Health, Education and
  Welfare
P.O. Box 1182
Washington, D.C. 20013

*IMPELL—Indian Migrant Project on
Education for Living and Learning*
IMPELL
P.O. Box 329
Toppenish, Wash. 98948

Interracial Books for Children Bulletin
The Council for Interracial Books for
  Children
1841 Broadway
New York, N.Y. 10023

National Child Protection Newsletter
The National Center for the Prevention
  and Treatment of Child Abuse and
  Neglect
Department of Pediatrics
University of Colorado Medical Center
1205 Oneida Street
Denver, Colo. 80220

Network—The Paper for Parents
National Committee for Citizens in
  Education
410 Wilde Lake Village Green
Columbia, Md. 21044

New Human Services Newsletter
New Careers
184 Fifth Avenue
New York, N.Y. 10010

New Schools Exchange Newsletter
New Schools Exchange
Pettigrew, Ark. 72752

*PEN—The Preschool Education
Newsletter*
Multimedia Education Inc.
11 West 42nd Street
New York, N.Y. 10036

*Now expanded to include "elementary" as well as "early childhood."
**Formerly called "Disadvantaged." Urban Education now includes disadvantaged.

Projecto LEER Bulletin
  Projecto LEER
  Books for the People Fund, Inc.
  1736 Columbia Road, NW, Suite 107
  Washington, D.C. 20009

The Publication
  The Publication
  P.O. Box 11173
  Pittsburgh, Pa. 15237

Re: Children
  Division of Public Education
  Office of Child Development
  Department of Health, Education
    and Welfare
  P.O. Box 1182
  Washington, D.C. 20013

Report on Educational Research
  Capitol Publications, Inc.
  2430 Pennsylvania, NW, Suite G–12
  Washington, D.C. 20037

Report on Preschool Education
  Capitol Publications, Inc.
  2430 Pennsylvania, NW, Suite G–12
  Washington, D.C. 20037

Reports on School Staffing
  Capitol Publications, Inc.
  2430 Pennsylvania, NW, Suite G–12
  Washington, D.C. 20037

Reports Magazine
  World Education
  1414 Sixth Avenue
  New York, N.Y. 10019

TEEM Exchange
  Tucson Early Education Model
  Research and Development Center
  Early Childhood Education Laboratory
  College of Education
  University of Arizona
  Tucson, Ariz. 85721

Today's Child
  Today's Child
  92A Nassau Street
  Princeton, N.J. 08540

Today's Child News Magazine
  Today's Child News Magazine
  Department 253
  Roosevelt, N.J. 08555

un nuevo dia
  un nuevo dia

  5410 West Mississippi
  Lakewood, Colo. 80226

Viewpoint
  Child Study Center
  Faculty of Education, U.B.C.
  2855 Acadia Road
  Vancouver 8, British Columbia
  Canada

Journals

*American Academy of Child Psychiatry
  Journal*
American Education
American Education Research Journal
American Journal of Orthopsychiatry
Child Care Quarterly
Children's House Magazine
Children Today (formerly Children)
Child Study Journal
*Compact (Education Commission of the
  States)*
Day Care and Early Education
Developmental Psychology
Early Child Development and Care
Early Childhood Education
Early Years
Educational Leadership
Educational Technology
The Elementary Principal
The Elementary School Journal
*Exceptional Child Education Resources
  (formerly Exceptional Child Education
  Abstracts)*
Exceptional Children
The Exceptional Parent
Focus on Exceptional Children
Human Development
Instructor
Journal of Child Language
*Journal of Child Psychology and
  Psychiatry and Allied Disciplines*
Journal of Educational Psychology
*Journal of Experimental Child
  Psychology*
*Journal of Genetic Psychology:
  Developmental and Clinical
  Psychology*

Journal of Nutrition Education

Journal of Open Education

Journal of Psychohistory (formerly
  History of Childhood Quarterly)

Merrill-Palmer Quarterly (or
  Merrill-Palmer Quarterly of Behavior
  and Development)

Phi Delta Kappan

School Review

Teacher

Today's Education

Unicef News

Appendix 5

Suppliers of Early Childhood Equipment, Books, and Materials

ABC School Supply Inc.
437 Armour Circle, NE
P.O. Box 13086
Atlanta, Ga. 30324

*Academy Press Limited
365 North Michigan Ave.
Chicago, Ill. 60601

Adaptive Therapeutic Systems, Inc.
683 Boston Park Rd.
Madison, Conn. 06443

Addison-Wesley Publishing Company
2725 Sand Hill Road
Menlo Park, Calif. 94025

*AFRO-AM Publishing Company, Inc.
1727 S. Indiana Avenue
Chicago, Ill. 60616

Alexander Steel Equipment Corp.
101 River Street
Waltham, Mass. 01254

Allyn and Bacon, Inc.
470 Atlantic Ave.
Boston, Mass. 02210

American Art Clay Company, Inc.
4717 West 16th Street
Indianapolis, Ind. 46222

*American Association of University
  Women
1056 Columbia Place
Boulder, Colo. 80303

American Book Company
A Division of Educational Publishing,
  Inc.
7625 Empire Drive
Florence, Ky. 41042

*American Friends Service Committee
112 South 16th Street
Philadelphia, Pa. 19102

American Guidance Service, Inc.
Publishers' Building
Circle Pines, Minn. 55014

American Playground Device Company
P.O. Drawer 2599
Anderson, Ind. 46011

American Science and Engineering, Inc.
20 Overland Street
Boston, Mass. 02215

Angeles Nursery Toys
5307 Lee Highway
Arlington, Va. 22207

Atheneum Publishers
122 East 42nd Street
New York, N.Y. 10017

B and T Learning Materials
1515 Broadway
New York, N.Y. 10036

Barnell Loft, Ltd.
958 Church Street
Baldwin, N.Y. 11510

Beckley-Cardy Company
1900 N. Narragansett Ave.
Chicago, Ill. 60639

Behavioral Research Laboratories, Inc.
Ladera Professional Center
P.O. Box 577
Palo Alto, Calif. 94302

Bellwether, Inc.
P.O. Box 457
Tuscaloosa, Ala. 35401

*Specializes in nonsexist, multicultural materials.

Binney and Smith, Inc.
1107 Broadway
New York, N.Y. 10010

Bobbs-Merrill Educational Publishing
4300 West 62nd Street
Indianapolis, Ind. 46206

Book-Lab, Inc.
1449 37th Street
Brooklyn, N.Y. 11218

Bowmar/Noble Publishers, Inc.
4563 Colorado Boulevard
Los Angeles, Calif. 90039

Caedmon Records, Inc.
505 8th Avenue
New York, N.Y. 10018

Cambosco Scientific Company
342 Western Avenue
Boston, Mass. 02135

*Change for Children
2558 Mission Street, No. 266
San Francisco, Calif. 94110

Charles E. Merrill Publishing Company
1300 Alum Creek Drive
Columbus, Ohio 43216

Child Bilt Systems
1512 Bay Street
Santa Cruz, Calif. 95060

Childcraft Education Corporation
20 Kilmer Road
Edison, N.J. 08817

Childhood Resources
5703 Lee Highway
Arlington, Va. 22207

Child Life Play Specialties, Inc.
55 Whitney Street
Holliston, Mass. 01746

Children's Music Center, Inc.
5373 W. Pico Boulevard
Los Angeles, Calif. 90019

*Child's Play
226 Atlantic Avenue
Brooklyn, N.Y. 11201

Child's World, Inc.
1556 Weatherstone Lane
Elgin, Ill. 60120

Community Playthings
Rifton, N.Y. 12471

Constructive Playthings
1040 E. 85th
Kansas City, Mo. 64131

Creative Playthings
A Division of Columbia Broadcasting
System, Inc.
Princeton, N.J. 08540

Cuisenaire Company of America, Inc.
12 Church Street
New Rochelle, N.Y. 10805

David C. Cook Publishing Company
Elgin, Ill. 60120

Delmar Publishers
50 Wolf Road
Albany, N.Y. 12205

Developmental Learning Materials
7440 Natchez Avenue
Niles, Ill. 60648

Dick Blick Company
P.O. Box 1267
Galesburg, Ill. 61401

Didax Distributors of Teaching Aids
and Educational Materials
3 Dearborn Road
P.O. Box 2258
Peabody, Mass. 01960

The Economy Company
P.O. Box 25308
1901 North Walnut
Oklahoma City, Okla. 73125

EDC Workshop Store
55 Chapel Street
Newton, Mass. 02160

Edmark Associates
P.O. Box 3903
Bellevue, Wash. 98009

Educational Activities, Inc.
P.O. Box 392
Freeport, N.Y. 11520

Educational Media, Inc.
3191 Westover Dr., SE
Washington, D.C. 20020

Educational Reading Services
320 Route 17
Mahwah, N.J. 07430

Educational Record Center
155 Sycamore Street
P.O. Box 1161
Decatur, Ga. 30030

Educational Teaching Aids
159 W. Kimzie Street
Chicago, Ill. 60610

Education Development Center
15 Mifflin Place
Cambridge, Mass. 02138

Educator's Service Center, Inc.
1100 W. Capitol, Box 203
Little Rock, Ark. 72203

Encyclopedia Britannica
    Educational Corporation
425 N. Michigan Avenue
Chicago, Ill. 60611

ERTL
805 13th Avenue,SE
Dyersville, Iowa 52040

Eye Gate Media
146-01 Archer Avenue
Jamaica, N.Y. 11435

Family Affair of Florida, Inc.
903 E. New Haven Avenue
Melbourne, Fla. 32901

Fearon-Pitman Publishers, Inc.
6 Davis Drive
Belmont, Calif. 94002

*Feminist Book Mart
162-119th Avenue
Flushing, N.Y. 11357

*Feminist for Equal Education
 Box 185
Saxonville Station
Framingham, Mass. 01701

*Feminist Resources for Equal Education
P.O. Box 3185
Framingham, Mass. 01701

Fisher-Price Toys
East Aurora, N.Y. 14052

Flex Products, Inc.
445 Industrial Road
Carlstadt, N.J. 07072

Folkways Records
43 W. 61st Street
New York, N.Y. 10023

Follett Publishing Company
1010 W. Washington Boulevard
Chicago, Ill. 60607

Funtastic, Inc.
5902 Farrington Avenue
Alexandria, Va. 22304

Gabriel Industries, Inc.
200 5th Avenue, Suite 1256
New York, N.Y. 10010

Game Time, Inc.
900 Anderson Road
Litchfield, Mich. 49252

Ginn and Company
P.O. Box 2649
Columbus, Ohio 43216

Grosset and Dunlap, Inc.
51 Madison Avenue
New York, N.Y. 10010

*Gryphon House
P.O. Box 274
Mt. Rainer, Md. 20822

Harper and Row Publishers, Inc.
10 East 53rd Street
New York, N.Y. 10022

Herder and Herder
232 Madison Avenue
New York, N.Y. 10016

Holt, Rinehart and Winston
383 Madison Avenue
New York, N.Y. 10017

Homer Debo-Fox Blocks Company
24401 Redwood Highway
Cloverdale, Calif. 95425

Houghton-Mifflin Company
One Beacon Street
Boston, Mass. 02107

Ideal School Supply Company
11000 S. Lavergne Avenue
Oak Lawn, Ill. 60453

Instructional Industries, Inc.
Executive Park
Ballston Lake, N.Y. 12019

The Instructo Corporation
Paoli, Pa. 19301

Instructor Curriculum Materials
Dansville, N.Y. 14437

J.A. Preston Corporation
71 Fifth Avenue
New York, N.Y. 10003

The Judy Company
250 James Street
Morristown, N.J. 07960

Judy Publishing Company
Main P.O., Box 5270
Chicago, Ill. 60680

Kenworthy Educational Service, Inc.
138 Allen Street
P.O. Box 3031
Buffalo, N.Y. 14205

Kenner Products
Cincinnati, Ohio 45202

Kimbo Educational
P.O. Box 477
Long Branch, N.J. 07740

Knickerbocker Toy Company
1107 Broadway
New York, N.Y. 10010

LaPine Scientific Company
375 Chestnut Street
Norwood, N.J. 07648

Lakeshore Curriculum Materials
    Company
16463 Phoebe Street
LaMirada, Calif. 90637

Learning Resource Center, Inc.
10655 S.W. Greensburg Road
P.O. Box 23077
Portland, Ore. 97223

*Learn Me, Inc.
642 Grand Avenue
St. Paul, Minn. 55105

Lego Systems, Inc.
555 Taylor Road
Enfield, Conn. 06082

Love Publishing Company
6635 E. Villanova Place
Denver, Colo. 80222

Lyons
530 Riverview Avenue
Elkhart, Ind. 46514

Mafex Associates, Inc.
90 Cherry Street
Box 519
Johnstown, Pa. 15907

Magnamusic—Baton
6394 Delmar Boulevard
St. Louis, Mo. 63130

Maple Wood Products Company, Inc.
60 Merimac Street
Amesbury, Mass. 01913

Markham Distributors
507 Fifth Avenue
New York, N.Y. 10017

Mattel, Inc.
Hawthorne, Calif. 90250

McGraw-Hill Book Company
Webster Division
1221 Avenue of the Americas
New York, N.Y. 10020

Mead Educational Services
1391 Chattahoochee Avenue, NW
Atlanta, Ga. 30318

Melody House Publishing Company
819 N.W. 92nd Street
Oklahoma City, Okla. 73114

Miller-Brody Productions, Inc
342 Madison Avenue, Dept. 78
New York, N.Y. 10017

Milton Bradley Company
Springfield, Mass. 01101

Modern Education Corporation
P.O. Box 721
Tulsa, Okla. 74101

NASCO
901 Janesville Avenue
Fort Atkinson, Wisc. 53538

Novo Educational Toy and
    Equipment Corporation
124 W. 24th Street
New York, N.Y. 10011

*The Open Book
1025 Second Avenue
Salt Lake City, Utah 84103

Open Court Publishing Company
LaSalle, Ill. 61301

Parker Brothers
50 Dunham Road
Beverly, Mass. 01915

Perma Bound
Vandalia Road
Jacksonville, Ill. 62650

Platt and Munk
10055 Bronx River Avenue
Bronx, N.Y. 10472

Play-Art Educational Equipment
    Company
20 W. Armat Street
Philadelphia, Pa. 19144

Playground Corporation of America
29-24 40th Avenue
Long Island City, N.Y. 11101

PlayLearn Products/Theraplay Products
Division of PCA Industries, Inc.
2298 Grissom Drive
St. Louis, Mo. 63141

Playskool
4501 W. Augusta Boulevard
Chicago, Ill. 60651

Playworld Systems
P.O. Box 227
New Berlin, Pa. 17855

Prentice-Hall, Inc.
Englewood Cliffs, N.J. 07632

The Psychological Corporation
757 Third Avenue
New York, N.Y. 10017

Responsive Environment Corp.
200 Sylvan Ave.
Englewood Cliffs, N.J. 07632

Rhythm Productions
Whitney Building, Box 34485
Los Angeles, Calif. 90034

Scholastic
904 Sylvan Avenue
Englewood Cliffs, N.J. 07632

Science Research Associates, Inc.
259 E. Erie Street
Chicago, Ill. 60611

Scott, Foresman and Company
1900 E. Lake Avenue
Glenview, Ill. 60025

SEE (Selective Educational Equipment,
    Inc.)
3 Bridge Street
Newton, Mass. 02195

Selrite
School Equipment Corporation
225 West 34th Street
New York, N.Y. 10001

Simplex Toys
Steinmeier and Company
Gestelsestraat 7,
Aalst, N.B. Holland

Skill Development Equipment Company
1340 N. Jefferson
Anaheim, Calif. 92807

St. Regis Paper Company
150 E. 42nd Street
New York, N.Y. 10017

Teaching Resources
100 Boylston Street
Boston, Mass. 02116

Thomas Y. Crowell Company
10 East 53rd Street
New York, N.Y. 10022

3-7 Playways
1233 W. Country Road "E"
St. Paul, Minn. 55112

Timber Toys
P.O. Box 551
Broken Arrow, Okla. 74012

Tonka Toys, Division of Tonka
    Corporation
5300 Shoreline
Mound, Md. 55364

Tot Toys
Box 87
Wadena, Minn. 56482

*Toys That Care and Other Items, Inc.
P.O. Box 81
Briarcliff Manor, N.Y. 10510

Transparent Products Corporation
1727 West Pico Boulevard
Los Angeles, Calif. 90015

TREND Enterprises, Inc.
P.O. Box 43073
St. Paul, Minn. 55164

Troll Associates
320 Rt 17
Mahwah, N.J. 07430

United Canvas and Sling, Inc.
155 State Street
Hackensack, N.J. 07601

United Learning
6633 West Howard Street
Niles, Ill. 60648

Webster's International Tutoring
   Systems, Inc.
Suite 205, 2416 Hillsboro Road
Nashville, Tenn. 37212

Western Publishing Company, Inc.
150 Parish Drive
Wayne, N.J. 07470

Wollensack 3M Company
3M Center
St. Paul, Minn. 55101

*Women on Words and Images
Box 2163
Princeton, N.J. 08540

*Women's Action Alliance, Inc.
Non-Sexist Child Development Project
370 Lexington Avenue
New York, N.Y. 10017

Workshop for Learning Things
5 Bridge Street
Watertown, Mass. 02172

Xerox Education Publications
1250 Fairwood Avenue
P.O. Box 2639
Columbus, Ohio 43216

Zaner-Bloser
612 North Park Street
Columbus, Ohio 43215

Appendix 6

Instructional Kits and Sets

Learning Skills and/or Multicurricular Areas
(All kits are listed alphabetically by kit names.)

Witty, Paul A. *Adventures in Discovery*. Bobbs-Merrill Company, Inc.
Structured activities to help three- through six-year-olds develop general readiness skills, oral language, science and nature concepts, and creativity. Children engage in gamelike tasks and work in activity books. Materials, available separately or as a unit, include manual, teacher's resource book, activity books, and picture books.

Young, Ethel (Project's Coordinator). *The Amazing Life Games Theatre*. Houghton Mifflin Co.
Activities and materials for preprimary through first grade in social studies, the arts, communication skills, science, and mathematics. Children engage in gamelike activities, complete work sheets, and enjoy books and films. Materials, available separately, include manual, activity cards, patterns and instructions for making games, film preview poster, books, films, and other teaching resources.

*·†Lewis, L., and T.D. Yawkey. *Assessing Children for Early Prescriptive Teaching*. The Economy Company.
Computerized diagnostic program to identify and prescribe for individual developmental lags in social-emotional, perceptual-motor, and cognitive areas. ACEPT isolates individual areas in which a child should profit from additional experience, then recommends prescriptive activities. Test results are submitted to the Center for Educational Assessment, where they are measured against appropriate performance levels; a computer then provides individualized prescriptive activities. Components of program, some available separately, include assessment instrument, handbook, manipulative kit, prescriptive activities, record keeping system, and duplicating masters.

*Bridges, C. *Awareness of the World Around You: Part 1*. Imperial Educational Resources (Lakeland, Fla.)
Geared for ages 2 through 5, including visually handicapped, for developing concepts in health, safety, social behavior, community, nature, and ecology. Kit consists of posters, audiotape cassettes, and guides; sold as a unit. Part 2 available for primary-grade children.

*·†*Beginning Concepts*. Scholastic Book Services.
Helps preprimary through early primary children learn concepts of size, color, number,

*Handicapped
†Educationally disadvantaged

shape, texture, position, time, opposites, parts of the body, and growth. Children view sound filmstrips and engage in discussions and gamelike activities. Materials include manual, filmstrips, records, fold-out books, and minibooks. Two units, one for each semester, sold separately.

*Thurston, Thelma G., and D.L. Lillie. *Beginning to Learn: Fine Motor Skills.* Science Research Associates.
Designed for preschool, kindergarten, and first grade. Materials used to develop the eye-hand coordination needed for writing: finger speed, hand-and-finger dexterity, arm steadiness, and arm-and-hand precision. Learning methods are cutting, tracing, connecting dots, aiming, coloring, pasting, and completing figures. Materials, sold separately, include manual, workbooks, plastic templates, tracing boards, and transparencies for overhead projector.

Bold Beginning in Early Learning. Ideal School Supply Company.
Thirty-six-week developmental program designed to present thinking skills and concepts in all major curricular areas. Lesson plans and activities introduced through weekly topics, such as "Family," "Transportation," "Animal Homes," "Good Manners," "Clouds," and "Health." Children engage in learning games and activities with hand and face puppets; puppet house; vocabulary, numeral, alphabet, color, and color graduation cards; picture and activity books; number blocks; flannel board family; alphabet stick-on letters; pattern stencils; and measuring tapes. Comprehensive Teacher's Guide. Materials may be purchased separately.

Cheves, R. *Cheves Program.* Teaching Resources.
Designed for preprimary functional level; includes simple puzzles, form puzzles, geometric shapes and association cards, phonics puzzles and games, quantity and number relationships activities, and numerical progression and time activities. Available as a unit, or component parts can be purchased separately.

*Mevedeff, E., and B. Dearth. *CHILD.* Ideal School Supply Company.
Comprehensive program of assessment–teaching–learning materials to assist in early identification and treatment of possible learning problems. An Early Identification Screening Inventory utilizes a behavioral checklist. Three individually administered diagnostic instruments: Motor Perceptual Diagnostic Inventory, Fine Visual Motor Screening Inventory, and Perceptual Organization Screening Inventory. Prescriptive components link findings of diagnostic tools to specific elements of the curriculum designed to provide corrective activities. Sold as a unit. A special training program is available for individual or group in-service training; materials for the training program are sold separately.

*,†*Conceptos basicos.* EDL/McGraw-Hill.
Teaches basic skills (color, shapes, classification, numbers) to Spanish-speaking kindergarten and grade 1 children, including mentally handicapped, emotionally disturbed, and learning disabled. Materials include activity books, picture books, audiotape cassettes, cards, shapes, and guide with dual-culture resource section. Sold as a unit.

Welch, K.A., J.W. Cole, T.D. Yawkey, and F. Sucher. *Crossties.* The Economy Company.
Basic discovery program. Childhood education. Children develop social-emotional, cognitive, and perceptual motor skills with presentation of specific information and concepts. Classroom may be organized for large-group, small-group, and individual activities. Components, separately, include *Grand Central Books,* teacher's manual,

Little Trolley Books and accompanying tapes, discovery cards, duplicating masters, teacher's evaluation record, and some materials from *Kindergarten Keys*.

*Gould, Lawrence N. *Detect Tactile*. Science Research Associates.
Designed to develop perceptual and cognitive abilities through sense of touch, in preschool through second grade. In gamelike, manipulative, and paper-and-pencil tasks, children classify geometric forms by shape, size, and texture; draw geometric forms according to symbolic prescriptions; and follow verbal and symbol directions for moving shapes. Materials, available separately, include manual, game board, plastic forms, and workbooks.

*Gould, Lawrence. *Detect Visual*. Science Research Associates.
Designed to develop perceptual and cognitive abilities through sense of sight, in preprimary through second grade. Children verbally describe and reproduce these images: linear pictures, geometric forms, patterns of forms, alphabet letters, and numerals. Materials include manual, tachistoscopic adapter (a device for flashing images with use of any overhead projector), transparencies, and workbooks, available separately.

*Janiak, W. *Developing Everyday Skills for Early Childhood and Special Education*. Kimbo Educational. (Long Branch, NJ)
Series of phonograph records designed to develop sense of rhythm, self-expression, coordination, and ability to follow directions in preschool and kindergarten children, including mentally and language handicapped. Six albums and guides available separately.

Lavatelli, Celia. *Early Childhood Curriculum: A Piaget Program*. American Science and Engineering.
Designed to develop logical thinking ability in four- through six-year-olds. Fosters development of intellectual skills in three areas: classification; number, measurement, and space; and seriation. Each training session requires child to physically and/or mentally manipulate data and use appropriate words to describe the manipulation. Gamelike activities used in conjunction with free play and other activities. Materials include manual, objects, and pictures. Each of the three units available separately. Staff training material is C.S. Lavatelli's *Piaget's Theory Applied to an Early Childhood Curriculum* (a book on the rationale behind the *Early Childhood Curriculum*).

*Karnes, Merle B. (Director). *Early Childhood Enrichment Units*. Educational Teaching Aids.
Each unit has a specific purpose: Unit 1, "Toys to Develop Perceptual Skills," emphasizes visual discrimination skills. Unit 2, "Learning to Develop Language Skills," focuses on labeling skills, associative qualities, and divergent and convergent responses. Unit 3, "Development of Number Readiness," emphasizes matching, sorting and grouping, patterning, one-to-one relationships, and building equivalent and nonequivalent sets. Unit 4, "Development of Readiness to Read," focuses on verbal, visual and auditory skills, ability to sequence, and logical relationships. All units programmed, and have gamelike and verbal tasks for three- through five-year-olds. Materials include manual, objects, and pictures; each unit sold separately.

Curry, N., R. Jaynes, M. Crune, and R. Radlaver. *Early Childhood Series*. Bowmar/Noble Publishers, Inc.
Helps prekindergarten through third-grade children develop concepts in language arts and social science understandings. Three basic themes: positive self-concept; awareness of physical environment; social awareness. Children listen to stories and records,

view filmstrips, and study prints. Materials, available separately, include manual, books, records, filmstrips, and study prints.

*Fairbanks, J.S., and J. Robinson. *Fairbanks-Robinson Program*, Revised Edition. Teaching Resources.
Designed to develop preacademic skills in handicapped, and for reinforcement and remedial work in kindergarten and first grade. Covers preacademic skills of line reproduction, shape and size perception, coloring, cutting, spatial relationships, figure-ground discrimination, sequencing, and parts-to-whole relationship. Two levels available, and sold separately: Level 1, preschool and early kindergarten functional level; Level 2, kindergarten functional level. Worksheet refills available.

*Forsdale, J. *Film Learning to Increase Cognitive Skill* (FLICS) Prentice-Hall.
Mentally handicapped, emotionally disturbed, and learning disabled kindergarten through fourth-grade children can use FLICS to develop perceptual and cognitive skills. Students interact with filmstrips and film loops, and perform supplemental activities. Kit consists of filmstrips, film loops, audiotape cassettes, plastic discs, and guides. Filmstrips and film loops sold separately.

*Sprigle, Herbert A. *Inquisitive Games: Discovering How to Learn*. Science Research Associates.
Designed to help preschool through first-grade children develop learning strategies, such as gathering information, classifying and organizing information and materials, processing information, making decisions, and solving problems. Eight sections: "Human Body," "Clothing," "Properties," "Food," "Furniture," "Animals," "Transportation," and "Applying Strategies and Knowledge." Children engage in gamelike activities. Materials sold as a unit; include manual, charts, games, and pictures cards.

Nale, N., M. Creekmore, T.L. Harris, and M.H. Greenman. *Kindergarten Keys*. The Economy Company.
Develops basic skills and concepts in prereading, science, social studies, language arts, mathematics, music, art, health and safety, and physical education, through gamelike and paper-and-pencil tasks. Includes testing—a General Inventory, Prereading Skills Test, and Mathematics Skills Test. Teacher's Guidebook contains daily plans for the program's 14 basic units. Two pupil-activity books with accompanying teacher's manuals have been added. The *Caterpillar Caper* is designed to develop skills used in beginning reading—visual discrimination, auditory discrimination, auditory-visual discrimination, comprehension skills, and fine motor skills. *Sand Dollar Shuffle* is a mathematics program for introducing children to geometric shapes, sets and comparisons of sets, numerals 0 to 10, number concepts, ordinal number words, measurement, telling time, and values of coins. Besides manuals and activity books, other materials are *The Language Development Cards*, calendar pocket chart, color chart, number chart, solid geometric shapes, and templates. A Parent/Paraprofessional Kit is available for use in home or class setting. Materials can be purchased separately.

Vanderslice, Margaret. *The Learning Board*. Bobbs-Merrill Company, Inc.
For early primary grades. Emphasizes skills such as sight vocabulary, word attack, phonics, handwriting, color perception, numbers, size relationships, time concepts, money values, and shapes. Skills introduced through gamelike activities. Materials sold as unit, including manual and Learning Board, and its accompanying materials.

Berger, C.F., G.D. Berkheimer, L.E. Lewis, Jr., H.T. Neuberger, and E.A. Wood. *Learning to Learn*. Houghton Mifflin.

Concentrates on science processes (observing, describing, manipulating, and investigating), while building readiness skills of eye-hand coordination, form perception, visual-aduitory-tactile discrimination, classification, seriation, and spatial relationships. Materials are purchased as audiovisual kit, equipment kit, pupil progress chart, and teacher's guide.

Thurstone, T.G. *The Learning to Think Series.* Science Research Associates.
Designed for training kindergarten and early primary grade children in primary mental abilities: verbal meaning, space thinking, reasoning, quantitative thinking, word fluency, memory, perception, and motor coordination. Children progress through four sequenced workbooks, each with charts and manual, in four semesters. Materials available separately.

*Insel, E., and A. Edson. *The Learning Well.* Educational Activities (Freeport, N.Y.)
For preschool, kindergarten, and primary grades, including mentally handicapped, emotionally disturbed, and learning disabled. Kit contains materials to teach multiple readiness activities such as color indentification, classification, size concepts, visual and auditory perception, and numbers. Materials, available separately, include sound filmstrips, audiotapes, activity cards to color on and wipe off, and guide.

Educational Testing Service. *Let's Look at Children.* Addison-Wesley Publishing Company.
Instructional and assessment kit for first grade, designed to foster intellectual development. Specifically, it is for assessing areas of language skills (learning to communicate and language for thinking); concepts of time and space (shapes and forms, spatial perspective, and notion of time); logical concepts (logical classification and concepts of relationships); mathematical concepts (one-to-one correspondence, number relations, and conservation of quantity); reasoning skills (understanding cause and effect, reasoning by association, and reasoning by inference); and general signs of development (growing awareness and responsiveness, direct activity, general knowledge, and developing imagination). Children engage in gamelike activities and paper-and-pencil tasks. Materials, available separately, include manual, worksheets, sequence and directions card games, and answer sheet.

Manipulative Learning Unit. Florida Imperial Educational Resources (Lakeland, Fla.)
Manipulative materials teach reading readiness, math concepts, and perceptual motor skill development in individualized, self-paced program. Materials are appropriate for preschool through third-grade mentally handicapped, emotionally disturbed, or learning disabled. Kit contains form boards, upper- and lower-case letters, numerals, mathematics problem strips, picture-word strips, tracing paper, and guide. Language and mathematics units and individual strip sets available separately.

Frostig, M. *Move·Grow·Learn.* Follett Publishing Company.
Provides movement education activities to enhance overall development of kindergarten and primary-age children by improving physical, creative, and perceptual development. Consists of activity cards in skill areas of body awareness, coordination, strength, flexibility, balance, agility, and creative movement. Materials sold as a unit, although *Teacher's Guide* and a specimen set may be purchased separately.

Open Court Headway Program, Level A. Open Court Publishing Company.
Systematically planned program for teaching basic physical, social and academic skills. Basic divisions, Language Skills and Thinking Skills, are reinforced by perceptual activities, basic vocabulary activities, and exercises in social development. Children engage in gamelike procedures and paper-and-pencil tasks. Materials include

teacher's manuals, workbooks, manipulative equipment, activity resource cards, big flip books, and progress charts. Optional materials, such as phonics cassettes, music records, a music workbook, and a music teacher's guide, are available. Materials sold separately.

*Ross, D.M., and S.A. Ross. *Pacemaker Primary Curriculum*. Fearon-Pitman Publishers. Lessons in "Academic Skills," "Cognitive Skills," "Social Skills," "Motor Skills," "Fine Arts," and "Independence Skills." Materials, available separately, include for each of four levels: lesson books, duplicating masters, and manual. Manipulable materials to complement lessons include full-color die-cut "Family Figures" and "Picture Pack." Teacher training film also available.

Dunn, L.M., L.T. Chun, D.C. Crowell, L.M. Dunn, L.G. Halevi, and E.R. Yackel. *Peabody Early Experiences Kit*. American Guidance Service.
Designed to help young children (average three-year-olds, advanced two-year-olds, and less mature four-year-olds) think more effectively and express thoughts and feelings more clearly. About 50 percent of the activities focus on cognitive development, 25 percent on affective development, and 25 percent on oral language development. Also body coordination and awareness activities. Materials include: teacher's guide, manuals, puppets, pocket charts, beads, rope sections, fishing pole, pictures, posters, small objects, templates, storycards, balls, bags, and carrying case. Component parts available separately.

*Shearer, David. *Portage Guide to Early Education*. Portage Project (Portage, Wisconsin). Individualized instruction kit for mental ages birth to 5 years, for use with the exceptional child, including profoundly handicapped—mentally handicapped, emotionally disturbed, learning disabled, physically handicapped, speech handicapped, and multiply handicapped. Emphasizes five developmental areas: cognitive, self-help, motor, language, and socialization. Kit includes a checklist of behaviors and card file of curriculum ideas; sold as a unit.

Project Mainstream. Educational Progress Corporation. (Tulsa, OK)
Designed to help children with mental handicaps, emotional disturbances, or learning disabilities in preschool through third grade. Three sets are: "Development of Aural Skills," "Development of Visual Skills," and "The Social/Emotional Development Skills." Materials include audiotape cassettes, activity worksheets, "Behavior Skills Inventories," class performance profiles, and guide. Each of the three sets available separately.

McLeod, P.H. *Readiness for Learning Clinic*. J.B. Lippincott Co.
Designed to help kindergarten and first-grade children develop physical and perceptual skills, specifically visual and auditory perception and gross motor skills. Children learn through large muscle, auditory, visual, and eye-hand coordination tasks. Materials, sold as a unit, include performance charts, visual-motor perception skill activity cards, auditory perception and verbal communication skill activity cards, workbooks for eye-hand coordination, matching cards, and tachistoscopes.

Sullivan Associates. *The Sullivan Academic Readiness Curriculum*. Behavioral Research Laboratories.
Designed to introduce basic skills of language arts, math, social language and concepts, and science. Children look at giant demonstration books, listen to cassette narratives, begin to read and do simple computations as they engage in activities and discussions. Materials, available separately, include 15 giant demonstration books

with accompanying manuals and cassettes, alphabet strips, word cards, picture cards, number cards and charts, handwriting workbooks, and beginning readers.

Teaching Resources' Basic Skills Curriculum Guide. Teaching Resources.
Skill areas are motor, perceptual, cognitive, prereading, language, and mathematics. Guide, sold separately, includes brief discussion of each skill and relationship to child's development, and list of activities to use with preprimary, primary, and special education children in developing that skill. Suggested materials for activities sold separately.

Manolakes, George, Robert Weltman, Marie Scian, and Louis Waldo. *Try.* Bowmar/Noble Publishers, Inc.
Develops basic readiness skills in children with mental ages 4.0 years through 7.0 years; readiness skills include visual and language skills, left-to-right and top-to-bottom orientation, and discrimination between shape and size. Children engage in perceptual tasks such as discriminating geometric shapes and forms and design patterns. Materials, sold separately, include manual, activity book, and set of three-dimensional, manipulative materials.

*Robinson, J., and B.A. Schmitt. *Vanguard School Program.* Teaching Resources.
Teaches body awareness, discrimination and classification, spatial relationships, and visual-motor integration activities for kindergarten through second grade. Remedial activities for five through fourteen years. Designed for small groups of students, followed by individual work. Materials include guide, workbooks, and acetates. Each of the four areas available separately; also additional workbooks.

Language Arts and Reading

Sanford, A. *Audio Reading Progress Laboratory* (Level A). Tulsa, Oklahoma Educational Progress Company.
Multisensory approach to teaching left-to-right progression, listening, following directions, matching, comprehension, vocabulary, rhyming, and vowels and consonants. Teacher-directed lessons designed for ages 4 to 6. Kit, sold as a unit, includes audiotape cassettes, learning activity packages, manipulative materials, and manual.

Thurstone, T.E., and D.L. Lillie. *Beginning to Learn: Perceptual Skills.* Science Research Associates.
Develops perceptual abilities of selection, accuracy and speed, flexibility and analysis to maximun level of efficiency in kindergarten or first grade. Materials, sold separately, include spirit masters, transparencies, filmstrips, and manual.

Rowland, J.T. *Beginning to Read, Write, and Listen.* J.B. Lippincott Co.
Moves kindergarten through first-grade children from readiness to independent reading. Correlated program covers areas of handwriting, auditory skills, language activities, art projects, spelling, and reading. Children engage in gamelike tasks, rhythmic activities, singing, art projects, and listening. Materials include manual, "Letterbooks," taped cassette lessons, duplicating masters, three-dimensional pop-out cards, "Startwrite" chalk, magic slate, alphabet cards, etc.

Scarry, Richard. *Best Word Program Ever.* Educational Insights.
Preprimary through third-grade; develops skills in naming and describing objects, making comparisons, introduces sight vocabulary. Children learn by viewing pictures,

listening, picture reading, and reading words. Materials, purchased as a unit, consist of manual and pictures mounted on boards with word list on reverse side.

*Children's Songs Sound Filmstrip Set. Bowmar Publishing Company.
Stimulates language development and provides "reading" activity for kindergarten and first-grade children, including mentally handicapped, emotionally disturbed, and learning disabled. Materials, sold as a unit, include filmstrips, phonograph record, 10 copies of booklet, and guide. A Children's Song Reading Readines Kit is available, containing verse cards, sentence strips, study prints, audiotape cassettes, vocabulary cards, and guide.

Bridwell, Norman. Clifford, The Big Red Dog. Scholastic Coach Book Service.
Helps kindergarten through third-grade children develop positive attitudes toward literature; specifically, helps children learn to listen effectively, recognize main ideas, retell a story sequence, distinguish between fact and fantasy, develop basic values, recognize spatial concepts, understand the alphabet, read for different purposes, increase vocabulary, and use language effectively. Children learn by listening to and telling stories, art work, music, dramatization, and flannel board activities. Suggestions for supplementary experiences and for evaluation listed in manual. Besides manual, materials include paperback books, recorded narrations of stories, and recorded interviews with authors. Sold as unit, with one unit per grade level.

Concepts for Communication. Teaching Resources.
Aids in developing receptive, associative, and expressive language skills. Three units available: "Listening with Understanding," "Concept Building," and "Communication." Materials differ for each unit; may be purchased individually. Some materials are matrix cards, picture books, activity books, cassettes, and manuals. In addition to regular classroom use, program is helpful for children with language or learning disabilities and children learning English as a second language.

*Karnes, M.B. Development of Readiness to Read. Milton Bradley Company.
For visually impaired preschool, kindergarten, and first-grade; individual or group instruction. Teaches reading readiness through verbal, visual, and auditory skills, and use of logical relationships. Kit includes games, pictures, manuscript letters, puzzles, and flannel board materials; sold as a unit.

*Directionality Program. Bowmar Publishing Corp.
Teaches concepts of directionality, location, and positions in space to visually impaired preschool, kindergarten, primary grade children. With filmstrips and audiotape cassette, child locates and tracks large images as they are projected. Sold as a unit.

†Engelmann, S., J. Osborn, and T. Engelmann. Distar Language, second edition. Science Research Associates.
Basal language program for preschool through third grade. Focuses on language of instruction used in school. Children learn through physical actions, responding to pictures, and verbal give-and-take. Materials, available separately, include take-home books, workbooks, student textbook, behavioral objectives, and guides.

†Engelmann, S., and E.C. Bruner. Distar Reading, second edition. Science Research Associates.
Basal reading program for preschool through third grade. Scripted lessons for teaching reading. Materials, available separately, include storybooks, take-home books, behavioral objectives, student readers, workbooks, and manuals. Preservice and inservice training program and Distar Library Series of additional books also available.

Dubnoff, B., I. Chambers, and F. Schaefer. *Dubnoff School Program.* Teaching Resources.
Prewriting program for kindergarten or supplemental and reinforcement program for
first grade. Each level has guide, child's workbook, crayons, acetates, and felt markers.
Each of three levels available separately, as well as four sets of "Dubnoff write-on
Cards," to use as supplemental materials.

*Liddle, W. *Early Approaches to Reading Skills.* The Economy Company.
Individualized program to develop auditory comprehension skills in kindergarten and
primary grade children, including mentally handicapped, emotionally disturbed, and
learning disabled. Materials include audiotape cassettes, response booklets, and guide.
Response booklets are consumable, and thus purchased separately.

*Halton, D.A., F.J. Pizzat, and J.M. Pelkowski. *Erie Program.* Teaching Resources.
Preschool or kindergarten level, or for primary-grade children with visual-perceptual
problems. Each set of visual-perceptual activities has carefully controlled progression
of difficulty. Program may be purchased as a unit, or each of four parts available
separately.

*Borton, T. *Find Your Own Way: Experiences in Language.* Harcourt Brace Jovanovich.
Helps with self-identity and communication skills in preschool through second-grade
children, including mentally handicapped, emotionally disturbed, and learning disabled. Children participate in art and craft work, discussions, and written activities.
Materials consist of filmstrips, audiotape cassettes, activity books, activity cards, and
guide. Activity books are consumable, and thus may be purchased separately.

Frostig, M. *The Frostig Developmental Program, Revised: Pictures and Patterns.* Follett
Publishing Company.
For preschool through third-grade children. Sequentially arranged paper-and-pencil
exercises to develop five skill areas of visual perception: visual-motor coordination,
figure-ground perception, perceptual constancy, perception of position in space, and
perception of spatial relationships. The separate teacher's guide and three student's
books (Beginning, Intermediate, and Advanced) available separately. Transparent acetate overlays also available.

*Frostig, M., D. Horne, and P. Maslow. *The Frostig Remediation Program.* Follett Publishing Company.
Paper-and-pencil exercises for preschool through third-grade children to facilitate
remedial training in five skill areas of visual perception: visual-motor coordination,
figure-ground perception, perceptual constancy, perception of position in space, and
perception of spatial relationships. Section on transitional exercises focuses child's
attention on underlying structural features that distinguish letters from each other.
Materials may be purchased as a unit, or materials for each of the five skill areas
available separately.

*Karnes, M.B. *Goal: Level 1 Language Development.* Milton Bradley.
Develops language processing skills in children 3 to 5 years of age, including mentally
handicapped and learning disabled. Self-paced material follows rationale of the *Illinois
Test of Psycholinguistic Abilities.* Materials are in game format, and include games,
puzzles, puppets, cards, manual, and lesson plans. Sold as a unit.

Goldman, R., and M.E. Lynch. *Goldman-Lynch Sounds and Symbols Development Kit.*
American Guidance Service.
Guides preschool through first-grade children in making association between sounds
and their written symbols. Program uses puppets, songs, pictures and posters, story-

books, sentence strips, word cards, and an alphabet of magnetic symbols. Materials available separately.

*Initial Consonant Learning Center. Illinois Society for Visual Education. (Chicago, Ill.)
Teaches letter-sound relationships of consonants to kindergarten through primary mentally handicapped, emotionally disturbed, learning disabled, and speech handicapped children. Components of kit, sold separately, include filmstrips, picture cards, audiotape cassettes, and guides.

*Initial Consonant Learning Module. Illinois Society for Visual Education. (Chicago, Ill.)
Teaches letter-sound relationships of consonants used in conjunction with any basic reading program. Designed for kindergarten through primary mentally handicapped, emotionally disturbed, learning disabled, and speech handicapped children. Components of kit, sold separately, include filmstrips, audiotape cassettes, picture cards, and games.

*Initial Consonants Learning Satellites. Illinois Society for Visual Education. (Chicago, Ill.)
Teaches and reviews letter-sound relationships of consonants. Kit is specified for remedial students, mentally handicapped, emotionally disturbed, learning disabled, and speech handicapped. Includes lotto game, "Consonant Race Board Game," "Consonant Jumble Floor Game," and guide. All components available separately.

*Initial Experiences Module. Reader's Digest Services.
Teaches recognizing and using narrative order, left-to-right progression, comparing size and order, and vocabulary development. For ages 3 through 5, and mentally handicapped, emotionally disturbed, and learning disabled. Blocks, picture cards, check list, and guide included; sold as a unit.

Pollack, Cecelia. Intersensory Reading Program. Book-Lab.
Purposes are: Phase 1—(kindergarten or early first grade), "Development of Auditory Perception and Phonic Readiness." Children expected to recognize phonic elements in simple words, understand that words are represented by symbols, and develop blending and word-building skills using objects. Phase 2—(first grade), "Learning with Letter Symbols." Phase 1 words again presented, but object symbols replaced by letter symbols. Phases 3 and 4—(first and second grades), "Reading and Writing." Phonic and linguistic patterns presented; children engage in gamelike tasks with kinesthetic reinforcement. Materials, sold separately, include manual, "Phonics Readiness Set," reading and writing books, manuscript and cursive writing forms, and "Game of Words."

Slepian, J., and A. Seidler. The Junior Listen-Hear Program. Follett Publishing Company.
For preschool through grade 2; program of auditory training sequenced from simple recognition and discrimination of gross environmental sounds to beginning auditory discrimination of speech sounds. Materials, sold as a unit, consist of five books, one record, three posters, and manual.

CEMREL, Inc. Lanuage and Thinking. Follett Publishing Company.
"Learning through experiencing" approach for teaching language, basic concepts, and critical thinking skills to three- through seven-year-olds. Materials, available separately, include multisensory packages ("Shapes," "Sizes," "Blends," "Action," "Functions," "Classification," and "Relevant Learning Experiences"), teacher's guide, student activity books, teacher orientation package, and spirit masters.

*,†Allen, R.V., and C. Allen. *Language Experiences in Early Childhood*. Encyclopedia
   Britannica Educational Corporation.
   Helps child build language skills by using his own interests and experiences to encourage communication. LEEC is a guide or sourcebook of creative ideas for organizing
   classroom and planning lessons. Parent participation is part of LEEC program; "Pupil–
   Parent Leaflets" describes home activities for parents and children; available in English
   or Spanish. For use in regular kindergarten classrooms and with slow learners, remedial or "special" classes, disadvantaged children, or those for whom English is a second
   language. "Resource Guide" and "Leaflets" sold as a unit; additional "Leaflets" available separately.

Allen, R.V., R.L. Venezky, and H.T. Hahn. *Language Experiences in Reading*. Encyclopedia Britannica Educational Corporation.
   Levels I, II, and III for first-, second-, and third-graders, respectively. Based on Allen's
   "language experience" approach to reading, which begins with child's oral language.
   Reading is thus only part of child's language experiences. Teacher's materials include
   daily lesson plan guides, resource guide, language study guide, and class record sheet.
   Children's materials include resource cards, filmstrips, records or cassettes, books,
   ditto sheets, activity books, and magazines and newspapers. Program centers around
   units. Except for student consumable materials, each level sold as complete unit.

*Karnes, M.B. *Language Learning at Home*. The Council for Exceptional Children.
   Stimulates language development of three- through five-year-olds at home, with or
   without correlated program. Includes four groups of lessons focusing on four basic skill
   areas: *Learning to Do* builds motor skills through manual expression; *Learning to Listen*
   builds auditory skills; *Learning to Look* builds visual skills; *Learning to Tell* builds
   verbal expression. There are 50 lessons in each category; each lesson includes four
   reinforcement and extension activities. Manual and Record of Progress forms included.
   Materials sold as a unit.

*Plunkett, P.L. *Language Patterns*. Milton Bradley Company.
   Sequenced lessons in audio-linguistic patterns, designed for nonreaders in preschool
   through grade 1, including mentally handicapped, emotionally disturbed, and learning
   disabled. Kit, sold as a unit, includes audiotape cassettes, picture worksheets, picture
   wheel card, and teacher's guide.

*Sprugel, Catherine C. *Learning to Develop Language Skills*. Milton Bradley Company.
   Increases vocabulary, auditory, and visual memory, and verbal fluency. Instructional
   levels include preschool through first grade and mentally handicapped, emotionally
   disturbed, learning disabled, and speech handicapped. Kit includes manipulative
   materials, posters, books, and guide; sold as a unit.

Let's Look For. Bowmar Publishing Corp.
   Helps kindergarten and primary children, including visually impaired, identify objects
   and receive figure-ground training. Materials, sold as a unit (except for an evaluation
   filmstrip) include filmstrips used in conjunction with a rear view projection screen,
   audiotape cassettes, and manual.

Linguistic Readiness Program. Charles E. Merrill Publishing Company
   Prereading and prehandwriting program designed to develop readiness competencies
   in many language art skills areas. Suitable for kindergarten, first grade, or any children

needing preparation for reading. Materials include survey test, diagnostic tests, pupil record cards, filmstrips and cassettes with spirit duplicating masters, linguistic readiness cards, activity sheets, alphabet cards, and program manual. Sold as a unit or separately.

Listen and Say. EDL/McGraw-Hill.
Twenty listening lessons to develop listening comprehension and auditory discrimination for kindergarten and grade 1, including mentally hanicapped, emotionally disturbed, learning disabled, and physically handicapped. Kit includes picture cards, audiotape cassettes, and guide; sold as a unit.

Slepian, J., and A. Seidler. *The Listen-Hear Program.* Follett Publishing Company.
Auditory, speech, and language stimulation activities for kindergarten through grade 3. Troublesome sounds of s, l, r, th, k, and f used at beginning, in middle, and at end of words, and in blends. Materials, sold as a unit, consist of six books and manual.

Mother Goose Songs Sound Filmstrip Set. Bowmar Publishing Corp.
Stimulates language development and provides "reading" activity for kindergarten and grade 1 children, including mentally handicapped, emotionally disturbed, and learning disabled. Materials, sold as a unit, include filmstrips, phonograph record, 10 copies of a booklet, and guide. *Mother Goose Songs Reading Readiness Kit* also available, containing verse cards, sentence strips, study prints, audiotape cassettes, vocabulary cards, and guide.

Dunn, L., and J.O. Smith. *Peabody Language Development Kits.* American Guidance Service.
Focuses on reception through senses, vocal and motor expression, and divergent, convergent, and associative thinking involved in conceptualization. Intent is overall language development rather than specific training in particular psycholinguistic processes. Divided into four levels: Level #P (M.A. 3–5); Level #1 (M.A. 4.6–6.6); Level #2 (M.A. 6–8); Level #3 (M.A. 7.6–9.6). Some materials are: manual, various cards, fruits and vegetables, templates, posters, records, puppets, manikins, geometric shapes, color chips, and carrying case. Component parts available separately.

*Scott, R.T., and M. Meyer. *Perceptual Skills.* Reader's Digest Service, Inc.
Develops perceptual abilities needed for general learning (recognition of geometric forms, classifying, sequencing, responding to positional concepts). Designed for mentally handicapped and hearing impaired. Materials, sold as a unit, include photographs, picture cards, geometric shapes, boad games, phonograph records, tests and evaluation charts, and manual for teacher-directed and independent activities.

Perceptual Training: PAL System, Programmed Assistance to Learning Language Improvement to Facilitate Education. Instructional Industries, Inc.
Increases four- through six-year-old's ability to: discriminate and associate word composition and letters; visualize properties of size, shape, and color; visualize added and omitted features in pictures and figure-ground relations; understand positions-in-space and spatial relationships. Children learn through programmed filmstrips. Materials, available separately, include manual and four sets of filmstrips.

Prereading Module. Reader's Digest Services.
Teaches auditory discrimination, sound-letter correspondence, and position and sequence of sounds within words. Designed for ages 4 through 6; used with mentally handicapped, emotionally disturbed, and learning disabled. Kit, sold as a unit, consists of activity books, records, cards, charts, games, and guide.

University of Wisconsin Research and Development Center for Cognitive Learning. *Pre-reading Skills Program.* Encyclopedia Britannica Educational Corporation.
Teaches five skills necessary for learning to read effectively: attending to letter order, attending to letter orientation, attending to word detail, sound matching, and sound blending. "Teacher's Guide Folder," "Sound Schedule," and "Visual Schedule" give sequence of instruction. Activities in schedules are keyed in "Teacher's Resource File." Instruction based on variety of games and activities involving cards, practice sheets, games, letters to parents, class charts, books, and record. Sold as a unit.

Buchanan, C.D., and M.W. Sullivan. *Reading Readiness Kits I and II.* Webster Division/ McGraw-Hill Book Company.
Programmed method of teaching reading readiness. Kit I teaches names of letters, colors, and directionality. Kit II uses corresponding materials to review and introduce new sounds and words. Materials, available separately, include "Big Books," cassettes, ditto masters, and manuals.

*Ross, S. *Rhyming Words.* Enrich Inc. (Sunnyvale, Calif.)
Self-pacing materials suitable for mentally handicapped, emotionally disturbed, and learning disabled in kindergarten through second grade. Kit includes tape cassettes, two visual cartridges with 20 picture frames each, duplication masters, and manual. Materials sold as a unit.

Wood, L. *Rhythms to Reading.* Bowmar/Noble Publishers Inc.
Helps preprimary through third grade children make transition from prereading to reading. Children participate in action songs and singing games, listen to stories, view art prints, and participate in gamelike activities in music and language arts. Materials, available separately, include books, long-playing records, and songbook.

*Semel, E. *Semel Auditory Processing Program.* Follett Publishing Company.
Remediation techniques for preschool through adolescence. Each of three levels may be used to assess and remediate auditory processing difficulties. Materials consist of activity cards, teacher's guide, and student response books. Teacher's guide and student response books available separately for each level; one specimen set may also be purchased separately.

Semel, E. *Sound·Order·Sense.* Follett Publishing Company.
Two-year auditory perceptual program teaches children to listen for: "Sound"—sounds that make-up speech; "Order"— sequence of sounds in words and words in groups; and "Sense"—attributes that give meaning to words. Level 1 recommended for first grade; Level 2 recommended for use after completion of Level 1. Each kit, sold as a unit for each level, contains activity cards, records, teacher's guide, and special markers. Pupil Response Books sold separately.

*Society for Visual Education, Inc. *Tall Tales of Cowboy Jack.* Illinois Society for Visual Education, Inc. (Chicago, Illinois)
Develops listening and response skills in kindergarten through grade 3. Adventures of Cowboy Jack and factual narrative of modern life in American West. Suitable for mentally handicapped, emotionally disturbed, and learning disabled. Kit, sold as a unit, consists of audiotape cassettes, picture cards, puppets, and guide.

Thinking Activity Series: PAL System, Programmed Assistance to Learning Language Improvement to Facilitate Education. Instructional Industries, Inc.
Assists four- through six-year-olds in areas of: memory for color, objects, and positions; sequencing by size; picture absurdities; classification; figural memory and transforms;

maze tracing; pattern analysis; visual closure and completion; what does not belong; picture rotations; camouflaged numerals, objects, and letters; whole/part analogies; and implications and deductions. Children learn with six sets of programmed filmstrips, available separately.

Toys to Develop Perceptual Skills (3rd edition). Milton Bradley Company.
Enrichment kit; reinforces colors, shapes, patterns, and dimensions for preschool and kindergarten children, including mentally handicapped, emotionally disturbed, and learning disabled. Kit, sold as a unit, includes beads, plastic shapes, various-sized discs, board game, objects to feel, picture cards, puzzles, and manual.

Treasure Tub. Ideal School Supply Company.
Multisensory reading readiness program emphasizing eight reading readiness skills: visual discrimination, auditory discrimination, tactile-kinesthetic skills, context clues, word configuration, initial sight vocabulary, left-right sequencing, and phonics readiness. Materials, sold as a unit, consist of several sets of alphabet letters and numerals, alphabet floor stick-on cards, color cards, color cubes and pattern sheets, picture cards, picture books, and manual.

Visual Perception Big Box. Developmental Learning Materials. (Niles, Ill.)
Eye-hand integration, spatial relations, copying geometric figures, part-whole relationships, symmetry, sequence, and visual memory activities for preschool through grade 3, including mentally handicapped, emotionally disturbed, and learning disabled. Cards, puzzles, books, and guide each sold separately.

*Baum, L.F. *The Wizard of Oz.* Illinois Society for Visual Education, Inc. (Chicago, Ill.)
Stimulates listening and creative skills in preschool through grade 3 mentally handicapped, emotionally disturbed, and learning disabled. Adaptation of *The Wizard of Oz* and factual narration of life in the Midwest presented via audiotape cassettes, pictures cards, puppets, and guide. Sold as a unit.

Mathematics

*Cruickshank,W.M. *Basic Materials Kit—Foundations for Mathematics.* Boston, Massachusetts Teaching Resources.
Concrete materials for teaching units 1, 2, and 4 in the *Foundations for Mathematics* programs. Units focus on color and shape (unit 1), size and sequence (unit 2), and sets (unit 4). Materials include acetate protectors for writing on worksheets, flannel boards, geometric figures, worksheets, and manual. Sold as a unit; specified for use with mentally handicapped, emotionally disturbed, and learning disabled.

†Englemann, S., and D. Carnine. *Distar Arithmetic,* second edition. Science Research Associates.
Basal arithmetic program for preschool through grade 3. Scripted lessons teach precise strategies for analyzing and solving problems. Materials, sold separately, include take-home books, workbooks, behavioral objectives, and manuals.

Wilson, J.W., and A.E. Upichard. *Fundamentals Underlying Number.* Teaching Resources.
Helps three- through six-year-olds understand basic concepts underlying number. Can be used before or with any other math program. Three major concepts, each containing sixteen levels: one-to-one correspondence; greater/lesser than; and equivalence class and order. Up to six children can engage in noncompetitive and self-correcting group

games. Materials are purchased as a unit, and include manual, spinner cloth, set boards, cubes, blocks, numeral caps, numerals and numeral word cards, counting boards, and order-class columns.

*Karnes, Merle B. *Goal: Mathematical Concepts.* Milton Bradley Company.
Concepts of geometric shapes, one-to-one correspondence and sets, whole numbers and rational counting, numerals, addition and subtraction, measurement, patterns, and progressions. Kit with cards, flannel boards, games, charts, manipulatives, and guide was developed for preschool through grade 1, including mentally handicapped, emotionally disturbed, and learning disabled. Sold as a unit.

*Sprigle, Herbert A. *Inquisitive Games: Exploring Number and Space.* Science Research Associates.
Assists preprimary through first grade children develop mathematics fundamentals. Children participate in gamelike tasks to explore concepts of: spatial judgments; classification; seriation; addition and subtraction; more/less than; recognition of numerals and sets of objects for which they stand; and equivalence. Materials, sold as a unit, include manual, games, and modular plastic sticks.

*International Educational Films. *Let's Tell Time.* AIMS Instructional Media Services. (Hollywood, CA)
Learning package for hearing impaired; helps primary age children learn to tell time. Materials, sold as a unit, include: filmstrips, 40 clock faces, teacher's clock, overhead transparency with moveable hands, and study guide.

Number Concepts Module. Reader's Digest Services.
Introduces number concepts and skills ages 4 through 6. Suitable for mentally handicapped, emotionally disturbed, and learning disabled. Materials, sold as a unit, include activity books, picture cards, puzzle, and guides.

Crawley, J.F. *Project Math.* Educational Progress Corporation. (Tulsa, Okla.)
Materials for math activities in 6 areas: patterns, geometry, measurement, sets, numbers, and fractions. Designed for kindergarten through grade 2, including mentally handicapped, emotionally disturbed, and learning disabled. Includes activity books, manipulatives (blocks and geoboards), guide cards, progress record cards, and guides. Some components available separately, as well as kit for each of the 6 areas.

Real Math Program. Open Court Publishing Company.
Teaches basic skills and understandings needed for elementary school mathematics: ability to count intelligently in variety of concrete situations, with solid understanding of what one is doing; skill in simple measurement and estimation, using counting units; ability to recognize and write legibly numerals 0 through 10; and ability to increase or decrease numbers by 1, a prelude to addition and subtraction. Lively and enjoyable activities, with balance between concrete "hands on" activities and more verbal, reflective activities. Emphasis on thinking and problem solving. Materials include workbook and manipulative material; available separately.

Social Studies

Barlett, Elsa Jaffe, and Anne Gray Kaback. *Adventures in Living.* Bobbs-Merrill Company, Inc.
Helps kindergarten through third graders in perceptual, sensory, communication, and cognitive skills, in social studies context. Four units: "The Classroom," "The Country,"

"The Neighborhood," "The City." Children learn by viewing books, through gamelike tasks, and through discussions. Materials, available separately, include manual, stand-up mural, picture and storybooks, and activity cards.

Beginning Concepts/People Who Work. Scholastic Book Services.
Helps young people learn how important work is to the individual and to the community as a whole. Occupations visited are toymaker, architect, doctor, quiltmaker, fisherman, baker. Each of two units contains filmstrips, records or cassettes, hats, finger puppets, and manual. Each unit available separately.

*Career Kits for Kids. Encyclopedia Britannica Educational Corp.
Teaches preschool, kindergarten, and primary grade children, including mentally handicapped, emotionally disturbed, and learning disabled, about social and personal aspects of six careers: construction worker, fire fighter, taxi driver, nurse, letter carrier, and baker. Includes filmstrips, phonograph recordings, hats, posters, duplicating masters, and guides. Materials for each career available separately, or entire kit available as a unit.

Five Children and Five Families. Scholastic Book Services.
Helps preprimary and early primary children perceive similarities in family needs and differences in family life styles in the United States. Children view filmstrips and engage in gamelike activities and in discussion. Materials include manual, filmstrips, long-playing records or cassettes, and poster. Each two-semester unit sold separately.

Davis, D.E. *My Friends and Me.* American Guidance Service.
Helps teachers and parents encourage healthy personal and social development. Group activities sequenced in spiral order (i.e., themes addressed many times in gradually increasing complexity) around cluster themes of social, emotional, physical, intellectual and creative, cooperation, consideration for others, ownership and sharing, and dependence and help. Materials, available separately, include teacher's guide, activity manuals, carrying case, activity board, magnetic shapes, storybooks, song cards, activity pictures, dolls, cassettes or records, duplicating masters, print box, and activity board equipment.

People in Action. Holt, Rinehart and Winston.
Photographs stimulate verbal and action responses through use of role-playing and discussion. Level A contains 12 picture cards for preschool and primary grade children. Levels B through E each contain eight photo-problems for primary grade children. Teacher's guides provided. Each level sold separately.

Michaelis, John, and Ruth H. Grossman. *Schools, Families, Neighborhoods.* Field Educational Publications.
Helps kindergarten through third graders develop two kinds of sociocultural concepts: those leading to self-understanding (perception, identification, needs, attitudes); and those concerning interaction of people in groups (interdependence, change, roles, authority, responsibility). Children learn by asking and answering questions, viewing study prints and shortstrips (soundless six-frame filmstrips), viewing and listening to filmstrips and accompanying records, role playing and pantomiming, model building, taking field trips, and using a variety of inquiry processes (observing, recalling, comparing, classifying, analyzing, interpreting, inferring, generalizing, hypothesizing, predicting, evaluating, synthesizing). Materials include manual, study prints, filmstrips with accompanying records, wall charts, and shortstrips. Components sold as a unit; but two subkits make it possible to replace part of materials without replacing all.

*,†McLaughlin, R., and L. Wood. *Sing a Song of People*. Bowmar/Noble Publishers, Inc.
   Helps prekindergarten through third grades understand basic social studies concepts of
   home, neighborhood, community, and world; also develops concepts of self and
   positive value system. Children learn by manipulating felt board figures, singing, and
   viewing filmstrips. Sets, sold as unit, include manual, felt figures, songbook, long-
   playing records, filmstrips, and minibooks.

Hansen, H.S., R.M. Hansen, and F.L. Ryan. *Windows On Our World: Me*. Houghton
   Mifflin.
   Provides opportunity to practice manipulative and thinking skills, coordination, shape
   and sound discrimination, following directions, and oral expression. Units relate to
   children's experiences of "Me," "My Family," "My School," "My Tools." Materials are
   purchased as the media kit, activity sheets, and manual.

Science

Beginning Concepts/Science. Scholastic Books Service.
   Two-unit program exploring physical science concepts (energy, earth science, matter)
   and life science concepts (adaptation, ecology, life of plants and animals). Emphasizes
   questioning, observing, and experimenting. Each unit consists of filmstrips, records or
   cassettes, and manual.

Piltz, A., G. Blough, A. Costa, R. Roche, and R.A. Van Beever. *Discovering Science: A
   Readiness Book*. Charles E. Merrill Publishing Company.
   Helps children at readiness level develop fundamental thinking and investigative skills
   for use throughout life. The book (part of a series) combines process skills, concepts,
   and inquiry activities in science setting. Content includes principles of energy and
   matter, life, and earth and space science. Materials, sold separately, include pupil's
   book (also available in Spanish) and teacher's edition with behavioral objectives guide.

Our Animal Friends. Coronet Instructional Media. (Chicago, Ill.)
   Appropriate for preschool through primary grade children, including mentally handicapped, emotionally disturbed, and learning disabled. Materials include film loops
   and guides. Each film loop, with story of one animal, available separately.

Sullivan Associates. *Sullivan Adventures in Science*. Behavioral Research Laboratories.
   Real world of science complemented by fantasy world of child's imagination. In Level
   1, curious lamb tries to imitate physical and behavioral characteristics of other animals.
   In Level 2, trio of inquisitive characters experience evaporation, condensation, and
   other water phenomena while traveling through the water cycle. Children look at
   giant demonstration books, listen to cassette narratives, watch demonstrations, and
   participate in discussions and experiments. Materials include four manuals and
   four giant books with accompanying cassettes. Each kit, two for each of two levels,
   available separately.

Fisher, Aileen, *The Way of Animals*. Bowmar/Noble Publishers, Inc.
   Helps prekindergarten through third graders understand animal behavior, adaptation,
   life cycles, habitats. Children view filmstrips and look at books. Materials available
   separately, include manual, books, and filmstrips.

Art

Mandlin, D., and H. Mandlin. *Bowmar Art Worlds*. Bowmar/Noble Publishers, Inc.
   Encourages prekindergarten through third graders perceptual awareness, manipula-

tion of art materials, and creative desires; specifically, children develop visual and self-awareness and graphic expression by viewing filmstrips and art visuals, singing, and engaging in creative art and language activities. Materials, available separately, include manual, filmstrips, records, posters, and art visuals.

Dagley, C.S. *Idea: Developmental Experiences through Art*. Follett Publishing Company. For preschool through grade 2. Activities cover: "Basic Art Skills"; Colors, Shapes, and Sizes"; "The Senses"; "Letters and Numbers"; "Stories, Rhymes, and Words"; "Animals"; "People"; "Nature Study"; "Holiday and Special Days"; "Popular Projects." Activity cards and teacher's guide sold as a unit.

Self-concept

*Cohen, S. *Accepting Individual Differences*. Teaching Resources.
Based on premise that handicaps are extensions of individual characteristics found in all groups of people. Four teacher's guides treat visual impairments, hearing impairments, mental retardation, and learning disabilities. Each guide divided into instructor's section about the specific disability and suggestions for simulation, reading, and conferences; and student activities (discussions and game-like activities). Materials, available separately for each handicap, include guides, spiral-bound flip book with photographs and narratives. Audio cassette of deaf children learning to speak included for "The Hearing Impairments Unit" only.

Body and Self Awareness Big Box. Teaching Resources.
Helps develop positive self-concepts and learn to express feelings and reactions to people and things encountered in daily life. Activity cards and manipulative materials available separately.

Body Image, Levels I and II. Bowmar Publishing Corp.
For kindergarten and primary grades, including visually impaired. Children learn to name parts of the body and answer the question, "Who Am I?" with Body Image, Level I; about basic body movements with Body Image, Level II. Levels I and II sold as separate units; include filmstrips used in conjunction with rear view projection screen, audiotape cassettes, and manual.

Dinkmeyer, Don. *Developing Understanding of Self and Others*. American Guidance Service.
Two kits; kit D-1 helps kindergarten and lower primary children develop healthy self-concept. Unit themes are "Understanding and Accepting Self," "Understanding Feelings," "Understanding Others," "Understanding Independence," "Understanding Goals and Purposeful Behavior," "Understanding Mastery, Competence, and Resourcefulness," "Understanding Choices and Consequences." Children learn by listening, inquiry, discussion, role playing, puppetry, and activities in reading, art, and music. Materials, sold as a unit, include manual, storybooks, posters with easel, records or cassettes, puppets, puppet props, activity cards, and discussion cards. More advanced DUSO Kit D-2 available for upper primary and grade 4.

Nardine, E. *Discover: Self and Society*. Follett Publishing Company and Advanced Learning Concepts, Inc.
Encourages preschool through grade 2 children in developing self-awareness and exploring the world of relationships. Kit, sold as a unit except for the manual, consists of full-color photographic study prints, filmstrip, and manual.

Anderson, Judith, Carole Lang, and Virginia Scott. *Focus on Self-Development: Awareness.* Science Research Associates.

Helps kindergarten through second graders develop understanding of self and others and of environment and its effects on them; self-concept, sensorial awareness of environment; and socialization processes. Children engage in discussions, games, role playing, viewing filmstrips and photoboards, and answering open-ended sentences. Materials, available separately, include manual, filmstrips and records, story/activity records, photoboards, activity books, and counselor's guide. Stage Two: Responding, also available for grades 2–4.

·†Free to Be—You and Me. McGraw-Hill.

Affective development for preschool through grade 3, including mentally handicapped and emotionally disturbed. Multimedia kit centers on themes of independence, exceptions, friendship, and cooperation. Components include filmstrips, audiotape cassettes, picture books, poster, games, and guide; available separately.

How Are You Feeling Today? Bowman Publishing Corp.

Helps kindergarten and primary grade children, including visually impaired, identify basic emotions (happiness, sadness, anger, fear). Materials, sold as a unit, include filmstrips used in conjunction with a rear view projection screen, audiotape cassettes, and manual.

Kindle. Scholastic Book Services.

Helps preprimary through early primary children develop positive self-image. Five units: concept of self, concept of learning, concept of interrelationships, problem of relating, and nonverbal communication. Children participate in gamelike activities, discussions, and view filmstrips. Materials include manual, filmstrips, and long-playing records. Each available separately.

Schaefer, F., I. Chambers, S. Rafkin, J. Maybrook, L. Cormack, L. Wipff, M. Heilig, and S. Rubin. *Project Me.* Bowmar/Noble Publishers, Inc.

For preprimary through early primary; presents four units:

1. "Body Image" (Level 1) helps children discover and name parts of the body.
2. "Bods Image" (Level 2) focuses on more difficult to learn body parts—facial features and body joints.
3. "Let's Look For," a visual perception program, helps children find common objects and gives figure-ground training.
4. "How Are You Feeling Today?" is effective program emphasizing recognition of emotions from facial and body cues.

Children are involved in gamelike activities, singing, and viewing filmstrips. Materials, available separately, include manual, filmstrips with cassettes, and floor-based rear projection screen.

Outreach and Development Division of the Exceptional Child Center, Utah State University. Training For Independence. Developmental Learning Materials.

Fundamental self-care and functional training for daily living. Intended for trainable, low educable, preschool, and Head Start children. Each of seven skill-programs contains pre-check assessment to determine readiness, series of sequential lessons leading to development of independent skills, and follow-up activities. Practical techniques for modifying and establishing appropriate behavior explained in reference book, *When a Child Misbehaves.* Each skill-program, reference book, and pressure-sensitive reward badges, available separately.

Appendix 7

Parent's Handbook

Hubbard's Suburb

Kindergarten-Primary School

CONTENTS

Our School
Entrance Requirements
Registration, Supplies,
   and Clothing
Attendance, Session Times,
   and Early Dismissal
Lunch and Milk
A Child Stays Home
Everyday Experiences
Special Experiences
How Parents Can Help
Your Child's Progress
Parent's Check List
In Appreciation
Forms

NOTE: Because of space limitations, pages of the Parent's Handbook are indicated by rules and page numbers. In making your school's handbook, arrange materials attractively on each page, a short paragraph can be centered; drawings, and so forth, can be added.

1

Our School

Dear Mom and Dad,

It's going to be four months before I can start kindergarten. I went to see my school today, so I could find out about kindergarten. That way I'll be ready to go in September.

My school is in a big building with very few interior walls. I like that, because I can see just about everything. I've never seen so many toys, books, and records. And, they even have hamsters and lots of other animals—almost like a zoo!

My teacher's name is _____ I asked her lots of questions and found out all about kindergarten. My school is a kindergarten-primary school. The kids will be five, six, seven, and eight years old. My teacher said there will be plenty of things for all of us to do. At first, I'll have easy things to do. Then as I learn, I'll get harder things to do. My teacher said that most children go to school here four years, but a few go three years and a few stay five years. It's called a "continuous progress" approach. I don't understand what that means, but you will hear about it in the Spring Orientation meeting tomorrow.

2

Entrance Requirements

Age

Little kids can't go to kindergarten. I'm big now. I'm five! This was printed in our newspaper:

> A child may attend kindergarten if he or she is five years old on or before November first.

Birth Certificate

Our state requires that children have a legal birth certificate to enter school. I have to bring it when I register. You have mine, but the teacher said that Mary's parents will have to write to:

The Bureau of Vital Statistics

State Capitol Building

_____ ,   _____   _____
       (Capital City)   (State)   (Zip Code)

The charge is $ _____ .

Emergency Information Form

You always give me lots of good food, put me to bed early, and let me play outside. I'm very careful because skinned knees hurt. My teacher will take care of me while I'm at school and will need an "emergency information form," in case I get sick or hurt. It's in the back of this book. I'll get your pen and you can give my teacher the information.

Health History,

Physical Examination,

Immunizations,

and Dental Examination

My teacher says that I must be healthy and strong in kindergarten. You will have to call my doctor and dentist soon, because they're so busy. They have to write on all the other forms in the back of this handbook. Will I need to get a pen for the doctor and the dentist? I'll bring one, just in case.

3

Registration, Supplies, and Clothing

Registration

I am assigned to the school in the school attendance area in which I live. You found out where my class was by calling the Elementary School Director's Office. About two weeks before school starts, our town's newspaper will tell all about the school attendance areas and when to register.

The newspaper will also tell you about bus routes and the times the bus will pick me up and bring me back home, if I am to ride the bus.

Supplies

My teacher gave me a list of supplies. Here is a copy.

---

1 box of large washable crayons.

1 20 in. × 48 in. plastic mat stitched crosswise in several sections.

1 terry cloth apron with snap fasteners.

These supplies are sold in our three variety stores and our two discount stores.

Clothing

With so many children and with so much for each of us to do in kindergarten, the teacher says these are good qualities for school clothes:

1. Labeled for identification
2. Easy to handle (large buttons and buttonholes; underwear convenient for toileting; boots the child can put on and remove; loops on coats and sweaters for hanging)
3. Washable
4. Sturdy
5. Not too tight
6. Shoes with composition or rubber soles

4

Attendance, Session Times, and Early Dismissal

Attendance

Our school has attendance regulations. My teacher says it is important that I go to school every day, so I'll get to do all the fun things with my friends.

Session Times

Our kindergarten starts at _____ and closes at _____ . I should arrive at school no more than ten minutes before school starts. If you bring me to school in the car, we should drive in the circular driveway and I should enter the school at the side door. I should never leave our car at the curb by the street. You can pick me up at the same place right after school.

Early Dismissal

My teacher says that I'm not to leave early unless there is an emergency. These are the rules parents have to follow:

1. Only the principal can dismiss a student.
2. A student cannot be excused by a telephone call without verification of the telephone call.
3. A student can be dismissed only to a parent or a person properly identified.

5

Lunch and Milk

I want to eat lunch and drink milk with the other kids. Here's a note that tells all about it.

A hot lunch will be served in the cafeteria every day. It costs _____ ¢ a day or you may pay $_____ . _____ . a week. Checks may be made payable to _____ . If your child wishes to bring his lunch, milk will cost him _____ ¢ a day. Those who wish to inquire whether their children qualify for free or reduced-cost lunches may secure forms in the central office.

When sending money to school, place it in an envelope and write the child's name and the teacher's name on the envelope.

6

A Child Stays Home

When Ill

I'm supposed to stay home if I'm sick. Here is a list of reasons.

chills	fever—99.2° and over
communicable disease	headache, severe
coughing	joints, red or swollen
diarrhea	listlessness
earache	nausea or vomiting
eyes, inflamed or swollen	skin rash or sores
face, flushed or unusual pallor	sore throat

During Family Emergency

I may stay home if there is a death or serious illness in our family.

During Extremely Inclement Weather

Mom and Dad, you must decide if the weather is too bad for me to go to school. Sometimes there will be no school during bad weather. The following radio and TV stations carry school closing announcements: WKID, WKDG-TV, and WBUG-TV.

Bring a Note

I'm supposed to bring a note when I come back to school telling my teacher why I've been absent. If I've been to the doctor, he must sign my note before I return.

7

Everyday Experiences

When I visited the kindergarten at my school, I saw children doing many things in the building and outdoors. Some of the children were singing in the music room, two boys were feeding the hamsters, a girl was walking on a balance beam, and one big boy was reading a story to a little boy. My teacher said that in the kindergarten-primary school we do all those things and much more, like counting, painting, working with clay, reading books, learning about ourselves and people near and far, and visiting places in our town. We even eat together at lunch and get two snacks, one in the morning and one in the afternoon.

8

Special Experiences

Field Trips

When our class plans a field trip, the school asks our parents if we can go. The teacher will send a note to you each time we go on such a trip, and you will have to sign it. If I forget to get it signed, the teacher says I can't go *even if you call*. I'll have to be very careful not to lose the notes.

Parties and Treats

Birthdays are a lot of fun. When it is my birthday, I can share some treats with my class. My teacher will give you a list of all the rules about birthday treats. Even grown-ups have rules!

We will have five holiday parties. My teacher will send a note to you. Maybe you can sign-up to help with a party.

At our school we do not exchange gifts at Christmas (or on any holiday). We just say, "Merry Christmas!" We can give cards on Valentine's Day. My teacher will send you a list of names.

Bringing Things to School

Sometimes I can share one of my books, games, pictures, objects from nature, and souvenirs from trips. You can help me choose what to bring so that I don't bring fragile, valuable (i.e., expensive or family treasure), or sharp-edged objects.

9

How Parents Can Help

Guess what? My teacher at school says that all the kids' parents are teachers, too! There are lots of teachers. Here is a letter from my school teacher to my parent teacher.

Dear Parents,

As parents you have been responsible for the early teaching of your child. Although he/she is now old enough for school, you will still be the most important teachers in your child's life. Here are some ways you can help your child in school.

1. Attend individual and group conferences as often as you can.
2. Read and answer all notes from the school.
3. Give special help to your kindergartener by:

   promoting good health and safety habits
   praising your child for things done well
   talking about everyday experiences
   planning family activities
   reading stories
   watching children's television shows with your child
   providing materials for cutting, coloring, and building
   helping your child start a collection
   teaching your child to take care of toileting needs, to dress (outdoor clothing),
       and to put away toys.

10

Your Child's Progress

Our school doesn't send home report cards, but you can always find out how I'm doing in school. My teacher will get together with you several times this year, and you will talk about how I'm doing in just about everything.

You can talk with my teacher anytime, and you can see me in school after I've been there one month. My school will also have some special meetings for you. I've got a list of the meetings the teacher planned. There's a blank space by each one. You can write the time in when you get a note or telephone call from my teacher.

Get-acquainted conference (approximately
two weeks after the beginning of school) _____

Fall individual conference (November) _____

Spring individual conference (April) _____

11

Parent's Check List

Here's a "Parent's Check List" to make sure everything is done.

Have you read this handbook?   _____

Does your child have a legal birth certificate?   _____

Have you completed and signed the emergency information form?   _____

Have you completed and signed the health history form?   _____

Has your physician completed and signed the physical examination
    form?   _____

Has your physician completed and signed the immunization record form?_____

Has your dentist signed the dental report?   _____

Do you know the date of registration?   _____

Have you obtained the school supplies?   _____

Are all outdoor clothes labeled?   _____

Does your child have the right type of school clothes?   _____

Are you following the suggestions given in the section,
    "How Parents Can Help"?   _____

List any questions you would like to discuss with the staff.

_____

_____

_____

12

In Appreciation

Here is a note from my teacher.

Dear Parents,

The following lines from an anonymous source express my appreciation to you.

"Thank you for lending me your child today.

All the years of loving care and training which you have given him have stood him in good stead in his work and in his play.

I send him home to you today.

I hope a little stronger, a little taller, a little freer, a little nearer his goal.

Lend him to me again tomorrow I pray you

In my care of him I shall show my gratitude."

Sincerely yours,

_____

(Teacher's signature)

13

Forms

Remember those forms that are part of the entrance requirements? Here they are, and you will have to take them when I go to school the first day.

Emergency Information

Child's name _____

Home address _____Phone number _____

Father's name _____

Place of business _____Phone number _____

Mother's name _____

Place of business _____

Phone number _____

Give name of another person to be called in case of
    emergency, if parents cannot be reached:

Name _____Phone number _____

Address _____Relationship _____

Physician to be called in case of emergency:

1st choice: _____Phone number _____

2nd choice: _____Phone number _____

Name of hospital to be used in emergency:

1st choice: _____

2nd choice: _____

Other comments: _____

_____

_____

_____

Date _____ Signed _____
                              (Parent or guardian)

Health History

Child's name _____

General evaluation of family's health: _____

_____

Family deaths (causes): _____

_____

Child's illnesses. If your child has had any of these diseases, please state the age at which he had them.

_____ measles   _____ smallpox
_____ mumps   _____ diabetes
_____ whooping cough   _____ heart disease
_____ poliomyelitis   _____ Chorea (St. Vitus Dance)
_____ rheumatic fever   _____ epilepsy (convulsions)
_____ scarlet fever   _____ chicken pox
_____ diptheria   _____ pneumonia
_____ serious accident   _____ asthma, hay fever

Has your child ever had tests for tuberculosis? _____

Skin test? _____ Date _____ Chest X ray? _____ Date _____

Please check any of the following which you have noted recently.

_____ frequent sore throat   _____ shortness of breath
_____ persistent cough   _____ frequent nose bleed
_____ frequent headache   _____ allergy
_____ poor vision   _____ frequent urination
_____ dizziness   _____ fainting spells
_____ frequent styes   _____ abdominal pain
_____ dental defects   _____ loss of appetite
_____ speech difficulty   _____ hard of hearing
_____ tires easily   _____ four or more colds per year

Describe your child socially and emotionally _____

_____

_____

Are there any matters which you would like to discuss with the school staff? _____

Date _____ Signed: _____
                               (Parent or guardian)

15

Physical Examination

Child's name _____

Comment on any significant findings:

Eyes: Right _____ Left _____ Squint _____

Ears: Right _____ Left _____ Discharge _____

Nose _____ Throat _____

Glands _____ Tonsils _____

Heart and Circulation _____

Lungs _____

Abdomen _____

Bones and joints _____

Reflexes _____

Nutrition _____

Posture _____

Hernia _____ Neurological _____

Hemoglobin (if physician indicates) _____

Urinalysis (if physician indicates) _____

Does the school program need to be adjusted for this

child? _____

_____

_____

Date _____ Signed: _____ M.D.
                                                        D.O.

Immunization Record

Child's name _____

Diphtheria-Tetanus (since age 3)

_____ _____ _____

     (1st date)   (2nd date)   (Booster)

Poliomyelitis (since age 3)

_____ _____ _____ _____

   (1st date)   (2nd date)   (3rd date)   (Booster)

Measles (Rubeola): Disease or Immunization _____
                                                 (date)

T.B. Test
   Tine _____ Reaction: Pos. _____ Date: _____

   Mantoux _____ Neg. _____ Date: _____

   Chest X-Ray _____ Results: _____ Date: _____

Date _____ Signed: _____ M.D.
                                                                       D.O.

Dental Report

Child's name _____

Cavities _____ Gums _____

Malocclusion _____

Please explain any abnormal findings or deformities _____

_____

_____

Please indicate care given:

Prophylaxis _____ Cavities filled _____

Extractions _____ Orthondontics _____

What additional care do you plan for this child? _____

_____

_____

_____

Date _____ Signed: _____ D.D.S.

Appendix 8
Tests
Aptitude

ADMINISTRATION	CONTENT	MATERIALS	TEST DATA
THE ABC INVENTORY TO DETERMINE KINDERGARTEN AND SCHOOL READINESS Adair, N., and G. Blesch Educational Studies and Development			
Administrator: teacher Age range: 3.3 to 6.6 years Time required; 30 minutes Individual Verbal, paper-and-pencil, and manipulative	Covers general information (properties of objects such as color and size), eye-hand coordination (drawing), repeating digits, number concepts, and draw-a-man.	Administrator: manual test sheets class data sheet Each child: test sheet pencil pre-cut paper square	Raw score Readiness age equivalent
AMERICAN SCHOOL INTELLIGENCE TESTS Pratt, W.E., M.R. Trabue, R.B. Porter, and G.A.W. Stouffer, Jr. Bobbs-Merrill Co.			
Administrator: teacher Grade range Primary battery— kindergarten through third grade	Measures general mental ability. Selected factors: 1. comprehension 2. similarities 3. picture completion 4. form 5. arithmetic 6. discrimination 7. opposites	Administrator: test booklet manual Each child: test booklet pencil paper marker (for kindergarten children)	Raw score Percentile Stanine Mental age Ratio IQ

389

ADMINISTRATION	CONTENT	MATERIALS	TEST DATA
Time required: not timed Group and individual test Paper-and-pencil			
AMERICAN SCHOOL READING READINESS TEST Pratt, W.E., and G.A.W. Stouffer, Jr. Bobbs-Merrill Co.			
Administrator: teacher Grade range: beginning of first grade Time required: not timed, approximately 30 minutes Group and individual test Paper-and-pencil	Predicts readiness to read; includes 1. visual discrimination (discrimination between letters, letter combinations, word forms, and geometric forms) 2. vocabulary (ability to recognize simple objects) 3. memory-copying of simple geometric forms 4. ability to follow directions Auditory discrimination not included because of effects of variations in administration.	Administrator: test booklet manual Each child: test booklet pencil	Raw score Percentile rank Stanine Predicted reading grade
ANTON BRENNER DEVELOPMENTAL GESTALT TEST OF SCHOOL READINESS Brenner, A. Western Psychological Services			

Administrator:
  teacher

Age range:
  5 through 6 years

Time required:
  10 minutes or less

Individual

Verbal and
  paper-and-pencil

Qualitative and quantitative test of school readiness; measures perceptual and conceptual differentiation.

Administrator:
  manual
  BGT Protocol
    Booklet
  Number Recognition
    Forms
  15 to 20 ½-inch
    cubes of the same
    color

Each child:
  pencil
  black or blue crayon

Raw score
BGT total score
Readiness evaluation
  based on BGT total
  score

ARIZONA ARTICULATION PROFICIENCY SCALE (Revised)
Fudala, J.B.
Western Psychological Services

Administrator:
  speech clinician

Age range:
  3 through 11 years

Time required:
  10 minutes

Individual

Verbal

AAPS uses numerical scale to test articulatory proficiency (i.e., numerical values for sounds are related to probable frequency of occurrence in American speech). Scale may be used for screening and for determining progress. "Picture Test Cards" used with younger children; "The Sentence Test" with older children and adults.

Administrator:
  manual
  "Picture Test Cards"
  "The Sentence Test"
  "The Protocol
    Booklet"
  "The Survey Form"

Total consonant score
Total vowel score
Total Sound score
AAPS Total Score
  (percentage of
  individual's
  articulation which is
  correct)

Average AAPS Score
  for each age level
Interpretive Values of
  AAPS Total Scores

ADMINISTRATION	CONTENT	MATERIALS	TEST DATA
AUDITORY DISCRIMINATION TEST (revised edition) Wepman, Joseph M. Language Research Associates Administrator: teacher Age range: 5 to 8 years Time required: 5 minutes Individual test	Tests ability to recognize fine differences that exist between phonemes in English speech. Child indicates whether each pair of words is same or different. (Each word pair equated for length; therefore, child evaluated on audition only.)	Administrator: test manual test booklet pencil	Raw score Rating scale (5 point rating scale—+2 indicates "very good development" through −2 "below threshold of adequacy")
THE BAYLEY SCALES OF INFANT DEVELOPMENT Bayley, Nancy The Psychological Corp. Administrator: psychometrist Age range: 2 to 30 months Time required: not timed, approximately 45 minutes Individual test Manipulative	Divided into three parts: 1. Mental Scale designed to measure child's sensory responses, understandings of "object constancy," ability to learn and remember, vocalizations and verbal communication, and ability to generalize and classify. 2. Motor Scale is designed to assess child's general body control and large and small muscle skills. 3. Behavior Record contains ratings of child's social and object orientation, goal directedness, general emotional tone, and interest in sensory areas.	Administrator: kit of materials record forms for each of the three scales manual	Raw score "Mental Development Index" "Psychomotor Development Index" "Infant Behavior Record" (descriptive rating scales)

BENDER-GESTALT TEST FOR YOUNG CHILDREN
Koppitz, E.
Grune and Stratton

Administrator:
  psychometrist
Age range:
  5 to 10 years
Time required:
  Not timed; however, record is kept of time child uses in completing task. Average time is 5 minutes for a 5-year-old and 6 minutes for an older child.

Individual
Paper-and-pencil

Measures development level, intellectual functioning, brain damage, mental retardation, and emotional disturbances in young children.

Administrator:
  Bender cards (nine design cards)
  Scoring Manual for the Developmental Bender Scoring System
Each child:
  Paper
  Pencil with eraser

Raw score
Percentile
Age equivalent
Grade equivalent
Level of maturation in visual-motor perception

BOEHM TEST OF BASIC CONCEPTS
Boehm, A.E.
The Psychological Corp.

Administrator:
  teacher
Grade range:
  kindergarten through second grade (difficult for prekindergarten children)

Evaluates child's knowledge of terms selected from directions and other portions of curriculum materials in reading, arithmetic, and science.
Terms selected:
1. Those which occurred with considerable frequency;
2. Those which were seldom clearly defined, or defined in simpler forms than used in complex forms without adequate transitions; and

Administrator:
  manual
  demonstration copy of both test booklets
  class record form
Each child:
  booklets 1 and 2
  pencil or crayon

Raw score
Percentile
Class record sheet
Recommended instructional methods

ADMINISTRATION	CONTENT	MATERIALS	TEST DATA
Time required: not timed, approximately 30–40 minutes Group and individual test Paper-and-pencil	3. Those which were abstract.		Percentage passing for each item Class average

BRUININKS-OSERETSKY TEST OF MOTOR PROFICIENCY
Bruininks, R.H.
American Guidance Service

ADMINISTRATION	CONTENT	MATERIALS	TEST DATA
Administrator: teacher, occupational therapists, psychologists Age range: 4.6 through 14.6 years Time required: Complete battery; 40 to 60 minutes; Short form; 15 to 20 minutes Individual Motor activities	Measures gross and fine motor development. Subtests are: 1. Running speed and agility 2. Balance 3. Bilateral coordination 4. Strength 5. Upper-limb coordination 6. Response speed 7. Visual-motor control 8. Upper-limb speed and dexterity	Administrator: manual individual record form equipment for testing children	Complete battery Raw scores Standard scores (Gross Motor Composite; Fine Motor Composite; Battery Composite) Percentile ranks Stanines Age equivalents Short form Raw scores Standard scores Percentile ranks Stanines

California Short-Form Test of Mental Maturity
Sullivan, E.T., W.W. Clark, and E.W. Tiegs
CTB/McGraw-Hill

Administrator:
teacher

Grade range:
Level 0: preprimary (kindergarten through low first grade)
Level 1: primary grades

Time required: timed, 34 minutes

Group and individual test

Paper-and-pencil

Assesses language and nonlanguage aspects of mental ability. Total of seven test units grouped according to four factors:
1. Factor 1: Logical Reasoning
   test 1—opposites
   test 2—similarities
   test 3—analogies
2. Factor 2: Numerical Reasoning
   test 4—numerical values
   test 5—numerical problems
3. Factor 3: Verbal Concepts
   test 6—verbal comprehension
4. Factor 4: Memory
   test 7—delayed recall

Administrator:
test booklet
manual
stopwatch
Each child:
test booklet
pencil or crayon
paper marker

Raw and standard scores
Percentile rank
Stanine
Mental age
Deviation IQ
Profile
"Intellectual Status Index" (reflects pupil performance in relation to national norm population for grade placement)

The Cassel Developmental Record
Cassel, R.N.
Psychologists and Educators, Inc.

Administrator:
teacher

Age range:
birth to senility

Time required:
5 minutes

Individual

Paper-and-pencil check list

Psychological profile; graph is plotted beginning with chronological age and ending with "average total development." Recorded areas include physiological, emotional, psycho-sexual, intellectual, social, and educational development.

Administrator:
manual
profile sheet
felt-tip pin

Profile
Description of typical, under-development, and over-development patterns

ADMINISTRATION	CONTENT	MATERIALS	TEST DATA
CLYMER-BARRETT PREREADING BATTERY Clymer, T., and T.C. Barrett Personnel Press			
Administrator: teacher	Forms A & B consist of six tasks organized in three categories:	Administrator: battery booklet directions for administering test	Raw score Percentile rank Stanine
Grade range: after middle of kindergarten year or first weeks of first grade	1. Category 1: Visual Discrimination task 1—recognition of lower case and capital letters task 2—matching words	Each child: battery booklet pencil	Class record sheet Suggestions given for using test results
Time required: Long form, 90 minutes (3 sittings); Short form, 30 minutes (only Form A has both times)	2. Category 2: Auditory Discrimination task 3—discrimination of beginning sounds in words task 4—discrimination of ending sounds in words		
Group and individual test	3. Category 3: Visual-Motor Coordination task 5—geometric shape completion task 6—copy a sentence		
Paper-and-pencil			
COGNITIVE ABILITIES TEST Thorndike, R.L., E. Hagen, and I. Lorge Houghton Mifflin Co.			
Administrator: teacher	Provides information on development of generalized thinking skills. Primary I and Primary II use pictorial materials and oral instructions to measure:	Administrator: test booklet manual scoring key	Grade Percentile based on USS (form 3) Raw score (forms 1 and 3)
Grade range: Primary I: last half of kindergarten and	1. Oral vocabulary 2. Relational concepts		

first grade
Primary II: second and third grades

Time required:
54 minutes; short version, 48 minutes on form 1 only

Group and individual test

Paper-and-pencil

3. Multi-mental ("one that doesn't belong")
4. Quantitative concepts

A shortened version of Primary I is available.

Each child:
test booklet
record sheet
pencil

Percentile rank (forms 1 and 3)
Standard Age Score (form 3)
Stanine (form 1)
Stanine for SAS (form 3)
Deviation IQ (form 1)
Grade equivalent (form 1)
Intelligence quotient equivalent (form 1)
Universal Scale Score (form 3)

COGNITIVE SKILLS ASSESSMENT BATTERY
Boehm, A.E., and B.R. Slater
Teachers College Press

Administrator: teacher

Grade range: prekindergarten through kindergarten

Time required: 20 to 25 minutes

Individual

Verbal and paper-and-pencil

Provides profile of strengths and weaknesses of prekindergartener in cognitive skills area. May also be used as a class profile. Child's level of functioning measured in criterion-referenced items in areas of "orientation toward and familiarity with one's environment" (e.g., basic information and body parts) "large muscle and visual-motor coordination," "discrimination of similarities and differences," "auditory, visual, picture, and story memory," and "comprehension and concept formation."

Administrator:
card manual (picture material and instructions)
interpretive manual
pupil response sheet (checked by teachers)
8 blocks of same color, shape, and size
class record sheet

Percentages of children responding to each option by grade and socioeconomic status

Level of response (e.g., "elaborated statements," "partial descriptions," and "incorrect or irrelevant responses")

ADMINISTRATION	CONTENT	MATERIALS	TEST DATA
		Each child: pupil response sheet (handled by child for copying shapes) pencil	
COMPREHENSIVE IDENTIFICATION PROCESS (CIP) Zehrbach, R. Reid Scholastic Testing Service			
Administrator: teacher or trained paraprofessional Age range: 2.6 through 5.6 years Time required: approximately 40 minutes Individual Paper-and-pencil, verbal, and manipulative	Screening instrument for identifying preschool handicapped children. Areas screened include fine motor, gross motor, cognitive-verbal, speech and expressive language (articulation, voice fluency, and expressive language), social affective behavior, medical history, hearing, and vision.	Administrator: manual manipulatives "Parent Interview" "Child Record Folder" "Speech and Expressive Language Record" "Observation of Behavior Form"	Manual refers to three possibilities for each area screened: (1) Pass—Normal for age; (2) Refer—for a specific problem such as hearing, vision, speech; and (3) Evaluate—a complete diagnostic evaluation by professional interdisciplinary team
CONCEPT ASSESSMENT KIT—CONSERVATION Goldschmid, Marcel L., and P.M. Bentler Educational and Industrial Testing Service			

Administrator:
teacher

Grade range:
kindergarten
through third or
fourth grade

Time required:
Forms A and B, 15
minutes; Form C, 10
minutes

Individual

Verbal and
manipulative

Measures concept of conservation, the essential construct that moves child mentally from Piagetian preoperational stage to concrete operations. Items in Forms A and B measure conservation of two-dimensional space, number, substance, quantity, weight, and discontinuous quantity. Items in Form C measure conservation of area and length. The parallel forms (A and B) may be used for pretest and posttest in experimental studies.

Administrator:
manual
kit materials
(typical Piagetian
materials—balls,
glasses, eggs and
egg cups)
recording forms

Raw Score
Scored as correct or incorrect for "behavior" (i.e., child indicates objects, amounts, etc. are same) and "explanation" (i.e., child can verbalize principle)

DETROIT TEST OF LEARNING APTITUDE
Baker, H.J., and B. Leland
Bobbs-Merrill

Administrator:
psychometrist

Age range:
3 through 15 years

Time required:
approximately 45
minutes; some items
timed

Individual

Verbal and drawing

Subtests for 3- through 6-year-olds include: auditory attention span, oral commissions, social adjustment, visual attention span (words), pictorial absurdities, pictorial opposites, orientation, free association, memory design, motor speed and precision, and number ability.

Administrator:
manual
book of
"Pictorial
Material"
pupil's record book

Raw score
Mental age
Ratio IQ
Profile

Administration	Content	Materials	Test Data
Developmental Activities Screening Inventory DuBose, R.F., and M.B. Langley Teaching Resources			
Administrator: teacher Age range: 6 through 60 months Time required: untimed, approximately 30 to 60 minutes Individual Oral and manipulative	Items include manipulation of objects, copying forms, making bead patterns, counting, identifying colors, matching pictures by association, and matching numerals and words.	Administrator: manipulative items with exception of common items such as pull toy, rubber squeeze toys, etc. manual response form	Developmental level
Developmental Test of Visual-Motor Integration Barry, Keith, and Norman A. Buktenica Follett Publishing Co.			
Administrator: teacher Age range: approximately 2 through 15 years (designed for preschool and early primary grades)	Determines degree to which visual perception and motor behavior are integrated in young children. Short test form (with 15 geometric figures) is suitable for ages 2–8). Long test form (with 24 figures) intended for with children ages 2–15. Child copies the following geometric figures: 1. vertical line 2. horizontal line 3. circle 4. vertical-horizontal cross	Administrator: manual Each child: test booklet (short form or long form) pencil	Raw score Age equivalent Recommended instructional methods ("Monograph & Stimulus Cards" and "Assessment Worksheets")

400

Time required:
not timed,
approximately
15–20 minutes

Group and individual
test

Paper-and-pencil

5. right oblique line
6. square
7. left oblique line
8. oblique cross
9. triangle
10. open square and circle
11. three-line cross
12. directional arrows
13. two-dimensional rings
14. six-circle triangle
15. circle and tilted square
16. vertical diamond
17. tilted triangles
18. eight dot circle
19. Wertheimer's hexagons
20. horizontal diamond
21. three-dimensional rings
22. Necker's cube
23. tapered box
24. three-dimensional star

Developmental
comments given for
purposes of making
scorer aware of
certain
developments
and deviations

EDUCATIONAL ABILITY SERIES
(available only as an optional component of SRA Achievement Series)
Science Research Associates

Administrator:
teacher

Grade range:
Level A: K.5
through 1.5

Time required:
approximately 30
minutes

Measure of students' general learning ability. Level A
has four subtests:
1. picture vocabulary (identifying the picture named);
2. number (applying basic quantitative concepts);
3. picture grouping (finding the picture that does not
belong); and
4. spatial (visualizing relation of one shape to
another).

Administrator:
manual
user's guide
practice sheet
test booklet

Each child:
practice sheet
test booklet

Raw scores
Percentiles
Growth scale values
Quotient
Stanines

ADMINISTRATION	CONTENT	MATERIALS	TEST DATA
Group Paper-and-pencil		pencil with eraser place marker	
FIRST GRADE SCREENING TEST Pate, John E., and Warren W. Webb American Guidance Service, Inc.			
Administrator: teacher Grade range: end of kindergarten through first grade Time required: 45 minutes in kindergarten (2 sittings); 30 minutes in first grade (1 sitting) Group Paper-and-pencil	Predicts difficulty child may encounter in first grade. Scores may be used as basis for referral for special help or for initial grouping for instruction.	Administrator: manual test booklet Each child: test booklet (boy's or girl's) pencil with eraser	Raw score Percentile Cutting score Other suggested uses
FULL-RANGE PICTURE VOCABULARY TEST Ammons, **R.B.**, and H.S. Ammons Psychological Test Specialists			
Administrator: teacher Age range: 2.0 years through adult	Individual test of intelligence based on verbal comprehension; individual indicates which cartoon-like drawing best illustrates meaning of a given word.	Administrator: manual record sheets test plates	Raw score IQ Mental age Percentiles

Time required:
5 to 10 minutes

Individual

Verbal

Raw score

Percentile rank

GOLDMAN-FRISTOE TEST OF ARTICULATION
Goldman, Ronald, and Macalyne Fristoe
American Guidance Service, Inc.

Administrator:
speech clinician

Age range:
2 to 16+ years

Time required:
not timed,
approximately 10 to
15 minutes

Individual test

Verbal

Assesses articulation; includes three subtests:
1. "Sounds-in-Words" assesses child's articulation of major speech sounds in initial, medial, and final position.
2. "Sounds-in-Sentences" appraises child's articulation of connected speech.
3. "Stimulability" measures syllable, word, and sentence articulation.

Administrator:
test plates
manual
response forms
(filmstrip available as alternate testing method

GOLDMAN-FRISTOE-WOODCOCK TEST OF AUDITORY DISCRIMINATION
Goldman, R., M. Fristoe, and R.W. Woodcock
American Guidance Service, Inc.

Administrator:
individual with
minimum
preparation (see list
of materials)

Age range:
3.8 years to adult

Measures speech-sound discrimination ability. Auditory discrimination measured under ideal listening conditions and in presence of controlled background noise.

Administrator:
manual
training and test plates,
spiral-bound into an easel kit
magnetic tape recording

Raw score
Standard Score
Percentile
Total error scores on voiced sounds, unvoiced sounds, plosives,

Administration	Content	Materials	Test Data
Time required: training procedure, approximately 15 minutes; testing procedure, 7½ minutes Individual Verbal		response forms "Large Training Plates" (for administrator training use—optional)	continuants, and nasals can be obtained for clinical use only
GOODENOUGH-HARRIS DRAWING TEST Harris, D.B. Harcourt, Brace and World Administrator: teacher Age range: 3 through 15 years Time required: approximately 10 to 15 minutes Individual (preschool) and group (kindergarten and primary) Paper-and-pencil	Estimates child's general ability level. Correlation between individual intelligence tests and Goodenough-Harris score is substantial, especially for children between 5 and 10 years.	Administrator: manual, test booklet Each child: test booklet, pencil	Raw score Standard score
HISKEY-NEBRASKA TEST OF LEARNING APTITUDE Hiskey, M.S. University of Nebraska			

Administrator:
  psychometrist

Age range:
  3 through 16 years

Time required:
  45 to 50 minutes (2 sittings for young children)

Individual

Paper-and-pencil and manipulative

Evaluates abilities in:
1. Visual-motor coordination and integration
2. Sequential memory
3. Visual retention
4. Visual discrimination and matching
5. Visual association

May be used with hearing and deaf children.

Administrator:
  manual
  test record blank
  kit (cubes, beads, pictures, etc.)
  stop watch

Each child:
  pencil

Raw score
Deviation IQ
Median MA (deaf)
Learning age and Learning quotient (deaf)

HUMAN FIGURE DRAWINGS
Koppitz, E.M.
Grune and Stratton

Administrator:
  psychometrist

Age range:
  5 to 12 years

Time required:
  not timed: usually less than 10 minutes

Individual (preferable) or group

Paper-and-pencil

Child's drawing of "a whole person" scored quantitatively and qualitatively on both developmental and emotional indicator items.

Administrator:
  Koppitz's Psychological Evaluation of Human Figure Drawings

Each child:
  8½" × 11" blank sheet of paper
  #2 pencil with eraser

Raw score
Estimated intelligence quotient (verbal description)
Quartiles
Discussion of emotional indicators, school achievement, psychosomatic complaints, etc.

ADMINISTRATION	CONTENT	MATERIALS	TEST DATA
ILLINOIS TEST OF PSYCHOLINGUISTIC ABILITIES Kirk, S.A., J.J. McCarthy, and W.D. Kirk University of Illinois Press Administrator: psychometrist Age range: 2 to 10 years Time required: not timed, approximately 1 hour Individual test Verbal	Evaluates abilities in: 1. Channels of communication (auditory-vocal and visual-motor) 2. Psycholinguistic processes (receptive, organizing, and expressive) 3. Organization levels (automatic, representational) The twelve subtests are: auditory reception, visual reception, auditory association, visual association, verbal expression, manual expression, grammatic closure, visual closure, auditory sequential memory, visual sequential memory, auditory closure, and sound blending.	Administrator: kit of materials record forms picture strips	Raw score "Composite Psycholinguistic Age" "Psycholinguistic Quotient"
IPAT–CULTURE FAIR INTELLIGENCE TEST Institute for Personality and Ability Testing Administrator: teacher Age range: 4 to 8 years Time required: 40 to 60 minutes gross time; 22 minutes testing time Group and individual test (4 subtests each)	Attempts to eliminate "pseudo-intelligence" that is carried largely by language and scholastic skills and measured by some intelligence tests. Scale not wholly nonverbal. Four subtests administered individually, four to the group. I.Q. estimate can be obtained from the group administerable subtests alone.	Administrator: handbook scoring key "Classification Test Cards" test booklet Each child: test booklets pencils	Raw score Mental age Deviation IQ

Verbal, manipulative, and paper-and-pencil

Raw score
Stanine

KINDERGARTEN EVALUATION OF LEARNING POTENTIAL
Roebeck, M.C., and John A.R. Wilson
Webster Division McGraw-Hill Book Company

Administrator:
teacher

Grade range:
end of kindergarten

Time required:
20 to 30 minutes for each of 3 levels (3 sittings)

Group test

Paper-and-pencil, manipulative, and verbal

Summary test checks for conventional readiness skills (auditory discrimination, sequencing, and number relationships) and creative abilities.

Administrator:
manual
test booklet
"Calendar Paste-ons"
(candles, dates, days)
1 sheet for paste-ons
paste
1 box crayons

Each child:
test booklet
pencil with eraser

Raw score
Stanine

KOHS BLOCK DESIGN TEST
Kohs, S.C.
Stoelting Company

Administrator:
psychometrist

Age range:
3 to 19 years

Time required:
30 to 45 minutes

Uses design cubes to obtain intelligence quotient; eliminates language factor involved in most intelligence tests.

Administrator:
Blocks (16 cubes)
Design cards (17)
Score cards
(examiner records time and number of moves)

Raw score
Mental age equivalent

ADMINISTRATION	CONTENT	MATERIALS	TEST DATA
Individual			
Manipulative			
KUHLMANN-ANDERSON TEST (7th ed.)			
Personnel Press			
Administrator: teacher	Measures intelligence. Level K includes:	Administrator: test booklet	Raw score
Age range: Booklet K: 5 through 7 years	1. Missing parts of pictures 2. Story completion 3. Vocabulary	manual class record sheet keys for scoring technical manual	Percentile rank Stanine Deviation IQ
Time required: timed, approximately 75–90 minutes (several sittings)	4. Form completion 5. Visual discrimination 6. Number concepts 7. Auditory patterns 8. Memory drawing	Each child: test booklet pencil	Grade equivalent (for all levels except K)
Group and individual test			
Paper-and-pencil			
MATURITY LEVEL FOR SCHOOL ENTRANCE AND READING READINESS			
Banham, Katharine M.			
American Guidance Service, Inc.			
Administrator: teacher	Measures general readiness for school entrance and more specific area of reading readiness. "Maturity for	Administrator: manual	Raw score
Age and grade range: age 6, end of kindergarten or early first grade	School Entrance" measured in areas of bodily coordination, eye-hand coordination, speech and language comprehension, personal independence, and social cooperation. "Reading Readiness" measured in	individual record sheet	Cutting scores for "Maturity Level for School Entrance" and "Reading Readiness"

Time required:
5 minutes

Individual

Teacher check list

sections on eye-hand coordination and speech and language comprehension.

The McCarthy Scales of Children's Abilities
McCarthy, Dorothea
The Psychological Corp.

Administrator:
psychometrist

Age range:
2.6 through 8.6 years

Time required:
not timed, approximately 40–50 minutes for children under 5 years and approximately 1 hour for older children.

Individual test

Paper-and-pencil and verbal, drawing and manipulative

Measures total development; three subtests are:
1. "Verbal Scale" items, assessing pictorial memory, word knowledge, verbal memory, verbal fluency, and opposite analogies;
2. "Quantitative Scale" items, measuring numerical memory, counting and sorting, and number questions; and
3. "Perceptual-Performance Scale" items, evaluating ability to reason with concrete materials and conceptualize without words.

Administrator:
kit materials
manual
record forms
drawing booklets

Raw score
"General Cognitive Index," a combination of the three scales, indicates child's intellectual functioning

ADMINISTRATION	CONTENT	MATERIALS	TEST DATA

McCarthy Screening Test
McCarthy, D.
The Psychological Corp.
 	
Administrator: teacher
Age range: 4.0 to 6.6 years
Time required: 20 minutes
Individual
Paper-and-pencil, verbal, and manipulative
	Designed to identify children as "at risk" or "not at risk." Measures cognitive, sensorimotor functions necessary for successful school performance. Includes: verbal memory, right-left orientation, leg coordination, draw-a-design, numerical memory, and conceptual grouping.	Administrator:
		  manual
		  record forms
		  "Drawing Booklets"
		  kit materials ("Roger Cards," "Tape," "White Card," and "Conceptual Grouping Blocks in Box")
		
		With exception of the Tape, materials are not interchangeable with those of full McCarthy Scales.
			Raw Score
			"General Cognitive Index"

The Merrill-Palmer Scale of Mental Test
Stutsman, Ruth
Stoelting Co.
 	
Administrator: psychometrist
Age range: 18 to 65 months
	Tests mental ability in such areas as language and gross and fine motor skills. Designed as supplement to or substitute for Stanford-Binet. (Does not contain any items from the Binet, as does the California Preschool Mental Scale and the Minnesota Preschool Scale.)	Administrator:
		  manual
		  kit materials (nested cubes, form boards, scissors, pegboard, etc.)
		  record blanks
			Raw score
			Percentile rank
			Mental age
			Ratings of Personality Traits in Mental Test Situation

Time required:
total test
approximately 45
minutes; certain
items timed

Individual test

Verbal and
manipulative

METROPOLITAN READINESS TESTS
Nurss, J., and M.E. McGauvran
Harcourt Brace Jovanovich

Administrator:
teacher

Grade range:
Level I, beginning
through middle
kindergarten;
Level II, end of
kindergarten
through beginning
first grade

Time required:
Level I, 80 minutes
(7 sittings);
Level II, 90 minutes
(5 sittings);
Levels I and II,
"Practice
Booklet," 15
minutes; "Copying

Level I assesses prereading skill development in:

1. Auditory Memory—tests ability to remember and associate sounds with visual symbols
2. Rhyming—evaluates ability to discriminate among medial and final sounds in rhyming context
3. Letter recognition—evaluates ability to recognize upper- and lower-case letters
4. Visual Matching assesses visual-perceptual skills in matching words, numerals, etc.
5. School Language and Listening—measures basic concepts and grammatical structure
6. Quantitative Language—evaluates size, shape, number-quality relationships

Level II assesses skills needed in begining reading and math:

1. Beginning Consonants—assesses ability to discriminate among initial sounds of words
2. Sound-Letter Correspondence—evaluates ability to associate sound-symbol relationship in words

Administrator:
Practice Booklet
test booklet
manual (parts I and II)
Copying Sheet
Class Analysis Chart

Each child:
Practice booklet
test booklet
Copying Sheet
crayon or pencil without eraser

Other materials:
The Handbook of Skill Development Activities for Young Children

Raw score
Percentile rank
Stanine
"Performance Ratings," such as high, average, and low, based on stanines
Scaled scores

Administration	Content	Materials	Test Data
Test" (optional), 5 minutes Group and individual test Paper-and-pencil	3. Visual Matching assesses ability to match letters, numerals, and letter-like forms 4. Finding Patterns—measures ability to locate letter-groups, words, and numerals embedded in layer groupings of similar content 5. School Language—tests basic concepts and grammatical structure 6. Listening—evaluates ability to integrate and reorganize information, to draw inferences, and to analyze material 7. Quantitave Operations—measures ability to do rational counting and simple operations (adding, subtracting) (optional) Levels I and II "Copying"—measures fine visual-motor coordination needed in writing (optional)	Parent-Teacher Conference Report Early School Inventory	

MINNESOTA PRESCHOOL SCALE
Goodenough, F.L., and K.M. Maurer
American Guidance Service, Inc.

Administration	Content	Materials	Test Data
Administrator: teacher Age range: 1.6 through 6.0 years Time required: not timed, approximately 30 minutes	Measures verbal and nonberbal (perceptual-motor) ability. Required behaviors are pointing out parts of the body and objects in pictures, copying drawings, block building, telling stories about pictures, following directions, discrimination of geometric forms, completing picture puzzles, digit span, absurdities, paper folding, vocabulary, clock-time concepts, and opposites.	Administrator: printed materials (provided) set of materials to be collected (given in manual) individual record for each child	Raw score Percentile IQ equivalent C score or a measure increasing by grades about equal in difficulty from one unit to the next

Individual test
Verbal and manipulative

NORTHWESTERN SYSTEX SCREENING TEST
Lee, L.L.
Northwestern University Press, 1735 Benson Ave., Evanston, Ill. 60201

Adminstrator:
speech clinician

Age range:
3 to 8 years

Time required:
15 minutes

Individual
Verbal and picture
selection

Twenty sentence pairs identified receptively by
picture selection and 20 similar pairs produced in
response to stimulus pictures.

Administrator:
manual
stimulus pictures
answer forms

Raw score
Percentiles by age

PEABODY PICTURE VOCABULARY TEST
Dunn, Lloyd M.
American Guidance Service Inc.

Administrator
teacher

Age range:
3.3 years to
adulthood

Time required:
not timed,
approximately
10–15 minutes

Provides estimate of verbal intelligence by measuring
hearing vocabulary.

Administrator:
series of plates
manual
individual test
records

Raw score
Percentile
Mental age
Deviation IQ

ADMINISTRATION	CONTENT	MATERIALS	TEST DATA
PICTORIAL TEST OF INTELLIGENCE French, Joseph L. Houghton Mifflin Co.			
Individual test Verbal Administrator: pyschometrist Age range: 3 through 8 years Time required: not timed, approximately 45 minutes	Measures various facets of mental functioning; six subtests: 1. Picture vocabulary 2. Information and comprehension 3. Form discrimination 4. Similarities 5. Size and number 6. Immediate recall	Administrator: kit of test materials additional packages of record forms	Raw score Percentile rank Mental age Deviation IQ
PREP (PARENT READINESS EVALUATION OF PRESCHOOLERS) Ahr, A.E. Priority Innovations, Inc.			
Individual test Verbal Administrator: parent Age range: 3.9 to 5.8 years Time required: Each of two sessions takes 30 to 45 minutes	Samples skills and abilities such as comprehension, opposities, identification, verbal associations, verbal descriptions, listening, language, visual-motor association, motor-coordination, visual interpretation, memory, and concepts needed for academic achievement.	Administrator: test manual test booklet objects described in test manual for use in identification and verbal description	Range of average raw scores by chronological age for subtests and combined categories

Individual
Verbal and
  paper-and-pencil

Each child:
  test booklet
  pencil

PRESCHOOL ATTAINMENT RECORD
Doll, Edgar A.
American Guidance Service Inc.

Administrator
  experienced
  interviewer

Age range:
  6 months through 7
  years

Time required:
  not timed,
  approximately
  20–30 minutes

Observation of child
Paper-and-pencil
  interview with
  parent

Three parts:
1. Physical—appraises ambulation and manipulation;
2. Social—provides information regarding rapport, communication, and responsibility;
3. Intellectual—assesses information, ideation, and creativity.

Administrator:
  manual
  score sheets

Raw score
Profile
Attainment age
"Attainment quotient"

PRESCHOOL INVENTORY (revised)
Addison-Wesley Testing Service

Administrator:
  teacher

Age range:
  3.0 through 6.5
  years

Four subtests:
1. "Personal-Social Responsiveness" items measure child's knowledge of world and ability to get along with and respond to communications of adults;
2. "Associate Vocabulary" items evaluate child's ability to demonstrate awareness of connotation of a word;

Administrator:
  manual
  answer folders
  blank paper
  3 small cars (1 each red, yellow and blue)

Raw scores
Percentile rank

ADMINISTRATION	CONTENT	MATERIALS	TEST DATA
Time required: not timed Individual test Verbal	3. "Concept Activation-Numerical" items test child's ability to name quantities, make judgments of more and less, and recognize positions when objects are seriated; 4. "Concept Activation-Sensory" items measure child's awareness of sensory properties of objects and ability to execute visual-motor responses (Spanish and English editions available).	8 large crayons—red, orange, yellow, brown, green, blue, purple and black 10 red or black checkers (not mixed) 3 cardboard boxes	

PRESCHOOL LANGUAGE SCALE KIT, (rev. ed.)
Zimmerman, I.L., V. G. Steiner, & R. Evatt Pond
Charles E. Merrill Publishing Co.
Kit order number 8262–5; extra record forms 8261–7 (English), 8087–8 (Spanish)

ADMINISTRATION	CONTENT	MATERIALS	TEST DATA
Administrator: teacher Age range: 1½–7 years Time required: unspecified Individual Auditory, verbal: bilingual	A screening test for assessing a child's receptive and expressive language. One section evaluates whether the child can receive auditory information. Child shows response nonverbally. Another section measures vocabulary, verbalized memory span, concrete and abstract thinking ability, concept development, articulation, and understanding and use of syntax. Test allows comparison between auditory and verbal aspects of language development.	Administrator: Kit—1 manual ("How to Do It" expands on each test question), 1 picture book, 1 record form. More forms can be ordered. Needed materials: 12 1" blocks small piece coarse sandpaper set of coins stopwatch or clock	Test results: Recommended teaching methods Scores for each area and areas combined (point, current age, quotient, base age, ceiling age)

416

	Description	Materials	Scoring
PRIMARY MENTAL ABILITIES (K-1) Thurstone, T.G. Science Research Associates Adminsistrator: teacher Grade range: kindergarten through first grade Time required: approximately 1 hour Group and individual test Paper-and-pencil	Determines maturity in five areas: 1. Auditory Discrimination (distinguishing between pairs of words differing in beginning, middle, or ending sounds) 2. Verbal Meaning (understanding ideas expressed in words) 3. Perceptual Speed (recognizing likenesses and differences between pictures of objects or symbols) 4. Number Facility (working with numbers) 5. Spatial Relations (visualizing objects in space and seeing relationships among them)	Administrator: test booklets manual PMA Profile folder stopwatch Each child: test booklets pencil place marker PMA profile folder	Raw score Student profiles
THE PUPIL RATING SCALE Myklebust, H.R. Grune and Stratton, Inc. Administrator: teacher Grade range: primary grades Time required: 10 minutes if behaviors have been observed Individual Teacher check list	24-item scale to screen for potential learning deficits. Children are rated on a 5-point scale in "auditory comprehension," "spoken language," "orientation," (e.g., time, spatial concepts, left-right, and cardinal directions). "motor coordination," and "personal-social behavior."	Administrator: manual check sheet	Mean, standard deviation, and range given for each item t-scores Cutting score of "3" (i.e., children with ratings below "3" should receive further evaluation)

417

Administration	Content	Materials	Test Data
THE PURDUE PERCEPTUAL-MOTOR INVENTORY Roach, E.G., and N.C. Kephart Charles E. Merrill Publishing Co.			
Administrator: teacher Age range: 6 through 10 years Time required: approximately 1 hour Individual Motor	Detects errors in perceptual-motor development. Qualitative scale designates areas for remediation. Areas checked: balance and posture; body image and differentiation; perceptual-motor match; form perception. Not designed for children with specific defects.	Administrator: manual summary sheet check list few pieces of equipment: walking board, penlight, chalkboard, and chalk	Rating scale Summary sheet with space for comments
QUICK SCREENING SCALE OF MENTAL DEVELOPMENT Banham, K.M. Psychometric Affiliates			
Administrator: teacher Age range: 6 months through 10 years Time required: 10 minutes Individual Paper-and-pencil check list	Check list of readily observable behavior. Items grouped into categories: bodily coordination; manual performance; speech and language; listening attention and number; play interests. Items within each category sequenced according to behavior of "typical" children at specified mental levels.	Administrator: manual checklist booklet pencil and writing paper or chalk and chalk board.	Developmental quotient Mental age for each category of behavior

Quick Test

Ammons, R.B., and C.H. Ammons
Psychological Test Specialists

Administrator:
  teacher
Age range:
  2.0 years through adult
Time required:
  3 to 10 minutes
Individual
Verbal

Individual intelligence test based on perceptual-verbal performance. Individual indicates which line drawing best illustrates meaning of a given word.

Administrator:
  manual
  record sheets
  test plates
  instruction cardboard and item cardboard

Raw scroes
IQ
Mental age
Percentiles

Ready or Not?

Austin, John G., and J. Clayton Lafferty
Research Concepts. A Division of Test Makers, Inc.

Administrator:
  parent
Grade range:
  kindergarten through first grade
Time required:
  approximately one hour, unless parent has already observed the skills and concepts in the child
Individual test
Paper-and-pencil

Assists parents in determining child's readiness for kindergarten ("The School Readiness Checklist") and for first grade ("The First Grade Readiness Checklist"). Readiness checked in counting, drawing, motor skills, taking care of oneself, and general knowledge.

Administrator:
  "Handbook for the School Readiness Checklist and The First Grade Readiness Checklist"
  "The School Readiness Checklist"
  "The First Grade Readiness Checklist"
  paper for drawing shapes

Raw score
Based on raw score, an approximate state of readiness for kindergarten or first grade is given and some suggestions for possible action.

ADMINISTRATION	CONTENT	MATERIALS	TEST DATA
		additional booklets and articles on readiness Each child: pencil paper for drawing shapes	

THE RILEY ARTICULATION AND LANGUAGE TEST (Revised)
Riley, G.O.
Western Psychological Services

ADMINISTRATION	CONTENT	MATERIALS	TEST DATA
Administrator: psychometrist Age range: 4 through 7 years Time required: 3 minutes Individual Verbal	Estimates language proficiency and intelligibility; provides objective articulation loss score, standardized language loss score, and language function score.	Administrator: manual "Protocol Booklet"	Articulation loss score (index of speech loss and speech function) Language loss score Language function score Cutting scores

RILEY PRESCHOOL DEVELOPMENTAL SCREENING INVENTORY
Riley, C.M.D.
Western Psychological Services

ADMINISTRATION	CONTENT	MATERIALS	TEST DATA
Administrator: psychometrist, counselor, or teacher with training	Indicates child's present developmental age and self-concept and provides information necessary for psychological referral. Items include drawing designs and draw-a-person.	Administrator: manual inventory booklet	Developmental age Recommendations for referral

Age range:
18 months through
7 years

Time required:
20 minutes

Individual

Paper-and-pencil

Each child:
inventory booklet
black crayon

RING AND PEG TESTS OF BEHAVIOR DEVELOPMENT (revised edition)
Banham, Katherine M.
Psychomotor Affiliates

Administrator:
teacher

Age range:
1 to 72 months

Time required:
not timed,
approximately 30
minutes

Individual

Paper-and-pencil,
verbal, and
manipulative

Assesses development in psychomotor, cognitive, and affective domains. Test items involve:
1. Ambulative (posture, balance, and locomotion)
2. Manipulative (form perception, eye-hand coordination)
3. Communicative (sound and time perception, speech, and language)
4. Social adaptive (sociability, independence, and cooperation)
5. Emotive (emotion, interest, drive, and motivation)

Administrator:
manual
"Point and Age
   Scale Scoring
   Sheet"
pencil
paper
black and white
   shoelaces
kit (8 rings, 3 pegs,
   and a base)

Raw score
Developmental
   Quotient
"Behavior-Age
   Equivalent"—
indicates rate of
   development:
   accelerated,
   retarded, or normal,
   in each category of
   behavior
"Whole Scale
   Behavior
   Age"—estimate of
   general
   developmental level

ADMINISTRATION	CONTENT	MATERIALS	TEST DATA
SCHOOL READINESS TEST Anderhalter, O.F. Scholastic Testing Service, Inc.			
Administrator: teacher Grade range: kindergarten or during second week of first grade (no "repeaters") Time required: approximately 1 hour (2 sittings); items timed Group test Paper-and-pencil	Measures readiness in word recognition, identifying letters, visual discrimination, auditory discrimination, comprehension and interpretation, handwriting readiness, and number readiness.	Administrator: manual test booklet Each child: test booklet pencil crayon	Raw score Percentile rank Class record sheet Verbal rating based on total score
SHORT FORM TEST OF ACADEMIC APTITUDE Derived from the CALIFORNIA TEST OF MENTAL MATURITY CTB/McGraw-Hill			
Administrator: teacher Grade range: Level 1: grades 1.5–2 Time required: timed,	Evaluates level of intellectual development and predicts potential rate of school progress and success. Two sections: 1. Language (vocabulary and memory) 2. Nonlanguage (analogies and sequences) At Level 1, all test items are either pictures, designs, letters, or numerals; thus, no reading required.	Administrator: manual test booklet stopwatch Each child: test booklet pencil with eraser	Raw and standard scores Percentile rank Stanine Mental age Deviation IQ

approximately 30 minutes

Group and individual test

Paper-and-pencil

paper marker

"Reference Scale Score," and expanded standard score

SHORT TEST OF EDUCATIONAL ABILITY
Science Research Associates

Administrator: teacher

Grade range:
Level 1: kindergarten through first grade

Time required: not timed, approximately 30 minutes

Group and individual test

Paper-and-pencil

Consists of three subtests:
1. "What would happen if . . ."
2. "How would you . . ."
3. "Spatial Relations"
Subtests 1 and 2 measure basic forms of logic and ability to understand cause and effect in dealing with actions and objects. Subtest 3 assesses ability to visualize relations of one shape to another.

Administrator:
test booklet
manual
interpretive manual

Each child:
test booklet
pencil, no. 2 with eraser
paper marker

Raw score
Percentile
Stanine
Grade-based Quotient

SLOSSON DRAWING COORDINATION TEST (SDCT) FOR CHILDREN AND ADULTS
Slosson, Richard T.
Slosson Educational Publications, Inc.

Administrator: psychometrist

Age range: 1 year to adult

Identifies individuals with various forms of brain dysfunctions or perceptual disorders involving eye-hand coordination. Author points out that any findings for children younger than six years are "tentative."

Administrator:
manual
test sheet

Each child:
test sheet
pencil

Raw score
"Accuracy score" (any child scoring below 85% should be referred for further evaluation)

ADMINISTRATION	CONTENT	MATERIALS	TEST DATA
Time required: not timed, approximately 10 to 15 minutes Group test Paper-and-pencil			Indepth recommendations about interpretation of test

SLOSSON INTELLIGENCE TEST (SIT) FOR CHILDREN AND ADULTS
Slosson, Richard L.
Slosson Educational Publications, Inc.

ADMINISTRATION	CONTENT	MATERIALS	TEST DATA
Administrator: teacher Age range: 1 month through adult Time required: 10 to 30 minutes Individual Paper-and-pencil, verbal, and manipulative	Quick screening of intellectual ability.	Administrator: manual score sheet pencil paper book 6 small blocks or spools, rubber balls, rattle, spoon, and cup (for testing infants) Each child: paper pencil	Raw score Mental age Ratio IQ

SOUTHERN CALIFORNIA SENSORY INTEGRATION TESTS
Ayres, A.J.
Western Psychological Services

Administrator: psychometrist

Age range: 4 through 10 years for some tests (More normative data available for 6 through 9 years)

Time required: 90 minutes (2 sittings)

Individual (for some subsections) and group (for other subsections)

Paper/pencil, manipulative, and verbal (only 2 items on left-right discrimination)

The Southern California Sensory Integration Tests (SCSIT) include the former Ayres Space Test, Southern California Motor Accuracy Test, Southern California Figure-Ground Visual Perception Test, Southern California Kinesthesia and Tactile Perception Tests, and the Southern California Perceptual-Motor Tests. Two new tests are: Position in Space and Design Copying. SCSIT identifies four types of sensory integrative disorders or dysfunctions in the neural system that subserves the following categories: form and space perceptions, praxis, postural integration, and bilateral integration.

Administrator:
manual
protocol sheet
test plates
form boards
stimulus cards
blocks
pegs
centimeter ruler
kinesthesia chart
geometric forms
printed cardboard with 12 forms
pencils with erasers
stopwatch
Each child:
test sheet
pencil

Raw score
t values
Age equivalent

STANFORD-BINET INTELLIGENCE SCALE
Terman, L.M., and M.A. Merrill
Houghton Mifflin Co.

Administrator: certified examiner

Age range: 2 years through adult

Time required: not timed, approximately

Measures general mental ability. Items included for ages 2 to 5 are identification of parts of the body, picture vocabulary, delayed response, identifying objects by name and by use, repeating digits, obeying commands, block building, paper folding, and geometric figures, comprehension of sentences, sorting objects, size comparisons, analogies, memory

Administrator:
kit materials (includes manual and printed card material)
record booklets, forms, and objects

Raw scores
Mental age
Deviation IQ

ADMINISTRATION	CONTENT	MATERIALS	TEST DATA
30–40 minutes for young children Individual test Verbal	for sentences, pictorial similarities and differences, discrimination of forms, and stringing beads.		

STAR (SCREENING TEST FOR ACADEMIC READINESS)
Ahr, A.E.
Priority Innovations, Inc.

ADMINISTRATION	CONTENT	MATERIALS	TEST DATA
Administrator: teacher Age range: 4 to 6.5 Time required: 1 hour, including breaks; each item timed Group Paper-and-pencil	Screening test with subtests in picture vocabulary, letters, picture completion, copying, picture description, human figure drawing, relationships, and number.	Administrator: manual test booklet "STAR Record Form" "Class Record List" stopwatch Each child: test booklet pencil	Raw score Deviation intelligence quotient "Potential Academic Ability,"—prorated raw score "Experimental Deficit Index" (indication of extent to which environmental circumstances have depressed child's level of functioning)

START (SCREENING TEST FOR THE ASSIGNMENT OF REMEDIAL TREATMENTS)
Ahr, A.E.
Priority Innovations, Inc.

ADMINISTRATION	CONTENT	MATERIALS	TEST DATA
Administrator: teacher	Assesses development of visual-memory, auditory memory, visual-motor coordination and visual discrimination.	Administrator: manual test booklet	Raw score (subtests and total)

Age range:
4.6 to 6.5 years

Time required:
1 hour, including breaks; each item timed

Group

Paper-and-pencil

scoring form
"Class Record List"
"Visual Memory Flash Cards"

Each child:
test booklet
pencil

Stanine (subtests and total)

THE STEINBACH TEST OF READING READINESS
Steinbach, M. Nila
Scholastic Testing Service

Administrator:
teacher

Grade range:
end of kindergarten or during second week of first grade

Time required:
approximately 40 minutes (2 sittings)

Group test

Paper-and-pencil

Administrator:
manual
test booklet
mounted words
stopwatch

Each child:
test booklet
2 pencils or crayons
2 markers

Indicates areas of strength and weakness (visual acuity, memory of word or letter forms, ability to relate sounds and pictures) and predicts end-of-first-grade reading level.

Raw score
Stanine
Class median
Class record sheet
Suggestions for grouping children

SYSTEM OF MULTICULTURAL PLURALISTIC ASSESSMENT (SOMPA)
Mercer, J.R., and J.F. Lewis
The Psychological Corp.

Administrator:
trained professional:
"Parent Interview"

Administrator:
manual
"Parent Interview

Useful with children of multicultures. Assesses level at which children function in cognitive, perceptual-motor, and adaptive behavior. "Parent

Raw score
Percentile

ADMINISTRATION	CONTENT	MATERIALS	TEST DATA
psychometrist: WISC-R and Bender Visual Motor Gestalt health specialist: Physical Dexterity Tasks, Visual Acuity, and Weight by Height Age range: 5 through 11 years Time required: parent interview: 1 hour; aptitude tests: 1 hour; health tests: 1 hour Individual Paper-and-pencil rating scale, verbal, manipulative	Interview" takes place in the home, and is conducted in Spanish or English. Three measures administered: 1. Adaptive Behavior Inventory for Children—measures interpersonal relations with family, peers, and other adults and ability to care for own physical needs 2. Sociocultural Scales—measures social, cultural, and economic characteristics of child's family 3. Health History Inventory—deals with child's past and present health conditions Student Assessment involves: 1. Wechsler Intellectual Scale for children—Revised and Bender Visual Motor Gestalt Test. (See descriptions in this appendix) 2. Physical Dexterity Tasks—measures fine and gross motor coordination and balance 3. Visual Acuity—the Snellen Test 4. Auditory Acuity—conducted by an audiometrist 5. Weight by Height—indicates health and overall well-being	Record Form" "Student Assessment Record Form"	Scaled scores Typical visual and auditory screening scores (See types of data obtained on WISC-R and Bender Visual Motor Gestalt Test in Appendix 4) "Estimated Learning Potential" (ELP): verbal, performance, and full scale
TESTS OF BASIC EXPERIENCES Moss, Margaret H. CTB/McGraw-Hill Administrator: teacher Grade range Level K: preschool and kindergarten	Four curriculum-oriented tests: 1. Mathematics Test—measures fundamental mathematical concepts, terms used, and ability to see relationships between objects. 2. Language Tests—assesses vocabulary, sentence	Administrator: test booklet for level used manual for level used	Raw and standard scores Percentile rank Stanine

Level L: kindergarten and first grade

Time required: not timed, approximately 1 hour for long form (4 sittings) and approximately 25 minutes for short form

Group and individual test

Paper-and-pencil

structure, verb tense, sound-symbol relationships, letter recognition, listening skills, and the concept that symbols carry meaning

3. Science Test—measures scientific observations

4. Social Studies Test—has items concerning social groups, social roles, social customs, safety, and human emotions.

General Concepts Test, short form of *Tests of Basic Experiences*, is composed of selected items from the four curriculum-oriented tests.

instructions
class evaluation record

Each child:
booklet for each test in level used
pencil

Class record sheet
Class difficulty level for each item
Class average
Reference-group difficulty level for each item

TORRANCE TESTS OF CREATIVE THINKING
Torrance, E. Paul
Personnel Press

Administrator: teacher

Grade range: kindergarten through graduate school

Time required: Verbal test: 45 minutes; Figural test: 30 minutes

Individual test

Verbal and paper-and-pencil

Consists of a verbal and figural test. Measures following aspects of creative thinking:

1. Fluency—measures aptitude to originate ideas about and solutions to problems

2. Flexibility—measures adaptability to changing directions, emancipation from normal constraints in thinking, and capability of using several means of access to solutions

3. Originality—measures talent for providing uncommon answers and ingenious or clever calculations

4. Elaboration—measures knack of executing and embellishing an idea

Administrator:
test booklets
scoring worksheets
manual
examiner's kit
booklet of norms and technical information

Raw score
Scores for "fluency," "flexibility," "originality," and "elaboration" are obtained
Norms are available for these scores

429

ADMINISTRATION	CONTENT	MATERIALS	TEST DATA
UTAH TEST OF LANGUAGE DEVELOPMENT (revised) Mecham, M.J., and J.D. Jones Communication Research Associates, Inc. (P.O. Box 11012, Salt Lake City, Utah 84147)			
Administrator: speech pathologist Age range: 1.6 to 15.0 years Time required: 20 to 30 minutes Individual Verbal	Measures milestones of communication development in receptive and expressive language. Emphasis on semantics and audiolinguistic processing ability.	Administrator: manual scoring forms object kit picture plates	Raw scores Percentiles Age equivalent Stanines Standard deviations and means for each age level
VERBAL LANGUAGE DEVELOPMENT SCALE Mecham, Merlin J. American Guidance Service, Inc.			
Administrator: teacher Age range: birth through 15 years Time required: not timed Individual test Interview	Items from various standardized sources felt primarily to measure language facility. Assesses: 1. Verbal facility 2. Listening Comprehension 3. Reading ability 4. Writing (legibility and style) 5. Use of language in communication	Administrator: manual score sheets	Raw score "Language Age Equivalent"
VOCABULARY COMPREHENSION SCALE Bangs, Tina E. Teaching Resources			

430

Administrator teacher or speech clinician Age range: 2 through 6 years Time required: 20 minutes Individual Manipulative	Comprehension of pronouns and words of position, size, quality, and quantity.	Administrator: manipulative items manual scoring form	Age equivalent

WATSON NUMBER-READINESS TEST
Watson, G.M.
The Book Society of Canada, Limited

Administrator: teacher Grade range: kindergarten through first grade Time required: 45 minutes Group Paper-and-pencil	Divided into subjective and objective parts. Subjective test measures social, emotional, and psychological readiness in relationship to number work. Objective test measures concepts of position in space, relationship and concepts of size, knowledge of money, advanced numerical items (e.g., forming sets), and interpretation of symbols. Manual includes advanced power test to be used a year later to verify prognostication of readiness test.	Administrator: manual test booklet Each child: test booklet pencil	Raw score Percentage Suggested cutting score

WATSON READING-READINESS TEST
Watson, G.M.
The Book Society of Canada, Limited

Administrator: teacher	Two parts: (1) Subjective Test—child's physical, social, emotional, and psychological readiness quantitatively scored by teacher	Administrator: manual test booklet	Raw score Suggested cutting scores for placing

ADMINISTRATION	CONTENT	MATERIALS	TEST DATA
Grade range: end of kindergarten or during first two weeks of first grade	(2) Objective Test—measures child's visual discrimination and eye-hand coordination	Each child: test booklet pencil or crayon marker	child in reading situation or reading-readiness group
Time required: 60 to 90 minutes (4 sittings)			
Group			
Paper-and-pencil			
WECHSLER PRESCHOOL AND PRIMARY SCALE OF INTELLIGENCE Wechsler, David The Psychological Corp.			
Administrator: psychometrist	Two subtests: 1. Verbal tests include "information," "vocabulary," "similarities," "comprehension" and "arithmetic." "Sentences" is an alternate test. 2. Performance tests include "animal house," "picture completion," "mazes," "geometric design" and "block design."	Administrator: kit of materials manual record forms maze test geometric design sheets	Raw score Verbal, performance and full-scale IQs
Age range: 4.0 through 6.6 years			
Time required: not timed, time ranges between 45 and 75 minutes (2 or more sittings)			
Individual test			
Verbal and manipulative			

WEISS COMPREHENSIVE ARTICULATION TEST (WCAT)
Weiss, C.E.
Teaching Resources

Administrator:
speech clinician
Age range:
3 through adult
Time required:
approximately 20
minutes
Individual
Verbal

1. Determines whether articulation disorder or delay is present
2. Identifies kind of misarticulation patterns that exist
3. Identifies other problems or features present in child's articulation

Administrator:
comprehensive flip book with 85 pictures
pictures or sentences
response forms

Articulation score
Articulation age
Intelligibility score
Stimulability score
Number of errors

WOODCOCK-JOHNSON PSYCHO-EDUCATIONAL BATTERY
Woodcock, R.W., and M.B. Johnson
Teaching Resources

Administrator:
teacher
Age range: 3.0 years through adult
Time required:
2 hours
Individual

Three parts:
1. Cognitive Ability—picture vocabulary, spatial relationships, memory for sentences, blending
2. Tests for Achievement—letter-word identification, word attack, passage comprehension, calculation
3. Tests of Interest Level—reading interests, math interests, language interests, physical interests, social interests

Administrator:
2 flip-page books
response booklets
cassette tape
technical manual

Basal ceiling rules are applied
Scores are plotted as confidence bands or bands of expected performance
Special methods of interpreting scores include "Relative Performance Indexes" and "Suggested Instructional Ranges"

433

ADMINISTRATION	CONTENT	MATERIALS	TEST DATA

YELLOW BRICK ROAD
Kallstrom, C.
Teaching Resources
 	
Administrator:
  teacher
Age range:
  5 through 6 years
Time required:
  45 minutes for
    individual test
  2 hours for group
    test in several
    sittings
Individual and group
Verbal, manipulative,
  and
  paper-and-pencil
	Items include imitation of body positions, identification of body parts, visual tracking and visual discrimination exercises, sequencing, categorizing, associating, and articulating within the four batteries of motor, visual, auditory, and language.	Administrator:
		  manipulative
		  materials with the
		  exception of
		  common items
		  such as masking
		  tape, yardstick,
		  paper and pencil
		  manual
		  test forms
			Four battery scores with indication of adequate/inadequate functioning levels

Achievement

ADMINISTRATION	CONTENT	MATERIALS	TEST DATA

AMERICAN SCHOOL ACHIEVEMENT TESTS
Pratt, W.W., R.V. Young, and M.E. Wilt
Bobbs-Merrill Co.
 	
Administrator:
  teacher
	Measures achievement in reading and mathematics. Items divided into three categories:
	1. Word recognition items assess ability to recognize words common to reading vocabularies at this level.
		Administrator:
		  manual
		  test booklet
		  stopwatch
			Raw score
			Grade and age
			  equivalents

Grade range:
primary Battery I;
first grade

Time required:
approximately 35
minutes (2 sittings)

Group and individual
test

Paper-and-pencil

2. Word Meaning items measure recognition and
comprehension of words common to reading
vocabularies at this level.
3. Number items evaluate child's concepts of size
relationships, cardinal and ordinal numbers,
numerals, fraction parts, and time concepts.

Each child:
test booklet
pencil

ASSESSMENT PROGRAM OF EARLY LEARNING LEVELS
Cochran, Eleanor V., and James L. Shannon
Ecodyne Corp.

Administrator:
teacher

Grade range:
preschool,
kindergarten, first
grade

Time required:
approximately 1
hour (2 or 4 sittings)

Group and individual
test

Paper-and-pencil

Covers specific skills (performance objectives)
necessary for entrance into primary reading and
mathematics programs. Assesses three areas:
1. Pre-Reading (visual discrimination, auditory
association, letter names)
2. Pre-Math (discrimination of attributes, number
concepts, and number facts)
3. Language (nouns, pronouns, verbs, adjectives,
plurals, and prepositions)

Administrator:
teacher's edition of
manual

Each child:
nonconsumable
plastic student
test booklets
"Student Response"
cards

Raw score
Profile
Class record sheet

435

ADMINISTRATION	CONTENT	MATERIALS	TEST DATA
BILINGUAL SYNTAX MEASURE Burt, M.K., H.C. Dulay, and E.H. Ch. Harcourt Brace Jovanovich, Inc.			
Administrator: teacher Grade range: kindergarten through second grade Time required: 10 to 15 minutes Individual Verbal	Identifies child's control over basic oral syntactic structures in both English and Spanish. Cartoon-type pictures and simple questions elicit responses. BSM may be used for placement decisions as well as summative and formative evaluation.	Administrator: manual picture books response booklets class record technical handbook	Level of language proficiency
BOBBS-MERRILL ARITHMETIC ACHIEVEMENT TEST Kline, W.F., and H.J. Baker Bobbs-Merrill Co.			
Administrator: teacher Grade range: Level 1: grade 1; Level 2: grade 2; Level 3: grade 3 Time required: 40 minutes (2 sittings)	Measures achievement in arithmetic; divided into two parts: Part I measures knowledge of concepts and ability to solve statement problems applying those concepts. Part II evaluates computation, free of any verbal factor.	Administrator: manual test booklet stopwatch scoring plate Each child: test booklet 2 sheets of scratch paper 2 pencils with erasers	Raw score Percentile Stanine Grade equivalent

Group and individual test

Paper-and-pencil

THE CALIFORNIA ACHIEVEMENT TESTS, LEVEL 10
CTB/McGraw-Hill

Administrator:
teacher

Grade range:
Level 10: K.0
through 1.3

Time required:
Practice Test, 15
minutes; Battery,
approximately 3
hours (7 sittings)

Group

Paper-and-pencil

Norm-referenced and criterion-referenced. Level 10 has 7 tests: listening for information, letter forms, letter names, letter sounds, visual discrimination, sound matching, mathematics. Levels 10, 11, and 12 for use with primary grade students. (Only Level 10 is described here, because Levels 11 and 12 are somewhat the same except for more advanced reading and mathematics questions, and are used after child has spent several months in formal reading and mathematics programs.)

Administrator:
manual
practice test
test book
"Group Information Sheet"
stopwatch

Each child:
practice test (optional)
test book
pencils with erasers
scratch paper
place marker

Additional material:
"Test Coordinator's Handbook"
"Class Management Guide"
"Norms Tables"
"Technical Bulletin"

Raw scores
Percentile ranks
Stanines
Scale scores
Grade equivalent
Normal curve equivalents

ADMINISTRATION	CONTENT	MATERIALS	TEST DATA
CIRCUS Educational Testing Service Addison-Wesley Publishing Company			
Administrator: teacher Grade range: preschool through 3.5 Time required: not timed, approximately 30 minutes Group test Verbal, manipulative, and paper-and-pencil	Circus A used with children entering kindergarten; B used with children during last months of kindergarten and beginning first grade. A and B cover: 1. Language (comprehension, productive language, auditory discrimination) 2. Math (quantitative concepts) 3. Perception (visual discrimination, perceptual-motor coordination, recognition of letters and numerals) 4. Information processing and experience (general information, visual and associative memory, classifying) 5. Divergent production (divergent picture production) 6. Attitudes and interests (behavior inventory and attitudes inventory). C and D used with primary grade children; cover reading, mathematics, listening, and writing skills.	Administrator: "Technical Report" teacher's edition of test booklet cassette tape "Activities Inventory" "Behavior Inventory" "Educational Environment Questionnaire" "After the Circus" (instructional booklet) Each child: test booklet pencil	Levels A and B: Percentiles Sentence descriptions Levels C and D: Percentiles Stanines Standard scores "Grade Level Indicators"
COMPREHENSIVE TESTS OF BASIC SKILLS (expanded edition) CTB/McGraw-Hill			
Administrator: teacher Grade range: Level A,	Measures skills necessary for studying and learning in school. Level A has eight tests: "letter forms," "letter names," "listening for information," "letter sounds," "visual discrimination," "sound matching," "language," and "mathematics." Level B also has 8	Administrator: manual practice test test book stopwatch	Raw score Standard score (Scale score) Stanine

438

			Grade equivalent Profile Class record sheet
kindergarten through 1.3; Level B, K.6 through 1.9 Time required: Level A, approximately 3½ hours (8 sittings); Level B, approximately 4 hours (8 sittings) Group test Paper-and-pencil	tests: "letter sounds," "word recognition I and II," "reading comprehension," "language I and II," mathematics concepts and applications, and math computation.	"Class Record Sheet" "Individual Test Record" Each child: practice test test book pencil with eraser place marker	

THE COOPERATIVE PRIMARY TESTS
Cooperative Test and Services

			Raw score Percentile rank Recommended instructional methods
Administrator: teacher Grade range: end of first grade through third grade Time required: timed, approximately 3 hours (2 tests per day suggested) Group and individual test Paper-and-pencil	Surveys language, reading, and mathematics skills: 1. Listening items—comprehension, recall, and interpretation 2. Reading items—words, sentences, and paragraphs 3. Word Analysis items—measure understanding of phonetic and structural properties of words. 4. Writing Skill items—spelling, punctuation, capitalization, and grammar (second and third grades only) 5. Mathematics items—major mathematics concepts of number, symbolism, operation, function and relation, approximation and estimation, proof, measurement, and geometry Pilot test of ten items gives children practice with format and kinds of questions and responses they will encounter in the other subtest.	Administrator: manual test booklet scoring key Each child: test booklet pencil	

ADMINISTRATION	CONTENT	MATERIALS	TEST DATA

DOREN DIAGNOSTIC READING TEST OF WORD RECOGNITION SKILLS
Doren, Margaret
American Guidance Service

ADMINISTRATION	CONTENT	MATERIALS	TEST DATA
Administrator: teacher	Diagnoses reading difficulties regardless of basic reading program used. Assesses:	Administrator: manual test booklet class composite sheet key	Raw score Recommended remedial activities Individual score sheet
Grade range: primary grades	1. Letter recognition (identity, case, and forms)		
Time required: approximately 1 to 3 hours	2. Beginning sounds (sound identity, context selection)	Each child: test booklet pencil	
Group or individual test	3. Whole word recognition (word identity and similarity)		
Paper-and-pencil	4. Words within words (compound and hidden words, discrimination)		
	5. Speech consonants (auditory, visual)		
	6. Ending sounds (consonant, variant, and plural)		
	7. Blending (consonant blends)		
	8. Rhyming (auditory and visual rhyming, similar nonrhyming, dissimilar rhyming)		
	9. Vowels (word choices, vowel identities, vowel rules, vowel sounds, rule exceptions, double vowel choices, double vowel sounds, diphthongs, sound exceptions)		
	10. Discrimination guessing (riddles, common expressions, homonyms)		
	11. Spelling (phonetic and nonphonetic words)		
	12. Sight words		

GATES-MACGINITIE READING TESTS—READINESS SKILLS
Gates, A.I., and W.H. MacGinitie
Teachers College Press

Administrator:
teacher

Grade range:
kindergarten or
during second
week of first
grade

Time required:
2 hours (4
sittings)

Group

Paper-and-pencil

Measures readiness skills in:
1. Listening comprehension
2. Auditory discrimination
3. Visual discrimination
4. Following directions
5. Letter recognition
6. Visual-motor coordination
7. Auditory blending
8. Word recognition

Administrator:
manual
test booklet
scoring key and
overlay
"Class Record
Sheet"
"Technical
Supplement"

Each child:
test booklet
pencil

Raw score
Percentile
Stanine
Weighted score for
each subtest (i.e.,
weight given to each
subtest in order to
provide the best
prediction of later
reading
achievement)
Total weighted
score
Discussion on
interpretation
and use of
scores

IOWA TESTS OF BASIC SKILLS
Hieronymus, A.N., and E.F. Lindquist
Houghton Mifflin Co.

Administrator:
teacher

Age and grade
range:
Level 7, age 7,
grades 1.7
through 2.5;
Level 6, age 6,
grades K.8–1.9;

Level 7 measures growth in fundamental skills:
listening, vocabulary, word analysis, reading, the
mechanics of writing, methods of study, and
mathematics. A shorter form of the test is available in
Level 7 only. Levels 5 and 6 do not have methods of
study. Level 5 does not have reading.

Administrator:
test booklet
guide
manual

Each child:
test booklet
pencil

Raw score
Percentile rank
Stanine
Grade equivalent
Recommended
instructional
methods
Age equivalent

441

ADMINISTRATION	CONTENT	MATERIALS	TEST DATA
Level 5, age 5, grades K.1–1.5			Scaled score Item Analysis
Time required: timed, basic edition, 3 hours and five minutes; standard edition, 4 hours and 45 minutes; Level 6, 3 hours and 25 minutes; Level 5, 2 hours and 30 minutes			
Group and individual test			
Paper-and-pencil			
KEY MATH DIAGNOSTIC ARITHMETIC TEST Connally, Austin J., William Nachtman, and E. Milo Pritchett American Guidance Service			
Administrator: teacher Grade range: preschool through sixth grade, no upper limit for remedial use	Measures three areas of arithmetic: 1. Content (numeration, fractions, geometry and symbols) 2. Operations (addition, subtraction, multiplication, division, mental computation, numerical reasoning) 3. Applications (word problems, missing elements, money, measurement, and time)	Administrator: kit materials (test plates, diagnostic records, and manual) diagnostic records manual	Raw score Diagnostic profile Description of each item's content and an indication of whether the child has mastered it

442

			Normal curve equivalents available for grades 2–6
Time required: approximately 30 minutes			
Individual test			
Verbal			

KRANER PRESCHOOL MATH INVENTORY
Kraner, R.E.
Teaching Resources

Administrator: teacher	Counting, understanding of cardinal numbers, quantities, sequence, position, direction, size, and form concepts.	Administrator: manual scoring forms	Mastery age for each item
Age range: 3 through 6.6 years			
Time required: untimed, approximately 30 to 60 minutes			
Individual			
Painting responses and oral			

THE NEW DEVELOPMENTAL READING TESTS
Bond, G.L., B. Balow, and C.J. Hoyt
Lyons and Carnahan

| Administrator: teacher | Measures and diagnoses general reading growth. Specifically measures word recognition and comprehension of ideas and instructions | Administrator: manual test booklet scoring key | Raw score Grade equivalent Recommended instructional methods |
| Grade range: first grade and first half of second grade | | | |

443

ADMINISTRATION	CONTENT	MATERIALS	TEST DATA
Time required: timed, 40 minutes (3 sittings) Group and individual test Paper-and-pencil		Each child: test booklet pencil with eraser	

PEABODY INDIVIDUAL ACHIEVEMENT TEST
Dunn, Lloyd M., and Frederick C. Markwardt, Jr.
American Guidance Service, Inc.

ADMINISTRATION	CONTENT	MATERIALS	TEST DATA
Administrator: teacher Age range: kindergarten through adult Time required: approximately 30–40 minutes Individual test Verbal	Surveys level of educational attainment in basic skills and knowledge. Five subtests: 1. Mathematics 2. Reading recognition 3. Reading comprehension 4. Spelling 5. General information	Administrator: test plates manual record blooklets "Training Tape" containing accepted pronunciations	Raw scores Percentile rank Grade and age equivalents Standard scores

PRESCRIPTIVE READING INVENTORY
CTB/McGraw-Hill

ADMINISTRATION	CONTENT	MATERIALS	TEST DATA
Administrator: teacher Grade range: grade 1.5 through	Covers ninety behavioral objectives in areas of: 1. Recognition of sound and symbol 2. Phonic analysis 3. Structural analysis	Administrator: "Individual Study Guide" "Class Diagnostic	Raw score Profile Class record sheet

grade 6.0 (4 test levels)

Time required: untimed, approximately 3 hours (30–40 minute sittings)

Group and individual test

Paper-and-pencil

4. Translation
5. Literal comprehension
6. Interpretive comprehension
7. Critical comprehension

Map,
"Class Grouping Report"
"Program Reference Guide" manual

Each child:
test booklet
"Individual Diagnostic Map"
pencil

Recommended instructional methods

"Individual Study Guide," and the "Program Reference Guide" lists the pages in texts, teacher's editions, and workbooks where each objective is taught

REVISED PRE-READING SCREENING PROCEDURES
Slingerland, Beth H.
Educational Publishing Service, Inc.

Administrator: teacher

Grade range: end of kindergarten or entering first grade

Time required: 20 to 30 minutes for each of 3 sittings, suggested time for each item

Group test

Paper-and-pencil

Screens children of average to superior intelligence who show difficulties in auditory, visual, or kinesthetic modalities. These weaknesses call for specific instruction to prevent failure.

Administrator:
"Pre-Reading Screening Procedures Folder" ("Teacher Observation Sheet" and "Summary Sheet")
1 per child
practice page
test booklet

Each child:
practice page
test booklet
pencil without eraser
cardboard marker

Raw score
Verbal ratings from "high" to "low." Child is rated as above or below average in each section.

Administration	Content	Materials	Test Data
SLOSSON ORAL READING TEST (SORT) Slosson, Richard L. Slosson Educational Publications			
Administrator: teacher Grade range: first grade through high school Time required: 3 minutes Individual Verbal	Checks ability to pronounce words at different levels of difficulty.	Administrator: manual list of words score sheet Each child: list of words	Raw score Grade equivalent Recommended instructional methods
SRA ACHIEVEMENT SERIES Science Research Associates			
Administrator: teacher Grade range Level A: K.5 through 1.5 Time required: 2 hours, 15 minutes (5 sittings) Group Paper-and-pencil	Level A, forms 1 and 2, measures achievement in five areas: 1. Visual discrimination (letter features, letter forms, word forms) 2. Auditory discrimination (same word, beginning sounds, vowels, ending sounds) 3. Letters and sounds (letter matching, letter recognition, initial and final consonants) 4. Listening comprehension (understanding directions, grouping details, summarizing, perceiving relationships, drawing conclusions, understanding vocabulary) 5. Mathematics concepts (numbers and numerals, geometry and measurement, problem solving)	Administrator: manual user's guide practice sheet test booklet Each child: practice sheet test booklet pencil with eraser place marker	Raw scores Percentiles Growth scale values Grade equivalents Normal curve equivalents Percentage correct and ratios Stanines

446

STANFORD EARLY SCHOOL ACHIEVEMENT TEST (Level I)
Madden, R., and E.F. Gardner
Harcourt Brace Jovanovich, Inc.

Administrator:
teacher with
assistant

Grade range:
kindergarten
through
entrance to first
grade

Time required:
approximately 90
minutes (5 sittings)

Group and individual
test

Paper-and-pencil

Measures achievement in science, social studies, mathematics, language arts, and reading. Level I:
1. Environment items—measure child's knowledge of social and natural environments;
2. Mathematics items—evaluate conservation of number, space, and volume; measurement; numeration; counting; classification; algorithms;
3. Letter and Sound items—appraise ability to recognize upper and lower case letters and auditory perception of initial sounds;
4. Aural Comprehension items—evaluate ability to pay attention to, organize, interpret, infer, and retain verbal communication.

Administrator:
test booklet
manual scoring key
class record sheet
chart of practice
sheet

Each child:
test booklet
crayon or pencil
paper marker

Raw score
Percentile
Stanine
Grade equivalent
Scaled score

STANFORD EARLY SCHOOL ACHIEVEMENT TEST (Level II)
Madden, R., and E. Gardner
Harcourt Brace Jovanovich, Inc.

Administrator:
teacher

Grade range:
last month of
kindergarten
through last month
of first grade

Time required:
approximately 2

Measures achievement in science, social studies, mathematics, language arts, and reading. Level II:
1. Environment items—taken almost equally from social and natural sciences;
2. Mathematics items—measure conservation of number and space, counting, measurement, numeration, classification, simple operations;
3. Letter and Sound items—measure recognition of printed symbols and auditory perception of beginning sounds.

Administrator:
test booklet
manual
class record sheet
scoring key

Each child:
test booklet
pencil

Raw score
Percentile rank
Stanine
Grade equivalent
Scaled score

ADMINISTRATION	CONTENT	MATERIALS	TEST DATA
hours and 20 minutes (7 sittings)	4. Aural Comprehension items—require ability to pay attention to, organize, interpret, infer, and retain verbal communication.		
Group and individual test	5. Word Reading items—require child to recognize words from reading tests		
Paper-and-pencil	6. Sentence Reading items—require child to identify sentence that tells about a picture. (Three sentences about each picture are read before child identifies appropriate sentence.)		

THE WIDE RANGE ACHIEVEMENT TEST (revised edition)
Jastak, J.F., and S.R. Jastak
Guidance Associates of Delaware, Inc.

ADMINISTRATION	CONTENT	MATERIALS	TEST DATA
Administrator: teacher	Three subtests:	Administrator: manual test blank	Raw score
Age range: Level 1, five to 12 years	1. Reading—recognizing and naming letters and pronouncing words (out of context)	Each child: test blank pencil	Standard score Percentile Stanine
Time required: 20 to 30 minutes	2. Spelling—copying "marks" and writing words		Scaled score T score
Group (arithmetic and spelling) and individual (reading) test	3. Arithmetic—counting, reading math symbols, and solving problems		Manual contains a discussion of the use of WRAT as a diagnostic tool and some suggestions for follow-up.
Paper-and-pencil and verbal			

448

WOODCOCK READING MASTERY TESTS
Woodcock, Richard W.
American Guidance Service, Inc.

Administrator:
  teacher

Grade range:
  kindergarten
  through twelfth
  grade

Time required:
  approximately
  20–30 minutes

Individual test

Verbal

Measures:
  1. Letter identification
  2. Word identification
  3. Word attack
  4. Word comprehension
  5. Passage comprehension

Administrator:
  kit materials
  test plates (form
  A or B), 25
  response forms
  manual
  response forms

Raw and standard
  scores
Percentile rank
Mastery scale scores
Mastery profile
Normal curve
  equivalents
  available for
  grades 2–6.
Grade and age
  equivalents
"SES" (socioeconomic
  status are adjusted
  norms based on
  communities having
  similar SES
  characteristics to the
  local community)

Personal-Social Adjustment

ANIMAL CRACKERS: A TEST OF MOTIVATION TO ACHIEVE
Adkins, Dorothy C., and Bonnie L. Ballif
CTB/McGraw-Hill

Administrator:
  teacher

Motivation to achieve assessed by determining:
  1. School enjoyment (child experts to feel pleasure as
     a result of school achievement)

Administrator:
  manual
  administration

Raw score
Percentile rank

ADMINISTRATION	CONTENT	MATERIALS	TEST DATA
Grade range: preschool, kindergarten, or first grade Time required: 10 minutes practice; test time approximately 20–45 minutes Group (paper-and-pencil part) and individual (verbal part) test Verbal and paper-and-pencil	2. Self-Confidence (child sees himself as an individual who can achieve) 3. Purposiveness (child sets up purposes and goals to direct his behavior) 4. Instrumental activity (child knows how to accomplish purposes and goals efficiently) 5. Self-Evaluation (child can evaluate his school performance)	booklet item card test booklet individual and group performance records Each child: test booklet pencil with eraser	Recommended instructional methods
BLACKY PICTURES Blum, G.S. Psychodynamic Instruments Administrator: psychometrist Age range: 5 years through adult Timed required: 30 to 45 minutes Individual Verbal	Measures personality dynamics. Child tells stories about events in the life of Blacky, a cartooned dog; also answers questions and indicates preferences for cartoons.	Administrator: manual pictures inquiry booklet record blank research guide	Psychosexual variables are assessed

450

BRISTOL SOCIAL ADJUSTMENT GUIDES (fifth edition)
Stott, D.H.
Hodder and Stoughton Educational

Administrator:
teacher

Age range:
5 to 6 years

Time required:
15 minutes per child

Teacher rating

Teacher measures social adjustment in areas of "unforthcomingness" (lack of self assertion); "withdrawal" (indifferences or defensiveness about human affiliations); "depression" (lack of normal response to stimuli); "inconsequence" (failure to inhibit first response-impulses which come to mind); and "hostility" (desire to break or not to form an affectional relationship by means of attack or avoidance). "Unforthcomingness," "withdrawal," and "depression" are considered under-reacting behavior ("unract") and "inconsequence" and "hostility as over-reacting behavior ("ovract"). In addition to core syndromes, child receives scores in associated groupings that support or are closely related to core syndromes.

Administrator:
Bristol Social Adjustment Guides-Manual (fifth edition)
"The Child in School-Boy" (1 per boy) and "The Child in School-Girl" (1 per girl)
"The Child in School-Diagnostic Form"
pencil
transparent template for scoring
(Other form available for children in residential setting and in family setting)

Raw score
Percentile rank
Per cent at each score

451

CALIFORNIA TEST OF PERSONALITY
Willis, W., and E.W. Tiegs
CTB/McGraw-Hill

Administrator:
teacher

Determines effectiveness with which individual meets personal and social problems. Also measures

Administrator:
manual

Raw score
Percentile

ADMINISTRATION	CONTENT	MATERIALS	TEST DATA
Grade range: Primary Form, kindergarten through third grade

Time required: 45 minutes

Individual (if children cannot read) or group (if children can read)

Paper-and-pencil | indirectly how he impresses his fellows. "Personal Adjustment" subtest measures self-reliance, sense of personal worth, sense of personal freedom, feeling of belonging, withdrawing tendencies, and nervous symptoms. "Social Adjustment" subtest measures social standards, social skills, anti-social tendencies, family relations, school relations, and community relations. | test booklet profile sheet "Class Record Sheet"

Each child: (if children are mature enough to mark their own tests): test booklet pencil | rank (test and subsections) Recommended guidance methods |
| **THE CHILD BEHAVIOR RATING SCALE (CBRS)** Cassel, R.N. Western Psychological Services | | | |
| Administrator: teacher

Grade range: kindergarten through third grade

Time required: approximately 30 minutes

Individual

Teacher check list | Standardized for objective assessment of personality adjustment. Ratings on specific child can be compared with typical children and emotionally-handicapped children. Measures adjustment in five areas: self-adjustment, home adjustment, social adjustment, school adjustment, physical adjustment. Each item rated on six-point scale that indicates degree to which child presents a specific behavior to the rater. | Administrator: manual rating book | Weighted score for each area of adjustment "Personality Total Adjustment Score" (sum of weighted scores in self, home and school adjustment)

T scores |

452

CHILDREN'S APPERCEPTION TEST (CAT)
Bellak, L., and S.S. Bellak
C.P.S., Inc.

Administrator:
psychometrist

Age range:
3 through 10 years

Time required:
approximately 30
minutes

Individual

Verbal and
manipulative

Measures personality adjustment. Based on Thematic Apperception Test; however, Bellak and Bellak believe children respond to animal pictures on the CAT more readily than to the stimulus pictures used on the TAT. For each stimulus picture, child expresses his conceptions of interpersonal relationships.

Administrator:
manual
stimulus pictures
scoring key

Profile—compares scores with T scores of typical children and with atypical children

Projective pictures

DETROIT ADJUSTMENT INVENTORY—DELTA FORM
Baker, H.J.
Bobbs-Merrill Co.

Administrator:
teacher

Age range:
5 through 8 years

Two-dimensional inventory; determines (1) self-status, self-social, self-emotional, and self-ethical; (2) school-status, school-social, school-emotional, and school-ethical; (3) community-status, community-social, community-emotional, and community-ethical; and (4) home-status, home-social, home-emotional, and home-ethical reactions.

Administrator:
manual
test booklet
record blank
and scoring
key

Raw score
Descriptive
evaluations
Remedial
leaflets are
provided for

453

ADMINISTRATION	CONTENT	MATERIALS	TEST DATA
Time required: approximately 30 minutes Individual Paper-and-pencil			use by teachers and parents
DRAW-A-CLASSROOM TEST (DAC) Wright, E.N. The Board of Education for the city of Toronto			
Administrator: teacher (administers) psychometrist (interprets) Age range: 4 through 10 years Time required: approximately 10 minutes Group Paper-and-pencil and verbal	Synthesis of elements of Goodenough Harris Draw-A-Man Test and Lowenfeld Draw-a-World Test reoriented toward child's view of his school. Child draws picture of his classroom then discusses his drawing.	Administrator: Completed copies are sent to: Research Department, Toronto Board of Education Each child: 12 × 18″ newsprint crayons	Analysis is done in terms of space, people, and objects
DRISCOLL PLAY KIT Driscoll, G.P. The Psychological Corp.			
Administrator: psychometrist	Provides standardized situation for investigating dynamics of personality development and adjustment	Administrator: manual	Projective doll play

454

Age range:
2 to 10 years

Time required:
approximately 30 minutes

Individual

Verbal and manipulative

carrying case which opens to form an apartment of five rooms and bath, furnished with 27 pieces of furniture, and inhabited by a family of five dolls

EARLY SCHOOL PERSONALITY QUESTIONNAIRE
Institute for Personality and Ability Testing

Administrator:
teacher

Age range:
6 to 8 years

Time required:
approximately 30–40 minutes

Group and individual test

Paper-and-pencil

Assesses personality development in 14 factor, analytically defined dimensions. Dimensions are

1. Reserved—outgoing
2. Less intelligent—more intelligent
3. Affected by feeling—emotionally stable
4. Phlegmatic—excitable
5. Obedient—assertive
6. Sober—happy-go-lucky
7. Expedient—conscientious
8. Shy—venturesome
9. Tough-minded—tender-minded
10. Vigorous—doubting
11. Forthright—shrewd
12. Placid—apprehensive
13. Casual—controlled
14. Relaxed—tense

Administrator:
test manual with norms
test booklet
scoring stencils

Each child:
answer sheet

Raw score
Profile
Standard Ten Score (STEN)
Ability to identify clinical problems
Identification, prediction, and understanding of disciplinary problems
Prediction of academic potential

ADMINISTRATION	CONTENT	MATERIALS	TEST DATA
HOLTZMAN INKBLOT TECHNIQUE Holtzman, W.H. The Psychological Corp. Administrator: psychometrist Age range: 5 years through adult Individual and group Verbal	Aids clinician in diagnosis of behavior pathologies. Set of 45 inkblots used to elicit and appraise projective-expressive responses.	Administrator: manual scoring guide inkblots record forms materials for group administration	Percentile norms
PASS (PRIMARY ACADEMIC SENTIMENT SCALE) Thompson, G.R. Priority Innovations, Inc. Administrator: teacher Grade range: kindergarten through first grade Time required: not timed; takes approximately 1 hour, including breaks Group Paper-and-pencil	Evaluates child's motivation for learning, relative maturity, and independence from parents.	Administrator: manual test booklet "Pass Scoring Form "Class Record Sheet" Each child: test booklet pencil	"Dependency Stanine" "Sentiment Quotient"
THE PIKUNAS GRAPHOSCOPIC SCALE (PGS: FORMS I AND II Pikunas, J. University of Detroit Press			

Administrator:
 psychometrist

Age range:
 5 to 18 years

Time required:
 30 to 50 minutes

Individual and group

Drawing

Personality test assessing intelligence, self-expressive balance, many diagnostic variables. Child completes drawing on ten plates.

Administrator:
 manual
 test blank
 scoring sheets

IQ
Self-expressive balance index
Creativity index
Adjustment index
Total rating

THE PRESCHOOL RACIAL ATTITUDE MEASURE II (PRAM) AND COLOR MEANING TEST II (CMT) (revised)
Williams, J.E., and D.L. Best
Department of Psychology, Wake Forrest University, Winston-Salem, N.C. 27109

Administrator:
 teacher

Age range:
 3 through 9 years

Time required:
 PRAM II, 20 minutes; CMT II, 15 minutes

Individual

Verbal

PRAM II assesses children's attitudes toward Euro-American and Afro-American persons. Also elicits views on sex roles. CMT II, a companion measure, assesses attitudes toward black and white.

Administrator:
 manuals
 stimulus pictures and stories
 scoring form

Cutting scores indicating: (1) pro-Afro/anti-Euro bias, pro-Euro/anti-Afro bias, or no bias; (2) high sex role awareness or no sex role awareness; (3) pro-white/anti-black attitude; pro-black/anti-white attitude; no consistent color range

---

PRESCHOOL SELF-CONCEPT PICTURE TEST (PS-CPT)
Woolner, R.B.
Author. 3551 Aurora, Memphis, TN 38111

ADMINISTRATION	CONTENT	MATERIALS	TEST DATA
Administrator: teacher Age range: 4 through 6 years Time required: approximately 20 minutes Individual Verbal	Picture test composed of four separate subtests for Negro and Caucasian children. Child is presented plates with paired pictures representing characteristics preschool children recognize as sharing and not-sharing, etc. Examines opinions children have of themselves: (1) as they perceive themselves to be (self-concept); (2) as they think they would prefer to be (ideal self-concept). Also provides measure of degree of variability between the foregoing. Positive and negative characteristics selected for use on picture plates related to needs, concerns, characteristics, and developmental tasks.	Administrator: manual, answer sheets, pencil	The child is compared to himself and not to others

ROCK-A-BYE BABY: A GROUP PROJECTIVE TEST FOR CHILDREN
Haworth, M.R., and A.G. Woltomann
Psychological Cinema Register
(The Pennsylvania State University)

ADMINISTRATION	CONTENT	MATERIALS	TEST DATA
Administrator: psychometrist Age range: 5 through 10 years Time required: approximately 1 hour Group and individual Verbal and drawing	Group projective technique. 35-minute filmed puppet show reveals presence of baby in the family. Film may also be used to diagnose self-concept, jealousy index, aggression to parents, guilt index, anxiety index, and index of obsessive trends.	Administrator: manual, filmed two-act puppet show, record blank; Each child: drawing paper and crayons (used to get additional information if verbal	Age and sex norms were determined; High scores indicating deviations are given for each index; Test behavior also recorded; Children whose protocols reveal

responses are meager)

deviations should be selected for further clinical study

ROSENZWEIG PICTURE-FRUSTRATION STUDY: CHILDREN'S FORM
Rosenzweig, S.
Rana House, 8029 Washington St., St. Louis, MO 63114

Administrator: teacher with supervision Age range: 4 through 13 years Time required: 15 through 25 minutes Individual (if verbal) or group (if paper-and-pencil) Paper-and-pencil or verbal	Involves response to 24 cartoon-like pictures, representing an everyday frustrating situation involving two persons. One cartooned character is shown saying something; subject is asked to complete caption box or ballon above the second character. Half the cartoons involve an adult frustrating the child, other half involve frustration by a peer.	Administrator: basic manual supplementary manual scoring sheet examination leaflet Each child: examination leaflet pencil (if group, paper-and-pencil exam)	Raw score based on type of aggression and direction of aggression Percentiles by age

---

SELF-CONCEPT AND MOTIVATION INVENTORY (SCAMIN): PRESCHOOL KINDERGARTEN FORM
Milchus, N.J., G.A. Farrah, and N. Reitz
Person-o-metrics, Inc.

Administrator: teacher Age and grade range: 4 through 6 years, preschool and kindergarten	Students are asked "What Face Would You Wear?" if certain things happened. Item content on teachers, parents, peers/siblings, self, and school academic and social climates are balanced throughout the factors. Factors measured are Achievement Investment and Self-Concept. Inventory's structure and nonintrusive	Administrator: manual response sheet Each child: response sheet pencil paper marker	Raw score Stanines

ADMINISTRATION	CONTENT	MATERIALS	TEST DATA
Time required: approximately 25 minutes Group Paper-and-pencil	content interface with Early Elementary SCAMIN Form (grades 1–3).		

SOUTH AFRICAN PICTURE ANALYSIS TEST
Nel, B.F., and A.J.K. Pelser
Swets and Zeitlinger, Amsterdam

ADMINISTRATION	CONTENT	MATERIALS	TEST DATA
Administrator: psychometrist Age range: 5 to 13 years Time required: approximately 1 hour Individual Verbal	Measures personality dynamics and adjustment. According to authors, test was developed to fill gap between Thematic Apperception Test and Children's Apperception Test. Children describe 10 pictures; their stories are analyzed for such things as condition of hero (secure or insecure); environmental pressure (inferiority, parents, home, and school); needs (dominance and security reactions); and characteristics of story (tone, endings, kind of story, value).	Administrator: manual pictures (12) analysis sheet	Analysis based on frequency of occurrence of same conditions, needs, reactions, etc., and frequency of these factors in most significant stories.

STAMP BEHAVIOR STUDY TECHNIQUE (BST)
Stamp, I.M.
Australian Council for Educational Research, Frederick Street, Hawthorne, Australia 3122

ADMINISTRATION	CONTENT	MATERIALS	TEST DATA
Administrator: teacher describes behavior, psychometrist scores	Describes and evaluates behavior. Screens behavioral problems in: (1) attitudes toward self and others; (2) expression of negative feelings; (3) use of powers; and (4) integration of home and kindergarten life. Form is multiple-choice questionnaire, requiring observer to	Administrator: teacher: (1) teacher's guide and (2)questionnaire	Percentages of children described in various categories

Age range:
3 through 5 years

Time required:
approximately 45 minutes

Individual

Teacher checklist

select behavior most typical of the child in different situations.

psychologist:
(1) manual,
(2) questionnaire, and (3) scoring key

VINELAND SOCIAL MATURITY SCALE
Doll, Edgar A.
American Guidance Service, Inc.

Administrator:
Skilled interviewer

Age range:
birth through maturity

Time required:
approximately 20–30 minutes

Individual test

Verbal

Measures ability to look after one's own practical needs. Categories include
1. Self-help general
2. Self-help eating
3. Self-help dressing
4. Self-direction
5. Occupation
6. Communication
7. Locomotion
8. Socialization

Administrator:
manual
scoring sheets
record blanks
Textbook,
  Measurement
  of Social
  Competence

Raw score
"Social Quotient"
"Social Age
  Equivalent"

ZULLIGER INDIVIDUAL AND GROUP TEST (ZT)
Zulliger, H.
International Universities Press, Inc.

Administrator:
psychometrist

Age range:
3 years through adult

Form-interpretation test in keeping with Rorschach and Behn-Rorschach Tests.

Administrator:
The Zulliger
  Individual
  and Group
  Test

Psychogram is developed

Each item evaluated according to

ADMINISTRATION	CONTENT	MATERIALS	TEST DATA
Time required: approximately 20 minutes Individual (with younger children) Verbal		3 cards paper for writing stories and actions	formula developed by Rorschach

Parent Scales

ADMINISTRATION	CONTENT	MATERIALS	TEST DATA
APPRAISAL OF PARENT BEHAVIOR Baldwin, A., J. Kalhorn, and F.H. Breese The American Psychological Association, Inc.			
Administrator: trained rater Age range: parents of preschoolers rated every 6 months Time required: Each visit, approximately 2 hours Paper-and-pencil rating scale	Thirty scales variables are on a continuum, and include: 1. Warmth—home in which parent genuinely likes and enjoys child and is approving of child's personality; 2. Intellectual objectivity toward child—parent able to divorce his behavior from his immediate mood; 3. Control employed by parent—restrictive to lax discipline.	Administrator: manual rating scale (10 different children are rated on a single variable)	Raw score T-score (referred to as a sigma index by the Fels Researchers) Rater places an x on a 90-millimeter rating line at or near the cue which best describes the parent's behavior toward the child

462

Index

Academically oriented approaches,
  28–29, 32–33, 39–41
Academically Oriented Preschool, 21
Accident insurance, pupil, 212
Accreditation, 53–54, 68, 82
Achievement and diagnostic tests, 268,
  389–462
Achievement records, 272–73
Acoustics, 128–30, 132, 140
Activity centers. *See* Interest (activity)
  centers
Administration, nature and importance
  of, 1, 12–13, 48
Administrative functions, 47–48
Administrator qualifications, 76–77
Admission of children, 195–96, 212,
  270–71
Advocacy, 36, 302, 310–12, 314
The Alliance of Child Development
  Associations, 77, 89, 330–31
Ameliorative Preschool Program
  (Champaign, Ill.), 30–31, 218
American Academy of Pediatrics, the,
  88–89, 212
American Association of
  Elementary-Kindergarten, Nursery
  Educators, 79, 100
American Dietetic Association 91, 209

American Montessori Society, Inc., 51,
  80–81, 331–32
Anecdotal records, 271
Aptitude tests, 268, 389–462
Art materials, 165–66
Assessment
  definition of, 256–57
  disadvantages of, 256–59
  informal methods of
    interviews, 260–61
    observations, 259–60
    samples of children's work, 261–62,
      269, 273, 277
    staff-constructed tests, 262–63
  standardized tests
    achievement and diagnostic, 268,
      389–462
    advantages and disadvantages of,
      263–64
    aptitude, 268
    considerations in, 264–65
    definition of, 263
    personal-social adjustment tests,
      268, 389–462
    technical terms in, 258, 265–67
  steps in planning, 257–59, 264
  trends in, 264
  value of, 37, 257, 263

Assistant teachers. *See* Staff, teachers and assistant teachers
Association for Childhood Education, International, 9, 90, 332–33
Audiovisual equipment, 158–59
Autotelic Responsive Environment, 186

Background information records, 260–61, 270–71
Bank Street Early Childhood Center (New York), 21, 29, 33, 219
Bereiter-Englemann program, 30–32, 36
Birthday celebration plans, 198, 240–41
Blocks and building structures, 161–62
Bloom, Benjamin S., 2
Blow, Susan E., 2, 9
Board of education (directors or advisors)
  policies required by state, 49
  regulations of, 53, 76
  responsibilities of local, 22–23, 49, 51, 65–66, 88, 237–38, 291, 305–6
Boiler and machinery insurance, 147
British Infant Schools, 21, 36, 185
Bruner, Jerome, 2
Budget
  defined, 305
  developing, 306–8
  format, 306
  regulations governing, 305–6
Budgeting procedures, 154–55, 305–8
Building. *See* Housing
Bushell Applied Behavior Analysis, 29, 32–33

Care-givers. *See* Staff, child care personnel
Carpet, 127–31
Caseworkers, 92
Ceilings, 131–32, 139
Certification
  administrators, 76–77, 119
  agencies (Appendix 1), 317–19
  Child Development Associate credential, 81
  supervisors, 119
  teachers of handicapped, 78–91
  teachers, Montessori, 80–81
  teachers, private programs, 80–90
  teachers, public school, 77–80, 89–90
Chain, 51, 95

Chain-of-command. *See* Communication, lines of
Check sheets, 279
Child and Family Resource Program, 8
Child care personnel. *See* Staff, child care personnel
Child Development Associate (CDA), 8, 77, 81, 89–90
Child-staff ratio, 59, 85, 91, 218–19
Child Welfare League of America, Inc., 50, 55, 82
Civil Rights Act of 1964, 53, 74–75
Code of ethics, 313–14
Communication
  defined, 93
  flow of, 94
  lines of, 49, 94–95
  process of, 93–94
Community resources, 179–80
Computer-Assisted Instruction (Suppes), 186
Conferences with parents, 217, 225–26, 229–34, 246–47, 260–61, 277
Contract and terms of employment, 104
Cooking materials, 164
Corporations, 4, 50, 64–67
Costs
  computing, 304–5
  of programs, 288–90
  to families, 290
Criterion-referenced measure, 258
Cubbies, 134–35, 141
Cumulative records, 274
Curriculum, 26

Day care
  defined and history of, 5–7, 56
  licensing of, 55–64
  types of
    after-school programs, 6, 288
    drop-in centers, 7
    family day-care homes, 7, 54–55, 64, 288
    infant group-care programs, 7
    parent cooperatives, 7, 11
    play schools, 7
    public school centers, 7
Demonstration and Research Center for Early Education (Nashville, Tenn.), 21, 31–32, 219, 243, 245
Developmental Continuity Project, 8

Developmental theories, 18–19, 27–28

Diagnostic tests. *See* Achievement and diagnostic tests

Dietitians, 61, 91, 206, 209

Dining area, 136–37

Director. *See* Staff, director

"Discovery" approaches, 21, 28–29, 32–34, 39–41

Drinking fountain, 61, 136, 141

Early childhood programs
administrative organizational patterns, 48–51
definition of, 4, 36
enrollment statistics of, 3–4, 9–10
factors influencing, 1–3, 27
federal, 51, 292–99
financing of, 3–5, 292–99
Montessori School, 51
need for, 2–3
private, 49–51
public school, 49
status of, 3–4
theoretical models of 19–22
types of, 4–12

Early identification and screening, 72

Education for All Handicapped Children Act. *See* P. L. 94–142

Education, formal, 97

Educational Development Center, 21, 29, 32–33

Education Professions Development Act, 3

"Electric Company," 34–35

Emergency information, 212, 376–88

Englemann-Becker Distar Program, 29–30, 33, 186

Environmental control, 60, 138–40

Entrance requirements, 195–96, 224–25

Entry-exit area, 124, 141

Equipment and materials
arranging, 155
caring for, 156–57
inventory of, 155, 210
licensing requirements for, 60–61
purchasing, guidelines and procedure for, 151–55, 209
safety of, 153, 156–57
sources of
community resources, 179–80
free and inexpensive, 178

Equipment and materials *(cont.)*
kits and sets, 176–77, 357–75
miscellaneous, 178–79
professional library, 180
raw or primitive, 177
staff-made, 177–78
suppliers, (Appendix 5), 351–56
texts and workbooks, 175–76
types of
art, 165–66
audiovisual, 158–59
blocks and building structures, 161–62
cooking, 164
furniture, 157–58
handicapped, 172–74
housekeeping and dramatic play, 162–63
infants and toddlers, 168–72
language arts, 159–60
large-muscle activity, 167–68
manipulative activity, 166–67
mathematics, 160
music, 165
science, 163–64
social studies, 160–61
water, sand, and mud play, 164
woodworking or carpentry, 164–65. *See also* Storage and display facilities

Evaluation, children's. *See* Assessment

Evaluation, program
formative, 42, 257
need for, 41–43
summative, 41–42, 257

Evaluation, staff, 100–3

Facilities. *See* housing

Fair Labor Standards Act, 75

Family Day Care Homes, 7, 54–55, 64

Family Educational Rights and Privacy Act of 1974 (P.L. 93–380). *See* P.L 93–380

Far West Laboratory for Educational Research and Development (Berkeley, California), 218–19

Federal Interagency Day Care Regulations
"Appropriateness Study," 69–70
content of, 69–85
history of, 23, 69

Federal Interagency (cont.)
  programs regulated by 68–69
Federal funds
  agencies funding, 202–99
  obtaining, 299–302
Federal programs
  financing, 51, 292–302
  regulations, 48, 68–70
Fees, 23, 304
Fencing. See Outdoor space
Fergus/Florissant Home-School Program
    for Four-Year-Olds (St. Louis
    County, Mo.), 218
FICA, 105
Field trip destinations, 179–80
Field trip form, example of, 197, 240
Field trip plans, 196–98, 240
Financing, 287–305
Fire insurance, 146–47
Fire safety and sanitation requirements,
    53, 60, 74
First day plans, 195–96
Floor covering, 127–32
Floor planes, wells and platforms, 127,
    132
Floor plans, 130, 131, 144–46
Floors, 127–32, 135–37
Florida Parent-Infant Education Project,
    244
Follow Through, 5, 7–8, 29, 32, 36, 219
Foundation support, 302–3
Franchise, 51
Free materials, 178
Froebel, Friedrich, 2, 9, 217
Funding agencies, 37–38. See also
    Funding sources
Funding sources
  federal agencies, 202–300
  fees and tuition, 304
  foundations, 302–3
  local, 291
  miscellaneous, 304–5
  state, 291–92

Furniture, 157–58

General office personnel, 92
Gordon Parent Education Model, 29
Grants
  preproposal planning of, 299–300
  writing the proposal, 301–2

Grievance procedures, 95
Grouping
  ability, 186
  departmentalized, 185–86
  horizontal, 185–86
  individualized, 186
  self-contained, 185
  team teaching or care-giving, 186
  vertical, 184–85
Guidance and placement records,
    273–74

Hall, G. Stanley, 9
Handicapped (exceptional and
    educationally disadvantaged)
    children
  child-staff ratio needed, 59
  costs of programs, 289–90
  housing for, 123, 140
  legislation on behalf of, 38, 54, 70–73,
      86–87, 123. See also P.L. 94–142
  materials for, 172–74, 258, 264
  programs for, 34, 36, 39–41, 204
  statistics on, 2
  supportive services needed, 86–87
  teachers of, 78, 86–87, 98
Head Start
  definition of, 5, 7–8, 36
  funding, 3–4, 6–7, 237–38, 292
  research on, 29–31, 34, 36, 42, 219
Head Start Performance Objectives, 70
Health and safety codes, 54, 60–62
Health education of staff and parents,
    213–14
Health history form, 212, 270–71,
    376–88
Health insurance and hospital-medical
    insurance, 106
Health services
  developing adult education program,
      213–14
  developing policies, 211–13
Heating, cooling, and ventilating, 140
Hill, Patty S., 2, 9, 11
Holiday celebration plans, 198, 240–41
Home Start, 8, 34, 243
Home visits, 234, 245–46
Housekeeping and dramatic play,
    162–63
Housing
  adult areas, 60, 137–38, 223–24

Housing (cont.)
  basic considerations in, 122–24
  children's activity room, 125–34, 137
  dining area, 136–37
  directional orientation, 125
  entry-exit area, 124
  isolation, 137
  kitchen, 60
  licensing, 60
  napping, 137
  resource room, 134
  restrooms, 60–61, 135–36
  room arrangement, 126
  shared activity areas, 134
  size of, 60, 125–26
  steps in planning, 122–24
Hunt, J. McV, 2

Immunizations, 61, 212, 376–88. See
  also Health services
Incorporation, 65–67
Individually Prescribed Instruction
  System, 186
Infant and toddler programs
  equipment and materials for, 168–72,
    264
  licensing regulations, 62
  research on, 29, 34
  schedule, example of, 193–94
Infant Education Research Project
  (Washington, D.C.), 219
Infant Schools, 5
Inservice education, 97–99, 118, 205,
  213–14, 239–40
Insurance, crime coverage, 106
Insurance and retirement plans, 105–6.
  See also Boiler and machinery
  insurance; Fire insurance; Health
  insurance and hospital medical
  insurance; Insurance, crime
  coverage; Liability vehicle insurance;
  Workman's compensation insurance
Interest (activity) centers
  arrangement of, 126–30
  materials for, 159–67
  planning activities for, 187–89
  specific centers
    animal and plant, 130
    art, 62, 129
    block, 62, 128
    concept and manipulative, 62, 130

Interest (activity) centers (cont.)
    dramatic play, 62, 128
    music, 62, 129
    sand play, 129
    water play, 130
Internal Revenue Service Regulations,
  75–76
Interviews
  children, 260–61
  staff, 96–97
Inventory, 152, 210
Isolation area (illness), 60, 137, 213

Job descriptions, need for, 104–5. See
  also Staff

Kindergarten, definition and history of,
  5, 8–10, 78
Kitchen, 61, 136–37
Kits and sets, 176–77, 357–75

Language arts materials, 159–60
Large-muscle activity materials, 167–68
Learning episodes, planning activities
  for, 187–88
"Least restrictive environment," 73
Letters
  achievement reporting, 277–78
  class newsletters, 236–37
Liability insurance, 105
Library, professional, 180
Licensing
  agency issuing, 55, 317–19
  characteristics of laws, 57–64
    curricular content, 62
    discipline of children, 62–63
    equipment, 61
    health and safety, 61–62
    necessity for statement of
      organizational plan, 58, 238
    personnel needed and qualifications,
      58–62, 90–91
    physical plant and equipment,
      60–61
    procedure for application, 57–58
  child care programs included in, 56,
    67
  definition of, 54
  history of, 55
  policies required by agencies, 58,
    103–4

Licensing (cont.)
  purposes, 54–55
  requirements, 54–64
  upgrading attempts, 63–64
Lighting, 128, 130, 138–39
Local board regulations, 68, 76, 291
Locker, children's, 134–35, 141
Lounge, staff/parent, 138

Mainstreaming, 73, 86, 98, 289–90
Maintenance staff, 92
Manipulative activity materials, 166–67
Manuals, 175
Mathematics materials, 160
McMillan, Margaret, 2, 11
McMillan, Rachel, 2, 11
Meals and snacks. See Nutrition program
Medical care, licensing and, 62
Medical examination, 212, 270, 376–88
Medical staff, 59–60, 62, 91–92
Montessori, Maria, 2, 10, 80–81
Montessori schools, 4–5, 10–11, 20–21,
    30–32, 88, 185
Music materials, 165

Napping area, 137
National Association for the Education of
    Young Children, 79, 337–38
National Association of Child Care
    Administrators, 77, 89, 338–39
National Kindergarten Association,
    79–80, 100
Nimnicht Responsive Model, 21, 29, 33
Nonsexist education, 38
Norm-referenced measure, 258
Nursery schools, definition and history
    of, 5–6, 10–11
Nutrition program
  equipment for, 209
  food purchasing for, 209–10
  importance of, 202–3
  licensing of, 62
  objectives for, 203–5
  parent education, 205
  planning meals and snacks
    example of meal and snack plans,
        207–8
    general suggestions, 207, 209
    infants, 206
    young children, 206–9
  regulations regarding, 62, 205–6
  sanitation and, 210–11

Oberlin, Jean, 2
Observation room, 137–38, 224
Observing children, 259–60
Office, 60, 138
Office of Child Development, U.S., 19
Office workers, 92
Open house, 217, 235
Orientation, parents, 224–25, 239–40,
    244–45
Orientation, staff, 97–99, 118, 239
Outdoor space
  active play areas in, 142–44
  arrangement of, 61, 141–44
  basic considerations of, 140–41
  fencing, 61, 141
  interest (activity) areas, 142–44
  locating, 61, 141
  passive play areas in, 142–44
  shelter in, 142
  size of, 61, 141
  storage in, 144, 145
  surfacing, types of, 61, 141

Parent-Child Center Program, 3–4, 6, 8,
    34, 245
Parent communication
  first individual visit, 225–26, 260–61
  handbook, 224, 226–29, 376–88
  home visits, 234
  individual conferences, 225–26,
      230–33, 277
  large-group conferences, 229–30,
      246–47
  letters, 236–37, 277–78
  non-scheduled individual conferences,
      234, 260–61, 277
  "Open House," 217, 235
  orientation, 224–25, 244–45
  small-group conferences, 230, 246–47
  telephone conversations, 236
  visitation of program, 234–35
Parent Cooperative Preschools
    International, 222
Parent education
  effects of, 243–44
  purposes of, 242
  types of, 244–50
Parent Education Program of the Institute
    for Development of Human
    Resources (University of Florida),
    218

Parent information
    child care and education, 219, 223–25,
        246–47
    health education, 213–14, 223–24
    nutrition, 205
    self-improvement, 249–50
Parent involvement
    as teachers/aides, 218, 239–40
    benefits of, and obstacles to, 218–20
    legal rights, 221–22
    making instructional materials, 218,
        240
    parent educator, 225
    policy-determining roles, 36, 218, 223,
        237–38
    resource people, 218, 241–42
Parent handbook, 224, 226–29, 376–88
Parent-reception area, 137–38, 223–24
Parent Self-Improvement Programs,
    249–50
Parent-Teachers Association (PTA), 222,
    244
Partnerships, 4, 50, 64–65
Peabody, Elizabeth, 2, 9
Permission slip, 196–98
Personal-social adjustment tests, 268,
    389–462
Personnel. See Staff
Personnel services and records, 60,
        103–7. See also Insurance and
        retirement plans; Job descriptions,
        need for
Philosophy
    definition of, 16
    developmental theories of, 18–19
    importance of, 17–18, 122–24, 152,
        184, 256–57, 276, 287
    selection of, 16–22
Physical facilities. See Housing
Piaget, Jean, 2, 21, 28
Piagetian Based Cognitively Oriented
    Curriculum, 30
P.L. 93–380, 24, 275–76
P.L. 93–579, 107
P.L. 94–142
    history of, 38, 70–71
    provisions of, 54, 71–73, 123, 140, 222
Plant. See Housing
Playground. See Outdoor space
Pluralistic education, 38, 41, 264
Policies, 16, 22–25, 58, 310–12

Primary schools, 5, 12
Principal. See Staff, director
Privacy rights. See P.L. 93–380; P.L.
    93–579
Private programs
    administrative personnel, 50–51
    financing, 292–305
    regulations, 48–51
Professional contributions
    advocacy, 36, 310–12, 314
    developing a "code of ethics," 313–14
    helping others find a place in the
        profession, 314–15
    research, 28–36, 312–13
Professional organizations, 99–100,
    330–50
Program
    defined, 26
    factors determining, 28–35
    research on, 28–35
Proposals. See Grants
Proprietorships, 4, 36, 50, 64–65
Psychologist, 60, 92
Public school programs
    administrative personnel, 49
    financing, 290–92
    regulations, 48–49, 67–68
Pupil accident insurance, 212
Purchasing, 151–55, 209–10

Rambusch, Nancy McCormick, 10
Raw or primitive materials, 177
Records
    achievement, 272–73
    anecdotal, 271
    background information, 270–71
    cumulative, 274
    defined, 268
    guidance and placement, 273–74
    hazards involved in, 268–69
    privacy rights, 275–76
    referral, 274
    values of, 269–70
Referral records, 274
Registration requirements, 64
Regulations, definition and
        characteristics of, 53. See also
        Budget; Civil Rights Act of 1964,
        Title VI; Federal programs,
        regulations; Fire safety and
        sanitation requirements; Local board

Regulations *(cont.)*
  regulations; Nutrition program;
  Parent involvement,
  policy-determining roles; Private
  programs, regulations; Public school
  programs, regulations; Teacher and
  paraprofessional qualifications;
  Transportation regulations; Zoning
  regulations
Report cards, 279–84
Reporting children's progress
  methods of
    check sheets, 279
    individual parent-staff conferences,
      277. *See also* Conferences with
      parents
    informal conferences, 277
    report cards, 279–84
    report letters, 277–78
  purposes of, 276–77
  trends in, 276
Research
  need for, 36, 312–13
  problems in, 35
  programmatic, 28–35
  trends in, 313
Resource people, 218, 241–42, 246
Resource centers for parents, 247–48
Resource room, 134
Resource teachers, 90–91
Responsive Environment Corp., 29
Resting, 137
Restrooms
  adult, 138
  children, 135–36
Retirement programs, 106
Revenue sources, 287–305

Safety. *See* Health and safety codes;
  Health education of staff and
  parents; Health services
Samples of children's work, 261–62
Schedules, examples of, 190–94
Scheduling
  basic considerations in, 62, 187
  characteristics of, 189–90
  class celebrations, 198, 240–41
  coordination of staff responsibilities
    in, 194
  examples of schedules, 190–94
  field trips, 196–98, 240

Scheduling *(cont.)*
  first days, 195–96
  planning activities for interest centers
    and learning episodes, 187–89
  rationale for, 62, 183–84
  session length, 189
Schurz, Margarethe Meyer (Mrs. Carl), 9
Science materials, 163–64
"Sesame Street," 34–35, 246
Session length, 189, 217
Snacks. *See* Nutrition program
Social Studies materials, 160–61
Special Food Service Program for
  Children (1968), 205–6
Spring or autumn orientation, 224–25
Staff
  "burnout," 194
  caseworkers, 60, 92
  character of, 60
  child care personnel
    definition of, 89
    qualifications for, 59, 77–81, 88–91
    responsibilities, 49, 77, 89
  determining need for, 95–96
  dietitians and food service personnel,
    91, 209
  Director
    definition of, 51, 88
    qualifications for, 59, 76–77, 88–89
    responsibilities, 49, 51, 59, 65, 88
  evaluating, 100–3, 113–14
  general office personnel, 92
  health of, 60–61
  inservice education of, 97–99, 118,
    239–40
  maintenance, 92
  medical, 59–60, 91–92
  men on, 86–87
  meetings, 94
  non-program personnel, 91–93
  orientation of, 97–99, 118
  personnel qualifications. *See*
    Administrator qualifications;
    American Montessori Society, Inc.;
    Certification; Child Development
    Associate; Licensing,
    characteristics of laws; Teacher
    and paraprofessional qualifications
  program personnel, 87–91
  psychologist, 60, 92
  qualifications, general, 59

Staff (*cont.*)
  records, 106–7
  recruiting of, 96–97
  resource teachers, 90–91
  selection of, 95–103
  substitutes, 198–200
  supervisors
    defined, 112
    qualifications, 118–19
    responsibilities, 112–18
  teachers and assistant teachers, 35–36,
      59, 89–91
  transportation personnel, 92
  trends in, 85–87
  upgrading qualifications of, 97–103
  volunteers, 100–3, 113–14, 239–42
Staff-constructed tests, 262–63
Staff-made materials, 177–78, 240
Standardized tests, 260–68, 389–462
State Task Force, 37
State Unemployment Insurance, 105
Storage and display facilities, 127–29,
      131, 133, 136–38, 144–45, 155–56,
      158
Superintendent. *See* Staff, director
Supervising
  functions of, 112–13
  history of, 111–12
  problems in, 114–17
  methods of, 117–18
Supervisors, 49, 88, 118–19

Teacher and paraprofessional
      qualifications, 77–81
Teachers. *See* Staff, teachers and
      assistant teachers
Teacher's Centers, 118
Telephone conferences with parents, 236

Tests
  staff-constructed, 262–63
  standardized, 263–68, 389–462
Textbooks, 175–76
Theoretical models, 19–22
"Traditional" Approaches, 21, 30–32, 36,
      39–41
Transportation personnel, 62, 74, 92
Transportation regulations, 53, 62
Tucson Early Education Model, 29–33

University laboratory schools, 4, 48
University of Pittsburgh Individually
      Prescribed Instruction, 29

Vehicle insurance, 147
Vinyl or resilient flooring, 129, 132,
      135–36
Visitation of program, 234–35
Volunteers. *See* Staff, volunteers

Walls, 127, 129, 133, 135, 139
Water, sand, and mud play materials,
      164
Weikart Cognitively Oriented
      Curriculum, 21
Weikart's High Scope Model, 29, 33
Wiggin, Kate, 2
Woodworking or carpentry materials,
      164–65
Workbooks, 175–76
Workman's Compensation Insurance, 105
Workroom 138
Worksheets, 175–76

Ypsilanti Home Teaching Project, 246

Zoning regulations, 53, 60, 74